Java™ Servlet Programming

Second Edition

Jason Hunter
with William Crawford

O'REILLY®

Beijing • Cambridge • Farnham • Köln • Paris • Sebastopol • Taipei • Tokyo

Java Servlet Programming, Second Edition
by Jason Hunter with William Crawford

Published by O'Reilly & Associates, Inc., 1005 Gravenstein Highway North, Sebastopol, CA 95472.

Editors: Robert Eckstein and Paula Ferguson

Production Editor: Colleen Gorman

Cover Designer: Hanna Dyer

Printing History:

October 1998:	First Edition.
April 2001:	Second Edition.

ISBN: 0-596-00040-5

[M] [9/03]

Table of Contents

Preface

Since I wrote the first edition of this book, servlets and the server-side Java platform have grown in popularity beyond everyone's wildest expectations. Adoption is pervasive. Web server vendors now offer servlet support as a standard feature. The Java 2, Enterprise Edition (J2EE), specification has included servlets as a core component, and application server vendors wouldn't be caught dead without a scalable servlet implementation. It's more than just vendor-driven hype too. Servlets have become the basis for JavaServer Pages (JSP) and other frameworks, and servlet technology now supports such high-traffic sites as ESPN.com and AltaVista.com.

Not surprisingly, the servlet landscape looks somewhat different today than it did when the first edition went to print. The Servlet API has undergone two revisions, with a third revision on the way. The familiar startup companies Live Software and New Atlanta that once made money selling the JRun and ServletExec servlet engines (now called *servlet containers*) have gotten themselves noticed and were purchased by larger web-focused companies, Allaire and Unify, respectively. They now offer features above and beyond basic servlet support in an effort to differentiate themselves.

Amazingly, the official `javax.servlet` and `javax.servlet.http` packages have been the first Java classes to be officially released as open source. They were transferred to the Apache Software Foundation (ASF) and now reside at *http://jakarta.apache.org*. The packages continue to follow the Servlet API specification, but bug fixes and specification updates can now be handled by a set of trusted open source developers—including yours truly, who recently had the chance to fix a bug to improve conditional GET request handling in `HttpServlet`. In addition, the server that acts as the Servlet API reference implementation was also transferred to the ASF and made available as open source under the name Apache Tomcat.

Tomcat has since become one of the most popular servlet containers. For more information, see *http://opensource.org*.

The servlet world has changed, and this book brings you up-to-date. It explains everything you need to know about Java servlet programming, from start to finish. The first five chapters cover the basics: what servlets are, what they do, and how they work. The following 15 chapters are where the true meat is—they explore the things you are likely to do with servlets and the tools you're likely to use. You'll find numerous examples, several suggestions, a few warnings, and even a couple of true hacks that somehow made it past technical review.

Servlet API 2.2

This edition of the book covers Version 2.2 of the Servlet API, which went to "public release" status in August 1999 and to "final release" status in December 1999. The first edition of this book covered Version 2.0. Changes between Versions 2.0 and 2.2 have been substantial:

- Rules have been provided that define how servlets can be distributed across multiple backend servers.
- Servlets now make use of pluggable web applications, which can be configured and deployed in a server-independent manner.
- Servlet security has been greatly improved.
- Servlets can now delegate request handling to other server components.
- Servlets can now share information using their `ServletContext`.
- There's a way to abstract servlet resources to support distributed access.
- Servlets now have more control over session management.
- Response output buffering has added.
- Control over HTTP headers has been enhanced.
- More advanced error handling can now be used.
- The API has been "cleaned up" to make method names more consistent and predictable.
- The Servlet API is now defined by a formal specification document, with future API updates managed by the formal Java Specification Request (JSR) process.
- Servlets are now integrated into the umbrella Java 2 platform, Enterprise Edition (J2EE), specification.

All these changes, and many other more minor changes, are fully explained in this new edition. This second edition also has extensive coverage of the most exciting area of servlet development: techniques for building on the servlet base to easily and efficiently create dynamic content for real-world sites. In this edition you'll find tutorials on five of the most popular open source servlet-based content creation technologies:

- JavaServer Pages (JSP), the Sun standard, developed and released in conjunction with servlets
- Tea, created by the Walt Disney Internet Group (formerly GO.com), used for high-traffic sites like ESPN.com, NFL.com, Disney.com, DisneyLand.com, GO.com, and Movies.com
- WebMacro, created by Semiotek and used by the search engine AltaVista
- XMLC, created by Lutris Technologies to leverage the power of XML technology for the Web, used by innovative sites like customatix.com
- The Element Construction Set (ECS), created by Apache to handle the most demanding programming needs

This second edition also introduces WAP, the Wireless Application Protocol, and explains how to create servlet-based web applications for wireless devices.

Servlet API 2.3

At the time of the writing, Servlet API 2.3 is under development. However, it has not yet been finalized. Consequently, the text in this edition includes in various places a brief mention of the changes expected in the Servlet API 2.3. In addition, the final chapter of this book takes a thorough look at the October 2000 draft specification of the Servlet API 2.3, which should help you become familiar with the latest features that the Servlet API 2.3 will offer. We should point out, however, that these specifications are still subject to change, and the released version may differ slightly from the material presented here.

Readers of the First Edition

Readers of *Java Servlet Programming, 1st ed.* will find this book comprehensively updated for Servlet API 2.2 and, where possible, Servlet 2.3. Every chapter has enjoyed substantial improvement from the first edition, and there are six new chapters covering servlet-based content creation techniques, as well a seventh new chapter, *Enterprise Servlets and J2EE*, that explains how servlets integrate into the J2EE platform.

Due to the significant impact the pluggable *web application* model has made across all aspects of servlet programming, we recommend readers of the first edition read each chapter of interest and take note of the new mechanisms that exist for accomplishing the traditional tasks. For readers whose time is limited, we include for your convenience a list of the most significant changes in the "Organization" section later.

Audience

Is this book for you? It is if you're interested in developing applications to be deployed on the Web. Specifically, this book was written to help:

J2EE programmers
: Servlets are an integral part of the Java 2, Enterprise Edition, standard. Programmers developing for J2EE servers can learn how best to integrate servlets into other backend technologies.

JSP programmers
: JavaServer Pages (JSP) are built on top of servlets. To take full advantage of JSP requires an understanding of servlets, which this book provides. This book also includes a tutorial on JSP as well as the four leading alternatives to JSP.

Java applet programmers
: It has always been difficult for an applet to talk to a server. Servlets make it easier by giving the applet an easy-to-connect-to, Java-based agent on the server.

CGI programmers
: CGI is a popular method of extending the functionality of a web server. Servlets provide an elegant, efficient alternative.

Other server-side programmers
: There are many CGI alternatives including FastCGI, PHP, NSAPI, WAI, ISAPI, ASP, and now ASP+. Each of these has limitations regarding portability, security, performance, and/or integration with backend data sources. Servlets tend to excel in each of these areas.

What You Need to Know

When we first started writing this book, we found to our surprise that one of the hardest things was determining what to assume about you, the reader. Are you familiar with Java? Have you done CGI or other web application programming before? Or are you getting your feet wet with servlets? Do you understand HTTP and HTML, or do those abbreviations seem perfectly interchangeable? No matter what experience level we imagined, it was sure to be too simplistic for some and too advanced for others.

In the end, this book was written with the notion that it should contain predominantly original material: it could leave out exhaustive descriptions of topics and concepts that are well described online or in other books. Scattered throughout the text, you'll find several references to these external sources of information.

Of course, external references only get you so far. This book expects you are comfortable with the Java programming language and basic object-oriented programming techniques. If you are coming to servlets from another language, we suggest you prepare yourself by reading a book on general Java programming, such as *Learning Java*, by Patrick Niemeyer and Jonathan Knudsen (O'Reilly). You may want to skim quickly the sections on applets and Swing (graphical) programming and spend extra time on network and multithreaded programming. If you want to get started with servlets right away and learn Java as you go, we suggest you read this book with a copy of *Java in a Nutshell*, by David Flanagan (O'Reilly), or another Java reference book at your side.

This book does not assume you have extensive experience with web programming, HTTP, and HTML. But neither does it provide a full introduction to or exhaustive description of these technologies. We'll cover the basics necessary for effective servlet development and leave the finer points (such as a complete list of HTML tags and HTTP 1.1 headers) to other sources.

About the Examples

In this book you'll find more than a hundred servlet examples. The code for these servlets is all contained within the text, but you may prefer to download the examples rather than type them in by hand. You can find the code online and packaged for download at *http://www.oreilly.com/catalog/jservlet2*. You can also see many of the servlets in action at *http://www.servlets.com*.

All the examples have been tested using the Apache Tomcat 3.2 server running in standalone mode, using the Java Virtual Machine (JVM) bundled with the Java Development Kit (JDK) 1.1.8 and 1.2.2, on both Windows and Unix. A few advanced examples require features that Tomcat does not support in standalone mode; in these cases the examples were tested against various other servers as noted in the text. The Apache Tomcat server is the official Servlet API reference implementation, available for free under an open source license from *http://jakarta.apache.org*.

This book also contains a set of utility classes—they are used by the servlet examples, and you may find them helpful for your own general-purpose servlet development. These classes are contained in the `com.oreilly.servlet` package. Among other things, there are classes to help servlets parse parameters, handle file uploads, generate multipart responses (server push), negotiate locales for internationalization, return files, manage socket connections, and act as RMI servers, as well as a class to help applets communicate with servlets. Since the first edition, there are also new classes to help servlets send email messages, cache responses, and autodetect servlet API support. The source code for most of the `com.oreilly.servlet` package is contained within the text; and the complete latest version is also available online (with *javadoc* documentation) for download from *http://www.servlets.com.**

Organization

This book consists of 20 chapters and 6 appendixes, as follows:

Chapter 1, *Introduction*
: Explains the role and advantage of Java servlets in web application development. The second edition has been updated with additional server information.

Chapter 2, *HTTP Servlet Basics*
: Provides a quick introduction to HTTP and the things an HTTP servlet can do. Demonstrates basic web page generation and introduces the notion of pluggable web applications. The second edition covers web applications and their XML-based deployment descriptors.

Chapter 3, *The Servlet Lifecycle*
: Explains the details of how and when a servlet is loaded, how and when it is executed, how threads are managed, and how to handle the synchronization issues in a multithreaded system. Persistent state capabilities are also covered. The second edition includes new rules for context reloading and registering servlets, a new section on server-side caching, and a new sidebar on `super.init(config)`.

Chapter 4, *Retrieving Information*
: Introduces the most common methods a servlet uses to receive information—about the client, the server, the client's request, and itself. Also demonstrates a reusable class to handle file uploads. The second edition discusses setting information in the deployment descriptor, getting a servlet's name, accessing temporary directories, handling context init parameters, determining the Servlet API version, assigning servlet mappings, and accessing abstract resources. It also demonstrates an improved, more flexible file upload component.

* This book does not come with a CD-ROM. Bundling a CD-ROM increases the cost of production and the cost to you. It's our belief anyone reading this book has access to an Internet connection, and you'd rather save your money and simply download the example code off the Web. Plus, we don't see much point in bundling evaluation copies of the various web and application servers. Considering the breakneck pace of innovation in the servlet market, the bundled servers would be obsolete before the book went to press. The same evaluation versions are available online, and we recommend you download the latest releases yourself. Just remember, if you plan to read the book offline, you might want to download the example code and a copy of the Apache Tomcat web server the next chance you get. The download links are at *http://www.servlets.com.*

Chapter 5, *Sending HTML Information*

Describes how a servlet can generate HTML, return errors and other status codes, buffer responses, redirect requests, write data to the server log, and send custom HTTP header information. The second edition contains new coverage of response buffering, a truly useful redirection example, and new sections on configuring error pages and error handling.

Chapter 6, *Sending Multimedia Content*

Looks at some of the interesting things a servlet can return: WAP/WML content for wireless devices, dynamically generated images, compressed content, and multipart responses. The second edition adds the WAP/WML coverage, welcome file lists, a discussion of PNG, an improved server-side image cache, and more details on generating compressed content.

Chapter 7, *Session Tracking*

Shows how to build a sense of state on top of the stateless HTTP protocol. The first half of the chapter demonstrates the traditional session-tracking techniques used by CGI developers; the second half shows how to use the built-in support for session tracking in the Servlet API. The second edition includes the rules for web application sessions, material on new session method names, a discussion of how to manage timeouts, and applet-based session tracking.

Chapter 8, *Security*

Explains the security issues involved with distributed computing. Demonstrates how to make use of standard servlet hooks for user account management and how to build a more powerful system using custom authentication and authorization. Also explains a servlet's role in secure SSL communication. Has been updated in its entirety in this second edition.

Chapter 9, *Database Connectivity*

Shows how servlets can be used for high-performance web-database connectivity. Includes a tutorial on JDBC. The second edition contains a demonstration of configuring connections with a properties file, a new guestbook example, and a new section on JDBC 2.0.

Chapter 10, *Applet-Servlet Communication*

Describes how servlets can be leveraged by an applet that needs to communicate with the server. Updated for this second edition.

Chapter 11, *Servlet Collaboration*

Discusses why servlets need to communicate with one another and how they can collaborate by sharing information or making calls on one another. Has been updated in its entirety in this second edition.

Chapter 12, *Enterprise Servlets and J2EE*

Discusses advanced servlet features needed for enterprise sites: distribution of load and J2EE component integration. New in the second edition.

Chapter 13, *Internationalization*

Shows how a servlet can read and generate multilingual content. The second edition explains how to use *javac* to manage encodings and how to use new API methods to manage locales.

Chapter 14, *The Tea Framework*

Demonstrates the Tea framework, an elegant yet powerful templating engine. New in the second edition.

Chapter 15, *WebMacro*

Discusses the WebMacro framework, similar to Tea but with several different design decisions. New in the second edition.

Chapter 16, *Element Construction Set*

Gives short coverage on ECS, an object-oriented approach to page creation. New in the second edition.

Chapter 17, *XMLC*

Provides an overview of XMLC, a page creation approach with an XML bent. New in the second edition.

Chapter 18, *JavaServer Pages*

Explains JSP, the Sun standard technology in which web pages are autocompiled into servlets. New in the second edition.

Chapter 19, *Odds and Ends*

Presents a junk drawer full of useful servlet examples and tips that don't really belong anywhere else. The second edition includes a localized parameter parser, a new email class, an updated regular expression section, a new third-party tool section, and additional performance tips.

Chapter 20, Changes in the Servlet 2.3 API

Illustrates the upcoming changes in the 2.3 version of the Servlets API, which is expected to be released in mid-2001. New in the second edition.

Appendix A, *Servlet API Quick Reference*

Contains a full description of the classes, methods, and variables in the `javax.servlet` package. The second edition has been updated for Servlet API 2.2.

Appendix B, *HTTP Servlet API Quick Reference*

Contains a full description of the classes, methods, and variables in the `javax.servlet.http` package. The second edition has been updated for Servlet API 2.2.

Appendix C, *Deployment Descriptor DTD Reference*
: Presents an annotated reference for the *web.xml* deployment descriptor's Document Type Definition. New in the second edition.

Appendix D, *HTTP Status Codes*
: Lists the status codes specified by HTTP, along with the mnemonic constants used by servlets.

Appendix E, *Character Entities*
: Lists the character entities defined in HTML, along with their equivalent Unicode escape values.

Appendix F, *Charsets*
: Lists the suggested charsets servlets may use to generate content in several different languages.

Please feel free to read the chapters of this book in whatever order you like. Reading straight through from front to back ensures that you won't encounter any surprises, as efforts have been made to avoid forward references. If you want to skip around, however, you can do so easily enough, especially after Chapter 5—the rest of the chapters all tend to stand alone. One last suggestion: read the "Debugging" section of Chapter 19 if at any time you find a piece of code that doesn't work as expected.

Conventions Used in This Book

Italic is used for:

- Pathnames, filenames, and program names.
- New terms where they are defined.
- Internet addresses, such as domain names and URLs.

Boldface is used for:

- Particular keys on a computer keyboard.
- Names of user interface buttons and menus.

`Constant width` is used for:

- Anything that appears literally in a Java program, including keywords, datatypes, constants, method names, variables, class names, and interface names.
- All Java code listings.
- HTML documents, tags, and attributes.

`Constant width italic` is used for:

- General placeholders that indicate that an item is replaced by some actual value in your own program.

`Constant width bold` is used for:

- Command-line entries.

Request for Comments

Please help us to improve future editions of this book by reporting any errors, inaccuracies, bugs, misleading or confusing statements, and plain old typos that you find anywhere in this book. Email your bug reports and comments to us at: *bookquestions@oreilly.com.* (Before sending a bug report, however, you may want to check for an errata list at *http://www.oreilly.com/catalog/jservlet2* to see if the bug has already been submitted.)

Please also let us know what we can do to make this book more useful to you. We take your comments seriously and will try to incorporate reasonable suggestions into future editions.

Acknowledgments

While I was working on this second edition, a friend said to me, "It must be easier for you to write a second edition; you already wrote the book once." I thought about that for a minute, laughed, and replied, "It is easier, but not nearly as easy as I'd hoped!"

Looking back, I believe the reason has little to do with books and more to do with technology. The first edition covered Servlet API 2.0, a specification developed over about two years. This second edition covers Servlet API 2.2 and 2.3, representing roughly two years of additional design work. So it only makes sense from that perspective that if the first edition took a year of active writing, then the second edition should take something similar. And, in fact, it did: about nine months.

There are many who have helped in the writing of this book to whom I am profoundly indebted. First and foremost are the book's technical reviewers: James Duncan Davidson, Servlet API Specification lead for APIs 2.1 and 2.2, and Danny Coward, lead for the upcoming API 2.3. I can't say enough good things about James and Danny. Not only have they provided me with invaluable assistance and advice throughout the writing of the book, they have given us all a wonderful platform for web programming.

My thanks also to the many developers who donated their expertise to help with the content creation chapters (and in many cases actually created the technology being discussed): Reece Wilton and Brian O'Neill for Tea, Justin Wells for WebMacro, Jon Stevens for ECS, Mark Diekhans and Christian Cryder for XMLC, and Hans Bergsten and Craig McClanahan for JSP.

I'd also like to thank Bob Eckstein, the book's editor, whose handwritten edits were always insightful, if sometimes unreadable. Bob took over editing duties from Paula Ferguson after she became responsible for managing O'Reilly's web and scripting books.

My thanks also to Jim Grisham, who helped locate all varieties of machine and browser types for testing examples; Magnus Stenman of Orion, who explained how the Orion Server implements J2EE; Justyna Horwat, called by some the Tag Library Goddess, for answering questions about JSP tag libraries; and Ethan Henry, who helped with suggestions on servlet performance tuning.

I can't forget Brett McLaughlin, author of *Java and XML* (O'Reilly) and the cocreator of JDOM. His cooperating with me on JDOM actually slowed down the book, but the speed with which he writes inspires me, and besides, with the acknowledgment he gave to me in his book, I have to say *something* here!

And finally, thanks to my girlfriend, Kathlyn Bautista, who didn't complain if I worked Sundays but made me never want to.

Jason Hunter
November 2000

Acknowledgments from the First Edition

In a sense, this book began March 20, 1997, at the Computer Literacy bookstore in San Jose, California. There—after a hilarious talk by Larry Wall and Randall Schwartz, where Larry explained how he manages to automate his house using Perl—I met the esteemed Tim O'Reilly for the first time. I introduced myself and brazenly told him that someday (far in the future, I thought) I had plans to write an O'Reilly book. I felt like I was telling Steven Spielberg I planned to star in one of his movies. To my complete and utter surprise, Tim replied, "On what topic?" So began the rollercoaster ride that resulted in this book.

There have been several high points I fondly remember: meeting my editor (cool, she's young too!), signing the official contract (did you know that all of O'Reilly's official paper has animals on it?), writing the first sentence (over and over), printing the first chapter (and having it look just like an O'Reilly book), and then watching as the printouts piled higher and higher, until eventually there was nothing more to write (well, except the acknowledgments).

There have been a fair number of trying times as well. At one point, when the book was about half finished, I realized the Servlet API was changing faster than I could keep up. I believe in the saying, "If at first you don't succeed, ask for help," so after a quick talent search I asked William Crawford, who was already working on *Java Enterprise in a Nutshell*, if he could help speed the book to completion. He graciously agreed and in the end helped write two chapters, as well as portions of the appendixes.

There are many others who have helped in the writing of this book, both directly and indirectly. I'd like to say thank you to Paula Ferguson, the book's editor, and Mike Loukides, the Java series editor, for their efforts to ensure (and improve) the quality of this book. And to Tim O'Reilly for giving me the chance to fulfill a dream.

Thanks also to my managers at Silicon Graphics, Kathy Tansill and Walt Johnson, for providing more encouragement and flexibility than I had any right to expect.

I can't say thank you enough to the engineers at Sun who were tremendously helpful in answering questions, keeping me updated on changes in the Servlet API and promptly fixing almost every bug I reported: James Duncan Davidson (who looks the spitting image of James Gosling), Jim Driscoll, Rob Clark, and Dave Brownell.

Thanks also to the members of the jserv-interest mailing list, whose questions and answers have shaped the content of this book; Will Ramey, an old friend who didn't let friendship blind his critical eye; Mike Engber, the man to whom I turned when I had run out of elegant workarounds and was ready to accept the crazy things he comes up with; Dave Vandegrift, the first person to read many of the chapters; Bill Day, author of *Java Media Players*, who helped intangibly by going through the book writing process in parallel with me; Michael O'Connell and Jill Steinberg, editors at *JavaWorld*, where I did my first professional writing; Doug Young, who shared with me the tricks he learned writing seven technical books of his own; and Shoji Kuwabara, Mieko Aono, Song Yung, Matthew Kim, and Alexandr Pashintsev for their help translating "Hello World" for Chapter 13.

I'd like to say a big thank you to the book's technical reviewers, whose constructive criticism has done much to improve this work: Mike Slinn, Mike Hogarth, James Duncan Davidson, Dan Pritchett, Dave McMurdie, and Rob Clark. I'm still in shock that it took one reviewer just three days to read what took us a full year to write!

Finally, thanks to Mom and Dad, for your love and support and for the time you spent long ago teaching me the basics of writing. And thanks to Kristi Taylor, who made the small time away from work a pleasure.

And Grandpa, I wish you could have seen this.

Jason Hunter
June 1998

First and foremost, thanks to Shelley Norton, Dr. Isaac Kohane, Dr. James Fackler, and Dr. Richard Kitz (plus a supporting cast whose contributions were invaluable), whose assistance and early support have made everything since possible. Also, to Martin Streeter of Invantage, Inc., for his support during this project.

Without Rob Leith, Roger Stacey, and Fred Strebeigh, I would probably still be stuck in the passive voice. Dale Dougherty offered me money in exchange for words, a twist of events that I still haven't gotten over. Andy Kwak, Joel Pomerantz, and Matthew Proto, brave souls all, were willing to read drafts and listen to complaints at one o'clock in the morning.

And, of course, to Mom and Dad for their years of support, and to my sister Faith for (usually) letting me get away with being a nerd.

William Crawford
July 1998

In this chapter:
- *History of Web Applications*
- *Support for Servlets*
- *The Power of Servlets*

1 Introduction

The rise of server-side Java applications—everything from standalone servlets to the full Java 2, Enterprise Edition (J2EE), platform—has been one of the most exciting trends to watch in Java programming. The Java language was originally intended for use in small, embedded devices. It was first hyped as a language for developing elaborate client-side web content in the form of applets. But until the last few years, Java's potential as a server-side development platform had been sadly overlooked. Now, Java has come to be recognized as a language ideally suited for server-side development.

Businesses in particular have been quick to recognize Java's potential on the server—Java is inherently suited for large client/server applications. The cross-platform nature of Java is extremely useful for organizations that have a heterogeneous collection of servers running various flavors of the Unix and Windows (and increasingly Mac OS X) operating systems. Java's modern, object-oriented, memory-protected design allows developers to cut development cycles and increase reliability. In addition, Java's built-in support for networking and enterprise APIs provides access to legacy data, easing the transition from older client/server systems.

Java servlets are a key component of server-side Java development. A servlet is a small, pluggable extension to a server that enhances the server's functionality. Servlets allow developers to extend and customize any Java-enabled web or application server with a hitherto unknown degree of portability, flexibility, and ease. But before we go into any more detail, let's put things into perspective.

History of Web Applications

While servlets can be used to extend the functionality of any Java-enabled server, they are most often used to extend web servers, providing a powerful, efficient replacement for CGI scripts. When you use a servlet to create dynamic content for a web page or otherwise extend the functionality of a web server, you are in effect creating a web application. While a web page merely displays static content and lets the user navigate through that content, a web application provides a more interactive experience. A web application can be as simple as a keyword search on a document archive or as complex as an electronic storefront. Web applications are being deployed on the Internet and on corporate intranets and extranets, where they have the potential to increase productivity and change the way that companies, large and small, do business.

To understand the power of servlets, we need to step back and look at some of the other approaches that can be used to create web applications.

Common Gateway Interface

The Common Gateway Interface, normally referred to as CGI, was one of the first practical techniques for creating dynamic content. With CGI, a web server passes certain requests to an external program. The output of this program is then sent to the client in place of a static file. The advent of CGI made it possible to implement all sorts of new functionality in web pages, and CGI quickly became a de facto standard, implemented on dozens of web servers.

It's interesting to note that the ability of CGI programs to create dynamic web pages is a side effect of its intended purpose: to define a standard method for an information server to talk with external applications. This origin explains why CGI has perhaps the worst life cycle imaginable. When a server receives a request that accesses a CGI program, it must create a new process to run the CGI program and then pass to it, via environment variables and standard input, every bit of information that might be necessary to generate a response. Creating a process for every such request requires time and significant server resources, which limits the number of requests a server can handle concurrently. Figure 1-1 shows the CGI life cycle.

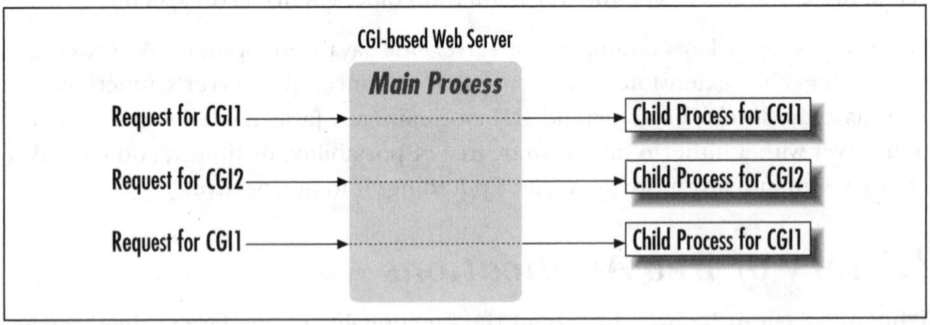

Figure 1-1. The CGI life cycle

Even though a CGI program can be written in almost any language, the Perl programming language has become the predominant choice. Perl's advanced text-processing capabilities are a big help in managing the details of the CGI interface. Writing a CGI script in Perl gives it a semblance of platform independence, but it also requires that each request start a separate Perl interpreter, which takes even more time and requires extra resources.

Another often-overlooked problem with CGI is that a CGI program cannot interact with the web server or take advantage of the server's abilities once it begins execution, because it is running in a separate process. For example, a CGI script cannot write to the server's log file. For more information on CGI programming, see *CGI Programming on the World Wide Web* by Shishir Gundavaram (O'Reilly).

FastCGI

A company named Open Market developed an alternative to standard CGI named FastCGI. In many ways, FastCGI works just like CGI—the important difference is that FastCGI creates a single persistent process for each FastCGI program, as shown in Figure 1-2. This eliminates the need to create a new process for each request.

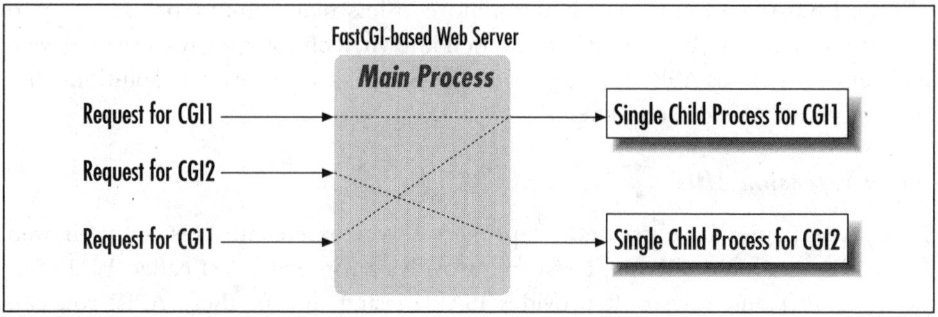

Figure 1-2. The FastCGI life cycle

Although FastCGI is a step in the right direction, it still has a problem with process proliferation: there is at least one process for each FastCGI program. If a FastCGI program is to handle concurrent requests, it needs a pool of processes, one per request. Considering that each process may be executing a Perl interpreter, this approach does not scale as well as you might hope. (Although, to its credit, FastCGI can distribute its processes across multiple servers.) Another problem with FastCGI is that it does nothing to help the FastCGI program more closely interact with the server. Finally, FastCGI programs are only as portable as the language in which they're written. For more information on FastCGI, see *http://www.fastcgi.com*.

PerlEx

PerlEx, developed by ActiveState, improves the performance of CGI scripts written in Perl that run on Windows NT web servers (Microsoft's Internet Information Server, O'Reilly's WebSite Professional, and iPlanet's FastTrack Server and Enterprise Server). It has advantages and disadvantages similar to FastCGI. For more information on PerlEx, see *http://www.activestate.com/plex.*

mod_perl

If you are using the Apache web server, another option for improving CGI performance is using mod_perl. mod_perl is a module for the Apache server that embeds a copy of the Perl interpreter into the Apache executable, providing complete access to Perl functionality within Apache. The effect is that your CGI scripts are precompiled by the server and executed without forking, thus running much more quickly and efficiently. The downside is that the application can be deployed only on the Apache server. For more information on mod_perl, see *http://perl.apache.org.*

Other Solutions

CGI/Perl has the advantage of being a more-or-less platform-independent way to produce dynamic web content. Other well-known technologies for creating web applications, such as ASP and server-side JavaScript, are proprietary solutions that work only with certain web servers.

Server extension APIs

Several companies have created proprietary server extension APIs for their web servers. For example, iPlanet/Netscape provides an internal API called WAI (formerly NSAPI) and Microsoft provides ISAPI. Using one of these APIs, you can write server extensions that enhance or change the base functionality of the server, allowing the server to handle tasks that were once relegated to external CGI programs. As you can see in Figure 1-3, server extensions exist within the main process of a web server.

Because server-specific APIs use linked C or C++ code, server extensions can run extremely fast and make full use of the server's resources. Server extensions, however, are not a perfect solution by any means. Besides being difficult to develop and maintain, they pose significant security and reliability hazards: a crashed server extension can bring down the entire server; a malicious server extension could steal user passwords and credit card numbers. And, of course, proprietary server extensions are inextricably tied to the server API for which they were written—and often tied to a particular operating system as well.

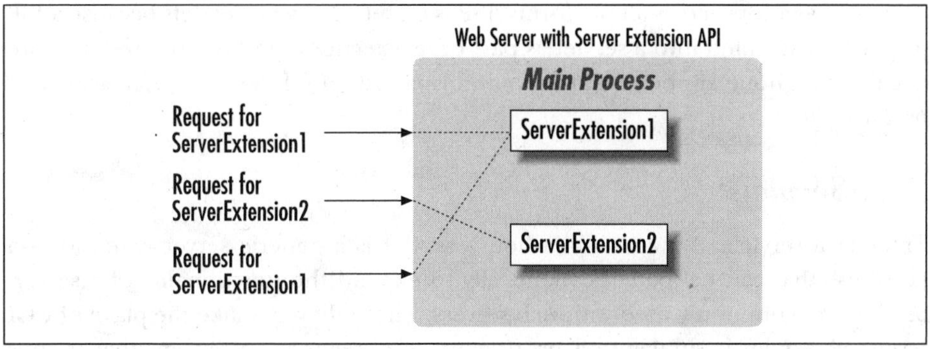

Figure 1-3. The server extension life cycle

Server-side JavaScript

iPlanet/Netscape also has a technique for server-side scripting, which it calls *server-side JavaScript,* or *SSJS* for short. Like ASP, SSJS allows snippets of code to be embedded in HTML pages to generate dynamic web content. The difference is that SSJS uses JavaScript as the scripting language. With SSJS, web pages are pre-compiled to improve performance. Support for server-side JavaScript is available only with iPlanet/Netscape servers. For more information on programming with server-side JavaScript, see *http://developer.netscape.com/tech/javascript/ssjs/ssjs.html.*

Active Server Pages

Microsoft has a technique for generating dynamic web content called *Active Server Pages,* or sometimes just *ASP.* With ASP, an HTML page on the web server can contain snippets of embedded code (usually VBScript or JScript—although it's possible to use nearly any language). This code is read and executed by the web server before it sends the page to the client. ASP is optimized for generating small portions of dynamic content, using COM components to do the heavy lifting.

Support for ASP is built into Microsoft Internet Information Server Version 3.0 and above, available for free from *http://www.microsoft.com/iis.* Support for other web servers is available as a commercial product from Chili!Soft at *http://www.chilisoft.com.* Beware that ASP pages running on a non-Windows platform may have a hard time performing advanced tasks without the Windows COM library. For more information on programming Active Server Pages, see *http://www.microsoft.com/workshop/server/default.asp* and *http://www.activeserverpages.com/.*

JavaServer Pages

JavaServer Pages, commonly called just *JSP,* is a Java-based alternative to ASP, invented and standardized by Sun. JSP uses a syntax similar to ASP except the scripting language is Java. Unlike ASP, JSP is an open standard implemented by dozens of vendors across all platforms. JSP is closely tied with servlets because a JSP page is transformed into a servlet as part of its execution. JSP is discussed in more detail throughout this book. For more information on JSP, see *http://java.sun.com/products/jsp*.

Java Servlets

Enter Java servlets. As was said earlier, a servlet is a generic server extension—a Java class that can be loaded dynamically to expand the functionality of a server. Servlets are commonly used with web servers, where they can take the place of CGI scripts. A servlet is similar to a proprietary server extension, except that it runs inside a Java Virtual Machine (JVM) on the server (see Figure 1-4), so it is safe and portable. Servlets operate solely within the domain of the server: unlike applets, they do not require support for Java in the web browser.

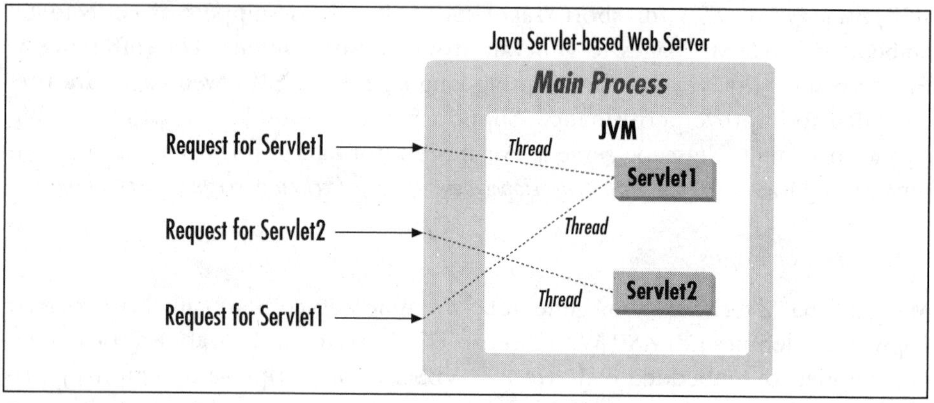

Figure 1-4. The servlet life cycle

Unlike CGI and FastCGI, which must use multiple processes to handle separate programs and/or separate requests, servlets can all be handled by separate threads within the same process or by threads within multiple processes spread across a number of backend servers. This means that servlets are also efficient and scalable. Because servlets run with bidirectional communication to the web server, they can interact very closely with the server to do things that are not possible with CGI scripts.

Another advantage of servlets is that they are portable: both across operating systems as we are used to with Java and also across web servers. As you'll see shortly, all of the major web servers and application servers support servlets. We believe that Java servlets offer the best possible platform for web application development, and we'll have much more to say about this later in the chapter.

Support for Servlets

Like Java itself, servlets were designed for portability. Servlets are supported on all platforms that support Java, and servlets work with all the major web servers.* Java servlets, as defined by the Java Software division of Sun Microsystems (formerly known as JavaSoft), are an *Optional Package* to Java (formerly known as a *Standard Extension*). This means that servlets are officially blessed by Sun and are part of the Java language, but they are not part of the core Java API. Instead, they are now recognized as part of the J2EE platform.

To make it easy for you to develop servlets, Sun and Apache have made available the API classes separately from any web engine. The `javax.servlet` and `javax.servlet.http` packages constitute this Servlet API. The latest version of these classes is available for download from *http://java.sun.com/products/servlet/download.html*.† All web servers that support servlets must use these classes internally (although they could use an alternate implementation), so generally this JAR file can also be found somewhere within the distribution of your servlet-enabled web server.

It doesn't much matter where you get the servlet classes, as long as you have them on your system, since you need them to compile your servlets. In addition to the servlet classes, you need a servlet runner (technically called a *servlet container*, sometimes called a *servlet engine*), so that you can test and deploy your servlets. Your choice of servlet container depends in part on the web server(s) you are running. There are three flavors of servlet containers: *standalone*, *add-on*, and *embeddable*.

Standalone Servlet Containers

A standalone servlet container is a server that includes built-in support for servlets. Such a container has the advantage that everything works right out of the box. One disadvantage, however, is that you have to wait for a new release of the web server to get the latest servlet support. Another disadvantage is that server vendors generally support only the vendor-provided JVM. Web servers that provide standalone support include those in the following list.

* Note that several web server vendors have their own server-side Java implementations, some of which have also been given the name *servlets*. These are generally incompatible with the Java servlets as defined by Sun. Most of these vendors are converting their Java support to standard servlets or are introducing standard servlet support in parallel, to allow backward compatibility.

† At one point it was planned for these classes to come bundled as part of JDK 1.2. However, it was later decided to keep the servlet classes separate from the JDK, to better allow for timely revisions and corrections to the Servlet API.

- Apache's Tomcat Server, the official reference implementation for how a servlet container should support servlets. Written entirely in Java, and freely available under an open source license. All the source code is available and anyone can help with its development. This server can operate standalone or as an add-on providing Apache or other servers with servlet support. It can even be used as an embedded container. Along with Tomcat, Apache develops the standard implementation of the `javax.servlet` and `javax.servlet.http` packages. At the time of this writing servlets are the only `java.*` or `javax.*` packages officially maintained as open source.* See *http://jakarta.apache.org*.
- iPlanet (Netscape) Web Server Enterprise Edition (Version 4.0 and later), perhaps the most popular web server to provide built-in servlet support. Some benchmarks show this server to have the fastest servlet implementation. Beware that, while Versions 3.51 and 3.6 of this server had built-in servlet support, those servers supported only the early Servlet API 1.0 and suffered from a number of bugs so significant the servlet support was practically unusable. To use servlets with Netscape 3.x servers, use an add-on servlet container. See *http://www.iplanet.com*.
- O'Reilly's WebSite Professional, with similar functionality to iPlanet Enterprise Server for a lower price. See *http://website.oreilly.com*.
- Zeus Web Server, a web server some consider the fastest available. Its feature list is quite long and includes servlet support. See *http://www.zeus.co.uk*.
- Caucho's Resin, an open source container that prides itself on performance. It can run in standalone mode or as an add-on to many servers. See *http://www.caucho.com*.
- Gefion Software's LiteWebServer, a small (just over 100K) servlet container intended for uses, such as bundling with demos, where small size matters. See *http://www.gefionsoftware.com/LiteWebServer*.
- World Wide Web Consortium's Jigsaw Server, open source and written entirely in Java. See *http://www.w3.org/Jigsaw*.
- Sun's Java Web Server, the server that started it all. This server was the first server to implement servlets and acted as the effective reference implementation for Servlet API 2.0. It's written entirely in Java (except for two native code libraries that enhance its functionality but are not needed). Sun has discontinued development on the server, concentrating now on iPlanet/Netscape products as part of the Sun-Netscape Alliance. See *http://java.sun.com/products*.

* Having a standard open source implementation of `javax.servlet` and `javax.servlet.http` has resulted in numerous helpful bug fixes (for example, Jason committed a fix to `HttpServlet` improving the behavior of conditional GET) and no incompatibility concerns. We hope this track record helps encourage more official Java packages to be released as open source.

Application servers are a growing area of development. An application server offers server-side support for developing enterprise-based applications. Most Java-based application support servlets and the rest of the Java 2, Enterprise Edition, (J2EE) specification. These servers include:

- BEA System's WebLogic Application Server, one of the first and most famous Java-based application servers. See *http://www.beasys.com/products/weblogic.*
- Orion Application Server, a high-end but relatively low-priced server, written entirely in Java. See *http://www.orionserver.com.*
- Enhydra Application Server, an open source server from Lutris. See *http://www.enhydra.org.*
- Borland Application Server 4, a server with a special emphasis on CORBA. See *http://www.borland.com/appserver.*
- IBM's WebSphere Application Server, a high-end server based partially on Apache code. See *http://www-4.ibm.com/software/webservers.*
- ATG's Dynamo Application Server 3, another high-end server written entirely in Java. See *http://www.atg.com.*
- Oracle's Application Server, a server designed for integration with an Oracle database. See *http://www.oracle.com/appserver.*
- iPlanet Application Server, the J2EE-compliant big brother to the iPlanet Web Server Enterprise Edition. See *http://www.iplanet.com/products/infrastructure/app_servers/nas.*
- GemStone/J Application Server, a Java server from a company previously known for its Smalltalk server. See *http://www.gemstone.com/products/j.*
- Allaire's JRun Server (formerly from Live Software), a simple servlet container that grew to an advanced container providing many J2EE technologies including EJB, JTA, and JMS. See *http://www.allaire.com/products/jrun.*
- Silverstream Application Server, a fully compliant J2EE server that also started with a servlet focus. See *http://www.silverstream.com.*

Add-on Servlet Containers

An add-on servlet container functions as a plug-in to an existing server—it adds servlet support to a server that was not originally designed with servlets in mind or to a server with a poor or outdated servlet implementation. Add-on servlet containers have been written for many servers including Apache, iPlanet's FastTrack Server and Enterprise Server, Microsoft's Internet Information Server and Personal Web

Server, O'Reilly's WebSite, Lotus Domino's Go Webserver, StarNine's WebSTAR, and Apple's AppleShare IP. Add-on servlet containers include the following:

- New Atlanta's ServletExec, a plug-in designed to support servlets on all the popular web servers on all the popular operating systems. Includes a free debugger. See *http://www.servletexec.com*.
- Allaire's JRun (formerly from Live Software), available as a plug-in to support servlets on all the popular web servers on all the popular operating systems. See *http://www.allaire.com/products/jrun/*.
- The Java-Apache project's JServ module, a freely available open source servlet container that adds servlet support to the extremely popular Apache server. Development has completed on JServ, and the Tomcat Server (acting as a plug-in) is the replacement for JServ. See *http://java.apache.org/*.
- Apache's Tomcat Server, as discussed previously, Tomcat may be plugged into other servers including Apache, iPlanet/Netscape, and IIS.

Embeddable Servlet Containers

An embeddable container is generally a lightweight servlet deployment platform that can be embedded in another application. That application becomes the true server. Embeddable servlet containers include the following:

- Apache's Tomcat Server, while generally used standalone or as an add-on, this server also can be embedded into another application when necessary. Because this server is open source, development on most other embeddable containers has stopped.
- Anders Kristensen's Nexus Web Server, a freely available servlet runner that implements most of the Servlet API and can be easily embedded in Java applications. See *http://www-uk.hpl.hp.com/people/ak/java/nexus/*.

Additional Thoughts

Before proceeding, we feel obliged to point out that not all servlet containers are created equal. So, before you choose a servlet container (and possibly a server) with which to deploy your servlets, take it out for a test drive. Kick its tires a little. Check the mailing lists. Always verify that your servlets behave as they do in the Tomcat reference implementation. Also, you may want to check what development tools are provided, which J2EE technologies are supported, and how quickly you can get a response on the support lines. With servlets, you don't have to worry about the lowest-common-denominator implementation, so you should pick a servlet container that has the features you want.

For a complete, up-to-date list of available servlet containers, complete with current pricing information, see *http://www.servlets.com*.

The Power of Servlets

So far, we have portrayed servlets as an alternative to other dynamic web content technologies, but we haven't really explained why we think you should use them. What makes servlets a viable choice for web development? We believe that servlets offer a number of advantages over other approaches, including portability, power, efficiency, endurance, safety, elegance, integration, extensibility, and flexibility. Let's examine each in turn.

Portability

Because servlets are written in Java and conform to a well-defined and widely accepted API, they are highly portable across operating systems and across server implementations. You can develop a servlet on a Windows NT machine running the Tomcat server and later deploy it effortlessly on a high-end Unix server running the iPlanet/Netscape Application Server. With servlets, you can truly "write once, serve everywhere."

Servlet portability is not the stumbling block it so often is with applets, for two reasons. First, servlet portability is not mandatory. Unlike applets, which have to be tested on all possible client platforms, servlets have to work only on the server machines that you are using for development and deployment. Unless you are in the business of selling your servlets, you don't have to worry about complete portability. Second, servlets avoid the most error-prone and inconsistently implemented portion of the Java language: the Abstract Windowing Toolkit (AWT) that forms the basis of Java graphical user interfaces, including Swing.

Power

Servlets can harness the full power of the core Java APIs: networking and URL access, multithreading, image manipulation, data compression, database connectivity (JDBC), object serialization, internationalization, remote method invocation (RMI), and legacy integration (CORBA). Servlets can also take advantage of the J2EE platform that includes support for Enterprise JavaBeans (EJBs), distributed transactions (JTS), standardized messaging (JMS), directory lookup (JNDI), and advanced database access (JDBC 2.0). The list of standard APIs available to servlets continues to grow, making the task of web application development faster, easier, and more reliable.

As a servlet author, you can also pick and choose from a plethora of third-party Java classes and JavaBeans components. Servlets can use third-party code to handle tasks such as regular expression searching, data charting, custom database access, advanced networking, XML parsing, and XSLT translations.

Servlets are also well suited for enabling client/server communication. With a Java-based applet and a Java-based servlet, you can use RMI and object serialization in your client/server communication, which means that you can leverage the same custom code on the client as on the server. Using languages other than Java on the server side is much more complicated, as you have to develop your own custom protocols to handle the communication.

Efficiency and Endurance

Servlet invocation is highly efficient. Once a servlet is loaded, it remains in the server's memory as a single object instance. Thereafter, the server invokes the servlet to handle a request using a simple, lightweight method invocation. Unlike with CGI, there's no process to spawn or interpreter to invoke, so the servlet can begin handling the request almost immediately. Multiple, concurrent requests are handled by separate threads, so servlets are highly scalable.

Servlets are naturally enduring objects. Because a servlet stays in the server's memory as a single object instance, it automatically maintains its state and can hold on to external resources, such as database connections, that may otherwise take several seconds to establish.

Safety

Servlets support safe programming practices on a number of levels. Because they are written in Java, servlets inherit the strong type safety of the Java language. In addition, the Servlet API is implemented to be type-safe. While most values in a CGI program, including a numeric item like a server port number, are treated as strings, values are manipulated by the Servlet API using their native types, so a server port number is represented as an integer. Java's automatic garbage collection and lack of pointers mean that servlets are generally safe from memory management problems like dangling pointers, invalid pointer references, and memory leaks.

Servlets can handle errors safely, due to Java's exception-handling mechanism. If a servlet divides by zero or performs some other illegal operation, it throws an exception that can be safely caught and handled by the server, which can politely log the error and apologize to the user. If a C++-based server extension were to make the same mistake, it could potentially crash the server.

A server can further protect itself from servlets through the use of a Java security manager or access controller. A server can execute its servlets under the watch of a strict access controller that, for example, enforces a security policy designed to prevent a malicious or poorly written servlet from damaging the server filesystem.

Elegance

The elegance of servlet code is striking. Servlet code is clean, object oriented, modular, and amazingly simple. One reason for this simplicity is the Servlet API itself, which includes methods and classes to handle many of the routine chores of servlet development. Even advanced operations, like cookie handling and session tracking, are abstracted into convenient classes. A few more advanced but still common tasks were left out of the API, and, in those places, we have tried to step in and provide a set of helpful classes in the `com.oreilly.servlet` package.

Integration

Servlets are tightly integrated with the server. This integration allows a servlet to cooperate with the server in ways that a CGI program cannot. For example, a servlet can use the server to translate file paths, perform logging, check authorization, and perform MIME type mapping. Server-specific extensions can do much of this, but the process is usually much more complex and error-prone.

Extensibility and Flexibility

The Servlet API is designed to be easily extensible. As it stands today, the API includes classes with specialized support for HTTP servlets. But at a later date, it could be extended and optimized for another type of servlets, either by Sun or by a third party. It is also possible that its support for HTTP servlets could be further enhanced.

Servlets are also quite flexible in how they create content. They can generate simple content using `out.println()` statements, or they can generate complicated sets of pages using a template engine. They can create an HTML page by treating the page as a set of Java objects, or they can create an HTML page by performing an XML-to-HTML transformation. Servlets can even be built upon to create brand new technologies like JavaServer Pages. Who knows what they (or you) will come up with next.

2

In this chapter:
- *HTTP Basics*
- *The Servlet API*
- *Page Generation*
- *Web Applications*
- *Moving On*

HTTP Servlet Basics

This chapter provides a short tutorial on how to write and execute a simple HTTP servlet. Then it explains how to deploy the servlet in a standard web application and how to configure the servlet's behavior using an XML-based deployment descriptor.

Unlike the first edition, this chapter does *not* cover servlet-based server-side includes (SSI) or servlet chaining and filtering. This is because those techniques, as useful as they were and despite the fact they were implemented in the Java Web Server, have not been officially endorsed by the servlet specification (which came out after the first edition of this book was published). SSI has been replaced by new techniques for doing programmatic includes. Servlet chaining has been decreed too inelegant for official endorsement, although the basic idea seems likely to reappear in Servlet API 2.3 as part of an official general-purpose pre- and post-filtering mechanism.

Note that the code for each of the examples in this chapter and throughout the book is available for download in both source and compiled form (as described in the Preface). However, for this first chapter, we suggest that you deny yourself the convenience of the Internet and take the time to type in the examples. It should help the concepts seep into your brain. Don't be alarmed if we seem to skim lightly over some topics in this chapter. Servlets are powerful and, at times, complicated. The point here is to give you a general overview of how things work, before jumping in and overwhelming you with all of the details. By the end of this book, we promise that you'll be able to write servlets that do everything but make tea.

HTTP Basics

Before we can even show you a simple HTTP servlet, we need to make sure that you have a basic understanding of how the protocol behind the Web, HTTP, works. If you're an experienced CGI programmer (or if you've done any serious server-side web programming), you can safely skip this section. Better yet, you might skim it to refresh your memory about the finer points of the GET and POST methods. If you are new to the world of server-side web programming, however, you should read this material carefully, as the rest of the book is going to assume that you understand HTTP. For a more thorough discussion of HTTP and its methods, see *HTTP Pocket Reference* by Clinton Wong (O'Reilly).

Requests, Responses, and Headers

HTTP is a simple, stateless protocol. A client, such as a web browser, makes a request, the web server responds, and the transaction is done. When the client sends a request, the first thing it specifies is an HTTP command, called a *method*, that tells the server the type of action it wants performed. This first line of the request also specifies the address of a document (a URL) and the version of the HTTP protocol it is using. For example:

```
GET /intro.html HTTP/1.0
```

This request uses the GET method to ask for the document named *intro.html*, using HTTP Version 1.0. After sending the request, the client can send optional header information to tell the server extra information about the request, such as what software the client is running and what content types it understands. This information doesn't directly pertain to what was requested, but it could be used by the server in generating its response. Here are some sample request headers:

```
User-Agent: Mozilla/4.0 (compatible; MSIE 4.0; Windows 95)
Accept: image/gif, image/jpeg, text/*, */*
```

The `User-Agent` header provides information about the client software, while the `Accept` header specifies the media (MIME) types that the client prefers to accept. (We'll talk more about request headers in the context of servlets in Chapter 4, *Retrieving Information.*) After the headers, the client sends a blank line, to indicate the end of the header section. The client can also send additional data, if appropriate for the method being used, as it is with the POST method that we'll discuss shortly. If the request doesn't send any data, it ends with an empty line.

After the client sends the request, the server processes it and sends a response. The first line of the response is a status line specifing the version of the HTTP protocol the server is using, a status code, and a description of the status code. For example:

```
HTTP/1.0 200 OK
```

This status line includes a status code of 200, which indicates that the request was successful, hence the description OK. Another common status code is 404, with the description Not Found—as you can guess, this means that the requested document was not found. Chapter 5, *Sending HTML Information,* discusses common status codes and how you can use them in servlets, while Appendix D, *HTTP Status Codes,* provides a complete list of HTTP status codes.

After the status line, the server sends response headers that tell the client things like what software the server is running and the content type of the server's response. For example:

```
Date: Saturday, 23-May-00 03:25:12 GMT
Server: Tomcat Web Server/3.2
MIME-version: 1.0
Content-type: text/html
Content-length: 1029
Last-modified: Thursday, 7-May-00 12:15:35 GMT
```

The `Server` header provides information about the server software, while the `Content-type` header specifies the MIME type of the data included with the response. (We'll also talk more about response headers in Chapter 5.) The server sends a blank line after the headers, to conclude the header section.

If the request was successful, the requested data is then sent as part of the response. Otherwise, the response may contain human-readable data that explains why the server couldn't fulfill the request.

GET and POST

When a client connects to a server and makes an HTTP request, the request can be of several different types, called methods. The most frequently used methods are GET and POST. Put simply, the GET method is designed for getting information (a document, a chart, or the results from a database query), while the POST method is designed for posting information (a credit card number, some new chart data, or information that is to be stored in a database). To use a bulletin board analogy, GET is for reading and POST is for tacking up new material. GET is the method used when you type a URL directly into your browser or click on a hyperlink; either GET or POST can be used when submitting an HTML form.

The GET method, although it's designed for reading information, can include as part of the request some of its own information that better describes what to get—such as an x, y scale for a dynamically created chart. This information is passed as a sequence of characters appended to the request URL in what's called a *query string.* Placing the extra information in the URL in this way allows the page to be bookmarked or emailed like any other. Because GET requests theoretically shouldn't need to send large amounts of information, some servers limit the length of URLs and query strings to about 240 characters.

The POST method uses a different technique to send information to the server because in some cases it may need to send megabytes of information. A POST request passes all its data, of unlimited length, directly over the socket connection as part of its HTTP request body. The exchange is invisible to the client. The URL doesn't change at all. Consequently, POST requests cannot be bookmarked or emailed or, in some cases, even reloaded. That's by design—information sent to the server, such as your credit card number, should be sent only once. POST also provides a bit of extra security when sending sensitive information because the server's access log that records all URL accesses won't record the submitted POST data.

In practice, the use of GET and POST has strayed from the original intent. It's common for long parameterized requests for information to use POST instead of GET to work around problems with overly long URLs. It's also common for simple forms that upload information to use GET because, well—why not, it works! Generally, this isn't much of a problem. Just remember that GET requests, because they can be bookmarked so easily, should not be allowed to cause a change on the server for which the client could be held responsible. In other words, GET requests should not be used to place an order, update a database, or take an explicit client action in any way.

Other Methods

In addition to GET and POST, there are several other lesser-used HTTP methods. There's the HEAD method, which is sent by a client when it wants to see only the headers of the response, to determine the document's size, modification time, or general availability. There's also PUT, to place documents directly on the server, and DELETE, to do just the opposite. These last two aren't widely supported due to complicated policy issues. The TRACE method is used as a debugging aid—it returns to the client the exact contents of its request. Finally, the OPTIONS method can be used to ask the server which methods it supports or what options are available for a particular resource on the server.

The Servlet API

Now that you have a basic understanding of HTTP, we can move on and talk about the Servlet API that you'll be using to create HTTP servlets, or any kind of servlets, for that matter. Servlets use classes and interfaces from two packages: `javax.servlet` and `javax.servlet.http`. The `javax.servlet` package contains classes and interfaces to support generic, protocol-independent servlets. These classes are extended by the classes in the `javax.servlet.http` package to add HTTP-specific functionality. The top-level package name is `javax` instead of the familiar `java`, to indicate that the Servlet API is an *Optional Package* (formerly called a *Standard Extension*).

Every servlet must implement the `javax.servlet.Servlet` interface. Most servlets implement this interface by extending one of two special classes: `javax.servlet.GenericServlet` or `javax.servlet.http.HttpServlet`. A protocol-independent servlet should subclass `GenericServlet`, while an HTTP servlet should subclass `HttpServlet`, which is itself a subclass of `GenericServlet` with added HTTP-specific functionality.

Unlike a regular Java program, and just like an applet, a servlet does not have a `main()` method. Instead, certain methods of a servlet are invoked by the server in the process of handling requests. Each time the server dispatches a request to a servlet, it invokes the servlet's `service()` method.

A generic servlet should override its `service()` method to handle requests as appropriate for the servlet. The `service()` method accepts two parameters: a request object and a response object. The request object tells the servlet about the request, while the response object is used to return a response. Figure 2-1 shows how a generic servlet handles requests.

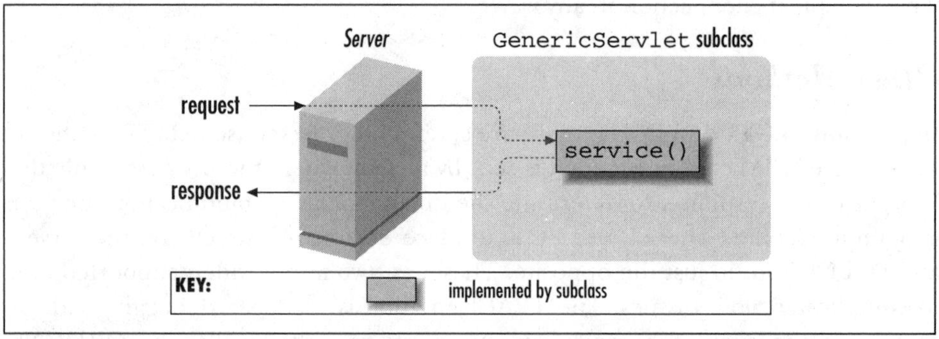

Figure 2-1. A generic servlet handling a request

In contrast, an HTTP servlet usually does not override the `service()` method. Instead, it overrides `doGet()` to handle GET requests and `doPost()` to handle POST requests. An HTTP servlet can override either or both of these methods, depending on the type of requests it needs to handle. The `service()` method of `HttpServlet` handles the setup and dispatching to all the `do`*`XXX`*`()` methods, which is why it usually should not be overridden. Figure 2-2 shows how an HTTP servlet handles GET and POST requests.

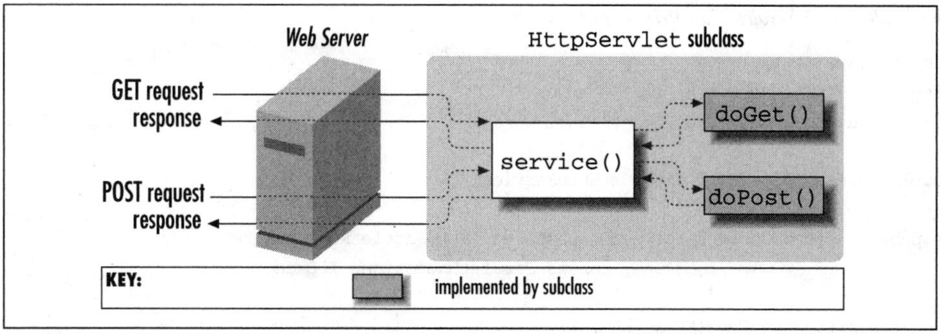

Figure 2-2. An HTTP servlet handling GET and POST requests

An HTTP servlet can override the `doPut()` and `doDelete()` methods to handle PUT and DELETE requests, respectively. However, HTTP servlets generally don't touch `doTrace()` or `doOptions()`. For these, the default implementations are almost always sufficient.

The remainder in the `javax.servlet` and `javax.servlet.http` packages are largely support classes. For example, the `ServletRequest` and `ServletResponse` classes in `javax.servlet` provide access to generic server requests and responses, while `HttpServletRequest` and `HttpServletResponse` in `javax.servlet.http` provide access to HTTP requests and responses. The `javax.servlet.http` package also contains an `HttpSession` class that provides built-in session tracking functionality and a `Cookie` class that allows you to quickly set up and process HTTP cookies.

Page Generation

The most basic type of HTTP servlet generates a full HTML page. Such a servlet has access to the same information usually sent to a CGI script, plus a bit more. A servlet that generates an HTML page can be used for all the tasks for which CGI is used currently, such as for processing HTML forms, producing reports from a database, taking orders, checking identities, and so forth.

Writing Hello World

Example 2-1 shows an HTTP servlet that generates a complete HTML page. To keep things as simple as possible, this servlet just says "Hello World" every time it is accessed via a web browser.*

* Fun trivia: the first instance of a documented "Hello World" program appeared in *A Tutorial Introduction to the Language B,* written by Brian Kernighan in 1973. For those too young to remember, B was a precursor to C. You can find more information on the B programming language and a link to the tutorial at *http://cm.bell-labs.com/who/dmr/bintro.html.*

Example 2-1. A Servlet That Prints "Hello World"

```
import java.io.*;
import javax.servlet.*;
import javax.servlet.http.*;

public class HelloWorld extends HttpServlet {

  public void doGet(HttpServletRequest req, HttpServletResponse res)
                               throws ServletException, IOException {

    res.setContentType("text/html");
    PrintWriter out = res.getWriter();

    out.println("<HTML>");
    out.println("<HEAD><TITLE>Hello World</TITLE></HEAD>");
    out.println("<BODY>");
    out.println("<BIG>Hello World</BIG>");
    out.println("</BODY></HTML>");
  }
}
```

This servlet extends the `HttpServlet` class and overrides the `doGet()` method inherited from it. Each time the web server receives a GET request for this servlet, the server invokes this `doGet()` method, passing it an `HttpServletRequest` object and an `HttpServletResponse` object.

The `HttpServletRequest` represents the client's request. This object gives a servlet access to information about the client, the parameters for this request, the HTTP headers passed along with the request, and so forth. Chapter 4 explains the full capabilities of the request object. For this example, we can completely ignore it. After all, this servlet is going to say "Hello World" no matter what the request!

The `HttpServletResponse` represents the servlet's response. A servlet can use this object to return data to the client. This data can be of any content type, though the type should be specified as part of the response. A servlet can also use this object to set HTTP response headers. Chapter 5 and Chapter 6, *Sending Multimedia Content*, explain everything a servlet can do as part of its response.

Our servlet first uses the `setContentType()` method of the response object to set the content type of its response to `text/html`, the standard MIME content type for HTML pages. Then, it uses the `getWriter()` method to retrieve a `PrintWriter`, the international-friendly counterpart to a `PrintStream`. `PrintWriter` converts Java's Unicode characters to a locale-specific encoding. For an English locale, it behaves the same as a `PrintStream`. Finally, the servlet uses this `PrintWriter` to send its `HelloWorld` HTML to the client.

That's it! That's all the code needed to say hello to everyone who "surfs" to our servlet.

Running Hello World

When developing servlets you need two things: the Servlet API class files, which are used for compiling, and a servlet container such as a web server, which is used for running the servlets. All popular servlet containers provide the Servlet API class files so you can satisfy both requirements with one download.

There are dozens of servlet containers available for servlet deployment, several of which are listed in Chapter 1, *Introduction.* Just be sure when selecting a server to find one that supports Version 2.2 of the Servlet API or later. This was the first Servlet API version to provide support for web applications as discussed in this chapter. A current list of servlet containers and what API level they support is available at *http://www.servlets.com.*

So, what do we do with our code to make it run in a web server? Well, it depends on the web server. The examples in this book use the Apache Tomcat 3.2 server, the Servlet API reference implementation, written entirely in Java and available under an open source license from *http://jakarta.apache.org.* The Tomcat server includes plenty of documentation explaining the use of the server, so while we discuss the general concepts involved with managing the server, we're leaving the details to the server's own documentation. If you choose to use another web server, these instructions should work for you, but we cannot make any guarantees.

If you are using the Apache Tomcat server, you should put the source code for the servlet in the *server_root/webapps/ROOT/WEB-INF/classes* directory (where *server_root* is the directory where you installed your server). This is a standard location for servlet class files. We'll talk about the reason servlets go in this directory later in the chapter.

Once you have the `HelloWorld` source code in the right location, you need to compile it. The standard *javac* compiler (or your favorite graphical Java development environment) can do the job. Just be sure you have the `javax.servlet` and `javax.servlet.http` packages in your classpath. With the Tomcat server, all you have to do is include *server_root/lib/servlet.jar* (or a future equivalent) somewhere in your classpath. The filename and location is server dependent, so look to your server's documentation if you have problems. If you see an error message that says something like `Package javax.servlet not found in import` that means the servlet packages aren't being found by your compiler; fix your classpath and try again.

Now that you have your first servlet compiled, there is nothing more to do but start your server and access the servlet! Starting the server is easy. Look for the *startup.sh* script (or *startup.bat* batch file under Windows) in the *server_root/bin* directory. This should start your server if you're running under Solaris or Windows. On other operating systems, you may need to make small edits to the startup scripts. In the default configuration, the server listens on port 8080.

There are several ways to access a servlet. For this example, we'll do it by explicitly accessing a URL with */servlet/* prepended to the servlet's class name. You can enter this URL in your favorite browser: *http://`server`:8080/servlet/HelloWorld.* Replace *`server`* with the name of your server machine or with `localhost` if the server is on your local machine. You should see a page similar to the one shown in Figure 2-3.

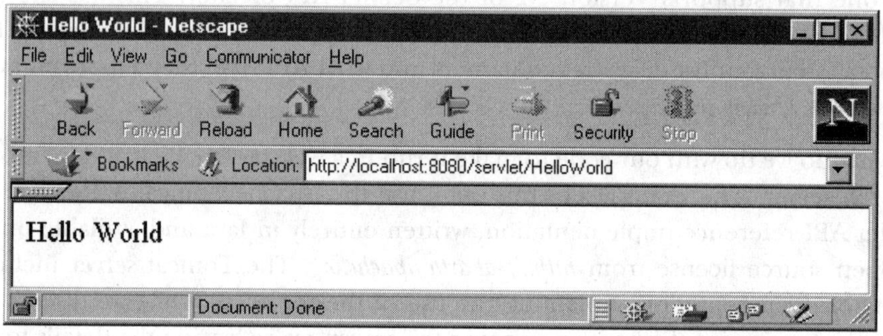

Figure 2-3. The Hello World servlet

If the servlet were part of a package, it would need to be placed in *server_root/webapps/ROOT/WEB-INF/package/name* and referred to with the URL *http://`server`:8080/servlet/package.name.HelloWorld.*

Not all servers by default allow servlets to be accessed using the generic */servlet/* prefix. This feature may be turned off for security reasons, to ensure servlets are accessed only via specific URLs set up during the server administration. Check your server's documentation for details on how to turn on and off the */servlet/* prefix.

Handling Form Data

The "Hello World" servlet is not very exciting, so let's try something slightly more ambitious. This time we'll create a servlet that greets the user by name. It's not hard. First, we need an HTML form that asks the user for his or her name. The following page should suffice:

```
<HTML>
<HEAD>
<TITLE>Introductions</TITLE>
</HEAD>
```

```
<BODY>
<FORM METHOD=GET ACTION="/servlet/Hello">
If you don't mind me asking, what is your name?
<INPUT TYPE=TEXT NAME="name"><P>
<INPUT TYPE=SUBMIT>
</FORM>
</BODY>
</HTML>
```

Figure 2-4 shows how this page appears to the user.

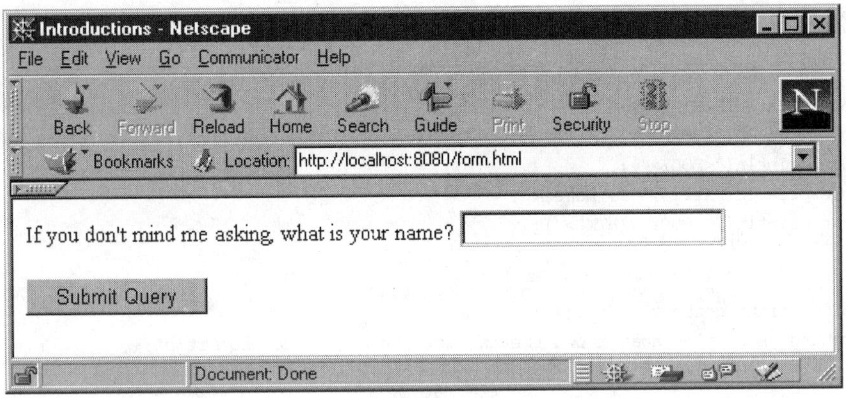

Figure 2-4. An HTML form

This form should go in an HTML file under the server's *document_root* directory. This is the location where the server looks for static files to serve. For the Tomcat server, this directory is *server_root/webapps/ROOT*. By putting the file in this directory, it can be accessed directly as *http://*`server`*:8080/form.html*.

When the user submits this form, his name is sent to the Hello servlet because we've set the ACTION attribute to point to the servlet. The form is using the GET method, so any data is appended to the request URL as a query string. For example, if the user enters the name "Inigo Montoya," the request URL is *http://*`server`*:8080/servlet/Hello?name=Inigo+Montoya*. The space in the name is specially encoded as a plus sign by the browser because URLs cannot contain spaces.

A servlet's `HttpServletRequest` object gives it access to the form data in its query string. Example 2-2 shows a modified version of our `Hello` servlet that uses its request object to read the `name` parameter.

Example 2-2. A Servlet That Knows to Whom It's Saying Hello

```
import java.io.*;
import javax.servlet.*;
import javax.servlet.http.*;

public class Hello extends HttpServlet {

  public void doGet(HttpServletRequest req, HttpServletResponse res)
                               throws ServletException, IOException {

    res.setContentType("text/html");
    PrintWriter out = res.getWriter();

    String name = req.getParameter("name");
    out.println("<HTML>");
    out.println("<HEAD><TITLE>Hello, " + name + "</TITLE></HEAD>");
    out.println("<BODY>");
    out.println("Hello, " + name);
    out.println("</BODY></HTML>");
  }

  public String getServletInfo() {
    return "A servlet that knows the name of the person to whom it's" +
           "saying hello";
  }
}
```

This servlet is nearly identical to the `HelloWorld` servlet. The most important change is that it now calls `req.getParameter("name")` to find out the name of the user and that it then prints this name instead of the harshly impersonal (not to mention overly broad) "World." The `getParameter()` method gives a servlet access to the parameters in its query string. It returns the parameter's decoded value or `null` if the parameter was not specified. If the parameter was sent but without a value, as in the case of an empty form field, `getParameter()` returns the empty string.

This servlet also adds a `getServletInfo()` method. A servlet can override this method to return descriptive information about itself, such as its purpose, author, version, and/or copyright. It's akin to an applet's `getAppletInfo()`. The method is used primarily for putting explanatory information into a web server administration tool. You'll notice we won't bother to include it in future examples because it is clutter in the way of learning.

The servlet's output looks something like what is shown in Figure 2-5.

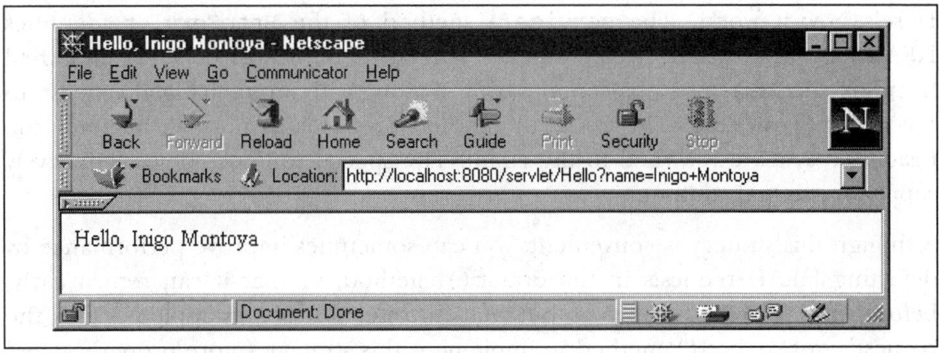

Figure 2-5. The Hello servlet using form data

Handling POST Requests

You've now seen two servlets that implement the doGet() method. Now let's change our Hello servlet so that it can handle POST requests as well. Because we want the same behavior with POST as we had for GET, we can simply dispatch all POST requests to the doGet() method with the following code:

```
public void doPost(HttpServletRequest req, HttpServletResponse res)
                              throws ServletException, IOException {
  doGet(req, res);
}
```

Now the Hello servlet can handle form submissions that use the POST method:

```
<FORM METHOD=POST ACTION="/servlet/Hello">
```

In general, it is best if a servlet implements either doGet() or doPost(). Deciding which to implement depends on what sort of requests the servlet needs to be able to handle, as discussed earlier. The code you write to implement the methods is almost identical. The major difference is that doPost() has the added ability to accept large amounts of input.

You may be wondering what would have happened had the Hello servlet been accessed with a POST request before we implemented doPost(). The default behavior inherited from HttpServlet for both doGet() and doPost() is to return an error to the client saying the requested URL does not support that method.

Handling HEAD Requests

A bit of under-the-covers magic makes it trivial to handle HEAD requests (sent by a client when it wants to see only the headers of the response). There is no doHead() method to write. Any servlet that subclasses HttpServlet and implements the doGet() method automatically supports HEAD requests.

Here's how it works. The `service()` method of the `HttpServlet` identifies HEAD requests and treats them specially. It constructs a modified `HttpServletResponse` object and passes it, along with an unchanged request, to the `doGet()` method. The `doGet()` method proceeds as normal, but only the headers it sets are returned to the client. The special response object effectively suppresses all body output.

Although this strategy is convenient, you can sometimes improve performance by detecting HEAD requests in the `doGet()` method, so that it can return early, before wasting cycles writing output that no one will see. Example 2-3 uses the request's `getMethod()` method to implement this strategy (more properly called a *hack*) in our `Hello` servlet.

Example 2-3. The Hello Servlet Modified to Return Quickly in Response to HEAD Requests

```
import java.io.*;
import javax.servlet.*;
import javax.servlet.http.*;

public class Hello extends HttpServlet {
  public void doGet(HttpServletRequest req, HttpServletResponse res)
                               throws ServletException, IOException {

    // Set the Content-Type header
    res.setContentType("text/html");

    // Return early if this is a HEAD
    if (req.getMethod().equals("HEAD")) return;

    // Proceed otherwise
    PrintWriter out = res.getWriter();
    String name = req.getParameter("name");
    out.println("<HTML>");
    out.println("<HEAD><TITLE>Hello, " + name + "</TITLE></HEAD>");
    out.println("<BODY>");
    out.println("Hello, " + name);
    out.println("</BODY></HTML>");
  }
}
```

Notice that we set the `Content-Type` header, even if we are dealing with a HEAD request. Headers such as these are returned to the client. Some header values, such as `Content-Length`, may not be available until the response has already been calculated. If you want to be accurate in returning these header values, the effectiveness of this shortcut is limited.

Make sure that you end the request handling with a return statement. Do not call `System.exit()`. If you do, you risk exiting the web server.

Web Applications

A *web application* (sometimes shortened to *web app*) is a collection of servlets, JavaServer Pages (JSPs), HTML documents, images, templates, and other web resources that are set up in such a way as to be portably deployed across any servlet-enabled web server. By having everyone agree on exactly where files in a web application are to be placed and agreeing on a standard configuration file format, a web app can be transferred from one server to another easily without requiring any extra server administration. Gone are the days of detailed instruction sheets telling you how to install third-party web components, with different instructions for each type of web server.

All the files under *server_root/webapps/ROOT* belong to a single web application (the root one). To simplify deployment, these files can be bundled into a single archive file and deployed to another server merely by placing the archive file into a specific directory. These archive files have the extension *.war*, which stands for *web application archive*. WAR files are actually JAR files (created using the *jar* utility) saved with an alternate extension. Using the JAR format allows WAR files to be stored in compressed form and have their contents digitally signed. The *.war* file extension was chosen over *.jar* to let people and tools know to treat them differently.

The file structure inside a web app is strictly defined. Example 2-4 shows a possible file listing.

Example 2-4. The File Structure Inside a Web Application

```
index.html
feedback.jsp
images/banner.gif
images/jumping.gif
WEB-INF/web.xml
WEB-INF/lib/bhawk4j.jar
WEB-INF/classes/MyServlet.class
WEB-INF/classes/com/mycorp/frontend/CorpServlet.class
WEB-INF/classes/com/mycorp/frontend/SupportClass.class
```

This hierarchy can be maintained as separate files under some server directory or they can be bundled together into a WAR file. On install, this web application can be mapped to any URI prefix path on the server. The web application then handles all requests beginning with that prefix. For example, if the preceding file structure were installed under the prefix */demo*, the server would use this web app to handle all requests beginning with */demo*. A request for */demo/index.html* would serve the *index.html* file from the web app. A request for */demo/feedback.jsp* or */demo/images/banner.gif* would also serve content from the web app.

The WEB-INF Directory

The *WEB-INF* directory is special. The files there are not served directly to the client; instead, they contain Java classes and configuration information for the web app. The directory behaves like a JAR file's *META-INF* directory: it contains meta-information about the archive contents.

The *WEB-INF/classes* directory contains the class files for this web app's servlets and support classes. *WEB-INF/lib* contains classes stored in JAR files. For convenience, server class loaders automatically look to *WEB-INF/classes* and *WEB-INF/lib* when loading classes—no extra install steps are necessary.

The servlets in this web app can be invoked using URIs like */demo/servlet/MyServlet* and */demo/servlet/com.mycorp.frontend.CorpServlet*. Notice how every request for this web app begins with */demo*, even requests for servlets.

With the Tomcat server, *server_root/webapps/ROOT* is the default context mapped to the root path "/". This means that servlets placed under *server_root/webapps/ROOT/WEB-INF/classes* can be accessed, as we saw earlier, using the path */servlet/HelloWorld*. With Tomcat, this default context mapping can be changed and new mappings can be added by editing the *server_root/conf/server.xml* serverwide configuration file. Other servers configure mappings in different ways; see your server's documentation for details.

The *web.xml* file in the *WEB-INF* directory is known as a *deployment descriptor*. This file contains configuration information about the web app in which it resides. It's an XML file with a standardized DTD. The DTD contains more than 50 tags, allowing full control over the web app's behavior. The deployment descriptor file controls servlet registration, URL mappings, welcome files, and MIME types, as well as advanced features like page-level security constraints and how a servlet should behave in a distributed environment. We'll discuss the contents of this file throughout the book. The full annotated DTD is available in Appendix C, *Deployment Descriptor DTD Reference*.

The structure of the *web.xml* file is not in itself important at this point; what's important is the fact that having a deployment descriptor file allows configuration information to be specified in a server-independent manner, greatly simplifying the deployment process. Because of deployment descriptors, not only are simple servlets portable, but you can now transfer whole self-contained subsections of your site between servers.

Over time it's likely that a commercial market for WAR files will develop. WAR files will become pluggable web components, capable of being downloaded and installed and put to work right away—no matter what your operating system or web server.

XML and DTDs

XML stands for Extensible Markup Language.[a] It's a universal syntax for structuring data, created as an activity of the World Wide Web Consortium (W3C) beginning in 1996. Since its standardization early in 1998 it has taken the Web by storm.

XML is similar to HTML in that both take content and "mark it up" using tags that begin and end with angle brackets, such as `<title>` and `</title>`. XML serves a different purpose than HTML, however. The tags in an XML document don't define how the text should be displayed but rather explain the meaning of the text. It's an "extensible" markup language because new tags can be created with their own meaning, as appropriate for the document being written. XML works especially well as a flat file format because it's a standard, well-defined, platform-independent technique for describing hierarchical data, and there are numerous tools to support the reading, writing, and manipulation of XML files.

The rules for writing XML are more strict than for HTML. First, XML tags are case sensitive. `<servlet>` and `<SERVLET>` are not the same. Second, all tags that begin must end. If there's a begin tag `<servlet>` there must be an end tag `</servlet>`—although for convenience the empty tag syntax `<servlet/>` may be substituted as a synonym for an immediate begin and end tag pairing `<servlet></servlet>`. Third, nested elements must not overlap. So it's legal to have `<outside><inside>data</inside></outside>` while it's illegal to have `<outside><inside>data</outside></inside>`. Fourth and finally, all attribute values must be surrounded by quotes, either single or double. This means `<servlet id="0"/>` is fine while `<servlet id=0/>` is not. Documents that follow these rules are called *well-formed* and will be successfully parsed by automated tools.

Beyond these rules, there are ways to explicitly declare a structure for the tags within an XML file. A specification of this sort is called a Document Type Definition, or DTD. A DTD explicitly states what tags are allowed in a compliant XML file, what type of data those tags are to contain, as well as where in the hierarchy the tags can (or must) be placed. Each XML file can be declared to follow a certain DTD. Files that perfectly conform to their declared DTD are called *valid*.

XML is used with servlets as the storage format for configuration files. XML also can be used by servlets to help with content creation, as described in Chapter 17, *XMLC*.

For more information on XML, see *http://www.w3.org/XML/* and the book *Java and XML* by Brett McLaughlin (O'Reilly).

---

a. XML was nearly named MAGMA. See *http://www.xml.com/axml/notes/TheCorrectTitle.html*.

Deployment descriptors also provide web-hosting companies with a convenient way to support multiple customers on the same server. Customers can be given control over their individual domains. They can individually manage servlet registration, URL mappings, MIME types, and page-level security constraints—without needing general access to the web server.

The Deployment Descriptor

A simple deployment descriptor file is shown in Example 2-5. For this file to describe Tomcat's default web application, it should be placed in *server_root/webapps/ROOT/WEB-INF/web.xml.*

Example 2-5. A Simple Deployment Descriptor

```
<?xml version="1.0" encoding="ISO-8859-1"?>

<!DOCTYPE web-app
    PUBLIC "-//Sun Microsystems, Inc.//DTD Web Application 2.2//EN"
    "http://java.sun.com/j2ee/dtds/web-app_2_2.dtd">

<web-app>
    <servlet>
        <servlet-name>
            hi
        </servlet-name>
        <servlet-class>
            HelloWorld
        </servlet-class>
    </servlet>
</web-app>
```

The first line declares this is an XML 1.0 file containing characters from the standard ISO-8859-1 (Latin-1) charset. The second line specifies the DTD for the file, allowing a tool reading the file to verify the file is *valid* and conforms to the DTD's rules. All deployment descriptor files begin with these two lines or very similar ones.

The rest of the text, everything between <web-app> and </web-app>, provides information to the server about this web application. This simple example registers our HelloWorld servlet under the name hi (surrounding whitespace is trimmed). The registered name is held between the <servlet-name> tags; the class name is placed within the <servlet-class> tags. The <servlet> tag holds the <servlet-name> and <servlet-class> tags together. It's true that the deployment descriptor's XML syntax appears better optimized for automated reading than direct human authoring. For this reason most commercial server vendors provide graphical tools to help the *web.xml* creation process. There also are several XML editors on the market that help with XML creation.

Watch Out for Tag Order

Beware that the tags in a *web.xml* are order dependent. For example, the `<servlet-name>` tag must come before `<servlet-class>` to ensure everything works. This is the order in which they are declared in the DTD. Validating parsers will enforce this ordering and will declare the document invalid if elements are out of order. Some servers, even without validating parsers, may simply expect this ordering and may get confused with any other ordering. To be safe, ensure all `<web-app>` tags are placed in the proper order. Some tags are optional, but every tag that is present must be placed in the proper order. Fortunately, tools help simplify this task. See the DTD in Appendix C for more information.

After this registration, upon restarting the server, we can access the `HelloWorld` servlet at the URL *http://*`server`*:8080/servlet/hi*. You may wonder why anyone would bother registering a servlet under a special name. The short answer is that it allows the server to remember things about the servlet and give it special treatment.

One example of such special treatment is that we can set up URL patterns that will invoke the registered servlet. The requested URL may look to the client like any other URL; however, the server can then detect that the request matches a given pattern mapping and thus should be handled by a particular servlet. For example, we can choose to have *http://*`server`*:8080/hello.html* invoke the `HelloWorld` servlet. Using servlet mappings in this way can help hide a site's use of servlets. It also lets a servlet seamlessly replace an existing page at any given URL, so all bookmarks and links to the page continue to work.

URL patterns are configured using the deployment descriptor, as shown in Example 2-6.

Example 2-6. Adding a Servlet Mapping

```
<?xml version="1.0" encoding="ISO-8859-1"?>

<!DOCTYPE web-app
    PUBLIC "-//Sun Microsystems, Inc.//DTD Web Application 2.2//EN"
    "http://java.sun.com/j2ee/dtds/web-app_2_2.dtd">

<web-app>
    <servlet>
        <servlet-name>
```

Example 2-6. Adding a Servlet Mapping (continued)

```
            hi
        </servlet-name>
        <servlet-class>
            HelloWorld
        </servlet-class>
    </servlet>
    <servlet-mapping>
        <servlet-name>
            hi
        </servlet-name>
        <url-pattern>
            /hello.html
        </url-pattern>
    </servlet-mapping>
</web-app>
```

This deployment descriptor adds a `<servlet-mapping>` entry indicating to the server that the servlet named `hi` should handle all URLs matching the pattern */hello.html*. If this web app is mapped to the root path "/", this lets the `HelloWorld` servlet handle requests for *http://*`server`*:8080/hello.html*. If the web app is instead mapped to the prefix path */greeting*, the `Hello` servlet will handle requests made to *http://*`server`*:8080/greeting/hello.html*.

Various URL mapping rules can be specified in the deployment descriptor. There are four types of mappings, searched in the following order:

- Explicit mappings, like */hello.html* or */images/chart.gif*, containing no wildcards. This mapping style is useful when replacing an existing page.
- Path prefix mappings, such as */lite/**, */dbfile/**, or */catalog/item/**. These mappings begin with a /, end with a /*, and handle all requests beginning with that prefix (not counting the context path). This mapping style allows a servlet to control an entire virtual hierarchy. For example, the servlet handling */dbfile/** may serve files from a database, while the servlet handling */lite/** may serve files from the filesystem automatically gzipped.
- Extension mappings, such as **.wm* or **.jsp*. These mappings begin with a * and handle all requests ending with that prefix. This mapping style lets a servlet operate on all files of a given extension. For example, a servlet can be assigned to handle files ending in **.jsp* to support JavaServer Pages. (In fact, this is an implicit mapping mandated by the servlet specification.)
- The default mapping, /. This mapping specifies the default servlet for the web app, to be used if no other matches occur. It's identical to the reduced path prefix mapping (/*) except this mapping matches after extension mappings. This gives control over how basic files are served—a powerful ability, but one that should not be used lightly.

When there's a collision between mappings, exact matches take precedence over path prefix matches, and path prefix matches take precedence over extension matches. The default mapping is invoked only if no other matches occur. Longer string matches within a category take precedence over shorter matches within a category.

The deployment descriptor snippet in Example 2-7 shows various mappings that can be used to access the `HelloWorld` servlet.

Example 2-7. So Many Ways to Say Hello

```
<!-- ... -->
<servlet-mapping>
    <servlet-name>
        hi
    </servlet-name>
    <url-pattern>
        /hello.html
    </url-pattern>
</servlet-mapping>
<servlet-mapping>
    <servlet-name>
        hi
    </servlet-name>
    <url-pattern>
        *.hello
    </url-pattern>
</servlet-mapping>
<servlet-mapping>
    <servlet-name>
        hi
    </servlet-name>
    <url-pattern>
        /hello/*
    </url-pattern>
</servlet-mapping>
<!-- ... -->
```

With these mappings, the `HelloWorld` servlet can be invoked using any of the following list:

```
/servlet/HelloWorld
/servlet/hi
/hello.html
/well.hello
/fancy/meeting/you/here.hello
/hello/to/you
```

We'll see more practical servlet mappings throughout the rest of the book.

Moving On

We realize this chapter has been a whirlwind introduction to servlets, web applications, and XML configuration files. By now, we hope you have an idea of how to write a simple servlet, install it on your server, and tell the server the paths for which you want it to be executed. Of course, servlets can do far more than say "Hello World" and greet users by name. Now that you've got your feet wet, we can dive into the details and move on to more interesting applications.

In this chapter:

- *The Servlet Alternative*
- *Servlet Reloading*
- *Init and Destroy*
- *Single-Thread Model*
- *Background Processing*
- *Load on Startup*
- *Client-Side Caching*
- *Server-Side Caching*

3

The Servlet Lifecycle

The servlet lifecycle is one of the most exciting features of servlets. This lifecycle is a powerful hybrid of the lifecycles used by CGI programming and lower-level WAI/NSAPI and ISAPI programming, as discussed in Chapter 1, *Introduction.*

The Servlet Alternative

The servlet lifecycle allows servlet containers to address both the performance and resource problems of CGI and the security concerns of low-level server API programming. A common way to execute servlets is for the servlet container to run all its servlets in a single Java Virtual Machine (JVM). By placing all the servlets into the same JVM, the servlets can efficiently share data with one another, yet they are prevented by the Java language from accessing one another's private data. Servlets can persist between requests inside the JVM as object instances. This takes up far less memory than full-fledged processes, yet servlets still are able to efficiently maintain references to external resources.

The servlet lifecycle is highly flexible. The only hard and fast rule is that a servlet container must conform to the following lifecycle contract:

1. Create and initialize the servlet.
2. Handle zero or more service calls from clients.
3. Destroy the servlet and then garbage collect it.

It's perfectly legal for a servlet to be loaded, created, and instantiated in its own JVM, only to be destroyed and garbage collected without handling any client requests or after handling just one request. Any servlet container that makes this a habit, however, probably won't last long on the open market. In this chapter we describe the most common and most sensible lifecycle implementations for HTTP servlets.

A Single Java Virtual Machine

Most servlet containers want to execute all servlets in a single JVM to maximize the ability of servlets to share information. (The exception being high-end containers that support distributed servlet execution across multiple backend servers, as discussed in Chapter 12, *Enterprise Servlets and J2EE*.) Where that single JVM executes can differ depending on the server:

- With a server written in Java, such as the Apache Tomcat server, the server itself can execute inside a JVM right alongside its servlets.
- With a single-process, multithreaded web server written in another language, the JVM can often be embedded inside the server process. Having the JVM be part of the server process maximizes performance because a servlet becomes, in a sense, just another low-level server API extension. Such a server can invoke a servlet with a lightweight context switch and can provide information about requests through direct method invocations.
- A multiprocess web server (which runs several processes to handle requests) doesn't really have the choice to embed a JVM directly in its process because there is no one process. This kind of server usually runs an external JVM that its processes can share. With this approach, each servlet access involves a heavyweight context switch reminiscent of FastCGI. All the servlets, however, still share the same external process.

Fortunately, from the perspective of the servlet (and thus from your perspective, as a servlet author), the server's implementation doesn't really matter because the server always behaves the same way.

Instance Persistence

We said earlier that servlets persist between requests as object instances. In other words, at the time the code for a servlet is loaded, the server creates a single instance. That single instance handles every request made of the servlet. This improves performance in three ways:

- It keeps the memory footprint small.
- It eliminates the object creation overhead that would otherwise be necessary to create a new servlet object. A servlet can already be loaded in a virtual machine when a request comes in, letting it begin executing right away.
- It enables persistence. A servlet can have already loaded anything it's likely to need during the handling of a request. For example, a database connection

can be opened once and used repeatedly thereafter. The connection can even be used by a group of servlets. Another example is a shopping cart servlet that loads in memory the price list along with information about its recently connected clients. Yet another servlet may choose to cache entire pages of output to save time if it receives the same request again.

Not only do servlets persist between requests, but so do any threads created by servlets. This perhaps isn't useful for the run-of-the-mill servlet, but it opens up some interesting possibilities. Consider the situation in which one background thread performs some calculation while other threads display the latest results. It's quite similar to an animation applet in which one thread changes the picture and another one paints the display.

A Simple Counter

To demonstrate the servlet lifecycle, we'll begin with a simple example. Example 3-1 shows a servlet that counts and displays the number of times it has been accessed. For simplicity's sake, it outputs plain text. (Remember, the code for all the examples is available online. See the Preface.)

Example 3-1. A Simple Counter

```
import java.io.*;
import javax.servlet.*;
import javax.servlet.http.*;

public class SimpleCounter extends HttpServlet {

  int count = 0;

  public void doGet(HttpServletRequest req, HttpServletResponse res)
                               throws ServletException, IOException {
    res.setContentType("text/plain");
    PrintWriter out = res.getWriter();
    count++;
    out.println("Since loading, this servlet has been accessed " +
                count + " times.");
  }
}
```

The code is simple—it just prints and increments the instance variable named count—but it shows the power of persistence. When the server loads this servlet, the server creates a single instance to handle every request made of the servlet. That's why this code can be so simple. The same instance variables exist between invocations and for all invocations.

A Simple Synchronized Counter

From the servlet developer's perspective, each client is another thread that calls the servlet via the `service()`, `doGet()`, or `doPost()` methods, as shown in Figure 3-1.*

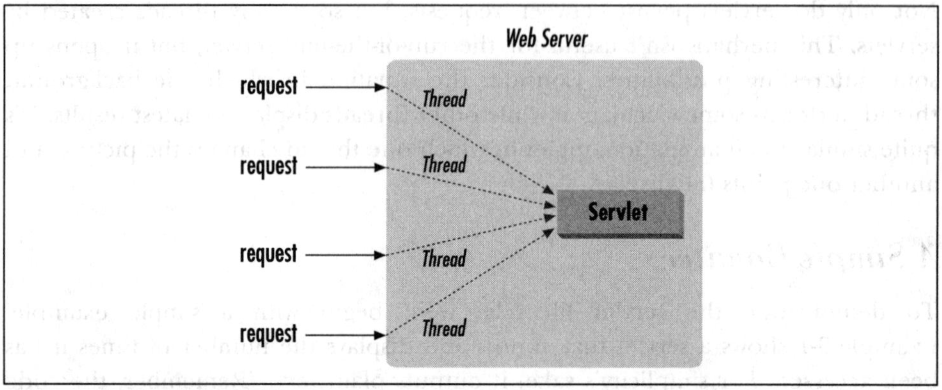

Figure 3-1. Many threads, one servlet instance

If your servlets only read from the request, write to the response, and save information in local variables (that is, variables declared within a method), you needn't worry about the interaction among these threads. Once any information is saved in nonlocal variables (that is, variables declared within a class but outside any specific method), however, you must be aware that each of these client threads has the ability to manipulate a servlet's nonlocal variables. Without precautions, this may result in data corruption and inconsistencies. For example, the `SimpleCounter` servlet makes a false assumption that the counter incrementation and output occur atomically (immediately after one another, uninterrupted). It's possible that if two requests are made to `SimpleCounter` around the same time, each will print the same value for `count`. How? Imagine that one thread increments the count and just afterward, before the first thread prints the count, the second thread also increments the count. Each thread will print the same count value, after effectively increasing its value by 2.†

---

* Does it seem confusing how one servlet instance can handle multiple requests at the same time? If so, it's probably because when we picture an executing program we often see object instances performing the work, invoking one another's methods and so on. But, although this model works for simple cases, it's not how things actually work. In reality, all real work is done by threads. The object instances are nothing more than data structures manipulated by the threads. Therefore, if there are two threads running, it's entirely possible that both are using the same object at the same time.

† Odd factoid: if `count` were a 64-bit `long` instead of a 32-bit `int`, it would be theoretically possible for the increment to be only half-performed at the time it is interrupted by another thread. This is because Java uses a 32-bit-wide stack.

The order of execution goes something like this:

```
count++            // Thread 1

count++            // Thread 2

out.println        // Thread 1

out.println        // Thread 2
```

Now, in this case, the inconsistency is not a real problem, but many other servlets have more serious opportunities for errors. To prevent these types of problems and the inconsistencies that come with them, we can add one or more synchronized blocks to the code. Anything inside a synchronized block or a synchronized method is guaranteed not to be executed concurrently by another thread. Before any thread begins to execute synchronized code, it must obtain a *monitor* (*lock*) on a specified object instance. If another thread already has that monitor—because it is already executing the same synchronized block or some other block with the same monitor—the first thread must wait. The whole thing works like a gas station bathroom with the door key (generally attached to a large wooden plank) as the monitor. All this is handled by the language itself, so it's very easy to use. Synchronization, however, should be used only when necessary. On some platforms, it requires a fair amount of overhead to obtain the monitor each time a synchronized block is entered. More importantly, during the time one thread is executing synchronized code, the other threads may be blocked waiting for the monitor to be released.

For `SimpleCounter`, we have four options to deal with this potential problem. First, we could add the keyword synchronized to the `doGet()` signature:

```
public synchronized void doGet(HttpServletRequest req,
                               HttpServletResponse res)
```

This guarantees consistency by synchronizing the entire method, using the servlet instance as the monitor. In general, though, this is not the right approach because it means the servlet can handle only one GET request at a time.

Our second option is to synchronize just the two lines we want to execute atomically:

```
PrintWriter out = res.getWriter();
synchronized(this) {
  count++;
  out.println("Since loading, this servlet has been accessed " +
              count + " times.");
}
```

This approach works better because it limits the amount of time this servlet spends in its synchronized block, while accomplishing the same goal of a consistent count. Of course, for this simple example, it isn't much different than the first option.

Our third option is to create a synchronized block that performs all the work that needs to be done serially, then to use the results outside the synchronized block. For our counter servlet, we can increment the count in a synchronized block, save the incremented value to a local variable (a variable declared inside a method), then print the value of the local variable outside the synchronized block:

```
PrintWriter out = res.getWriter();
int local_count;
synchronized(this) {
  local_count = ++count;
}
out.println("Since loading, this servlet has been accessed " +
            local_count + " times.");
```

This change shrinks the synchronized block to be as small as possible, while still maintaining a consistent count.

Our last option is to decide that we are willing to suffer the consequences of ignoring synchronization issues. Sometimes the consequences are quite acceptable. For this example, ignoring synchronization means that some clients may receive a count that's a bit off. Not a big deal, really. If this servlet were supposed to return unique numbers, however, it would be a different story.

Although it's not possible with this example, an option that exists for other servlets is to change instance variables into local variables. Local variables are not available to other threads and thus don't need to be carefully protected from corruption. At the same time, however, local variables are not persistent between requests, so we can't use them to store the persistent state of our counter.

A Holistic Counter

Now, the "one-instance-per-servlet" model is a bit of a gloss-over. The truth is that each registered name (but not each URL pattern match) for a servlet is associated with one instance of the servlet. The name used to access the servlet determines which instance handles the request. This makes sense because the impression to the client should be that differently named servlets operate independently. The separate instances are also a requirement for servlets that accept initialization parameters, as discussed later in this chapter.

Our `SimpleCounter` example uses the count instance variable to track the number of times it has been accessed. If, instead, it needed to track the count for all instances (and thus all registered names), it can use a class, or static, variable.

These variables are shared across all instances of a class. Example 3-2 demonstrates with a servlet that counts three things: the times it has been accessed, the number of instances created by the server (one per name), and the total times all of them have been accessed.

Example 3-2. A More Holistic Counter

```
import java.io.*;
import java.util.*;
import javax.servlet.*;
import javax.servlet.http.*;

public class HolisticCounter extends HttpServlet {

  static int classCount = 0;  // shared by all instances
  int count = 0;              // separate for each servlet
  static Hashtable instances = new Hashtable();  // also shared

  public void doGet(HttpServletRequest req, HttpServletResponse res)
                               throws ServletException, IOException {
    res.setContentType("text/plain");
    PrintWriter out = res.getWriter();

    count++;
    out.println("Since loading, this servlet instance has been accessed " +
                count + " times.");

    // Keep track of the instance count by putting a reference to this
    // instance in a hashtable. Duplicate entries are ignored.
    // The size() method returns the number of unique instances stored.
    instances.put(this, this);
    out.println("There are currently " +
                instances.size() + " instances.");

    classCount++;
    out.println("Across all instances, this servlet class has been " +
                "accessed " + classCount + " times.");
  }
}
```

This `HolisticCounter` tracks its own access count with the `count` instance variable, the shared count with the `classCount` class variable, and the number of instances with the `instances` hashtable (another shared resource that must be a class variable). Sample output is shown in Figure 3-2.

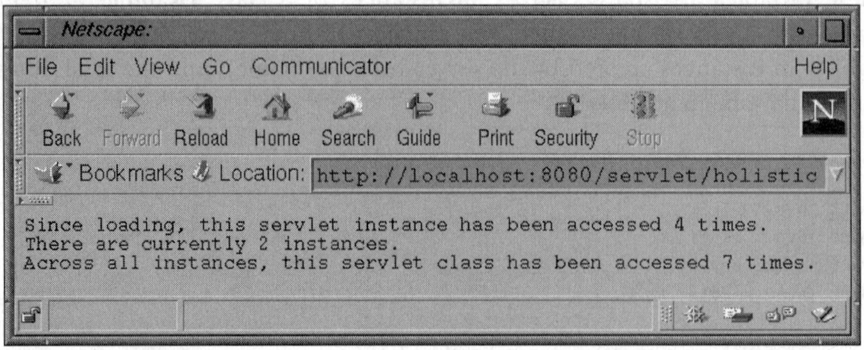

Figure 3-2. Output from HolisticCounter

Servlet Reloading

If you tried using these counters for yourself, you may have noticed that any time you recompiled one, its count automatically began again at 1. Trust us—it's not a bug, it's a feature. Most servers automatically reload a servlet after its class file (under the default servlet directory, such as *WEB-INF/classes*) changes. It's an on-the-fly upgrade procedure that greatly speeds up the development-test cycle—and allows for long server uptimes.

Servlet reloading may appear to be a simple feature, but it's quite a trick—and requires quite a hack. `ClassLoader` objects are designed to load a class just once. To get around this limitation and load servlets again and again, servers use custom class loaders that load servlets from special directories such as *WEB-INF/classes*.

When a server dispatches a request to a servlet, it first checks whether the servlet's class file has changed on disk. If it has changed, the server abandons the class loader used to load the old version and creates a new instance of the custom class loader to load the new version. Some servers improve performance by checking modification timestamps only after some timeout since the previous check or upon explicit administrator request.

In Servlet API versions before 2.2, this class loader trick resulted in different servlets being loaded by different class loaders, a situation that would sometimes cause a `ClassCastException` to be thrown when the servlets shared information (because a class loaded by one class loader is not the same as the class loaded by a second class loader, even if the underlying class data is identical). Beginning in Servlet API 2.2, it's mandated that these `ClassCastException` problems must not occur for servlets inside the same context. So most server implementations now load each web application context within a single class loader and use a new class loader to reload the entire context when any servlet in the context changes. Since all servlets and support classes in the context always have the same class loader, there will be no unexpected `ClassCastException` during execution. Reloading the entire context causes a slight performance penalty, but one that occurs only during development.

Class reloading is not performed when only a support class changes. For efficiency, servers check only the servlet class timestamp to determine whether to reload a context. Support classes in *WEB-INF/classes* may be reloaded when a context is reloaded, but if the support class is the only class to change, the server most likely won't notice.

Servlet reloading also is not performed for any classes (servlet or otherwise) that are found in the server's classpath. These classes are loaded by the core, primordial class loader, not the custom class loader necessary to do the reloading. Such classes are loaded once and retained in memory even when their class files change.

It's generally best to put global support classes (such as the utility classes in `com.oreilly.servlet`) somewhere in the server's classpath where they don't get reloaded. This speeds the reload process and allows servlets in different contexts to share instances of these objects without hitting a `ClassCastException`.

Init and Destroy

Just like applets, servlets can define `init()` and `destroy()` methods. The server calls a servlet's `init()` method after the server constructs the servlet instance and before the servlet handles any requests. The server calls the `destroy()` method after the servlet has been taken out of service and all pending requests to the servlet have completed or timed out.*

Depending on the server and the web application configuration, the `init()` method may be called at any of these times:

- When the server starts
- When the servlet is first requested, just before the `service()` method is invoked
- At the request of the server administrator

In any case, `init()` is guaranteed to be called and completed before the servlet handles its first request.

* Early drafts of the upcoming Servlet API 2.3 specification promise to add additional lifecycle methods that allow servlets to listen when a context or session is created or shut down, as well as when an attribute is bound or unbound to a context or session.

The `init()` method is typically used to perform servlet initialization—creating or loading objects that are used by the servlet in the handling of its requests. During the `init()` method a servlet may want to read its initialization (init) parameters. These parameters are given to the servlet itself and are not associated with any single request. They can specify initial values, like where a counter should begin counting, or default values, perhaps a template to use when not specified by the request. Init parameters for a servlet are set in the *web.xml* deployment descriptor, although some servers have graphical interfaces for modifying this file. See Example 3-3.

Example 3-3. Setting init Parameters in the Deployment Descriptor

```
<?xml version="1.0" encoding="ISO-8859-1"?>

<!DOCTYPE web-app
    PUBLIC "-//Sun Microsystems, Inc.//DTD Web Application 2.2//EN"
    "http://java.sun.com/j2ee/dtds/web-app_2_2.dtd">


<web-app>
    <servlet>
        <servlet-name>
            counter
        </servlet-name>
        <servlet-class>
            InitCounter
        </servlet-class>
        <init-param>
            <param-name>
                initial
            </param-name>
            <param-value>
                1000
            </param-value>
            <description>
                The initial value for the counter  <!-- optional -->
            </description>
        </init-param>
    </servlet>
</web-app>
```

Multiple `<init-param>` entries can be placed within the `<servlet>` tag. The existence of the `<description>` tag is optional and intended primarily for graphical tools. The full Document Type Definition for the *web.xml* file can be found in Appendix F, *Charsets.*

In the `destroy()` method, a servlet should free any resources it has acquired that will not be garbage collected. The `destroy()` method also gives a servlet a chance to write out its unsaved cached information or any persistent information that should be read during the next call to `init()`.

A Counter with Init

Init parameters can be used for anything. In general, they specify initial values or default values for servlet variables, or they tell a servlet how to customize its behavior in some way. Example 3-4 extends our `SimpleCounter` example to read an init parameter (named `initial`) that stores the initial value for our counter. By setting the initial count to a high value, we can make our page appear more popular than it really is.

Example 3-4. A Counter That Reads init Parameters

```
import java.io.*;
import javax.servlet.*;
import javax.servlet.http.*;

public class InitCounter extends HttpServlet {

  int count;

  public void init() throws ServletException {
    String initial = getInitParameter("initial");
    try {
      count = Integer.parseInt(initial);
    }
    catch (NumberFormatException e) {
      count = 0;
    }
  }

  public void doGet(HttpServletRequest req, HttpServletResponse res)
                               throws ServletException, IOException {
    res.setContentType("text/plain");
    PrintWriter out = res.getWriter();
    count++;
    out.println("Since loading (and with a possible initialization");
    out.println("parameter figured in), this servlet has been accessed");
    out.println(count + " times.");
  }
}
```

The `init()` method uses the `getInitParameter()` method to get the value for the init parameter named `initial`. This method takes the name of the parameter as a `String` and returns the value as a `String`. There is no way to get the value as any other type. This servlet therefore converts the `String` value to an `int` or, if there's a problem, defaults to a value of `0`. Remember, if you test this example you may need to restart your server for the *web.xml* changes to take effect, and you need to refer to the servlet using its registered name.

What Happened to super.init(config)?

In Servlet API 2.0, a servlet implementing the `init()` method had to implement a form of `init()` that took a `ServletConfig` parameter and had to call `super.init(config)` first thing:

```
public void init(ServletConfig config) throws ServletException {
  super.init(config);
  // Initialization code follows
}
```

The `ServletConfig` parameter provided configuration information to the servlet, and the `super.init(config)` call passed the config object to the `GenericServlet` superclass where it was stored for use by the servlet. Specifically, the `GenericServlet` class used the passed-in config parameter to implement the `ServletConfig` interface itself (passing all calls to the delegate config), thus allowing a servlet to invoke `ServletConfig` methods on itself for convenience.

The whole operation was fairly convoluted, and in Servlet API 2.1 it was simplified so that a servlet now needs only to implement the `init()` no-argument version and the `ServletConfig` and `GenericServlet` handling will be taken care of in the background.

Behind the scenes, the `GenericServlet` class supports the no-arg `init()` method with code similar to this:

```
public class GenericServlet implements Servlet, ServletConfig {

  ServletConfig _config = null;

  public void init(ServletConfig config) throws ServletException {
    _config = config;
    log("init called");
    init();
  }

  public void init() throws ServletException { }

  public String getInitParameter(String name) {
    return _config.getInitParameter(name);
  }

  // etc...
}
```

—Continued—

> Notice the web server still calls a servlet's `init(ServletConfig config)` method at initialization time. The change in 2.1 is that `GenericServlet` now passes on this call to the no-arg `init()`, which you can override without worrying about the `config`.
>
> If backward compatibility is a concern, you should continue to override `init(ServletConfig config)` and call `super.init(config)`. Otherwise you may end up wondering why your no-arg `init()` method is never called.
>
> As a side note to this sidebar, some programmers find it useful to call `super.destroy()` first thing when implementing `destroy()`. This calls the `GenericServlet` implementation of `destroy()`, which writes a note to the log that the servlet is being destroyed.

A Counter with Init and Destroy

Up until now, the counter examples have demonstrated how servlet state persists between accesses. This solves only part of the problem. Every time the server is shut down or the servlet is reloaded, the count begins again. What we really want is persistence across loads—a counter that doesn't have to start over.

The `init()` and `destroy()` pair can accomplish this. Example 3-5 further extends the `InitCounter` example, giving the servlet the ability to save its state in `destroy()` and load the state again in `init()`. To keep things simple, assume this servlet is not registered and is accessed only as *http://server:port/servlet/InitDestroyCounter*. If it were registered under different names, it would have to save a separate state for each name.

Example 3-5. A Fully Persistent Counter

```
import java.io.*;
import javax.servlet.*;
import javax.servlet.http.*;

public class InitDestroyCounter extends HttpServlet {

  int count;

  public void init() throws ServletException {
    // Try to load the initial count from our saved persistent state
    FileReader fileReader = null;
    BufferedReader bufferedReader = null;
    try {
      fileReader = new FileReader("InitDestroyCounter.initial");
      bufferedReader = new BufferedReader(fileReader);
      String initial = bufferedReader.readLine();
```

Example 3-5. A Fully Persistent Counter (continued)

```
        count = Integer.parseInt(initial);
        return;
      }
      catch (FileNotFoundException ignored) { }  // no saved state
      catch (IOException ignored) { }            // problem during read
      catch (NumberFormatException ignored) { }  // corrupt saved state
      finally {
        // Make sure to close the file
        try {
          if (bufferedReader != null) {
            bufferedReader.close();
          }
        }
        catch (IOException ignored) { }
      }

      // No luck with the saved state, check for an init parameter
      String initial = getInitParameter("initial");
      try {
        count = Integer.parseInt(initial);
        return;
      }
      catch (NumberFormatException ignored) { }  // null or non-integer value

      // Default to an initial count of "0"
      count = 0;
    }

    public void doGet(HttpServletRequest req, HttpServletResponse res)
                                 throws ServletException, IOException {
      res.setContentType("text/plain");
      PrintWriter out = res.getWriter();
      count++;
      out.println("Since the beginning, this servlet has been accessed " +
                  count + " times.");
    }

    public void destroy() {
      super.destroy();  // entirely optional
      saveState();
    }

    public void saveState() {
      // Try to save the accumulated count
      FileWriter fileWriter = null;
      PrintWriter printWriter = null;
      try {
        fileWriter = new FileWriter("InitDestroyCounter.initial");
```

Example 3-5. A Fully Persistent Counter (continued)

```
      printWriter = new PrintWriter(fileWriter);
      printWriter.println(count);
      return;
    }
    catch (IOException e) {  // problem during write
      // Log the exception. See Chapter 5.
    }
    finally {
      // Make sure to close the file
      if (printWriter != null) {
        printWriter.close();
      }
    }
  }
}
```

Each time this servlet is unloaded, it saves its state in a file named *InitDestroyCounter.initial*. In the absence of a supplied path, the file is saved in the server process's current directory, usually the startup directory. Ways to specify alternate locations are discussed in Chapter 4, *Retrieving Information*.* This file contains a single integer, saved as a string, that represents the latest count.

Each time the servlet is loaded, it tries to read the saved count from the file. If, for some reason, the read fails (as it does the first time the servlet runs because the file doesn't yet exist), the servlet checks if an init parameter specifies the starting count. If that too fails, it starts fresh with zero. You can never be too careful in `init()` methods.

Servlets can save their state in many different ways. Some may use a custom file format, as was done here. Others may save their state as serialized Java objects or put it into a database. Some may even perform *journaling*, a technique common to databases and tape backups, where the servlet's full state is saved infrequently while a journal file stores incremental updates as things change. Which method a servlet should use depends on the situation. In any case, you should always be watchful that the state being saved isn't undergoing any change in the background.

Right now you're probably asking yourself, "What happens if the server crashes?" It's a good question. The answer is that the `destroy()` method will not be called.† This doesn't cause a problem for `destroy()` methods that only have to free

---

* The location of the current user directory can be found with `System.getProperty("user.dir")`.

† Unless you're so unlucky that your server crashes while in the `destroy()` method. In that case, you may be left with a partially written state file—garbage written on top of your previous state. To be perfectly safe, a servlet should save its state to a temporary file and then copy that file on top of the official state file in one command.

resources; a rebooted server does that job just as well (if not better). But it does cause a problem for a servlet that needs to save its state in its `destroy()` method. For these servlets, the only guaranteed solution is to save state more often. A servlet may choose to save its state after handling each request, such as a "chess server" servlet should do, so that even if the server is restarted, the game can resume with the latest board position. Other servlets may need to save state only after some important value has changed—a "shopping cart" servlet needs to save its state only when a customer adds or removes an item from her cart. Last, for some servlets, it's fine to lose a bit of the recent state changes. These servlets can save state after some set number of requests. For example, in our `InitDestroyCounter` example, it should be satisfactory to save state every 10 accesses. To implement this, we can add the following line at the end of `doGet()`:

```
if (count % 10 == 0) saveState();
```

Does this addition make you cringe? It should. Think about synchronization issues. We've opened up the possibility for data loss if `saveState()` is executed by two threads at the same time and the possibility for `saveState()` to not be called at all if count is incremented by several threads in a row before the check. Note that this possibility did not exist when `saveState()` was called only from the `destroy()` method: the `destroy()` method is called just once per servlet instance. Now that `saveState()` is called in the `doGet()` method, however, we need to reconsider. If by some chance this servlet is accessed so frequently that it has more than 10 concurrently executing threads, it's likely that two servlets (10 requests apart) will be in `saveState()` at the same time. This may result in a corrupted datafile. It's also possible the two threads will increment count before either thread notices it was time to call `saveState()`. The fix is easy: move the count check into the synchronized block where count is incremented:

```
int local_count;
synchronized(this) {
  local_count = ++count;
  if (count % 10 == 0) saveState();
}
out.println("Since loading, this servlet has been accessed " +
            local_count + " times.");
```

The moral of the story is harder: always be vigilant to protect servlet code from multithreaded access problems.

Single-Thread Model

Although the normal situation is to have one servlet instance per registered servlet name, it is possible for a servlet to elect instead to have a pool of instances created for each of its names, all sharing the duty of handling requests. Such servlets indicate this desire by implementing the `javax.servlet.SingleThreadModel` interface. This is an empty, "tag" interface that defines no methods or variables and serves only to flag the servlet as wanting the alternate lifecycle.

A server that loads a `SingleThreadModel` servlet must guarantee, according to the Servlet API documentation, "that no two threads will execute concurrently in the servlet's service method." To accomplish this, each thread uses a free servlet instance from the pool, as shown in Figure 3-3. Thus, any servlet implementing `SingleThreadModel` can be considered thread safe and isn't required to synchronize access to its instance variables. Some servers allow the number of instances per pool to be configured, others don't. Some servers use pools with just one instance, causing behavior identical to a synchronized `service()` method.

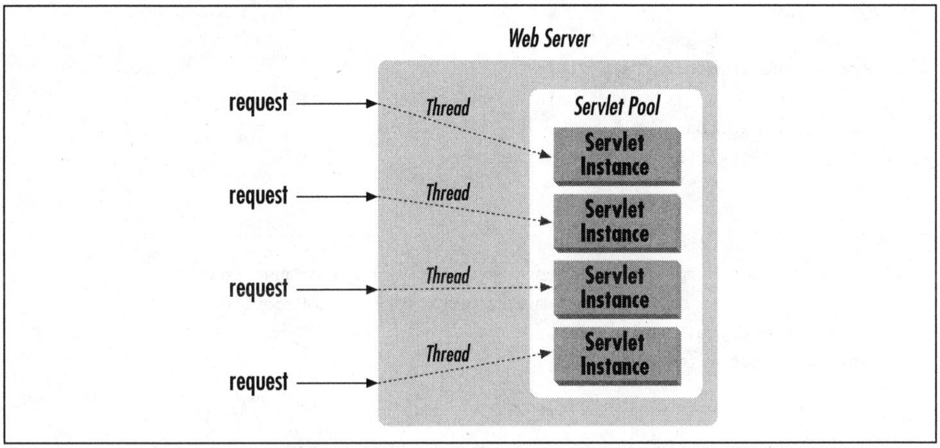

Figure 3-3. The single-thread model

A `SingleThreadModel` lifecycle is pointless for a counter or other servlet application that requires central state maintenance. The lifecycle can be of some use, however, in avoiding synchronization while still performing efficient request handling.

For example, a servlet that connects to a database sometimes needs to perform several database commands atomically as part of a single transaction. Each database transaction requires a dedicated database connection object, so the servlet somehow needs to ensure no two threads try to access the same connection at the same time. This could be done using synchronization, letting the servlet manage just one request at a time. By instead implementing `SingleThreadModel` and having one "connection" instance variable per servlet, a servlet can easily handle concurrent requests because each instance has its own connection. The skeleton code is shown in Example 3-6.

Example 3-6. Handling Database Connections Using SingleThreadModel

```
import java.io.*;
import java.sql.*;
import java.util.*;
import javax.servlet.*;
import javax.servlet.http.*;

public class SingleThreadConnection extends HttpServlet
                                    implements SingleThreadModel {

  Connection con = null;  // database connection, one per pooled instance

  public void init() throws ServletException {
    // Establish the connection for this instance
    try {
      con = establishConnection();
      con.setAutoCommit(false);
    }
    catch (SQLException e) {
      throw new ServletException(e.getMessage());
    }
  }

  public void doGet(HttpServletRequest req, HttpServletResponse res)
                               throws ServletException, IOException {
    res.setContentType("text/plain");
    PrintWriter out = res.getWriter();

    try {
      // Use the connection uniquely assigned to this instance
      Statement stmt = con.createStatement();

      // Update the database any number of ways

      // Commit the transaction
      con.commit();
    }
    catch (SQLException e) {
      try { con.rollback(); } catch (SQLException ignored) { }
    }
  }

  public void destroy() {
    if (con != null) {
      try { con.close(); } catch (SQLException ignored) { }
    }
  }
```

Example 3-6. Handling Database Connections Using SingleThreadModel (continued)

```
  private Connection establishConnection() throws SQLException {
    // Not implemented.  See Chapter 9.
  }
}
```

In reality, `SingleThreadModel` is not the best choice for an application such as this. A far better approach would be for the servlet to use a dedicated `ConnectionPool` object, held as an instance or class variable, from which it could "check out" and "check in" connections. The "checked-out" connection can be held as a local variable, ensuring dedicated access. An external pool provides the servlet more control over the connection management. The pool can also verify the health of each connection, and the pool can be configured to always create some minimum number of connections but never create more than some maximum. When using `SingleThreadModel`, the server might create many more instances (and thus more connections) than the database can handle.

Conventional wisdom now is to avoid using `SingleThreadModel`. Most any servlet using `SingleThreadModel` could be better implemented using synchronization and/or external resource pools. It's true the interface does provide some comfort to programmers not familiar with multithreaded programming; however, while `SingleThreadModel` makes the servlet itself thread safe, the interface does not make the system thread safe. The interface does not prevent synchronization problems that result from servlets accessing shared resources such as static variables or objects outside the scope of the servlet. There will always be threading issues when running in a multithreaded system, with or without `SingleThreadModel`.

Background Processing

Servlets can do more than simply persist between accesses. They can also execute between accesses. Any thread started by a servlet can continue executing even after the response has been sent. This ability proves most useful for long-running tasks whose incremental results should be made available to multiple clients. A background thread started in `init()` performs continuous work while request-handling threads display the current status with `doGet()`. It's a similar technique to that used in animation applets, where one thread changes the picture and another paints the display.

Example 3-7 shows a servlet that searches for prime numbers above one quadrillion. It starts with such a large number to make the calculation slow enough to adequately demonstrate caching effects—something we need for the next section. The algorithm it uses couldn't be simpler: it selects odd-numbered candidates and attempts to divide them by every odd integer between 3 and their square root. If none of the integers evenly divides the candidate, it is declared prime.*

Example 3-7. On the Hunt for Primes

```
import java.io.*;
import java.util.*;
import javax.servlet.*;
import javax.servlet.http.*;

public class PrimeSearcher extends HttpServlet implements Runnable {

  long lastprime = 0;                    // last prime found
  Date lastprimeModified = new Date();   // when it was found
  Thread searcher;                       // background search thread

  public void init() throws ServletException {
    searcher = new Thread(this);
    searcher.setPriority(Thread.MIN_PRIORITY);  // be a good citizen
    searcher.start();
  }

  public void run() {
    //               QTTTBBBMMMTTTOOO
    long candidate = 1000000000000001L;  // one quadrillion and one

    // Begin loop searching for primes
    while (true) {                       // search forever
      if (isPrime(candidate)) {
        lastprime = candidate;           // new prime
        lastprimeModified = new Date();  // new "prime time"
      }
      candidate += 2;                    // evens aren't prime

      // Between candidates take a 0.2 second break.
      // Another way to be a good citizen with system resources.
      try {
        searcher.sleep(200);
      }
      catch (InterruptedException ignored) { }
    }
  }

  private static boolean isPrime(long candidate) {
    // Try dividing the number by all odd numbers between 3 and its sqrt
```

* Why do we look only for factors below the square root? Because any factor above the square root would need to correspond to a factor below the square root. If there are no factors before the square root, we know there can be none above.

Example 3-7. On the Hunt for Primes (continued)

```
    long sqrt = (long) Math.sqrt(candidate);
    for (long i = 3; i <= sqrt; i += 2) {
      if (candidate % i == 0) return false;  // found a factor
    }

    // Wasn't evenly divisible, so it's prime
    return true;
  }

  public void doGet(HttpServletRequest req, HttpServletResponse res)
                               throws ServletException, IOException {
    res.setContentType("text/plain");
    PrintWriter out = res.getWriter();
    if (lastprime == 0) {
      out.println("Still searching for first prime...");
    }
    else {
      out.println("The last prime discovered was " + lastprime);
      out.println(" at " + lastprimeModified);
    }
  }

  public void destroy() {
    searcher.stop();
  }
}
```

The searcher thread begins its search in the `init()` method. Its latest find is saved in `lastprime`, along with the time it was found in `lastprimeModified`. Each time a client accesses the servlet, the `doGet()` method reports the largest prime found so far and the time it was found. The searcher runs independently of client accesses; even if no one accesses the servlet it continues to find primes silently. If several clients access the servlet at the same time, they all see the same current status.

Notice that the `destroy()` method stops the searcher thread.* This is very important! If a servlet does not stop its background threads, they continue to run until the virtual machine exits. Even when a servlet is reloaded (either explicitly or because its class file changed), its threads won't be stopped. Instead, it's likely that the new servlet will create extra copies of the background threads.

* Stopping threads using the `stop()` method as shown here is deprecated in JDK 1.2 in favor of a safer flag-based system, where a thread must periodically examine a `flag` variable to determine when it should stop, at which point it can clean up and return from its `run()` method. See the JDK documentation for details.

Load on Startup

To have the PrimeSearcher start searching for primes as quickly as possible, we can configure the servlet's web application to load the servlet at server start. This is accomplished by adding the <load-on-startup> tag to the <servlet> entry of the deployment descriptor, as shown in Example 3-8.

Example 3-8. Loading a Servlet on Startup

```
<?xml version="1.0" encoding="ISO-8859-1"?>

<!DOCTYPE web-app
    PUBLIC "-//Sun Microsystems, Inc.//DTD Web Application 2.2//EN"
    "http://java.sun.com/j2ee/dtds/web-app_2_2.dtd">

<web-app>
    <servlet>
        <servlet-name>
            ps
        </servlet-name>
        <servlet-class>
            PrimeSearcher
        </servlet-class>
        <load-on-startup/>
    </servlet>
</web-app>
```

This tells the server to create an instance of PrimeSearcher under the registered name ps and init() the servlet during the server's startup sequence. The servlet can then be accessed at the URL */servlet/ps*. Note that the servlet instance handling the URL */servlet/PrimeSearcher* is not loaded at startup.

The <load-on-startup> tag shown in Example 3-8 is empty. The tag can also contain a positive integer indicating the order in which the servlet should be loaded relative to other servlets in the context. Servlets with lower numbers are loaded before those with higher numbers. Servlets with negative values or noninteger values may be loaded at any time in the startup sequence, with the exact order depending on the server. For example, the *web.xml* shown in Example 3-9 guarantees first is loaded before second, while anytime could be loaded anytime during the server startup.

Example 3-9. A Little Servlet Parade

```
<?xml version="1.0" encoding="ISO-8859-1"?>

<!DOCTYPE web-app
    PUBLIC "-//Sun Microsystems, Inc.//DTD Web Application 2.2//EN"
    "http://java.sun.com/j2ee/dtds/web-app_2_2.dtd">
```

Example 3-9. A Little Servlet Parade (continued)

```
<web-app>
    <servlet>
        <servlet-name>
            first
        </servlet-name>
        <servlet-class>
            First
        </servlet-class>
        <load-on-startup>10</load-on-startup>
    </servlet>
    <servlet>
        <servlet-name>
            second
        </servlet-name>
        <servlet-class>
            Second
        </servlet-class>
        <load-on-startup>20</load-on-startup>
    </servlet>
    <servlet>
        <servlet-name>
            anytime
        </servlet-name>
        <servlet-class>
            Anytime
        </servlet-class>
        <load-on-startup/>
    </servlet>
</web-app>
```

Client-Side Caching

By now, we're sure you've learned that servlets handle GET requests with the `doGet()` method. And that's almost true. The full truth is that not every request really needs to invoke `doGet()`. For example, a web browser that repeatedly accesses `PrimeSearcher` should need to call `doGet()` only after the searcher thread has found a new prime. Until that time, any call to `doGet()` just generates the same page the user has already seen, a page probably stored in the browser's cache. What's really needed is a way for a servlet to report when its output has changed. That's where the `getLastModified()` method comes in.

Most web servers, when they return a document, include as part of their response a `Last-Modified` header. An example `Last-Modified` header value might be:

```
Tue, 06-May-98 15:41:02 GMT
```

This header tells the client the time the page was last changed. That information alone is only marginally interesting, but it proves useful when a browser reloads a page.

Most web browsers, when they reload a page, include in their request an `If-Modified-Since` header. Its structure is identical to the `Last-Modified` header:

```
Tue, 06-May-98 15:41:02 GMT
```

This header tells the server the `Last-Modified` time of the page when it was last downloaded by the browser. The server can read this header and determine if the file has changed since the given time. If the file has changed, the server must send the newer content. If the file hasn't changed, the server can reply with a simple, short response that tells the browser the page has not changed, and it is sufficient to redisplay the cached version of the document. For those familiar with the details of HTTP, this response is the 304 Not Modified status code.

This technique works great for static pages: the server can use the filesystem to find out when any file was last modified. For dynamically generated content, though, such as that returned by servlets, the server needs some extra help. By itself, the best the server can do is play it safe and assume the content changes with every access, effectively eliminating the usefulness of the `Last-Modified` and `If-Modified-Since` headers.

The extra help a servlet can provide is implementing the `getLastModified()` method. A servlet should implement this method to return the time it last changed its output. Servers call this method at two times. The first time the server calls the method is when the server returns a response, so that the server can set the response's `Last-Modified` header. The second time occurs in handling GET requests that include the `If-Modified-Since` header (usually reloads), so the server can intelligently determine how to respond. If the time returned by `getLastModified()` is equal to or earlier than the time sent in the `If-Modified-Since` header, the server returns the Not Modified status code. Otherwise, the server calls `doGet()` and returns the servlet's output.*

Some servlets may find it difficult to determine their last modified time. For these situations, it's often best to use the "play-it-safe" default behavior. Many servlets, however, should have little or no problem. Consider a "bulletin board" servlet where people post carpool openings or the need for racquetball partners. It can record and return when the bulletin board's contents were last changed. Even if the same servlet manages several bulletin boards, it can return a different modified time

* A servlet can directly set its `Last-Modified` header inside `doGet()`, using techniques discussed in Chapter 5, *Sending HTML Information*. However, by the time the header is set inside `doGet()`, it's too late to decide whether to call `doGet()`.

depending on the board given in the parameters of the request. Here's a `getLastModified()` method for our `PrimeSearcher` example that returns when the last prime was found:

```
public long getLastModified(HttpServletRequest req) {
  return lastprimeModified.getTime() / 1000 * 1000;
}
```

Notice that this method returns a long value that represents the time as a number of milliseconds since midnight, January 1, 1970, GMT. This is the same representation used internally by Java to store time values. Thus, the servlet uses the `getTime()` method to retrieve `lastprimeModified` as a `long`.

Before returning this time value, the servlet rounds it down to the nearest second by dividing by 1000 and then multiplying by 1000. All times returned by `getLastModified()` should be rounded down like this. The reason is that the `Last-Modified` and `If-Modified-Since` headers are given to the nearest second. If `getLastModified()` returns the same time but with a higher resolution, it may erroneously appear to be a few milliseconds later than the time given by `If-Modified-Since`. For example, let's assume `PrimeSearcher` found a prime exactly 869,127,442,359 milliseconds since the beginning of the Disco Decade. This fact is told to the browser, but only to the nearest second:

```
Thu, 17-Jul-97 09:17:22 GMT
```

Now let's assume that the user reloads the page and the browser tells the server, via the `If-Modified-Since` header, the time it believes its cached page was last modified:

```
Thu, 17-Jul-97 09:17:22 GMT
```

Some servers have been known to receive this time, convert it to exactly 869,127,442,000 milliseconds, find that this time is 359 milliseconds earlier than the time returned by `getLastModified()`, and falsely assume that the servlet's content has changed.* This is why, to play it safe, `getLastModified()` should always round down to the nearest thousand milliseconds.

The `HttpServletRequest` object is passed to `getLastModified()` in case the servlet needs to base its results on information specific to the particular request. The generic bulletin board servlet can make use of this to determine which board was being requested, for example.

* This bug actually existed in the official version of the `javax.servlet.http.HttpServlet` class for some time. Jason had the honor of fixing it after the code was available as open source.

Server-Side Caching

The `getLastModified()` method can be used, with a little trickery, to help manage a server-side cache of the servlet's output. Servlets implementing this trick can have their output caught and cached on the server side, then automatically resent to clients as appropriate according to the servlet's `getLastModified()` method. This can greatly speed servlet page generation, especially for servlets whose output takes a significant time to produce but changes only rarely, such as servlets that display database results.

To implement this server-side caching behavior, a servlet must:

- Extend `com.oreilly.servlet.CacheHttpServlet` instead of `HttpServlet`
- Implement a `getLastModified(HttpServletRequest)` method as usual

Example 3-10 shows a servlet taking advantage of `CacheHttpServlet`. It's a guestbook servlet that displays user-submitted comments. The servlet stores the user comments in memory as a `Vector` of `GuestbookEntry` objects. We'll see a version of this servlet running off a database in Chapter 9, *Database Connectivity*. For now, to simulate reading from a slow database, the display loop has a half-second delay per entry. As the entry list gets longer, the rendering of the page gets slower. However, because the servlet extends `CacheHttpServlet`, the rendering only has to occur during the first GET request after a new comment is added. All later GET requests send the cached response. Sample output is shown in Figure 3-4.

Example 3-10. A Guestbook Using CacheHttpServlet

```
import java.io.*;
import java.util.*;
import javax.servlet.*;
import javax.servlet.http.*;

import com.oreilly.servlet.CacheHttpServlet;

public class Guestbook extends CacheHttpServlet {

  private Vector entries = new Vector();  // User entry list
  private long lastModified = 0;          // Time last entry was added

  // Display the current entries, then ask for a new entry
  public void doGet(HttpServletRequest req, HttpServletResponse res)
                               throws ServletException, IOException {
    res.setContentType("text/html");
    PrintWriter out = res.getWriter();

    printHeader(out);
    printForm(out);
    printMessages(out);
```

Example 3-10. A Guestbook Using CacheHttpServlet (continued)

```
    printFooter(out);
  }

  // Add a new entry, then dispatch back to doGet()
  public void doPost(HttpServletRequest req, HttpServletResponse res)
                                throws ServletException, IOException {
    handleForm(req, res);
    doGet(req, res);
  }

  private void printHeader(PrintWriter out) throws ServletException {
    out.println("<HTML><HEAD><TITLE>Guestbook</TITLE></HEAD>");
    out.println("<BODY>");
  }

  private void printForm(PrintWriter out) throws ServletException {
    out.println("<FORM METHOD=POST>");  // posts to itself
    out.println("<B>Please submit your feedback:</B><BR>");
    out.println("Your name: <INPUT TYPE=TEXT NAME=name><BR>");
    out.println("Your email: <INPUT TYPE=TEXT NAME=email><BR>");
    out.println("Comment: <INPUT TYPE=TEXT SIZE=50 NAME=comment><BR>");
    out.println("<INPUT TYPE=SUBMIT VALUE=\"Send Feedback\"><BR>");
    out.println("</FORM>");
    out.println("<HR>");
  }

  private void printMessages(PrintWriter out) throws ServletException {
    String name, email, comment;

    Enumeration e = entries.elements();
    while (e.hasMoreElements()) {
      GuestbookEntry entry = (GuestbookEntry) e.nextElement();
      name = entry.name;
      if (name == null) name = "Unknown user";
      email = entry.email;
      if (name == null) email = "Unknown email";
      comment = entry.comment;
      if (comment == null) comment = "No comment";
      out.println("<DL>");
      out.println("<DT><B>" + name + "</B> (" + email + ") says");
      out.println("<DD><PRE>" + comment + "</PRE>");
      out.println("</DL>");

      // Sleep for half a second to simulate a slow data source
      try { Thread.sleep(500); } catch (InterruptedException ignored) { }
    }
  }
```

Example 3-10. A Guestbook Using CacheHttpServlet (continued)

```
  private void printFooter(PrintWriter out) throws ServletException {
    out.println("</BODY>");
  }

  private void handleForm(HttpServletRequest req,
                          HttpServletResponse res) {
    GuestbookEntry entry = new GuestbookEntry();

    entry.name = req.getParameter("name");
    entry.email = req.getParameter("email");
    entry.comment = req.getParameter("comment");

    entries.addElement(entry);

    // Make note we have a new last modified time
    lastModified = System.currentTimeMillis();
  }

  public long getLastModified(HttpServletRequest req) {
    return lastModified;
  }
}

class GuestbookEntry {
  public String name;
  public String email;
  public String comment;
}
```

The `CacheHttpServlet` source is shown in Example 3-11. The code is fairly complicated, especially at this point in the book. If you're interested, you may want to read the code for this class after completing Chapter 5.

Before handling a request, `CacheHttpServlet` class checks the value of `getLastModified()`. If the output cache is at least as current as the servlet's last modified time, the cached output is sent without calling the servlet's `doGet()` method.

In order to be safe, if this class detects that the servlet's query string, extra path info, or servlet path has changed, the cache is invalidated and re-created. However, this class does not invalidate the cache based on differing request headers or cookies; for servlets that vary their output based on these values (i.e., a session- tracking servlet), this class should probably not be used, or the `getLastModified()` method should take the headers and cookies into consideration. No caching is performed for POST requests.

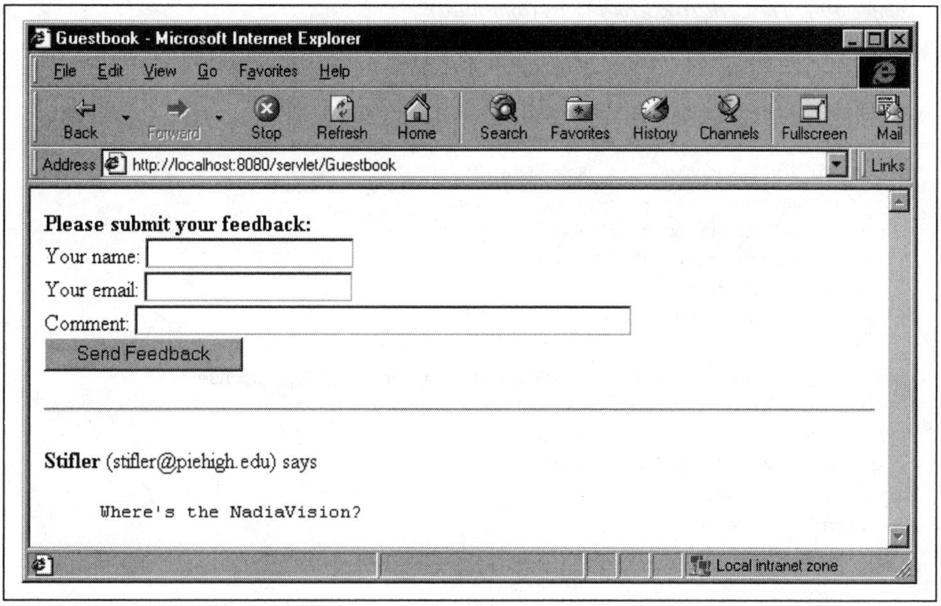

Figure 3-4. Guestbook output

`CacheHttpServletResponse` and `CacheServletOutputStream` are helper classes to the class and should not be used directly. The class has been built against Servlet API 2.2. Using it with previous Servlet API versions works fine; using it with future API versions likely won't work, because the `HttpServletResponse` interface that `CacheHttpServletResponse` must implement will probably change and leave some interface methods unimplemented. If you encounter such a problem, a current version of this class is always available at *http://www.servlets.com.*

It's interesting how `CacheHttpServlet` catches the request for early processing. It implements the `service(HttpServletRequest, HttpServletResponse)` method that the server calls to pass request-handling control to the servlet. The standard `HttpServlet` implementation of this method dispatches the request to the `doGet()`, `doPost()`, and other methods depending on the HTTP method of the request. `CacheHttpServlet` overrides that implementation and thus gains first control over the request handling. When the class has finished its processing, it can pass control back to the `HttpServlet` dispatch implementation with a `super.service()` call.

Example 3-11. The CacheHttpServlet Class

```
package com.oreilly.servlet;

import java.io.*;
import java.util.*;
import javax.servlet.*;
```

Example 3-11. The CacheHttpServlet Class (continued)

```
import javax.servlet.http.*;

public abstract class CacheHttpServlet extends HttpServlet {

  CacheHttpServletResponse cacheResponse;
  long cacheLastMod = -1;
  String cacheQueryString = null;
  String cachePathInfo = null;
  String cacheServletPath = null;
  Object lock = new Object();

  protected void service(HttpServletRequest req, HttpServletResponse res)
      throws ServletException, IOException {
    // Only do caching for GET requests
    String method = req.getMethod();
    if (!method.equals("GET")) {
      super.service(req, res);
      return;
    }

    // Check the last modified time for this servlet
    long servletLastMod = getLastModified(req);

    // A last modified of -1 means we shouldn't use any cache logic
    if (servletLastMod == -1) {
      super.service(req, res);
      return;
    }

    // If the client sent an If-Modified-Since header equal or after the
    // servlet's last modified time, send a short "Not Modified" status code
    // Round down to the nearest second since client headers are in seconds
    if ((servletLastMod / 1000 * 1000) <=
            req.getDateHeader("If-Modified-Since")) {
      res.setStatus(res.SC_NOT_MODIFIED);
      return;
    }

    // Use the existing cache if it's current and valid
    CacheHttpServletResponse localResponseCopy = null;
    synchronized (lock) {
      if (servletLastMod <= cacheLastMod &&
              cacheResponse.isValid() &&
              equal(cacheQueryString, req.getQueryString()) &&
              equal(cachePathInfo, req.getPathInfo()) &&
              equal(cacheServletPath, req.getServletPath())) {
        localResponseCopy = cacheResponse;
      }
```

Example 3-11. The CacheHttpServlet Class (continued)

```
    }
    if (localResponseCopy != null) {
      localResponseCopy.writeTo(res);
      return;
    }

    // Otherwise make a new cache to capture the response
    localResponseCopy = new CacheHttpServletResponse(res);
    super.service(req, localResponseCopy);
    synchronized (lock) {
      cacheResponse = localResponseCopy;
      cacheLastMod = servletLastMod;
      cacheQueryString = req.getQueryString();
      cachePathInfo = req.getPathInfo();
      cacheServletPath = req.getServletPath();
    }
  }

  private boolean equal(String s1, String s2) {
    if (s1 == null && s2 == null) {
      return true;
    }
    else if (s1 == null || s2 == null) {
      return false;
    }
    else {
      return s1.equals(s2);
    }
  }
}

class CacheHttpServletResponse implements HttpServletResponse {
  // Store key response variables so they can be set later
  private int status;
  private Hashtable headers;
  private int contentLength;
  private String contentType;
  private Locale locale;
  private Vector cookies;
  private boolean didError;
  private boolean didRedirect;
  private boolean gotStream;
  private boolean gotWriter;

  private HttpServletResponse delegate;
  private CacheServletOutputStream out;
  private PrintWriter writer;
```

Example 3-11. The CacheHttpServlet Class (continued)

```
  CacheHttpServletResponse(HttpServletResponse res) {
    delegate = res;
    try {
      out = new CacheServletOutputStream(res.getOutputStream());
    }
    catch (IOException e) {
      System.out.println(
        "Got IOException constructing cached response: " + e.getMessage());
    }
    internalReset();
  }

  private void internalReset() {
    status = 200;
    headers = new Hashtable();
    contentLength = -1;
    contentType = null;
    locale = null;
    cookies = new Vector();
    didError = false;
    didRedirect = false;
    gotStream = false;
    gotWriter = false;
    out.getBuffer().reset();
  }

  public boolean isValid() {
    // We don't cache error pages or redirects
    return didError != true && didRedirect != true;
  }

  private void internalSetHeader(String name, Object value) {
    Vector v = new Vector();
    v.addElement(value);
    headers.put(name, v);
  }

  private void internalAddHeader(String name, Object value) {
    Vector v = (Vector) headers.get(name);
    if (v == null) {
      v = new Vector();
    }
    v.addElement(value);
    headers.put(name, v);
  }

  public void writeTo(HttpServletResponse res) {
    // Write status code
```

Example 3-11. The CacheHttpServlet Class (continued)

```
    res.setStatus(status);
    // Write convenience headers
    if (contentType != null) res.setContentType(contentType);
    if (locale != null) res.setLocale(locale);
    // Write cookies
    Enumeration enum = cookies.elements();
    while (enum.hasMoreElements()) {
      Cookie c = (Cookie) enum.nextElement();
      res.addCookie(c);
    }
    // Write standard headers
    enum = headers.keys();
    while (enum.hasMoreElements()) {
      String name = (String) enum.nextElement();
      Vector values = (Vector) headers.get(name); // may have multiple values
      Enumeration enum2 = values.elements();
      while (enum2.hasMoreElements()) {
        Object value = enum2.nextElement();
        if (value instanceof String) {
          res.setHeader(name, (String)value);
        }
        if (value instanceof Integer) {
          res.setIntHeader(name, ((Integer)value).intValue());
        }
        if (value instanceof Long) {
          res.setDateHeader(name, ((Long)value).longValue());
        }
      }
    }
    // Write content length
    res.setContentLength(out.getBuffer().size());
    // Write body
    try {
      out.getBuffer().writeTo(res.getOutputStream());
    }
    catch (IOException e) {
      System.out.println(
        "Got IOException writing cached response: " + e.getMessage());
    }
  }

  public ServletOutputStream getOutputStream() throws IOException {
    if (gotWriter) {
      throw new IllegalStateException(
        "Cannot get output stream after getting writer");
    }
    gotStream = true;
    return out;
```

Example 3-11. The CacheHttpServlet Class (continued)

```
  }

  public PrintWriter getWriter() throws UnsupportedEncodingException {
    if (gotStream) {
      throw new IllegalStateException(
        "Cannot get writer after getting output stream");
    }
    gotWriter = true;
    if (writer == null) {
      OutputStreamWriter w =
        new OutputStreamWriter(out, getCharacterEncoding());
      writer = new PrintWriter(w, true);  // autoflush is necessary
    }
    return writer;
  }

  public void setContentLength(int len) {
    delegate.setContentLength(len);
    // No need to save the length; we can calculate it later
  }

  public void setContentType(String type) {
    delegate.setContentType(type);
    contentType = type;
  }

  public String getCharacterEncoding() {
    return delegate.getCharacterEncoding();
  }

  public void setBufferSize(int size) throws IllegalStateException {
    delegate.setBufferSize(size);
  }

  public int getBufferSize() {
    return delegate.getBufferSize();
  }

  public void reset() throws IllegalStateException {
    delegate.reset();
    internalReset();
  }

  public boolean isCommitted() {
    return delegate.isCommitted();
  }

  public void flushBuffer() throws IOException {
```

Example 3-11. The CacheHttpServlet Class (continued)

```
    delegate.flushBuffer();
  }

  public void setLocale(Locale loc) {
    delegate.setLocale(loc);
    locale = loc;
  }

  public Locale getLocale() {
    return delegate.getLocale();
  }

  public void addCookie(Cookie cookie) {
    delegate.addCookie(cookie);
    cookies.addElement(cookie);
  }

  public boolean containsHeader(String name) {
    return delegate.containsHeader(name);
  }

  /** @deprecated */
  public void setStatus(int sc, String sm) {
    delegate.setStatus(sc, sm);
    status = sc;
  }

  public void setStatus(int sc) {
    delegate.setStatus(sc);
    status = sc;
  }

  public void setHeader(String name, String value) {
    delegate.setHeader(name, value);
    internalSetHeader(name, value);
  }

  public void setIntHeader(String name, int value) {
    delegate.setIntHeader(name, value);
    internalSetHeader(name, new Integer(value));
  }

  public void setDateHeader(String name, long date) {
    delegate.setDateHeader(name, date);
    internalSetHeader(name, new Long(date));
  }

  public void sendError(int sc, String msg) throws IOException {
```

Example 3-11. The CacheHttpServlet Class (continued)

```
    delegate.sendError(sc, msg);
    didError = true;
  }

  public void sendError(int sc) throws IOException {
    delegate.sendError(sc);
    didError = true;
  }

  public void sendRedirect(String location) throws IOException {
    delegate.sendRedirect(location);
    didRedirect = true;
  }

  public String encodeURL(String url) {
    return delegate.encodeURL(url);
  }

  public String encodeRedirectURL(String url) {
    return delegate.encodeRedirectURL(url);
  }

  public void addHeader(String name, String value) {
    internalAddHeader(name, value);
  }

  public void addIntHeader(String name, int value) {
    internalAddHeader(name, new Integer(value));
  }

  public void addDateHeader(String name, long value) {
    internalAddHeader(name, new Long(value));
  }

  /** @deprecated */
  public String encodeUrl(String url) {
    return this.encodeURL(url);
  }

  /** @deprecated */
  public String encodeRedirectUrl(String url) {
    return this.encodeRedirectURL(url);
  }
}

class CacheServletOutputStream extends ServletOutputStream {

  ServletOutputStream delegate;
```

Example 3-11. The CacheHttpServlet Class (continued)

```
  ByteArrayOutputStream cache;

  CacheServletOutputStream(ServletOutputStream out) {
    delegate = out;
    cache = new ByteArrayOutputStream(4096);
  }

  public ByteArrayOutputStream getBuffer() {
    return cache;
  }

  public void write(int b) throws IOException {
    delegate.write(b);
    cache.write(b);
  }

  public void write(byte b[]) throws IOException {
    delegate.write(b);
    cache.write(b);
  }

  public void write(byte buf[], int offset, int len) throws IOException {
    delegate.write(buf, offset, len);
    cache.write(buf, offset, len);
  }
}
```

4

In this chapter:
- *The Servlet*
- *The Server*
- *The Client*

Retrieving Information

To build a successful web application, you often need to know a lot about the environment in which it is running. You may need to find out about the server that is executing your servlets or the specifics of the client that is sending requests. And no matter what kind of environment the application is running in, you most certainly need information about the requests that the application is handling.

A number of methods provide servlets access to this information. For the most part, each method returns one specific result. Compared this to the way environment variables are used to pass a CGI program its information, the servlet approach has several advantages:

- Stronger type checking. Servlets get more help from the compiler in catching errors. A CGI program uses one function to retrieve its environment variables. Many errors cannot be found until they cause runtime problems. Let's look at how a CGI program and a servlet find the port on which its server is running.

  A CGI script written in Perl calls:

  ```
  $port = $ENV{'SERVER_PORT'};
  ```

  where `$port` is an untyped variable. A CGI program written in C calls:

  ```
  char *port = getenv("SERVER_PORT");
  ```

  where `port` is a pointer to a character string. The chance for accidental errors is high. The environment variable name could be misspelled (it happens often enough) or the datatype might not match what the environment variable returns.

  A servlet, on the other hand, calls:

  ```
  int port = req.getServerPort()
  ```

This eliminates a lot of accidental errors because the compiler can guarantee there are no misspellings and each return type is as it should be.

- Delayed calculation. When a server launches a CGI program, the value for each and every environment variable must be precalculated and passed, whether the CGI program uses it or not. A server launching a servlet has the option to improve performance by delaying these calculations and performing them on demand as needed.
- More interaction with the server. Once a CGI program begins execution, it is untethered from its server. The only communication path available to the program is its standard output. A servlet, however, can work with the server. As discussed in the previous chapter, a servlet operates either within the server (when possible) or as a connected process outside the server (when necessary). Using this connectivity, a servlet can make ad hoc requests for calculated information that only the server can provide. For example, a servlet can have its server do arbitrary path translations, taking into consideration the server's aliases and virtual paths.

If you're coming to servlets from CGI, Table 4-1 is a "cheat sheet" you can use for your migration. It lists each CGI environment variable and the corresponding HTTP servlet method.

Table 4-1. CGI Environment Variables and the Corresponding Servlet Methods

CGI Environment Variable	HTTP Servlet Method
`SERVER_NAME`	`req.getServerName()`
`SERVER_SOFTWARE`	`getServletContext().getServerInfo()`
`SERVER_PROTOCOL`	`req.getProtocol()`
`SERVER_PORT`	`req.getServerPort()`
`REQUEST_METHOD`	`req.getMethod()`
`PATH_INFO`	`req.getPathInfo()`
`PATH_TRANSLATED`	`req.getPathTranslated()`
`SCRIPT_NAME`	`req.getServletPath()`
`DOCUMENT_ROOT`	`getServletContext().getRealPath("/")`
`QUERY_STRING`	`req.getQueryString()`
`REMOTE_HOST`	`req.getRemoteHost()`
`REMOTE_ADDR`	`req.getRemoteAddr()`
`AUTH_TYPE`	`req.getAuthType()`
`REMOTE_USER`	`req.getRemoteUser()`
`CONTENT_TYPE`	`req.getContentType()`
`CONTENT_LENGTH`	`req.getContentLength()`

Table 4-1. CGI Environment Variables and the Corresponding Servlet Methods (continued)

CGI Environment Variable	HTTP Servlet Method
HTTP_ACCEPT	req.getHeader("Accept")
HTTP_USER_AGENT	req.getHeader("User-Agent")
HTTP_REFERER	req.getHeader("Referer")

In the rest of this chapter, we'll see how and when to use these methods—and many other methods that have no CGI counterparts. Along the way, we'll put the methods to use in some real servlets.

The Servlet

Each registered servlet name can have specific initialization (init) parameters associated with it. Init parameters are available to the servlet at any time; they are set in the *web.xml* deployment descriptor and generally used in `init()` to set initial or default values for a servlet or to customize the servlet's behavior in some way. Init parameters are more fully explained in Chapter 3, *The Servlet Lifecycle.*

Getting a Servlet Init Parameter

A servlet uses the `getInitParameter()` method for access to its init parameters:

```
public String ServletConfig.getInitParameter(String name)
```

This method returns the value of the named init parameter or `null` if it does not exist. The return value is always a single `String`. It is up to the servlet to interpret the value.

The `GenericServlet` class implements the `ServletConfig` interface and thus provides direct access to the `getInitParameter()` method. This means the method can be called like this:

```
public void init() throws ServletException {
  String greeting = getInitParameter("greeting");
}
```

A servlet that needs to establish a connection to a database can use its init parameters to define the details of the connection. We can assume a custom `establishConnection()` method to abstract away the details of JDBC, as shown in Example 4-1.

Example 4-1. Using init Parameters to Establish a Database Connection

```
java.sql.Connection con = null;

public void init() throws ServletException {
  String host = getInitParameter("host");
```

Example 4-1. Using init Parameters to Establish a Database Connection (continued)

```
    int port = Integer.parseInt(getInitParameter("port"));
    String db = getInitParameter("db");
    String user = getInitParameter("user");
    String password = getInitParameter("password");
    String proxy = getInitParameter("proxy");

    con = establishConnection(host, port, db, user, password, proxy);
  }
```

There's also another more advanced and standard abstraction model available to servlets designed for Java 2, Enterprise Edition (J2EE). See Chapter 12, *Enterprise Servlets and J2EE.*

Getting Servlet Init Parameter Names

A servlet can examine all its init parameters using `getInitParameterNames()`:

```
public Enumeration ServletConfig.getInitParameterNames()
```

This method returns the names of all the servlet's init parameters as an `Enumeration` of `String` objects or an empty `Enumeration` if no parameters exist. It's most often used for debugging.

The `GenericServlet` class additionally makes this method directly available to servlets. Example 4-2 shows a servlet that prints the name and value for all of its init parameters.

Example 4-2. Getting init Parameter Names

```
import java.io.*;
import java.util.*;
import javax.servlet.*;

public class InitSnoop extends GenericServlet {

  // No init() method needed

  public void service(ServletRequest req, ServletResponse res)
                              throws ServletException, IOException {
    res.setContentType("text/plain");
    PrintWriter out = res.getWriter();

    out.println("Init Parameters:");
    Enumeration enum = getInitParameterNames();
    while (enum.hasMoreElements()) {
      String name = (String) enum.nextElement();
```

Example 4-2. Getting init Parameter Names (continued)

```
      out.println(name + ": " + getInitParameter(name));
    }
  }
}
```

Notice that this servlet directly subclasses `GenericServlet`, showing that init parameters are available to servlets that aren't HTTP servlets. A generic servlet can be used in a web server even though it lacks any support for HTTP-specific functionality.

Getting a Servlet's Name

Also in the `ServletConfig` interface there's a method that returns the servlet's registered name:

```
public String ServletConfig.getServletName()
```

If the servlet is unregistered, the method returns the servlet's class name. This method proves useful when writing to logs and when storing a servlet instance's state information into a shared resource such as a database or the servlet's `SessionContext` that we'll learn about shortly.

As an example, the following code demonstrates how to use the servlet's name to retrieve a value from the servlet context, using the name as part of the lookup key:

```
public void doGet(HttpServletRequest req, HttpServletResponse res)
                        throws ServletException, IOException {
  String name = getServletName();
  ServletContext context = getServletContext();
  Object value = context.getAttribute(name + ".state");
}
```

Using the servlet name in the key, each servlet instance can easily keep a separate attribute value within the shared context.

The Server

A servlet can find out much about the server in which it is executing. It can learn the hostname, listening port, and server software, among other things. A servlet can display this information to a client, use it to customize its behavior based on a particular server package, or even use it to explicitly restrict the machines on which the servlet will run.

Getting Information About the Server

A servlet gains most of its access to server information through the `ServletContext` object in which it executes. Before API 2.2, the

`ServletContext` was generally thought of as a reference to the server itself. Since API 2.2 the rules have changed and there now must be a different `ServletContext` for each web application on the server. The `ServletContext` has become a reference to the web application, not a reference to the server. For simple server queries, there's not much difference.

There are five methods that a servlet can use to learn about its server: two that are called using the `ServletRequest` object passed to the servlet and three that are called from the `ServletContext` object in which the servlet is executing.

A servlet can get the name of the server and the port number for a particular request with `getServerName()` and `getServerPort()`, respectively:

```
public String ServletRequest.getServerName()
public int ServletRequest.getServerPort()
```

These methods are attributes of `ServletRequest` because the values can change for different requests if the server has more than one name (a technique called *virtual hosting*). The returned name might be something like `www.servlets.com` while the returned port might be something like `8080`.

The `getServerInfo()` and `getAttribute()` methods of `ServletContext` provide information about the server software and its attributes:

```
public String ServletContext.getServerInfo()
public Object ServletContext.getAttribute(String name)
```

`getServerInfo()` returns the name and version of the server software, separated by a slash. The string returned might be something like `Tomcat Web Server/3.2`. Some servers add extra information at the end describing the server operating environment.

`getAttribute()` returns the value of the named server attribute as an `Object` or `null` if the attribute does not exist. Servers have the option to place hardcoded attributes in the context for use by servlets. You can think of this method as a back door through which a servlet can get extra information about its server. For example, a server could make available statistics on server load, a reference to a shared resource pool, or any other potentially useful information. The only mandatory attribute a server must make available is an attribute named `javax.servlet.context.tempdir`, which provides a `java.io.File` reference to a directory private to this context.

Servlets can also add their own attributes to the context using the `setAttribute()` method as discussed in Chapter 11, *Servlet Collaboration*. Attribute names should follow the same convention as package names. The package names `java.*` and `javax.*` are reserved for use by the Java Software division of Sun Microsystems, and `com.sun.*` is reserved for use by Sun Microsystems. You can see your server's documentation for a list of its attributes. A listing of all current attributes stored by the server and other servlets can be obtained using `getAttributeNames()`:

```
public Enumeration ServletContext.getAttributeNames()
```

Because these methods are attributes of the `ServletContext` in which the servlet is executing, you have to call them through that object:

```
String serverInfo = getServletContext().getServerInfo();
```

The most straightforward use of information about the server is an "About This Server" servlet, as shown in Example 4-3.

Example 4-3. Snooping the Server

```
import java.io.*;
import java.util.*;
import javax.servlet.*;

public class ServerSnoop extends GenericServlet {

  public void service(ServletRequest req, ServletResponse res)
                              throws ServletException, IOException {
    res.setContentType("text/plain");
    PrintWriter out = res.getWriter();

    ServletContext context = getServletContext();
    out.println("req.getServerName(): " + req.getServerName());
    out.println("req.getServerPort(): " + req.getServerPort());
    out.println("context.getServerInfo(): " + context.getServerInfo());
    out.println("getServerInfo() name: " +
                getServerInfoName(context.getServerInfo()));
    out.println("getServerInfo() version: " +
                getServerInfoVersion(context.getServerInfo()));
    out.println("context.getAttributeNames():");
    Enumeration enum = context.getAttributeNames();
    while (enum.hasMoreElements()) {
      String name = (String) enum.nextElement();
      out.println("  context.getAttribute(\"" + name + "\"): " +
                     context.getAttribute(name));
    }
  }

  private String getServerInfoName(String serverInfo) {
    int slash = serverInfo.indexOf('/');
    if (slash == -1) return serverInfo;
    else return serverInfo.substring(0, slash);
  }

  private String getServerInfoVersion(String serverInfo) {
```

Example 4-3. Snooping the Server (continued)

```
    // Version info is everything between the slash and the space
    int slash = serverInfo.indexOf('/');
    if (slash == -1) return null;
    int space = serverInfo.indexOf(' ', slash);
    if (space == -1) space = serverInfo.length();
    return serverInfo.substring(slash + 1, space);
  }
}
```

This servlet also directly subclasses `GenericServlet`, demonstrating that all the information about a server is available to servlets of any type. The servlet outputs simple raw text. When accessed, this servlet prints something like:

```
req.getServerName(): localhost
req.getServerPort(): 8080
context.getServerInfo(): Tomcat Web Server/3.2 (JSP 1.1; Servlet 2.2; ...)
getServerInfo() name: Tomcat Web Server
getServerInfo() version: 3.2
context.getAttributeNames():
  context.getAttribute("javax.servlet.context.tempdir"): work/localhost_8080
```

Writing to a Temporary File

The `javax.servlet.context.tempdir` attribute maps to a temporary directory where short-lived working files can be stored. Each context receives a different temporary directory. For the previous example, the directory is *server_root/work/localhost_8080*. Example 4-4 shows how to write to a temporary file in the temporary directory.

Example 4-4. Creating a Temporary File in a Temporary Directory

```
public void doGet(HttpServletRequest req, HttpServletResponse res)
                      throws ServletException, IOException {
  // The directory is given as a File object
  File dir = (File) getServletContext()
                      .getAttribute("javax.servlet.context.tempdir");

  // Construct a temp file in the temp dir (JDK 1.2 method)
  File f = File.createTempFile("xxx", ".tmp", dir);

  // Prepare to write to the file
  FileOutputStream fout = new FileOutputStream(f);

  // ...
}
```

First, this servlet locates its temporary directory. Then, it uses the `createTempFile()` method to create a temporary file in that directory with an `xxx` prefix and `.tmp` suffix. Finally, it constructs a `FileOutputStream` to write to the temporary file. Files that must persist between server restarts should not be placed in the temporary directory.

Locking a Servlet to a Server

There are many ways to put this server information to productive use. Let's assume you've written a servlet and you don't want it running just anywhere. Perhaps you want to sell it and, to limit the chance of unauthorized copying, you want to lock the servlet to your customer's machine with a software license. Or, alternatively, you've written a license generator as a servlet and want to make sure it works only behind your firewall. This can be done relatively easily because a servlet has instant access to the information about its server.

Example 4-5 shows a servlet that locks itself to a particular server IP address and port number. It requires an init parameter key that is appropriate for its server IP address and port before it unlocks itself and handles a request. If it does not receive the appropriate key, it refuses to continue. The algorithm used to map the key to the IP address and port (and vice versa) must be secure.

Example 4-5. A Servlet Locked to a Server

```
import java.io.*;
import java.net.*;
import java.util.*;
import javax.servlet.*;

public class KeyedServerLock extends GenericServlet {

  // This servlet has no class or instance variables
  // associated with the locking, so as to simplify
  // synchronization issues.

  public void service(ServletRequest req, ServletResponse res)
                             throws ServletException, IOException {
    res.setContentType("text/plain");
    PrintWriter out = res.getWriter();

    // The piracy check shouldn't be done in init
    // because name/port are part of request.
    String key = getInitParameter("key");
    String host = req.getServerName();
    int port = req.getServerPort();

    // Check if the init parameter "key" unlocks this server.
```

Example 4-5. A Servlet Locked to a Server (continued)

```
    if (! keyFitsServer(key, host, port)) {
      // Explain, condemn, threaten, etc.
      out.println("Pirated!");
    }
    else {
      // Give 'em the goods
      out.println("Valid");
      // etc...
    }
  }

  // This method contains the algorithm used to match a key with
  // a server host and port. This example implementation is extremely
  // weak and should not be used by commercial sites.
  //
  private boolean keyFitsServer(String key, String host, int port) {

    if (key == null) return false;

    long numericKey = 0;
    try {
      numericKey = Long.parseLong(key);
    }
    catch (NumberFormatException e) {
      return false;
    }

    // The key must be a 64-bit number equal to the logical not (~)
    // of the 32-bit IP address concatenated with the 32-bit port number.

    byte hostIP[];
    try {
      hostIP = InetAddress.getByName(host).getAddress();
    }
    catch (UnknownHostException e) {
      return false;
    }

    // Get the 32-bit IP address
    long servercode = 0;
    for (int i = 0; i < 4; i++) {
      servercode <<= 8;
      servercode |= hostIP[i];
    }

    // Concatentate the 32-bit port number
    servercode <<= 32;
    servercode |= port;
```

Example 4-5. A Servlet Locked to a Server (continued)

```
    // Logical not
    long accesscode = ~numericKey;

    // The moment of truth: Does the key match?
    return (servercode == accesscode);
  }
}
```

This servlet refuses to perform unless given the correct key. To really make it secure, however, the simple `keyFitsServer()` logic should be replaced with a strong algorithm and the whole servlet should be run through an obfuscator to prevent decompiling. Example 4-13 later in this chapter provides the code used to generate keys. If you try this servlet yourself, it's best if you access the server with its actual name, rather than `localhost`, so the servlet can determine the web server's true name and IP address.

Getting a Context Init Parameter

Servlet init parameters, as discussed earlier, are passed to individual servlets. When multiple servlets should receive the same init parameter values, those values may be assigned as a *context* init parameter. The `ServletContext` class has two methods—`getInitParameter()` and `getInitParameterNames()`—for retrieving contextwide initialization information:

```
public String ServletContext.getInitParameter(String name)
public Enumeration ServletContext.getInitParameterNames()
```

These methods are modeled after their counterparts in `ServletConfig`. `getInitParameter(String name)` returns the string value of the specified parameter. `getInitParameterNames()` returns an `Enumeration` containing the names of all the init parameters available to the web application, or an empty `Enumeration` if there were none.

The init parameters for a context are specified in the *web.xml* deployment descriptor for the context using the `<context-param>` tag as shown in Example 4-6.

Example 4-6. Setting Context Init Parameters in the Deployment Descriptor

```
<?xml version="1.0" encoding="ISO-8859-1"?>

<!DOCTYPE web-app
    PUBLIC "-//Sun Microsystems, Inc.//DTD Web Application 2.2//EN"
    "http://java.sun.com/j2ee/dtds/web-app_2.2.dtd">

<web-app>
    <context-param>
```

Example 4-6. Setting Context Init Parameters in the Deployment Descriptor (continued)

```
        <param-name>
            rmihost
        </param-name>
        <param-value>
            localhost
        </param-value>
    </context-param>
    <context-param>
        <param-name>
            rmiport
        </param-name>
        <param-value>
            1099
        </param-value>
    </context-param>
</web-app>
```

Any servlet within this web application can read the context init parameters to locate the shared RMI registry, as shown in Example 4-7.

Example 4-7. Finding the Registry Using Context Init Parameters

```
import java.io.*;
import java.rmi.registry.*;
import javax.servlet.*;
import javax.servlet.http.*;

public class RmiDemo extends HttpServlet {

  public void doGet(HttpServletRequest req, HttpServletResponse res)
                    throws ServletException, IOException {
    res.setContentType("text/plain");
    PrintWriter out = res.getWriter();

    try {
      ServletContext context = getServletContext();
      String rmihost = context.getInitParameter("rmihost");
      int rmiport = Integer.parseInt(context.getInitParameter("rmiport"));

      Registry registry = LocateRegistry.getRegistry(rmihost, rmiport);
      // ...
    }
    catch (Exception e) {
      // ...
    }
  }
}
```

There's no standard mechanism to create global init parameters visible across all contexts.

Determining the Servlet Version

A servlet can also ask the server what Servlet API version the server supports. Besides being useful for debugging, a servlet can use this information to decide whether to use a new approach to solve a task or an older, perhaps less efficient, approach. Servlet API 2.1 introduced two methods to return the version information:

```
public int ServletContext.getMajorVersion()
public int ServletContext.getMinorVersion()
```

For API 2.1, `getMajorVersion()` returns 2 and `getMinorVersion()` returns 1. Of course, these methods work only for servlets executing in servers supporting Servlet API 2.1 and later. To determine the current Servlet API version across all servers, you can use `com.oreilly.servlet.VersionDetector`. This class doesn't ask the server for the version; instead, it looks at the classes and variables available in the runtime and based on knowledge of the Servlet API history can calculate the current version, from 1.0 to 2.3. Because the class doesn't call `getMajorVersion()` or `getMinorVersion()`, it not only works across all versions of the API, but also compiles across all versions. The `VersionDetector` class also can determine the current JDK version, from 1.0 to 1.3, using the same technique. This turns out to be more reliable across JVM vendor implementations than querying the `System` class. Example 4-8 shows the `VersionDetector` class. Updates to the class to support future Servlet API and JDK versions will be posted to *http://www.servlets.com.*

Example 4-8. The VersionDetector Class

```
package com.oreilly.servlet;

public class VersionDetector {

  static String servletVersion;
  static String javaVersion;

  public static String getServletVersion() {
    if (servletVersion != null) {
      return servletVersion;
    }

    // javax.servlet.http.HttpSession was introduced in Servlet API 2.0
    // javax.servlet.RequestDispatcher was introduced in Servlet API 2.1
    // javax.servlet.http.HttpServletResponse.SC_EXPECTATION_FAILED was
    //   introduced in Servlet API 2.2
    // javax.servlet.Filter is slated to be introduced in Servlet API 2.3
```

Example 4-8. The VersionDetector Class (continued)

```
    String ver = null;
    try {
      ver = "1.0";
      Class.forName("javax.servlet.http.HttpSession");
      ver = "2.0";
      Class.forName("javax.servlet.RequestDispatcher");
      ver = "2.1";
      Class.forName("javax.servlet.http.HttpServletResponse")
                   .getDeclaredField("SC_EXPECTATION_FAILED");
      ver = "2.2";
      Class.forName("javax.servlet.Filter");
      ver = "2.3";
    }
    catch (Throwable t) {
    }

    servletVersion = ver;
    return servletVersion;
  }

  public static String getJavaVersion() {
    if (javaVersion != null) {
      return javaVersion;
    }

    // java.lang.Void was introduced in JDK 1.1
    // java.lang.ThreadLocal was introduced in JDK 1.2
    // java.lang.StrictMath was introduced in JDK 1.3
    String ver = null;
    try {
      ver = "1.0";
      Class.forName("java.lang.Void");
      ver = "1.1";
      Class.forName("java.lang.ThreadLocal");
      ver = "1.2";
      Class.forName("java.lang.StrictMath");
      ver = "1.3";
    }
    catch (Throwable t) {
    }

    javaVersion = ver;
    return javaVersion;
  }
}
```

The class works by attempting to load classes and access variables until a `NoClassDefFoundError` or `NoSuchFieldException` halts the search. At that point, the current version is known. Example 4-9 demonstrates a servlet that snoops the servlet and Java version.

Example 4-9. Snooping Versions

```
import java.io.*;
import javax.servlet.*;
import javax.servlet.http.*;

import com.oreilly.servlet.VersionDetector;

public class VersionSnoop extends HttpServlet {

  public void doGet(HttpServletRequest req, HttpServletResponse res)
                         throws ServletException, IOException {
    res.setContentType("text/plain");
    PrintWriter out = res.getWriter();

    out.println("Servlet Version: " + VersionDetector.getServletVersion());
    out.println("Java Version: " + VersionDetector.getJavaVersion());
  }
}
```

The Client

For each request, a servlet has the ability to find out about the client machine and, for pages requiring authentication, about the actual user. This information can be used for logging access data, associating information with individual users, or restricting access to certain clients.

Getting Information About the Client Machine

A servlet can use `getRemoteAddr()` and `getRemoteHost()` to retrieve the IP address and hostname of the client machine, respectively:

```
public String ServletRequest.getRemoteAddr()
public String ServletRequest.getRemoteHost()
```

Both values are returned as `String` objects. The information comes from the socket that connects the server to the client, so the remote address and hostname may be that of a proxy server. An example remote address might be `192.26.80.118` while an example remote host might be `dist.engr.sgi.com`.

The IP address or remote hostname can be converted to a `java.net.InetAddress` object using `InetAddress.getByName()`:

```
InetAddress remoteInetAddress = InetAddress.getByName(req.getRemoteAddr());
```

Restricting Access

Due to the United States government's policy restricting the export of strong encryption, some web sites must be careful about who they let download certain software. Servlets, with their ability to find out about the client machine, are well suited to enforce this restriction. These servlets can check the client machine and provide links for download only if the client appears to be coming from a permitted country.

In the first edition of this book, permitted countries were only the United States and Canada, and this servlet was written to allow downloads only for users from these two countries. In the time since that edition, the United States government has loosened its policy on exporting strong encryption, and now most encryption software can be downloaded by anyone except those from the "Terrorist 7" countries of Cuba, Iran, Iraq, North Korea, Libya, Syria, and Sudan. Example 4-10 shows a servlet that permits downloads from anyone outside these seven countries.

Example 4-10. Can They Be Trusted?

```
import java.io.*;
import java.net.*;
import java.util.*;
import javax.servlet.*;
import javax.servlet.http.*;

public class ExportRestriction extends HttpServlet {

  public void doGet(HttpServletRequest req, HttpServletResponse res)
                               throws ServletException, IOException {
    res.setContentType("text/html");
    PrintWriter out = res.getWriter();

    // ...Some introductory HTML...

    // Get the client's hostname
    String remoteHost = req.getRemoteHost();

    // See if the client is allowed
    if (! isHostAllowed(remoteHost)) {
      out.println("Access <BLINK>denied</BLINK>");
    }
    else {
      out.println("Access granted");
      // Display download links, etc...
    }
  }

  // Disallow hosts ending with .cu, .ir, .iq, .kp, .ly, .sy, and .sd.
```

Example 4-10. Can They Be Trusted? (continued)

```
  private boolean isHostAllowed(String host) {
    return (!host.endsWith(".cu") &&
            !host.endsWith(".ir") &&
            !host.endsWith(".iq") &&
            !host.endsWith(".kp") &&
            !host.endsWith(".ly") &&
            !host.endsWith(".sy") &&
            !host.endsWith(".sd"));
  }
}
```

This servlet gets the client hostname with a call to `req.getRemoteHost()` and, based on its suffix, decides if the client came from any of the denied countries. Of course, be sure to get high-priced legal counsel before making any cryptographic code available for download.

Getting Information About the User

What do you do when you need to restrict access to some of your web pages but want to have a bit more control over the restriction than this country-by-country approach? Say, for example, you publish an online magazine and want only paid subscribers to read the articles. Well (prepare yourself), you don't need servlets to do this.

Nearly every HTTP server has a built-in capability to restrict access to some or all of its pages to a given set of registered users. How you set up restricted access is covered in Chapter 8, *Security*, but here's how it works mechanically. The first time a browser attempts to access one of these pages, the HTTP server replies that it needs special user authentication. When the browser receives this response, it usually pops open a window asking the user for a name and password appropriate for the page, as shown in Figure 4-1.

Once the user enters his information, the browser again attempts to access the page, this time attaching the user's name and password along with the request. If the server accepts the name/password pair, it happily handles the request. If, on the other hand, the server doesn't accept the name/password pair, the browser is again denied and the user swears under his breath about forgetting yet another password.

How does this involve servlets? When access to a servlet has been restricted by the server, the servlet can get the name of the user that was accepted by the server, using the `getRemoteUser()` method:

```
public String HttpServletRequest.getRemoteUser()
```

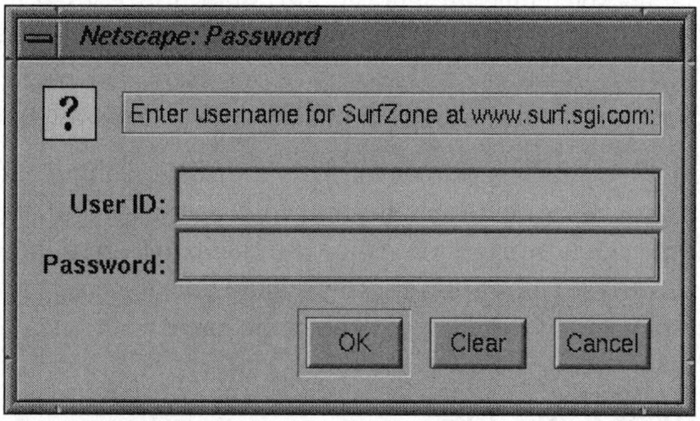

Figure 4-1. Login window for restricted page

Note that this information is retrieved from the servlet's `HttpServletRequest` object, the HTTP-specific subclass of `ServletRequest`. This method returns the name of the user making the request as a `String` or `null` if access to the servlet was not restricted. There is no comparable method to get the remote user's password (although it can be manually determined, as shown in Example 8-2 in Chapter 8). An example remote user might be `jhunter`.

A servlet can also use the `getAuthType()` method to find out what type of authorization was used:

```
public String HttpServletRequest.getAuthType()
```

This method returns the type of authentication used or `null` if access to the servlet was not restricted. The types may be `BASIC`, `DIGEST`, `FORM`, or `CLIENT-CERT`. See Chapter 8 for more information on the various types of authentication.

By the time the servlet calls `getRemoteUser()`, the server has already determined that the user is authorized to invoke the servlet, but that doesn't mean the remote user's name is worthless. The servlet could perform a second authorization check, more restrictive and dynamic than the server's. For example, it could return sensitive information about someone only if that person made the request, or it could enforce a rule that each user can make only 10 accesses per day.*

Then again, the client's name can simply tell the servlet who is accessing it. After all, the remote host is not necessarily unique to one user. Unix servers often host hundreds of users, and gateway proxies can act on behalf of thousands. But bear in mind that access to the client's name comes with a price. Every user must be registered with your server and, before accessing your site, must enter her name and

* Want to know how to say "access denied" for the 11th access attempt? It's in the next chapter.

password. Generally speaking, authentication should not be used just so a servlet can know to whom it is talking. Chapter 7, *Session Tracking*, describes some better, lower-maintenance techniques for knowing about users. However, if a servlet is already protected and has the name easily available, the servlet might as well use it.

With the remote user's name, a servlet can save information about each client. Over the long term, it can remember each individual's preferences. For the short term, it can remember the series of pages viewed by the client and use them to add a sense of state to a stateless HTTP protocol. The session-tracking tricks from Chapter 7 may be unnecessary if the servlet already knows the name of the client user.

A Personalized Welcome

A simple servlet that uses `getRemoteUser()` can greet its clients by name and remember when each last logged in, as shown in Example 4-11.

Example 4-11. Hey, I Remember You!

```
import java.io.*;
import java.util.*;
import javax.servlet.*;
import javax.servlet.http.*;

public class PersonalizedWelcome extends HttpServlet {

  Hashtable accesses = new Hashtable();

  public void doGet(HttpServletRequest req, HttpServletResponse res)
                              throws ServletException, IOException {
    res.setContentType("text/html");
    PrintWriter out = res.getWriter();

    // ...Some introductory HTML...

    String remoteUser = req.getRemoteUser();

    if (remoteUser == null) {
      out.println("Welcome!");
    }
    else {
      out.println("Welcome, " + remoteUser + "!");
      Date lastAccess = (Date) accesses.get(remoteUser);
      if (lastAccess == null) {
        out.println("This is your first visit!");
      }
      else {
        out.println("Your last visit was " + accesses.get(remoteUser));
      }
```

Example 4-11. Hey, I Remember You! (continued)

```
      if (remoteUser.equals("PROFESSOR FALKEN")) {
        out.println("Shall we play a game?");
      }

      accesses.put(remoteUser, new Date());
    }

    // ...Continue handling the request...
  }
}
```

This servlet uses a `Hashtable` to save the last access time for each remote user. The first thing it does for each request is greet the person by name and tell him the time of his last visit. Then it records the time of this visit, for use next time. After that, it continues handling the request.

The Request

We've seen how the servlet finds out about the server and about the client. Now it's time to move on to the really important stuff: how a servlet finds out what the client wants.

Request Parameters

Each access to a servlet can have any number of request parameters associated with it. These parameters are typically name/value pairs that tell the servlet any extra information it needs to handle the request. Please don't confuse these request parameters with servlet init parameters, which are associated with the servlet itself.

An HTTP servlet gets its request parameters as part of its query string (for GET requests) or as encoded POST data (for POST requests), or sometimes both. Fortunately, every servlet retrieves its parameters the same way, using `getParameter()` and `getParameterValues()`:

```
public String ServletRequest.getParameter(String name)
public String[] ServletRequest.getParameterValues(String name)
```

`getParameter()` returns the value of the named parameter as a `String` or `null` if the parameter was not specified.* The value is guaranteed to be in its normal, decoded form. If there's any chance a parameter could have more than one value,

* The `getParameter()` method was deprecated in the Java Web Server 1.1 in favor of `getParameterValues()`. However, after quite a lot of public protest, Sun took `getParameter()` off the deprecation list in the final release of Servlet API 2.0. It was the first Java method to be undeprecated!

you should use the `getParameterValues()` method instead. This method returns all the values of the named parameter as an array of `String` objects or `null` if the parameter was not specified. A single value is returned in an array of length 1. If you call `getParameter()` on a parameter with multiple values, the value returned is the same as the first value returned by `getParameterValues()`.

One word of warning: if the parameter information came in as encoded POST data, it will not be available if the POST data has already been read manually using the `getReader()` or `getInputStream()` method of `ServletRequest` (because POST data can be read only once).

The possible uses for request parameters are unlimited. They are a general-purpose way to tell a servlet what to do, how to do it, or both. For a simple example, let's look at how a dictionary servlet might use `getParameter()` to find out the word it needs to look up.

An HTML file could contain this form asking the user for a word to look up:

```
<FORM METHOD=GET ACTION="/servlet/Dictionary">
Word to look up: <INPUT TYPE=TEXT NAME="word"><P>
<INPUT TYPE=SUBMIT><P>
</FORM>
```

The following code retrieves the word parameter:

```
String word = req.getParameter("word");
String definition = getDefinition(word);
out.println(word + ": " + definition);
```

This code handles only one value per parameter. Some parameters have multiple values, such as when using <SELECT>:

```
<FORM METHOD=POST ACTION="/servlet/CarOrder">
Please select the Honda S2000 features you would like:<BR>
<SELECT NAME="features" MULTIPLE>
<OPTION VALUE="aero"> Aero Screen </OPTION>
<OPTION VALUE="cd"> CD Changer </OPTION>
<OPTION VALUE="spoiler"> Trunk Spoiler </OPTION>
</SELECT><BR>
<INPUT TYPE=SUBMIT VALUE="Add to shopping cart">
</FORM>
```

A servlet can use the `getParameterValues()` method to handle this form:

```
String[] features = req.getParameterValues("features");
if (features != null) {
  for (int i = 0; i < features.length; i++) {
    cart.add(features[i]);
  }
}
```

In addition to getting parameter values, a servlet can access parameter names using `getParameterNames()`:

```
public Enumeration ServletRequest.getParameterNames()
```

This method returns all the parameter names as an `Enumeration` of `String` object or an empty `Enumeration` if the servlet has no parameters. The method is most often used for debugging. The order of names will not necessarily match the order in the form.

Finally, a servlet can retrieve the raw query string of the request with `getQueryString()`:

```
public String ServletRequest.getQueryString()
```

This method returns the raw query string (encoded GET parameter information) of the request or `null` if there was no query string. This low-level information is rarely useful for handling form data. It's best for handling a single unnamed value, as in `/servlet/Sqrt?576`, where the returned query string is `576`.

Example 4-12 shows the use of these methods with a servlet that prints its query string, then prints the name and value for all its parameters.

Example 4-12. Snooping Parameters

```
import java.io.*;
import java.util.*;
import javax.servlet.*;
import javax.servlet.http.*;

public class ParameterSnoop extends HttpServlet {

  public void doGet(HttpServletRequest req, HttpServletResponse res)
                               throws ServletException, IOException {
    res.setContentType("text/plain");
    PrintWriter out = res.getWriter();

    out.println("Query String:");
    out.println(req.getQueryString());
    out.println();

    out.println("Request Parameters:");
    Enumeration enum = req.getParameterNames();
    while (enum.hasMoreElements()) {
      String name = (String) enum.nextElement();
      String values[] = req.getParameterValues(name);
      if (values != null) {
        for (int i = 0; i < values.length; i++) {
```

Example 4-12. Snooping Parameters (continued)

```
          out.println(name + " (" + i + "): " + values[i]);
        }
      }
    }
  }
}
```

This servlet's output is shown in Figure 4-2.

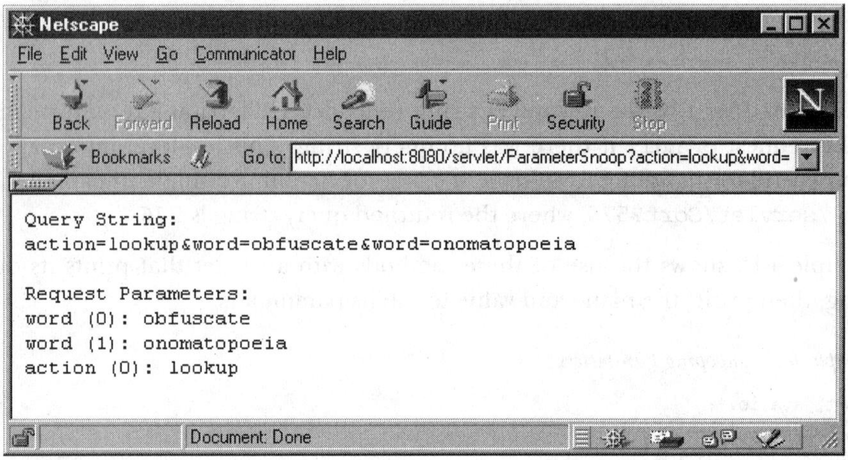

Figure 4-2. The snooped parameters

Beginning with Servlet API 2.2, you can create a POST form with an action URL that contains a query string. When you do this, the aggregated parameter information will be made available via the `getParameter()` methods, with query string parameter values coming before POST values in the case of name collisions. For example, if a request has a query string of `a=hokey` and POST data of `a=pokey`, the `req.getParameterValues("a")` method would return the array `{ "hokey", "pokey" }`.

Generating a License Key

Now we're ready to write a servlet that generates a `KeyedServerLock` license key for any given host and port number. A key from this servlet can be used to unlock the `KeyedServerLock` servlet. So, how will this servlet know the host and port number of the servlet it needs to unlock? Why, with request parameters, of course. Example 4-13 shows the code.

Example 4-13. Unlocking KeyedServerLock

```
import java.io.*;
import java.net.*;
import java.util.*;
import javax.servlet.*;
import javax.servlet.http.*;

public class KeyedServerUnlock extends HttpServlet {

  public void doGet(HttpServletRequest req, HttpServletResponse res)
                               throws ServletException, IOException {
    PrintWriter out = res.getWriter();

    // Get the host and port
    String host = req.getParameter("host");
    String port = req.getParameter("port");

    // If no host, use the current host
    if (host == null) {
      host = req.getServerName();
    }

    // Convert the port to an integer, if none use current port
    int numericPort;
    try {
      numericPort = Integer.parseInt(port);
    }
    catch (NumberFormatException e) {
      numericPort = req.getServerPort();
    }

    // Generate and print the key
    // Any KeyGenerationException is caught and displayed
    try {
      long key = generateKey(host, numericPort);
      out.println(host + ":" + numericPort + " has the key " + key);
    }
    catch (KeyGenerationException e) {
      out.println("Could not generate key: " + e.getMessage());
    }
  }

  // This method contains the algorithm used to match a key with
  // a server host and port. This example implementation is extremely
  // weak and should not be used by commercial sites.
  //
  // Throws a KeyGenerationException because anything more specific
  // would be tied to the chosen algorithm.
  //
```

Example 4-13. Unlocking KeyedServerLock (continued)

```
  private long generateKey(String host, int port) throws KeyGenerationException {

    // The key must be a 64-bit number equal to the logical not (~)
    // of the 32-bit IP address concatenated by the 32-bit port number.

    byte hostIP[];
    try {
      hostIP = InetAddress.getByName(host).getAddress();

    }
    catch (UnknownHostException e) {
      throw new KeyGenerationException(e.getMessage());
    }

    // Get the 32-bit IP address
    long servercode = 0;
    for (int i = 0; i < 4; i++) {
      servercode <<= 8;
      servercode |= hostIP[i];
    }

    // Concatentate the 32-bit port number
    servercode <<= 32;
    servercode |= port;

    // The key is the logical not
    return ~servercode;
  }
}

class KeyGenerationException extends Exception {

  public KeyGenerationException() {
    super();
  }

  public KeyGenerationException(String msg) {
    super(msg);
  }
}
```

You can use the output from this servlet to assign `KeyedServerLock` a special "key" instance variable:

```
<servlet>
  <servlet-name>
    ksl
  </servlet-name>
```

```
    <servlet-class>
      KeyedServerLock
    </servlet-class>
    <init-param>
      <param-name>
        key
      </param-name>
      <param-value>
        -9151314447111823249
      </param-value>
    </init-param>
  </servlet>
```

Remember to change the `generateKey()` logic before any real use.

Path Information

In addition to parameters, an HTTP request can include something called *extra path information* or a *virtual path.* Commonly, this extra path information is used to indicate a file on the server that the servlet should use for something. This path information is encoded in the URL of an HTTP request. An example URL looks like this:

```
http://server:port/servlet/ViewFile/index.html
```

This invokes the `ViewFile` servlet, passing `/index.html` as extra path information. A servlet can access this path information, and also translate the `/index.html` string into the real path of the *index.html* file. What is the real path of `/index.html`? It's the full file-system path to the file—what the server would return if the client asked for `/index.html` directly. This probably turns out to be *document_root/index.html*, but, of course, the server could have special aliasing that changes this.

Besides being specified explicitly in a URL, this extra path information can also be encoded in the `ACTION` parameter of an HTML form:

```
<FORM METHOD=GET ACTION="/servlet/Dictionary/dict/definitions.txt">
Word to look up: <INPUT TYPE=TEXT NAME="word"><P>
<INPUT TYPE=SUBMIT><P>
</FORM>
```

This form invokes the `Dictionary` servlet to handle its submissions and passes the `Dictionary` the extra path information `/dict/definitions.txt`. The `Dictionary` servlet can then know to look up word definitions using the *definitions.txt* file, the same file the client would see if it requested `/dict/definitions.txt`, on Tomcat probably `server_root/webapps/ROOT/dict/definitions.txt`.

Why Extra Path Information?

Why does HTTP have special support for extra path information? Isn't it enough to pass the servlet a path parameter? The answer is yes. Servlets don't need the special support, but CGI programs do.

A CGI program cannot interact with its server during execution, so it has no way to receive a path parameter, let alone ask the server to map it to a real filesystem location. The server has to somehow translate the path before invoking the CGI program. This is why there needs to be support for special "extra path information." Servers know to pretranslate this extra path and send the translation to the CGI program as an environment variable. It's a fairly elegant workaround to a shortcoming in CGI.

Of course, just because servlets don't need the special handling of extra path information, it doesn't mean they shouldn't use it. It provides a simple, convenient way to attach a path along with a request.

Getting path information

A servlet can use the `getPathInfo()` method to get extra path information:

```
public String HttpServletRequest.getPathInfo()
```

This method returns the extra path information associated with the request (URL decoded if necessary) or `null` if none was given. An example path is `/dict/definitions.txt`. The path information by itself, however, is only marginally useful. A servlet usually needs to know the actual filesystem location of the file given in the path information, which is where `getPathTranslated()` comes in:

```
public String HttpServletRequest.getPathTranslated()
```

This method returns the extra path information translated to a real filesystem path (URL decoded if necessary) or `null` if there is no extra path information. The method also returns `null` if the path could not be translated to a reasonable file path, such as when the web application is executing from a WAR archive, a remote filesystem not available locally, or a database. The returned path does not necessarily point to an existing file or directory. An example translated path is `C:\tomcat\webapps\ROOT\dict\definitions.txt`.

Example 4-14 shows a servlet that uses these two methods to print the extra path information it receives and the resulting translation to a real path.

Example 4-14. Showing Where the Path Leads

```
import java.io.*;
import java.util.*;
import javax.servlet.*;
import javax.servlet.http.*;

public class FileLocation extends HttpServlet {

  public void doGet(HttpServletRequest req, HttpServletResponse res)
                               throws ServletException, IOException {
    res.setContentType("text/plain");
    PrintWriter out = res.getWriter();

    if (req.getPathInfo() != null) {
      out.println("The file \"" + req.getPathInfo() + "\"");
      out.println("Is stored at \"" + req.getPathTranslated() + "\"");
    }
    else {
      out.println("Path info is null, no file to lookup");
    }
  }
}
```

Some example output of this servlet might be:

```
The file "/index.html"
Is stored at "/usr/local/tomcat/webapps/ROOT/index.html"
```

Ad hoc path translations

Sometimes a servlet needs to translate a path that wasn't passed in as extra path information. You can use the `getRealPath()` method for this task:

```
public String ServletContext.getRealPath(String path)
```

This method returns the real path of any given *virtual path* or `null` if the translation cannot be performed. If the given path is /, the method returns the document root (the place where documents are stored) for the server. If the given path is `getPathInfo()`, the method returns the same real path as would be returned by `getPathTranslated()`. This method can be used by generic servlets as well as HTTP servlets. There is no CGI counterpart.

Getting the context path

As we learned in Chapter 2, *HTTP Servlet Basics*, web applications are mapped to URI prefixes on the server. A servlet can determine the URI prefix of the context in which it's running using the `getContextPath()` method in `ServletRequest`:

```
public String ServletRequest.getContextPath()
```

This method returns a `String` representing the URI prefix of the context handling the request. The value starts with /, has no ending /, and, for the default context, is empty. For a request to */catalog/books/servlet/BuyNow*, for example, the `getContextPath()` would return `/catalog/books`.

You can use this method to help ensure your servlets will work regardless of what context path they're mapped to. For example, when generating a link to the home page for a context, you should refrain from hardcoding the context path and use generic code instead:

```
out.println("<a href=\"" + req.getContextPath() + "/index.html\">Home</a>");
```

Getting MIME types

Once a servlet has the path to a file, it often needs to discover the type of the file. Use `getMimeType()` to do this:

```
public String ServletContext.getMimeType(String file)
```

This method returns the MIME type of the given file, based on its extension, or `null` if it isn't known. Common MIME types are `text/html`, `text/plain`, `image/gif`, and `image/jpeg`. The following code fragment finds the MIME type of the extra path information:

```
String type = getServletContext().getMimeType(req.getPathTranslated())
```

Servers generally have knowledge about a core set of file-extension-to-mime-type mappings. These can be enhanced or overridden by entries in the *web.xml* deployment descriptor, giving each context a configurable behavior, as in Example 4-15.

Example 4-15. Everyone Loves a Mime

```
<?xml version="1.0" encoding="ISO-8859-1"?>

<!DOCTYPE web-app
    PUBLIC "-//Sun Microsystems, Inc.//DTD Web Application 2.2//EN"
    "http://java.sun.com/j2ee/dtds/web-app_2.2.dtd">

<web-app>
    <!-- ..... -->
    <mime-mapping>
        <extension>
            java
        </extension>
        <mime-type>
            text/plain
        </mime-type>
    </mime-mapping>
    <mime-mapping>
        <extension>
            cpp
```

Example 4-15. Everyone Loves a Mime (continued)

```
        </extension>
        <mime-type>
            text/plain
        </mime-type>
    </mime-mapping>
</web-app>
```

Serving Files

The Tomcat Server itself uses servlets to handle every request. Besides being a showcase for the ability of servlets, this gives the server a modular design that allows the wholesale replacement of certain aspects of its functionality. For example, all files are served by the `org.apache.tomcat.core.DefaultServlet` servlet, charged with the responsibility to handle the / path (meaning it's the default handler for requests). But there's nothing to say that the `DefaultServlet` cannot be replaced. In fact, it can be by changing the / URL pattern to use another servlet. Furthermore, it's not all that hard to write a primitive replacement for the `DefaultServlet`, using the methods we've just seen.

Example 4-16 shows a `ViewFile` servlet that uses the `getPathTranslated()` and `getMimeType()` methods to return the file is given by the extra path information.

Example 4-16. Dynamically Returning Static Files

```
import java.io.*;
import java.util.*;
import javax.servlet.*;
import javax.servlet.http.*;

import com.oreilly.servlet.ServletUtils;

public class ViewFile extends HttpServlet {

  public void doGet(HttpServletRequest req, HttpServletResponse res)
                               throws ServletException, IOException {
    // Use a ServletOutputStream because we may pass binary information
    ServletOutputStream out = res.getOutputStream();

    // Get the file to view
    String file = req.getPathTranslated();

    // No file, nothing to view
    if (file == null) {
      out.println("No file to view");
      return;
    }
```

Example 4-16. Dynamically Returning Static Files (continued)

```
    // Get and set the type of the file
    String contentType = getServletContext().getMimeType(file);
    res.setContentType(contentType);

    // Return the file
    try {
      ServletUtils.returnFile(file, out);
    }
    catch (FileNotFoundException e) {
      out.println("File not found");
    }
    catch (IOException e) {
      out.println("Problem sending file: " + e.getMessage());
    }
  }
}
```

This servlet first uses `getPathTranslated()` to get the name of the file it needs to display. Then it uses `getMimeType()` to find the content type of this file and sets the response content type to match. Last, it returns the file using the `returnFile()` method found in the `com.oreilly.servlet.ServletUtils` utility class:

```
// Send the contents of the file to the output stream
public static void returnFile(String filename, OutputStream out)
                        throws FileNotFoundException, IOException {
  // A FileInputStream is for bytes
  FileInputStream fis = null;
  try {
    fis = new FileInputStream(filename);
    byte[] buf = new byte[4 * 1024];  // 4K buffer
    int bytesRead;
    while ((bytesRead = fis.read(buf)) != -1) {
      out.write(buf, 0, bytesRead);
    }
  }
  finally {
    if (fis != null) fis.close();
  }
}
```

The servlet's error handling is basic—it returns a page that describes the error. This is acceptable for our simple example (and really more than many programs seem capable of), but we'll learn a better way using status codes in the next chapter. This servlet can be used directly with a URL like this:

```
http://server:port/servlet/ViewFile/index.html
```

Or, if you assign this servlet to handle the default URL pattern:

```
<servlet>
    <servlet-name>
        vf
    </servlet-name>
    <servlet-class>
        ViewFile
    </servlet-class>
</servlet>
<servlet-mapping>
    <servlet-name>
        vf
    </servlet-name>
    <url-pattern>
        /
    </url-pattern>
</servlet-mapping>
```

Then `ViewFile` is automatically invoked even for a URL like this:

```
http://server:port/index.html
```

Just beware that this servlet is a "proof-of-concept" example and does not have the full functionality of `DefaultServlet`.

Reading from an Abstract Resource

The `getPathTranslated()` method has some unfortunate limitations. First, it doesn't work for content served from WAR files because there's no direct file to access. Second, it doesn't work in a distributed load-balanced environment where there might exist a direct file but not on the server currently executing the servlet. To get around these limitations, Servlet API 2.1 introduced a technique for resource abstraction, which allows servlets to access a resource without knowing where the resource resides. A servlet gains access to an abstract resource using `getResource()`:

```
public URL ServletContext.getResource(String uripath)
```

This method returns a URL that can be used to investigate the specified resource and read its content. How the URI path parameter maps to an actual resource (file, WAR entry, database entry, or other) is determined by the web server. The two restrictions are that the path must be absolute (beginning with a slash) and that the URI should not be an active resource such as another servlet or CGI program. The `getResource()` method is intended to support only reading of static content (no dynamic content and no writing of content).

When using the context object to request resources, it's important to remember *not* to include the context path in the request. After all, the context knows its own path, and by not specifying the path in code, you ensure that the application can be moved to a different path prefix without recompiling. The following code fetches and prints the */includes/header.html* file for the current context:

```
URL url = getServletContext().getResource("/includes/header.html");
if (url != null) {
  ServletUtils.returnURL(url, out);
}
```

The *header.html* file may exist in an archive file on a server machine other than the one hosting the servlet, but conveniently that doesn't matter. The code uses the `returnURL()` convenience method from the `com.oreilly.servlet.ServletUtils` class:

```
// Sends URL contents to an OutputStream
public static void returnURL(URL url, OutputStream out) throws IOException {
  InputStream in = url.openStream();
  byte[] buf = new byte[4 * 1024];  // 4K buffer
  int bytesRead;
  while ((bytesRead = in.read(buf)) != -1) {
    out.write(buf, 0, bytesRead);
  }
}

// Sends URL contents to a PrintWriter
public static void returnURL(URL url, PrintWriter out) throws IOException {
  // Determine the URL's content encoding
  URLConnection con = url.openConnection();
  con.connect();
  String encoding = con.getContentEncoding();

  // Construct a Reader appropriate for that encoding
  BufferedReader in = null;
  if (encoding == null) {
    in = new BufferedReader(
         new InputStreamReader(url.openStream()));
  }
  else {
    in = new BufferedReader(
         new InputStreamReader(url.openStream(), encoding));
  }
  char[] buf = new char[4 * 1024];  // 4Kchar buffer
  int charsRead;
  while ((charsRead = in.read(buf)) != -1) {
    out.write(buf, 0, charsRead);
  }
}
```

As shown in the second `returnURL()` method in the preceding code, you can use the URL object to investigate the attributes of the abstract resource. Not all servers and Java runtimes support this functionality. Here's code that examines the home page for the current context:

```
URL url = getServletContext().getResource("/index.html"); // context home page
URLConnection con = url.openConnection();
con.connect();
int contentLength = con.getContentLength();      // not all support
String contentType = con.getContentType();       // not all support
long expiration = con.getExpiration();           // not all support
long lastModified = con.getLastModified();       // not all support
// etc...
```

Remember, the content served for the / URI path is entirely determined by the server. To access resources from another context, you can use `getContext()`:

```
public ServletContext ServletContext.getContext(String uripath)
```

This method returns a reference to the `ServletContext` for the given URI, subject to possible server-imposed security constraints. Here's how to get the default context:

```
getServletContext().getContext("/");
```

And here's how to get a reference to the web server's home page:

```
getServletContext().getContext("/").getResource("/index.html");
```

Be aware that `getResource()` does not necessarily follow the welcome file list, so `getResource"/"` may not return usable content.

There's a convenient method—`getResourceAsStream()`—for reading resources as a stream:

```
public InputStream ServletContext.getResourceAsStream(String uripath)
```

It behaves essentially the same as `getResource().openStream()`. For backward compatibility and to ease the transition to servlets for CGI programmers, the Servlet API will continue to include methods for file access, such as `getPathTranslated()`. Just remember that anytime you access a resource using a `File` object you're tying yourself to a particular machine.

Serving Resources

Using abstract resources, we can write an improved version of `ViewFile` that works even when the content is served from a WAR file or when the content resides on a machine different than the machine executing the servlet. The `UnsafeViewResource` servlet is shown in Example 4-17. It's labeled "unsafe" because it provides no protection of resources and it blindly serves files under *WEB-INF* and *.jsp* source.

Example 4-17. Serving an Abstract Resource, Unsafely

```
import java.io.*;
import java.net.*;
import java.util.*;
import javax.servlet.*;
import javax.servlet.http.*;

import com.oreilly.servlet.ServletUtils;

public class UnsafeViewResource extends HttpServlet {

  public void doGet(HttpServletRequest req, HttpServletResponse res)
                              throws ServletException, IOException {
    // Use a ServletOutputStream because we may pass binary information
    ServletOutputStream out = res.getOutputStream();
    res.setContentType("text/plain");  // sanity default

    // Get the resource to view
    String file = req.getPathInfo();
    if (file == null) {
      out.println("Extra path info was null; should be a resource to view");
      return;
    }

    // Convert the resource to a URL
    // WARNING: This allows access to files under WEB-INF and .jsp source
    URL url = getServletContext().getResource(file);
    if (url == null) {  // some servers return null if not found
      out.println("Resource " + file + " not found");
      return;
    }

    // Connect to the resource
    URLConnection con = null;
    try {
      con = url.openConnection();
      con.connect();
    }
    catch (IOException e) {
      out.println("Resource " + file + " could not be read: " + e.getMessage());
      return;
    }

    // Get and set the type of the resource
    String contentType = con.getContentType();
```

Example 4-17. Serving an Abstract Resource, Unsafely (continued)

```
    res.setContentType(contentType);

    // Return the resource
    // WARNING: This returns files under WEB-INF and .jsp source files
    try {
      ServletUtils.returnURL(url, out);
    }
    catch (IOException e) {
      res.sendError(res.SC_INTERNAL_SERVER_ERROR,
              "Problem sending resource: " + e.getMessage());
    }
  }
}
```

This servlet views files only within its own context. Any files outside its context are inaccessible from the `getServletContext().getResource()` method. This servlet also provides no protection of resources so files under *WEB-INF* and *.jsp* source may be served directly. Example 4-18 demonstrates a safer version of the class using the `ServletUtils.getResource()` method from `com.oreilly.servlet`.

Example 4-18. Serving an Abstract Resource, Safely

```
import java.io.*;
import java.net.*;
import java.util.*;
import javax.servlet.*;
import javax.servlet.http.*;

import com.oreilly.servlet.ServletUtils;

public class ViewResource extends HttpServlet {

  public void doGet(HttpServletRequest req, HttpServletResponse res)
                              throws ServletException, IOException {
    // Use a ServletOutputStream because we may pass binary information
    ServletOutputStream out = res.getOutputStream();
    res.setContentType("text/plain");  // sanity default

    // Get the resource to view
    URL url = null;
    try {
      url = ServletUtils.getResource(getServletContext(), req.getPathInfo());
    }
    catch (IOException e) {
      res.sendError(
        res.SC_NOT_FOUND,
        "Extra path info must point to a valid resource to view: " +
        e.getMessage());
```

Example 4-18. Serving an Abstract Resource, Safely (continued)

```
      return;
    }

    // Connect to the resource
    URLConnection con = url.openConnection();
    con.connect();

    // Get and set the type of the resource
    String contentType = con.getContentType();
    res.setContentType(contentType);

    // Return the resource
    try {
      ServletUtils.returnURL(url, out);
    }
    catch (IOException e) {
      res.sendError(res.SC_INTERNAL_SERVER_ERROR,
              "Problem sending resource: " + e.getMessage());
    }
  }
}
```

The `ServletUtils.getResource()` method wraps the `context.getResource()` method and adds three convenient security checks: Resources are not served if they contain double dots, end with a slash or dot, end with *.jsp*, or begin with *WEB-INF* or *META-INF*. The code follows:

```
public static URL getResource(ServletContext context, String resource)
                                    throws IOException {
  // Short-circuit if resource is null
  if (resource == null) {
    throw new FileNotFoundException(
      "Requested resource was null (passed in null)");
  }

  if (resource.endsWith("/") ||
      resource.endsWith("\\") ||
      resource.endsWith(".")) {
    throw new MalformedURLException("Path may not end with a slash or dot");
  }

  if (resource.indexOf("..") != -1) {
    throw new MalformedURLException("Path may not contain double dots");
  }

  String upperResource = resource.toUpperCase();
  if (upperResource.startsWith("/WEB-INF") ||
      upperResource.startsWith("/META-INF")) {
```

```
        throw new MalformedURLException(
          "Path may not begin with /WEB-INF or /META-INF");
      }

      if (upperResource.endsWith(".JSP")) {
        throw new MalformedURLException(
          "Path may not end with .jsp");
      }

      // Convert the resource to a URL
      URL url = context.getResource(resource);
      if (url == null) {
        throw new FileNotFoundException(
          "Requested resource was null (" + resource + ")");
      }

      return url;
    }
```

Serving Resources for Download

The `ViewResource` servlet has more than just academic use. If the `ViewResource` servlet hardcodes the `Content-Type` of the response to `application/octet-stream`, the servlet can act as a generic file downloader. Most browsers when they receive content of `application/octet-stream` offer the user a pop-up window asking where to save the content. The exception is Microsoft Internet Explorer, which, if it recognizes the content type empirically, ignores the server-assigned content type and displays the content normally. This "feature" precludes downloading GIF, JPEG, HTML, and other file types to an Internet Explorer browser.

Determining What Was Requested

A servlet can use several methods to find out exactly what file or servlet the client requested. After all, only the most conceited servlet would always assume itself to be the direct target of a request. A servlet may be nothing more than the handler for some other content.

No method directly returns the original Uniform Resource Locator (URL) used by the client to make a request. The `javax.servlet.http.HttpUtils` class, however, provides a `getRequestURL()` method that does about the same thing:*

```
public static StringBuffer HttpUtils.getRequestURL(HttpServletRequest req)
```

* Why isn't there a method that directly returns the original URL shown in the browser? Because the browser never sends the full URL. The port number, for example, is used by the client to make its HTTP connection, but it isn't included in the request made to the web server answering on that port.

This method reconstructs the request URL based on information available in the `HttpServletRequest` object. It returns a `StringBuffer` that includes the scheme (such as HTTP), server name, server port, and extra path information. The reconstructed URL should look almost identical to the URL used by the client. Differences between the original and reconstructed URLs should be minor (that is, a space encoded by the client as `%20` might be encoded by the server as a `+`). Because this method returns a `StringBuffer`, the request URL can be modified efficiently (for example, by appending query parameters). This method is often used for creating redirect messages and reporting errors.

Most of the time, however, a servlet doesn't really need the request URL. It just needs the request URI, which is returned by `getRequestURI()`:

```
public String HttpServletRequest.getRequestURI()
```

This method returns the Universal Resource Identifier (URI) of the request, before any URL decoding. For normal HTTP servlets, a request URI can be thought of as a URL minus the scheme, host, port, and query string, but including any extra path information. In other words, it's the context path plus the servlet path plus the path info.* Table 4-2 shows the request URIs for several request URLs.

Table 4-2. URLs and Their URIs

Request URL	Its URI Component
http://server:port/servlet/Classname	*/servlet/Classname*
http://server:port/servlet/registeredName	*/servlet/registeredName*
http://server:port/servlet/Classname?var=val	*/servlet/Classname*
http://server:port/servlet/Classname/pathinfo	*/servlet/Classname/pathinfo*
http://server:port/servlet/Classname/pathinfo?var=val	*/servlet/Classname/pathinfo*
http://server:port/servlet/Classname/path%20info[a]	*/servlet/Classname/path%20info*
http://server:port/alias.html (alias to a servlet)	*/alias.html*
http://server:port/context/path/servlet/Classname	*/context/path/servlet/Classname*

[a] *%20* is an encoded space

In some situations it is enough for a servlet to know the servlet name under which it was invoked. You can retrieve this information with `getServletPath()`:

```
public String HttpServletRequest.getServletPath()
```

* Technically, what is referred to here as a request URI could more formally be called a *request URL path*. This is because a URI is, in the most precise sense, a general-purpose identifier for a resource. A URL is one type of URI; a URN (Uniform Resource Name) is another. For more information on URIs, URLs, and URNs, see RFC 1630 at *http://www.ietf.org/rfc/rfc1630.txt*.

This method returns the part of the URI that refers to the servlet being invoked (URL decoded if necessary) or `null` if the URI does not directly point to a servlet. The servlet path does not include extra path information or the context path. Table 4-3 shows the servlet names for several request URLs.

Table 4-3. URLs and Their Servlet Paths

Request URL	Its Servlet Path
http://server:port/servlet/Classname	*/servlet/Classname*
http://server:port/servlet/registeredName	*/servlet/registeredName*
http://server:port/servlet/Classname?var=val	*/servlet/Classname*
http://server:port/servlet/Classname/pathinfo	*/servlet/Classname*
http://server:port/servlet/Classname/pathinfo?var=val	*/servlet/Classname*
http://server:port/servlet/Classname/path%20info	*/servlet/Classname*
http://server:port/alias.html (alias to a servlet)	*/alias.html*
http://server:port/context/path/servlet/Classname	*/servlet/Classname*

Here's a helpful trick in remembering path information:

```
decoded(getRequestURI) ==
              decoded(getContextPath) + getServletPath + getPathInfo
```

How It Was Requested

Besides knowing what was requested, a servlet has several ways of finding out details about how it was requested. The `getScheme()` method returns the scheme used to make this request:

```
public String ServletRequest.getScheme()
```

Examples include `http`, `https`, and `ftp`, as well as the newer Java-specific schemes `jdbc` and `rmi`. There is no direct CGI counterpart (though some CGI implementations have a `SERVER_URL` variable that includes the scheme). For HTTP servlets, this method indicates whether the request was made over a secure connection using the *Secure Sockets Layer (SSL)*, as indicated by the scheme `https`, or if it was an insecure request, as indicated by the scheme `http`.

The `getProtocol()` method returns the protocol and version number used to make the request:

```
public String ServletRequest.getProtocol()
```

The protocol and version number are separated by a slash. The method returns `null` if no protocol could be determined. For HTTP servlets, the protocol is usually

`HTTP/1.0` or `HTTP/1.1`. HTTP servlets can use the protocol version to determine if it's okay with the client to use the new features in HTTP Version 1.1.

To find out what method was used for a request, a servlet uses `getMethod()`:

```
public String HttpServletRequest.getMethod()
```

This method returns the HTTP method used to make the request. Examples include `GET`, `POST`, and `HEAD`. The `service()` method of the `HttpServlet` implementation uses this method in its dispatching of requests.

Request Headers

HTTP requests and responses can have a number of associated HTTP *headers*. These headers provide some extra information about the request or the response. The HTTP Version 1.0 protocol defines literally dozens of possible headers; the HTTP Version 1.1 protocol includes even more. A description of all the headers extends beyond the scope of this book; we discuss only the headers most often accessed by servlets. For a full list of HTTP headers and their uses, we recommend *HTTP Pocket Reference* by Clinton Wong (O'Reilly) or *Webmaster in a Nutshell* by Stephen Spainhour and Robert Eckstein (O'Reilly).

A servlet rarely needs to read the HTTP headers accompanying a request. Many of the headers associated with a request are handled by the server itself. Take, for example, how a server restricts access to its documents. The server uses HTTP headers, and servlets need not know the details. When a server receives a request for a restricted page, it checks that the request includes an appropriate `Authorization` header that contains a valid username and a password. If it doesn't, the server itself issues a response containing a `WWW-Authenticate` header, to tell the browser its access to a resource was denied. When the client sends a request that includes the proper `Authorization` header, the server grants the access and gives any servlet invoked access to the user's name via the `getRemoteUser()` call.

Other headers are used by servlets, but indirectly. A good example is the `Last-Modified` and `If-Last-Modified` pair discussed in Chapter 3. The server itself sees the `If-Last-Modified` header and calls the servlet's `getLastModified()` method to determine how to proceed.

There are a few HTTP headers that a servlet may want to read on occasion. These are listed in Table 4-4.

Table 4-4. Useful HTTP Request Headers

Header	Usage
`Accept`	Specifies the media (MIME) types the client prefers to accept, separated by commas. Some older browsers send a separate header for each media type. Each media type is divided into a type and subtype given as *`type/subtype`*. An asterisk (`*`) wildcard is allowed for the subtype (*type*/`*`) or for both the type and subtype (`*/*`). For example: `Accept: image/gif, image/jpeg, text/*, */*` A servlet can use this header to help determine what type of content to return. If this header is not passed as part of the request, the servlet can assume the client accepts all media types.
`Accept-Language`	Specifies the language or languages that the client prefers to receive, using the ISO-639 standard language abbreviations with an optional ISO-3166 country code. For example: `Accept-Language: en, es, de, ja, zh-TW` This indicates the client user reads English, Spanish, German, Japanese, and Chinese appropriate for Taiwan. By convention, languages are listed in order of preference. See Chapter 13, *Internationalization*, for more information on language negotiation.

`User-Agent`	Gives information about the client software. The format of the returned string is relatively free-form but often includes the browser name and version as well as information about the machine on which it is running. Netscape 4.7 on an SGI Indy running IRIX 6.2 reports:
	`User-Agent: Mozilla/4.7 [en] (X11; U; IRIX 6.2 IP22)`
	Microsoft Internet Explorer 4.0 running on a Windows 95 machine reports:
	`User-Agent: Mozilla/4.0 (compatible; MSIE 4.0; Windows 95)`
	A servlet can use this header to keep statistics or to customize its response based on browser type.

`Referer`	Gives the URL of the document that refers to the requested URL (that is, the document that contains the link the client followed to access this document).[a] For example: `Referer: http://developer.java.sun.com/index.html` A servlet can use this header to keep statistics or, if there's some error in the request, to keep track of the documents with errors.
`Authorization`	Provides the client's authorization to access the requested URI, including a username and password encoded in Base64. Servlets can use this for custom authorization, as discussed in Chapter 8.

[a] A dictionary would spell the word `Referrer`. However, we have to conform to the HTTP specification spelling `Referer`.

Accessing header values

HTTP header values are accessed through the `HttpServletRequest` object. A header value can be retrieved as a `String`, a `long` (representing a `Date`), or an `int`, using `getHeader()`, `getDateHeader()`, and `getIntHeader()`, respectively:

```
public String HttpServletRequest.getHeader(String name)
public long HttpServletRequest.getDateHeader(String name)
public int HttpServletRequest.getIntHeader(String name)
```

`getHeader()` returns the value of the named header as a `String` or `null` if the header was not sent as part of the request. The name is case insensitive, as it is for all these methods. Headers of all types can be retrieved with this method.

`getDateHeader()` returns the value of the named header as a `long` (representing a `Date`) that specifies the number of milliseconds since the epoch) or `-1` if the header was not sent as part of the request. This method throws an `IllegalArgumentException` when called on a header whose value cannot be converted to a `Date`. The method is useful for handling headers like `Last-Modified` and `If-Modified-Since`.

`getIntHeader()` returns the value of the named header as an `int` or `-1` if the header was not sent as part of the request. This method throws a `NumberFormatException` when called on a header whose value cannot be converted to an `int`.

A servlet can also get the names of all the headers it can access using `getHeaderNames()`:

```
public Enumeration HttpServletRequest.getHeaderNames()
```

This method returns the names of all the headers as an `Enumeration` of `String` objects. It returns an empty `Enumeration` if there were no headers. The Servlet API gives servlet container implementations the right to not allow headers to be accessed in this way, in which case this method returns `null`.

Some headers, like `Accept` and `Accept-Language`, support multiple values. Normally these values are passed in a single header separated by spaces, but some browsers prefer to send multiple values via multiple headers:

```
Accept-Language: en
Accept-Language: fr
Accept-Language: ja
```

To read a header with multiple values, servlets can use the `getHeaders()` method:

```
public Enumeration HttpServletRequest.getHeaders(String name)
```

This method returns all the values for the given header as an `Enumeration` of `String` objects or an empty `Enumeration` if the header was not sent as part of the request. If the servlet container does not allow access to header information, the call returns `null`. There is no `getDateHeaders()` or `getIntHeaders()` method.

Example 4-19 demonstrates the use of these methods in a servlet that prints information about its HTTP request headers.

Example 4-19. Snooping Headers

```
import java.io.*;
import java.util.*;
import javax.servlet.*;
import javax.servlet.http.*;

public class HeaderSnoop extends HttpServlet {

  public void doGet(HttpServletRequest req, HttpServletResponse res)
                               throws ServletException, IOException {
    res.setContentType("text/plain");
    PrintWriter out = res.getWriter();

    out.println("Request Headers:");
    out.println();
    Enumeration names = req.getHeaderNames();
    while (names.hasMoreElements()) {
      String name = (String) names.nextElement();
      Enumeration values = req.getHeaders(name);  // support multiple values
      if (values != null) {
        while (values.hasMoreElements()) {
          String value = (String) values.nextElement();
          out.println(name + ": " + value);
        }
      }
    }
  }
}
```

Some example output from this servlet might look like this:

```
Request Headers:

Connection: Keep-Alive
If-Modified-Since: Thursday, 17-Feb-00 23:23:58 GMT; length=297
User-Agent: Mozilla/4.7 [en] (WinNT; U)
Host: localhost:8080
Accept: image/gif, image/x-xbitmap, image/jpeg, image/pjpeg, image/png, */*
Accept-Language: en
Accept-Language: es
```

```
Accept-Charset: iso-8859-1,*,utf-8
Cookie: JSESSIONID=q1886xlc31
```

Wading the Input Stream

Each request handled by a servlet has an input stream associated with it. Just as a servlet can write to a `PrintWriter` or `OutputStream` associated with its response object, it can read from a `Reader` or `InputStream` associated with its request object. The data read from the input stream can be of any content type and of any length. The input stream has two purposes:

- To pass an HTTP servlet the content associated with a POST request
- To pass a non-HTTP servlet the raw data sent by the client

To read character data from the input stream, you should use `getReader()` to retrieve the input stream as a `BufferedReader` object:

```
public BufferedReader ServletRequest.getReader() throws IOException
```

The advantage of using a `BufferedReader` for reading character-based data is that it should translate charsets as appropriate. This method throws an `IllegalStateException` if `getInputStream()` has been called before on this same request. It throws an `UnsupportedEncodingException` if the character encoding of the input is unsupported or unknown.

To read binary data from the input stream, use `getInputStream()` to retrieve the input stream as a `ServletInputStream` object:

```
public ServletInputStream ServletRequest.getInputStream() throws IOException
```

A `ServletInputStream` is a direct subclass of `InputStream` and can be treated as a normal `InputStream`, with the added ability to efficiently read input a line at a time into an array of bytes. The method throws an `IllegalStateException` if `getReader()` has been called before on this same request. Once you have the `ServletInputStream`, you can read a line from it using `readLine()`:

```
public int ServletInputStream.readLine(byte b[], int off, int len)
  throws IOException
```

This method reads bytes from the input stream into the byte array `b`, starting at an offset in the array given by `off`. It stops reading when it encounters an `\n` or when it has read `len` number of bytes.* The ending `\n` character is read into the buffer as well. The method returns the number of bytes read or `-1` if the end of the stream is reached.

* Servlet API 2.0 implementations of `readLine()` suffered from a bug where the passed-in `len` parameter was ignored, causing problems including an `ArrayIndexOutOfBoundsException` if the line length exceeded the buffer size. This bug is fixed in Servlet API 2.1 and later.

A servlet can additionally check the content type and the length of the data being sent via the input stream, using `getContentType()` and `getContentLength()`, respectively:

```
public String ServletRequest.getContentType()
public int ServletRequest.getContentLength()
```

`getContentType()` returns the media type of the content being sent via the input stream or `null` if the type is not known (such as when there is no data). `getContentLength()` returns the length, in bytes, of the content being sent via the input stream or `-1` if this is not known.

Handling POST requests using the input stream

It is a rare occurrence when a servlet handling a POST request is forced to use its input stream to access the POST data. Typically, the POST data is nothing more than encoded parameter information, which a servlet can conveniently retrieve with its `getParameter()` method.

A servlet can identify this type of POST request by checking the content type of the input stream. If it is of type `application/x-www-form-urlencoded`, the data can be retrieved with `getParameter()` and similar methods.

A servlet may wish to call the `getContentLength()` method before calling `getParameter()` to prevent denial-of-service attacks. A rogue client may send an absurdly large amount of data as part of a POST request, hoping to slow the server to a crawl as the servlet's `getParameter()` method churns over the data. A servlet can use `getContentLength()` to verify that the length is reasonable, perhaps less than 4K, as a preventive measure.

Receiving files using the input stream

A servlet can also receive a file upload using its input stream. Before we see how, it's important to note that file uploading is experimental and not supported in all browsers. Netscape first supported file uploads with Netscape Navigator 3; Microsoft first supported it with Internet Explorer 4.

The full file upload specification is contained in experimental RFC 1867, available at *http://www.ietf.org/rfc/rfc1867.txt*, with additions in RFC 2388 at *http://www.ietf.org/rfc/rfc2388.txt*. The short summary is that any number of files and parameters can be sent as form data in a single POST request. The POST request is formatted differently than standard `application/x-www-form-urlencoded` form data and indicates this fact by setting its content type to `multipart/form-data`.

It's fairly simple to write the client half of a file upload. The HTML in Example 4-20 generates a form that asks for a user's name and a file to upload. Note the addition of the `ENCTYPE` attribute and the use of a `FILE` input type.

Example 4-20. A Form for Choosing a File to Upload

```
<FORM ACTION="/servlet/UploadTest" ENCTYPE="multipart/form-data" METHOD=POST>
What is your name? <INPUT TYPE=TEXT NAME=submitter> <BR>
Which file do you want to upload? <INPUT TYPE=FILE NAME=file> <BR>
<INPUT TYPE=SUBMIT>
</FORM>
```

A user receiving this form sees a page that looks something like Figure 4-3. A filename can be entered in the text area, or it can be selected by browsing. Multiple `<INPUT TYPE=FILE>` fields can be used, but current browsers support uploading only one file per field. After selection, the user submits the form as usual.

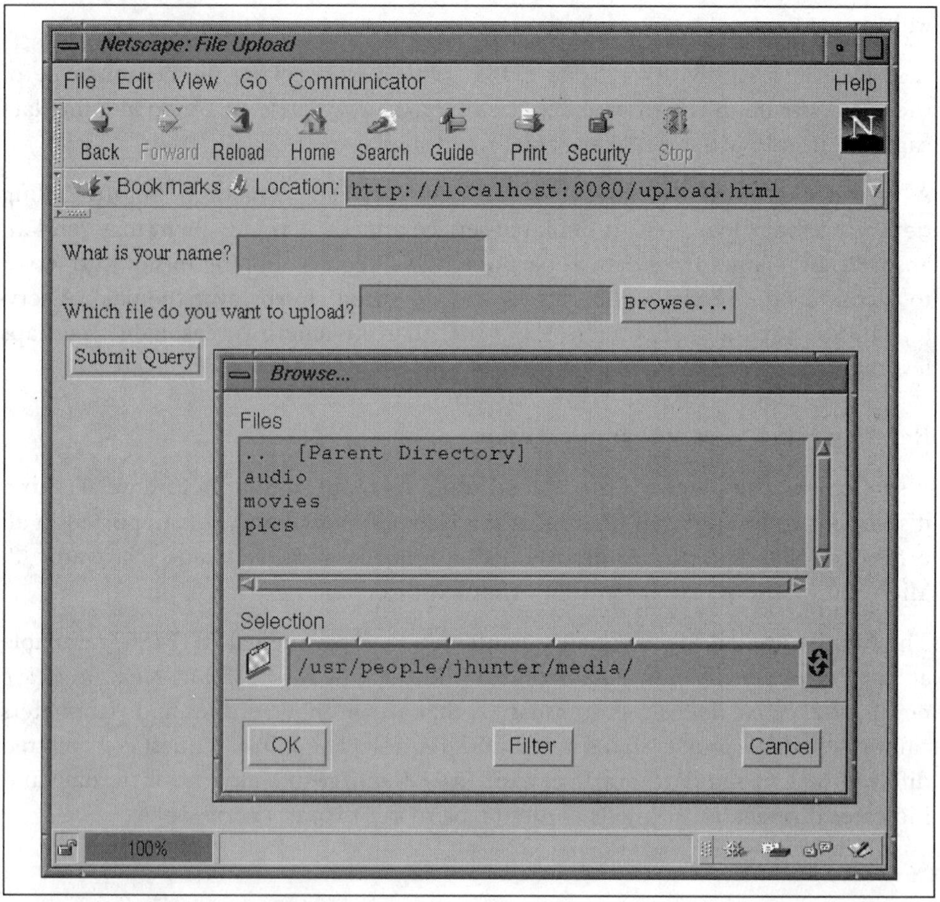

Figure 4-3. Choosing a file to upload

The server's responsibilities during a file upload are slightly more complicated. From the receiving servlet's perspective, the submission is nothing more than a raw data stream in its input stream—a data stream formatted according to the `multipart/form-data` content type given in RFC 1867. The Servlet API provides no methods to aid in the parsing of the data. To simplify your life (and ours since we don't want to explain RFC 1867), Jason has written a utility class that does the work for you. It's named `MultipartRequest` and is shown in Example 4-22 later in this section.

`MultipartRequest` wraps around a `ServletRequest` and presents a simple API to the servlet programmer. The class has two constructors:

```
public MultipartRequest(HttpServletRequest request, String saveDirectory,
                        int maxPostSize) throws IOException
public MultipartRequest(HttpServletRequest request,
                        String saveDirectory) throws IOException
```

Each of these methods creates a new `MultipartRequest` object to handle the specified request, saving any uploaded files to `saveDirectory`. Both constructors actually parse the `multipart/form-data` content and throw an `IOException` if there's any problem (so servlets using this class must refrain from reading the input stream themselves). The constructor that takes a `maxPostSize` parameter also throws an `IOException` if the uploaded content is larger than `maxPostSize`. The second constructor assumes a default `maxPostSize` of 1 MB.

Note that a server has two choices when receiving an upload whose content length is too large: first, try to send an error page, wait for the client to disconnect, and while waiting silently consume all uploaded content. This follows the HTTP/1.1 specification in RFC 2616, Section 8.2.2, which dictates a client should listen for an "error status" during its upload (see *http://www.ietf.org/rfc/rfc2616.txt*) and halt the upload should it receive an error. This ensures every client sees a proper error message, but for the many browsers which don't listen for an error status, this approach wastes server bandwidth as the client continues the full upload. For this reason many servers implement a second option: try to send an error page, and forcefully disconnect if necessary. This leaves some clients without a polite error message, but it assuredly stops the upload.

The `MultipartRequest` class has seven public methods that let you get at information about the request. You'll notice that many of these methods are modeled after `ServletRequest` methods. Use `getParameterNames()` to retrieve the names of all the request parameters:

```
public Enumeration MultipartRequest.getParameterNames()
```

This method returns the names of all the parameters as an `Enumeration` of `String` objects or an empty `Enumeration` if there are no parameters.

To get the value of a named parameter, use `getParameter()` or `getParameterValues()`:

```
public String MultipartRequest.getParameter(String name)
```

This method returns the value of the named parameter as a `String` or `null` if the parameter was not given. The value is guaranteed to be in its normal, decoded form. If the parameter has multiple values, only the last one is returned.

```
public String[] MultipartRequest.getParameterValues(String name)
```

This method returns all the values of the named parameter as an array of `String` objects or `null` if the parameter was not given. A single value is returned in an array of length `1`.

Use `getFileNames()` to get a list of all the uploaded files:

```
public Enumeration MultipartRequest.getFileNames()
```

This method returns the names of all the uploaded files as an `Enumeration` of `String` objects, or an empty `Enumeration` if there are no uploaded files. Note that each filename is the name specified by the HTML form's name attribute, not by the user. Once you have the name of a file, you can get its filesystem name using `getFilesystemName()`:

```
public String MultipartRequest.getFilesystemName(String name)
```

This method returns the filesystem name of the specified file or `null` if the file was not included in the upload. A filesystem name is the name specified by the user. It is also the name under which the file is actually saved. You can get the content type of the file with `getContentType()`:

```
public String MultipartRequest.getContentType(String name)
```

This method returns the content type of the specified file (as supplied by the client browser) or `null` if the file was not included in the upload. Finally, you can get a `java.io.File` object for the file with `getFile()`:

```
public File MultipartRequest.getFile(String name)
```

This method returns a `File` object for the specified file saved on the server's filesystem or `null` if the file was not included in the upload.

Example 4-21 shows how a servlet uses `MultipartRequest`. The servlet does nothing but display the statistics for what was uploaded. Notice that it does not delete the files it saves.

Example 4-21. Handling a File Upload

```
import java.io.*;
import java.util.*;
import javax.servlet.*;
import javax.servlet.http.*;

import com.oreilly.servlet.MultipartRequest;

public class UploadTest extends HttpServlet {

  public void doPost(HttpServletRequest req, HttpServletResponse res)
                                throws ServletException, IOException {
    res.setContentType("text/html");
    PrintWriter out = res.getWriter();

    try {
      // Blindly take it on faith this is a multipart/form-data request

      // Construct a MultipartRequest to help read the information.
      // Pass in the request, a directory to save files to, and the
      // maximum POST size we should attempt to handle.
      // Here we (rudely) write to the current dir and impose 5 Meg limit.
      MultipartRequest multi =
        new MultipartRequest(req, ".", 5 * 1024 * 1024);

      out.println("<HTML>");
      out.println("<HEAD><TITLE>UploadTest</TITLE></HEAD>");
      out.println("<BODY>");
      out.println("<H1>UploadTest</H1>");

      // Print the parameters we received
      out.println("<H3>Params:</H3>");
      out.println("<PRE>");
      Enumeration params = multi.getParameterNames();
      while (params.hasMoreElements()) {
        String name = (String)params.nextElement();
        String value = multi.getParameter(name);
        out.println(name + " = " + value);
      }
      out.println("</PRE>");

      // Show which files we received
      out.println("<H3>Files:</H3>");
      out.println("<PRE>");
      Enumeration files = multi.getFileNames();
      while (files.hasMoreElements()) {
        String name = (String)files.nextElement();
        String filename = multi.getFilesystemName(name);
        String type = multi.getContentType(name);
```

Example 4-21. Handling a File Upload (continued)

```
        File f = multi.getFile(name);
        out.println("name: " + name);
        out.println("filename: " + filename);
        out.println("type: " + type);
        if (f != null) {
          out.println("length: " + f.length());
        }
        out.println();
      }
      out.println("</PRE>");
    }
    catch (Exception e) {
      out.println("<PRE>");
      e.printStackTrace(out);
      out.println("</PRE>");
    }
    out.println("</BODY></HTML>");
  }
}
```

The servlet passes its request object to the `MultipartRequest` constructor, along with a directory relative to the server root where the uploaded files are to be saved (because large files may not fit in memory) and a maximum POST size of 5 MB. The servlet then uses `MultipartRequest` to iterate over the parameters that were sent. Notice that the `MultipartRequest` API for handling parameters matches that of `ServletRequest`. Finally, the servlet uses its `MultipartRequest` to iterate over the files that were sent. For each file, it gets the file's name (as specified on the form), filesystem name (as specified by the user), and content type. It also gets a `File` reference and uses it to display the length of the saved file. If there are any problems, the servlet reports the exception to the user.

Example 4-22 shows the code for `MultipartRequest`. You'll notice the `MultipartRequest` class actually uses `com.oreilly.servlet.multipart.MultipartParser` behind the scenes to handle the task of parsing the request. The `MultipartParser` class provides low-level access to the upload by walking the request piece by piece. This allows, for example, direct uploading of files into a database or checking that a file passes certain criteria before saving. The code and documentation for `MultipartParser` is available at *http://www.servlets.com.* (My thanks to Geoff Soutter for the factoring-out work necessary to create the parser.)

Be aware that many server vendors don't adequately test their server for file upload use, and it's not uncommon for this class to uncover server bugs. If you have problems using the class try another server (such as Tomcat) to identify if it's a server-specific issue and if so contact your server vendor.

Example 4-22. The MultipartRequest Class

```
package com.oreilly.servlet;

import java.io.*;
import java.util.*;
import javax.servlet.*;
import javax.servlet.http.*;

import com.oreilly.servlet.multipart.MultipartParser;
import com.oreilly.servlet.multipart.Part;
import com.oreilly.servlet.multipart.FilePart;
import com.oreilly.servlet.multipart.ParamPart;

// A utility class to handle <code>multipart/form-data</code> requests.
public class MultipartRequest {

  private static final int DEFAULT_MAX_POST_SIZE = 1024 * 1024;  // 1 Meg

  private Hashtable parameters = new Hashtable();  // name - Vector of values
  private Hashtable files = new Hashtable();       // name - UploadedFile

  public MultipartRequest(HttpServletRequest request,
                          String saveDirectory) throws IOException {
    this(request, saveDirectory, DEFAULT_MAX_POST_SIZE);
  }

  public MultipartRequest(HttpServletRequest request,
                          String saveDirectory,
                          int maxPostSize) throws IOException {
    // Sanity check values
    if (request == null)
      throw new IllegalArgumentException("request cannot be null");
    if (saveDirectory == null)
      throw new IllegalArgumentException("saveDirectory cannot be null");
    if (maxPostSize <= 0) {
      throw new IllegalArgumentException("maxPostSize must be positive");
    }

    // Save the dir
    File dir = new File(saveDirectory);

    // Check saveDirectory is truly a directory
    if (!dir.isDirectory())
      throw new IllegalArgumentException("Not a directory: " + saveDirectory);

    // Check saveDirectory is writable
    if (!dir.canWrite())
```

Example 4-22. The MultipartRequest Class (continued)

```
      throw new IllegalArgumentException("Not writable: " + saveDirectory);

    // Parse the incoming multipart, storing files in the dir provided,
    // and populate the meta objects which describe what we found
    MultipartParser parser = new MultipartParser(request, maxPostSize);

    Part part;
    while ((part = parser.readNextPart()) != null) {
      String name = part.getName();
      if (part.isParam()) {
        // It's a parameter part, add it to the vector of values
        ParamPart paramPart = (ParamPart) part;
        String value = paramPart.getStringValue();
        Vector existingValues = (Vector)parameters.get(name);
        if (existingValues == null) {
          existingValues = new Vector();
          parameters.put(name, existingValues);
        }
        existingValues.addElement(value);
      }
      else if (part.isFile()) {
        // It's a file part
        FilePart filePart = (FilePart) part;
        String fileName = filePart.getFileName();
        if (fileName != null) {
          // The part actually contained a file
          filePart.writeTo(dir);
          files.put(name, new UploadedFile(
                      dir.toString(), fileName, filePart.getContentType()));
        }
        else {
          // The field did not contain a file
          files.put(name, new UploadedFile(null, null, null));
        }
      }
    }
  }

  // Constructor with an old signature, kept for backward compatibility.
  public MultipartRequest(ServletRequest request,
                          String saveDirectory) throws IOException {
    this((HttpServletRequest)request, saveDirectory);
  }

  // Constructor with an old signature, kept for backward compatibility.
  public MultipartRequest(ServletRequest request,
                          String saveDirectory,
                          int maxPostSize) throws IOException {
```

Example 4-22. The MultipartRequest Class (continued)

```
    this((HttpServletRequest)request, saveDirectory, maxPostSize);
  }

  public Enumeration getParameterNames() {
    return parameters.keys();
  }

  public Enumeration getFileNames() {
    return files.keys();
  }

  public String getParameter(String name) {
    try {
      Vector values = (Vector)parameters.get(name);
      if (values == null || values.size() == 0) {
        return null;
      }
      String value = (String)values.elementAt(values.size() - 1);
      return value;
    }
    catch (Exception e) {
      return null;
    }
  }

  public String[] getParameterValues(String name) {
    try {
      Vector values = (Vector)parameters.get(name);
      if (values == null || values.size() == 0) {
        return null;
      }
      String[] valuesArray = new String[values.size()];
      values.copyInto(valuesArray);
      return valuesArray;
    }
    catch (Exception e) {
      return null;
    }
  }

  public String getFilesystemName(String name) {
    try {
      UploadedFile file = (UploadedFile)files.get(name);
      return file.getFilesystemName();  // may be null
    }
    catch (Exception e) {
      return null;
```

Example 4-22. The MultipartRequest Class (continued)

```
    }
  }

  public String getContentType(String name) {
    try {
      UploadedFile file = (UploadedFile)files.get(name);
      return file.getContentType();  // may be null
    }
    catch (Exception e) {
      return null;
    }
  }

  public File getFile(String name) {
    try {
      UploadedFile file = (UploadedFile)files.get(name);
      return file.getFile();  // may be null
    }
    catch (Exception e) {
      return null;
    }
  }
}


// A class to hold information about an uploaded file.
class UploadedFile {

  private String dir;
  private String filename;
  private String type;

  UploadedFile(String dir, String filename, String type) {
    this.dir = dir;
    this.filename = filename;
    this.type = type;
  }

  public String getContentType() {
    return type;
  }

  public String getFilesystemName() {
    return filename;
  }

  public File getFile() {
    if (dir == null || filename == null) {
```

Example 4-22. The MultipartRequest Class (continued)

```
      return null;
    }
    else {
      return new File(dir + File.separator + filename);
    }
  }
}
```

`MultipartRequest` is production quality and, unlike many other file upload libraries, supports arbitrarily large uploads. Can you figure out why the class doesn't implement the `HttpServletRequest` interface? It's because to do so would limit its forward compatibility. If the class implemented `HttpServletRequest` and Servlet API 2.3 were to add a method to the interface, this class would no longer fully implement the interface, causing compiles of servlets using the class to fail.

Extra Attributes

Sometimes a servlet needs to know something about a request that's not available via any of the previously mentioned methods. In these cases, there is one last alternative, the `getAttribute()` method. Remember how `ServletContext` has a `getAttribute()` method that returns server-specific attributes about the server itself? `ServletRequest` also has a `getAttribute()` method:

```
public Object ServletRequest.getAttribute(String name)
```

This method returns the value of a server-specific attribute for the request or `null` if the server does not support the named request attribute. This method allows a server to provide a servlet with custom information about a request. Servers are free to provide whatever attributes they choose, or even no attributes at all. The only rules are that attribute names should follow the same convention as package names, with the package names `java.*` and `javax.*` reserved for use by the Java Software division of Sun Microsystems and `com.sun.*` reserved for use by Sun Microsystems. You should see your server's documentation for a description of its attributes, and remember that using any server-specific attributes restricts your application's portability.

Servlets can also add their own attributes to the request using the `setAttribute()` method as discussed in Chapter 11. A listing of all current attributes, hard-coded by the server or placed there by servlets, can be obtained with `getAttributeNames()`:

```
public Enumeration ServletRequest.getAttributeNames()
```

The following code displays all current attributes:

```
Enumeration enum = req.getAttributeNames();
while (enum.hasMoreElements()) {
```

```
    String name = (String) enum.nextElement();
    out.println("  req.getAttribute(\"" + name + "\"): " +
                   req.getAttribute(name));
  }
```

Several standard attributes exist involving included requests (see Chapter 11) and client-side digital certificates (see Chapter 8).

In this chapter:

- *The Structure of a Response*
- *Sending a Normal Response*
- *Using Persistent Connections*
- *Response Buffering*
- *Status Codes*
- *HTTP Headers*
- *When Things Go Wrong*
- *Six Ways to Skin a Servlet Cat*

5

Sending HTML Information

In the previous chapter, we learned that a servlet has access to all sorts of information—information about the client, about the server, about the request, and even about itself. Now it's time to look at what a servlet can do with that information, by learning how it sets and sends information.

The chapter begins with a review of how a servlet returns a normal HTML response, fully explaining some methods we glossed over in previous examples. Next we cover how to reduce the overhead involved in returning a response by keeping alive a connection to the client, and we look at how to use response buffering to help this. Then we explore the extra things you can do with HTML and HTTP, including returning errors and other status codes, sending custom header information, redirecting the request, using client pull, handling servlet exceptions, detecting when the user disconnects, and writing data to the server log.

Unlike the first edition, this chapter does *not* go into detail on generating HTML within servlets. Instead, at the end of the chapter, we introduce the concept of a content-creation architecture, which can be layered on top of servlets and provides a more effective way of generating HTML content. This is an introduction to later chapters in the book in which we discuss a number of individual frameworks.

The Structure of a Response

An HTTP servlet can return three kinds of things to the client: a single status code, any number of HTTP headers, and a response body. A *status code* is an integer value that describes, as you would expect, the status of the response. The status code can indicate success or failure, or it can tell the client software to take further action to finish the request. The numerical status code is often accompanied by a *reason phrase* that describes the status in prose better understood by a human. Usually, a status code works behind the scenes and is interpreted by the browser software. Sometimes, especially when things go wrong, a browser may show the status code to the user. The most famous status code is probably the 404 Not Found code, sent by a web server when it cannot locate a requested URL.

We saw HTTP headers in the previous chapter when clients used them to send extra information along with a request. In this chapter, we'll see how a servlet can send HTTP headers as part of its response.

The response body is the main content of the response. For an HTML page, the response body is the HTML itself. For a graphic, the response body contains the bytes that make up the image. A response body can be of any type and of any length; the client knows what to expect by reading and interpreting the HTTP headers in the response.

A generic servlet is much simpler than an HTTP servlet—it returns only a response body to its client. It's possible, however, for a subclass of `GenericServlet` to present an API that divides this single response body into a more elaborate structure, giving the appearance of returning multiple items. In fact, this is exactly what HTTP servlets do. At the lowest level, a web server sends its entire response as a stream of bytes to the client. Any methods that set status codes or headers are abstractions above that.

It's important to understand this because even though a servlet programmer doesn't have to know the details of the HTTP protocol, the protocol does affect the order in which a servlet can call its methods. Specifically, the HTTP protocol specifies that the status code and headers must be sent before the response body. A servlet, therefore, must be careful to always set its status code and headers before sending any response body to the client. A servlet can buffer its response body to give it some extra flexibility, but once any response body has been sent the response is considered *committed* and the status code and headers cannot be altered.

Sending a Normal Response

Let's begin our discussion of servlet responses with another look at the first servlet in this book, the `HelloWorld` servlet, shown in Example 5-1. We hope it looks a lot simpler to you now than it did back in Chapter 2, *HTTP Servlet Basics.*

Example 5-1. Hello Again

```
import java.io.*;
import javax.servlet.*;
import javax.servlet.http.*;
```

Example 5-1. Hello Again (continued)

```
public class HelloWorld extends HttpServlet {

  public void doGet(HttpServletRequest req, HttpServletResponse res)
                               throws ServletException, IOException {

    res.setContentType("text/html");
    PrintWriter out = res.getWriter();

    out.println("<HTML>");
    out.println("<HEAD><TITLE>Hello World</TITLE></HEAD>");
    out.println("<BODY>");
    out.println("<BIG>Hello World</BIG>");
    out.println("</BODY></HTML>");
  }
}
```

This servlet uses two methods and a class that have been only briefly mentioned before. The `setContentType()` method of `ServletResponse` sets the content type of the response to be the specified type:

```
public void ServletResponse.setContentType(String type)
```

In an HTTP servlet, this method sets the `Content-Type` HTTP header.

The `getWriter()` method returns a `PrintWriter` for writing character-based response data:

```
public PrintWriter ServletResponse.getWriter() throws IOException
```

The writer encodes the characters according to whatever charset is given in the content type. If no charset is specified, as is generally the case, the writer uses the ISO-8859-1 (Latin-1) encoding appropriate for Western European languages. Charsets are covered in depth in Chapter 13, *Internationalization,* so for now just remember that it's good form to always set the content type before you get a `PrintWriter`. This method throws an `IllegalStateException` if `getOutputStream()` has already been called for this response; and this method throws an `UnsupportedEncodingException` if the encoding of the output stream is unsupported or unknown.

In addition to using a `PrintWriter` to return a response, a servlet can use a special subclass of `java.io.OutputStream` in order to write binary data—the `ServletOutputStream`, which is defined in `javax.servlet`. You can get a `ServletOutputStream` with `getOutputStream()`:

```
public ServletOutputStream ServletResponse.getOutputStream() throws IOException
```

This method returns a `ServletOutputStream` for writing binary (byte-at-a-time) response data. No encoding is performed. This method throws an

`IllegalStateException` if `getWriter()` has already been called for this response.

The `ServletOutputStream` class resembles the standard Java `PrintStream` class. In the Servlet API Version 1.0, this class was used for all servlet output, both textual and binary. In the Servlet API Version 2.0 and later, however, it has been relegated to handling binary output only. As a direct subclass of `OutputStream`, it makes available the `write()`, `flush()`, and `close()` methods of the `OutputStream` class. To these it adds its own `print()` and `println()` methods for writing most of the primitive Java datatypes (see Appendix A, *Servlet API Quick Reference,* for a complete list). The only difference between the `ServletOutputStream` interface and that of a `PrintStream` is the `print()` and `println()` methods of `ServletOutputStream` inexplicably cannot directly print parameters of type `Object` or `char[]`.

Using Persistent Connections

Persistent connections (sometimes called *keep-alive connections*) can be used to optimize the way servlets return content to the client. To understand how this optimization works, you first need to understand how HTTP connections work. We'll keep this at a high level and go only as low as is necessary to explain the basic idea. The details are well covered in Clinton Wong's *HTTP Pocket Reference* (O'Reilly).

When a client, such as a browser, wants to request a web document from a server, it begins by establishing a socket connection to the server. Over this connection, the client makes its request and then receives the server's response. The client indicates it has finished its request by sending a blank line; the server, in turn, indicates that the response is complete by closing the socket connection.

So far, so good. But what if the retrieved page contains `<IMG>` tags or `<APPLET>` tags that require the client to retrieve more content from the server? Well, another socket connection is used. If a page contains 10 graphics along with an applet made up of 25 classes, that's 36 connections needed to transfer the page. No wonder some people say WWW stands for the World Wide Wait! This approach is like ordering a pizza, but making a separate phone call for each topping.

A better approach is to use the same socket connection to retrieve more than one piece of a page, something called a persistent connection. The trick with a persistent connection is that the client and server must somehow agree on where the server's response ends and where the client's next request begins. They could try to use a token like a blank line, but what if the response itself contains a blank line? The way persistent connections work is that the server just tells the client how big the response body will be by setting the `Content-Length` header as part of the response. The client then knows that after that much response body, it has control of the socket again.

Most servers internally manage the `Content-Length` header for the static files they serve; the `Content-Length` is set to match the file's length. To determine the content length of servlet-generated output, a server requires the servlet's assistance. A servlet can set the response `Content-Length` and gain the advantages of a persistent connection for its dynamic content by using the `setContentLength()` method:

```
public void ServletResponse.setContentLength(int len)
```

This method sets the length (in bytes) of the content being returned by the server. In an HTTP servlet, the method sets the HTTP `Content-Length` header. Note that using this method is optional. If you use it, however, your servlets will be able to take advantage of persistent connections when they are available. The client will also be able to display an accurate progress monitor during the download.

If you do call `setContentLength()`, there are two caveats: a servlet must call this method before sending the response body, and the given length must be exact. If it's off by even one byte, you have the potential for problems.

Response Buffering

Beginning with Servlet API 2.2, a servlet has control over whether the server buffers its response and may dictate how large a buffer the server can use. In previous versions of the API, most web servers implemented response buffering as a way to improve performance; exactly how large that buffer was depended on the server. Generally, servers had buffers in the neighborhood of 8K.

A response buffer allows a servlet to write some amount of output with a guarantee that the response won't be immediately committed. If the servlet finds an error, the status code and headers can still be changed so long as the buffer has not been flushed.

Response buffering also provides a simple way to avoid the potentially difficult content length precalculation. A servlet can use buffering to automatically calculate the content length, as shown in Example 5-2.

Example 5-2. A Servlet Using Buffering to Support Persistent Connections

```
import java.io.*;
import javax.servlet.*;
import javax.servlet.http.*;

public class KeepAlive extends HttpServlet {
```

Example 5-2. A Servlet Using Buffering to Support Persistent Connections (continued)

```
  public void doGet(HttpServletRequest req, HttpServletResponse res)
                               throws ServletException, IOException {

    res.setContentType("text/html");

    // Ask for a 16K byte response buffer; do not set the content length
    res.setBufferSize(16 * 1024);

    PrintWriter out = res.getWriter();
    out.println("<HTML>");
    out.println("<HEAD><TITLE>Hello World</TITLE></HEAD>");
    out.println("<BODY>");
    out.println("<BIG>Less than 16K of response body</BIG>");
    out.println("</BODY></HTML>");
  }
}
```

This servlet calls `setBufferSize()` to request a 16K-byte minimum response buffer, then sends its response body as usual. The server uses an internal buffer at least 16,384 bytes large to hold the response body and waits to send the content to the client until either the buffer fills or the servlet requests a buffer flush. Should the full response body fits within the buffer, the server can (but is not required to) automatically set the response `Content-Length` header.

It is important to note that buffering responses comes with a price. Buffering all the output and sending it all in one batch requires extra memory, and it may delay the time at which a client begins receiving data. For servlets with short responses, persistent connections make sense, but for servlets with long responses, the memory overhead and delay probably outweigh the benefit of opening fewer connections.

It is also important to note that not all servers and not all clients support persistent connections. That said, it's still appropriate for a servlet to set its content length or buffer its output so the server can determine the length. The content length information will be used by those servers and clients that support persistent connections and ignored by the others.

Controlling the Response Buffer

Five methods in `ServletResponse` provide control over response buffering. You can use `setBufferSize()` to tell the server the minimum buffer size (in bytes) that your servlet will accept:

```
public void ServletResponse.setBufferSize(int size)
  throws IllegalStateException
```

The server may provide a larger buffer than requested—it may want to keep buffers in 8K blocks, for example, to facilitate reuse. A larger buffer allows more content to be written before anything is actually sent, thus providing the servlet with more time to set appropriate status codes and headers. A smaller buffer decreases server memory load and allows the client to start receiving data more quickly. This method must be called before any response body content is written; if content has been written, this method throws an `IllegalStateException`. Use `getBufferSize()` to determine the size of the buffer:

```
public int ServletResponse.getBufferSize()
```

This method returns an `int` indicating how large the current buffer actually is or 0 in the unlikely event no buffering is used.

You can call `isCommitted()` to determine whether any part of the response has actually been sent:

```
public boolean ServletResponse.isCommitted()
```

If this method returns `true`, it's too late to change the status code and headers, and the `Content-Length` cannot be automatically calculated.

If you need to start over with your response, you can call `reset()` to clear the response buffer and the currently assigned status code and response headers:

```
public void ServletResponse.reset() throws IllegalStateException
```

This method must be called before the response has been committed, otherwise it throws an `IllegalStateException`. The `sendError()` and `sendRedirect()` methods, discussed later, behave similar to this and clear the response buffer, however those methods don't touch the response headers.

You can also force any content in the buffer to be written to the client by calling `flushBuffer()`, allowing the client to begin receiving the content immediately:

```
public void ServletResponse.flushBuffer() throws IOException
```

Calling this method automatically commits the response, meaning the status code and headers will be written and a `reset()` will no longer be possible.

Example 5-3 shows a servlet using the `reset()` method to write and then clear content. It prints the default buffer size but to the log instead of the client so that it won't be `reset()` away.

Example 5-3. Managing the Response Buffer

```
import javax.servlet.*;
import javax.servlet.http.*;
import java.io.*;
```

Example 5-3. Managing the Response Buffer (continued)

```
public class Buffering extends HttpServlet {

  public void doGet(HttpServletRequest req, HttpServletResponse res)
                               throws ServletException, IOException {
    res.setBufferSize(8 * 1024); // 8K buffer
    res.setContentType("text/html");
    PrintWriter out = res.getWriter();

    int size = res.getBufferSize(); // returns 8096 or greater

    // Record the default size, in the log
    log("The default buffer size is " + size);

    out.println("The client won't see this");
    res.reset();
    out.println("Nor will the client see this!");
    res.reset();
    out.println("And this won't be seen if sendError() is called");
    if (req.getParameter("important_parameter") == null) {
      res.sendError(res.SC_BAD_REQUEST, "important_parameter needed");
    }
  }
}
```

Status Codes

Until now, our servlet examples have not set HTTP response status codes. We've been taking advantage of the fact that if a servlet doesn't specifically set the status code, the server steps in and sets its value to the default 200 OK status code. That's a useful convenience when we are returning normal successful responses. However, by using status codes, a servlet can do more with its response. For example, it can redirect a request or report a problem.

The most common status code numbers are defined as mnemonic constants (`public final static int` fields) in the `HttpServletResponse` class. A few of these are listed in Table 5-1. The complete list is available in Appendix D, *HTTP Status Codes.*

Table 5-1. HTTP Status Codes

Mnemonic Constant	Code	Default Message	Meaning
SC_OK	200	OK	The client's request was successful, and the server's response contains the requested data. This is the default status code.

Table 5-1. HTTP Status Codes (continued)

Mnemonic Constant	Code	Default Message	Meaning
SC_NO_CONTENT	204	No Content	The request succeeded but there was no new response body to return. Browsers receiving this code should retain their current document view. This is a useful code for a servlet when it accepts data from a form but wants the browser view to stay at the form, as it avoids the "Document contains no data" error message.
SC_MOVED_PERMANENTLY	301	Moved Permanently	The requested resource has permanently moved to a new location. Future references should use the new URL in requests. The new location is given by the `Location` header. Most browsers automatically access the new location.
SC_MOVED_TEMPORARILY	302	Moved Temporarily	The requested resource has temporarily moved to another location, but future references should still use the original URL to access the resource. The new location is given by the `Location` header. Most browsers automatically access the new location.
SC_UNAUTHORIZED	401	Unauthorized	The request lacked proper authorization. Used in conjunction with the `WWW-Authenticate` and `Authorization` headers.
SC_NOT_FOUND	404	Not Found	The requested resource was not found or is not available.
SC_INTERNAL_SERVER_ERROR	500	Internal Server Error	An unexpected error occurred inside the server that prevented it from fulfilling the request.
SC_NOT_IMPLEMENTED	501	Not Implemented	The server does not support the functionality needed to fulfill the request.
SC_SERVICE_UNAVAILABLE	503	Service Unavailable	The service (server) is temporarily unavailable but should be restored in the future. If the server knows when it will be available again, a `Retry-After` header may also be supplied.

Setting a Status Code

A servlet can use `setStatus()` to set a response status code:

```
public void HttpServletResponse.setStatus(int sc)
```

This method sets the HTTP status code to the given value. The code can be specified as a number or with one of the `SC_XXX` codes defined within `HttpServletResponse`. Remember, the `setStatus()` method should be called before the response is committed, otherwise the call is ignored.

If a servlet sets a status code that indicates an error during the handling of the request, it can call `sendError()` instead of `setStatus()`:

```
public void HttpServletResponse.sendError(int sc)
  throws IOException, IllegalStateException
public void HttpServletResponse.sendError(int sc, String sm)
  throws IOException, IllegalStateException
```

The `sendError()` method causes the server to generate and send an appropriate server-specific page describing the error, letting the servlet error page have a similar appearance to other server error pages. Calling `setStatus()` on an error leaves a servlet with the responsibility of generating the error page. When the two-argument version of this method is used, the status message parameter may be included directly in the body of the response, depending on the server's implementation. This method should be called before the response is committed, otherwise it will throw an `IllegalStateException`. This method performs an implicit reset on the response buffer before generating the error page. Headers set before `sendError()` remain set.

Improving ViewFile Using Status Codes

So far, we haven't bothered calling any of these methods to set a response's status code. We've simply relied on the fact that the status code defaults to `SC_OK`. But there are times when a servlet needs to return a response that doesn't have the `SC_OK` status code—when the response does not contain the requested data. As an example, think back to how the `ViewFile` servlet in Chapter 4, *Retrieving Information*, handled the `FileNotFoundException`:

```
// Return the file
try {
  ServletUtils.returnFile(file, out);
}
catch (FileNotFoundException e) {
  out.println("File not found");
}
```

Without setting a status code, the best this servlet can do is write out an explanation of the problem, ironically sending the explanation as part of a page that is supposed to contain the file's contents. With status codes, however, it can do exactly what the `DefaultServlet` does: set the response code to `SC_NOT_FOUND` to indicate that the requested file was not found and cannot be returned. Here's the improved version:

```
// Return the file
try {
  ServletUtils.returnFile(file, out);
}
catch (FileNotFoundException e) {
  res.sendError(res.SC_NOT_FOUND);
}
```

The appearance of the page generated by a `sendError()` call is server dependent but generally appears identical to the server's normal error page. For the Apache/Tomcat server, this call generates the Apache server's own 404 Not Found page, complete with the Apache footer (as shown in Figure 5-1). Note that this page is indistinguishable from every other Apache 404 Not Found page, providing the servlet the ability to blend in with the server.

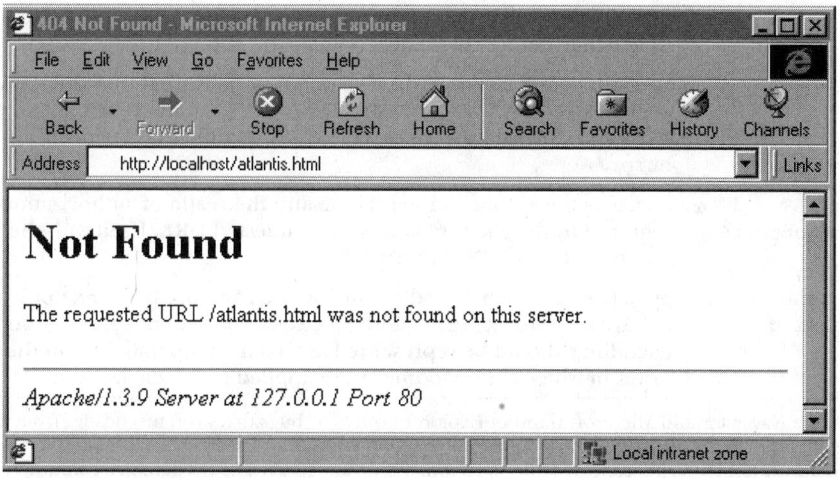

Figure 5-1. The Apache/Tomcat "404 Not Found" page

HTTP Headers

A servlet can set HTTP headers to provide extra information about its response. As we said in Chapter 4, a full discussion of all the possible HTTP 1.0 and HTTP 1.1 headers is beyond the scope of this book. Table 5-2 lists the HTTP headers that are most often set by servlets as a part of a response.

Table 5-2. HTTP Response Headers

Header	Usage
`Cache-Control`	Specifies any special treatment a caching system should give to this document. The most common values are `no-cache` (to indicate this document should not be cached), `no-store` (to indicate this document should not be cached or even stored by a proxy server, usually due to its sensitive contents), and `max-age=`*`seconds`* (to indicate how long before the document should be considered stale). This header was introduced in HTTP 1.1.[a]
`Pragma`	This is the HTTP 1.0 equivalent of `Cache-Control`, with `no-cache` as its only possible value. It's wise to use `Pragma` in conjunction with `Cache-Control` to support older browsers.
`Connection`	Used to indicate whether the server is willing to maintain an open (persistent) connection to the client. If so, its value is set to `keep-alive`. If not, its value is set to `close`. Most web servers handle this header on behalf of their servlets, automatically setting its value to `keep-alive` when a servlet sets its `Content-Length` header or when the server can automatically determine the content length.
`Retry-After`	Specifies a time when the server can again handle requests, used with the `SC_SERVICE_UNAVAILABLE` status code. Its value is either an `int` that represents the number of seconds or a date string that represents an actual time.
`Expires`	Specifies a time when the document may change or when its information will become invalid. It implies that it is unlikely the document will change before that time.
`Location`	Specifies a new location of a document, usually used with the status codes `SC_CREATED`, `SC_MOVED_PERMANENTLY`, and `SC_MOVED_TEMPORARILY`. Its value must be an fully qualified URL (including `http://`).
`WWW-Authenticate`	Specifies the authorization scheme and the realm of authorization required by the client to access the requested URL. Used with the status code `SC_UNAUTHORIZED`.
`Content-Encoding`	Specifies the scheme used to encode the response body. Example values are `gzip` (or `x-gzip`) and `compress` (or `x-compress`). Multiple encodings should be represented as a comma-separated list in the order in which the encodings were applied to the data.

[a] Netscape Navigator and Microsoft Internet Explorer both have bugs that keep this header from always being obeyed. When you must absolutely guarantee servlet output isn't cached, each request to the servlet should use a slightly different URL, perhaps with a little added extraneous parameter information.

Setting an HTTP Header

The `HttpServletResponse` class provides a number of methods to assist servlets in setting HTTP response headers. Use `setHeader()` to set the value of a header:

```
public void HttpServletResponse.setHeader(String name, String value)
```

This method sets the value of the named header as a `String`. The name is case insensitive, as it is for all these methods. If the header had already been set, the new value overwrites the previous one. Headers of all types can be set with this method.

If you need to specify a timestamp for a header, you can use `setDateHeader()`:

```
public void HttpServletResponse.setDateHeader(String name, long date)
```

This method sets the value of the named header to a particular date and time. The method accepts the date value as a `long` that represents the number of milliseconds since the epoch (midnight, January 1, 1970, GMT). If the header has already been set, the new value overwrites the previous one.

Finally, you can use `setIntHeader()` to specify an integer value for a header:

```
public void HttpServletResponse.setIntHeader(String name, int value)
```

This method sets the value of the named header as an `int`. If the header had already been set, the new value overwrites the previous one.

The `containsHeader()` method provides a way to check if a header already exists:

```
public boolean HttpServletResponse.containsHeader(String name)
```

This method returns `true` if the named header has already been set, `false` if not.

For the relatively rare cases when a servlet has to send multiple values for the same header, there are additional methods.

```
public void HttpServletResponse.addHeader(String name, String value)
public void HttpServletResponse.addDateHeader(String name, long value)
public void HttpServletResponse.addIntHeader(String name, int value)
```

These methods set the header to the given value, but while the traditional `setHeader()` method would replace any existing value or values, `addHeader()` leaves current settings alone and just sets an additional value.

Finally, the HTML 3.2 specification defines an alternate way to set header values using the `<META HTTP-EQUIV>` tag inside the HTML page itself:

```
<META HTTP-EQUIV="name" CONTENT="value">
```

This tag must be sent as part of the `<HEAD>` section of the HTML page. This technique does not provide any special benefit to servlets; it was developed for use with static documents, which do not have access to their own headers.

Redirecting a Request

One of the useful things a servlet can do using status codes and headers is redirect a request. This is done by sending instructions for the client to use another URL in the response. Redirection is generally used when a document moves (to send the client to the new location), for load balancing (so one URL can distribute the load to several different machines), or for simple randomization (choosing a destination at random).

Example 5-4 shows a servlet that performs a random redirect, sending a client to a random site selected from its site list. Depending on the site list, a servlet like this could have many uses. As it stands now, it's just a jump-off point to a selection of cool servlet sites. With a site list containing advertising images, it can be used to select the next ad banner.

Example 5-4. Random Redirector

```
import java.io.*;
import java.util.*;
import javax.servlet.*;
import javax.servlet.http.*;

public class SiteSelector extends HttpServlet {

  Vector sites = new Vector();
  Random random = new Random();

  public void init() throws ServletException {
    sites.addElement("http://www.oreilly.com/catalog/jservlet2");
    sites.addElement("http://www.servlets.com");
    sites.addElement("http://java.sun.com/products/servlet");
    sites.addElement("http://www.newInstance.com");
  }

  public void doGet(HttpServletRequest req, HttpServletResponse res)
                               throws ServletException, IOException {
    res.setContentType("text/html");
    PrintWriter out = res.getWriter();

    int siteIndex = Math.abs(random.nextInt()) % sites.size();
    String site = (String)sites.elementAt(siteIndex);

    res.setStatus(res.SC_MOVED_TEMPORARILY);
    res.setHeader("Location", site);
  }
}
```

The actual redirection happens in two lines:

```
res.setStatus(res.SC_MOVED_TEMPORARILY);
res.setHeader("Location", site);
```

The first line sets the status code to indicate a redirection is to take place, while the second line gives the new location. To guarantee they will work, you must call these methods before the response is committed. Remember, the HTTP protocol sends status codes and headers before the content body. Also, HTTP dictates the new site must be given as an absolute URL (for example, *http://server:port/path/file.html*). Anything less than that may confuse the client.

These two lines can be simplified to one using the `sendRedirect()` convenience method:

```
public void HttpServletResponse.sendRedirect(String location)
  throws IOException, IllegalStateException
```

For our example, the two lines become simply:

```
res.sendRedirect(site);
```

This method redirects the response to the specified location, automatically setting the status code and `Location` header. In addition, to support clients without redirect capabilities or that do not recognize the `SC_MOVED_TEMPORARILY` status code, the method writes a short response body that contains a hyperlink to the new location. Consequently, do not write your own response body when using this method. The `sendRedirect()` method can, beginning with Servlet API 2.2, accept a relative URL. The HTTP specification dictates that all redirect URLs must be absolute; however, this method will transform a relative URL to an absolute form (automatically prepending the current protocol, server, and port—but not the context path, do that yourself if necessary) before sending it to the client. Pretty slick! Make sure to call this method before the response is committed, otherwise it will throw an `IllegalStateException`. This method performs an implicit reset on the response buffer before generating the redirect page. Headers set before `sendRedirect()` remain set.

Watching Links to Other Sites

Redirection can also be used to learn where clients go when they leave your site. Assume you have several pages containing lists of links to other sites. Instead of linking directly to the external site, you can link to a redirecting servlet that can record each time an external link is selected. The HTML looks like this:

```
<a href="/goto/http://www.servlets.com">Servlets.com</a>
```

A servlet can be registered to handle the */goto/** path prefix where it will receive the selected URL as extra path info and redirect the client to that location after making a note in the server log. The GoTo servlet code is shown in Example 5-5.

Example 5-5. Where Do You Think You're Going?

```
import java.io.*;
import java.util.*;
import javax.servlet.*;
import javax.servlet.http.*;

public class GoTo extends HttpServlet {

  public void doGet(HttpServletRequest req, HttpServletResponse res)
                               throws ServletException, IOException {
    // Determine the site where they want to go
    String site = req.getPathInfo();
    String query = req.getQueryString();

    // Handle a bad request
    if (site == null) {
      res.sendError(res.SC_BAD_REQUEST, "Extra path info required");
    }

    // Cut off the leading "/" and append the query string
    // We're assuming the path info URL is always absolute
    String url = site.substring(1) + (query == null ? "" : "?" + query);

    // Log the requested URL and redirect
    log(url);  // or write to a special file
    res.sendRedirect(url);
  }
}
```

A servlet similar to this could handle aliasing so that */goto/servlets* would automatically redirect to *http://www.servlets.com.* Selling aliases such as this is the business model for *http://go.to* and *http://i.am.*

Client Pull

Client pull is similar to redirection, with one major difference: the browser actually displays the content from the first page and waits some specified amount of time before retrieving and displaying the content from the next page. It's called *client pull* because the client is responsible for pulling the content from the next page.

Why is this useful? For two reasons. First, the content from the first page can explain to the client that the requested page has moved before the next page is automatically loaded. Second, pages can be retrieved in sequence, making it possible to present a slow-motion page animation.

Client pull information is sent to the client using the `Refresh` HTTP header. This header's value specifies the number of seconds to display the page before pulling the next one, and it optionally includes a URL string that specifies the URL from which to pull. If no URL is given, the same URL is used. Here's a call to `setHeader()` that tells the client to reload this same servlet after showing its current content for three seconds:

```
setHeader("Refresh", "3");
```

And here's a call that tells the client to display Netscape's home page after the three seconds:

```
setHeader("Refresh", "3; URL=http://home.netscape.com");
```

Example 5-6 shows a servlet that uses client pull to display the current time, updated every 10 seconds.

Example 5-6. The Current Time, Kept Current

```
import java.io.*;
import java.util.*;
import javax.servlet.*;
import javax.servlet.http.*;

public class ClientPull extends HttpServlet {

  public void doGet(HttpServletRequest req, HttpServletResponse res)
                               throws ServletException, IOException {
    res.setContentType("text/plain");
    PrintWriter out = res.getWriter();

    res.setHeader("Refresh", "10");
    out.println(new Date().toString());
  }
}
```

This is an example of a text-based animation—we'll look at graphical animations in the next chapter. Note that the `Refresh` header is nonrepeating. It is not a directive to load the document repeatedly. For this example, however, the `Refresh` header is specified on each retrieval, creating a continuous display.

The use of client pull to retrieve a second document is shown in Example 5-7. This servlet redirects requests for one host to another host, giving an explanation to the client before the redirection.

Example 5-7. An Explained Host Change

```
import java.io.*;
import java.util.*;
import javax.servlet.*;
import javax.servlet.http.*;

public class ClientPullMove extends HttpServlet {

  static final String NEW_HOST = "http://www.oreilly.com";

  public void doGet(HttpServletRequest req, HttpServletResponse res)
                               throws ServletException, IOException {
    res.setContentType("text/html");
    PrintWriter out = res.getWriter();

    String newLocation = NEW_HOST + req.getRequestURI();

    res.setHeader("Refresh", "10; URL=" + newLocation);

    out.println("The requested URI has been moved to a different host.<BR>");
    out.println("Its new location is " + newLocation + "<BR>");
    out.println("Your browser will take you there in 10 seconds.");
  }
}
```

This servlet generates the new location from the requested URI, which allows it to redirect any requests made to the old server to the same path on the new server. Using the *web.xml* deployment descriptor, this servlet could be configured to handle every request, to gradually transition clients to the new location.

When Things Go Wrong

All right, let's face it. Sometimes things go wrong. Sometimes the dog bites, and sometimes the bee stings. There are any number of possible causes: bad parameters, missing resources, and (gasp!) actual bugs. The point here is that a servlet has to be prepared for problems, both expected and unexpected. There are two points of concern when things go wrong:

- Limiting damage to the server
- Properly informing the client

Because servlets are written in Java, the potential damage they can cause to their server is greatly minimized. A server can safely embed servlets (even within its process), just as a web browser can safely embed downloaded applets. This safety is built on Java's security features, including the use of protected memory, exception handling, and security managers. Java's memory protection guarantees that servlets cannot accidentally (or intentionally) access the server's internals. Java's exception handling lets a server catch every exception raised by a servlet. Even if a servlet accidentally divides by zero or calls a method on a null object, the server can continue to function. Java's security manager mechanism provides a way for servers to place untrusted servlets in a sandbox, limiting their abilities and keeping them from intentionally causing problems.

You should be aware that trusted servlets executing outside a security manager's sandbox are given abilities that could potentially cause damage to the server. For example, a servlet can overwrite the server's file space or even call `System.exit()`. It is also true that a trusted servlet should never cause damage except by accident, and it's hard to accidentally call `System.exit()`. Still, if it's a concern, even trusted servlets can be (and often are) run inside a fairly lenient but sanity-checking security manager.

Properly describing a problem to the client cannot be handled by Java language technology alone. There are many things to consider:

How much to tell the client?
: Should the servlet send a generic status code error page, a prose explanation of the problem, or (in the case of a thrown exception) a detailed stack trace? What if the servlet is supposed to return nontextual content, such as an image?

How to record the problem?
: Should it be saved to a file, written to the server log, sent to the client, or ignored?

How to recover?
: Can the same servlet instance handle subsequent requests? Or is the servlet corrupted, meaning that it needs to be reloaded?

The answers to these questions depend on the servlet and its intended use, and they should be addressed for each servlet you write on a case-by-case basis. How you handle errors is up to you and should be based on the level of reliability and robustness required for your servlet. What we'll look at next is an overview of the servlet error-handling mechanisms that you can use to implement whatever policy you select.

Status Codes

The simplest (and arguably best) way for a servlet to report an error is to use the `sendError()` method to set the appropriate 400 series or 500 series status code. For example, when the servlet is asked to return a file that does not exist, it can return `SC_NOT_FOUND`. When it is asked to do something beyond its capabilities, it can return SC_NOT_IMPLEMENTED. And when the entirely unexpected happens, it can return SC_INTERNAL_SERVER_ERROR.

By using `sendError()` to set the status code, the server can replace the servlet's response body with a server-specific page that explains the error. If the error is such that a servlet ought to provide its own explanation to the client in the response body, it can set the status code with `setStatus()` and send the appropriate body—which could be text based, a generated image, or whatever is appropriate.

A servlet must be careful to catch and handle any errors before the response is committed. As you probably recall (because we've mentioned it several times), HTTP specifies that the status code and HTTP headers must be sent before the response body. Once you have sent any data down the wire to the client, it's too late to change your status code or your HTTP headers. The best way to guarantee you don't find yourself in this "too late" situation is to check for errors early and use buffering to postpone the sending of data to the client.

Configuring Error Pages

Sometimes, instead of using the server-standard error pages, you may want to develop a set of standard error pages for a web application, pages to be used no matter where the application is deployed. For example, a web application could be configured with a 404 error page containing a search engine entry field should the user want help locating the Not Found resource. You could accomplish this directly by using `setStatus()` and having every servlet generate an identical error page, but a better approach is to set up an `<error-page>` rule in the *web.xml* deployment descriptor. Example 5-8 demonstrates.

Example 5-8. Configuring 400 and 404 Error Pages

```
<?xml version="1.0" encoding="ISO-8859-1"?>

<!DOCTYPE web-app
    PUBLIC "-//Sun Microsystems, Inc.//DTD Web Application 2.2//EN"
    "http://java.sun.com/j2ee/dtds/web-app_2.2.dtd">

<web-app>
    <!-- ..... -->
    <error-page>
        <error-code>
            400
        </error-code>
        <location>
            /400.html
        </location>
    </error-page>
```

Example 5-8. Configuring 400 and 404 Error Pages (continued)

```
    <error-page>
        <error-code>
            404
        </error-code>
        <location>
            /404.html
        </location>
    </error-page>
</web-app>
```

These two `<error-page>` entries tell the server that any call to `sendError()` with a 400 status code should display the contents of the `/400.html` resource, and any 404 should display `/404.html`. It's common for web servers to support error page customization similar to this, however entries in the *web.xml* file override the default server configuration and provide a mechanism for a web application to mandate a set of standard error pages to be used across all server implementations. Servers are required to respect the `<error-page>` rules for all content served from the web application, even static files.

Some things to remember: the value of the `<location>` must begin with a slash, is treated as based in the context root, and must refer to a resource within the context. To reference a resource outside the current context, you can point to an HTML file within the context that contains an immediate redirect outside the context:

```
<META HTTP-EQUIV="Refresh" CONTENT="0; URL=http://www.errors.com/404.html">
```

The `<location>` target can be a dynamic resource, such as a servlet or JSP. For dynamic resources the server makes available two special request attributes telling information about the error:

`javax.servlet.error.status_code`
: An `Integer` telling the error status code. The type was initially unspecified and some early server implementations may return the code as a `String`.

`javax.servlet.error.message`
: A `String` telling the status message, generally passed as the second argument to `sendError()`.

These attributes allow us to write a general-purpose error page display servlet, as is shown in Example 5-9. In order to use this servlet, assign it as the path for the `<location>` tag.

Example 5-9. Dynamically Creating a Status Code Error Page

```
import java.io.*;
import javax.servlet.*;
import javax.servlet.http.*;

public class ErrorDisplay extends HttpServlet {

  public void doGet(HttpServletRequest req, HttpServletResponse res)
                               throws ServletException, IOException {
    res.setContentType("text/html");
    PrintWriter out = res.getWriter();

    Object codeObj = req.getAttribute("javax.servlet.error.status_code");
    Object messageObj = req.getAttribute("javax.servlet.error.message");

    // The code and message should never be null on API 2.2 compliant servers
    String code = (codeObj != null ?
                   codeObj.toString() : "Missing Status Code");
    String message = (messageObj != null ?
                      messageObj.toString() : "Missing Error Message");

    out.println("<HTML>");
    out.println("<HEAD><TITLE>" + code + ": " + message + "</TITLE></HEAD>");
    out.println("<BODY>");
    out.println("<H1>" + code + "</H1>");
    out.println("<H2>" + message + "</H2>");
    out.println("<HR>");
    out.println("<I>Error accessing " + req.getRequestURI() + "</I>");
    out.println("</BODY></HTML>");
  }
}
```

A path to this servlet can be configured as the target for any error codes that need a simple error page rendering. An advanced version of this servlet could generate a more interesting page and could track the error codes being generated to detect odd trends, such as an abundance of 404 errors for the same URI, probably indicating a newly posted bad link somewhere that should be fixed.

To summarize, here's the cheat sheet for sending error status codes. The `setStatus()` method allows you to set an error status code and retain full control of the response. The `sendError()` method lets you set an error status code and pass control of page creation to the server. By default the server will send its standard error page for that code. With an `<error-page>` entry you can tell the server to send a special error page.

Logging

Servlets have the ability to write their actions and their errors to a log file using the `log()` method:

```
public void GenericServlet.log(String msg)
public void GenericServlet.log(String msg, Throwable t)
```

The single-argument method writes the given message to a servlet log, which is usually an event log file. The two-argument version writes the given message and the `Throwable`'s stack trace to a servlet log. The exact output format and location of the log are server-specific but generally include a timestamp and the registered name of the servlet.

The `log()` method aids debugging by providing a way to track a servlet's actions. It also offers a way to save a complete description of any errors encountered by the servlet. The description can be the same as the one given to the client, or it can be more exhaustive and detailed.

Now we can go back and improve `ViewFile` further, so that it uses `log()` to record on the server when requested files do not exist, while returning a simple 404 Not Found page to the client:

```
// Return the file
try {
  ServletUtils.returnFile(file, out);
}
catch (FileNotFoundException e) {
  log("Could not find file: " + e.getMessage());
  res.sendError(res.SC_NOT_FOUND);
}
```

For more complicated errors, a servlet can log the complete stack trace, as shown here:

```
// Return the file
try {
  ServletUtils.returnFile(file, out);
}
catch (FileNotFoundException e) {
  log("Could not find file: " + e.getMessage());
  res.sendError(res.SC_NOT_FOUND);
}
catch (IOException e) {
  log("Problem sending file", e);
  res.sendError(res.SC_INTERNAL_SERVER_ERROR);
}
```

Reporting

In addition to logging errors and exceptions for the server administrator, during development it's often convenient to print a full description of the problem along with a stack trace. Unfortunately, an exception cannot return its stack trace as a `String`—it can print its stack trace only to a `PrintStream` or `PrintWriter`. To retrieve a stack trace as a `String`, we have to jump through a few hoops. We need to let the `Exception` print to a special `PrintWriter` built around a `ByteArrayOutputStream`. That `ByteArrayOutputStream` can catch the output and convert it to a `String`. The `com.oreilly.servlet.ServletUtils` class has a `getStackTraceAsString()` method that does just this:

```
public static String getStackTraceAsString(Throwable t) {
  ByteArrayOutputStream bytes = new ByteArrayOutputStream();
  PrintWriter writer = new PrintWriter(bytes, true);
  t.printStackTrace(writer);
  return bytes.toString();
}
```

Here's how `ViewFile` can provide information that includes an `IOException` stack trace:

```
// Return the file
try {
  ServletUtils.returnFile(file, out);
}
catch (FileNotFoundException e) {
  log("Could not find file: " + e.getMessage());
  res.sendError(res.SC_NOT_FOUND);
}
catch (IOException e) {
  log("Problem sending file", e);
  res.sendError(res.SC_INTERNAL_SERVER_ERROR,
                ServletUtils.getStackTraceAsString(e));
}
```

The output for a sample exception is shown in Figure 5-2.

Exceptions

As we said before, any exception that is thrown but not caught by a servlet is caught by its server. How the server handles the exception is server dependent: it may pass the client the message and the stack trace, or it may not. It may automatically log the exception, or it may not. It may even call `destroy()` on the servlet and reload it, or it may not.

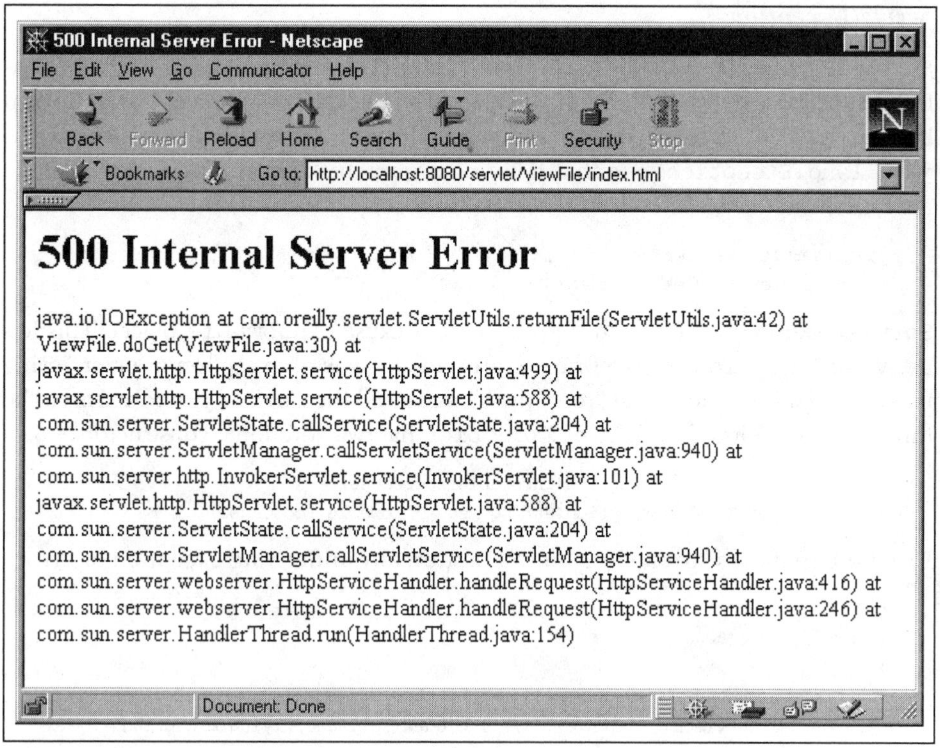

Figure 5-2. Keeping the client well informed

Servlets designed and developed to run with a particular server can optimize for that server's behavior. A servlet designed to interoperate across several servers cannot expect any particular exception handling on the part of the server. If such a servlet requires special exception handling, it must catch its own exceptions and handle them accordingly.

There are some types of exceptions a servlet has no choice but to catch itself. A servlet can propagate to its server only those exceptions that subclass `IOException`, `ServletException`, or `RuntimeException`. The reason has to do with method signatures. The `service()` method of `Servlet` declares in its `throws` clause that it throws `IOException` and `ServletException` exceptions. For it (or the `doGet()` and `doPost()` methods it calls) to throw and not catch anything else causes a compile-time error. The `RuntimeException` is a special-case exception that never needs to be declared in a `throws` clause. A common example is a `NullPointerException`.

The `init()` and `destroy()` methods have their own signatures as well. The `init()` method declares that it throws only `ServletException` exceptions, and `destroy()` declares that it throws no exceptions.

ServletException

`ServletException` is a subclass of `java.lang.Exception` that is specific to servlets—the class is defined in the `javax.servlet` package. This exception is thrown by a servlet to indicate a general servlet problem. It has the same constructors as `java.lang.Exception`: one that takes no arguments and one that takes a single message string:

```
javax.servlet.ServletException()
javax.servlet.ServletException(String msg)
```

`ServletException` can also support a "root cause" `Throwable` object. This lets `ServletException` act as a wrapper around any type of exception or error, giving the server a way to know what "root" problem caused the `ServletException` to be thrown. To support this, `ServletException` has two additional constructors:

```
javax.servlet.ServletException(Throwable rootCause)
javax.servlet.ServletException(String msg, Throwable rootCause)
```

Using the root cause capability you can pass on any underlying exception or error:

```
try {
  thread.sleep(60000);
}
catch (InterruptedException e) {
  throw new ServletException(e);  // includes full underlying exception
}
```

The server can retrieve and examine the underlying exception, stack trace and all, by calling `getRootCause()`:

```
public Throwable ServletException.getRootCause()
```

The call returns `null` if there is no nested exception.

UnavailableException

The `javax.servlet` package defines one subclass of `ServletException`, `UnavailableException`, although you can, of course, add your own. This exception indicates a servlet is unavailable, either temporarily or permanently.

Permanent unavailability means that the servlet instance throwing the `UnavailableException` cannot recover from the error. The servlet might be misconfigured, or the state of the servlet may be corrupted.

A servlet that throws a permanent `UnavailableException` during request handling will be removed from service, and a new instance will be created to handle requests. If no "available" servlet instance can be created, the client will receive an error. A servlet that throws a permanent `UnavailableException` (or a regular `ServletException`) during its `init()` method will never enter into service; instead, the server will attempt to initialize a new instance to handle future requests.

Temporary unavailability means the servlet cannot handle requests for some duration due to a systemwide problem. For example, a third-tier server might not be accessible, or there may be insufficient memory or disk storage to handle requests. The problem may be self-correcting, such as those due to excessive load, or an administrator may need to take corrective action.

During the unavailability, the server handles requests for the servlet by returning an `SC_SERVICE_UNAVAILABLE` (503) status code with a `Retry-After` header telling the client the estimated end time of the unavailability. If a servlet throws a temporary `UnavailableException` exception during its `init()` method, the servlet will never enter into service, and the server will attempt to initialize a new instance after the period of unavailability. For simplicity's sake, servers are allowed to treat temporary unavailability like permanent unavailability.

`UnavailableException` has two constructors:

```
javax.servlet.UnavailableException(String msg)
javax.servlet.UnavailableException(String msg, int seconds)
```

The one-argument constructor creates a new exception that indicates the servlet is permanently unavailable, with an explanation given by `msg`. The two-argument version creates a new exception that indicates the servlet is temporarily unavailable, with an explanation given by `msg`. A well-written servlet should include in the explanation the reason for the problem and any corrective action the server administrator should perform to let the servlet become available. The duration of its unavailability is given by seconds. This time is only an estimate. If no estimate can be made, a nonpositive value may be used. `UnavailableException` provides the `isPermanent()` and `getUnavailableSeconds()` methods to retrieve information about an exception.

Configuring Exception Pages

The full behavior when a server catches a servlet exception varies based on the server, however a web application can indicate, via its deployment descriptor, a set of error pages for handling particular kinds of exceptions. The error pages are specified using the `<error-page>` tag, just as with status codes, except we replace `<error-code>` with `<exception-type>`. See Example 5-10.

Example 5-10. Configuring Exception Error Pages

```
<?xml version="1.0" encoding="ISO-8859-1"?>

<!DOCTYPE web-app
    PUBLIC "-//Sun Microsystems, Inc.//DTD Web Application 2.2//EN"
    "http://java.sun.com/j2ee/dtds/web-app_2.2.dtd">

<web-app>
    <!-- ..... -->
    <error-page>
        <exception-type>
            javax.servlet.ServletException
        </exception-type>
        <location>
            /servlet/ErrorDisplay
        </location>
    </error-page>
</web-app>
```

This entry indicates that any `ServletException` thrown to the server should be displayed using the `ErrorDisplay` servlet. Note that the `<exception-type>` must be fully qualified with the package name; `ServletException` alone will not work. Also, this rule applies to all `ServletException` subclasses like `UnavailableException`, unless there's a more specific `UnavilableException`-handling rule in the deployment descriptor that takes precedence.

For dynamic `<location>` targets, the server makes available two request attributes to describe the thrown exception:

`javax.servlet.error.exception_type`
: A `java.lang.Class` instance telling the exception type. The attribute type was initially unspecified and some early server implementations may return a `String` form of the class name.

`javax.servlet.error.message`
: A `String` telling the exception message, passed to the exception constructor. There exists no way to get the exception or its stack trace.

Using these attributes we can enhance `ErrorDisplay` from Example 5-9 to act as a general error display resource, supporting the display of both error status codes and exceptions, as shown in Example 5-11.

Example 5-11. Dynamically Creating a General-Purpose Error Page

```
import java.io.*;
import javax.servlet.*;
import javax.servlet.http.*;
```

Example 5-11. Dynamically Creating a General-Purpose Error Page (continued)

```
public class ErrorDisplay extends HttpServlet {

  public void doGet(HttpServletRequest req, HttpServletResponse res)
                               throws ServletException, IOException {
    res.setContentType("text/html");
    PrintWriter out = res.getWriter();

    String code = null, message = null, type = null;
    Object codeObj, messageObj, typeObj;

    // Retrieve the three possible error attributes, some may be null
    codeObj = req.getAttribute("javax.servlet.error.status_code");
    messageObj = req.getAttribute("javax.servlet.error.message");
    typeObj = req.getAttribute("javax.servlet.error.exception_type");

    // Convert the attributes to string values
    if (codeObj != null) code = codeObj.toString();
    if (messageObj != null) message = messageObj.toString();
    if (typeObj != null) type = typeObj.toString();

    // The error reason is either the status code or exception type
    String reason = (code != null ? code : type);

    out.println("<HTML>");
    out.println("<HEAD><TITLE>" + reason + ": " + message + "</TITLE></HEAD>");
    out.println("<BODY>");
    out.println("<H1>" + reason + "</H1>");
    out.println("<H2>" + message + "</H2>");
    out.println("<HR>");
    out.println("<I>Error accessing " + req.getRequestURI() + "</I>");
    out.println("</BODY></HTML>");
  }
}
```

Unfortunately, only the exception type and message—not the exception's stack trace—are available to the `ErrorDisplay` servlet, limiting the usefulness of the exception error page. To guarantee display or logging of the exception stack trace, you must catch the exception within the original servlet and deal with the exception before it propagates to the server. You'll have to write a little extra code, but by handling exceptions yourself you can guarantee consistent and proper error handling. It's expected a new request attribute containing the exception itself will be added in Servlet API 2.3 using the name `javax.servlet.error.exception`.

Knowing when no one's listening

Sometimes clients hang up on servlets. Sure, it's rude, but it happens. Sometimes the client makes a mistake and goes to the wrong page. Sometimes the servlet takes too long to respond. Remember, all the while a servlet is preparing its response, the user is being tempted by the browser's big, glowing Stop button that is just begging to be clicked. You may be wondering, just what happens to the servlet once that button is pushed?

Unfortunately, a servlet is not given any immediate indication that the user has clicked the Stop button—there is no interrupt that tells it to stop processing. The servlet discovers the client has stopped the request only when it tries to send output to the nonexistent client, at which point an error condition occurs.

A servlet that sends information using a `ServletOutputStream` sees an `IOException` when it tries to write output. For servers that buffer their output, the `IOException` is thrown when the buffer fills up and its contents are flushed.

Because an `IOException` may be thrown any time a servlet tries to output, a well-written servlet frees its resources in a `finally` block. (The `finally` block is an optional part of a `try/catch/finally` construct. It comes after zero or more `catch` blocks, and its code is executed once regardless of how the code in the `try` block executes.) Here's a version of the `returnFile()` method from the `ViewFile` servlet that uses a `finally` block to guarantee the closure of its `FileInputStream`:

```
void returnFile(String filename, OutputStream out)
                          throws FileNotFoundException, IOException {
  FileInputStream fis = null;
  try {
    fis = new FileInputStream(filename);
    byte[] buf = new byte[4 * 1024];  // 4K buffer
    int bytesRead;
    while ((bytesRead = fis.read(buf)) != -1) {
      out.write(buf, 0, bytesRead);
    }
  }
  finally {
    if (fis != null) fis.close();
  }
}
```

The addition of a `finally` block does not change the fact that this method propagates all exceptions to its caller, but it does guarantee that, before that propagation, the method gets a chance to close the open `FileInputStream`.

A servlet sending character data using a `PrintWriter` doesn't get an `IOException` when it tries to write output, because the methods of `PrintWriter` never throw exceptions. Instead, a servlet that sends character data has to call the `checkError()` method of `PrintWriter`. This method flushes the output—committing the response—and returns a `boolean` that indicates if there was a problem writing to the underlying `OutputStream`. It returns `true` if the client has stopped the request.

A long-running servlet that doesn't mind committing the response early should call `checkError()` regularly to determine if it can halt processing before completion. If there hasn't been any output since the last check, a servlet can send filler content. For example:

```
out.println("<H2>Here's the solution for your differential equation:</H2>");
if (out.checkError()) return;

preliminaryCalculation();

out.print(" "); // filler content, extra whitespace is ignored in HTML
if (out.checkError()) return;

additionalCalculation();
```

It's important to note that a server is not required to throw an `IOException` or set the error flag of the `PrintWriter` after the client disconnects. A server may elect to let the response run to completion with its output ignored. Generally this does not cause a problem, but it does mean that a servlet running inside such a server should always have a set end point and should not be written to continuously loop until the user hits Stop.

Six Ways to Skin a Servlet Cat

In the time since the first edition of this book, servlets have become the de facto standard for Java-based server-side web development. The Darwinistic battle between servlets, server-side applets, and other Java-based pluggable architectures has effectively ended and servlets have been declared the winner, supported today in every web server and application server. The new area of active innovation can be found above the servlet layer, at the presentation and framework levels, where individuals and companies are exploring how best to build on top of servlets to create effective web sites.

Such solutions are needed because the simple approach to generating markup content, having the servlet programmer write an `out.println()` call for each content line, has proven to be a serious problem for real-world use. With the `out.println()` approach, markup content has to be created within code, and that becomes an onerous and time-consuming task for long pages. In addition, page creators have to ask developers to make all site changes.

The goal nearly all content creation architectures share is to "separate content from presentation." The term *content* here means the raw data of the site and the manipulation of that data. A better term perhaps would be *data processing*, but to "separate data processing from presentation" doesn't seem to have the right ring to it. The term *presentation* means the representation of the data given to the end user (often HTML, although with the growth of web-connected devices it's increasingly likely to be WML, the Wireless Markup Language). Separating content from presentation gives several advantages, primarily easier site creation and maintenance because the *content* of the page (controlled by a programmer) can be developed and changed independently of the *presentation* of the page (controlled by a designer or producer). Some refer to this separation as a Model-View-Controller (MVC) architecture. The *model* is synonymous with *content*, the *view* is synonymous with *presentation*, and the *controller* squeezes in at various places depending on the technology.

Later in the book, we'll take a closer look at a number of popular alternatives for servlet-based content creation. For each alternative we'll provide some background on the tool, demonstrate how to use the tool, and examine where the tool works best. Because of space and time considerations and the fact that every project mentioned is a quickly moving target, we cannot provide a full tutorial for each alternative. One thing to be clear about: these are more than just five different implementations of the same idea. Each alternative approaches the content creation problem from a different angle, and as a result the techniques for solving the problem vary widely. A tool that works well in one situation might not work so well in another situation. One size does not fit all here. So don't read the examples in these chapters looking for the best technology. Look instead for the best technology for your project.

We have avoided discussion of proprietary commercial solutions because of the inherent risk in tying to a single-vendor solution influenced by the financial motivations of the commercial vendor.* The alternatives discussed later in the book are as follows:

JavaServer Pages
: JavaServer Pages (JSP) is a technology created by Sun Microsystems and closely tied to servlets. As with servlets, Sun releases a JSP specification, and third-party vendors compete on their implementation of that standard. Being

* We learned this the hard way. In the first edition of this book we covered the commercial htmlKona package from WebLogic because there was no similar alternative and because we were assured by WebLogic that it would remain available at a reasonable price. After WebLogic was purchased by BEA Systems, that assurance could not be counted upon, and in fact htmlKona became a minor footnote on the BEA Systems price sheet. Happily, htmlKona was reimplemented as the open source Element Construction Set (ECS) Project through the Apache Jakarta Project and will now be available and maintained as long as people are interested in the project.

released by Sun puts JSP in a very privileged position, and had JSP solved a sufficient number of user problems it would probably have won the market before there were any other viable entries. As is, a surprising number of users are disenchanted with JSP and alternatives are gaining popularity. See Chapter 18, *JavaServer Pages*, and *http://java.sun.com/products/jsp*.

Tea

Tea is a newly open sourced product from the Walt Disney Internet Group (formerly GO.com), created internally over the years to solve their tremendous web production needs for sites such as ESPN.com. It's similar to JSP although it avoids many of JSP's problems and already has terrific tools support. See Chapter 14, *The Tea Framework*, and *http://opensource.go.com*.

WebMacro

WebMacro is a template engine created by Semiotek, Inc., as part of the Shimari project and possibly merging into the Apache Jakarta Project. Many template engines could be discussed, however WebMacro has the largest mindshare, has been used on extraordinarily high-traffic commercial sites such as AltaVista.com, has been integrated in open source frameworks such as Turbine and Melati, and has been used in prominent open source projects such as JetSpeed. In addition, see Chapter 15, *WebMacro*, and *http://webmacro.org* and *http://jakarta.apache.org/velocity*.

Element Construction Set

The Element Construction Set (ECS) package from the Apache Jakarta Project is a set of classes modeled after the htmlKona product from WebLogic (now BEA Systems). ECS has many limitations, but it solves a certain class of problems, and looking at the ECS approach provides a good base for discussing the more flexible XMLC. See Chapter 16, *Element Construction Set*, and *http://jakarta.apache.org/ecs*.

XMLC

XMLC makes use of XML to get nearly all the power of ECS without many of its limitations. It was created by Lutris as part of their open source Enhydra Application Server and can be used as a separate component. See Chapter 17, *XMLC*, and *http://xmlc.enhydra.org*.

Cocoon

Cocoon is another XML-based alternative created by the XML Apache Project. Cocoon uses XML and XSLT to manage content and create what has often been referred to as a *web publishing framework*. Cocoon is a servlet-driven framework whereby XML content, either static or dynamically created, is run through an XSLT filter before presentation to the client. That filter may format the content as any content type including HTML, XML, WML, or PDF—and the framework may choose different filters depending on the client. We won't discuss Cocoon at length in this book because it has more to do with XSLT programming than Java programming, and because (at least right now) it's generally not the tool of choice for writing interactive web applications. It's better suited for large scale mostly static sites that want to allow multiple views on their content. For more information on Cocoon see *http://xml.apache.org* and the book *Java and XML* by Brett McLaughlin (O'Reilly). The *Java and XML* chapter covering Cocoon is available online for free at *http://www.oreilly.com/catalog/javaxml/chapter/ch09.html.*

If your favorite tool, or a popular tool, isn't mentioned, it's not surprising. Look at the date of your tool's creation: it's probably after this book went to press. The innovation taking place in this area is tremendous, and with XML providing us with new abilities and web-enabled devices making demands for new features, this area is ripe for new entries. Also, please understand that enhancements to these tools are coming at a breakneck pace. Each tutorial chapter is sure to be at least slightly out of date by the time you read this. To help you stay current, be sure to check out *http://www.servlets.com.*

In this chapter:
- *WAP and WML*
- *Images*
- *Compressed Content*
- *Server Push*

6

Sending Multimedia Content

Until now, every servlet we've written has returned a standard HTML page. The web consists of more than HTML, though, so in this chapter we'll look at some of the more interesting things a servlet can return. We'll start by looking at the new WAP protocol and the WML markup language used by cell phones and mobile devices and see how servlets can use this new technology. Then we'll show how to generate images dynamically from a servlet to create charts and manipulate pictures. Toward the end of the chapter we'll explore when and how to send a compressed response and examine using multipart responses to implement server push.

WAP and WML

The *Wireless Application Protocol* (WAP, pronounced like *whap*) is a de facto standard for providing Internet communications to mobile phones, pagers, and personal digital assistants (PDAs) on wireless networks across the world. It was created in 1998 by Ericsson, Nokia, Motorola, and Phone.com (formerly Unwired Planet) who wisely desired to create a standard protocol rather than competing proprietary protocols. Together the four companies founded the WAP Forum (*http://www.wapforum.org*), a democratically organized group whose participation has since grown to more than 400 members.

WAP consists of a set of specifications for developing applications to run on wireless networks. The WAP Protocols covers both the application level (the WML markup language and the WMLScript scripting language, collectively known as the Web Application Environment or WAE) and the underlying network transport layers (the WDP, WTLS, WTP, and WSP protocols). The WAP stack parallels the web protocol stack, as shown in Figure 6-1.

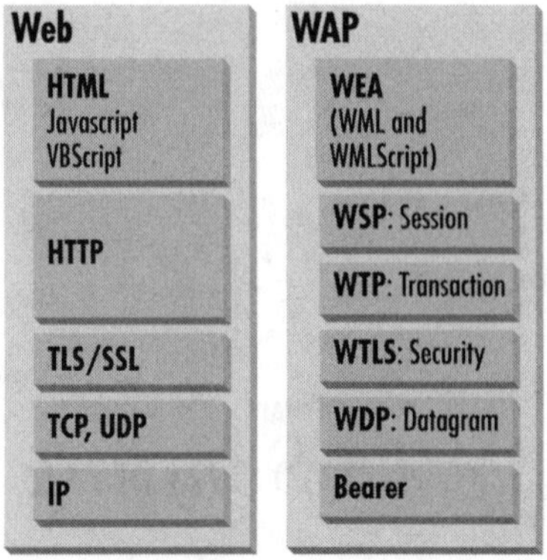

Figure 6-1. Web and WAP stacks

The primary difference is that WAP is optimized for low-bandwidth wireless communication. For example, WAP uses a binary format for request and response structure instead of the text format used by the Web.

A *WAP Gateway* acts as an intermediary between the WAP network and the Web. A gateway converts a WAP request into a web request, and the following web response into a WAP response. You can think of a WAP Gateway as a "protocol stack converter."* WAP Gateways give WAP devices access to standard web servers. Figure 6-2 demonstrates.

The short story is, as a wireless developer, you can ignore the WAP transport layer. A WAP Gateway takes care of making a device's request look like an HTTP request. The layer where you must concentrate is the application layer, where instead of generating HTML you instead generate WML.

WML

Portable devices are far more limited than PCs. They have slow processors, tiny amounts of memory, small displays, and extremely limited bandwidth. Because of these limitations, WAP devices don't interact with normal HTML and image content. Instead, they use the Wireless Markup Language (WML) for text content, the WMLScript language for scripting, and the Wireless Bitmap (WBMP) monochromatic image format for graphics.

WML is an application of XML, similar to HTML but with far fewer tags. It follows the metaphor of a deck of cards. Each card represents a screen or page, and each

* WAP Gateways are normally provided transparently by the bearer of a wireless network. For those interested in setting up their own gateway or in learning how a gateway operates, there's an open source WAP Gateway named Kannel available at *http://www.wapgateway.org*.

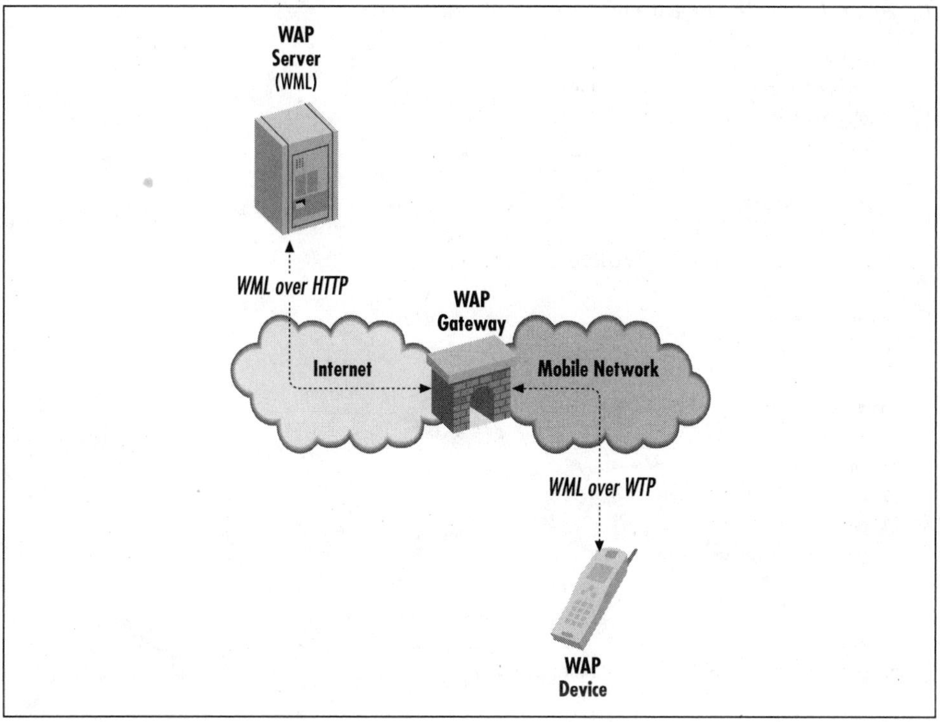

Figure 6-2. The role of a WAP Gateway

deck is a collection of cards that can be transferred at once. Sending content a deck at a time instead of a card at a time reduces the latency (how long it takes to view the next card) when accessing content.

Example 6-1 shows a static WML document that acts as a minibartender. It provides a list of drinks to choose from, then displays the ingredients of the selected drink.* Notice the document is XML with a well-known DTD.

Example 6-1. A WML Minibartender, drinks.wml

```
<?xml version="1.0"?>

<!DOCTYPE wml PUBLIC
  "-//WAPFORUM//DTD WML 1.1//EN"
  "http://www.wapforum.org/DTD/wml_1.1.xml">

<wml>
  <card id="Bartender" title="Select a Drink">
    <p>
    Select a Drink:
```

* A full implementation of this idea is available to the public at *http://www.wap2bar.com/index.wml.*

Example 6-1. A WML Minibartender, drinks.xml (continued)

```
    <anchor>
      Kamikaze <go href="#Kamikaze" />
    </anchor><br/>
    <anchor>
      Margarita <go href="#Margarita" />
    </anchor><br/>
    <anchor>
      Boilermaker <go href="#Boilermaker" />
    </anchor><br/>
    </p>
  </card>

  <card id="Kamikaze" title="Kamikaze">
    <p>
    To make a Kamikaze:<br/>
    1 part Vodka<br/>
    1 part Triple Sec<br/>
    1 part Lime Juice<br/>
    </p>
  </card>

  <card id="Margarita" title="Margarita">
    <p>
    To make a Margarita:<br/>
    1 1/2 oz Tequila<br/>
    1/2 oz Triple Sec<br/>
    1 oz Lime Juice<br/>
    Salt<br/>
    </p>
  </card>

  <card id="Boilermaker" title="Boilermaker">
    <p>
    To make a Boilermaker:<br/>
    2 oz Whiskey<br/>
    10 oz Beer<br/>
    </p>
  </card>
</wml>
```

The document contains four cards. The first card, displayed by default, provides a short list of drinks. Each drink name is a hyperlink to another card in the document, with the card name given with the `#Cardname` syntax. The later cards each display the ingredients for a given drink. The entire document can be transferred to a device in a single step, even though only parts are available at any point in time.

WAP Device Simulators

To make it possible to execute WAP applications without taking to the airwaves, various companies have created WAP-enabled phone simulators, software to run on a PC that acts like (and even looks like!) a phone. Figure 6-3 shows how the document appears on the Phone.com UP.Simulator (*http://www.phone.com*). Other simulators and WAP development kits can be found at *http://www.nokia.com*, *http://www.ericsson.com*, *http://www.motorola.com*, and many more sites. Some standard web browsers, including Opera, also support WML.

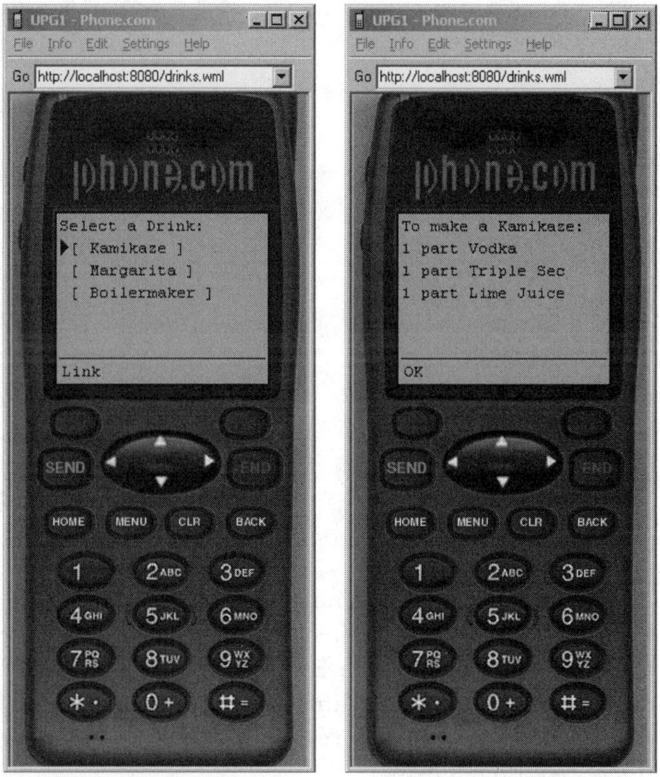

Figure 6-3. Don't drink and dial

Serving WAP Content

For WAP content to be served correctly, the server must send the WML file with the explicit content type `text/vnd.wap.wml`. Some servers set this content type automatically for *.wml* files. Others have to be told about the new type. A server can be told about WAP-related content types with the following `<mime-mapping>` elements in the server's *web.xml* deployment descriptor. The *web.xml* snippet in

Example 6-2 adds the proper content types for WML, WMLScript, and Wireless Bitmap files.

Example 6-2. Adding WAP Mime Types to web.xml

```
<!-- ... -->
<mime-mapping>
    <extension>
        wml
    </extension>
    <mime-type>
        text/vnd.wap.wml
    </mime-type>
</mime-mapping>
<mime-mapping>
    <extension>
        wmls
    </extension>
    <mime-type>
        text/vnd.wap.wmlscript
    </mime-type>
</mime-mapping>
<mime-mapping>
    <extension>
        wbmp
    </extension>
    <mime-type>
        image/vnd.wap.wbmp
    </mime-type>
</mime-mapping>
<!-- ... -->
```

In addition, some web application programmers find it useful to add *index.wml* to the default list of files to search in a directory, known as the *welcome file list.* The *web.xml* deployment descriptor block in Example 6-3 sets the welcome file list to *index.html, index.htm,* and *index.wml,* in that order. This indicates to the server a request for *http://localhost/wap* should resolve to *http://localhost/wap/index.wml* if *index.html* and *index.htm* do not exist.

Example 6-3. Adding WAP Welcome Files to web.xml

```
<!-- ... -->
<welcome-file-list>
  <welcome-file>
    index.html
  </welcome-file>
  <welcome-file>
    index.htm
  </welcome-file>
```

Example 6-3. Adding WAP Welcome Files to web.xml (continued)

```
  <welcome-file>
    index.wml
  </welcome-file>
</welcome-file-list>
<!-- ... -->
```

The `<welcome-file-list>` feature comes in handy for non-WAP uses as well. For example, a web application that for historical reasons uses *home.html* as the default welcome file can add *home.html* to the welcome file list and safely deploy across any servlet-enabled server.

Dynamic WAP Content

There's almost no technical difference in how a servlet serves dynamic WAP content and how a servlet serves dynamic web content. To serve WAP a servlet must simply change the response content type to `text/vnd.wap.wml` and the response content from HTML to WML. To a servlet the request is normal HTTP; the external WAP Gateway handles the WAP and web protocol stack conversion. But while the technical difference is slight, the occasion when it's appropriate to use a servlet for dynamic content generation can be more limited.

On the Web, there's usually little performance penalty in contacting the server for minor tasks and page updates. With WAP the performance penalty can be more noticeable. As a result, simple tasks such as card navigation and form data validation, which on the Web might involve a servlet, are best performed in WAP using the WML deck metaphor and the WMLScript client-side scripting ability. For example, the previous bartender uses a set of WML cards to serve its drinks without contacting the server.

Servlets still have their place of course. A servlet (or other server script) is needed to generate a deck of cards containing dynamic information pulled from a database. A servlet is also necessary to handle queries against data too large to fit on a set of cards. Devices are often limited to storing just 1400 bytes of compiled page data.

Example 6-4 and Example 6-5 demonstrate with a WML form and WML-generating servlet that together provide an area code lookup application. A client may enter a telephone area code into the form, submit it to the servlet, and learn which state or region contains that code. People with WAP-enabled phones can use this application to physically locate any Caller ID number.

Example 6-4. Using WML to Ask for an Area Code

```
<?xml version="1.0"?>

<!DOCTYPE wml PUBLIC
  "-//WAPFORUM//DTD WML 1.1//EN"
  "http://www.wapforum.org/DTD/wml_1.1.xml">

<wml>
  <card id="AreaCode" title="Enter an Area Code">
    <do type="accept" label="Enter">
      <go href="servlet/AreaCode?code=$(code)"/>
    </do>
    <p>
    Enter an Area Code: <input type="text" name="code"/>
    </p>
  </card>
</wml>
```

This WML document holds a simple form with a text input area. Whatever area code is entered gets sent to the `AreaCode` servlet as the `code` parameter. We use the `$(code)` variable substitution syntax to construct the query string manually.

Example 6-5. Using WAP to Locate an Area Code

```
import java.io.*;
import java.util.*;
import javax.servlet.*;
import javax.servlet.http.*;

public class AreaCode extends HttpServlet {

  Properties lookup = new Properties();

  public void init() {
    // Transfer raw data from below into a fast-lookup Properties list
    for (int i = 0; i < data.length; i++) {
      Object[] record = data[i];
      String state = (String) record[0];
      int[] codes = (int[]) record[1];
      for (int j = 0; j < codes.length; j++) {
        lookup.put(String.valueOf(codes[j]), state);
      }
    }
  }

  public void doGet(HttpServletRequest req, HttpServletResponse res)
                              throws ServletException, IOException {
    res.setContentType("text/vnd.wap.wml");
    PrintWriter out = res.getWriter();
```

Example 6-5. Using WAP to Locate an Area Code (continued)

```
    String msg = null;

    String code = req.getParameter("code");
    String region = null;
    if (code != null) {
      region = lookup.getProperty(code);
    }

    out.println("<?xml version=\"1.0\"?>");
    out.println("<!DOCTYPE wml PUBLIC " +
                "\"-//WAPFORUM//DTD WML 1.1//EN\" " +
                "\"http://www.wapforum.org/DTD/wml_1.1.xml\">");

    out.println("<wml>");
    out.println("<card id=\"Code\" title=\"Code\">");
    out.println("  <p>");
    out.println("  Area code '" + code + "'<br/>");
    if (region != null) {
      out.println("  is " + region + ".<br/>");
    }
    else {
      out.println("  is not valid.<br/>");
    }
    out.println("  </p>");
    out.println("</card>");
    out.println("</wml>");
  }

  // Raw area code data for each region
  private Object[][] data = new Object[][] {
    { "Toll Free", new int[] { 800, 855, 866, 877, 888 } },
    { "Alabama", new int[] { 205, 256, 334 } },
    { "Alaska", new int[] { 907 } },
    { "Alberta", new int[] { 403, 780 } },
    { "Arizona", new int[] { 480, 520, 602, 623 } },
    { "Arkansas", new int[] { 501, 870 } },
    { "British Columbia", new int[] { 250, 604 } },
    { "California", new int[] { 209, 213, 310, 323, 369, 408, 415, 424, 510,
      530, 559, 562, 619, 626, 627, 650, 661, 707, 714, 760, 805, 818, 831,
      858, 909, 916, 925, 949 } },
    { "Colorado", new int[] { 303, 719, 720, 970 } },
    { "Connecticut", new int[] { 203, 475, 860, 959 } },
    { "Deleware", new int[] { 302 } },
    { "District of Columbia", new int[] { 202 } },
    { "Florida", new int[] { 305, 321, 352, 407, 561, 727, 786, 813, 850, 863,
      904, 941, 954 } },
    { "Georgia", new int[] { 229, 404, 478, 678, 706, 770, 912 } },
    { "Hawaii", new int[] { 808 } },
```

Example 6-5. Using WAP to Locate an Area Code (continued)

```
{ "Idaho", new int[] { 208 } },
{ "Illinois", new int[] { 217, 224, 309, 312, 618, 630, 708, 773, 815,
  847 } },
{ "Indiana", new int[] { 219, 317, 765, 812 } },
{ "Iowa", new int[] { 319, 515, 712 } },
{ "Kansas", new int[] { 316, 785, 913 } },
{ "Kentucky", new int[] { 270, 502, 606, 859 } },
{ "Louisiana", new int[] { 225, 318, 337, 504 } },
{ "Maine", new int[] { 207 } },
{ "Manitoba", new int[] { 204 } },
{ "Maryland", new int[] { 240, 301, 410, 443 } },
{ "Massachusetts", new int[] { 413, 508, 617, 781, 978 } },
{ "Michigan", new int[] { 231, 248, 313, 517, 586, 616, 734, 810, 906 } },
{ "Minnesota", new int[] { 218, 320, 507, 612, 651, 763, 952 } },
{ "Mississippi", new int[] { 228, 601, 662 } },
{ "Missouri", new int[] { 314, 417, 573, 636, 660, 816 } },
{ "Montana", new int[] { 406 } },
{ "Nebraska", new int[] { 308, 402 } },
{ "Nevada", new int[] { 702, 775 } },
{ "New Brunswick", new int[] { 506 } },
{ "New Hampshire", new int[] { 603 } },
{ "New Jersey", new int[] { 201, 609, 732, 856, 908, 973 } },
{ "New Mexico", new int[] { 505 } },
{ "New York", new int[] { 212, 315, 347, 516, 518, 607, 631, 646, 716,
  718, 845, 914, 917 } },
{ "Newfoundland", new int[] { 709 } },
{ "North Carolina", new int[] { 252, 336, 704, 828, 910, 919, 980 } },
{ "North Dakota", new int[] { 701 } },
{ "Northwest Territories", new int[] { 867 } },
{ "Nova Scotia", new int[] { 902 } },
{ "Ohio", new int[] { 216, 234, 330, 419, 440, 513, 614, 740, 937 } },
{ "Oklahoma", new int[] { 405, 580, 918 } },
{ "Ontario", new int[] { 416, 519, 613, 647, 705, 807, 905 } },
{ "Oregon", new int[] { 503, 541, 971 } },
{ "Pennsylvania", new int[] { 215, 267, 412, 484, 570, 610, 717, 724, 814,
  878, 902 } },
{ "Puerto Rico", new int[] { 787 } },
{ "Quebec", new int[] { 418, 450, 514, 819 } },
{ "Rhode Island", new int[] { 401 } },
{ "Saskatchewan", new int[] { 306 } },
{ "South Carolina", new int[] { 803, 843, 864 } },
{ "South Dakota", new int[] { 605 } },
{ "Tennessee", new int[] { 423, 615, 865, 901, 931 } },
{ "Texas", new int[] { 210, 214, 254, 281, 361, 409, 469, 512, 682, 713,
  806, 817, 830, 832, 903, 915, 940, 956, 972 } },
{ "US Virgin Islands", new int[] { 340 } },
```

Example 6-5. Using WAP to Locate an Area Code (continued)

```
      { "Utah", new int[] { 435, 801 } },
      { "Vermont", new int[] { 802 } },
      { "Virginia", new int[] { 540, 571, 703, 757, 804 } },
      { "Washington", new int[] { 206, 253, 360, 425, 509, 564 } },
      { "West Virginia", new int[] { 304 } },
      { "Wyoming", new int[] { 307 } },
      { "Yukon Territory", new int[] { 867 } },
    };
}
```

This servlet receives the WAP request as a normal HTTP GET request. In its `doGet()` method the servlet sets the content type to `text/vnd.wap.wml`, fetches the `code` parameter, locates the corresponding region via the lookup table, and finally generates a WML document containing the region. The area code information comes from a manually entered `data` array that's converted to a `Properties` table on servlet initialization. A screen shot of the output is shown in Figure 6-4.

Figure 6-4. Using WAP to locate callers

And That's a WAP

If you're interested in learning more about how to create sites catering to WAP devices, see *Learning WML & WMLScript* by Martin Frost (O'Reilly). There are also many good resource sites including *http://www.wap-resources.net*, *http://www.AnywhereYouGo.com*, and *http://www.wirelessdevnet.com*. There's even a Sun-hosted *webjava-wireless* mailing list with archives at *http://archives.java.sun.com/archives/webjava-wireless.html*.

Images

People are visually oriented—they like to see, not just read, their information. Consequently, it's nearly impossible to find a web site that doesn't use images in some way, and those you do find tend to look unprofessional. To cite the well-worn cliche (translated into programmer-speak), "An image is worth a thousand words."

Luckily, it's relatively simple for a servlet to send an image as its response. In fact, we've already seen a servlet that does just this: the `ViewResource` servlet from Chapter 4, *Retrieving Information*. As you may recall, this servlet can return any file under the server's document root. When the file happens to be an image file, it detects that fact with the `getMimeType()` method and sets its response's content type with `setContentType()` before sending the raw bytes to the client.

This technique requires that we already have the needed image files saved on disk, which isn't always the case. Often, a servlet must generate or manipulate an image before sending it to the client. Imagine, for example, a web page that contains an image of an analog clock that displays the current time. Sure, someone could save 720 images (60 minutes times 12 hours) to disk and use a servlet to dispatch the appropriate one. But that someone isn't me, and it shouldn't be you. Instead, the wise servlet programmer writes a servlet that dynamically generates the image of the clock face and its hands—or as a variant, a servlet that loads an image of the clock face and adds just the hands. And, of course, the frugal programmer also has the servlet cache the image (for about a minute) to save server cycles.

There are many other reasons you might want a servlet to return an image. By generating images, a servlet can display things such as an up-to-the-minute stock chart, the current score for a baseball game (complete with icons representing the runners on base), or a graphical representation of the Cokes left in the Coke machine. By manipulating preexisting images, a servlet can do even more. It can draw on top of them; change their color, size, or appearance; or combine several images into one.

Image Generation

Suppose you have an image as raw pixel data that you want to send to someone. How do you do it? Let's assume it's a true-color, 24-bit image (3 bytes per pixel) and that it's 100 pixels tall and 100 pixels wide. You could take the obvious approach and send it one pixel at a time, in a stream of 30,000 bytes. But is that enough? How does the receiver know what to do with the 30,000 bytes he received? The answer is that he doesn't. You also need to say that you are sending raw, true-color pixel values, that you're beginning in the upper-left corner, that you're sending row by row, and that each row is 100 pixels wide. Yikes! And what if you decide to send fewer bytes by using compression? You have to say what kind of compression you are using, so the receiver can decompress the image. Suddenly this has become a complicated problem.

Fortunately this is a problem that has been solved, and solved several different ways. Each image format (GIF, JPEG, PNG, TIFF, etc.) represents one solution. Each image format defines a standard way to encode an image so that it can later be decoded for viewing or manipulation. Each encoding technique has certain advantages and limitations. For example, the compression used for GIF encoding excels at handling computer-generated images, but the GIF format is limited to just 256 colors. The compression used for JPEG encoding, on the other hand, works best on photo-realistic images that contain millions of colors, but it works so well because it uses "lossy" compression that can blur the photo's details. PNG (pronounced "ping") is a relatively new encoding intended to replace GIF because it's smaller, supports millions of colors, employs "lossless" compression, and has an alpha channel for great transparency effects—plus it's free from patent issues that have plagued GIF.*

Understanding image encoding helps you understand how servlets handle images. A servlet like `ViewResource` can return a preexisting image by sending its encoded representation unmodified to the client—the browser decodes the image for viewing. But a servlet that generates or modifies an image must construct an internal representation of that image, manipulate it, and then encode it, before sending it to the client.

A "Hello World" image

Example 6-6 gives a simple example of a servlet that generates and returns a GIF image. The graphic says "Hello World!," as shown in Figure 6-5.

* For more information on PNG, see *http://graphicswiz.com/png*.

Example 6-6. Hello World Graphics

```
import java.io.*;
import java.awt.*;
import javax.servlet.*;
import javax.servlet.http.*;

import Acme.JPM.Encoders.GifEncoder;

public class HelloWorldGraphics extends HttpServlet {

  public void doGet(HttpServletRequest req, HttpServletResponse res)
                               throws ServletException, IOException {
    ServletOutputStream out = res.getOutputStream();  // binary output!

    Frame frame = null;
    Graphics g = null;

    try {
      // Create an unshown frame
      frame = new Frame();
      frame.addNotify();

      // Get a graphics region, using the Frame
      Image image = frame.createImage(400, 60);
      g = image.getGraphics();

      // Draw "Hello World!" to the off-screen graphics context
      g.setFont(new Font("Serif", Font.ITALIC, 48));
      g.drawString("Hello World!", 10, 50);

      // Encode the off-screen image into a GIF and send it to the client
      res.setContentType("image/gif");
      GifEncoder encoder = new GifEncoder(image, out);
      encoder.encode();
    }
    finally {
      // Clean up resources
      if (g != null) g.dispose();
      if (frame != null) frame.removeNotify();
    }
  }
}
```

Although this servlet uses the `java.awt` package, it never actually displays a window on the server's display. Nor does it display a window on the client's display. It performs all its work in an off-screen graphics context and lets the browser display the image. The strategy is as follows: create an off-screen image, get its graphics

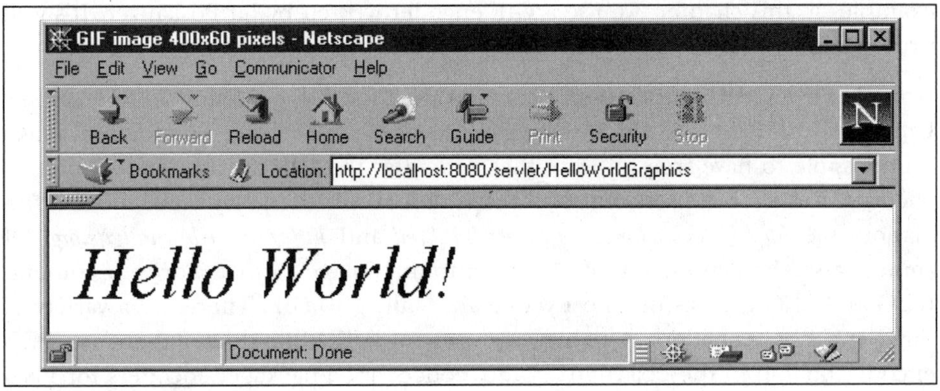

Figure 6-5. Hello World graphics

context, draw to the graphics context, and then encode the resulting image for transmission to the client.

Obtaining an off-screen image involves jumping through several hoops. In Java, an image is represented by the `java.awt.Image` class. Unfortunately, in JDK 1.1, an `Image` object cannot be instantiated directly through a constructor. It must be obtained through a factory method like the `createImage()` method of `Component` or the `getImage()` method of `Toolkit`. Because we're creating a new image, we use `createImage()`. Note that before a component can create an image, its native peer must already exist. Thus, to create our `Image` we must create a `Frame`, create the frame's peer with a call to `addNotify()`, and then use the frame to create our `Image`.*

In JDK 1.2, the process has been simplified and an `Image` can be created directly by constructing a new `java.awt.image.BufferedImage`. However, our examples in this chapter use the `frame.createImage()` technique for maximum portability across JDK versions.

Once we have an image, we draw onto it using its graphics context, which can be retrieved with a call to the `getGraphics()` method of `Image`. In this example, we just draw a simple string.

After drawing into the graphics context, we call `setContentType()` to set the MIME type to `image/gif` since we're going to use the GIF encoding. For the

* For web servers running on Unix systems, the frame's native peer has to be created inside an X server. Thus, for optimal performance, make sure the `DISPLAY` environment variable (which specifies the X server to use) is unset or set to a local X server. Also make sure the web server has been granted access to the X server, which may require the use of xhost or xauth. "Headless" server machines without an X server running can use Xvfb (X virtual frame buffer) to handle the graphics chores; just make sure to point the `DISPLAY` at the Xvfb server.

examples in this chapter, we use a GIF encoder written by Jef Poskanzer. It's well written and freely available with source from *http://www.acme.com.*

Note that the LZW compression algorithm used for GIF encoding is protected by Unisys and IBM patents which, according to the Free Software Foundation, make it impossible to have free software that generates the GIF format. The Acme GIF encoder uses LZ compression, so perhaps that avoids the patent. For more information, see *http://www.fsf.org/philosophy/gif.html* and *http://www.burnallgifs.org.* Of course, a servlet can encode its `Image` into any image format. For web content, JPEG and PNG exist as the most viable alternatives to GIF. There are a variety of JPEG and PNG encoders available. For users of JDK 1.2 and later there's a JPEG encoder built-in in the `com.sun.image.codec.jpeg` package; encoders for PNG and other formats are available for JDK 1.2 in the official Java Advanced Imaging API from *http://java.sun.com/products/java-media/jai.* . For users who need JDK 1.1 support as well, there's the Java Image Management Interface (JIMI) tool, formerly a commercial product from Activated Intelligence but now a Sun library available for free from *http://java.sun.com/products/jimi.*

To encode the image, we create a `GifEncoder` object, passing it the `Image` object and the `ServletOutputStream` for the servlet. When we call `encode()` on the `GifEncoder` object, the image is encoded and sent to the client.

After sending the image, the servlet does what all well-behaved servlets should do: it releases its graphical resources. These would be reclaimed automatically during garbage collection, but releasing them immediately helps on systems with limited resources. The code to release the resources is placed in a `finally` block to guarantee its execution, even when the servlet throws an exception.

A dynamically generated chart

Now let's look at a servlet that generates a more interesting image. Example 6-7 creates a bar chart that compares apples to oranges (who said it couldn't be done?), with regard to their annual consumption.

Example 6-7. A Chart Comparing Apples and Oranges

```
import java.awt.*;
import java.io.*;
import javax.servlet.*;
import javax.servlet.http.*;

import Acme.JPM.Encoders.GifEncoder;

import javachart.chart.*;  // from Visual Engineering

public class SimpleChart extends HttpServlet {
```

Example 6-7. A Chart Comparing Apples and Oranges (continued)

```
static final int WIDTH = 450;
static final int HEIGHT = 320;

public void doGet(HttpServletRequest req, HttpServletResponse res)
                             throws ServletException ,IOException {
  ServletOutputStream out = res.getOutputStream();

  Frame frame = null;
  Graphics g = null;

  try {
    // Create a simple chart
    BarChart chart = new BarChart("Apples and Oranges");

    // Give it a title
    chart.getBackground().setTitleFont(new Font("Serif", Font.PLAIN, 24));
    chart.getBackground().setTitleString("Comparing Apples and Oranges");

    // Show, place, and customize its legend
    chart.setLegendVisible(true);
    chart.getLegend().setLlX(0.4);  // normalized from lower left
    chart.getLegend().setLlY(0.75); // normalized from lower left
    chart.getLegend().setIconHeight(0.04);
    chart.getLegend().setIconWidth(0.04);
    chart.getLegend().setIconGap(0.02);
    chart.getLegend().setVerticalLayout(false);

    // Give it its data and labels
    double[] appleData = {950, 1005, 1210, 1165, 1255};
    chart.addDataset("Apples", appleData);

    double[] orangeData = {1435, 1650, 1555, 1440, 1595};
    chart.addDataset("Oranges", orangeData);

    String[] labels = {"1993", "1994", "1995", "1996", "1997"};
    chart.getXAxis().addLabels(labels);

    // Color apples red and oranges orange
    chart.getDatasets()[0].getGc().setFillColor(Color.red);
    chart.getDatasets()[1].getGc().setFillColor(Color.orange);

    // Name the axes
    chart.getXAxis().setTitleString("Year");
    chart.getYAxis().setTitleString("Tons Consumed");

    // Size it appropriately
    chart.resize(WIDTH, HEIGHT);
```

Example 6-7. A Chart Comparing Apples and Oranges (continued)

```
      // Create an unshown frame
      frame = new Frame();
      frame.addNotify();

      // Get a graphics region of appropriate size, using the Frame
      Image image = frame.createImage(WIDTH, HEIGHT);
      g = image.getGraphics();

      // Ask the chart to draw itself to the off screen graphics context
      chart.drawGraph(g);

      // Encode and return what it painted
      res.setContentType("image/gif");
      GifEncoder encoder = new GifEncoder(image, out);
      encoder.encode();
    }
    finally {
      // Clean up resources
      if (g != null) g.dispose();
      if (frame != null) frame.removeNotify();
    }
  }
}
```

Figure 6-6 shows the results. There's little need for this chart to be dynamically generated, but it lets us get the point across without too much code. Picture in your mind's eye, if you will, that the servlet is charting up-to-the-minute stock values or the server's recent load.

The basics are the same: create an off-screen image and get its graphics context, draw to the graphics context, and then encode the image for transmission to the client. The difference is that this servlet constructs a `BarChart` object to do the drawing. There are more than a dozen charting packages available in Java. The `BarChart` class from this example came from Visual Engineering's KavaChart (formerly JavaChart) package, available at *http://www.ve.com/kavachart*. It's a commercial product, but for readers of this book they have granted free permission to use the portion of the API presented in our example. The KavaChart package also includes a set of free chart-generating servlets at *http://www.ve.com/kavachart/servlets.html*. Another good charting package is JClass Chart from Sitraka at *http://www.sitraka.com* (formerly KL Group).

Image Composition

So far, we've drawn our graphics onto empty images. In this section, we discuss how to take preexisting images and either draw on top of them or combine them

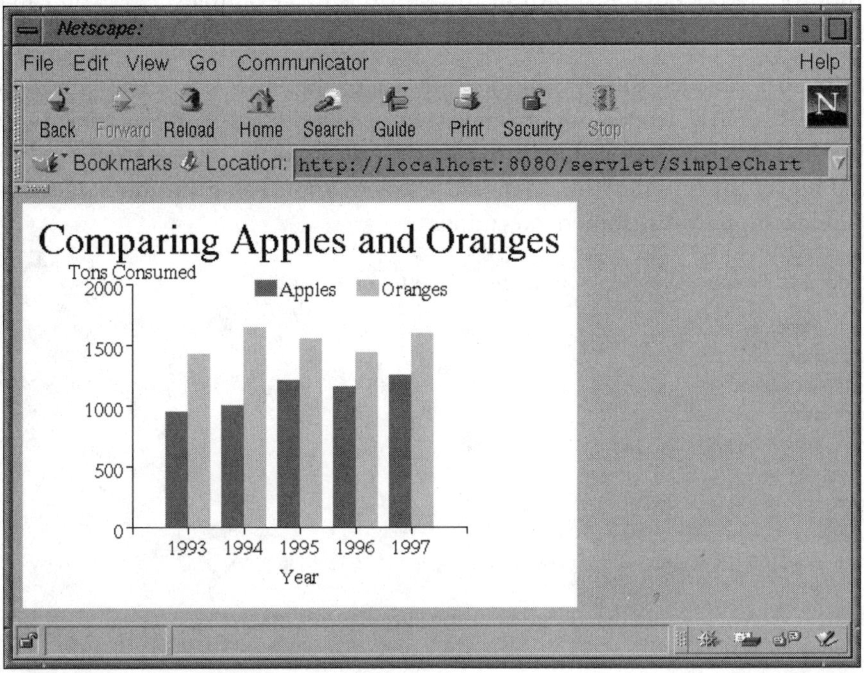

Figure 6-6. A chart comparing apples and oranges

to make conglomerate images. We also examine error handling in servlets that return images.

Drawing over an image

Sometimes it's useful for a servlet to draw on top of an existing image. A good example is a building locator servlet that knows where every employee sits. When queried for a specific employee, it can draw a big red dot over that employee's office.

One deceptively easy technique for drawing over a preexisting image is to retrieve the image with `Toolkit.getDefaultToolkit().getImage(imagename)`, get its graphics context with a call to the `getGraphics()` method of `Image`, and then use the returned graphics context to draw on top of the image. Unfortunately, it isn't quite that easy. The reason is that you cannot use `getGraphics()` unless the image was created with the `createImage()` method of `Component`. With the AWT, you always need to have a native peer in the background doing the actual graphics rendering.

Here's what you have to do instead: retrieve the preexisting image via the `Toolkit.getDefaultToolkit().getImage(imagename)` method and then tell it to draw itself into another graphics context created with the `createImage()`

method of `Component`, as shown in the previous two examples. Now you can use that graphics context to draw on top of the original image.

Example 6-8 clarifies this technique with an example. It's a servlet that writes "CONFIDENTIAL" over every image it returns. The image name is passed to the servlet as extra path information; the servlet will load the image from the corresponding location under the server's document root, using the `getResource()` method to support distributed execution.

Example 6-8. Drawing Over an Image to Mark It Confidential

```
import java.awt.*;
import java.io.*;
import java.net.*;
import javax.servlet.*;
import javax.servlet.http.*;

import com.oreilly.servlet.ServletUtils;

import Acme.JPM.Encoders.GifEncoder;

public class Confidentializer extends HttpServlet {

  Frame frame = null;

  public void init() throws ServletException {
    // Construct a reusable unshown frame
    frame = new Frame();
    frame.addNotify();
  }

  public void doGet(HttpServletRequest req, HttpServletResponse res)
                               throws ServletException, IOException {
    ServletOutputStream out = res.getOutputStream();
    Graphics g = null;

    try {
      // Get the image location from the path info
      // Use ServletUtils (Chapter 4) for safety
      URL source =
        ServletUtils.getResource(getServletContext(), req.getPathInfo());
      }

      // Load the image (from bytes to an Image object)
      MediaTracker mt = new MediaTracker(frame);  // frame acts as ImageObserver
      Image image = Toolkit.getDefaultToolkit().getImage(source);
      mt.addImage(image, 0);
      try {
        mt.waitForAll();
```

Example 6-8. Drawing Over an Image to Mark It Confidential (continued)

```
      }
      catch (InterruptedException e) {
        res.sendError(res.SC_INTERNAL_SERVER_ERROR,
                "Interrupted while loading image: " +
                ServletUtils.getStackTraceAsString(e));
        return;
      }

      // Get the width and height
      int w = image.getWidth(frame);
      int h = image.getHeight(frame);

      // Make sure we are reading valid image data
      if (w <= 0 || h <= 0) {
        res.sendError(res.SC_NOT_FOUND,
                "Extra path information must point to a valid image");
        return;
      }

      // Construct a matching-size off screen graphics context
      Image offscreen = frame.createImage(w, h);
      g = offscreen.getGraphics();

      // Draw the image to the off-screen graphics context
      g.drawImage(image, 0, 0, frame);

      // Write CONFIDENTIAL over its top
      g.setFont(new Font("Monospaced", Font.BOLD | Font.ITALIC, 30));
      g.drawString("CONFIDENTIAL", 10, 30);

      // Encode the off-screen graphics into a GIF and send it to the client
      res.setContentType("image/gif");
      GifEncoder encoder = new GifEncoder(offscreen, out);
      encoder.encode();
    }
    finally {
      // Clean up resources
      if (g != null) g.dispose();
    }
  }

  public void destroy() {
    // Clean up resources
    if (frame != null) frame.removeNotify();
  }
}
```

Some example output is shown in Figure 6-7.

Figure 6-7. Drawing over an image to mark it confidential

You can see that this servlet performs each step exactly as described earlier, along with some additional housekeeping. The servlet creates its unshown `Frame` in its `init()` method. Creating the `Frame` once and reusing it is an optimization previously left out for the sake of clarity. For each request, the servlet begins by retrieving the name of the preexisting image from the extra path information and converts the path to a resource using `getResource()`. Then it retrieves a reference to the image with the `getImage()` method of `Toolkit` and physically loads it into memory with the help of a `MediaTracker`. Normally it's fine for an image to load asynchronously with its partial results painted as it loads, but in this case we paint the image just once and need to guarantee it's fully loaded beforehand. Then the servlet gets the width and height of the loaded image and creates an offscreen image to match. Finally, the big moment: the loaded image is drawn on top of the newly constructed, empty image. After that it's old hat. The servlet writes its big "CONFIDENTIAL" and encodes the image for transmission.

Notice how this servlet handles error conditions by calling `sendError()`. When returning images, it's difficult to do much more. This approach allows the server to do whatever it deems appropriate.

Combining images

A servlet can also combine images into one conglomerate image. Using this ability, a building locator servlet could display an employee's smiling face, instead of a red dot, over her office. The technique used for combining images is similar to the one we used to draw over the top of an image: the appropriate images are loaded, they're drawn onto a properly created `Image` object, and that image is encoded for transmission.

Example 6-9 shows how to do this for a servlet that displays a hit count as a sequence of individual number images combined into one large image. The number images it uses are available at *http://www.geocities.com/SiliconValley/6742*, along with several other styles.

Example 6-9. Combining Images to Form a Graphical Counter

```
import java.awt.*;
import java.io.*;
import java.net.*;
import javax.servlet.*;
import javax.servlet.http.*;

import com.oreilly.servlet.ServletUtils;

import Acme.JPM.Encoders.GifEncoder;

public class GraphicalCounter extends HttpServlet {

  public static final String DIR = "/images/odometer";
  public static final String COUNT = "314159";

  public void doGet(HttpServletRequest req, HttpServletResponse res)
                              throws ServletException, IOException {
    ServletOutputStream out = res.getOutputStream();

    Frame frame = null;
    Graphics g = null;

    try {
      // Get the count to display, must be sole value in the raw query string
      // Or use the default
      String count = (String)req.getQueryString();
      if (count == null) count = COUNT;
```

Example 6-9. Combining Images to Form a Graphical Counter (continued)

```
    int countlen = count.length();
    Image images[] = new Image[countlen];

    for (int i = 0; i < countlen; i++) {
      URL imageSrc =
        getServletContext().getResource(DIR + "/" + count.charAt(i) + ".GIF");
      if (imageSrc == null) {
        imageSrc = new URL("file:");  // placeholder, handle errors later
      }
      images[i] = Toolkit.getDefaultToolkit().getImage(imageSrc);
    }

    // Create an unshown frame
    frame = new Frame();
    frame.addNotify();

    // Load the images
    MediaTracker mt = new MediaTracker(frame);
    for (int i = 0; i < countlen; i++) {
      mt.addImage(images[i], i);
    }
    try {
      mt.waitForAll();
    }
    catch (InterruptedException e) {
      res.sendError(res.SC_INTERNAL_SERVER_ERROR,
              "Interrupted while loading image: " +
              ServletUtils.getStackTraceAsString(e));
      return;
    }

    // Check for problems loading the images
    if (mt.isErrorAny()) {
      // We had a problem, find which image(s)
      StringBuffer problemChars = new StringBuffer();
      for (int i = 0; i < countlen; i++) {
        if (mt.isErrorID(i)) {
          problemChars.append(count.charAt(i));
        }
      }
      res.sendError(res.SC_INTERNAL_SERVER_ERROR,
              "Could not load an image for these characters: " +
              problemChars.toString());
      return;
    }

    // Get the cumulative size of the images
    int width = 0;
```

Example 6-9. Combining Images to Form a Graphical Counter (continued)

```
      int height = 0;
      for (int i = 0; i < countlen; i++) {
        width += images[i].getWidth(frame);
        height = Math.max(height, images[i].getHeight(frame));
      }

      // Get a graphics region to match, using the Frame
      Image image = frame.createImage(width, height);
      g = image.getGraphics();

      // Draw the images
      int xindex = 0;
      for (int i = 0; i < countlen; i++) {
        g.drawImage(images[i], xindex, 0, frame);
        xindex += images[i].getWidth(frame);
      }

      // Encode and return the composite
      res.setContentType("image/gif");
      GifEncoder encoder = new GifEncoder(image, out);
      encoder.encode();
    }
    finally {
      // Clean up resources
      if (g != null) g.dispose();
      if (frame != null) frame.removeNotify();
    }
  }
}
```

The output can be seen in Figure 6-8.

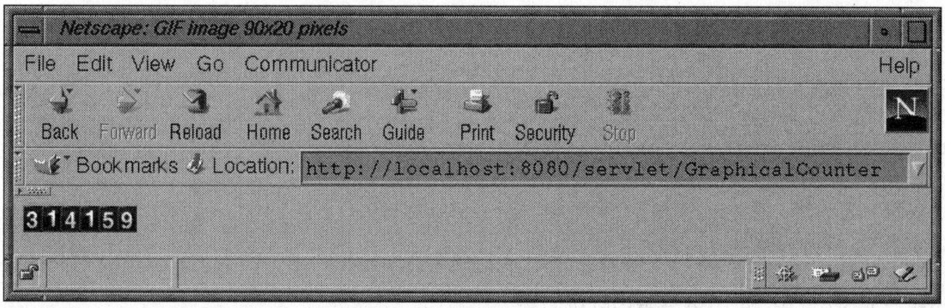

Figure 6-8. Combining images to form a graphical counter

This servlet receives the number to display by reading its raw query string. For each number in the count, it retrieves and loads the corresponding number image from the directory given by DIR. (DIR is always under the server's document root. It's given as a virtual path and converted to an abstract resource path.) Then it calculates the combined width and the maximum height of all these images and constructs an off-screen image to match. The servlet draws each number image into this off-screen image in turn from left to right. Finally, it encodes the image for transmission.

To be of practical use, this servlet must be called by another servlet that knows the hit count to be displayed and places the count in the query string. For example, it could be called by a JSP page or other dynamically created page using syntax like the following:

```
<IMG SRC="/servlet/GraphicalCounter?121672">
```

This servlet handles error conditions in the same way as the previous servlet, by calling `sendError()` and leaving it to the server to behave appropriately.

Image Effects

We've seen how servlets can create and combine images. In this section, we look at how servlets can also perform special effects on images. For example, a servlet can reduce the transmission time for an image by scaling down its size before transmission. Or it can add some special shading to an image to make it resemble a clickable button. As an example, let's look at how a servlet can convert a color image to grayscale.

Converting an image to grayscale

Example 6-10 shows a servlet that converts an image to grayscale before returning it. The servlet performs this effect without ever actually creating an off-screen graphics context. Instead, it creates the image using a special `ImageFilter`. (We'd show you before and after images, but they wouldn't look very convincing in a black-and-white book.)

Example 6-10. An Image Effect Converting an Image to Grayscale

```
import java.awt.*;
import java.awt.image.*;
import java.io.*;
import java.net.*;
import javax.servlet.*;
import javax.servlet.http.*;

import com.oreilly.servlet.ServletUtils;

import Acme.JPM.Encoders.*;

public class DeColorize extends HttpServlet {
```

Example 6-10. An Image Effect Converting an Image to Grayscale (continued)

```
public void doGet(HttpServletRequest req, HttpServletResponse res)
                              throws ServletException, IOException {
  res.setContentType("image/gif");
  ServletOutputStream out = res.getOutputStream();

  // Get the image location from the path info
  URL source = ServletUtils.getResource(getServletContext(),
                                        req.getPathInfo());
  if (source == null) {
    res.sendError(res.SC_NOT_FOUND,
           "Extra path information must point to an image");
    return;
  }

  // Construct an unshown frame
  // No addNotify() because its peer isn't needed
  Frame frame = new Frame();

  // Load the image
  Image image = Toolkit.getDefaultToolkit().getImage(source);
  MediaTracker mt = new MediaTracker(frame);
  mt.addImage(image, 0);
  try {
    mt.waitForAll();
  }
  catch (InterruptedException e) {
    res.sendError(res.SC_INTERNAL_SERVER_ERROR,
           "Interrupted while loading image: " +
           ServletUtils.getStackTraceAsString(e));
    return;
  }

  // Get the size of the image
  int width = image.getWidth(frame);
  int height = image.getHeight(frame);

  // Make sure we are reading valid image data
  if (width <= 0 || height <= 0) {
    res.sendError(res.SC_NOT_FOUND,
           "Extra path information must point to a valid image");
    return;
  }

  // Create an image to match, run through a filter
  Image filtered = frame.createImage(
    new FilteredImageSource(image.getSource(),
                            new GrayscaleImageFilter()));
```

Example 6-10. An Image Effect Converting an Image to Grayscale (continued)

```
    // Encode and return the filtered image
    GifEncoder encoder = new GifEncoder(filtered, out);
    encoder.encode();
  }
}
```

Much of the code for this servlet matches that of the `Confidentializer` example. The major difference is shown here:

```
    // Create an image to match, run through a filter
    Image filtered = frame.createImage(
      new FilteredImageSource(image.getSource(),
                              new GrayscaleImageFilter()));
```

This servlet doesn't use the `createImage(int, int)` method of `Component` we've used until now. It takes advantage of the `createImage(ImageProducer)` method of `Component` instead. The servlet creates an image producer with a `FilteredImageSource` that then passes the image through a `GrayscaleImageFilter`. This filter converts each color pixel to its grayscale counterpart. Thus, the image is converted to grayscale as it is being created. The code for the `GrayscaleImageFilter` is shown in Example 6-11.

Example 6-11. The GrayscaleImageFilter class

```
import java.awt.*;
import java.awt.image.*;

public class GrayscaleImageFilter extends RGBImageFilter {

  public GrayscaleImageFilter() {
    canFilterIndexColorModel = true;
  }

  // Convert color pixels to grayscale
  // The algorithm matches the NTSC specification
  public int filterRGB(int x, int y, int pixel) {

    // Get the average RGB intensity
    int red = (pixel & 0x00ff0000) >> 16;
    int green = (pixel & 0x0000ff00) >> 8;
    int blue = pixel & 0x000000ff;

    int luma = (int) (0.299 * red + 0.587 * green + 0.114 * blue);

    // Return the luma value as the value for each RGB component
```

Example 6-11. The GrayscaleImageFilter class (continued)

```
    // Note: Alpha (transparency) is always set to max (not transparent)
    return (0xff << 24) | (luma << 16) | (luma << 8) | luma;
  }
}
```

For each value in the colormap, this filter receives a pixel value and returns a new filtered pixel value. By setting the `canFilterIndexColorModel` variable to `true`, we signify that this filter can operate on the colormap and not on individual pixel values. The pixel value is given as a 32-bit `int`, where the first octet represents the alpha (transparency) value, the second octet the intensity of red, the third octet the intensity of green, and the fourth octet the intensity of blue. To convert a pixel value to grayscale, the red, green, and blue intensities must be set to identical values. We could average the red, green, and blue values and use that average value for each color intensity. That would convert the image to grayscale. Taking into account how people actually perceive color (and other factors), however, demands a weighted average. The 0.299, 0.587, 0.114 weighting used here matches that used by the National Television Systems Committee for black-and-white television. For more information, see Charles A. Poynton's book *A Technical Introduction to Digital Video* (Wiley) and the web site *http://www.color.org*.

Caching a converted image

The process of creating and encoding an image can be expensive, taking both time and server CPU cycles. Caching encoded images can often improve performance dramatically. Instead of doing all the work for every request, the results can be saved and resent for subsequent requests. The clock face idea that we mentioned earlier is a perfect example. The clock image needs to be created at most once per minute. Any other requests during that minute can be sent the same image. A chart for vote tabulation is another example. It can be created once and changed only as new votes come in.

The `com.oreilly.servlet.CacheHttpServlet` superclass from Chapter 3, *The Servlet Lifecycle*, provides a simple caching mechanism for images as well as text. A servlet generating the clock image could extend `CacheHttpServlet` and implement a `getLastModified()` method that returns the current time rounded down to the nearest minute. A servlet generating the vote tabulation chart could implement a `getLastModified()` method that returns the time the last vote was placed.

Our `DeColorize` example could extend `CacheHttpServlet` with a `getLastModified()` method that returns the time the image resource last changed. Unfortunately, `CacheHttpServlet` caches only the last response, providing little benefit in the likely scenario that `DeColorize` is called on more than one image. DeColorize should probably use a more sophisticated caching algorithm to handle multiple images. The servlet lifecycle makes this fairly simple. Our new DeColorize servlet can save each converted image as a byte array stored in a Hashtable keyed by the image name. First, our servlet needs to create a Hashtable instance variable. This must be declared outside doGet():

```
Hashtable gifs = new Hashtable();
```

To fill this hashtable, we need to capture the encoded graphics. So, instead of giving the GifEncoder the ServletOutputStream, we give it a ByteArrayOutputStream. Then, when we encode the image with encode(), the encoded image is stored in the ByteArrayOutputStream. Finally, we store the captured bytes in the hashtable and then write them to the ServletOutputStream to send the image to the client. Here's the new code to encode, store, and return the filtered image:

```
// Encode, store, and return the filtered image
ByteArrayOutputStream baos = new ByteArrayOutputStream(1024);  // 1K initial
GifEncoder encoder = new GifEncoder(filtered, baos);
encoder.encode();
gifs.put(source, baos);
baos.writeTo(out);
```

This fills the hashtable with encoded images keyed by image name. Now, earlier in the servlet, we can go directly to the cache when asked to return a previously encoded image. This code should go immediately after the code executed if source==null:

```
// Short circuit if it's been done before
if (gifs.containsKey(source)) {
  ByteArrayOutputStream baos = (ByteArrayOutputStream) gifs.get(source);
  baos.writeTo(out);
  return;
}
```

With these modifications, any image found in the cache is returned quickly, directly from memory.

Of course, caching multiple images tends to consume large amounts of memory. To cache a single image is rarely a problem, but a servlet such as this should use some method for cleaning house. For example, it could cache only the 100 most recently requested images. A more robust version of the servlet could also examine the file's timestamp to make sure the original image hasn't changed since the black-and-white version was cached.

Compressed Content

The `java.util.zip` package was introduced in JDK 1.1. This package contains classes that support reading and writing the ZIP and GZIP compression formats. Although this package was added to support Java Archive (JAR) files, they also provide a convenient, standard way for a servlet to send compressed content.

Compressed content doesn't look any different to the end user because it's decompressed by the browser before it's displayed. Yet, while it looks the same, it can improve the end user's experience by reducing the time required to download the content from the server. For heavily compressible content such as HTML, compression can reduce transmission times by an order of magnitude. Quite a trick! Just bear in mind that to compress content dynamically forces the server to perform extra work, so any speedup in transmission time has to be weighed against slower server performance.

By now you should be familiar with the idea that a servlet can send a `Content-Type` header as part of its response to tell the client the type of information being returned. To send compressed content, a servlet must also send a `Content-Encoding` header to tell the client the scheme by which the content has been encoded. Under the HTTP 1.1 specification, the possible encoding schemes are `gzip` (or `x-gzip`), `compress` (or `x-compress`), and `deflate`.

Not all clients understand all encodings. To tell the server which encoding schemes it understands, a client may send an `Accept-Encoding` header that specifies acceptable encoding schemes as a comma-separated list. Not all browsers—including a few that do support compressed encodings—provide this header. For now, a servlet has to decide that without the header it won't send compressed content, or it has to examine the `User-Agent` header to see if the browser is one that supports compression. Of the current popular browsers, most but not all support gzip encoding, none supports compress encoding, and only Microsoft Internet Explorer 4 and 5 on Windows support deflate encoding. To easily determine the capabilities of a browser, including whether it supports GZIP, try the BrowserHawk4J product from Cyscape. This commercial product detects GZIP support as well as dozens of other interesting browser properties including browser type, browser version, client operating system, installed plug-ins, browser width and height, client monitor width and height, disabled cookies, disabled JavaScript, and even connection speed. See *http://www.cyscape.com/products/bh4j*.*

Although negotiating which compression format to use can involve a fair amount of logic, actually sending the compressed content could hardly be simpler. The servlet just wraps its standard `ServletOutputStream` with a `GZIPOutputStream`

* Jason is proud that he was one of the principal developers hired to create BrowserHawk4J.

or `ZipOutputStream`. Be sure to call `out.close()` when your servlet is done writing output, so that the appropriate trailer for the compression format is written. Ah, the wonders of Java!

Example 6-12 shows the `ViewResource` servlet from Chapter 4 rewritten to send compressed content whenever possible. We'd show you a screen shot, but there's nothing new to see. As we said before, an end user cannot tell that the server sent compressed content to the browser—except perhaps with reduced download times.

Example 6-12. Sending Compressed Content

```
import java.io.*;
import java.net.*;
import java.util.*;
import java.util.zip.*;
import javax.servlet.*;
import javax.servlet.http.*;

import com.oreilly.servlet.ServletUtils;

public class ViewResourceCompress extends HttpServlet {

  public void doGet(HttpServletRequest req, HttpServletResponse res)
                               throws ServletException, IOException {
    OutputStream out = null;

    // Select the appropriate content encoding based on the
    // client's Accept-Encoding header. Choose GZIP if the header
    // includes "gzip". Choose ZIP if the header includes "compress".
    // Choose no compression otherwise. Make sure the Content-Encoding
    // uses the "x-" prefix if and only if the Accept-Encoding does.
    String encodings = req.getHeader("Accept-Encoding");
    if (encodings != null && encodings.indexOf("gzip") != -1) {
      // Go with GZIP
      if (encodings.indexOf("x-gzip") != -1) {
        res.setHeader("Content-Encoding", "x-gzip");
      }
      else {
        res.setHeader("Content-Encoding", "gzip");
      }
      out = new GZIPOutputStream(res.getOutputStream());
    }
    else if (encodings != null && encodings.indexOf("compress") != -1) {
      // Go with ZIP
      if (encodings.indexOf("x-compress") != -1) {
        res.setHeader("Content-Encoding", "x-compress");
      }
      else {
```

Example 6-12. Sending Compressed Content (continued)

```
        res.setHeader("Content-Encoding", "compress");
      }
      out = new ZipOutputStream(res.getOutputStream());
      ((ZipOutputStream)out).putNextEntry(new ZipEntry("dummy name"));
    }
    else {
      // No compression
      out = res.getOutputStream();
    }
    res.setHeader("Vary", "Accept-Encoding");

    // Get the resource to view
    URL url = null;
    try {
      url = ServletUtils.getResource(getServletContext(), req.getPathInfo());
    }
    catch (IOException e) {
      res.sendError(
        res.SC_NOT_FOUND,
        "Extra path info must point to a valid resource to view: " +
        e.getMessage());
    }

    // Connect to the resource
    URLConnection con = url.openConnection();
    con.connect();

    // Get and set the type of the resource
    String contentType = con.getContentType();
    res.setContentType(contentType);

    // Return the resource
    try {
      ServletUtils.returnURL(url, out);
    }
    catch (IOException e) {
      res.sendError(res.SC_INTERNAL_SERVER_ERROR,
              "Problem sending resource: " + e.getMessage());
    }

    // Write the compression trailer and close the output stream
    out.close();
  }
}
```

The servlet begins by declaring a `null` `OutputStream` and then setting this `OutputStream` to a `GZIPOutputStream`, or `ZipOutputStream`, or `ServletOutputStream`, depending on the received `Accept-Encoding` header.

As it selects which output stream to use, the servlet sets the `Content-Encoding` header accordingly. When sending compressed content, this header must be set for the client to run the appropriate decompression algorithm. The servlet also sets the `Vary` header to the value `Accept-Encoding` to be polite and indicate to the client that the servlet varies its output depending on the `Accept-Encoding` header. Most clients ignore this header.

After this early logic, the servlet can treat the output stream as just another `OutputStream`. It could wrap the stream with a `PrintStream` or `PrintWriter`, or it could pass it to a `GifEncoder`. But, no matter what it does, the servlet has to be sure to call `out.close()` when it's finished sending content. This call writes the appropriate trailer to the compressed stream.

There is some content that should not be compressed. For example, GIF and JPEG images are already compressed as part of their encoding, so there's not generally any benefit in compressing them again (and some browsers have a problem displaying images sent compressed). An improved version of the `FileViewCompressed` servlet would detect when it's returning an image and not bother with an attempt at further compression.

Server Push

Up until now, every page returned by a servlet has been just that: a page. Always one page with one content type. But why think in such limited terms? Why not have a servlet return several pages, each with a different content type, all in response to the same request? It may be hard to imagine—and sound even harder to implement—but it's actually quite easy using a technique known as *server push.*

It's called *server push* because the server sends, or pushes, a sequence of response pages to the client. Compare this to the client pull technique discussed in the last chapter, where it's left to the client to get, or pull, each page from the server. Although the results of each technique are similar to the end user—the appearance of a sequence of pages—the implementation details and the appropriate uses of the two techniques are quite different.

With server push, the socket connection between the client and the server remains open until the last page has been sent. This gives the server the ability to send page updates quickly and to control exactly when those updates are sent. As such, server push is ideal for pages that need frequent updates (such as rudimentary animations) or pages that need server-controlled but somewhat infrequent updates (such as live status updates). Note, however, that server push is not yet supported by Microsoft Internet Explorer, and extended use should be avoided, as it has been found to be harmful to the server's available socket count.

With client pull, the socket connection is broken after every page, so responsibility for page updates falls to the client. The client uses the `Refresh` header value sent by the server to determine when to perform its update, so client pull is the best choice for pages that require infrequent updates or have updates at known intervals.

Server push can come in handy for limited-length animations and for real-time status updates. For example, consider a servlet that could push the four latest satellite weather maps, creating a rudimentary animation. If you recall the `PrimeSearcher` servlet from Chapter 3, think about how we could use server push to notify a limited number of clients immediately as the servlet finds each new prime.

Example 6-13 shows a servlet that uses server push to display a countdown to a rocket launch. It begins by sending a series of pages that count down from 10 to 1. Every page replaces the previous page. When the countdown reaches 0, the servlet sends a picture of a launch. It uses the `com.oreilly.servlet.MultipartResponse` utility class (shown in Example 6-14) to manage the server push details.

Example 6-13. Countdown to a Rocket Launch

```
import java.io.*;
import javax.servlet.*;
import javax.servlet.http.*;

import com.oreilly.servlet.MultipartResponse;
import com.oreilly.servlet.ServletUtils;

public class Countdown extends HttpServlet {

  static final String LAUNCH = "/images/launch.gif";

  public void doGet(HttpServletRequest req, HttpServletResponse res)
                              throws ServletException, IOException {
    ServletOutputStream out = res.getOutputStream();  // some binary output

    // Prepare a multipart response
    MultipartResponse multi = new MultipartResponse(res);

    // First send a countdown
    for (int i = 10; i > 0; i--) {
      multi.startResponse("text/plain");
      out.println(i + "...");
      multi.endResponse();
      try { Thread.sleep(1000); } catch (InterruptedException e) { }
    }
```

Example 6-13. Countdown to a Rocket Launch (continued)

```
    // Then send the launch image
    multi.startResponse("image/gif");
    try {
      ServletUtils.returnFile(req.getRealPath(LAUNCH), out);
    }
    catch (FileNotFoundException e) {
      throw new ServletException("Could not find file: " + e.getMessage());
    }

    // Don't forget to end the multipart response
    multi.finish();
  }
}
```

The `MultipartResponse` class hides most of the nasty, dirty details involved in using server push. Feel free to use it in your own servlets. It is easy to use, as you can see from the previous example.

First, create a new `MultipartResponse` object, passing it the servlet's response object. `MultipartResponse` uses the response object to fetch the servlet's output stream and to set the response's content type. Then, for each page of content, begin by calling `startResponse()` and passing in the content type for that page. Send the content for the page by writing to the output stream as usual. A call to `endResponse()` ends the page and flushes the content, so the client can see it. At this point, you can add a call to `sleep()`, or some other kind of delay, until the next page is ready for sending. The call to `endResponse()` is optional, as the `startResponse()` method knows whether the previous response was ended and ends it if necessary. You should still call `endResponse()` if there's going to be a delay between the time one response ends and the next begins. This lets the client display the latest response while it is waiting for the next one. Finally, after all the response pages have been sent, a call to the `finish()` method finishes the multipart response and sends a code telling the client there will be no more responses.

Example 6-14 contains the code for the `MultipartResponse` class.

Example 6-14. The MultipartResponse Class

```
package com.oreilly.servlet;

import java.io.*;
import javax.servlet.*;
import javax.servlet.http.*;

public class MultipartResponse {
```

Example 6-14. The MultipartResponse Class (continued)

```
  HttpServletResponse res;
  ServletOutputStream out;
  boolean endedLastResponse = true;

  public MultipartResponse(HttpServletResponse response) throws IOException {
    // Save the response object and output stream
    res = response;
    out = res.getOutputStream();

    // Set things up
    res.setContentType("multipart/x-mixed-replace;boundary=End");
    out.println();
    out.println("--End");
  }

  public void startResponse(String contentType) throws IOException {
    // End the last response if necessary
    if (!endedLastResponse) {
      endResponse();
    }
    // Start the next one
    out.println("Content-Type: " + contentType);
    out.println();
    endedLastResponse = false;
  }

  public void endResponse() throws IOException {
    // End the last response, and flush so the client sees the content
    out.println();
    out.println("--End");
    out.flush();
    endedLastResponse = true;
  }

  public void finish() throws IOException {
    out.println("--End--");
    out.flush();
  }
}
```

7

In this chapter:
- *User Authentication*
- *Hidden Form Fields*
- *URL Rewriting*
- *Persistent Cookies*
- *The Session Tracking API*

Session Tracking

HTTP is a stateless protocol: it provides no built-in way for a server to recognize that a sequence of requests all originated from the same user. Privacy advocates may consider this a feature, but most web programmers see it as a major headache because web applications aren't stateless. Robust web applications need to interact back and forth with the user, remembering information about the user between requests. The shopping cart application is a classic example. A client has to be able to put items into his virtual cart, and the server has to remember his items until he checks out several page requests later, or sometimes even days later!

The HTTP state problem can best be understood if you imagine an online chat forum where you are the guest of honor. Picture dozens of chat users, all conversing with you at the same time. They are asking you questions, responding to your questions, and generally making you wish you had taken that typing course back in high school. Now imagine that when each participant writes to you, the chat forum doesn't tell you who's speaking! All you see is a bunch of questions and statements mixed in with each other. In this kind of forum, the best you can do is hold simple conversations, perhaps answering direct questions. If you try to do anything more, such as ask someone a question in return, you won't necessarily know when the answer comes back. This is exactly the HTTP state problem. The HTTP server sees only a series of requests—it needs extra help to know exactly who's making a request.*

The solution, as you may have already guessed, is for a client to introduce itself as it makes each request. Each client needs to provide a unique identifier that lets the server identify it, or it needs to give some information that the server can use

* If you're wondering why the HTTP server can't identify the client by the connecting machine's IP address, the answer is that the reported IP address could possibly be the address of a proxy server or the address of a server machine that hosts multiple users.

to properly handle the request. To use the chat example, a participant has to begin each of his sentences with something like "Hi, I'm Jason, and. . ." or "Hi, I just asked about your age, and. . ." As you'll see in this chapter, there are several ways for HTTP clients to send this introductory information with each request.

The first half of the chapter explores the traditional session-tracking techniques used by CGI developers: user authentication, hidden form fields, URL rewriting, and persistent cookies. The second half of the chapter demonstrates the built-in support for session tracking in the Servlet API. This support is built on top of the traditional techniques and it greatly simplifies the task of session tracking in your servlets. All the discussion in this chapter assumes the use of a single server. Chapter 12, *Enterprise Servlets and J2EE*, explains how to handle shared session state across multiple backend servers.

User Authentication

One way to perform session tracking is to leverage the information that comes with user authentication. We discussed user authentication back in Chapter 4, *Retrieving Information*, but, in case you've forgotten, it occurs when a web server restricts access to some of its resources to only those clients that log in using a recognized username and password. After the client logs in, the username is available to a servlet through `getRemoteUser()`.

We can use the username to track a client session. Once a user has logged in, the browser remembers her username and resends the name and password as the user views new pages on the site. A servlet can identify the user through her username and thereby track her session. For example, if the user adds an item to her virtual shopping cart, that fact can be remembered (in a shared class or external database, perhaps) and used later by another servlet when the user goes to the checkout page.

For example, a servlet that utilizes user authentication might add an item to a user's shopping cart with code like the following:

```
String name = req.getRemoteUser();
if (name == null) {
  // Explain that the server administrator should protect this page
}
else {
  String[] items = req.getParameterValues("item");
  if (items != null) {
    for (int i = 0; i < items.length; i++) {
      addItemToCart(name, items[i]);
    }
  }
}
```

Another servlet can then retrieve the items from a user's cart with code like this:

```
String name = req.getRemoteUser();
if (name == null) {
  // Explain that the server administrator should protect this page
}
else {
  String[] items = getItemsFromCart(name);
}
```

The biggest advantage of using user authentication to perform session tracking is that it's easy to implement. Simply tell the server to protect a set of pages (following the instructions in Chapter 8, *Security*), and use `getRemoteUser()` to identify each client. Another advantage is that the technique works even when the user accesses your site from different machines. It also works even if the user strays from your site or exits her browser before coming back.

The biggest disadvantage of user authentication is that it requires each user to register for an account and then log in each time she starts visiting your site. Most users will tolerate registering and logging in as a necessary evil when they are accessing sensitive information, but it's overkill for simple session tracking. Another downside is that HTTP's basic authentication provides no logout mechanism; the user has to exit her browser to log out. A final problem with user authentication is that a user cannot simultaneously maintain more than one session at the same site. We clearly need alternative approaches to support anonymous session tracking and to support authenticated session tracking with logout.

Hidden Form Fields

One way to support anonymous session tracking is to use hidden form fields. As the name implies, these are fields added to an HTML form that are not displayed in the client's browser. They are sent back to the server when the form that contains them is submitted. You include hidden form files with HTML like this:

```
<FORM ACTION="/servlet/MovieFinder" METHOD="POST">
...
<INPUT TYPE=hidden NAME="zip" VALUE="94040">
<INPUT TYPE=hidden NAME="level" VALUE="expert">
...
</FORM>
```

In a sense, hidden form fields define constant variables for a form. To a servlet receiving a submitted form, there is no difference between a hidden field and a visible field.

With hidden form fields, we can rewrite our shopping cart servlets so that users can shop anonymously until checkout time. Example 7-1 demonstrates the technique with a servlet that displays the user's shopping cart contents and lets the user choose to add more items or check out. An example screen for a bookworm is shown in Figure 7-1.

Example 7-1. Session Tracking Using Hidden Form Fields

```
import java.io.*;
import javax.servlet.*;
import javax.servlet.http.*;

public class ShoppingCartViewerHidden extends HttpServlet {

  public void doGet(HttpServletRequest req, HttpServletResponse res)
                               throws ServletException, IOException {
    res.setContentType("text/html");
    PrintWriter out = res.getWriter();

    out.println("<HEAD><TITLE>Current Shopping Cart Items</TITLE></HEAD>");
    out.println("<BODY>");

    // Cart items are passed in as the item parameter.
    String[] items = req.getParameterValues("item");

    // Print the current cart items.
    out.println("You currently have the following items in your cart:<BR>");
    if (items == null) {
      out.println("<B>None</B>");
    }
    else {
      out.println("<UL>");
      for (int i = 0; i < items.length; i++) {
        out.println("<LI>" + items[i]);
      }
      out.println("</UL>");
    }

    // Ask if the user wants to add more items or check out.
    // Include the current items as hidden fields so they'll be passed on.
    out.println("<FORM ACTION=\"/servlet/ShoppingCart\" METHOD=POST>");
    if (items != null) {
      for (int i = 0; i < items.length; i++) {
        out.println("<INPUT TYPE=HIDDEN NAME=\"item\" VALUE=\"" +
          items[i] + "\">");
      }
    }
    out.println("Would you like to<BR>");
    out.println("<INPUT TYPE=SUBMIT VALUE=\" Add More Items \">");
    out.println("<INPUT TYPE=SUBMIT VALUE=\" Check Out \">");
```

Example 7-1. Session Tracking Using Hidden Form Fields (continued)

```
    out.println("</FORM>");

    out.println("</BODY></HTML>");
  }
}
```

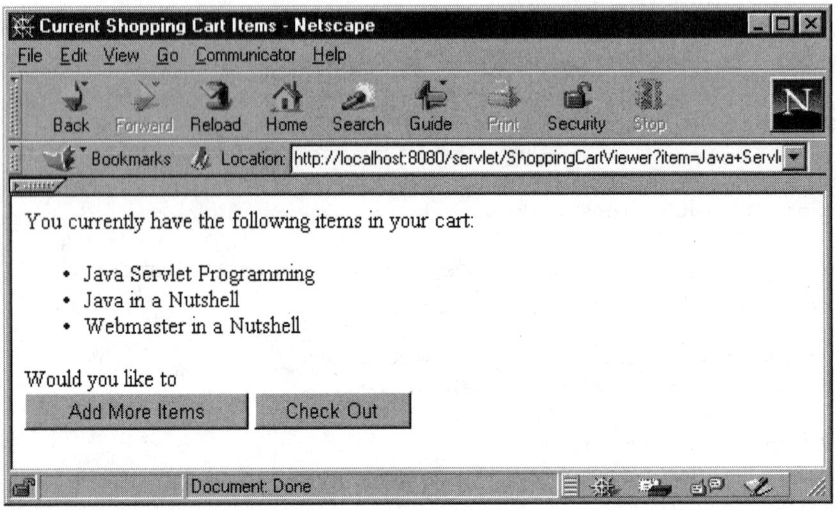

Figure 7-1. Shopping cart contents

This servlet first reads the items that are already in the cart using `getParameterValues("item")`. Presumably, the item parameter values were sent to this servlet using hidden fields. The servlet then displays the current items to the user and asks if he wants to add more items or check out. The servlet asks its question with a form that includes hidden fields, so the form's target (the `ShoppingCart` servlet) receives the current items as part of the submission.

As more and more information is associated with a client's session, it can become burdensome to pass it all using hidden form fields. In these situations, it's possible to pass on just a unique session ID that identifies a particular client's session. That session ID can be associated with complete information about the session that is stored on the server.

Beware that session IDs must be held as a server secret because any client with knowledge of another client's session ID can, with a forged hidden form field, assume the second client's identity. Consequently, session IDs should be generated so as to be difficult to guess or forge, and active session IDs should be protected—for example, don't make public the server's access log because the logged URLs may contain session IDs for forms submitted with GET requests.

Hidden form fields can be used to implement authentication with logout. Simply present an HTML form as the logon screen, and once the user has been authenticated by the server her identity can be associated with her particular session ID. On logout the session ID can be deleted (by not sending the ID to the client on later forms), or the association between ID and user can simply be forgotten. Chapter 8 demonstrates this approach in more detail.

The advantages of hidden form fields are their ubiquity and support for anonymity. Hidden fields are supported in all the popular browsers, they demand no special server requirements, and they can be used with clients that haven't registered or logged in. The major disadvantage with this technique, however, is that the session persists only through sequences of dynamically generated forms. The session cannot be maintained with static documents, emailed documents, bookmarked documents, or browser shutdowns.

URL Rewriting

URL rewriting is another way to support anonymous session tracking. With URL rewriting, every local URL the user might click on is dynamically modified, or rewritten, to include extra information. The extra information can be in the form of extra path information, added parameters, or some custom, server-specific URL change. Due to the limited space available in rewriting a URL, the extra information is usually limited to a unique session ID. For example, the following URLs have been rewritten to pass the session ID `123`:*

```
http://server:port/servlet/Rewritten                   original
http://server:port/servlet/Rewritten/123               extra path information
http://server:port/servlet/Rewritten?sessionid=123     added parameter
http://server:port/servlet/Rewritten;jsessionid=123    custom change
```

Each rewriting technique has its advantages and disadvantages. Using extra path information works on all servers, but it doesn't work well if a servlet has to use the extra path information as true path information. Using an added parameter works on all servers too, but it can cause parameter naming collisions. Using a custom, server-specific change works under all conditions for servers that support the change. Unfortunately, it doesn't work at all for servers that don't support the change.

Example 7-2 shows a revised version of our shopping cart viewer that uses URL rewriting in the form of extra path information to anonymously track a shopping cart.

* Remember, session ID values should be difficult to guess or forge. `123` does not qualify as a good session ID, except in a simple book example.

Example 7-2. Session Tracking Using URL Rewriting

```
import java.io.*;
import javax.servlet.*;
import javax.servlet.http.*;

public class ShoppingCartViewerRewrite extends HttpServlet {

  public void doGet(HttpServletRequest req, HttpServletResponse res)
                               throws ServletException, IOException {
    res.setContentType("text/html");
    PrintWriter out = res.getWriter();

    out.println("<HEAD><TITLE>Current Shopping Cart Items</TITLE></HEAD>");
    out.println("<BODY>");

    // Get the current session ID, or generate one if necessary
    String sessionid = req.getPathInfo();
    if (sessionid == null) {
      sessionid = generateSessionId();
    }

    // Cart items are associated with the session ID
    String[] items = getItemsFromCart(sessionid);

    // Print the current cart items.
    out.println("You currently have the following items in your cart:<BR>");
    if (items == null) {
      out.println("<B>None</B>");
    }
    else {
      out.println("<UL>");
      for (int i = 0; i < items.length; i++) {
        out.println("<LI>" + items[i]);
      }
      out.println("</UL>");
    }

    // Ask if the user wants to add more items or check out.
    // Include the session ID in the action URL.
    out.println("<FORM ACTION=\"/servlet/ShoppingCart/" + sessionid +
                "\" METHOD=POST>");
    out.println("Would you like to<BR>");
    out.println("<INPUT TYPE=SUBMIT VALUE=\" Add More Items \">");
    out.println("<INPUT TYPE=SUBMIT VALUE=\" Check Out \">");
    out.println("</FORM>");

    // Offer a help page. Include the session ID in the URL.
    out.println("For help, click <A HREF=\"/servlet/Help/" + sessionid +
                "?topic=ShoppingCartViewerRewrite\">here</A>");
```

Example 7-2. Session Tracking Using URL Rewriting (continued)

```
    out.println("</BODY></HTML>");
  }

  private static String generateSessionId() {
    String uid = new java.rmi.server.UID().toString();  // guaranteed unique
    return java.net.URLEncoder.encode(uid);  // encode any special chars
  }

  private static String[] getItemsFromCart(String sessionid) {
    // Not implemented
  }
}
```

This servlet first tries to retrieve the current session ID using `getPathInfo()`. If a session ID is not specified, it calls `generateSessionId()` to generate a new unique session ID using an RMI class designed specifically for this. The session ID is used to fetch and display the current items in the cart. The ID is then added to the form's `ACTION` attribute, so it can be retrieved by the `ShoppingCart` servlet. The session ID is also added to a new help URL that invokes the `Help` servlet. This wasn't possible with hidden form fields because the `Help` servlet isn't the target of a form submission.

The advantages and disadvantages of URL rewriting closely match those of hidden form fields. Both work with all browsers, allow anonymous access, and can be used to implement authentication with logout. The major difference is that URL rewriting works for all dynamically created documents, such as the `Help` servlet, not just forms. Plus, with the right server support, custom URL rewriting can even work for static documents. Unfortunately, actually performing the URL rewriting can be tedious.

Persistent Cookies

A fourth technique to perform session tracking involves persistent cookies. A cookie is a bit of information sent by a web server to a browser that can later be read back from that browser. When a browser receives a cookie, it saves the cookie and thereafter sends the cookie back to the server each time it accesses a page on that server, subject to certain rules. Because a cookie's value can uniquely identify a client, cookies are often used for session tracking.

Cookies were first introduced in Netscape Navigator. Although they were not part of the official HTTP specification, cookies quickly became a de facto standard supported in all the popular browsers including Netscape 0.94 Beta and up and Microsoft Internet Explorer 2 and up. Currently the HTTP Working Group of the Internet Engineering Task Force (IETF) is in the process of making cookies an official standard as written in RFC 2109. For more information on cookies see

Netscape's cookie specification at *http://home.netscape.com/newsref/std/cookie_spec.html* and RFC 2109 at *http://www.ietf.org/rfc/rfc2109.txt*. Another good site is *http://www.cookiecentral.com*.

Working with Cookies

The Servlet API provides the `javax.servlet.http.Cookie` class for working with cookies. The HTTP header details for the cookies are handled by the Servlet API. You create a cookie with the `Cookie()` constructor:

```
public Cookie(String name, String value)
```

This creates a new cookie with an initial name and value. The rules for valid names and values are given in Netscape's cookie specification and RFC 2109.

A servlet can send a cookie to the client by passing a `Cookie` object to the `addCookie()` method of `HttpServletResponse`:

```
public void HttpServletResponse.addCookie(Cookie cookie)
```

This method adds the specified cookie to the response. Additional cookies can be added with subsequent calls to `addCookie()`. Because cookies are sent using HTTP headers, they should be added to the response before the response has been committed. Browsers are only required to accept 20 cookies per site, 300 total per user, and they can limit each cookie's size to 4096 bytes.

The code to set a cookie looks like this:

```
Cookie cookie = new Cookie("ID", "123");
res.addCookie(cookie);
```

A servlet retrieves cookies by calling the `getCookies()` method of `HttpServletRequest`:

```
public Cookie[] HttpServletRequest.getCookies()
```

This method returns an array of `Cookie` objects that contains all the cookies sent by the browser as part of the request or an empty array if no cookies were sent. Servlet API versions before 2.1 had `getCookies()` return `null` if no cookies were sent. For maximum portability it's best to assume either a `null` or an empty array is legitimate.

The code to fetch cookies looks like this:

```
Cookie[] cookies = req.getCookies();
if (cookies != null) {
  for (int i = 0; i < cookies.length; i++) {
    String name = cookies[i].getName();
    String value = cookies[i].getValue();
  }
}
```

Lamentably, there's no method in the standard Servlet API to fetch a cookie value by name. You can set a number of attributes for a cookie in addition to its name and value. The following methods are used to set these attributes. As you can see in Appendix B, *HTTP Servlet API Quick Reference*, there is a corresponding get method for each set method. The get methods are rarely used, however, because when a cookie is sent to the server, it contains only its name, value, and version. If you set an attribute on a cookie received from the client, you must add it to the response for the change to take effect, and you should take care that all attributes except name, value, and version are reset on the cookie as well.

```
public void Cookie.setVersion(int v)
```

sets the version of a cookie. Servlets can send and receive cookies formatted to match either Netscape persistent cookies (Version 0) or the newer, somewhat experimental RFC 2109 cookies (Version 1). Newly constructed cookies default to Version 0 to maximize interoperability.

```
public void Cookie.setDomain(String pattern)
```

specifies a domain restriction pattern. A domain pattern specifies the servers that should see a cookie. By default, cookies are returned only to the host that saved them. Specifying a domain name pattern overrides this. The pattern must begin with a dot and must contain at least two dots. A pattern matches only one entry beyond the initial dot. For example, *.foo.com* is valid and matches *www.foo.com* and *upload.foo.com* but not *www.upload.foo.com.** For details on domain patterns, see Netscape's cookie specification and RFC 2109.

```
public void Cookie.setMaxAge(int expiry)
```

specifies the maximum age of the cookie in seconds before it expires. A negative value indicates the default, that the cookie should expire when the browser exits. A zero value tells the browser to delete the cookie immediately.

```
public void Cookie.setPath(String uri)
```

specifies a path for the cookie, which is the subset of URIs to which a cookie should be sent. By default, cookies are sent to the page that set the cookie and to all the pages in that directory or under that directory. For example, if */servlet/CookieMonster* sets a cookie, the default path is */servlet.* That path indicates the cookie should be sent to */servlet/Elmo* and to */servlet/subdir/BigBird*—but not to the */Oscar.html* servlet alias or to any CGI programs under */cgi-bin.* A path set to /

* Technically, according to the Netscape cookie specification, two dots are needed for the top-level domains of *.com, .edu, .net, .org, .gov, .mil,* and *.int,* while three dots are required for all other domains. This rule keeps a server from accidentally or maliciously setting a cookie for the domain *.co.uk* and passing the cookie to all companies in the United Kingdom, for example. Unfortunately, nearly all browsers ignore the three-dot rule! See *http://homepages.paradise.net.nz/~glineham/cookiemonster.html* for more information.

causes a cookie to be sent to all the pages on a server. A cookie's path must be such that it includes the servlet that set the cookie.

```
public void Cookie.setSecure(boolean flag)
```

indicates whether the cookie should be sent only over a secure channel, such as SSL. By default, its value is `false`.

```
public void Cookie.setComment(String comment)
```

sets the comment field of the cookie. A comment describes the intended purpose of a cookie. Web browsers may choose to display this text to the user. Comments are not supported by Version 0 cookies.

```
public void Cookie.setValue(String newValue)
```

assigns a new value to a cookie. With Version 0 cookies, values should not contain the following: whitespace, brackets, parentheses, equals signs, commas, double quotes, slashes, question marks, at signs, colons, and semicolons. Empty values may not behave the same way on all browsers.

Shopping Using Persistent Cookies

Example 7-3 shows a version of our shopping cart viewer that has been modified to maintain the shopping cart using persistent cookies.

Example 7-3. Session Tracking Using Persistent Cookies

```
import java.io.*;
import javax.servlet.*;
import javax.servlet.http.*;

public class ShoppingCartViewerCookie extends HttpServlet {

  public void doGet(HttpServletRequest req, HttpServletResponse res)
                               throws ServletException, IOException {
    res.setContentType("text/html");
    PrintWriter out = res.getWriter();

    // Get the current session ID by searching the received cookies.
    String sessionid = null;
    Cookie[] cookies = req.getCookies();
    if (cookies != null) {
      for (int i = 0; i < cookies.length; i++) {
        if (cookies[i].getName().equals("sessionid")) {
          sessionid = cookies[i].getValue();
          break;
        }
      }
    }
```

Example 7-3. Session Tracking Using Persistent Cookies (continued)

```
    // If the session ID wasn't sent, generate one.
    // Then be sure to send it to the client with the response.
    if (sessionid == null) {
      sessionid = generateSessionId();
      Cookie c = new Cookie("sessionid", sessionid);
      res.addCookie(c);
    }

    out.println("<HEAD><TITLE>Current Shopping Cart Items</TITLE></HEAD>");
    out.println("<BODY>");

    // Cart items are associated with the session ID
    String[] items = getItemsFromCart(sessionid);

    // Print the current cart items.
    out.println("You currently have the following items in your cart:<BR>");
    if (items == null) {
      out.println("<B>None</B>");
    }
    else {
      out.println("<UL>");
      for (int i = 0; i < items.length; i++) {
        out.println("<LI>" + items[i]);
      }
      out.println("</UL>");
    }

    // Ask if they want to add more items or check out.
    out.println("<FORM ACTION=\"/servlet/ShoppingCart\" METHOD=POST>");
    out.println("Would you like to<BR>");
    out.println("<INPUT TYPE=SUBMIT VALUE=\" Add More Items \">");
    out.println("<INPUT TYPE=SUBMIT VALUE=\" Check Out \">");
    out.println("</FORM>");

    // Offer a help page.
    out.println("For help, click <A HREF=\"/servlet/Help\" +
                "?topic=ShoppingCartViewerCookie\">here</A>");

    out.println("</BODY></HTML>");
  }

  private static String generateSessionId() {
    String uid = new java.rmi.server.UID().toString();  // guaranteed unique
    return java.net.URLEncoder.encode(uid);  // encode any special chars
  }
```

Example 7-3. Session Tracking Using Persistent Cookies (continued)

```
  private static String[] getItemsFromCart(String sessionid) {
    // Not implemented
  }
}
```

This servlet first tries to fetch the client's session ID by iterating through the cookies it received as part of the request. If no cookie contains a session ID, the servlet generates a new one using `generateSessionId()` and adds a cookie containing the new session ID to the response. The rest of this servlet matches the URL rewriting version, except that this version doesn't perform any rewriting.

Persistent cookies offer an elegant, efficient, easy way to implement session tracking. Cookies provide as automatic an introduction for each request as you could hope for. For each request, a cookie can automatically provide a client's session ID or perhaps a list of the client's preferences. In addition, the ability to customize cookies gives them extra power and versatility.

The biggest problem with cookies is that browsers don't always accept cookies. Sometimes this is because the browser doesn't support cookies. More often, it's because the user has specifically configured the browser to refuse cookies (out of privacy concerns, perhaps). WAP devices also don't currently accept cookies due to limited memory space, and only recently have WAP gateways begun to manage cookies on their devices' behalf. If any of your clients might not accept cookies, you have to fall back to the solutions discussed earlier in this chapter.

The Session Tracking API

Fortunately for us servlet developers, it's not always necessary for a servlet to manage its own sessions using the techniques we have just discussed. The Servlet API provides several methods and classes specifically designed to handle short-term session tracking on behalf of servlets. In other words, servlets have built-in session tracking.*

The Session Tracking API, as we call the portion of the Servlet API devoted to session tracking, should be supported in any web server that supports servlets. The level of support, however, depends on the server. Most servers support session tracking through the use of persistent cookies, with the ability to revert to using URL rewriting when cookies fail. Some servers allow session objects to be written to the server's disk or to a database as memory fills up or when the server shuts

* Yes, we do feel a little like the third grade teacher who taught you all the steps of long division, only to reveal later how you could use a calculator to do the same thing. But we believe, as your teacher probably did, that you better understand the concepts after first learning the traditional approach.

down. (The items you place in the session need to implement the `Serializable` interface to take advantage of this option.) See your server's documentation for details pertaining to your server. The rest of this section describes the lowest-common-denominator functionality required by Servlet API 2.2 for a nondistributed server. Remember, Chapter 12 discusses distributed session tracking.

Session-Tracking Basics

Session tracking is wonderfully elegant. Every user of a site is associated with a `javax.servlet.http.HttpSession` object that servlets can use to store or retrieve information about that user. You can save any set of arbitrary Java objects in a session object. For example, a user's session object provides a convenient location for a servlet to store the user's shopping cart contents or, as you'll see in Chapter 9, *Database Connectivity*, the user's database connection.

To allow web applications to operate independently, sessions are scoped at the web application level. This means each `ServletContext` maintains its own pool of `HttpSession` instances, and a servlet running inside one context cannot access session information saved by a servlet in another context.

A servlet uses its request object's `getSession()` method to retrieve the current `HttpSession` object:

```
public HttpSession HttpServletRequest.getSession(boolean create)
```

This method returns the current session associated with the user making the request. If the user has no current valid session, this method creates one if `create` is `true` or returns `null` if `create` is `false`. The standard use of the method is `getSession(true)`, so for simplicity Servlet API 2.1 introduced a no-argument version that assumes a `create` flag of `true`:

```
public HttpSession HttpServletRequest.getSession()
```

To ensure the session is properly maintained, the `getSession()` method must be called at least once before committing the response.

You can add data to an `HttpSession` object with the `setAttribute()` method:

```
public void HttpSession.setAttribute(String name, Object value)
```

This method binds the specified object value under the specified name. Any existing binding with the same name is replaced. To retrieve an object from a session, use `getAttribute()`:

```
public Object HttpSession.getAttribute(String name)
```

This methods returns the object bound under the specified name or `null` if there is no binding. You can also get the names of all of the objects bound to a session with `getAttributeNames()`:

```
public Enumeration HttpSession.getAttributeNames()
```

returns an `Enumeration` containing the names of all objects bound to this session as `String` objects or an empty `Enumeration` if there are no bindings. Finally, you can remove an object from a session with `removeAttribute()`:

```
public void HttpSession.removeAttribute(String name)
```

This method removes the object bound to the specified name or does nothing if there is no binding. Each of these methods can throw a `java.lang.IllegalStateException` if the session being accessed is invalid (we'll discuss invalid sessions in an upcoming section).

Note that Servlet API 2.2 changed these method names from `setValue()`, `getValue()`, `getValueNames()`, and `removeValue()` to the more standard names `setAttribute()`, `getAttribute()`, `getAttributeNames()`, and `removeAttribute()`. The `Value` methods still work but are deprecated.

A Hit Count Using Session Tracking

Example 7-4 shows a simple servlet that uses session tracking to count the number of times a client has accessed it, as shown in Figure 7-2. The servlet also displays all the bindings for the current session, just because it can.

Example 7-4. Session Tracking a Hit Count

```
import java.io.*;
import java.util.*;
import javax.servlet.*;
import javax.servlet.http.*;

public class SessionTracker extends HttpServlet {

  public void doGet(HttpServletRequest req, HttpServletResponse res)
                               throws ServletException, IOException {
    res.setContentType("text/html");
    PrintWriter out = res.getWriter();

    // Get the current session object, create one if necessary
    HttpSession session = req.getSession();

    // Increment the hit count for this page. The value is saved
    // in this client's session under the name "tracker.count".
    Integer count = (Integer)session.getAttribute("tracker.count");
    if (count == null)
```

Example 7-4. Session Tracking a Hit Count (continued)

```
      count = new Integer(1);
    else
      count = new Integer(count.intValue() + 1);
    session.setAttribute("tracker.count", count);

    out.println("<HTML><HEAD><TITLE>SessionTracker</TITLE></HEAD>");
    out.println("<BODY><H1>Session Tracking Demo</H1>");

    // Display the hit count for this page
    out.println("You've visited this page " + count +
      ((count.intValue() == 1) ? " time." : " times."));

    out.println("<P>");

    out.println("<H2>Here is your session data:</H2>");
    Enumeration enum = session.getAttributeNames();
    while (enum.hasMoreElements()) {
      String name = (String) enum.nextElement();
      out.println(name + ": " + session.getAttribute(name) + "<BR>");
    }
    out.println("</BODY></HTML>");
  }
}
```

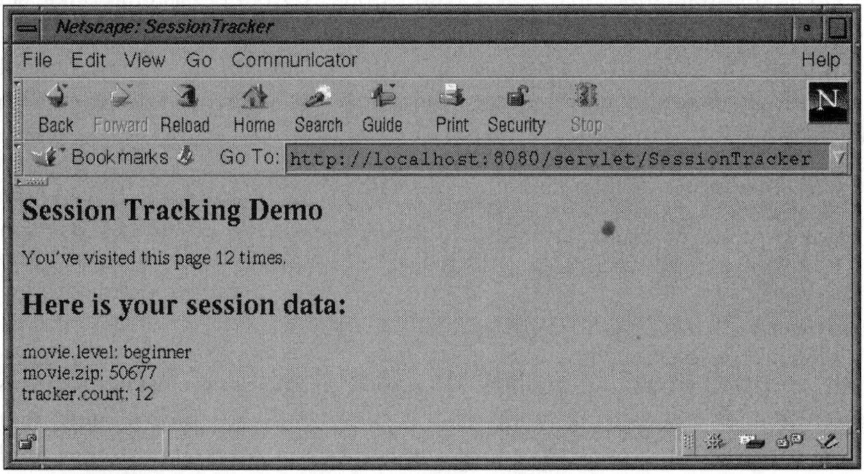

Figure 7-2. Counting client visits

This servlet first gets the `HttpSession` object associated with the current client. By using the no-argument version of `getSession()`, it asks for a session to be created if necessary. The servlet then gets the `Integer` object bound to the name `tracker.count`. If there is no such object, the servlet starts a new count. Otherwise, it replaces the `Integer` with a new `Integer` whose value has been incremented by one. Finally, the servlet displays the current count and all the current name/value pairs in the session.

The Session Lifecycle

Sessions do not last forever. A session either expires automatically, after a set time of inactivity (for the Tomcat Server the default is 30 minutes), or manually, when it is explicitly invalidated by a servlet. A server shutdown may or may not invalidate a session, depending on the capabilities of the server. When a session expires (or is invalidated), the `HttpSession` object and the data values it contains are removed from the system.

Beware that any information saved in a user's session object is lost when the session is invalidated. If you need to retain information beyond that time, you should keep it in an external location (such as a database) and provide your own mechanism for associating the user with his database entries. Common approaches are to require some form of login, set a long-term cookie that can be read for years, and/or provide the user with a rewritten URL to bookmark.

A real-life example is My Yahoo! where users login using an HTML form, have their login session tracked using an expire-at-browser-shutdown cookie, and (if they check the Remember My ID & Password box) have a persistent cookie set to record their identity until they explicitly log out. It's especially interesting that even though Yahoo may know the user's identity because of the persistent cookie, Yahoo still requires the user to enter her password before accessing email and other sensitive information.

The built-in session-tracking capability can still be used in conjunction with long-term sessions to manage the login session, store a handle to the external data, and/or hold a cached copy of the information in the database for quick retrieval.

Setting the Session Timeout

Ideally, a session would be invalidated as soon as the user closed his browser, browsed to a different site, or stepped away from his desk. Unfortunately, there's no way for a server to detect any of these events. Consequently, sessions live throughout some period of inactivity after which the server assumes the user must have left and it's not worth holding session state for him any more.

The default session timeout can be specified using the *web.xml* deployment descriptor; it applies to all sessions created in the given web application. See Example 7-5.

Example 7-5. Setting the Default Timeout to One Hour

```
<?xml version="1.0" encoding="ISO-8859-1"?>

<!DOCTYPE web-app
    PUBLIC "-//Sun Microsystems, Inc.//DTD Web Application 2.2//EN"
    "http://java.sun.com/j2ee/dtds/web-app_2.2.dtd">

<web-app>
    <!-- ..... -->
    <session-config>
        <session-timeout>
            60 <!-- minutes -->
        </session-timeout>
    </session-config>
</web-app>
```

The `<session-timeout>` tag holds a timeout value given in minutes. For this example, we specified that should 60 minutes pass without the user making any request to this web application, the server can invalidate the user's session and unbind the objects stored within. The servlet specification requires the timeout value be a "whole number," which precludes negative values, but some servers use a negative value to indicate sessions should never time out.

Timeout values can also be configured individually for a session. The `HttpSession` object has a `setMaxInactiveInterval()` method to support this fine-grained control:

```
public void HttpSession.setMaxInactiveInterval(int secs)
```

This method specifies the timeout value for this session, as given in *seconds*. A negative value for the interval indicates the session should never time out. Yes, the units don't match those of `<session-timeout>`, for no good reason except accident. To help you remember which units to use, think to yourself: "For fine-grained control I have fine-grained units."

The current timeout value can be retrieved using `getMaxInactiveInterval()`:

```
public int HttpSession.getMaxInactiveInterval()
```

This method returns the timeout value for this session, in seconds. If you don't specify a `<session-timeout>` you can call this method on a new session to determine the default timeout of your server.

Example 7-6 demonstrates these methods with a servlet that displays the current timeout value, then sets the new timeout value to two hours. On first execution, the current timeout displays the application-wide setting. On second execution, the current timeout displays two hours—because that's the timeout set during the first execution.

Example 7-6. Toying with the Timeout

```
import java.io.*;
import java.util.*;
import javax.servlet.*;
import javax.servlet.http.*;

public class SessionTimer extends HttpServlet {

  public void doGet(HttpServletRequest req, HttpServletResponse res)
                               throws ServletException, IOException {
    res.setContentType("text/html");
    PrintWriter out = res.getWriter();

    // Get the current session object, create one if necessary
    HttpSession session = req.getSession();

    out.println("<HTML><HEAD><TITLE>SessionTimer</TITLE></HEAD>");
    out.println("<BODY><H1>Session Timer</H1>");

    // Display the previous timeout
    out.println("The previous timeout was " +
                session.getMaxInactiveInterval());
    out.println("<BR>");

    // Set the new timeout
    session.setMaxInactiveInterval(2*60*60);  // two hours

    // Display the new timeout
    out.println("The newly assigned timeout is " +
                session.getMaxInactiveInterval());

    out.println("</BODY></HTML>");
  }
}
```

Choosing the right timeout

So we're armed with several ways to control session timeouts, but what timeout value is best to use? The answer, of course, is that it depends.

The first thing to remember is that the session timeout value does not determine how long a session lasts. It determines only how long the server will wait between requests before invalidating the session. A session with a half-hour timeout could easily last for hours.

Determining the proper period of inactivity requires a compromise between user convenience, user security, and server scalability. Longer timeouts provide the user more convenience because she can pause longer between requests, perhaps taking a phone call or checking her email, without losing her state. Shorter timeouts increase user security because it limits the time of vulnerability should a user forget to log out, and it increases server scalability because it lets the server free the objects in the session that much sooner.

For a starting point, ask yourself what is the maximum interval you would expect your users to pause between requests? A typical answer is a half-hour.

Now take your answer to that question and apply some rules of thumb:

- Secure web applications, such as online banking, should have shorter than usual timeouts to reduce the opportunity for an imposter to exploit an abandoned browser.
- Sessions that store "expensive" items (like database connections) should also have shorter than usual timeouts to allow the server to reclaim or release the items as quickly as possible.
- Sessions that store no "expensive" items can have longer than usual timeouts.
- Sessions that store shopping cart contents (expensive or not!) should have longer timeouts because users may not remember all of their cart contents, meaning an early invalidation will cost you money!
- Sessions that cache database information should have shorter timeouts if the cache is large, but longer timeouts if the database lookup is particularly slow.
- If you train your users to log out when they are finished, the default timeout can be set longer.

Finally, remember the timeout does not have to be the same for every user. You can use `setMaxInactiveInterval()` to set a custom timeout based on user preferences or even change the timeout during the session's lifetime—perhaps to make the timeout shorter after storing an "expensive" item.

Lifecycle Methods

There are several additional methods involved in managing the session lifecycle:

public boolean HttpSession.isNew()
: This method returns whether the session is new. A session is considered new if it has been created by the server but the client has not yet acknowledged joining the session.

public void HttpSession.invalidate()
: This method causes the session to be immediately invalidated. All objects stored in the session are unbound. Call this method to implement a "logout."

public long HttpSession.getCreationTime()
: This method returns the time at which the session was created, as a `long` value that represents the number of milliseconds since the epoch (midnight, January 1, 1970, GMT).

public long HttpSession.getLastAccessedTime( )

This method returns the time at which the client last sent a request associated with this session, as a `long` value that represents the number of milliseconds since the epoch. The current request does not count as the last request.

Each of these methods can throw a `java.lang.IllegalStateException` if the session being accessed is invalid.

Manually Invalidating a Stale Session

To demonstrate these methods, Example 7-7 shows a servlet that manually invalidates a session if it is more than a day old or has been inactive for more than an hour.

Example 7-7. Invalidating a Stale Session

```
import java.io.*;
import java.util.*;
import javax.servlet.*;
import javax.servlet.http.*;

public class ManualInvalidate extends HttpServlet {

  public void doGet(HttpServletRequest req, HttpServletResponse res)
                               throws ServletException, IOException {
    res.setContentType("text/html");
    PrintWriter out = res.getWriter();

    // Get the current session object, create one if necessary
    HttpSession session = req.getSession();

    // Invalidate the session if it's more than a day old or has been
    // inactive for more than an hour.
    if (!session.isNew()) {  // skip new sessions
      Date dayAgo = new Date(System.currentTimeMillis() - 24*60*60*1000);
      Date hourAgo = new Date(System.currentTimeMillis() - 60*60*1000);
      Date created = new Date(session.getCreationTime());
      Date accessed = new Date(session.getLastAccessedTime());

      if (created.before(dayAgo) || accessed.before(hourAgo)) {
        session.invalidate();
        session = req.getSession();  // get a new session
      }
    }

    // Continue processing...
  }
}
```

How Sessions Really Work

So, how does a web server implement session tracking? When a user first accesses a web application, that user is assigned a new `HttpSession` object and a unique session ID. The session ID identifies the user and is used to match the user with the `HttpSession` object in subsequent requests. Some servers use a single session ID for the entire server with each web application mapping that ID to a different `HttpSession` instance. Other servers assign a session ID per web application, as an extra precaution against a malicious web application helping an intruder impersonate you.

Behind the scenes, the session ID is usually saved on the client in a cookie called `JSESSIONID`. For clients that don't support cookies, the session ID can be sent as part of a rewritten URL, encoded using a `jsessionid` path parameter, e.g., *http://www.servlets.com/catalog/servlet/ItemDisplay;jsessionid=123?item=156592391X.* Other implementations, like using SSL (Secure Sockets Layer) sessions, are also possible.

A servlet can discover a session's ID with the `getId()` method:

```
public String HttpSession.getId()
```

This method returns the unique `String` identifier assigned to this session. For example, a Tomcat Server ID might be something like `awj4qyhsn2`. The method throws an `IllegalStateException` if the session is invalid.

Remember, the session ID should be treated as a server secret. Be careful what you do with this value.

The Deprecation of HttpSessionContext

In Servlet API 2.0, there existed an `HttpSessionContext` object that could be used for perusing the current sessions (and corresponding session IDs) managed by the server. Almost always the class was used for debugging, checking what sessions existed. The class still exists for binary compatibility, but beginning with Servlet API 2.1 it has been deprecated and defined to be empty. The reason is that session IDs must be carefully guarded, so they shouldn't be stored in an easily accessible single location, especially when the existence of that location doesn't provide any significant benefit beyond debugging.

Applet-Based Session Tracking

Almost every server that supports servlets implements cookie-based session tracking, where the session ID is saved on the client in a persistent cookie. The server reads the session ID from the `JSESSIONID` cookie and determines which session object to make available during each request.

For applet clients this can present a problem. Most applet environments implement `HttpURLConnection` in such a way that when an applet makes an HTTP connection, the environment automatically adds the containing browser's cookies to the request. This allows the applet to participate in the same session as other requests from the browser. The problem is that other applet environments, such as older versions of the Java Plug-In environment, do not have that integration with the browser and thus applet requests appear separate from the browser's normal session. The solution for the situation when applets need to run in such environments is to send the session ID to the applet and let the applet pass that ID back to the server as an artificially created `JSESSIONID` cookie. Chapter 10, *Applet-Servlet Communication*, includes an `HttpMessage` class to help with this. The applet can receive the session ID as a normal applet parameter (dynamically added to the HTML page containing the applet).

Noncookie Fallbacks

The servlet specification mandates web servers must also support session tracking for browsers that don't accept cookies, so many use URL rewriting as a fallback. This requires additional help from servlets that generate pages containing URLs. For a servlet to support session tracking via URL rewriting, it has to rewrite every local URL before sending it to the client. The Servlet API provides two methods—`encodeURL()` and `encodeRedirectURL()`—to perform this encoding:

`public String HttpServletResponse.encodeURL(String url)`
: This method encodes (rewrites) the specified URL to include the session ID and returns the new URL, or, if encoding is not needed or not supported, it leaves the URL unchanged. The rules used to decide when and how to encode a URL are server-specific. All URLs emitted by a servlet should be run through this method. Note that this `encodeURL()` method could more properly have been named `rewriteURL()` so as not to be confused with the URL encoding process that encodes special characters in URL strings.

`public String HttpServletResponse.encodeRedirectURL(String url)`
: This method encodes (rewrites) the specified URL to include the session ID and returns the new URL, or, if encoding is not needed or not supported, it leaves the URL unchanged. The rules used to decide when and how to encode a URL are server-specific. This method may use different rules than `encodeURL()`. All URLs passed to the `sendRedirect()` method of `HttpServletResponse` should be run through this method.

The following code snippet shows a servlet writing a link to itself that is encoded to contain the current session ID:

```
out.println("Click <A HREF=\"" +
            res.encodeURL(req.getRequestURI()) + "\">here</A>");
out.println("to reload this page.");
```

On servers that don't support URL rewriting or have URL rewriting turned off, the resulting URL remains unchanged. Now here's a code snippet that shows a servlet redirecting the user to a URL encoded to contain the session ID:

```
res.sendRedirect(res.encodeRedirectURL("/servlet/NewServlet"));
```

A servlet can detect whether the session ID used to identify the current `HttpSession` object came from a cookie or from an encoded URL using the `isRequestedSessionIdFromCookie()` and `isRequestedSessionIdFromURL()` methods:

```
public boolean HttpServletRequest.isRequestedSessionIdFromCookie()
public boolean HttpServletRequest.isRequestedSessionIdFromURL()
```

Determining if the session ID came from another source, such as an SSL session, is not currently possible.

A requested session ID may not match the ID of the session returned by the `getSession()` method, such as when the session ID is invalid. A servlet, though, can determine whether a requested session ID is valid using `isRequestedSessionIdValid()`:

```
public boolean HttpServletRequest.isRequestedSessionIdValid()
```

Finally, be aware when using session tracking based on URL rewriting that multiple browser windows can belong to different sessions or the same session, depending on how the windows were created and whether the link creating the windows was URL rewritten.

SessionSnoop

The `SessionSnoop` servlet shown in Example 7-8 uses most of the methods discussed thus far in the chapter to snoop information about the current session. Figure 7-3 shows a sample of its output.

Example 7-8. Snooping Session Information

```
import java.io.*;
import java.util.*;
import javax.servlet.*;
import javax.servlet.http.*;

public class SessionSnoop extends HttpServlet {
```

Example 7-8. Snooping Session Information (continued)

```
public void doGet(HttpServletRequest req, HttpServletResponse res)
                              throws ServletException, IOException {
  res.setContentType("text/html");
  PrintWriter out = res.getWriter();

  // Get the current session object, create one if necessary
  HttpSession session = req.getSession();

  // Increment the hit count for this page. The value is saved
  // in this client's session under the name "snoop.count".
  Integer count = (Integer)session.getAttribute("snoop.count");
  if (count == null)
    count = new Integer(1);
  else
    count = new Integer(count.intValue() + 1);
  session.setAttribute("snoop.count", count);

  out.println("<HTML><HEAD><TITLE>SessionSnoop</TITLE></HEAD>");
  out.println("<BODY><H1>Session Snoop</H1>");

  // Display the hit count for this page
  out.println("You've visited this page " + count +
    ((count.intValue() == 1) ? " time." : " times."));

  out.println("<P>");

  out.println("<H3>Here is your saved session data:</H3>");
  Enumeration enum = session.getAttributeNames();
  while (enum.hasMoreElements()) {
    String name = (String) enum.nextElement();
    out.println(name + ": " + session.getAttribute(name) + "<BR>");
  }

  out.println("<H3>Here are some vital stats on your session:</H3>");
  out.println("Session id: " + session.getId() +
              " <I>(keep it secret)</I><BR>");
  out.println("New session: " + session.isNew() + "<BR>");
  out.println("Timeout: " + session.getMaxInactiveInterval());
  out.println("<I>(" + session.getMaxInactiveInterval() / 60 +
              " minutes)</I><BR>");
  out.println("Creation time: " + session.getCreationTime());
  out.println("<I>(" + new Date(session.getCreationTime()) + ")</I><BR>");
  out.println("Last access time: " + session.getLastAccessedTime());
  out.println("<I>(" + new Date(session.getLastAccessedTime()) +
              ")</I><BR>");

  out.println("Requested session ID from cookie: " +
              req.isRequestedSessionIdFromCookie() + "<BR>");
```

Example 7-8. Snooping Session Information (continued)

```
    out.println("Requested session ID from URL: " +
                req.isRequestedSessionIdFromURL() + "<BR>");
    out.println("Requested session ID valid: " +
                 req.isRequestedSessionIdValid() + "<BR>");

    out.println("<H3>Test URL Rewriting</H3>");
    out.println("Click <A HREF=\"" +
                res.encodeURL(req.getRequestURI()) + "\">here</A>");
    out.println("to test that session tracking works via URL");
    out.println("rewriting even when cookies aren't supported.");

    out.println("</BODY></HTML>");
  }
}
```

This servlet begins with the same code as the `SessionTracker` servlet shown in Example 7-4. Then it continues on to display the current session's ID, whether it is a new session, the session's timeout value, the session's creation time, and the session's last access time. Next the servlet displays whether the requested session ID (if there is one) came from a cookie or a URL and whether the requested ID is valid. Finally, the servlet prints an encoded URL that can be used to reload this page to test that URL rewriting works even when cookies aren't supported.

Session Binding Events

Some objects may wish to perform an action when they are bound to or unbound from a session. For example, a database connection may begin a transaction when bound to a session and end the transaction when unbound. Any object that implements the `javax.servlet.http.HttpSessionBindingListener` interface is notified when it is bound to or unbound from a session. The interface declares two methods, `valueBound()` and `valueUnbound()`, that must be implemented:

```
public void HttpSessionBindingListener.valueBound(
            HttpSessionBindingEvent event)
public void HttpSessionBindingListener.valueUnbound(
            HttpSessionBindingEvent event)
```

The `valueBound()` method is called when the listener is bound into a session, and `valueUnbound()` is called when the listener is unbound from a session—by being removed or replaced or having the session become invalid.

The `javax.servlet.http.HttpSessionBindingEvent` argument provides access to the name under which the object is being bound (or unbound) with the `getName()` method:

```
public String HttpSessionBindingEvent.getName()
```

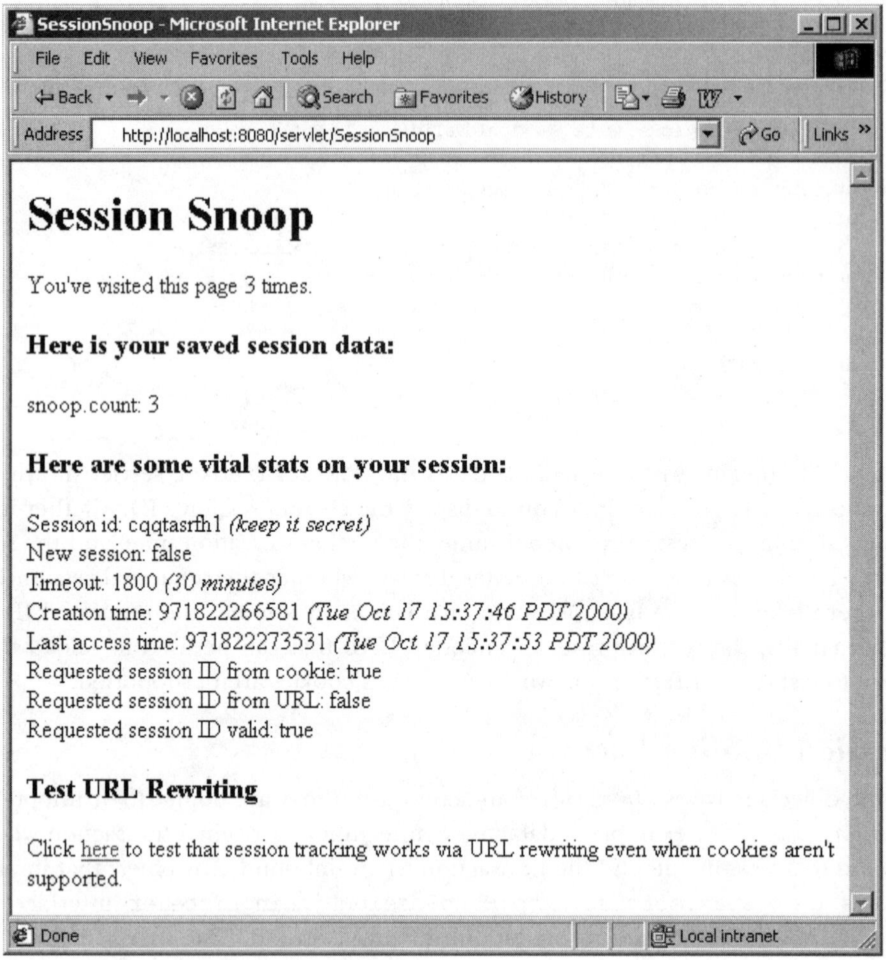

Figure 7-3. Example output from SessionSnoop

The `HttpSessionBindingEvent` object also provides access to the `HttpSession` object to which the listener is being bound (or unbound) with `getSession()`:

```
public HttpSession HttpSessionBindingEvent.getSession()
```

Example 7-9 demonstrates the use of `HttpSessionBindingListener` and `HttpSessionBindingEvent` with a listener that logs when it is bound to and unbound from a session.

Example 7-9. Tracking Session Binding Events

```
import java.io.*;
import java.util.*;
import javax.servlet.*;
import javax.servlet.http.*;

public class SessionBindings extends HttpServlet {

  public void doGet(HttpServletRequest req, HttpServletResponse res)
                               throws ServletException, IOException {
    res.setContentType("text/plain");
    PrintWriter out = res.getWriter();

    // Get the current session object, create one if necessary
    HttpSession session = req.getSession();

    // Add a CustomBindingListener
    session.setAttribute("bindings.listener",
                         new CustomBindingListener(getServletContext()));

    out.println("This page intentionally left blank");
  }
}

class CustomBindingListener implements HttpSessionBindingListener {

  // Save a ServletContext to be used for its log() method
  ServletContext context;

  public CustomBindingListener(ServletContext context) {
    this.context = context;
  }

  public void valueBound(HttpSessionBindingEvent event) {
    context.log("[" + new Date() + "] BOUND as " + event.getName() +
                " to " + event.getSession().getId());
  }

  public void valueUnbound(HttpSessionBindingEvent event) {
    context.log("[" + new Date() + "] UNBOUND as " + event.getName() +
                " from " + event.getSession().getId());
  }
}
```

Each time a `CustomBindingListener` object is bound to a session, its `valueBound()` method is called and the event is logged. Each time it is unbound from a session, its `valueUnbound()` method is called so that event too is logged. We can observe the sequence of events by looking at the server's event log.

Let's assume that this servlet is called once, reloaded 30 seconds later, and not called again for at least a half-hour. The event log would look something like this:

```
[Tue Sep 27 22:46:48 PST 2000]
  BOUND as bindings.listener to awj4qyhsn2
[Tue Sep 27 22:47:18 PST 2000]
  UNBOUND as bindings.listener from awj4qyhsn2
[Tue Sep 27 22:47:18 PST 2000]
  BOUND as bindings.listener to awj4qyhsn2
[Tue Sep 27 23:17:18 PST 2000]
  UNBOUND as bindings.listener from awj4qyhsn2
```

The first entry occurs during the first page request, when the listener is bound to the new session. The second and third entries occur during the reload, as the listener is unbound and rebound during the same `setAttribute()` call. The fourth entry occurs a half-hour later, when the session expires and is invalidated.

Shopping Using Session Tracking

Let's end this chapter with a look at how remarkably simple our shopping cart viewer servlet becomes when we use session tracking. Example 7-10 shows the viewer saving each of the cart's items in the user's session under the name `cart.items`. Notice the URLs in the page are rewritten to support clients that have cookies disabled.

Example 7-10. Using the Session Tracking API

```
import java.io.*;
import javax.servlet.*;
import javax.servlet.http.*;

public class ShoppingCartViewerSession extends HttpServlet {

  public void doGet(HttpServletRequest req, HttpServletResponse res)
                               throws ServletException, IOException {
    res.setContentType("text/html");
    PrintWriter out = res.getWriter();

    // Get the current session object, create one if necessary.
    HttpSession session = req.getSession();

    // Cart items are maintained in the session object.
    String[] items = (String[])session.getAttribute("cart.items");

    out.println("<HTML><HEAD><TITLE>SessionTracker</TITLE></HEAD>");
    out.println("<BODY><H1>Session Tracking Demo</H1>");
```

Example 7-10. Using the Session Tracking API (continued)

```
    // Print the current cart items.
    out.println("You currently have the following items in your cart:<BR>");
    if (items == null) {
      out.println("<B>None</B>");
    }
    else {
      out.println("<UL>");
      for (int i = 0; i < items.length; i++) {
        out.println("<LI>" + items[i]);
      }
      out.println("</UL>");
    }

    // Ask if they want to add more items or check out.
    out.println("<FORM ACTION=\"" +
                res.encodeURL("/servlet/ShoppingCart") + "\" METHOD=POST>");
    out.println("Would you like to<BR>");
    out.println("<INPUT TYPE=SUBMIT VALUE=\" Add More Items \">");
    out.println("<INPUT TYPE=SUBMIT VALUE=\" Check Out \">");
    out.println("</FORM>");

    // Offer a help page. Encode it as necessary.
    out.println("For help, click <A HREF=\"" +
                res.encodeURL("/servlet/Help?topic=ShoppingCartViewer") +
                "\">here</A>");

    out.println("</BODY></HTML>");
  }
}
```

8

In this chapter:
- *HTTP Authentication*
- *Form-Based Authentication*
- *Custom Authentication*
- *Digital Certificates*
- *Secure Sockets Layer (SSL)*

Security

So far we have imagined that our servlets exist in a perfect world, where everyone is trustworthy and nobody locks their doors at night. Sadly, that's a 1950s fantasy world: the truth is that the Internet has its share of fiendish rogues. As companies place more and more emphasis on online commerce and begin to load their intranets with sensitive information, security has become one of the most important topics in web programming.

Security is the science of keeping sensitive information in the hands of authorized users. On the Web, this boils down to four important issues:

Authentication
: Being able to verify the identities of the parties involved

Authorization
: Limiting access to resources to a select set of users or programs

Confidentiality
: Ensuring that only the parties involved can understand the communication

Integrity
: Being able to verify that the content of the communication is not changed during transmission

It helps to think of this in context: a client wants to be sure that it is talking to a legitimate server (authentication), and it also wants to be sure that any information it transmits, such as credit card numbers, is not subject to eavesdropping (confidentiality). The server is also concerned with authentication and confidentiality, as well as authorization. If a company is selling a service or providing sensitive information to its own employees, it has a vested interest in making sure that nobody but an authorized user can access it. Finally, both sides need integrity to make sure that whatever information they send gets to the other party unaltered.

Authentication, authorization, confidentiality, and integrity are all linked by digital certificate technology. Digital certificates allow web servers and clients to use advanced cryptographic techniques to handle identification and encryption in a secure manner. Thanks to Java's built-in support for digital certificates, servlets are an excellent platform for deploying secure web applications that use digital certificate technology. We'll be taking a closer look at them later.

Security is also about making sure that crackers can't gain access to the sensitive data on your web server. Because Java was designed from the ground up as a secure, network-oriented language, it is possible to leverage the built-in security features and make sure that server add-ons from third parties are almost as safe as the ones you write yourself.

This chapter introduces the basics of web security and digital certificate technology in the context of using servlets. It also discusses how to maintain the security of your web server when running servlets from untrusted third parties. You'll notice that this chapter takes a higher-level approach and shows fewer examples than previous chapters. The reason is that many of the topics in this chapter require web server-specific administration to implement. The servlets just tag along for the ride.

Finally, a note of caution: we are just a couple of servlet programmers, and we disclaim all responsibility for any security-related incidents that might result from following our advice. For a much more complete overview of web security technology and procedures, see *Web Security & Commerce* by Simson Garfinkel with Gene Spafford (O'Reilly). Of course, they probably won't accept responsibility either.

HTTP Authentication

As we discussed briefly in Chapter 4, *Retrieving Information*, the HTTP protocol provides built-in authentication support—called *basic authentication*—based on a simple challenge/response, username/password model. With this technique, the web server maintains a database of usernames and passwords and identifies certain resources (files, directories, servlets, etc.) as protected. When a user requests access to a protected resource, the server responds with a request for the client's username and password. At this point, the browser usually pops up a dialog box where the user enters the information, and that input is sent back to the server as part of a second authorized request. If the submitted username and password match the information in the server's database, access is granted. The whole authentication process is handled by the server itself.

Basic authentication alone is very weak. It provides no confidentiality, no integrity, and only the most basic authentication. The problem is that passwords are transmitted over the network, thinly disguised by a well-known and easily reversed

Base64 encoding. Anyone monitoring the TCP/IP data stream has full and immediate access to all the information being exchanged, including the username and password, unless there is additional SSL encryption employed (as discussed later in the chapter). Plus, passwords are often stored on the server in clear text, making them vulnerable to anyone cracking into the server's filesystem. While it's certainly better than nothing, sites that rely exclusively on basic authentication cannot be considered really secure.

Digest authentication is a variation on the basic authentication scheme. Instead of transmitting a password over the network directly, a digest of the password is used instead. The digest is produced by taking a hash (using the very secure MD5 encryption algorithm) of the username, password, URI, HTTP request method, and a randomly generated *nonce* value provided by the server. Both sides of the transaction know the password and use it to compute digests. If the digests match, access is granted. Transactions are thus somewhat more secure than they would be otherwise because digests are valid for only a single URI request and nonce value. The server, however, must still maintain a database of the original passwords. And, as of this writing, digest authentication is not supported by very many browsers.

The moral of the story is that HTTP authentication can be useful in low-security environments. For example, a site that charges for access to content—say, an online newspaper—is more concerned with ease of use and administration than lock-tight security, so HTTP authentication is often sufficient.

Configuring HTTP Authentication

In versions of the Servlet API before 2.2, the technique for configuring authentication varied depending on the server. Beginning with API 2.2, the technique has been standardized and now configuration of security policies can be accomplished in a portable manner using the *web.xml* deployment descriptor.

Before we begin, there are two caveats to this portability. First, a web server is not required to implement the Servlet API 2.2 security mechanism to be considered Servlet API 2.2 compliant. Implementing the full security portion of the specification is quite involved, and a servlet container is allowed to implement only a portion of the security mechanism, or even none at all. The only servers required to implement the full security mechanism are those wishing to be compliant with the more advanced Java 2, Enterprise Edition (J2EE) specification, of which the Servlet API is but one part. Second, security is one of the newest and least understood aspects of Servlet API 2.2, and web servers have varied somewhat on their implementations of these mechanisms. Over time that will settle down, but in the meanwhile, to ensure your site remains secure, make sure you test everything at least once when migrating between servers.

Role-based authentication

Using tags in the web application deployment descriptor, security constraints can be set up to indicate that certain pages in the web application are to be accessed only by users with certain credentials. Servlets use role-based authorization to manage access. With this model, access permissions are granted to an abstract entity called a *security role*, and access is allowed only to users or groups of users who are part of that given role. For example, you might want to set up your site so that pages that display salary information are restricted to only those users who are in a "manager" role.

The deployment descriptor specifies the type of access granted to each role, but does not specify that role to user or group mapping. That's done during deployment of the application, using server-specific tools. The ultimate mapping may come from many locations—text files, database tables, the operating system, and so on.

Restricting access to a servlet

For a concrete example, let's assume we have a servlet that needs restricted access, as shown in Example 8-1. (Servlets aren't the only things that can be protected—static files and anything else can be as well—but somehow it seems appropriate in this book to use a servlet as our example.)

Example 8-1. Are You Sure You Have Permissions to Read This Example?

```
import java.io.*;
import javax.servlet.*;
import javax.servlet.http.*;

public class SalaryServer extends HttpServlet {

  public void doGet(HttpServletRequest req, HttpServletResponse res)
                              throws ServletException, IOException {
    res.setContentType("text/plain");
    PrintWriter out = res.getWriter();

    out.println("Top-secret information:");
    out.println("Everyone else gets paid more than you!");
  }
}
```

Let's also assume that you have a user database for your server that contains a list of usernames, passwords, and roles. Remember, not all servers provide this, and those that do are free to implement the user database however they see fit. For Tomcat 3.2 you specify users in the *conf/tomcat-users.xml* file as shown in

Example 8-2. (Future Tomcat versions are likely to have a more secure storage format than plain text in an XML file.)

Example 8-2. Tomcat's conf/tomcat-users.xml File

```
<tomcat-users>
  <user name="Dilbert"       password="dnrc"          roles="engineer" />
  <user name="Wally"         password="iluvalice"     roles="engineer,slacker" />
  <user name="MrPointyHair" password="MrPointyHair" roles="manager,slacker" />
</tomcat-users>
```

Notice `MrPointyHair` is the only user who belongs to the `manager` role. Assuming he figures out how to connect his Etch-A-Sketch computer to the Web, he should be the only employee with permission to access our secret servlet. We specify that rule with the *web.xml* file shown in Example 8-3.

Remember, the order of the tags in a *web.xml* file does matter. Always follow this order: `<security-constraint>`, `<login-config>`, then `<security-role>`. Order of the tags within these elements matters as well.

This example may look a bit complicated. Security is one place where it's often easiest to use a graphical tool as an aid in creating *web.xml* files.

Example 8-3. Restricting Access with Basic Authentication

```
<?xml version="1.0" encoding="ISO-8859-1"?>

<!DOCTYPE web-app
    PUBLIC "-//Sun Microsystems, Inc.//DTD Web Application 2.2//EN"
    "http://java.sun.com/j2ee/dtds/web-app_2_2.dtd">

<web-app>
    <servlet>
        <servlet-name>
            secret
        </servlet-name>
        <servlet-class>
            SalaryServer
        </servlet-class>
    </servlet>

    <security-constraint>
        <web-resource-collection>
            <web-resource-name>
                SecretProtection
            </web-resource-name>
            <url-pattern>
                /servlet/SalaryServer
            </url-pattern>
```

Example 8-3. Restricting Access with Basic Authentication (continued)

```
            <url-pattern>
                /servlet/secret
            </url-pattern>
            <http-method>
                GET
            </http-method>
            <http-method>
                POST
            </http-method>
        </web-resource-collection>
        <auth-constraint>
            <role-name>
                manager
            </role-name>
        </auth-constraint>
    </security-constraint>

    <login-config>
        <auth-method>
            BASIC       <!-- BASIC, DIGEST, FORM, CLIENT-CERT -->
        </auth-method>
        <realm-name>
            Default     <!-- optional, only useful for BASIC -->
        </realm-name>
    </login-config>

    <security-role>
        <role-name>
            manager
        </role-name>
    </security-role>
</web-app>
```

This deployment descriptor protects all GET and POST access to */servlet/secret* and */servlet/SalaryServer* so that only users in the role `manager` who have logged in using basic authentication are allowed access. The rest of the site remains unrestricted.

It works like this: the `<security-constraint>` tag protects a `<web-resource-collection>` so that access is granted only for roles in the `<auth-constraint>`. Each `<web-resource-collection>` contains a name, any number of URL patterns specifying the URLs to protect, and any number of HTTP methods for which access should be restricted. The name must be specified even though it's really useful only for tools. For URL patterns you can use the same wildcards you use for servlet mapping, as discussed in Chapter 2, *HTTP Servlet Basics.* For HTTP methods you should usually specify at least GET and POST; if no `<http-method>`

entries are specified, then all methods are protected. The `<auth-constraint>` tag holds any number of roles that are to be granted access to the resource collection.

The `<login-config>` tag specifies the login methodology to be used by this application. In this case, we specify basic authentication in the `Default` realm. The `<auth-method>` tag allows `BASIC`, `DIGEST`, `FORM`, and `CLIENT-CERT` values representing authentication types of Basic, Digest, form-based, and client-side certificates, respectively. We'll talk about form-based and client-side certificates later in the chapter. The `<realm-name>` tag specifies the login realm to use (since a server may manage different user lists for different realms); it has meaning only for Basic and Digest authentication.

Finally, the `<security-role>` tag holds a list of roles that may be used by this application. Explicitly declaring the roles to be used supports tool-based manipulations of the file.

The security rules are fairly limited. For example, there's no way to allow access by all users except those in a "blacklist" role. The closest solution would be to have an approved list role that the server mapped to all users not in some group.

Now that we have this *web.xml* file in place, the server will catch all requests for the given URL patterns that use the given HTTP methods and check for client credentials. If the credentials are valid and the user maps (in a server-specific way) to the `manager` role, then access is granted. If the credentials are invalid or if the user is not in the `manager` role, then access is denied and a browser pop-up window will ask the user to try again.

Retrieving Authentication Information

A servlet can retrieve information about the server's authentication using two methods introduced in Chapter 4: `getRemoteUser()` and `getAuthType()`. The Servlet API 2.2 also includes a new method, `getUserPrincipal()`, that returns an object implementing the `java.security.Principal` interface:

```
public java.security.Principal HttpServletRequest.getUserPrincipal()
```

A *principal* is the technical term for the entity being authenticated. It may be a user, group, corporation, or just a generic login ID. The `Principal` interface includes a `getName()` method that returns the principal's name. The `getUserPrincipal()` method is the preferred way to determine the authenticated user's identity, while `getRemoteUser()` is primarily for CGI compatibility. The `isUserInRole()` method was also introduced in Servlet API 2.2. This method returns `true` only if the authenticated user belongs to the specified role:

```
public boolean HttpServletRequest.isUserInRole(String role)
```

This method allows a certain amount of decision making to be done within a servlet itself. For example, assume a deployment descriptor allows access to a servlet by many different roles. Calling this method allows the servlet to vary its runtime behavior depending on the authenticated user's role.

Any number of role aliases can be created in the deployment descriptor, so that from a servlet's perspective, a query on the role `mgr` would be the same as a query on the role `manager`. This proves especially useful when integrating servlets from web applications that may use different role names than those in this web application. Aliases are configured per servlet, using the `<security-role-ref>` tag inside the `<servlet>` tag, as shown in the following *web.xml* snippet:

```
<servlet>
    <servlet-name>
        secret
    </servlet-name>
    <servlet-class>
        SalaryViewer
    </servlet-class>
    <security-role-ref>
        <role-name>
            mgr         <!-- name used by servlet -->
        </role-name>
        <role-link>
            manager     <!-- name used in deployment descriptor -->
        </role-link>
    </security-role-ref>
</servlet>
```

Any number of `<security-role-ref>` tags may exist for a servlet. Remember that these aliases are valid only when accessing the servlet under its registered name.

Example 8-4 shows a simple servlet that tells the client its name, its principal, the kind of authentication performed (`BASIC`, `DIGEST`, `FORM`, `CLIENT-CERT`), and whether the user is a `manager`. To see this servlet in action, you should install it in your web server and protect it with a security scheme as shown in the previous section (making sure to restrict access to this new `<url-pattern>`).

Example 8-4. Snooping the Authentication Information

```
import java.io.*;
import java.security.*;
import javax.servlet.*;
import javax.servlet.http.*;

public class AuthenticationSnoop extends HttpServlet {
```

Example 8-4. Snooping the Authentication Information (continued)

```
  public void doGet(HttpServletRequest req, HttpServletResponse res)
                               throws ServletException, IOException {
    res.setContentType("text/html");
    PrintWriter out = res.getWriter();

    out.println("<HTML><HEAD><TITLE>AuthenticationSnoop</TITLE></HEAD><BODY>");

    out.println("<H1>This is a password protected resource</H1>");
    out.println("<PRE>");
    out.println("User Name: " + req.getRemoteUser());
    String name = (req.getUserPrincipal() == null) ?
                  null : req.getUserPrincipal().getName();
    out.println("Principal Name: " + name);
    out.println("Authentication Type: " + req.getAuthType());
    out.println("Is a Manager: " + req.isUserInRole("manager"));
    out.println("</PRE>");
    out.println("</BODY></HTML>");
  }
}
```

The resulting output looks something like this:

```
This is a password protected resource
User Name: jhunter
Principal Name: jhunter
Authentication Type: BASIC
Is a Manager: false
```

Form-Based Authentication

Servlets can also perform authentication without relying on HTTP authentication, by using HTML forms instead. Using this technique allows users to enter your site through a well-designed, descriptive and friendly login page. For example, imagine you're developing an online banking site. Would you rather let the browser present a generic prompt for username and password or provide your customers with a custom login form that politely asks for specific banking credentials, as shown in Figure 8-1?

Many banks and other online services have chosen to use form-based authentication. Implementing such a system is relatively straightforward with servlets because form-based authentication is built into Servlet API 2.2. To change from basic authentication to form-based, replace the `<login-config>` section of the *web.xml* file in Example 8-3 with the `<login-config>` section shown in Example 8-5.

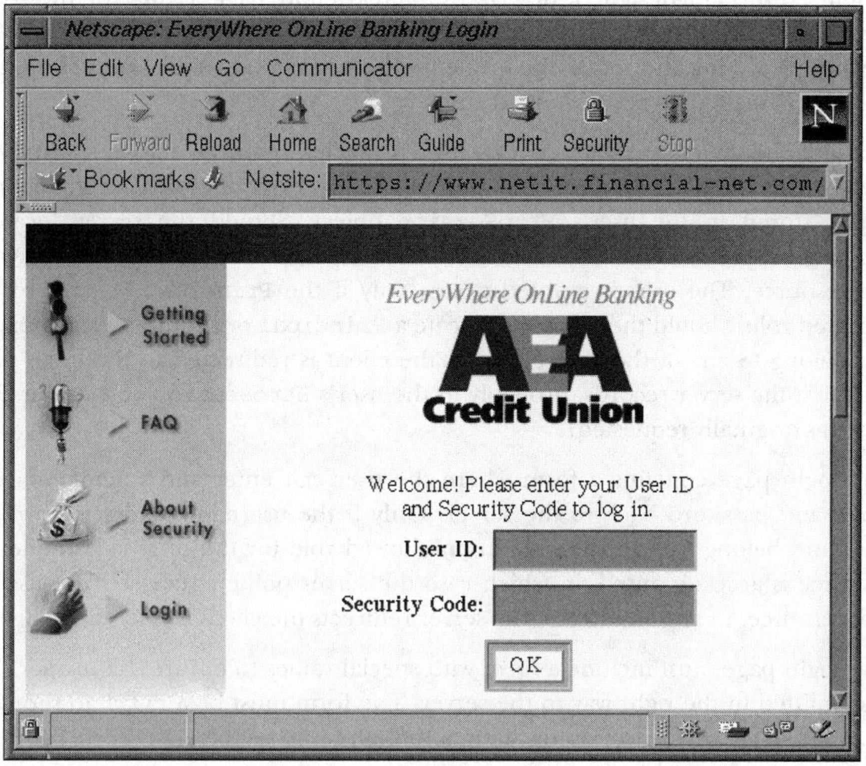

Figure 8-1. An online banking login screen

Example 8-5. Configuring Form-Based Authentication

```
<login-config>
    <auth-method>
        FORM       <!-- BASIC, DIGEST, FORM, CLIENT-CERT -->
    </auth-method>
    <form-login-config>  <!-- only useful for FORM -->
        <form-login-page>
            /loginpage.html
        </form-login-page>
        <form-error-page>
            /errorpage.html
        </form-error-page>
    </form-login-config>
</login-config>
```

Notice the `<auth-method>` has been changed from `BASIC` to `FORM`. This indicates that form-based authentication should be used for this web application. The `<realm-name>` tag has also been replaced with `<form-login-config>`. This tag specifies the login page and error page to use for authentication. The login page should be the well-designed, descriptive, and friendly page asking for the user's credentials. The error page should be the well-designed, descriptive, and possibly mean page telling the server the credentials are no good. Both URLs should be absolute paths rooted at the context root.

Any time the server receives a request for a protected resource, the server checks if the user has already logged in. For example, a server might look for a `Principal` object stored in the user's `HttpSession` object. Should the server locate a `Principal`, the roles of the `Principal` are compared to those required to access the resource. The user is granted access only if the `Principal` belongs to the required role. Should the server not locate a `Principal` or should the `Principal` not belong to any of the allowed roles, the client is redirected to the login page (but first the server records, probably in the user's `HttpSession` object, the URL that was originally requested).

The login page contains a form where the user can enter and submit his username and password back to the server. Only if the username and password are valid and belong to a `Principal` in an allowed role for the originally requested resource is access granted, in which case the server politely redirects the user to that resource. In any other case, the server redirects the client to the error page.

The login page must include a form with special values to ensure the proper data is submitted in the right way to the server. The form must be a POST to the URL `j_security_check` (no leading slash, although some servers have been known to erroneously require it) with a username sent as `j_username` and a password sent as `j_password`. For example:

```
<FORM METHOD=POST ACTION="j_security_check">
Username: <INPUT TYPE=TEXT NAME="j_username"><br>
Password: <INPUT TYPE=PASSWORD NAME="j_password"><br>
<INPUT TYPE=SUBMIT>
</FORM>
```

Example 8-6 shows a more realistic *loginpage.html* file that generates the form shown in Figure 8-2.

Example 8-6. The loginpage.html File

```
<HTML>
<TITLE>Login</TITLE>
<BODY>
<FORM METHOD=POST ACTION=j_security_check>
<CENTER>
<TABLE BORDER=0>
<TR><TD COLSPAN=2>
<P ALIGN=center>
Welcome!  Please enter your Name<br>
 and Password to log in.
```

Example 8-6. The loginpage.html File (continued)

```
</TD></TR>

<TR><TD>
<P ALIGN=right><B>Name:</B>
</TD>
<TD>
<P><INPUT TYPE=TEXT NAME="j_username" VALUE="" SIZE=15>
</TD></TR>

<TR><TD>
<P ALIGN=RIGHT><B>Password:</B>
</TD>
<TD>
<P><INPUT TYPE=PASSWORD NAME="j_password" VALUE="" SIZE=15>
</TD></TR>

<TR><TD COLSPAN=2>
<CENTER>
<INPUT TYPE=submit VALUE="  OK   ">
</CENTER>
</TD></TR>
</TABLE>
</FORM>
</BODY></HTML>
```

Figure 8-2 shows the form that is generated.

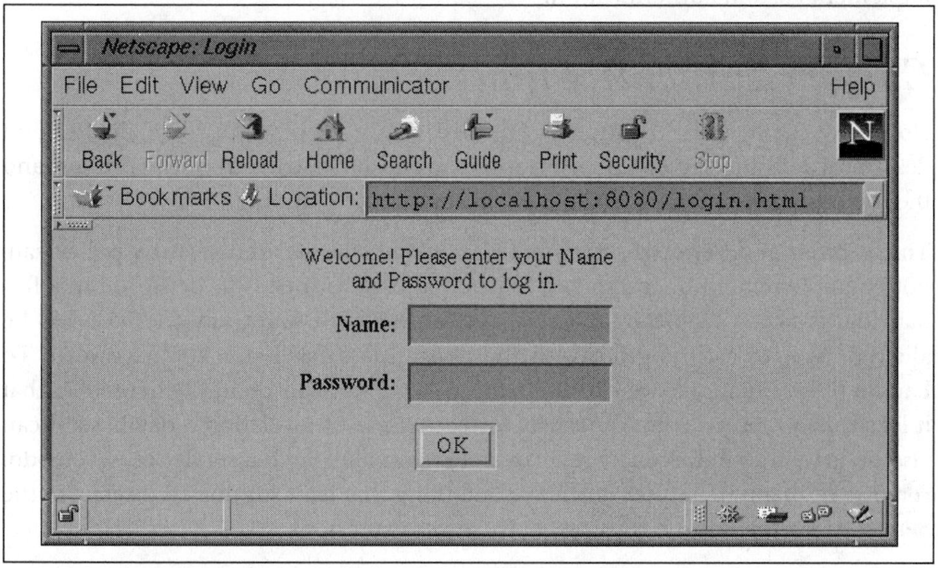

Figure 8-2. A friendly login form

The error page you specify in the `<login-config>` section of *web.xml* can be any HTML file. There are no special tags for it to include, nor unfortunately does it have access to any special information reporting why access was denied or even which page it should point the user at to try again! See Example 8-7 for a simple error page.

Example 8-7. The errorpage.html File

```
<HTML>
<TITLE>Login Denied</TITLE>
<BODY>
Sorry, your login was denied.
Please hit the Back button to try again.
</BODY></HTML>
```

Compared with basic authentication, form-based login has the advantage that the user can enter your site through a friendly and descriptive login page. It shares the problem with basic authentication that the password is transmitted in plain text unless the communication channel has been secured by other means.

Both Basic and form-based login also have the problem that they support no standard logout mechanism. Calling `session.invalidate()` is likely to have that effect for form-based login, but there are no guarantees. Both also rely on the server to validate users, even though there are cases where validation should be done in ways not supported by the server (for example, some banks require an account number, password, and PIN for access). To solve these problems, we can implement custom authentication.

Custom Authentication

Normally, client authentication is handled by the web server. The deployment descriptor tells the server which resources are to be restricted to which roles, and the server somehow manages the user/group to role mapping.

This is often good enough. Sometimes, however, the desired security policy cannot be implemented by the server. Maybe the user list needs to be stored in a format that is not readable by the server. Or maybe you want any username to be allowed, as long as it is given with the appropriate "skeleton key" password. To handle these situations, we can use servlets. A servlet can be implemented so that it learns about users from a specially formatted file or a relational database; it can also be written to enforce any security policy you like. Such a servlet can even add, remove, or manipulate user entries—something that isn't supported directly in the Servlet API, except through proprietary server extensions.

A servlet uses status codes and HTTP headers to manage its own basic authentication security policy. The servlet receives encoded user credentials in the `Authorization` header. If it chooses to deny those credentials, it does so by sending the `SC_UNAUTHORIZED` status code and a `WWW-Authenticate` header that describes the desired credentials. A web server normally handles these details without involving its servlets, but for a servlet to do its own authorization, it must handle these details itself, while the server is told not to restrict access to the servlet.

The `Authorization` header, if sent by the client, contains the client's username and password. With the basic authorization scheme, the `Authorization` header contains the string of *`username:password`* encoded in Base64. For example, the username of `webmaster` with the password `try2gueSS` is sent in an `Authorization` header with the value:

```
Authorization: BASIC d2VibWFzdGVyOnRyeTJndWVTUw
```

If a servlet needs to, it can send a `WWW-Authenticate` header to tell the client the authorization scheme and the realm against which users will be verified. A *realm* is simply a collection of user accounts and protected resources. For example, to tell the client to use basic authentication for the realm `Admin`, the `WWW-Authenticate` header is:

```
WWW-Authenticate: BASIC realm="Admin"
```

Example 8-8 shows a servlet that performs custom authorization, receiving an `Authorization` header and sending the `SC_UNAUTHORIZED` status code and `WWW-Authenticate` header when necessary. The servlet restricts access to its "top-secret stuff" to those users (and passwords) it recognizes in its user list. For this example, the list is kept in a simple `Hashtable` and its contents are hard-coded; this would, of course, be replaced with some other mechanism, such as an external relational database, for a production servlet.

To retrieve the Base64-encoded username and password, the servlet needs to use a Base64 decoder. Fortunately, there are several freely available decoders. For this servlet, we will use our own `com.oreilly.servlet.Base64Decoder` class, not shown here but available at *http://www.servlets.com*, along with `com.oreilly.servlet.Base64Encoder`. You can find the details of Base64 encoding in RFC 1521 at *http://www.ietf.org/rfc/rfc1521.txt*.*

* You could also use the `sun.misc.BASE64Decoder` class that accompanies the JDK. Because it is in the `sun.*` hierarchy means it's unsupported and subject to change, but it's likely already on your system.

Example 8-8. Security in a Servlet

```
import java.io.*;
import java.util.*;
import javax.servlet.*;
import javax.servlet.http.*;

import com.oreilly.servlet.Base64Decoder;

public class CustomAuth extends HttpServlet {

  Hashtable users = new Hashtable();

  public void init(ServletConfig config) throws ServletException {
    super.init(config);

    // Names and passwords are case sensitive!
    users.put("Wallace:cheese",      "allowed");
    users.put("Gromit:sheepnapper", "allowed");
    users.put("Penguin:evil",        "allowed");
  }

  public void doGet(HttpServletRequest req, HttpServletResponse res)
                               throws ServletException, IOException {
    res.setContentType("text/plain");
    PrintWriter out = res.getWriter();

    // Get Authorization header
    String auth = req.getHeader("Authorization");

    // Do we allow that user?
    if (!allowUser(auth)) {
      // Not allowed, so report he's unauthorized
      res.setHeader("WWW-Authenticate", "BASIC realm=\"users\"");
      res.sendError(res.SC_UNAUTHORIZED);
      // Could offer to add him to the allowed user list
    }
    else {
      // Allowed, so show him the secret stuff
      out.println("Top-secret stuff");
    }
  }

  // This method checks the user information sent in the Authorization
  // header against the database of users maintained in the users Hashtable.
  protected boolean allowUser(String auth) throws IOException {
    if (auth == null) return false;  // no auth
```

Example 8-8. Security in a Servlet (continued)

```
    if (!auth.toUpperCase().startsWith("BASIC "))
      return false;  // we only do BASIC

    // Get encoded user and password, comes after "BASIC "
    String userpassEncoded = auth.substring(6);

    // Decode it, using any base 64 decoder (we use com.oreilly.servlet)
    String userpassDecoded = Base64Decoder.decode(userpassEncoded);

    // Check our user list to see if that user and password are "allowed"
    if ("allowed".equals(users.get(userpassDecoded)))
      return true;
    else
      return false;
  }
}
```

Although the web server is told to grant any client access to this servlet, the servlet sends its top-secret output only to those users it recognizes. With a few modifications, it could allow any user with a trusted skeleton password. Or, like anonymous FTP, it could allow the "anonymous" username with any email address given as the password.

Custom authorization can be used for more than restricting access to a single servlet. Were we to add this logic to our `ViewResource` servlet, we could implement a custom access policy for an entire set of files; a URL prefix mapping rule could be created so that the secure `ViewResource` servlet served an entire directory structure of protected files. Were we to create a special subclass of `HttpServlet` and add this logic to that, we could easily restrict access to every servlet derived from that subclass. Our point is this: with custom authorization, the security policy limitations of the server do not limit the possible security policy implementations of its servlets.

Form-Based Custom Authorization

Servlets also have the ability to perform custom form-based authorization. By doing custom form-based login, a web application can use an elegant HTML login page, with the additional advantage that any security policy can be implemented, all in a completely portable manner. For example, several banking applications require more than a username and password for login; some require an account number, password, *and* PIN. Such a login can't be accomplished using `FORM` `<auth-method>` but can be accomplished with custom form-based authorization. The cost is additional complexity because the form-based login details have to be managed manually.

The steps are relatively straightforward. First, we need the login page. It can be written like any other HTML form. Example 8-9 shows a sample *login.html* file that generates the form shown in Figure 8-3.

Example 8-9. The login.html File

```
<HTML>
<TITLE>Login</TITLE>
<BODY>
<FORM ACTION=/servlet/LoginHandler METHOD=POST>
<CENTER>
<TABLE BORDER=0>
<TR><TD COLSPAN=2>
<P ALIGN=CENTER>
Welcome!<br>
Please enter your Account Number,<br>
 Password, and PIN to log in.
</TD></TR>

<TR><TD>
<P ALIGN=RIGHT><B>Account:</B>
</TD>
<TD>
<P><INPUT TYPE=TEXT NAME="account" VALUE="" SIZE=15>
</TD></TR>

<TR><TD>
<P ALIGN=RIGHT><B>Password:</B>
</TD>
<TD>
<P><INPUT TYPE=PASSWORD NAME="password" VALUE="" SIZE=15>
</TD></TR>

<TR><TD>
<P ALIGN=RIGHT><B>PIN:</B>
</TD>
<TD>
<P><INPUT TYPE=PASSWORD NAME="pin" VALUE="" SIZE=15>
</TD></TR>

<TR><TD COLSPAN=2>
<CENTER>
<INPUT TYPE=SUBMIT VALUE="  OK   ">
</CENTER>
</TD></TR>
</TABLE>
</FORM>
</BODY></HTML>
```

Figure 8-3 displays the form.

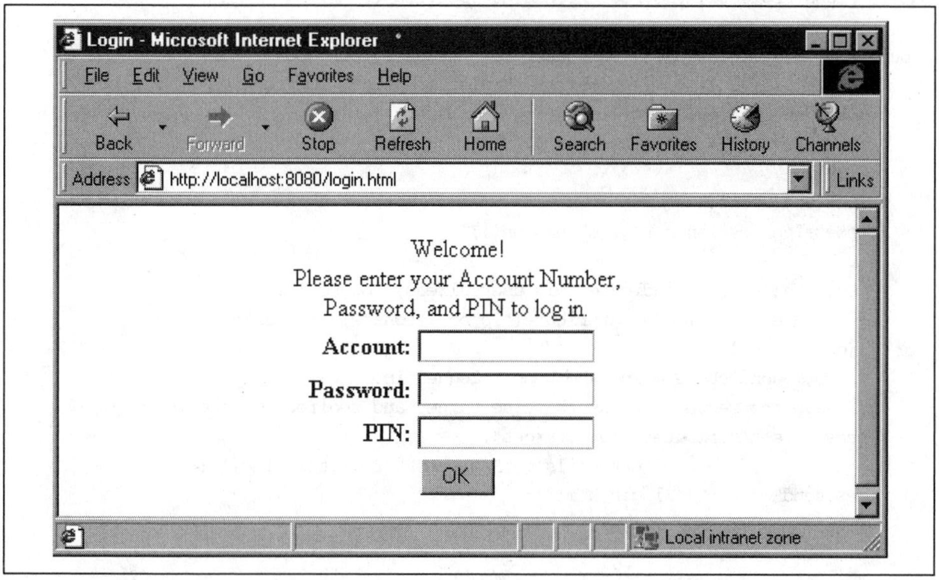

Figure 8-3. A friendly banking login form

This form asks the client for her account number, password, and PIN, then submits the information to the `LoginHandler` servlet that validates the login. We'll see the code for `LoginHandler` soon, but first we should ask ourselves, "When is the client going to see this login page?" It's clear she can browse to this login page directly, perhaps following a link on the site's front page. But what if she tries to access a protected resource directly without first logging in? In that case, she should be redirected to this login page and, after a successful login, be redirected back to the original target. The process should work as seamlessly as having the browser pop open a window—except in this case the site pops open an intermediary page.

Example 8-10 shows a servlet that implements this redirection behavior. It outputs its secret data only if the client's session object indicates she has already logged in. If she hasn't logged in, the servlet saves the request URL in her session for later use, and then redirects her to the login page for validation.

Example 8-10. A Protected Resource

```
import java.io.*;
import java.util.*;
import javax.servlet.*;
import javax.servlet.http.*;
```

Example 8-10. A Protected Resource (continued)

```
public class ProtectedResource extends HttpServlet {

  public void doGet(HttpServletRequest req, HttpServletResponse res)
                               throws ServletException, IOException {
    res.setContentType("text/plain");
    PrintWriter out = res.getWriter();

    // Get the session
    HttpSession session = req.getSession();

    // Does the session indicate this user already logged in?
    Object done = session.getAttribute("logon.isDone");  // marker object
    if (done == null) {
      // No logon.isDone means she hasn't logged in.
      // Save the request URL as the true target and redirect to the login page.
      session.setAttribute("login.target",
                           HttpUtils.getRequestURL(req).toString());
      res.sendRedirect("/login.html");
      return;
    }

    // If we get here, the user has logged in and can see the goods
    out.println("Unpublished O'Reilly book manuscripts await you!");
  }
}
```

This servlet sees if the client has already logged in by checking her session for an object with the name `logon.isDone`. If such an object exists, the servlet knows that the client has already logged in and therefore allows her to see the secret goods. If it doesn't exist, the client must not have logged in, so the servlet saves the request URL under the name `login.target` and then redirects the client to the login page. Under custom form-based authorization, all protected resources (or the servlets that serve them) have to implement this behavior. Subclassing, or the use of a utility class, can simplify this task.

Now for the login handler. After the client enters her information on the login form, the data is posted to the `LoginHandler` servlet shown in Example 8-11. This servlet checks the account number, password, and PIN for validity. If the client fails the check, she is told that access is denied. If the client passes, that fact is recorded in her session object and she is immediately redirected to the original target.

Example 8-11. Handling a Login

```
import java.io.*;
import java.util.*;
import javax.servlet.*;
import javax.servlet.http.*;
```

Example 8-11. Handling a Login (continued)

```
public class LoginHandler extends HttpServlet {

  public void doPost(HttpServletRequest req, HttpServletResponse res)
                                throws ServletException, IOException {
    res.setContentType("text/html");
    PrintWriter out = res.getWriter();

    // Get the user's account number, password, and pin
    String account = req.getParameter("account");
    String password = req.getParameter("password");
    String pin = req.getParameter("pin");

    // Check the name and password for validity
    if (!allowUser(account, password, pin)) {
      out.println("<HTML><HEAD><TITLE>Access Denied</TITLE></HEAD>");
      out.println("<BODY>Your login and password are invalid.<BR>");
      out.println("You may want to <A HREF=\"/login.html\">try again</A>");
      out.println("</BODY></HTML>");
    }
    else {
      // Valid login. Make a note in the session object.
      HttpSession session = req.getSession();
      session.setAttribute("logon.isDone", account);  // just a marker object

      // Try redirecting the client to the page she first tried to access
      try {
        String target = (String) session.getAttribute("login.target");
        if (target != null) {
          res.sendRedirect(target);
          return;
        }
      }
      catch (Exception ignored) { }

      // Couldn't redirect to the target. Redirect to the site's home page.
      res.sendRedirect("/");
    }
  }

  protected boolean allowUser(String account, String password, String pin) {
    return true;  // trust everyone
  }
}
```

The actual validity check in this servlet is quite simple: it assumes any user credentials are valid. That keeps things simple, so we can concentrate on how the servlet behaves when the login is successful. The servlet saves the user's account number (any old object will do) in the client's session under the name `logon.isDone`, as a marker that tells all protected resources this client is okay. It then redirects the client to the original target saved as `login.target`, seamlessly sending her where she wanted to go in the first place. If that fails for some reason, the servlet redirects the user to the site's home page.

Digital Certificates

Real applications require a higher level of security than simple basic and form-based authentication provides. They also need guaranteed confidentiality and integrity, as well as more reliable authentication. Digital certificate technology provides this.

The "key" concept is public key cryptography. In a public key cryptographic system, each participant has two keys that are used to encrypt or decrypt information. One is the public key, which is distributed freely. The other is a private key, which is kept secret. The keys are mathematically related, but one cannot be derived from the other. To demonstrate, assume Jason wants to send a secret message to Will. He finds Will's public key and uses it to encrypt the message. When Will gets the message, he uses his private key to decrypt it. Anyone intercepting the message in transit is confronted with indecipherable gibberish.

Public key encryption schemes have been around for several years and are quite well developed. Most are based on the RSA algorithm developed by Ron Rivest, Adi Shamir, and Leonard Adelman.* RSA uses very large prime numbers to generate a pair of asymmetric keys (i.e., each key can decode messages encoded with the other). Individual keys come in varying lengths, usually expressed in terms of the number of bits that make up the key. 1024- or 2048-bit keys are adequate for secure RSA communications.

Because keys are so large, it is not practical for a user to type one into his web browser for each request. Instead, public keys are stored on disk in the form of digital certificates, and private keys are stored encrypted on disk protected by a *passphrase*. Digital certificates can be generated by software like the PGP package, or they can be issued by a third party. The certificate files themselves can be loaded by most security-aware applications, such as servers, browsers, and email software.

Public key cryptography solves the confidentiality problem because the communication is encrypted. It also solves the integrity problem: Will knows that the message he received was not tampered with since it decodes properly. So far, though, it does not provide any authentication. Will has no idea whether Jason actually

* United States Patent No. 4,405,829. It expired September 20, 2000.

sent the message. This is where digital signatures come into play. Because public and private keys are asymmetric, Jason can first use his private key to encode a message and then use Will's public key to encode it again. When Will gets the message, he decodes it first with his private key, and then with Jason's public key. Because only Jason can encode messages with his private key—messages that can be decoded only with his public key—Will knows that the message was truly sent by Jason.

This is different from simpler symmetric key systems, where a single key is used for encoding and decoding. While asymmetric keys have the significant advantage of allowing secure communication without ever requiring a secure channel, they have the disadvantage of requiring much more computational muscle. As a compromise, many encryption systems use asymmetric public and private keys to identify each other and then confidentially exchange a separate symmetric key for encrypting the actual exchange. The symmetric key is usually based on DES (Data Encryption Standard).

U.S. government export restrictions have traditionally limited symmetric key size to 56 bits (about 72 quadrillion possible keys). Messages encrypted with a 56-bit key are difficult to decode, but by no means impossible—specialized machines have been used to decode such messages within a matter of hours. Within the United States, however, many systems use 128-bit DES keys (about 3.40282×10^{38} possible keys). Because there is no known way to decode a DES-encrypted message short of brute-force trial and error, messages sent using large keys are very, very secure.

This leaves one final problem—how does one user know that another user is who she says she is? Jason and Will know each other, so Will trusts that the public key Jason gave him in person is the real one.* On the other hand, if Lisa wants to give Jason her public key, but Jason and Lisa have never met, there is no reason for Jason to believe that Lisa is not actually Mark. But, if we assume that Will knows Lisa, we can have Will use his private key to sign Lisa's public key. Then, when Jason gets the key, he can detect that Will, whom he trusts, is willing to vouch for Lisa's identity. These introductions are sometimes called a *web of trust*.

In the real world, this third-party vouching is usually handled by a specially established certificate authority, such as VeriSign Corporation. Because VeriSign is a well-known organization with a well-known public key, keys verified and signed by VeriSign can be assumed to be trusted, at least to the extent that VeriSign received proper proof of the receiver's identity. VeriSign offers a number of classes of digital

* To be truthful, people almost never meet in dark alleys to exchange their full public keys. Instead, they exchange keys digitally (via email, perhaps) and in person simply compare a small fingerprint hash of the key.

IDs, each with an increasing level of trust and an increased price. You can get a Class 1 ID by simply filling out a form on the VeriSign web site and receiving an email. Higher classes are individually verified by VeriSign employees, using background checks and investigative services to verify identities.

When selecting a certificate authority, it is important to choose a firm with strong market presence. VeriSign certificates, for instance, are included in Netscape Navigator and Microsoft Internet Explorer, so virtually every user on the Internet will trust and accept them. The following firms provide certificate authority services:

- VeriSign (*http://www.verisign.com*)
- Thawte Consulting (*http://www.thawte.com*)
- Entrust Technologies (*http://www.entrust.com*)

For more abstract information about digital certificates, we recommend *Understanding Digital Signatures* by Gail L. Grant (McGraw-Hill), which provides an excellent introduction to the subject suitable for programmers and nonprogrammers alike. For more on cryptography as it is related to Java, we recommend *Java Cryptography* by Jonathan Knudsen (O'Reilly).

Secure Sockets Layer (SSL)

The Secure Sockets Layer protocol, or SSL, sits between the application-level protocol (in this case HTTP) and the low-level transport protocol (for the Internet, almost exclusively TCP/IP). It handles the details of security management using public key cryptography to exchange symmetric keys that encrypt all client/server communication. SSL was introduced by Netscape with Netscape Navigator 1. It has since become the de facto standard for secure online communications and forms the basis of the Transport Layer Security (TLS) protocol currently under development by the Internet Engineering Task Force. For more information on TLS, see *http://www.ietf.org/rfc/rfc2246.txt.*

SSL Version 2.0, the version first to gain widespread acceptance, includes support for server certificates only. It provides authentication of the server, confidentiality, and integrity. Here's how it works:

1. A user connects to a secure site using the HTTPS (HTTP plus SSL) protocol. (You can detect sites using the HTTPS protocol because their URLs begin with *https:* instead of *http:*.)
2. The server signs its public key with its private key and sends it back to the browser.
3. The browser uses the server's public key to verify that the same person who signed the key actually owns it.

4. The browser checks to see whether a trusted certificate authority signed the key. If one didn't, the browser asks the user if the key can be trusted and proceeds as directed.
5. The client generates a symmetric (DES) key for the session, which is encrypted with the server's public key and sent back to the server. This new key is used to encrypt all subsequent transactions. The symmetric key is used because of the high computational cost of public key cryptosystems.

All this is completely transparent to servlets and servlet developers. You just need to obtain an appropriate server certificate, install it, and configure your server appropriately. Information transferred between servlets and clients is now encrypted. Voila, security!

SSL Client Authentication

Our security toolbox now includes strong encryption and strong server authentication, but only weak client authentication. Of course, using SSL 2.0 puts us in better shape because SSL-equipped servers can use the basic authentication methods discussed at the beginning of this chapter without concern for eavesdropping. We still don't have proof of client identity, however—after all, anybody could have guessed or gotten hold of a client username and password.

SSL 3.0 fixes this problem by providing support for client certificates. These are the same type of certificates that servers use, but they are registered to clients instead. SSL 3.0 with client authentication works the same way as SSL 2.0, except that after the client has authenticated the server, the server requests the client's certificate. The client then sends its signed certificate, and the server performs the same authentication process the client did, comparing the client certificate to a library of existing certificates (or simply storing the certificate to identify the user on a return visit). As a security precaution, many browsers require the client user to enter a password before they will send the certificate.

Once a client has been authenticated, the server can allow access to protected resources such as servlets or files just as with HTTP authentication. The whole process occurs transparently, without inconveniencing the user. It also provides an extra level of authentication because the server knows the client with a John Smith certificate really is John Smith (and it can know which John Smith it is by reading his unique certificate). The disadvantages of client certificates are that users must obtain and install signed certificates, servers must maintain a database of all accepted public keys, and servers must support SSL 3.0 in the first place. As of this writing, most do.

Configuring SSL Security

A web application that requires SSL (HTTPS) security can indicate this fact to the server using its deployment descriptor. When SSL is required, the *web.xml* file should be modified so that the `<security-constraint>` tag contains a `<user-data-constraint>` tag indicating the security requirements. Example 8-12 demonstrates this.

Example 8-12. This Collection Requires a Secure Connection

```
<!-- ...etc... -->

<security-constraint>
    <web-resource-collection>
        <web-resource-name>
            SecretProtection
        </web-resource-name>
        <url-pattern>
            /servlet/SalaryServer
        </url-pattern>
        <url-pattern>
            /servlet/secret
        </url-pattern>
        <http-method>
            GET
        </http-method>
        <http-method>
            POST
        </http-method>
    </web-resource-collection>
    <auth-constraint>
        <role-name>
            manager
        </role-name>
    </auth-constraint>
    <user-data-constraint>
        <transport-guarantee>
            CONFIDENTIAL              <!-- INTEGRAL or CONFIDENTIAL -->
        </transport-guarantee>
    </user-data-constraint>
</security-constraint>

<!-- ...etc... -->
```

The addition of the `<user-data-constraint>` indicates that not only does this resource collection require its users belong to the manager role, but also the users must connect using a connection that is `CONFIDENTIAL`.

The <transport-guarantee> tag has two legal values: INTEGRAL and CONFIDENTIAL. INTEGRAL requires the data must be guaranteed not to change in transit. CONFIDENTIAL requires the data must be guaranteed not to have been read by an unauthorized third party in transit. A CONFIDENTIAL guarantee implies INTEGRAL. It's left to the server to decide what encryption algorithms qualify as INTEGRAL and what qualify as CONFIDENTIAL. Most common SSL algorithms qualify as both, although a server might treat 56-bit DES encryption as sufficient for INTEGRAL (because to be decoded it must not have changed) but not sufficient for CONFIDENTIAL (because it can be so easily cracked).* In practical terms on the Web today, there is very little difference between the two, and CONFIDENTIAL is the standard guarantee.

The <auth-constraint> and <user-data-constraint> tags can exist with or without the other. For example, a credit card processing page will require CONFIDENTIAL communication but can remain viewable by all users.

Configuring SSL Authentication

As SSL 3.0 gains in popularity, more sites may want to authenticate users using their client certificate. This provides an automatic and secure method to determine the identity of the client user. Depending on the trust level associated with the client certificate, this authentication mechanism may be considered secure enough to support legally binding contracts and even online voting.

As anyone reading the past *web.xml* comments should be able to predict, authentication based on client certificates can be specified with a change to the <login-config> tag:

```
<login-config>
    <auth-method>
      CLIENT-CERT <!-- client must be recognized using X.509 cert -->
    </auth-method>
</login-config>
```

This tells the server that all authentication for this web application will be done using client certificates, instead of the traditional basic or form-based alternatives. The client will never see a login page, although the browser will prompt for a password to unlock their certificate before it's sent to the server. If the browser does not have a client certificate, access is denied.

* A client/server connection across a secure Virtual Private Network (VPN) could meet the CONFIDENTIAL constraint, even without SSL being used.

Retrieving SSL Authentication Information

As with basic and digest authentication, all of the SSL details are handled by the server, transparent to servlets. In other words, there is nothing special a servlet must do to run inside a secure server! It is sometimes possible, though, for a servlet to retrieve useful SSL authentication information. For example, a servlet can ask if the connection to the client is secure using the `isSecure()` method:

```
public boolean ServletRequest.isSecure()
```

This method returns `true` if the server deems the connection secure. What strength of encryption constitutes "secure" depends on the server implementation; see your server's documentation for details. Unfortunately, there is no standard way for a servlet to request the actual encryption algorithm used for the connection or even the bit size (40, 56, 128) of the symmetric key used for encrypting. A server does have the option to make this available as a request attribute, but as of yet there is no standardized attribute name. Such a feature is expected in Servlet API 2.3 using the request attribute names `javax.servlet.request.cipher_suite` and `javax.servlet.request.key_size`.

When the client has been authenticated using `CLIENT-CERT`, the client principal name can be retrieved using the `getUserPrincipal()` method introduced earlier. The principal name is taken from the Distinguished Name field of the certificate.

Finally, anytime a client certificate is sent to the server (which can occur during the normal SSL 3.0 handshake process, even when `CLIENT-CERT` is not specified), a servlet can retrieve the client's certificate as a request attribute:

```
java.security.cert.X509Certificate cert =
  (java.security.cert.X509Certificate)
  req.getAttribute("javax.servlet.request.X509Certificate");
```

For any server running on J2SE 1.2 (JDK 1.2) or supporting J2EE 1.2, the request attribute `javax.servlet.request.X509Certificate` will return a `java.security.cert.X509Certificate` object representing an X.509v3 certificate (see your server's documentation for configuration instructions). Servers running JDK 1.1 that don't wish to be J2EE 1.2 compliant are not required to support this attribute (because JDK 1.1 alone does not include the `java.security.cert` package). The servlet in Example 8-13 prints the client's certificate chain, if available.

Example 8-13. Examining Client Certificates

```
import java.io.*;
import java.util.*;
import java.security.cert.*;
import javax.servlet.*;
import javax.servlet.http.*;
```

Example 8-13. Examining Client Certificates (continued)

```
public class X509Snoop extends HttpServlet {

  public void doGet(HttpServletRequest req, HttpServletResponse res)
                               throws ServletException, IOException {
    res.setContentType("text/plain");
    PrintWriter out = res.getWriter();

    X509Certificate[] certs = (X509Certificate[])
      req.getAttribute("javax.servlet.request.X509Certificate");
    if (certs != null) {
      for (int i = 0; i < certs.length; i++) {
        out.println("Client Certificate [" + i + "] = "
                        + certs[i].toString());
      }
    }
    else {
      if ("https".equals(req.getScheme())) {
        out.println("This was an HTTPS request, " +
                    "but no client certificate is available");
      }
      else {
        out.println("This was not an HTTPS request, " +
                    "so no client certificate is available");
      }
    }
  }
}
```

The `X509Certificate` returned can be picked apart and checked for validity, issuer, serial number, signature, and so forth. Printing each certificate as a `String` yields output as shown in Example 8-14. The first certificate is the user's public key. The second is VeriSign's signature that vouches for the authenticity of the first signature.

Example 8-14. The X.509 Certificate Chain for Ramesh Mandava

```
Client Certificate [0] = [
[
  Version: V3
  Subject: EmailAddress=rmandava@talentportal.com, CN=Ramesh Babu Mandava, OU=Digital
ID Class 1 -
Netscape, OU=Persona Not Validated, OU="www.verisign.com/repository/RPA Incorp. by
Ref.,LIAB.LTD(c)98",
OU=VeriSign Trust Network, O="VeriSign, Inc."
  Signature Algorithm: MD5withRSA, OID = 1.2.840.113549.1.1.4

  Key:  com.sun.net.ssl.internal.ssl.JSA_RSAPublicKey@5b5870e3
  Validity: [From: Tue Oct 10 17:00:00 PDT 2000,
```

Example 8-14. The X.509 Certificate Chain for Ramesh Mandava (continued)

```
               To: Sun Dec 10 15:59:59 PST 2000]
  Issuer: CN=VeriSign Class 1 CA Individual Subscriber-Persona Not Validated,
OU="www.verisign.com/repository/RPA Incorp. By Ref.,LIAB.LTD(c)98", OU=VeriSign Trust
Network,
O="VeriSign, Inc."
  SerialNumber: [    1ef11638 5ab8aaa1 bfa2b1b3 c0fb9cd9 ]

Certificate Extensions: 4
[1]: ObjectId: 2.16.840.1.113730.1.1 Criticality=false
NetscapeCertType [
   SSL client
]

[2]: ObjectId: 2.5.29.32 Criticality=false
Extension unknown: DER encoded OCTET string =
0000: 04 3D 30 3B 30 39 06 0B   60 86 48 01 86 F8 45 01  .=0;09..`.H...E.
0010: 07 01 08 30 2A 30 28 06   08 2B 06 01 05 05 07 02  ...0*0(..+......
0020: 01 16 1C 68 74 74 70 73   3A 2F 2F 77 77 77 2E 76  ...https://www.v
0030: 65 72 69 73 69 67 6E 2E   63 6F 6D 2F 72 70 61     erisign.com/rpa


[3]: ObjectId: 2.5.29.31 Criticality=false
Extension unknown: DER encoded OCTET string =
0000: 04 2C 30 2A 30 28 A0 26   A0 24 86 22 68 74 74 70  .,0*0(.&.$."http
0010: 3A 2F 2F 63 72 6C 2E 76   65 72 69 73 69 67 6E 2E  ://crl.verisign.
0020: 63 6F 6D 2F 63 6C 61 73   73 31 2E 63 72 6C        com/class1.crl


[4]: ObjectId: 2.5.29.19 Criticality=false
BasicConstraints:[
CA:false
PathLen: undefined
]

]
  Algorithm: [MD5withRSA]
  Signature:
0000: 5E EC 5C F9 96 D5 3F F6   19 8B 66 0A 46 DE 02 FC  ^.\...?...f.F...
0010: 52 4E 32 70 5E DA 8B 92   43 F4 19 51 C3 A3 36 7D  RN2p^...C..Q..6.
0020: 02 4A 5B 35 B6 76 05 F8   FE C0 4F D7 9C B1 5B BA  .J[5.v....O...[.
0030: EE 38 A7 98 C5 57 A7 6B   86 B9 B2 A1 4F 25 5F FF  .8...W.k....O%_.
0040: 0B 19 54 86 D7 14 7A F7   97 A1 E8 E7 D3 89 75 B0  ..T...z.......u.
0050: 72 4F 4B 77 E4 56 5D B2   40 D2 7E 69 26 77 DD F1  rOKw.V].@..i&w..
0060: E6 31 3D F2 EF 5A 11 22   78 23 47 C2 D6 ED DD 14  .1=..Z."x#G.....
0070: 2F E9 2E 46 73 D9 20 72   BF 9B 6C 04 12 0D 68 C7  /..Fs. r..l...h.

]
Client Certificate [1] = [
[
```

Example 8-14. The X.509 Certificate Chain for Ramesh Mandava (continued)

```
  Version: V3
  Subject: CN=VeriSign Class 1 CA Individual Subscriber-Persona Not Validated,
OU="www.verisign.com/repository/RPA Incorp. By Ref.,LIAB.LTD(c)98", OU=VeriSign Trust
Network,
O="VeriSign, Inc."
  Signature Algorithm: MD2withRSA, OID = 1.2.840.113549.1.1.2

  Key:  com.sun.net.ssl.internal.ssl.JSA_RSAPublicKey@9ae870e3
  Validity: [From: Mon May 11 17:00:00 PDT 1998,
               To: Mon May 12 16:59:59 PDT 2008]
  Issuer: OU=Class 1 Public Primary Certification Authority, O="VeriSign, Inc.", C=US
  SerialNumber: [    d2762e8d 140c3d7d b2a8255d afee0d75 ]

Certificate Extensions: 4
[1]: ObjectId: 2.16.840.1.113730.1.1 Criticality=false
NetscapeCertType [
   SSL CA
   S/MIME CA
]

[2]: ObjectId: 2.5.29.32 Criticality=false
Extension unknown: DER encoded OCTET string =
0000: 04 40 30 3E 30 3C 06 0B   60 86 48 01 86 F8 45 01  .@0>0<..`.H...E.
0010: 07 01 01 30 2D 30 2B 06   08 2B 06 01 05 05 07 02  ...0-0+..+......
0020: 01 16 1F 77 77 77 2E 76   65 72 69 73 69 67 6E 2E  ...www.verisign.
0030: 63 6F 6D 2F 72 65 70 6F   73 69 74 6F 72 79 2F 52  com/repository/R
0040: 50 41                                              PA


[3]: ObjectId: 2.5.29.15 Criticality=false
KeyUsage [
  Key_CertSign
  Crl_Sign
]

[4]: ObjectId: 2.5.29.19 Criticality=false
BasicConstraints:[
CA:true
PathLen:0
]

]
  Algorithm: [MD2withRSA]
  Signature:
0000: 88 B8 37 3B DD DA 94 37   00 AD AA 9F E1 81 01 71  ..7;...7.......q
0010: 1E 92 6A 6D 2F F6 F1 9D   D3 CA 64 38 DC 1B 98 0C  ..jm/.....d8....
0020: 07 86 5B 85 15 6A 0F B9   49 85 A4 95 F1 17 7D 67  ..[..j..I......g
0030: B4 7F 2D 2C DD 9A 42 9E   C3 3E B4 8E AA E5 0B 06  ..-,..B..>......
```

Example 8-14. The X.509 Certificate Chain for Ramesh Mandava (continued)

```
0040: DE F2 56 2A FA 33 C7 BE   19 D7 53 4C C3 BD C8 E3  ..V*.3....SL....
0050: 17 B5 A4 49 42 63 EC C2   A6 17 0F 5D 58 1A 49 3C  ...IBc.....]X.I<
0060: 90 5C 55 A3 65 20 00 FD   18 20 E5 5F 82 A6 B1 A8  .\U.e ... ._....
0070: 92 C5 58 6A C1 8D 03 3C   EB C3 CD 05 A2 90 AE 6E  ..Xj...<.......n

]
```

In this chapter:
- *Relational Databases*
- *The JDBC API*
- *Reusing Database Objects*
- *Transactions*
- *A Guestbook Servlet*
- *Advanced JDBC Techniques*
- *Beyond the Core*

9

Database Connectivity

It's hard to find a professional web site today that doesn't have some sort of database connectivity. Webmasters have hooked online frontends to all manner of legacy systems, including package tracking and directory databases, as well as many newer systems like online messaging, storefronts, and search engines. But web-database interaction comes with a price: database-backed web sites can be difficult to develop and can often exact heavy performance penalties. Still, for many web sites, database connectivity is just too useful to let go. More and more, databases are driving the Web.

This chapter introduces relational databases, the *Structured Query Language* (*SQL*) used to manipulate those databases, and the Java Database Connectivity (JDBC) API itself. Servlets, with their enduring lifecycle, and JDBC, a well-defined database-independent database connectivity API, are an elegant and efficient solution for webmasters who need to hook their web sites to backend databases. In fact, both of your authors started working with servlets specifically because of this efficiency and elegance. Although elsewhere in the book we have assumed that you are familiar with Java, this chapter breaks that assumption and begins with a quick course in JDBC.

The biggest advantage for servlets with regard to database connectivity is that the servlet lifecycle (explained in depth in Chapter 3, *The Servlet Lifecycle*) allows servlets to maintain pools of open database connections. An existing connection can trim several seconds from a response time, compared to a CGI script that has to reestablish its connection for every invocation. Exactly how to maintain the database connection depends on the task at hand, and this chapter demonstrates several techniques appropriate for different tasks.

Another advantage of servlets over CGI and many other technologies is that JDBC is database independent. A servlet written to access a Sybase database can, with a

Servlets in the Middle Tier

One common place for servlets, especially servlets that access a database, is in what's called the *middle tier*. A middle tier is something that helps connect one endpoint to another (an applet to a database, for example) and along the way adds a little something of its own.

The most compelling reason for putting a middle tier between a client and our ultimate data source is that software in the middle tier (commonly referred to as *middleware*) can include business logic. Business logic abstracts complicated low-level tasks (such as updating database tables) into high-level tasks (placing an order), making the whole operation simpler and safer.

Imagine a client application that places an order. Without middleware, the application has to connect directly to the database server that stores the order records and then change the database fields to reflect the order. If the database server changes in any way (by moving to a different machine, altering its internal table structure, or changing database vendors), the client may break. Even worse, if someone makes a minor change to the client (either intentionally or accidentally), it's possible for the database to record orders without first receiving payment or to reject perfectly valid entries.

Middleware uses business logic to abstract the ordering process. Middleware accepts information about the order (for example, name, address, item, quantity, and credit card number), sanity-checks the information, verifies that the credit card is valid, and enters the information into the database. Should the database change, the middleware can be updated without any changes in the client. Even if the orders database is temporarily replaced with a simple flat file order log, the middleware can present the same appearance to the client.

Middleware can improve efficiency by spreading the processing load across several backend servers (CPU servers, database servers, file servers, directory servers, etc.). Middleware can also make more efficient use of bandwidth: instead of having a client perform the back-and-forth communication with the server over what might be a slow network connection, the client can tell the middleware what it needs and the middleware can do the work using a fast network connection and probably pooled database connections.

On the Web, middle tiers are often implemented using servlets. Servlets provide a convenient way to connect clients built using HTML forms or applets to backend servers. A client communicates its requirements to the servlet using HTTP, and the business logic in the servlet handles the request by connecting to the backend server. (More information on applet-servlet communication is coming up in Chapter 10, *Applet-Servlet Communication*.)

—Continued—

> Servlets often use another middle tier behind the web server to connect to a database, such as Enterprise JavaBeans (EJBs). If a web browser sends an HTML form with order information to a servlet, that servlet may parse the information and make an RMI call to an EJB on another machine that has the responsibility for handling all orders—from servlets as well as standalone programs. In these cases, what was once three tiers is now four tiers.

two-line modification or a change in a properties file, begin accessing an Oracle database (assuming none of the database calls it makes are vendor-specific). In fact, you should notice that the examples in this chapter are written to access a variety of different databases, including ODBC data sources such as Microsoft Access, Oracle, and Sybase.

Relational Databases

In some earlier examples, we've seen servlets that used file storage on the local disk to store their persistent data. The use of a flat file is fine for a small amount of data, but it can quickly get out of control. As the amount of data grows, access times slow to a crawl. And just finding data can become quite a challenge: imagine retrieving the names, cities, and email addresses of all your customers from a text file. It works great for a company that is just starting out, but what happens when you have hundreds of thousands of customers and want to display a list of all your customers in Boston with email addresses ending in *aol.com*?

One of the best solutions to this problem is a Relational Database Management System (RDBMS). At the most basic level, an RDBMS organizes data into tables. These tables are organized into rows and columns, much like a spreadsheet. Particular rows and columns in a table can be related (hence the term *relational*) to one or more rows and columns in another table.

One table in a relational database might contain information about customers, another might contain orders, and a third might contain information about individual items within an order. By including unique identifiers (say, customer numbers and order numbers), orders from the orders table can be linked to customer records and individual order components. Figure 9-1 shows how this might look if we drew it out on paper.

Data in the tables can be read, updated, appended, and deleted using the Structured Query Language, or SQL, sometimes also referred to as the Standard Query Language. Java's JDBC API introduced in JDK 1.1 uses a specific subset of SQL known as ANSI SQL-2 Entry Level. Unlike most programming languages, SQL is declarative: you say what you want, and the SQL interpreter gives it to you. Other

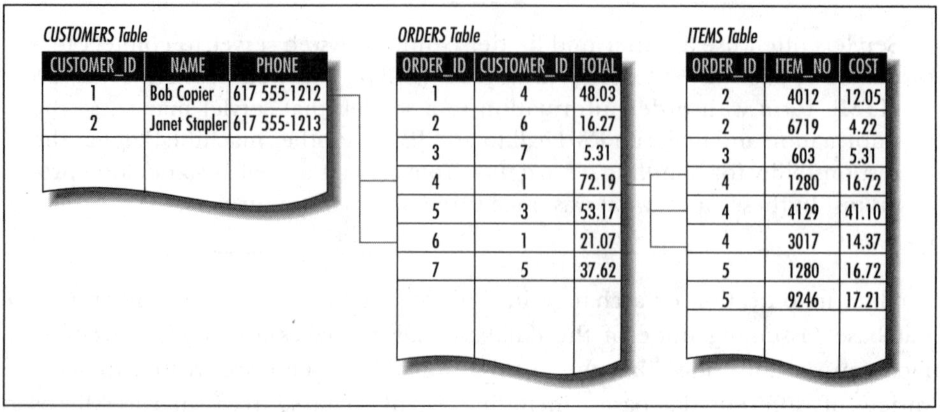
CUSTOMERS Table
CUSTOMER_ID NAME PHONE
1 Bob Copier 617 555-1212
2 Janet Stapler 617 555-1213
ORDERS Table
ORDER_ID CUSTOMER_ID TOTAL
1 4 48.03
2 6 16.27
3 7 5.31
4 1 72.19
5 3 53.17
6 1 21.07
7 5 37.62
ITEMS Table
ORDER_ID ITEM_NO COST
2 4012 12.05
2 6719 4.22
3 603 5.31
4 1280 16.72
4 4129 41.10
4 3017 14.37
5 1280 16.72
5 9246 17.21

Figure 9-1. Related tables

languages, like C, C++, and Java, by contrast, are essentially procedural, in that you specify the steps required to perform a certain task. SQL, while not prohibitively complex, is also rather too broad a subject to cover in great (or, indeed, merely adequate) detail here. In order to make the rest of the examples in this chapter comprehensible, though, we include here a brief tutorial. For a more extended primer on relational databases and SQL, we recommend *SQL for Dummies* by Allen Taylor (IDG Books Worldwide) as a tutorial book, and *SQL in a Nutshell* by Kevin Kline and Daniel Kline, Ph.D. (O'Reilly) as a reference book.

The simplest and most common SQL expression is the `SELECT` statement, which queries the database and returns a set of rows that matches a set of search criteria. For example, the following `SELECT` statement selects everything from the `CUSTOMERS` table:

```
SELECT * FROM CUSTOMERS
```

SQL keywords like `SELECT` and `FROM` and objects like `CUSTOMERS` are case insensitive but frequently written in uppercase. When run in Oracle's SQL*PLUS SQL interpreter, this query would produce something like the following output:

```
CUSTOMER_ID   NAME                            PHONE
------------- ------------------------------- ---------------
1             Bob Copier                      617 555-1212
2             Janet Stapler                   617 555-1213
3             Joel Laptop                     508 555-7171
4             Larry Coffee                    212 555-6525
```

More advanced statements might restrict the query to particular columns or include some specific limiting criteria:

```
SELECT ORDER_ID, CUSTOMER_ID, TOTAL FROM ORDERS
WHERE ORDER_ID = 4
```

This statement selects the ORDER_ID, CUSTOMER_ID, and TOTAL columns from all records where the ORDER_ID field is equal to 4. Here's a possible result:

```
ORDER_ID CUSTOMER_ID      TOTAL
--------- ----------- ---------
        4           1     72.19
```

A SELECT statement can also link two or more tables based on the values of particular fields. This can be either a one-to-one relationship or, more typically, a one-to-many relation, such as one customer to several orders:

```
SELECT CUSTOMERS.NAME, ORDERS.TOTAL FROM CUSTOMERS, ORDERS
WHERE ORDERS.CUSTOMER_ID = CUSTOMERS.CUSTOMER_ID AND ORDERS.ORDER_ID = 4
```

This statement connects (or, in database parlance, joins) the CUSTOMERS table with the ORDERS table via the CUSTOMER_ID field. Note that both tables have this field. The query returns information from both tables: the name of the customer who made order 4 and the total cost of that order. Here's some possible output:

```
NAME                                    TOTAL
--------------------------------------- ---------
Bob Copier                              72.19
```

SQL is also used to update the database. For example:

```
INSERT INTO CUSTOMERS (CUSTOMER_ID, NAME, PHONE)
  VALUES (5, "Bob Smith", "555 123-3456")

UPDATE CUSTOMERS SET NAME = "Robert Copier" WHERE CUSTOMER_ID = 1

DELETE FROM CUSTOMERS WHERE CUSTOMER_ID = 2
```

The first statement creates a new record in the CUSTOMERS table, filling in the CUSTOMER_ID, NAME, and PHONE fields with certain values. The second updates an existing record, changing the value of the NAME field for a specific customer. The last deletes any records with a CUSTOMER_ID of 2. Be very careful with all of these statements, especially DELETE. A DELETE statement without a WHERE clause will remove all the records in the table!

The JDBC API

Previously, we've assumed that you have a general working knowledge of the various Java APIs. Because even experienced Java programmers may have had relatively little experience with databases, this section provides a general introduction to JDBC. This chapter discusses primarily JDBC Version 1.2, the most widely supported version of JDBC. A small amount of coverage at the end of the chapter is given to JDBC Version 2.0.

If this is your first foray into the world of databases, we strongly recommend that you take a breather and find a book on general database and JDBC concepts. You may want to read *Database Programming with JDBC and Java*, by George Reese (O'Reilly), or *JDBC Database Access with Java*, by Graham Hamilton, Rick Cattell, and Maydene Fisher (Addison-Wesley). A quick overview is also presented in *Java Enterprise in a Nutshell* by David Flanagan et al. (O'Reilly). The official JDBC specification is available online at *http://java.sun.com/products/jdbc*.

JDBC is a SQL-level API—one that allows you to execute SQL statements and retrieve the results, if any. The API itself is a set of interfaces and classes designed to perform actions against any database. Figure 9-2 shows how JDBC programs interact with databases.

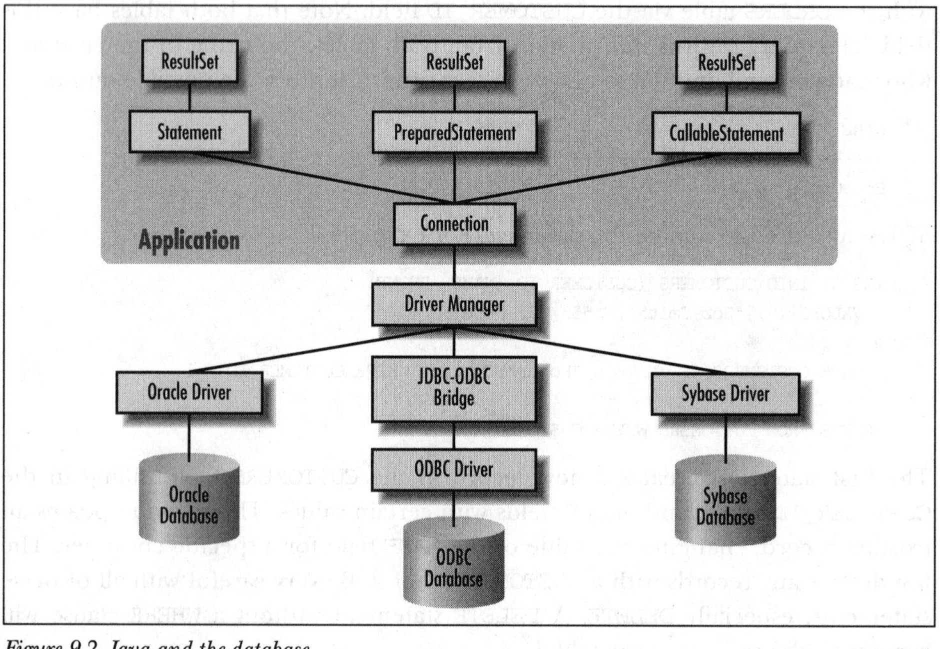

Figure 9-2. Java and the database

JDBC Drivers

The JDBC API, found in the `java.sql` package, contains only a few concrete classes. Much of the API is distributed as database-neutral interface classes that specify behavior without providing any implementation. The actual implementations are provided by third-party vendors.

An individual database system is accessed via a specific JDBC driver that implements the `java.sql.Driver` interface. Drivers exist for nearly all popular RDBMS systems, though not all are available for free. Sun bundles a free JDBC-ODBC bridge driver with the JDK to allow access to standard ODBC data sources, such as a Microsoft Access database. However, Sun advises against using the bridge driver for anything other than development and very limited deployment. Servlet developers in particular should heed this warning because any problem in the JDBC-ODBC bridge driver's native code section can crash the entire server, not just your servlets.

JDBC drivers are available for most database platforms, from a number of vendors and in a number of different flavors. There are four driver categories:

Type 1: JDBC-ODBC Bridge Driver
: Type 1 drivers use a bridge technology to connect a Java client to an ODBC database service. Sun's JDBC-ODBC bridge is the most common Type 1 driver. These drivers are implemented using native code.

Type 2: Native-API Partly Java Driver
: Type 2 drivers wrap a thin layer of Java around database-specific native code libraries. For Oracle databases, the native code libraries might be based on the OCI (Oracle Call Interface) libraries, which were originally designed for C/C++ programmers. Because Type 2 drivers are implemented using native code, in some cases they have better performance than their all-Java counterparts. They add an element of risk, however, because a defect in a driver's native code section can crash the entire server.

Type 3: Net-Protocol All-Java Driver
: Type 3 drivers communicate via a generic network protocol to a piece of custom middleware. The middleware component might use any type of driver to provide the actual database access. These drivers are all Java, which makes them useful for applet deployment and safe for servlet deployment.

Type 4: Native-Protocol All-Java Driver
: Type 4 drivers are the most direct of the lot. Written entirely in Java, Type 4 drivers understand database-specific networking protocols and can access the database directly without any additional software.

A list of currently available JDBC drivers can be found at *http://industry.java.sun.com/products/jdbc/drivers*.

Getting a Connection

The first step in using a JDBC driver to get a database connection involves loading the specific driver class into the application's JVM. This makes the driver available later, when we need it for opening the connection. An easy way to load the driver class is to use the `Class.forName()` method:

```
Class.forName("sun.jdbc.odbc.JdbcOdbcDriver");
```

When the driver is loaded into memory, it registers itself with the `java.sql.DriverManager` class as an available database driver.

The next step is to ask the `DriverManager` class to open a connection to a given database, where the database is specified by a specially formatted URL. The method used to open the connection is `DriverManager.getConnection()`. It returns a class that implements the `java.sql.Connection` interface:

```
Connection con =
  DriverManager.getConnection("jdbc:odbc:somedb", "user", "passwd");
```

A JDBC URL identifies an individual database in a driver-specific manner. Different drivers may need different information in the URL to specify the host database. JDBC URLs usually begin with `jdbc:`*`subprotocol`*`:`*`subname`*. For example, the Oracle JDBC-Thin driver uses a URL of the form of `jdbc:oracle:thin:@`*`dbhost`*`:`*`port`*`:`*`sid`*; the JDBC-ODBC bridge uses `jdbc:odbc:`*`datasourcename`*`;`*`odbcoptions`*.

During the call to `getConnection()`, the `DriverManager` object asks each registered driver if it recognizes the URL. If a driver says yes, the driver manager uses that driver to create the `Connection` object. Here is a snippet of code a servlet might use to load its database driver with the JDBC-ODBC bridge and create an initial connection:

```
Connection con = null;
try {
  // Load (and therefore register) the JDBC-ODBC Bridge
  // Might throw a ClassNotFoundException
  Class.forName("sun.jdbc.odbc.JdbcOdbcDriver");

  // Get a connection to the database
  // Might throw an SQLException
  con = DriverManager.getConnection("jdbc:odbc:somedb", "user", "passwd");

  // The rest of the code goes here.

}
catch (ClassNotFoundException e) {
  // Handle an error loading the driver
}
catch (SQLException e) {
  // Handle an error getting the connection
}
finally {
  // Close the Connection to release the database resources immediately.
  try {
    if (con != null) con.close();
  }
  catch (SQLException ignored) { }
}
```

There are actually three forms of `getConnection()` available. In addition to the preceding one shown, there's a simpler one that takes just a URL: `getConnection(String url)`. This method can be used when there are no login requirements or when the login information has to be placed in the URL. There's also one form that takes a URL and `Properties` object: `getConnection(String url, Properties props)`. This method provides the most flexibility. The `Properties` object (a `Hashtable` with all keys and values of type `String`) holds the standard `user` and `password` properties and in addition may hold any additional properties that might need to be passed to the underlying database driver. For example, some drivers respect the `cacherows` property specifying how many rows to cache at a time. Using this method makes it easy to establish a database connection based on an external *.properties* file.

For example, the driver, URL, and credentials to use can be specified in the following *sql.properties* file. This `name=value` format is standard for Java properties files:

```
connection.driver=sun.jdbc.odbc.JdbcOdbcDriver
connection.url=jdbc:odbc:somedb
user=user
password=passwd
```

The code shown in Example 9-1 establishes a database connection using the values stored within this *sql.properties* file. Note that the user and password properties are standard, the `connection.driver` and `connection.url` properties are special names used by the code, and any additional property values will just be passed on to the underlying driver as well.

Example 9-1. Using a Properties File to Open a Database Connection

```
// Get the properties for the database connection
Properties props = new Properties();
InputStream in = new FileInputStream("sql.properties");
props.load(in);
in.close();  // should really be in a finally block

// Load the driver
Class.forName(props.getProperty("connection.driver"));

// Get the connection
con = DriverManager.getConnection(
        props.getProperty("connection.url"), props);
```

First the `Properties` object is constructed and filled with the values read from the *sql.properties* file. Then the various properties are used to establish the database connection. Following this approach allows all database connection information to be changed without so much as a recompile of the Java code!

Getting a Connection from a Servlet

A servlet can use the same approach to load database connection information from a properties file stored under the web application's *WEB-INF* directory. The `getResourceAsStream()` method can retrieve the file's contents:

```
Properties props = new Properties();
InputStream in = getServletContext().getResourceAsStream(
                                       "/WEB-INF/sql.properties");
props.load(in);
in.close();
```

However, because servlets are often deployed using graphical deployment tools, we can go one step further and use the deployment tools to configure the database. One way to accomplish this is to place database connections inside a JNDI server where a servlet can locate the connection by name. This approach is generally employed by servlets designed to run inside J2EE servers. Chapter 12, *Enterprise Servlets and J2EE,* discusses this in more detail. Another approach that takes advantage of graphical deployment tools but doesn't require a JNDI server is to use context init parameters to hold configuration information. These init parameters can be configured using graphical deployment tools, then saved in the *web.xml* file for easy portable deployment. (For more information on context init parameters, see Chapter 4, *Retrieving Information.*)

The `ContextProperties` class shown in Example 9-2 makes the context init parameters available as a `Properties` object. This allows all the init parameter name/value pairs to be passed to the `DriverManager.getConnection()` method.

Example 9-2. The ContextProperties Class

```
import java.util.*;
import javax.servlet.*;
import javax.servlet.http.*;

public class ContextProperties extends Properties {

  public ContextProperties(ServletContext context) {
    Enumeration props = context.getInitParameterNames();
    while (props.hasMoreElements()) {
      String name = (String) props.nextElement();
      String value = (String) context.getInitParameter(name);
      put(name, value);
    }
  }
}
```

A servlet uses this class instead of loading data from *sql.properties*, as shown here:

```
// Get the context init params as a Properties object
ContextProperties props = new ContextProperties(getServletContext());

// Load the driver
Class.forName(props.getProperty("connection.driver"));

// etc...
```

Just set the context init parameters to the appropriate values for your database, either manually in the *web.xml* file or using a deployment tool, and everything's ready to go.

Executing SQL Queries

To really use a database, we need to have some way to execute queries. The simplest way to execute a query is to use the `java.sql.Statement` class. Statement objects are never instantiated directly; instead, a program calls the `createStatement()` method of `Connection` to obtain a new `Statement` object:

```
Statement stmt = con.createStatement();
```

A query that returns data can be executed using the `executeQuery()` method of `Statement`. This method executes the statement and returns a `java.sql.ResultSet` that encapsulates the retrieved data:

```
ResultSet rs = stmt.executeQuery("SELECT * FROM CUSTOMERS");
```

You can think of a `ResultSet` object as a representation of the query result returned one row at a time. You use the `next()` method of `ResultSet` to move from row to row. The `ResultSet` interface also boasts a multitude of methods designed for retrieving data from the current row. The `getString()` and `getObject()` methods are among the most frequently used for retrieving column values:

```
while(rs.next()) {
  String event = rs.getString("event");
  Object count = (Integer) rs.getObject("count");
}
```

You should know that the `ResultSet` is linked to its parent `Statement`. Therefore, if a `Statement` is closed or used to execute another query, any related `ResultSet` objects are closed automatically.

Example 9-3 shows a very simple servlet that uses the Oracle JDBC driver to perform a simple query, printing names and phone numbers for all employees listed in a database table. We assume that the database contains a table named `EMPLOYEES`, with at least two fields, `NAME` and `PHONE`.

Example 9-3. A JDBC-Enabled Servlet

```
import java.io.*;
import java.sql.*;
import javax.servlet.*;
import javax.servlet.http.*;

public class DBPhoneLookup extends HttpServlet {

  public void doGet(HttpServletRequest req, HttpServletResponse res)
                               throws ServletException, IOException {
    Connection con = null;
    Statement stmt = null;
    ResultSet rs = null;

    res.setContentType("text/html");
    PrintWriter out = res.getWriter();

    try {
      // Load (and therefore register) the Oracle Driver
      Class.forName("oracle.jdbc.driver.OracleDriver");

      // Get a Connection to the database
      con = DriverManager.getConnection(
        "jdbc:oracle:thin:@dbhost:1528:ORCL", "user", "passwd");

      // Create a Statement object
      stmt = con.createStatement();

      // Execute an SQL query, get a ResultSet
      rs = stmt.executeQuery("SELECT NAME, PHONE FROM EMPLOYEES");

      // Display the result set as a list
      out.println("<HTML><HEAD><TITLE>Phonebook</TITLE></HEAD>");
      out.println("<BODY>");
      out.println("<UL>");
      while(rs.next()) {
        out.println("<LI>" + rs.getString("name") + " " + rs.getString("phone"));
      }
      out.println("</UL>");
      out.println("</BODY></HTML>");
    }
    catch(ClassNotFoundException e) {
      out.println("Couldn't load database driver: " + e.getMessage());
    }
    catch(SQLException e) {
      out.println("SQLException caught: " + e.getMessage());
    }
    finally {
      // Always close the database connection.
```

Example 9-3. A JDBC-Enabled Servlet (continued)

```
      try {
        if (con != null) con.close();
      }
      catch (SQLException ignored) { }
    }
  }
}
```

This is about as simple a database servlet as you are likely to see. All `DBPhoneLookup` does is connect to the database, run a query that retrieves the names and phone numbers of everyone in the employees table, and display the list to the user.

Handling SQL Exceptions

`DBPhoneLookup` encloses most of its code in a `try/catch` block. This block catches two exceptions: `ClassNotFoundException` and `SQLException`. The former is thrown by the `Class.forName()` method when the JDBC driver class cannot be loaded. The latter is thrown by any JDBC method that has a problem. `SQLException` objects are just like any other exception type, with the additional feature that they can chain. The `SQLException` class defines an extra method, `getNextException()`, that allows the exception to encapsulate additional `Exception` objects. We didn't bother with this feature in the previous example, but here's how to use it:

```
catch (SQLException e) {
  out.println(e.getMessage());
  while((e = e.getNextException()) != null) {
    out.println(e.getMessage());
  }
}
```

This code displays the message from the first exception and then loops through all the remaining exceptions, outputting the error message associated with each one. In practice, the first exception will generally include the most relevant information.

Result Sets in Detail

Before we continue, we should take a closer look at the `ResultSet` interface and the related `ResultSetMetaData` interface. In Example 9-1, we knew what our query looked like and we knew what we expected to get back, so we formatted the output appropriately. But, if we want to display the results of a query in an HTML table, it would be nice to have some Java code that builds the table automatically from the `ResultSet` rather than having to write the same loop-and-display code over and over. As an added bonus, this kind of code makes it possible to change the contents of the table simply by changing the query.

The `ResultSetMetaData` interface provides a way for a program to learn about the underlying structure of a query result on the fly. We can use it to build an object that dynamically generates an HTML table from a `ResultSet`, as shown in Example 9-4. Many Java HTML content creation tools have a similar capability, as discussed in Chapters 14 through 18.

Example 9-4. A Class to Generate an HTML Table from a ResultSet Using ResultSetMetaData

```
import java.sql.*;

public class HtmlResultSet {

  private ResultSet rs;

  public HtmlResultSet(ResultSet rs) {
    this.rs = rs;
  }

  public String toString() {  // can be called at most once
    StringBuffer out = new StringBuffer();
    // Start a table to display the result set
    out.append("<TABLE>\n");

    try {
      ResultSetMetaData rsmd = rs.getMetaData();

      int numcols = rsmd.getColumnCount();

      // Title the table with the result set's column labels
      out.append("<TR>");
      for (int i = 1; i <= numcols; i++) {
        out.append("<TH>" + rsmd.getColumnLabel(i));
      }
      out.append("</TR>\n");

      while(rs.next()) {
        out.append("<TR>"); // start a new row
        for (int i = 1; i <= numcols; i++) {
          out.append("<TD>"); // start a new data element
          Object obj = rs.getObject(i);
          if (obj != null)
            out.append(obj.toString());
          else
            out.append(" ");
        }
```

Example 9-4. A Class to Generate an HTML Table from a ResultSet Using ResultSetMetaData (continued)

```
        out.append("</TR>\n");
      }

      // End the table
      out.append("</TABLE>\n");
    }
    catch (SQLException e) {
      out.append("</TABLE><H1>ERROR:</H1> " + e.getMessage() + "\n");
    }

    return out.toString();
  }
}
```

This example shows how to use two basic methods of `ResultSetMetaData`: `getColumnCount()` and `getColumnLabel()`. The first returns the number of columns in the `ResultSet`, while the second retrieves the name of a particular column in a result set based on its numerical index. Indexes in `ResultSet` objects follow the RDBMS standard rather than the C++/Java standard, which means they are numbered from 1 to *n* rather than from 0 to *n*-1.

This example also uses the `getObject()` method of `ResultSet` to retrieve the value of each column. All of the `get`*`XXX`*`()` methods work with column indexes as well as with column names. Accessing data this way is more efficient, and, with well-written SQL, is more portable. Here we use `getObject().toString()` instead of `getString()` to simplify the handling of null values, as discussed in the next section.

Table 9-1 shows the Java methods you can use to retrieve some common SQL datatypes from a database. No matter what the type, you can always use the `getObject()` method of `ResultSet`, in which case the type of the object returned is shown in the second column. You can also use a specific `get`*`XXX`*`()` method. These methods are shown in the third column, along with the Java datatypes they return. Remember that supported SQL datatypes vary from database to database.

Table 9-1. Methods to Retrieve Data from a ResultSet

SQL Data Type	Java Type Returned by getObject()	Recommended Alternative to getObject()
BIGINT	Long	long getLong()
BINARY	byte[]	byte[] getBytes()
BIT	Boolean	boolean getBoolean()
CHAR	String	String getString()

Table 9-1. Methods to Retrieve Data from a ResultSet (continued)

SQL Data Type	Java Type Returned by getObject( )	Recommended Alternative to getObject( )
DATE	java.sql.Date	java.sql.Date getDate()
DECIMAL	java.math.BigDecimal	java.math.BigDecimal getBigDecimal()
DOUBLE	Double	double getDouble()
FLOAT	Double	double getDouble()
INTEGER	Integer	int getInt()
LONGVARBINARY	byte[]	InputStream getBinaryStream()
LONGVARCHAR	String	InputStream getAsciiStream() InputStream getUnicodeStream()
NUMERIC	java.math.BigDecimal	java.math.BigDecimal getBigDecimal()
REAL	Float	float getFloat()
SMALLINT	Integer	short getShort()
TIME	Java.sql.Time	java.sql.Time getTime()
TIMESTAMP	Java.sql.Timestamp	java.sql.Timestamp getTimestamp()
TINYINT	Integer	byte getByte()
VARBINARY	byte[]	byte[] getBytes()
VARCHAR	String	String getString()

Handling Null Fields

A database field can be set to `null` to indicate that no value is present, in much the same way that a Java object can be set to `null`. Handling null database values with JDBC can be a little tricky. A method that doesn't return an object, like `getInt()`, has no way of indicating whether a column is `null` or whether it contains actual information. Any special value, like 0, might be a legitimate value. Therefore, JDBC includes the `wasNull()` method in `ResultSet`, which returns `true` or `false` depending on whether the last column read was a true database `null`. This means that you must read data from the `ResultSet` into a variable, call `wasNull()`, and proceed accordingly. It's not pretty, but it works. Here's an example:

```
int age = rs.getInt("age");
if (!rs.wasNull())
  out.println("Age: " + age);
```

Another way to check for null values is to use the `getObject()` method. If a column is `null`, `getObject()` always returns `null`. Using `getObject()` can eliminate the need to call `wasNull()` and result in simpler code, but the objects returned aren't easy-to-use primitives.

Updating the Database

Most database-enabled web sites need to do more than just perform queries. When a client submits an order or provides some kind of information, the data needs to be entered into the database. When you know you're executing a SQL UPDATE, INSERT, or DELETE statement and you know you don't expect a ResultSet, you can use the executeUpdate() method of Statement. It returns a count that indicates the number of rows modified by the statement. It's used like this:

```
int count =
  stmt.executeUpdate("DELETE FROM CUSTOMERS WHERE CUSTOMER_ID = 5");
```

If you are executing SQL that may return either a ResultSet or a count (say, if you're handling user-submitted SQL or building generic data-handling classes), use the generic execute() method of Statement. It returns a boolean whose value is true if the SQL statement produced one or more ResultSet objects or false if it resulted in an update count:

```
boolean b = stmt.execute(sql);
```

The getResultSet() and getUpdateCount() methods of Statement provide access to the results of the execute() method. Example 9-5 demonstrates the use of these methods with a new version of HtmlResultSet, named HtmlSQLResult, that creates an HTML table from any kind of SQL statement.

Example 9-5. A Class to Generate an HTML Table from a ResultSet Using ResultSetMetaData

```
import java.sql.*;

public class HtmlSQLResult {
  private String sql;
  private Connection con;

  public HtmlSQLResult(String sql, Connection con) {
    this.sql = sql;
    this.con = con;
  }

  public String toString() {  // can be called at most once
    StringBuffer out = new StringBuffer();

    // Uncomment the following line to display the SQL command at start of table
    // out.append("Results of SQL Statement: " + sql + "<P>\n");

    try {
      Statement stmt = con.createStatement();

      if (stmt.execute(sql)) {
        // There's a ResultSet to be had
```

Example 9-5. A Class to Generate an HTML Table from a ResultSet Using ResultSetMetaData (continued)

```
        ResultSet rs = stmt.getResultSet();
        out.append("<TABLE>\n");

        ResultSetMetaData rsmd = rs.getMetaData();

        int numcols = rsmd.getColumnCount();

        // Title the table with the result set's column labels
        out.append("<TR>");
        for (int i = 1; i <= numcols; i++)
          out.append("<TH>" + rsmd.getColumnLabel(i));
        out.append("</TR>\n");

        while(rs.next()) {
          out.append("<TR>");  // start a new row
          for(int i = 1; i <= numcols; i++) {
            out.append("<TD>");  // start a new data element
            Object obj = rs.getObject(i);
            if (obj != null)
              out.append(obj.toString());
            else
              out.append(" ");
            }
          out.append("</TR>\n");
        }

        // End the table
        out.append("</TABLE>\n");
      }
      else {
        // There's a count to be had
        out.append("<B>Records Affected:</B> " + stmt.getUpdateCount());
      }
    }
    catch (SQLException e) {
      out.append("</TABLE><H1>ERROR:</H1> " + e.getMessage());
    }

    return out.toString();
  }
}
```

This example uses `execute()` to execute whatever SQL statement is passed to the `HtmlSQLResult` constructor. Then, depending on the return value, it either calls `getResultSet()` or `getUpdateCount()`. Note that neither `getResultSet()` nor `getUpdateCount()` should be called more than once per query.

Using Prepared Statements

A PreparedStatement object is like a regular Statement object, in that it can be used to execute SQL statements. The important difference is that the SQL in a PreparedStatement is precompiled by the database for faster execution. Once a PreparedStatement has been compiled, it can still be customized by adjusting predefined parameters. Prepared statements are useful in applications that have to run the same general SQL command over and over.

Use the prepareStatement(String) method of Connection to create PreparedStatement objects. Use the ? character as a placeholder for values to be substituted later. For example:

```
PreparedStatement pstmt = con.prepareStatement(
  "INSERT INTO ORDERS (ORDER_ID, CUSTOMER_ID, TOTAL) VALUES (?,?,?)");

// Other code

pstmt.clearParameters();     // clear any previous parameter values
pstmt.setInt(1, 2);          // set ORDER_ID
pstmt.setInt(2, 4);          // set CUSTOMER_ID
pstmt.setDouble(3, 53.43); // set TOTAL
pstmt.executeUpdate();       // execute the stored SQL
```

The clearParameters() method removes any previously defined parameter values, while the set*XXX*() methods are used to assign actual values to each of the placeholder question marks. Once you have assigned values for all the parameters, call executeUpdate() to execute the PreparedStatement.

The PreparedStatement class has an important application in conjunction with servlets. When loading user-submitted text into the database using Statement objects and dynamic SQL, you must be careful not to accidentally introduce any SQL control characters (such as " or ') without escaping them in the manner required by your database. With a database like Oracle that surrounds strings with single quotes, an attempt to insert John d'Artagan into the database results in this corrupted SQL:

```
INSERT INTO MUSKETEERS (NAME) VALUES ('John d'Artagan')
```

As you can see, the string terminates twice. One solution is to manually replace the single quote (') with two single quotes (''), the Oracle escape sequence for one single quote. This solution requires you to escape every character that your database treats as special—not easy and not consistent with writing platform-independent code. A far better solution is to use a PreparedStatement and pass the string using its setString() method, as shown next. The PreparedStatement automatically escapes the string as necessary for your database:

```
PreparedStatement pstmt = con.prepareStatement(
  "INSERT INTO MUSKETEERS (NAME) VALUES (?)");
```

```
pstmt.setString(1, "John d'Artagan");
pstmt.executeUpdate();
```

Reusing Database Objects

In the introduction, we mentioned that the servlet lifecycle allows for extremely fast database access. After you've used JDBC for a short time, it will become evident that the major performance bottleneck often comes right at the beginning, when you are opening a database connection. This is rarely a problem for most applications and applets because they can afford a few seconds to create a `Connection` that is used for the life of the program. With servlets this bottleneck is more serious because we are creating and tearing down a new `Connection` for every page request. Luckily, the servlet lifecycle allows us to reuse the same connection for multiple requests, even concurrent requests, as `Connection` objects are required to be thread safe.

Reusing Database Connections

A servlet can create one or more `Connection` objects in its `init()` method and reuse them in its `service()`, `doGet()`, and `doPost()` methods. To demonstrate, Example 9-6 shows the phone lookup servlet rewritten to create its `Connection` object in advance. It also uses the `HtmlSQLResult` class from Example 9-5 to display the results. Note that this servlet uses the Sybase JDBC driver.

Example 9-6. An Improved Directory Servlet

```
import java.io.*;
import java.sql.*;
import javax.servlet.*;
import javax.servlet.http.*;

public class DBPhoneLookupReuse extends HttpServlet {

  private Connection con = null;

  public void init() throws ServletException {
    try {
      // Load (and therefore register) the Sybase driver
      Class.forName("com.sybase.jdbc.SybDriver");
      con = DriverManager.getConnection(
        "jdbc:sybase:Tds:dbhost:7678", "user", "passwd");
    }
    catch (ClassNotFoundException e) {
      throw new UnavailableException("Couldn't load database driver");
    }
    catch (SQLException e) {
```

Example 9-6. An Improved Directory Servlet (continued)

```
      throw new UnavailableException("Couldn't get db connection");
    }
  }

  public void doGet(HttpServletRequest req, HttpServletResponse res)
                               throws ServletException, IOException {
    res.setContentType("text/html");
    PrintWriter out = res.getWriter();

    out.println("<HTML><HEAD><TITLE>Phonebook</TITLE></HEAD>");
    out.println("<BODY>");

    HtmlSQLResult result =
      new HtmlSQLResult("SELECT NAME, PHONE FROM EMPLOYEES", con);

    // Display the resulting output
    out.println("<H2>Employees:</H2>");
    out.println(result);
    out.println("</BODY></HTML>");
  }

  public void destroy() {
    // Clean up.
    try {
      if (con != null) con.close();
    }
    catch (SQLException ignored) { }
  }
}
```

Reusing Prepared Statements

With a little care, you can speed servlet performance even more by creating other database-related objects ahead of time. The `PreparedStatement` object is an ideal candidate because it can precompile a SQL statement. This usually saves only a few milliseconds, but if your site gets a few hundred thousand hits a day, that can add up pretty quickly.

Note, however, that sharing objects other than connections poses a problem. Servlets must be thread safe, and accessing a `PreparedStatement` might require three or four method calls. If one thread calls the `clearParameters()` method of `PreparedStatement` right before another thread calls `execute()`, the results of `execute()` will be disastrous. Also, there's the limitation that a `Statement` can support only one query (and any associated result sets) at a time. One solution is to synchronize the sections of your code that use shared objects, as discussed in Chapter 3 and shown here:

```
synchronized (pstmt) {
  pstmt.clearParameters();
  pstmt.setInt(1, 2);
  pstmt.setInt(2, 4);
  pstmt.setDouble(3, 53.43);
  pstmt.executeUpdate();
}
```

Unfortunately, this solution is not without drawbacks. Entering a synchronization block on some platforms takes extra time, and synchronized objects can be used by only one thread at a time. However, some servlets already require a synchronization block, and in these cases the drawback is less of an issue. A good rule of thumb, then, is to create your connections ahead of time, along with any frequently used objects (such as `PreparedStatement` objects) that can be quickly used inside preexisting synchronization blocks.

For servlets written using the `SingleThreadModel` interface, these issues do not apply. On the other hand, you will have a number of copies of your servlet loaded at once, which could be just as detrimental to performance.

Transactions

So far, we have failed to mention one important feature of modern relational database systems: transactions. Most service-oriented web sites need to do more than run `SELECT` statements and insert single pieces of data. Let's look at an online banking application. To perform a transfer of $50,000 between accounts, your program needs to perform an operation that consists of two separate but related actions: credit one account and debit another. Now, imagine that for some reason or another, the SQL statement for the credit succeeds but the one for the debit fails. One account holder is $50,000 richer, but the other account has not been debited to match.

SQL failure is not the only potential problem. If another user checks the account balance in between the credit and the debit, she will see the original balance. The database is shown in an invalid state (more money is represented than actually exists). Granted, this kind of thing is unlikely to occur often, but in a universe of infinite possibilities, it will almost certainly happen sometime. This kind of problem is similar to the synchronization issues we discussed back in Chapter 3. This time, instead of concerning ourselves with the validity of data stored in a servlet, we are concerned with the validity of an underlying database. Simple synchronization is not enough to solve this problem: multiple servlets may be accessing the same database. For systems like banking software, chances are good that the database is being used by a number of entirely non-Java applications as well.

Sounds like a fairly tricky problem, right? Fortunately, it was a problem long before Java came along, so it has already been solved. Most major RDMBS systems support the concept of *transactions*. A transaction allows you to group multiple SQL statements together. Using a transaction-aware RDBMS, you can begin a transaction, perform any number of actions, and either commit the results to the database or roll back all of your SQL statements. If we build our online banking application with a transaction-based system, the credit will automatically be canceled if the debit fails.

A transaction is isolated from the rest of the database until finished. As far as the rest of the database is concerned, everything takes place at once (in other words, transactions are atomic). This means that other users accessing the database will always see a valid view of the data, although not necessarily an up-to-date view. If a user requests a report on widgets sold before your widget sales transaction is completed, the report will not include the most recent sale.

Using Transactions with JDBC

Transaction management with JDBC takes place via the `Connection` object. By default, new connections start out in *autocommit* mode. This means that every SQL statement is executed as an individual transaction that is immediately committed to the database. To control commitment yourself, thereby allowing you to group SQL statements into transactions, you call `setAutoCommit(false)` on the `Connection` object. You can check the status of autocommit with the `getAutoCommit()` method. Once you have completed all of your SQL statements, you call `commit()` to permanently record the transaction in the database. Or, if you encountered an error, you call `rollback()` to undo it.

Example 9-7 shows a servlet that uses transactions to do basic order processing. It assumes two tables in an ODBC database—`INVENTORY` (containing the product ID and amount in stock) and `SHIPPING` (containing a product ID, an order number, and the amount shipped). The servlet uses an unshown `chargeCard()` method that handles billing and throws an exception if the customer's credit card is invalid.

Example 9-7. Transaction-Based Order Management

```
import java.io.*;
import java.sql.*;
import javax.servlet.*;
import javax.servlet.http.*;

public class OrderHandler extends HttpServlet {

  public void doPost(HttpServletRequest req, HttpServletResponse res)
                                throws ServletException, IOException {
    res.setContentType("text/plain");
```

Example 9-7. Transaction-Based Order Management (continued)

```
    PrintWriter out = res.getWriter();

    Connection con = null;
    try {
      Class.forName("sun.jdbc.odbc.JdbcOdbcDriver");
      con = DriverManager.getConnection("jdbc:odbc:ordersdb", "user", "passwd");

      // Turn on transactions
      con.setAutoCommit(false);

      Statement stmt = con.createStatement();
      stmt.executeUpdate(
        "UPDATE INVENTORY SET STOCK = (STOCK - 10) WHERE PRODUCTID = 7");
      stmt.executeUpdate(
        "UPDATE SHIPPING SET SHIPPED = (SHIPPED + 10) WHERE PRODUCTID = 7");

      chargeCard();  // method doesn't actually exist...

      con.commit();
      out.println("Order successful!  Thanks for your business!");
    }
    catch (Exception e) {
      // Any error is grounds for rollback
      try {
        con.rollback();
      }
      catch (SQLException ignored) { }
      out.println("Order failed. Please contact technical support.");
    }
    finally {
      // Clean up.
      try {
        if (con != null) con.close();
      }
      catch (SQLException ignored) { }
    }
  }
}
```

Here are a few notes on this example. First, the order transaction logic is in `doPost()` since the client's action is definitely not safely repeatable. Second, because the example demonstrates transaction logic more than servlet logic, the servlet simply assumes the user is buying 10 units of item 7, rather than bothering to actually parse a form for credit card and order information. Finally, as the servlet runs, any exception thrown during driver initializing, connecting to the database, executing SQL, or charging the credit card causes execution to jump to the `catch()` block, where the `rollback()` method is called, undoing all our work.

Optimized Transaction Processing

Note that in the previous example the `Connection` object was created inside the `doPost()` method, giving up the performance improvements we gained earlier in the chapter by moving the creation up to `init()`. This is done because transactions are linked to connections and, therefore, connections using transactions cannot be shared. Imagine what would happen if another invocation of this servlet invoked the `commit()` method when our order had reached only the second SQL statement. Our `INVENTORY` table would be short 10 units!

So, how do we use transactions without having to connect to the database every time a page is requested? There are several possibilities:

- Synchronize the `doPost()` method. This means that each instance of the servlet deals with only one request at a time. This works well for very low traffic sites, but it does slow things down for your users because every transaction has to finish before the next can start. If you need to perform database-intensive updates and inserts, the delay will probably be unacceptable.
- Leave things as they are, but create a new `Connection` object for each transaction. If you need to update data only once in every few thousand page requests, this might be the simplest route.
- Create a pool of `Connection` objects in the `init()` method and hand them out as needed, as shown in Figure 9-3. This is probably the most efficient way to handle the problem, if done right. It can, however, become very complicated very quickly without third-party support classes.
- Implement session tracking in the servlet and use the `HttpSession` object to hold onto a `Connection` for each user. This allows you to go one step beyond the other solutions and extend a transaction across multiple page requests or even multiple servlets.

Connection Pooling

For a complicated servlet, creating a connection pool is the ideal approach. With a connection pool, we can duplicate only the resources we need to duplicate (that is, `Connection` objects). A connection pool can also intelligently manage the size of the pool and make sure each connection remains valid. A number of connection pool packages are currently available. Some, such as the `DbConnectionBroker` that is freely available from Java Exchange at *http://javaexchange.com*, work by creating an object that dispenses connections and connection IDs on request. Others, often called *pool drivers*, implement a new JDBC driver that handles a pool of connections to another JDBC driver. Using a pooling driver like this is the easiest way to implement connection pooling in your servlets. Pooling drivers, however, can have a

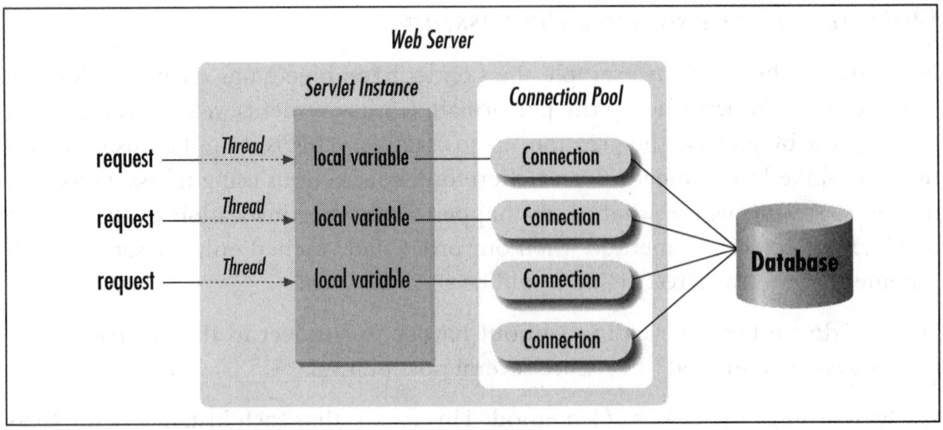

Figure 9-3. Servlets using a database connection pool

tiny bit more operational overhead than standard drivers because every JDBC class needs to be wrapped by another class.

Example 9-8 demonstrates a simple connection pooling system. A number of connections are created at startup and are handed out to methods as needed. If all the connections are in use, the servlet creates a new one. While our `ConnectionPool` class is fully functional, mission-critical deployments might benefit from one of the more complete third-party packages.

Example 9-8. The ConnectionPool Class

```
import java.sql.*;
import java.util.*;

public class ConnectionPool {
  private Hashtable connections = new Hashtable();
  private Properties props;

  public ConnectionPool(Properties props, int initialConnections)
                   throws SQLException, ClassNotFoundException {
    this.props = props;
    initializePool(props, initialConnections);
  }

  public ConnectionPool(String driverClassName, String dbURL,
                        String user, String password,
                        int initialConnections)
                   throws SQLException, ClassNotFoundException {
    props = new Properties();
    props.put("connection.driver", driverClassName);
    props.put("connection.url", dbURL);
    props.put("user", user);
```

Example 9-8. The ConnectionPool Class (continued)

```
    props.put("password", password);
    initializePool(props, initialConnections);
  }

  public Connection getConnection() throws SQLException {
    Connection con = null;

    Enumeration cons = connections.keys();

    synchronized (connections) {
      while(cons.hasMoreElements()) {
        con = (Connection)cons.nextElement();

        Boolean b = (Boolean)connections.get(con);
        if (b == Boolean.FALSE) {
          // So we found an unused connection.
          // Test its integrity with a quick setAutoCommit(true) call.
          // For production use, more testing should be performed,
          // such as executing a simple query.
          try {
            con.setAutoCommit(true);
          }
          catch(SQLException e) {
            // Problem with the connection, replace it.
            connections.remove(con);
            con = getNewConnection();
          }
          // Update the Hashtable to show this one's taken
          connections.put(con, Boolean.TRUE);
          // Return the connection
          return con;
        }
      }

      // If we get here, there were no free connections.  Make one more.
      // A more robust connection pool would have a maximum size limit,
      // and would reclaim connections after some timeout period
      con = getNewConnection();
      connections.put(con, Boolean.FALSE);
      return con;
    }
  }

  public void returnConnection(Connection returned) {
    if (connections.containsKey(returned)) {
      connections.put(returned, Boolean.FALSE);
    }
  }
```

Example 9-8. The ConnectionPool Class (continued)

```
  private void initializePool(Properties props, int initialConnections)
                  throws SQLException, ClassNotFoundException {
    // Load the driver
    Class.forName(props.getProperty("connection.driver"));

    // Put our pool of Connections in the Hashtable
    // The FALSE value indicates they're unused
    for(int i = 0; i < initialConnections; i++) {
      Connection con = getNewConnection();
      connections.put(con, Boolean.FALSE);
    }
  }

  private Connection getNewConnection() throws SQLException {
    return DriverManager.getConnection(
      props.getProperty("connection.url"), props);
  }
}
```

The `ConnectionPool` class maintains a `Hashtable`, using `Connection` objects as keys and `Boolean` objects as stored values. The `Boolean` value indicates whether a connection is in use. A program calls the `getConnection()` method of `ConnectionPool` to be assigned a `Connection` object it can use; it calls `returnConnection()` to give the connection back to the pool. This is a fairly simple model of a connection pool. For deployment, you probably want something that does a better job of maintaining the quality of the pool and does more verification of integrity than a simple call to `setAutoCommit()`.

Example 9-9 shows a revised version of the order processing servlet that uses the pooling class.

Example 9-9. Connection Pooling Transaction Servlet

```
import java.io.*;
import java.sql.*;
import javax.servlet.*;
import javax.servlet.http.*;

public class OrderHandlerPool extends HttpServlet {
  private ConnectionPool pool;

  public void init() throws ServletException {
    try {
      pool = new ConnectionPool("oracle.jdbc.driver.OracleDriver",
                         "jdbc:oracle:oci7:orders", "user", "passwd", 5);
    }
```

Example 9-9. Connection Pooling Transaction Servlet (continued)

```
    catch (Exception e) {
      throw new UnavailableException("Couldn't create connection pool");
    }
  }

  public void doPost(HttpServletRequest req, HttpServletResponse res)
                               throws ServletException, IOException {
    Connection con = null;

    res.setContentType("text/plain");
    PrintWriter out = res.getWriter();

    try {
      con = pool.getConnection();

      // Turn on transactions
      con.setAutoCommit(false);

      Statement stmt = con.createStatement();
      stmt.executeUpdate(
        "UPDATE INVENTORY SET STOCK = (STOCK - 10) WHERE PRODUCTID = 7");
      stmt.executeUpdate(
        "UPDATE SHIPPING SET SHIPPED = (SHIPPED + 10) WHERE PRODUCTID = 7");

      chargeCard();  // method doesn't actually exist...

      con.commit();
      out.println("Order successful!  Thanks for your business!");
    }
    catch (Exception e) {
      // Any error is grounds for rollback
      try {
        con.rollback();
      }
      catch (Exception ignored) { }
      out.println("Order failed. Please contact technical support.");
    }
    finally {
      if (con != null) pool.returnConnection(con);
    }
  }
}
```

Connections as Part of a Session

Session tracking, which we examined in detail back in Chapter 7, *Session Tracking*, gives us another way of handling transactions. Using sessions, we can create or allocate a dedicated database connection for individual users of a web site or intranet application. Example 9-10 demonstrates by showing a `ConnectionPerClient` servlet that associates a unique `Connection` with each client `HttpSession`. It wraps the `Connection` with a `ConnectionHolder` that is responsible for managing the connection's lifecycle.

Example 9-10. Associating a Connection with a Session

```
import java.io.*;
import java.sql.*;
import javax.servlet.*;
import javax.servlet.http.*;

class ConnectionHolder implements HttpSessionBindingListener {
  private Connection con = null;

  public ConnectionHolder(Connection con) {
    // Save the Connection
    this.con = con;
    try {
      con.setAutoCommit(false);  // transactions can extend between web pages!
    }
    catch(SQLException e) {
      // Perform error handling
    }
  }

  public Connection getConnection() {
    return con;  // return the cargo
  }

  public void valueBound(HttpSessionBindingEvent event) {
    // Do nothing when added to a Session
  }

  public void valueUnbound(HttpSessionBindingEvent event) {
    // Roll back changes when removed from a Session
    // (or when the Session expires)
    try {
      if (con != null) {
        con.rollback();  // abandon any uncomitted data
        con.close();
      }
    }
    catch (SQLException e) {
      // Report it
    }
  }
}
```

Example 9-10. Associating a Connection with a Session (continued)

```
/* Actual Servlet */

public class ConnectionPerClient extends HttpServlet {

  public void init() throws ServletException {
    try {
      Class.forName("oracle.jdbc.driver.OracleDriver");
    }
    catch (ClassNotFoundException e) {
      throw new UnavailableException("Couldn't load OracleDriver");
    }
  }

  public void doGet(HttpServletRequest req, HttpServletResponse res)
                              throws ServletException, IOException {
    res.setContentType("text/plain");
    PrintWriter out = res.getWriter();

    HttpSession session = req.getSession(true);
    Connection con;

    // Synchronize: Without this two holders might be created for one client
    synchronized (session) {
      // Try getting the connection holder for this client
      ConnectionHolder holder =
        (ConnectionHolder) session.getAttribute("servletapp.connection");

      // Create (and store) a new connection and holder if necessary
      if (holder == null) {
        try {
          holder = new ConnectionHolder(DriverManager.getConnection(
            "jdbc:oracle:oci7:ordersdb", "user", "passwd"));
          session.setAttribute("servletapp.connection", holder);
        }
        catch (SQLException e) {
          log("Couldn't get db connection", e);
        }
      }

      // Get the actual connection from the holder
      con = holder.getConnection();
    }

    // Now use the connection
    try {
      Statement stmt = con.createStatement();
      stmt.executeUpdate(
        "UPDATE INVENTORY SET STOCK = (STOCK - 10) WHERE PRODUCTID = 7");
```

Example 9-10. Associating a Connection with a Session (continued)

```
      stmt.executeUpdate(
        "UPDATE SHIPPING SET SHIPPED = (SHIPPED + 10) WHERE PRODUCTID = 7");

      // Charge the credit card and commit the transaction in another servlet
      res.sendRedirect(res.encodeRedirectURL(
        req.getContextPath() + "/servlet/CreditCardHandler"));
    }
    catch (Exception e) {
      // Any error is grounds for rollback
      try {
        con.rollback();
        session.removeAttribute("servletapp.connection");
      }
      catch (Exception ignored) { }
      out.println("Order failed. Please contact technical support.");
    }
  }
}
```

Rather than directly binding a connection to the session, we've created a simple holder class that implements the `HttpSessionBindingListener` interface. We do this because database connections are the most limited resource in a JDBC application and we want to make sure that they will be released properly when no longer needed. The wrapper class also allows us to roll back any uncommitted changes. If a user leaves our hypothetical online shopping system before checking out, his transaction is rolled back when the session expires.

Storing connections in sessions requires careful analysis of your application's needs. Most low-end and midrange database servers can max out at about 100 connections; desktop databases like Microsoft Access saturate even more quickly.

A Guestbook Servlet

To help the database concepts sink in, let's look at a real servlet. Example 9-11 shows the code for a typical database-backed "guestbook" servlet. This servlet manages a web page where visitors can enter comments and see what comments others have written. A screen shot is provided in Figure 9-4. All the visitor comments are held inside a database. In accessing the database, this servlet uses several of the techniques covered in this chapter including using a connection pool, using a prepared statement, and using `ContextProperties` to read database configuration information from context init parameters. The servlet even extends `com.oreilly.servlet.CacheHttpServlet` from Chapter 4 to optimize its output performance.

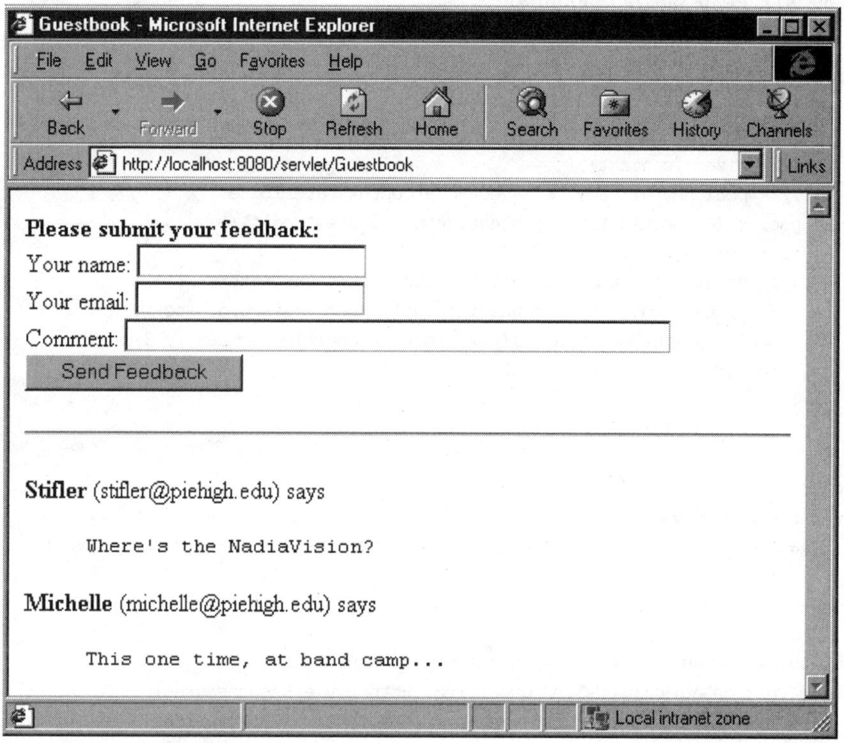

Figure 9-4. Guestbook output

Example 9-11. Please Sign In

```
import java.io.*;
import java.sql.*;
import java.util.*;
import javax.servlet.*;
import javax.servlet.http.*;

import com.oreilly.servlet.CacheHttpServlet;

public class Guestbook extends CacheHttpServlet {

  static final String SELECT_ALL =
    "SELECT name, email, cmt, id FROM guestlist ORDER BY id DESC";

  static final String INSERT =
    "INSERT INTO guestlist (id, name, email, cmt) " +
    "VALUES (?, ?, ?, ?)";

  private long lastModified = 0;  // Time database last changed
  private ConnectionPool pool;
```

Example 9-11. Please Sign In (continued)

```
  // Get a pointer to a connection pool
  public void init() throws ServletException {
    try {
      ServletContext context = getServletContext();
      synchronized (context) {
        // A pool may already be saved as a context attribute
        pool = (ConnectionPool) context.getAttribute("pool");
        if (pool == null) {
          // Construct a pool using our context init parameters
          // connection.driver, connection.url, user, password, etc
          pool = new ConnectionPool(new ContextProperties(context), 3);
          context.setAttribute("pool", pool);
        }
      }
    }
    catch (Exception e) {
      throw new UnavailableException(
      "Failed to fetch a connection pool from the context: " + e.getMessage());
    }
  }

  // Display the current entries, then ask for a new entry
  public void doGet(HttpServletRequest req, HttpServletResponse res)
                               throws ServletException, IOException {
    res.setContentType("text/html");
    PrintWriter out = res.getWriter();

    printHeader(out);
    printForm(out);
    printMessages(out);
    printFooter(out);
  }

  // Add a new entry, then dispatch back to doGet()
  public void doPost(HttpServletRequest req, HttpServletResponse res)
                               throws ServletException, IOException {
    handleForm(req, res);
    doGet(req, res);
  }

  private void printHeader(PrintWriter out) {
    out.println("<HTML><HEAD><TITLE>Guestbook</TITLE></HEAD>");
    out.println("<BODY>");
  }

  private void printForm(PrintWriter out) {
    out.println("<FORM METHOD=POST>");  // posts to itself
    out.println("<B>Please submit your feedback:</B><BR>");
```

Example 9-11. Please Sign In (continued)

```
    out.println("Your name: <INPUT TYPE=TEXT NAME=name><BR>");
    out.println("Your email: <INPUT TYPE=TEXT NAME=email><BR>");
    out.println("Comment: <INPUT TYPE=TEXT SIZE=50 NAME=comment><BR>");
    out.println("<INPUT TYPE=SUBMIT VALUE=\"Send Feedback\"><BR>");
    out.println("</FORM>");
    out.println("<HR>");
  }

  // Read the messages from the database, and print
  private void printMessages(PrintWriter out) throws ServletException {
    String name, email, comment;

    Connection con = null;
    Statement stmt = null;
    ResultSet rs = null;

    try {
      con = pool.getConnection();
      stmt = con.createStatement();
      rs = stmt.executeQuery(SELECT_ALL);

      while (rs.next()) {
        name = rs.getString(1);
        if (rs.wasNull() || name.length() == 0) name = "Unknown user";
        email = rs.getString(2);
        if (rs.wasNull() || email.length() == 0) name = "Unknown email";
        comment = rs.getString(3);
        if (rs.wasNull() || comment.length() == 0) name = "No comment";
        out.println("<DL>");
        out.println("<DT><B>" + name + "</B> (" + email + ") says");
        out.println("<DD><PRE>" + comment + "</PRE>");
        out.println("</DL>");
      }
    }
    catch (SQLException e) {
      throw new ServletException(e);
    }
    finally {
      try {
        if (stmt != null) stmt.close();
      }
      catch (SQLException ignored) { }
      pool.returnConnection(con);
    }
  }

  private void printFooter(PrintWriter out) {
    out.println("</BODY>");
  }
```

Example 9-11. Please Sign In (continued)

```
  // Save the new comment to the database
  private void handleForm(HttpServletRequest req,
                          HttpServletResponse res) throws ServletException {
    String name = req.getParameter("name");
    String email = req.getParameter("email");
    String comment = req.getParameter("comment");

    Connection con = null;
    PreparedStatement pstmt = null;
    try {
      con = pool.getConnection();
      // Use a prepared statement for automatic string escaping
      pstmt = con.prepareStatement(INSERT);
      long time = System.currentTimeMillis();
      pstmt.setString(1, Long.toString(time));
      pstmt.setString(2, name);
      pstmt.setString(3, email);
      pstmt.setString(4, comment);
      pstmt.executeUpdate();
    }
    catch (SQLException e) {
      throw new ServletException(e);
    }
    finally {
      try {
        if (pstmt != null) pstmt.close();
      }
      catch (SQLException ignored) { }
      pool.returnConnection(con);
    }

    // Make note we have a new last modified time
    lastModified = System.currentTimeMillis();
  }

  public long getLastModified(HttpServletRequest req) {
    return lastModified;  // supports CacheHttpServlet
  }
}
```

The SQL statements for accessing the database are given at the top of the class in static final variables. Separating the SQL makes future modifications much easier.

The `init()` method gets (or creates) a connection pool for this servlet to use. It first looks for a preexisting pool saved in as a `ServletContext` attribute under the name `pool`. If that attribute does not exist, the `init()` method constructs a new pool—using the `ContextProperties` class to specify database configuration information—and saves that pool to the context. To be honest, a connection pool isn't really needed for this servlet because there are no transactions and the bandwidth through a single reused Connection wouldn't be too great. In cases like this it makes sense to still use a connection pool but one that has the ability to return a shared Connection object for simultaneous use by multiple servlets.

The doGet() method prints the header, a form asking the user to comment, the previous comments retrieved from the database, and a footer. Techniques for more elegant HTML creation in cases like this are shown beginning with Chapter 14, *The Tea Framework*. For now this gets the job done.

The printMessages() method uses the pool to get a Connection, then executes the SELECT_ALL query using a Statement retrieved from that Connection. For each row in the ResultSet it prints a <DL> entry. In the finally block, the Connection goes back into the pool.

The doPost() method is called when a user submits comments using the form generated by doGet(). This method calls handleForm() to store the comment inside the database, then dispatches to doGet() to render the page. The handleForm() method retrieves the parameter's name, email, and comment and uses a PreparedStatement and the INSERT statement to save the parameter information in the database. By using a PreparedStatement to save the strings we automatically escape any special characters. A timestamp for the comment is also saved to the database, to provide a way to sort the comments and for possible later display.

At the bottom of the handleForm() method it sets lastModified to the current time. This allows the getLastModified() method to return the time the database was last updated. Because this servlet extends CacheHttpServlet, the last modified information will be used by the superclass to manage a cache of its output, changing the cache only after database updates.*

Advanced JDBC Techniques

Now that we've covered the basics, let's talk about a few advanced techniques that use servlets and JDBC. First, we'll examine how servlets can access stored database procedures. Then we'll look at how servlets can fetch complicated datatypes, such as binary data (images, applications, etc.), large quantities of text, or even executable database-manipulation code, from a database.

---

* Remember, though, there's no caching performed for POST requests, since they are not idempotent. This has an interesting side effect for the Guestbook example—if you do a page reload after submitting a new comment, you'll see the page generation will take some time even though it's the same page output you already viewed. This is because the submit was a POST request whose output was not cached.

Stored Procedures

Most RDBMS systems include some sort of internal programming language. One example is Oracle's PL/SQL. These languages allow database developers to embed procedural application code directly within a database and then call that code from other applications. RDBMS programming languages are often well suited to performing certain database actions; many existing database installations have a number of useful stored procedures already written and ready to go. Most introductions to JDBC tend to skip over this topic; we'll cover it here briefly.

The following code is an Oracle PL/SQL stored procedure:

```
CREATE OR REPLACE PROCEDURE sp_interest
(id IN INTEGER
bal IN OUT FLOAT) IS
BEGIN
SELECT balance
INTO bal
FROM accounts
WHERE account_id = id;

bal := bal + bal * 0.03;

UPDATE accounts
SET balance = bal
WHERE account_id = id;

END;
```

This procedure executes a SQL statement, performs a calculation, and executes another SQL statement. It would be fairly simple to write the SQL to handle this (in fact, the transaction example earlier in this chapter does something similar), so why bother with this at all? There are several reasons:

- Stored procedures are precompiled in the RDBMS, so they run faster than dynamic SQL.
- Stored procedures execute entirely within the RDBMS, so they can perform multiple queries and updates without network traffic.
- Stored procedures allow you to write database-manipulation code once and use it across multiple applications in multiple languages.
- Changes in the underlying table structures require changes only in the stored procedures that access them; applications using the database are unaffected.
- Many older databases already have a lot of code written as stored procedures, and it would be nice to be able to leverage that effort.

The Oracle PL/SQL procedure in our example takes an input value, in this case an account ID, and returns an updated balance. While each database has its own syntax for accessing stored procedures, JDBC creates a standardized escape sequence for accessing stored procedures using the `java.sql.CallableStatement` class. The syntax for a procedure that doesn't return a result is `{call procedure_name(?,?)}`. The syntax for a stored procedure that returns a result value is `{? = call procedure_name(?,?)}`. The parameters inside the parentheses are optional.

Using the `CallableStatement` class is similar to using the `PreparedStatement` class:

```
CallableStatment cstmt = con.prepareCall("{call sp_interest(?,?)}");
cstmt.registerOutParameter(2, java.sql.Types.FLOAT);
cstmt.setInt(1, accountID);
cstmt.execute();
out.println("New Balance: " + cstmt.getFloat(2));
```

This code first creates a `CallableStatement` using the `prepareCall()` method of `Connection`. Because this stored procedure has an output parameter, it uses the `registerOutParameter()` method of `CallableStatement` to identify that parameter as an output parameter of type `FLOAT`. Finally, the code executes the stored procedure and uses the `getFloat()` method of `CallableStatement` to display the new balance. The `get`*`XXX`*`()` methods in the `CallableStatement` interface are similar to those in the `ResultSet` interface.

Binaries and Books

Most databases support datatypes to handle text strings up to several gigabytes in size, as well as binary information like multimedia files. Different databases handle this kind of data in different ways, but the JDBC methods for retrieving it are standard. The `getAsciiStream()` method of `ResultSet` handles large text strings; `getBinaryStream()` works for large binary objects. Each of these methods returns an `InputStream`.

Support for large data types is one of the most common sources of JDBC problems. Make sure you test your drivers thoroughly, using the largest pieces of data your application will encounter. Oracle's JDBC driver is particularly prone to errors in this area.

Here's some code from a message board servlet that demonstrates reading a long ASCII string. We can assume that connections, statements, and so on have already been created:

```
try {
  ResultSet rs = stmt.executeQuery(
```

```
        "SELECT TITLE, SENDER, MESSAGE FROM MESSAGES WHERE MESSAGE_ID = 9");
      if (rs.next()) {
        out.println("<H1>" + rs.getString("title") + "</H1>");
        out.println("<B>From:</B> " + rs.getString("sender") + "<BR>");
        BufferedReader msgText = new BufferedReader(
          new InputStreamReader(rs.getAsciiStream("message")));
        while (msgText.ready()) {
          out.println(msgText.readLine());
        }
      }
    }
    catch (SQLException e) {
      // Report it
    }
```

While it is reading from the `InputStream`, this servlet doesn't get the value of any other columns in the result set. This is important because calling any other `getXXX()` method of `ResultSet` closes the `InputStream`.

Binary data can be retrieved in the same manner using `ResultSet.getBinaryStream()`. In this case, we need to set the content type as appropriate and write the output as bytes. Example 9-12 shows a servlet that returns a GIF file loaded from a database.

Example 9-12. Reading a Binary GIF Image from a Database

```
import java.io.*;
import java.sql.*;
import javax.servlet.*;
import javax.servlet.http.*;

public class DBGifReader extends HttpServlet {

  Connection con;

  public void init() throws ServletException {
    try {
      Class.forName("sun.jdbc.odbc.JdbcOdbcDriver");
      con = DriverManager.getConnection("jdbc:odbc:imagedb", "user", "passwd");
    }
    catch (ClassNotFoundException e) {
      throw new UnavailableException("Couldn't load JdbcOdbcDriver");
    }
    catch (SQLException e) {
      throw new UnavailableException("Couldn't get db connection");
    }
  }

  public void doGet(HttpServletRequest req, HttpServletResponse res)
                               throws ServletException, IOException {
```

Example 9-12. Reading a Binary GIF Image from a Database (continued)

```
    try {
      res.setContentType("image/gif");
      ServletOutputStream out = res.getOutputStream();

      Statement stmt = con.createStatement();
      ResultSet rs = stmt.executeQuery(
        "SELECT IMAGE FROM PICTURES WHERE PID = " + req.getParameter("PID"));

      if (rs.next()) {
        BufferedInputStream gifData =
          new BufferedInputStream(rs.getBinaryStream("image"));
        byte[] buf = new byte[4 * 1024];  // 4K buffer
        int len;
        while ((len = gifData.read(buf, 0, buf.length)) != -1) {
          out.write(buf, 0, len);
        }
      }
      else {
        res.sendError(res.SC_NOT_FOUND);
      }
    }
    catch(SQLException e) {
      // Report it
    }
  }
}
```

Beyond the Core

In addition to the core JDBC methods and techniques covered in this chapter, there are additional database APIs available that help in writing complicated database-access applications. One such API is JDBC 2.0, the follow-on to JDBC 1.2 discussed throughout this chapter.

At the time of this writing, JDBC 2.0 has yet to be widely implemented and used. To employ JDBC 2.0 requires both a database that supports its advanced features and a driver that grants access to those features. Luckily, you'll find JDBC 2.0 support in all J2EE servers because any server wishing to be J2EE complaint is required to provide access to a JDBC 2.0 database and driver. The J2EE reference implementation from Sun, for example, comes bundled with an evaluation copy of the Java-based Cloudscape database.

JDBC 2.0 comes in two parts. One part resides in the `java.sql` package of Java 2 and is required to be supported by any JDBC 2.0-compliant database and driver. The other part resides in the `javax.sql` package. This Optional Package contains several features which may be implemented by a JDBC 2.0-compliant database and driver but are not required.

Among the enhancements in the core `java.sql` package are scrollable and modifiable result sets. These two features allow the `ResultSet` cursor to be moved forward and backward arbitrarily (instead of just forward one row at a time), with the cursor able to change, insert, and delete rows along the way. Core support has also been added for new SQL3 data types (including `BLOB` for binary large objects, `CLOB` for character large objects, and `ARRAY` for arrays) and for batch updates that allow several update statements to be sent to the server with one network request.

The `javax.sql` Optional Package includes many features that are especially important to enterprise applications. One such feature is JNDI lookup support. This allows a database connection to be retrieved by name from a JNDI server. Another feature is built-in connection pooling, something that hardly changes the API but allows a preexisting connection to be retrieved. An extremely important optional feature in JDBC 2.0 is support for distributed transactions. This allows a transaction to be spread between multiple separate databases, updating both databases with one atomic operation. Finally, JDBC 2.0 includes support for `RowSet` objects that wrap `ResultSet` row data—allowing easy caching of data and easy transfer of data across a network, as well as standardized access to any tabular data source such as a spreadsheet or flat file.

More information on JDBC 2.0 features can be found in *Database Programming with JDBC and Java* by George Reese (O'Reilly) and *JDBC API Tutorial and Reference,*by Seth White et al. (Addison-Wesley) and in the online tutorials available at *http://java.sun.com/products/jdbc.*

Finally, for those who prefer to think in higher-level terms than JDBC provides, a company called Clear Ink sponsors an open source (Apache-license) library called Village that sits above JDBC 1.2 and exposes an API that simplifies interaction with the database. It's directly modeled after the dbKona commercial product from BEA/WebLogic. Others have built on top of Village to produce a more robust version named Town. Both Village and Town are available at *http://www.working-dogs.com.* (No news yet on City.)

In this chapter:
- *Communication Options*
- *Daytime Server*
- *Chat Server*

10

Applet-Servlet Communication

This chapter demonstrates several techniques by which applets can communicate with servlets. We're going to come at the topic from a slightly different angle than you might expect. Instead of assuming you have an applet and a servlet that need to communicate, we're going assume you have an applet that needs to talk to some entity on the server and explore why sometimes that entity should be a servlet.

To get the ball rolling, let's think about applets that need to communicate with the server. There are a number of good examples. Take a look at the administration applet that manages the Java Web Server. Think about how it works—it executes on the client, but it configures the server. To do this, the applet and the server need to be in near constant communication. As another example, take a look at one of the popular chat applets. One client says something, and all the rest see it. How does that work? They certainly don't communicate applet to applet. Instead, each applet posts its messages to a central server, and the server takes care of updating the other clients. Finally, imagine an applet that tracks the price of a set of stocks and offers continuous updates. How does the applet know the current stock prices, and, more importantly, how does it know when they change? The answer is that it talks with its server.

Communication Options

Our interest in stock trading rose along with the Dow, so let's continue with this hypothetical stock-tracking applet. We should warn you right now that this example will remain hypothetical. We'll use it solely as a reference point for discussing the issues involved in applet-server communication. But don't worry, there's plenty of code later in the chapter that demonstrates the techniques discussed here, just in somewhat simpler examples.

This stock-tracking applet of ours needs to get a stock feed from some server machine. Assuming it's a normal, untrusted applet, there's just one choice: the machine from which it was downloaded. Any attempt to connect to another machine results in a `SecurityException`, so let's assume the applet gets a stock feed from the server machine from which it was downloaded.* The question remains: how can the applet and the server communicate?

Trusted and Untrusted Applets

When a Java applet is embedded in a web page, a browser can download it and execute it automatically. If you think about it, that's a very dangerous thing to do. So, to protect the client, JDK 1.0 assumed all applets were untrusted and ran them under the watch of a `SecurityManager` that severely limited what they could do. For example, the security manager made sure applets couldn't write to the user's filesystem, read certain system properties, accept incoming socket connections, or establish outgoing socket connections to any host but the origin server. This protected the client, but it limited the usefulness of applets.

Consequently, JDK 1.1 introduced the concept of trusted applets—applets that can operate like normal applications with full access to the client machine. For an applet to be trusted, it has to be digitally signed by a person or company the client trusts (as marked in the client's browser). The signature authenticates the applet's origin and guarantees integrity during the transfer, so the client knows the applet code hasn't been surreptitiously changed. This allowed for more productive applets, but it was an all-or-nothing approach.

To give the client more control, JDK 1.2 introduced a fine-grained access control system. Under this new system, a digitally signed applet can be partially trusted, given certain abilities without being given free reign on the system. This promises to allow applets from unknown sources to be granted small privileges (such as writing to a single directory), without granting them the ability to wipe the client's hard drive. Browser vendors have been slow to provide integrated support for new JDK versions, but fortunately it's possible to upgrade a browser's JVM using the Java Plug-In, a free product available at *http://java.sun.com/products/plugin.*

HTTP and Raw Socket Connections

Before JDK 1.1 and servlets, there were two options for applet-server communication:

- Have the applet establish an HTTP connection to a CGI program on the server machine. The applet acts like a browser and requests a page, parsing the

* You may be wondering how the server machine itself got the stock feed. For the purposes of this example, it's magic.

response for its own use. The applet can provide information using a query string or POST data and can receive information from the returned page.

- Have the applet establish a raw socket connection to a non-HTTP server running on the server machine. The non-HTTP server can listen to a particular port and communicate with the applet using whatever custom protocol they agree upon.

Each of these approaches has advantages and disadvantages. Having an applet make an HTTP connection to a CGI program works well for these reasons:

- It's easy to write. The applet can take advantage of the `java.net.URL` and `java.net.URLConnection` classes to manage the communication channel, and the CGI program can be written like any other.
- It works even for applets running behind a firewall. Most firewalls allow HTTP connections but disallow raw socket connections.
- It allows a Java applet to communicate with a program written in any language. The CGI program doesn't have to be written in Java. It can be in Perl, C, C++, or any other language.
- It works with applets written using JDK 1.0, so it works with all Java-enabled browsers.
- It allows secure communication. An applet can communicate with a secure server using the encrypted HTTPS (HTTP + SSL) protocol.
- The CGI program can be used by browsers as well as applets. In the case of our stock-tracker example, the CGI program can do double duty, also acting as the backend for an HTML form-based stock quote service. This makes it especially convenient for an applet to leverage existing CGI programs.

But the HTTP connection to a CGI program also has some problems:

- It's slow. Because of the HTTP request/response paradigm, the applet and the CGI program cannot communicate interactively. They have to reestablish a new communication channel for each request and response. Plus, there is the standard delay while the CGI program launches and initializes itself to handle a request.
- It usually requires requests to be formed as an awkward array of name/value pairs. For example, when our stock-tracker applet asks for the daily high for Sun Microsystems' stock, it has to ask with an awkward query string like `stock=sunw&query=dailyhi`.
- It forces all responses to be formatted using some arbitrary, previously agreed upon standard. For example, when our stock-tracker applet receives the

response that contains a stock's daily high price, it needs to know exactly how to parse the data. Does the returned price begin with a dollar sign? Does the response include the time when the high occurred? And if so, where is the time specified and in what format?

- Only the applet can initiate communication. The CGI program has to wait passively for the applet to request something before it can respond. If a stock price changes, the applet can find out only when it asks the right question.

An applet and server can also communicate by having the applet establish a socket connection to a non-HTTP server process. This provides the following advantages over the HTTP-based approach:

- It allows bidirectional, sustained communication. The applet and servlet can use the same socket (or even several sockets) to communicate interactively, sending messages back and forth. For security reasons, the applet must always initiate the connection by connecting to a server socket on the server machine, but after a socket connection has been established, either party can write to the socket at any time. This allows our stock tracker to receive stock price updates as soon as they are available.
- It allows a more efficient program to run on the server side. The non-HTTP server can be written to handle a request immediately without launching an external CGI program to do the work.

But a socket connection also has disadvantages versus the HTTP-based approach:

- It fails for applets running behind firewalls. Most firewalls don't allow raw socket connections, and thus they disallow this sort of applet-server communication. Therefore, this mechanism should be used only when an applet is guaranteed to never run on the far side of a firewall, such as for an intranet application.
- It can be fairly complicated to write the code that runs on the server. There must always be some process (such as a stock quote server) listening on a well-known port on the server machine. Developing such an application in Java is easier than in C++, but it is still nontrivial.
- It may require the development of a custom protocol. The applet and server need to define the protocol they use for the communication. While this protocol may be simpler and more efficient than HTTP, it often has to be specially developed.
- The non-HTTP server cannot be conveniently connected to by a web browser. Browsers speak HTTP; they cannot communicate with a non-HTTP server.

The standard historical approach has been for applets to use HTTP to connect to CGI programs on the server. It's easy, and it works for all types of browsers, even browsers running behind firewalls. The use of raw socket connections has generally been reserved for situations in which it's absolutely necessary, such as when the applet and server require bidirectional communication. And, even in those cases, it's often possible to use HTTP connections to simulate bidirectional communication in order to pass through firewalls, as we'll see in a later example.

Servlets and Object Serialization

The recent introduction of Java servlets and object serialization has given new life to these traditional applet-server communication techniques. Servlets are replacing slow-starting CGI programs, improving the performance of HTTP-based applet-server communication and making frequent applet-server communication feasible. While it's true in the general case that the applet and the servlet still have to take time to reestablish their connection for each request and response, the applet no longer has to wait as the server launches a CGI program to handle each of its repeated requests.

Java object serialization has simplified the issues involved with formatting responses. With both applets and servlets written in Java, it's only natural that they should communicate by exchanging Java objects. For example, when our hypothetical stock-tracking applet asks our stock feed servlet the daily high value for Sun stock, it can receive the response as a serialized `StockPrice` object. From this, it can get the daily high value as a `float` and the time of the high value as a `Date`. It's convenient, and it provides easy type safety. But beware, object serialization works only with applets running inside browsers that support JDK 1.1 or later.

JDBC, RMI, and a Little CORBA

JDK 1.1 includes two additional features that have an impact on applet-server communication: JDBC and RMI. The JDBC (Java Database Connectivity) API, discussed in Chapter 9, *Database Connectivity*, allows a Java program to connect to a relational database on the same machine or on another machine. Java applets written to JDK 1.1 can use JDBC to communicate with a database on the server. This special-purpose communication doesn't generally require applet-servlet communication. However, it is often helpful for an applet (especially one written to JDK 1.0) to forgo connecting straight to the database (or to a pass-through proxy on the web server) and instead connect to a servlet that handles the database communication on the applet's behalf as explained in the "Servlets in the Middle Tier" sidebar in Chapter 9, *Database Connectivity*. For example, an applet that wants to look up a person's address can connect to a servlet using HTTP, pass the name of the person using HTTP parameters, and then receive the address as either a specially formatted string or a serialized object. This use of applet-servlet communication tends to piggyback on existing protocols like HTTP, so we aren't going to cover it in any more detail here.

The RMI (Remote Method Invocation) API allows an applet to invoke the methods of a Java object executing on the server machine, and, in some cases, it also allows the object on the server machine to invoke the methods of the applet. The advantages of RMI for applet-server communication are compelling:

- It allows applets and server objects to communicate using an elegant high-level, object-oriented paradigm. Requests can be made as method invocations, passing serialized object parameters if necessary. Responses can be received as serialized objects or even references to other remote objects. But to even use the words *request* and *response* shows we've been using HTTP too much! With RMI, there are no requests or responses, just method invocations. To go back to our stock-tracker example, the applet can get the daily high for Sun stock by calling `sunw.getDailyHigh()`, where `sunw` is a Java object that exists on the server.

- It allows server objects to make callbacks to the methods of the applet. For example, with our stock-tracking example, the server can notify interested applets that a stock price has changed by calling `applet.update(stock)`.

- It can be made to work through firewalls (though it doesn't like it, and current browsers don't support it very well). The RMI transport layer normally relies on direct socket connections to perform its work. When an applet executes behind a firewall, however, its socket connections fail. In this case, the RMI transport layer can automatically begin operating entirely within the HTTP protocol.*

This is not without cost, though. The HTTP overhead affects performance, and the HTTP request/response paradigm cannot support callbacks. The disadvantages of RMI are equally concerning:

- It's complicated. RMI communication uses special stub and skeleton classes for each remote object, and it requires a naming registry from which clients can obtain references to these remote objects.
- It's supported in few browsers. Of all the popular browsers available as of this writing, only Netscape Navigator 4 and above include RMI support. Neither

* For a description of the system properties necessary for an RMI client application to poke through a firewall, see John D. Mitchell's JavaWorld Java Tip 42 at *http://www.javaworld.com/javaworld/javatips/jw-javatip42.html*. (Unmentioned in the article but also important are the `socksProxySet`, `socksProxyHost`, and `socksProxyPort` properties necessary for SOCKS-based proxies.) All these system properties should be set automatically by web browsers, but unfortunately few web browsers currently do this, leaving their applets with no way to determine the proper settings and no way to use RMI through a firewall.

previous Netscape browser versions nor any versions of Microsoft's Internet Explorer support RMI without installing a special plug-in. (Although since the RMI classes are pure Java, people have had some success in adding RMI to Internet Explorer as if it were a third-party library.)

- It can be used only by Java clients. The server object can't be shared by a web browser or even a C++ client.

For more information on RMI programming, see *Java Network Programming* by Elliotte Rusty Harold (O'Reilly) and *Java Distributed Computing* by Jim Farley (O'Reilly).

CORBA (Common Object Request Broker Architecture) is a technology similar to RMI that enables communication between distributed objects written in various languages. With CORBA and its IIOP (Internet Inter-ORB Protocol) communication protocol, a C++ client can communicate with a Java servlet. Demonstrating this ability extends beyond the scope of this book. For more information, see *http://www.omg.org* and *http://java.sun.com/products/jdk/idl*.

The Hybrid Approach

Now that we've examined all the options, the question remains: how should our stock-tracking applet communicate with its stock feed server? The answer is: it depends.

If we can guarantee that all our potential clients support it, RMI's elegance and power make it an ideal choice. But currently that's like assuming all your friends enjoy your Star Trek jokes. It can be true if you carefully choose your friends (or your clients), but it's generally not the case in the real world.

When RMI isn't available, the bidirectional capabilities of the non-HTTP socket connection make it look fairly attractive. Unfortunately, that bidirectional communication becomes nonexistent communication when the applet ends up on the far side of a firewall.

There's always the old workhorse, HTTP communication. It's straightforward to implement and works on every Java-enabled client. And if you can guarantee that the client supports JDK 1.1 (and this is easier to guarantee than that the client support RMI), you can use object serialization.

Perhaps the best solution is to use every solution. Java makes it possible to combine the HTTP, non-HTTP, and RMI applet-server communication techniques, supporting them all for the same application. Why would anyone want to do this? Well, it's a handy technique when an applet wants to communicate using RMI or a non-HTTP protocol but needs to fall back to HTTP when necessary (such as when it finds itself behind a firewall). By using the same server to handle every client, the core server logic and the server state can be collected in one place. When you control your environment, of course, you can drop one or more of these protocols. But isn't it nice to know you don't have to?

For a complicated application running in an application server, the standard design is to make an RMI remote object available to support RMI clients, a socket listener available to support socket clients, and a servlet available to support HTTP clients. These objects all use a shared set of business logic classes to handle the client's requests (kind of like a take-out restaurant that can fulfill orders coming in by phone, fax, or email). For the remainder of this chapter, though, we'll simplify things somewhat and demonstrate RMI, socket, and HTTP communication being handled by a single servlet. One servlet, multiple access protocols.

Daytime Server

For a simple demonstration of each communication technique, we're going to write an applet that asks its server for the current time of day. The applet first uses an HTTP connection, then a non-HTTP socket connection, and finally an RMI connection. Of course, an applet can normally get the current time from the system on which it's running. To give this example an air of practicality, let's assume the applet needs an approximate timestamp for some event and cannot rely on the client machine to have a correctly set clock.

The Applet

We are going to be using the same example applet throughout this section. The skeleton code for this applet, `DaytimeApplet`, is shown in Example 10-1. At the moment, the applet just creates a user interface in which the times it retrieves can be displayed, as shown in Figure 10-1. As we proceed with this example, we will implement its `getDateUsingHttpText()`, `getDateUsingHttpObject()`, `getDateUsingSocketText()`, `getDateUsingSocketObject()`, and `getDateUsingRMIObject()` methods.

Note that the examples in this chapter use several JDK 1.0 methods that are deprecated in JDK 1.1. This is to maximize portability. You'll see deprecation warnings when compiling with new JDKs, but they can safely be ignored.

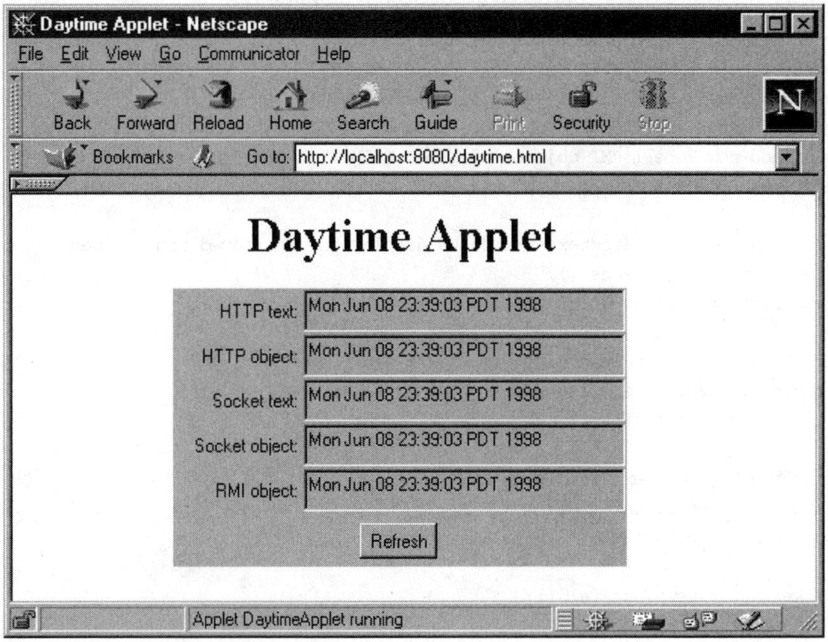

Figure 10-1. The DaytimeApplet user interface

Example 10-1. DaytimeApplet, Without all the Good Stuff

```
import java.applet.*;
import java.awt.*;
import java.io.*;
import java.util.*;

public class DaytimeApplet extends Applet {

  TextField httpText, httpObject, socketText, socketObject, RMIObject;
  Button refresh;

  public void init() {
    // Construct the user interface

    setLayout(new BorderLayout());

    // On the left create labels for the various communication
    // mechanisms
    Panel west = new Panel();
    west.setLayout(new GridLayout(5, 1));
```

Example 10-1. DaytimeApplet, Without all the Good Stuff (continued)

```
    west.add(new Label("HTTP text: ", Label.RIGHT));
    west.add(new Label("HTTP object: ", Label.RIGHT));
    west.add(new Label("Socket text: ", Label.RIGHT));
    west.add(new Label("Socket object: ", Label.RIGHT));
    west.add(new Label("RMI object: ", Label.RIGHT));
    add("West", west);

    // On the right create text fields to display the retrieved time values
    Panel center = new Panel();
    center.setLayout(new GridLayout(5, 1));

    httpText = new TextField();
    httpText.setEditable(false);
    center.add(httpText);

    httpObject = new TextField();
    httpObject.setEditable(false);
    center.add(httpObject);

    socketText = new TextField();
    socketText.setEditable(false);
    center.add(socketText);

    socketObject = new TextField();
    socketObject.setEditable(false);
    center.add(socketObject);

    RMIObject = new TextField();
    RMIObject.setEditable(false);
    center.add(RMIObject);

    add("Center", center);

    // On the bottom create a button to update the times
    Panel south = new Panel();
    refresh = new Button("Refresh");
    south.add(refresh);
    add("South", south);
  }

  public void start() {
    refresh();
  }

  private void refresh() {
    // Fetch and display the time values
    httpText.setText(getDateUsingHttpText());
```

Example 10-1. DaytimeApplet, Without all the Good Stuff (continued)

```
    httpObject.setText(getDateUsingHttpObject());
    socketText.setText(getDateUsingSocketText());
    socketObject.setText(getDateUsingSocketObject());
    RMIObject.setText(getDateUsingRMIObject());
  }

  private String getDateUsingHttpText() {
    // Retrieve the current time using an HTTP text-based connection
    return "unavailable";
  }

  private String getDateUsingHttpObject() {
    // Retrieve the current time using an HTTP object-based connection
    return "unavailable";
  }

  private String getDateUsingSocketText() {
    // Retrieve the current time using a non-HTTP text-based socket
    // connection
    return "unavailable";
  }

  private String getDateUsingSocketObject() {
    // Retrieve the current time using a non-HTTP object-based socket
    // connection
    return "unavailable";
  }

  private String getDateUsingRMIObject() {
    // Retrieve the current time using RMI communication
    return "unavailable";
  }

  public boolean handleEvent(Event event) {
    // When the refresh button is pushed, refresh the display
    // Use JDK 1.0 events for maximum portability
    switch (event.id) {
      case Event.ACTION_EVENT:
        if (event.target == refresh) {
          refresh();
          return true;
        }
    }
    return false;
  }
}
```

For this applet to be available for downloading to the client browser, it has to be placed under the server's document root, along with an HTML file referring to it. The HTML might look like this:

```
<HTML>
<HEAD><TITLE>Daytime Applet</TITLE></HEAD>
<BODY>
<CENTER><H1>Daytime Applet</H1></CENTER>
<CENTER><APPLET CODE=DaytimeApplet CODEBASE=/ WIDTH=300 HEIGHT=180>
</APPLET></CENTER>
</BODY></HTML>
```

The `CODEBASE` parameter indicates the directory (from the client's perspective) where the applet's class file has been placed. A `CODEBASE` of / indicates the class files will be retrieved from the document root for the default web application. If no `CODEBASE` is specified, its default value is the directory where the HTML file was found. Assuming the HTML file was named *daytime.html*, this applet can be viewed at the URL *http://server:port/daytime.html*, and the applet class will be pulled from *http://server:port/DaytimeApplet.class.*

Text-Based HTTP Communication

Let's start by implementing the lowest-common-denominator approach—text-based HTTP communication.

The servlet

For the `DaytimeApplet` to retrieve the current time from the server, it has to communicate with a servlet that returns the current time. Example 10-2 shows such a servlet. It responds to all GET and POST requests with a textual representation of the current time.

Example 10-2. The DaytimeServlet Supporting Basic HTTP Access

```
import java.io.*;
import java.util.*;
import javax.servlet.*;
import javax.servlet.http.*;

public class DaytimeServlet extends HttpServlet {

  public Date getDate() {
    return new Date();
  }

  public void doGet(HttpServletRequest req, HttpServletResponse res)
                               throws ServletException, IOException {
    res.setContentType("text/plain");
```

Example 10-2. The DaytimeServlet Supporting Basic HTTP Access (continued)

```
    PrintWriter out = res.getWriter();
    out.println(getDate().toString());
  }

  public void doPost(HttpServletRequest req, HttpServletResponse res)
                                throws ServletException, IOException {
    doGet(req, res);
  }
}
```

This servlet's class files should be placed in the standard location for servlets, *context_root/WEB-INF/classes.* Assuming they are placed in the default context, they can be accessed by any web browser using the URL *http://server:port/servlet/DaytimeServlet.*

Back to the applet

Now, for our `DaytimeApplet` to access this servlet, it must behave just like a browser and make an HTTP connection to the servlet URL, as the implementation of `getDateUsingHttpText()` in Example 10-3 shows.

Example 10-3. DaytimeApplet Getting the Time Using HTTP

```
import java.net.URL;                   // New addition
import com.oreilly.servlet.HttpMessage; // A support class, shown later

  private String getDateUsingHttpText() {
    try {
      // Construct a URL referring to the servlet
      URL url = new URL(getCodeBase(), "/servlet/DaytimeServlet");

      // Create a com.oreilly.servlet.HttpMessage to communicate with that URL
      HttpMessage msg = new HttpMessage(url);

      // Send a GET message to the servlet, with no query string
      // Get the response as an InputStream
      InputStream in = msg.sendGetMessage();

      // Wrap the InputStream with a DataInputStream
      DataInputStream result =
        new DataInputStream(new BufferedInputStream(in));

      // Read the first line of the response, which should be
      // a string representation of the current time
      String date = result.readLine();

      // Close the InputStream
      in.close();
```

Example 10-3. DaytimeApplet Getting the Time Using HTTP (continued)

```
      // Return the retrieved time
      return date;
    }
    catch (Exception e) {
      // If there was a problem, print to System.out
      // (typically the Java console) and return null
      e.printStackTrace();
      return null;
    }
  }
```

This method retrieves the current time on the server using a text-based HTTP connection. First, it creates a `URL` object that refers to the `DaytimeServlet` running on the server. The server host and port for this URL come from the applet's own `getCodeBase()` method. This guarantees that it matches the host and port from which the applet was downloaded. Then, the method creates an `HttpMessage` object to communicate with that URL. This object does all the dirty work involved in making the connection. The applet asks it to make a GET request of the `DaytimeServlet` and then reads the response from the returned `InputStream`.

The code for `HttpMessage` is shown in Example 10-4. It is loosely modeled after the `ServletMessage` class written by Rod McChesney.

Example 10-4. The HttpMessage Support Class

```
package com.oreilly.servlet;

import java.io.*;
import java.net.*;
import java.util.*;

public class HttpMessage {

  URL servlet = null;
  Hashtable headers = null;

  public HttpMessage(URL servlet) {
    this.servlet = servlet;
  }

  public InputStream sendGetMessage() throws IOException {
    return sendGetMessage(null);
  }

  public InputStream sendGetMessage(Properties args) throws IOException {
    String argString = "";  // default
```

Example 10-4. The HttpMessage Support Class (continued)

```
    if (args != null) {
      argString = "?" + toEncodedString(args);
    }
    URL url = new URL(servlet.toExternalForm() + argString);

    // Turn off caching
    URLConnection con = url.openConnection();
    con.setUseCaches(false);

    // Send headers
    sendHeaders(con);

    return con.getInputStream();
  }

  public InputStream sendPostMessage() throws IOException {
    return sendPostMessage(null);
  }

  public InputStream sendPostMessage(Properties args) throws IOException {
    String argString = "";  // default
    if (args != null) {
      argString = toEncodedString(args);  // notice no "?"
    }

    URLConnection con = servlet.openConnection();

    // Prepare for both input and output
    con.setDoInput(true);
    con.setDoOutput(true);

    // Turn off caching
    con.setUseCaches(false);

    // Work around a Netscape bug
    con.setRequestProperty("Content-Type",
                           "application/x-www-form-urlencoded");

    // Send headers
    sendHeaders(con);

    // Write the arguments as post data
    DataOutputStream out = new DataOutputStream(con.getOutputStream());
    out.writeBytes(argString);
    out.flush();
    out.close();
```

Example 10-4. The HttpMessage Support Class (continued)

```
    return con.getInputStream();
  }

  public InputStream sendPostMessage(Serializable obj) throws IOException {
    URLConnection con = servlet.openConnection();

    // Prepare for both input and output
    con.setDoInput(true);
    con.setDoOutput(true);

    // Turn off caching
    con.setUseCaches(false);

    // Set the content type to be application/x-java-serialized-object
    con.setRequestProperty("Content-Type",
                           "application/x-java-serialized-object");

    // Send headers
    sendHeaders(con);

    // Write the serialized object as post data
    ObjectOutputStream out = new ObjectOutputStream(con.getOutputStream());
    out.writeObject(obj);
    out.flush();
    out.close();

    return con.getInputStream();
  }

  public void setHeader(String name, String value) {
    if (headers == null) {
      headers = new Hashtable();
    }
    headers.put(name, value);
  }

  // Send the contents of the headers hashtable to the server
  private void sendHeaders(URLConnection con) {
    if (headers != null) {
      Enumeration enum = headers.keys();
      while (enum.hasMoreElements()) {
        String name = (String) enum.nextElement();
        String value = (String) headers.get(name);
        con.setRequestProperty(name, value);
      }
    }
  }
```

Example 10-4. The HttpMessage Support Class (continued)

```
  public void setCookie(String name, String value) {
    if (headers == null) {
      headers = new Hashtable();
    }
    String existingCookies = (String) headers.get("Cookie");
    if (existingCookies == null) {
      setHeader("Cookie", name + "=" + value);
    }
    else {
      setHeader("Cookie", existingCookies + "; " + name + "=" + value);
    }
  }

  public void setAuthorization(String name, String password) {
    String authorization = Base64Encoder.encode(name + ":" + password);
    setHeader("Authorization", "Basic " + authorization);
  }

  private String toEncodedString(Properties args) {
    StringBuffer buf = new StringBuffer();
    Enumeration names = args.propertyNames();
    while (names.hasMoreElements()) {
      String name = (String) names.nextElement();
      String value = args.getProperty(name);
      buf.append(URLEncoder.encode(name) + "=" + URLEncoder.encode(value));
      if (names.hasMoreElements()) buf.append("&");
    }
    return buf.toString();
  }
}
```

Some of you may have been expecting the `HttpMessage` class to establish a raw socket connection to the server and proceed to speak HTTP. This approach would certainly work, but it isn't necessary. The higher-level `java.net.URL` and `java.net.URLConnection` classes already provide this functionality in a convenient abstraction.

Let's do a quick walk-through of `HttpMessage`. `HttpMessage` is designed to communicate with just one URL, the URL given in its constructor. It can send multiple GET and/or POST requests to that URL, but it always communicates with just the one URL.

The code `HttpMessage` uses to send a GET message is fairly simple. First, `sendGetMessage()` creates a URL-encoded query string from the passed-in `java.util.Properties` list. It appends this query string to the saved URL, creating a new `URL` object. At this point, it could elect to use this new `URL` (named `url`) to communicate with the servlet. A call to `url.openStream()` would return an `InputStream` that contains the response. But, unfortunately for our purposes, by default all connections made using a `URL` object are cached. We don't want this—we want the current time, not the time of the last request. So `HttpMessage` has to turn caching off.*

The `URL` class doesn't directly support this low-level control, so `HttpMessage` gets the `URL` object's `URLConnection` and instructs it not to use caching. Finally, `HttpMessage` returns the `URLConnection` object's `InputStream`, which contains the servlet's response.

The code `HttpMessage` uses to send a POST request (`sendPostMessage()`) is similar. The major difference is that it directly writes the URL-encoded parameter information in the body of the request. This follows the protocol for how POST requests submit their information. The other difference is that `HttpMessage` manually sets the request's content type to `application/x-www-form-urlencoded`. This informs the server that the POST content contains parameter information.

We should mention that `HttpMessage` is a general-purpose class for HTTP communication. It doesn't have to be used by applets, and it doesn't have to connect to servlets. It's usable by any Java client that needs to connect to an HTTP resource. It's included in the `com.oreilly.servlet` package, though, because it's often useful for applet-servlet communication.

For the `HttpMessage` class to be usable by applets, it has to be made available for downloading along with the applet classes. This means it must be placed in the proper location under the web server's document root. For the Tomcat server, this location is *server_root/webapps/ROOT/com/oreilly/servlet*. We recommend you copy the class there from wherever you originally installed the `com.oreilly.servlet` package (perhaps *server_root/classes/com/oreilly/servlet*).

Note that `HttpMessage` has several set methods that can be used to send request headers, cookies, and basic authorization information to the server as part of the request. The `setHeader(String name, String value)` method adds a header to the request with the given name and value. If the header had been previously set, the new value replaces the old. The `setCookie(String name, String value)` method adds a request cookie with the given name and value. This method is particularly useful in getting around a session-tracking limitation for applets running within the Java Plug-In, as discussed in Chapter 7, *Session Tracking*. Lastly, the `setAuthorization(String name, String password)` method

* Actually, we could leave it up to the servlet to turn caching off, by having it set its `Pragma` header to `no-cache`. But it can't hurt to have it in the applet as well.

adds the given user credentials to the request, allowing applet access to password-protected pages. It uses the `com.oreilly.servlet.Base64Encoder` class not shown in this book but available at *http://www.servlets.com*. For all these methods, settings persist between requests, and the caller is responsible for ensuring there are no illegal characters in the name or value.

For secure communication from an applet, you can pass to `HttpMessage` a URL that begins `https`. It's that easy! (Just don't forget to have an HTTPS-enabled server listening on the server side.) This works only for applets, however, because the browser running the applet can help negotiate the HTTPS connection. For a nonapplet client the `URL` constructor will fail, complaining about an unknown HTTPS protocol. You can work around this by using the `com.oreilly.servlet.HttpsMessage` class available at *http://www.servlets.com*. It includes standalone HTTPS support contributed by Matt Towers. See *http://www.javaworld.com/javaworld/javatips/jw-javatip96.html* for a JavaWorld article describing its behavior.

Now, with all this code working together, we have an applet that retrieves the current time from its server using text-based HTTP applet-servlet communication. If you try it yourself, you should see the "HTTP text" date filled in, while the rest of the dates are still marked "unavailable."

Object-Based HTTP Communication

With a few modifications, we can have the `DaytimeApplet` receive the current time as a serialized `Date` object.

The servlet

For backward compatibility, let's change our `DaytimeServlet` to return a serialized `Date` only if the request asks for it by passing a `format` parameter with the value `object`. The code is given in Example 10-5.

Example 10-5. The DaytimeServlet Using HTTP to Serve an Object

```
import java.io.*;
import java.util.*;
import javax.servlet.*;
import javax.servlet.http.*;

public class DaytimeServlet extends HttpServlet {

  public Date getDate() {
    return new Date();
  }

  public void doGet(HttpServletRequest req, HttpServletResponse res)
                               throws ServletException, IOException {
```

Example 10-5. The DaytimeServlet Using HTTP to Serve an Object (continued)

```
    // If the client says "format=object" then
    // return the Date as a serialized object
    if ("object".equals(req.getParameter("format"))) {
      ObjectOutputStream out = new ObjectOutputStream(res.getOutputStream());
      out.writeObject(getDate());
    }
    // Otherwise send the Date as a normal string
    else {
      PrintWriter out = res.getWriter();
      out.println(getDate().toString());
    }
  }

  public void doPost(HttpServletRequest req, HttpServletResponse res)
                              throws ServletException, IOException {
    doGet(req, res);
  }
}
```

As the code shows, sending a serialized Java object is quite simple. This technique can be used to send any primitive types and/or any Java objects that implement the `Serializable` interface, including a `Vector` that contains `Serializable` objects. Multiple objects can also be written to the same `ObjectOutputStream`, as long as the class receiving the objects reads them in the same order and casts them to the same types.

You may notice that the servlet didn't set the content type of the response to indicate it contained a serialized Java object. The reason is that currently there are no standard MIME types to represent serialized objects. This doesn't really matter, though. A content type acts solely as an indication to the client of how to handle or display the response. If an applet already assumes it's receiving a specific serialized Java object, everything works fine. Sometimes, though, it's useful to use a custom MIME type (specific to your application), so that a servlet can indicate to an applet the contents of its response.

The applet

The applet code to retrieve the serialized `Date` object is very similar to the code to retrieve plain text. The `getDateUsingHttpObject()` method is shown in Example 10-6.

Example 10-6. The DaytimeApplet Using HTTP to Retrieve an Object

```
private String getDateUsingHttpObject() {
  try {
    // Construct a URL referring to the servlet
    URL url = new URL(getCodeBase(), "/servlet/DaytimeServlet");
```

Example 10-6. The DaytimeApplet Using HTTP to Retrieve an Object (continued)

```
      // Create a com.oreilly.servlet.HttpMessage to communicate with that URL
      HttpMessage msg = new HttpMessage(url);

      // Construct a Properties list to say format=object
      Properties props = new Properties();
      props.put("format", "object");

      // Send a GET message to the servlet, passing "props" as a query string
      // Get the response as an ObjectInputStream
      InputStream in = msg.sendGetMessage(props);
      ObjectInputStream result = new ObjectInputStream(in);

      // Read the Date object from the stream
      Object obj = result.readObject();
      Date date = (Date)obj;

      // Return the string representation of the Date
      return date.toString();
    }
    catch (Exception e) {
      // If there was a problem, print to System.out
      // (typically the Java console) and return null
      e.printStackTrace();
      return null;
    }
  }
```

There are two differences between this particular method and the `getDateUsingHttpText()` method. First, this method creates a `Properties` list to set the `format` parameter to the value `object`. This tells `DaytimeServlet` to return a serialized object. Second, the new method reads the returned content as an `Object`, using an `ObjectInputStream` and its `readObject()` method.

If the class being serialized is not part of the Java Core API (so it isn't already available to the applet), it too has to be made available in the proper location under the web server's document root. An applet can always receive an object's serialized contents, but it needs to download its class file to fully reconstruct the object.

Now the applet can retrieve the current time using both text-based and object-based HTTP communication. If you try it yourself now (with a web browser or applet viewer that supports JDK 1.1), you should see both the "HTTP text" and "HTTP object" fields filled in.

Posting a serialized object or file

Before we go on, we should look at one more (hitherto unmentioned) method from the `HttpMessage` class: `sendPostMessage(Serializable)`. This method helps an applet upload a serialized object to a servlet using the POST method. This object transfer isn't particularly useful to our daytime server example (and is kind of out of place here), but we mention it because it can come in handy when an applet needs to upload complicated data structures to its server. For example, an applet can upload a `Date` object, a `Person` object, or a `HighScore` array containing `Person` and `Date` objects. An applet can even upload an XML document, as a JDOM Document (*http://jdom.org*) or as a raw file. Just remember that when sending a file you should send the contents as a `byte[]` not a `File` object, because a `File` object holds only the file's name, not its contents. Example 10-7 contains the code for the `sendPostMessage(Serializable)` method.

Example 10-7. Posting a Serialized Object

```
// Uploads a serialized object with a POST request.
// Sets the content type to application/x-java-serialized-object.

public InputStream sendPostMessage(Serializable obj) throws IOException {
  URLConnection con = servlet.openConnection();

  // Prepare for both input and output
  con.setDoInput(true);
  con.setDoOutput(true);

  // Turn off caching
  con.setUseCaches(false);

  // Set the content type to be application/x-java-serialized-object
  con.setRequestProperty("Content-Type",
                         "application/x-java-serialized-object");

  // Write the serialized object as post data
  ObjectOutputStream out = new ObjectOutputStream(con.getOutputStream());
  out.writeObject(obj);
  out.flush();
  out.close();

  return con.getInputStream();
}
```

An applet uses `sendPostMessage(Serializable)` just as it uses `sendPostMessage(Properties)`. Here is the code for an applet that uploads any exceptions it encounters to a servlet:*

```
catch (Exception e) {
  URL url = new URL(getCodeBase(), "/servlet/ExceptionLogger");
```

* Normally whan an applet throws an unhandled exception, the browser records the exception stack trace to its Java console. This code has the applet effectively throw the exception to the server, where a server-side log of all exception stack traces can be stored and viewed by the applet's creator.

```
    HttpMessage msg = new HttpMessage(url);
    InputStream in = msg.sendPostMessage(e);
  }
```

The servlet, meanwhile, receives the `Exception` in its `doPost()` method like this:

```
ObjectInputStream objin = new ObjectInputStream(req.getInputStream());
Object obj = objin.readObject();
Exception e = (Exception) obj;
```

The servlet can receive the type of the uploaded object as the subtype (second half) of the content type. Note that this `sendPostMessage(Serializable)` method uploads just one object at a time and uploads only `Serializable` objects (that is, no primitive types).

Socket Communication

Now let's take a look at how an applet and servlet can communicate using non-HTTP socket communication.

The servlet

The servlet's role in this communication technique is that of a passive listener. Due to security restrictions, only the applet can initiate a socket connection. A servlet must be content to listen on a socket port and wait for an applet to connect. Generally speaking, a servlet should begin listening for applet connections in its `init()` method and stop listening in its `destroy()` method. In between, for every connection it receives, it should spawn a handler thread to communicate with the client.

With HTTP socket connections, these nitty-gritty details are managed by the web server. The server listens for incoming HTTP requests and dispatches them as appropriate, calling a servlet's `service()`, `doGet()`, or `doPost()` methods as necessary. But when a servlet opts not to use HTTP communication, the web server can't provide any help. The servlet acts, in essence, like its own server and thus has to manage the socket connections itself.

Okay, maybe we scared you a bit more than we had to there. The truth is that we can write a servlet superclass that abstracts away the details involved in managing socket connections. This class, which we call `DaemonHttpServlet`, can be extended by any servlet wanting to make itself available via non-HTTP socket communication.*

* The name *daemon* was chosen to refer to Unix daemons, programs that run in the background quietly handling certain events. And where did those programs get the daemon moniker? According to the *New Hacker's Dictionary*, it originally came "from the mythological meaning, [but was] later rationalized as the acronym 'Disk And Execution MONitor.'"

DaemonHttpServlet starts listening for client requests in its init() method and stops listening in its destroy() method. In between, for every connection it receives, it calls the abstract handleClient(Socket) method. This method should be implemented by any servlet that subclasses DaemonHttpServlet.

Example 10-8 shows how DaytimeServlet extends DaemonHttpServlet and implements handleClient() to make itself available via non-HTTP socket communication.

Example 10-8. HTTP Server

```
import java.io.*;
import java.net.*;
import java.util.*;
import javax.servlet.*;
import javax.servlet.http.*;

import com.oreilly.servlet.DaemonHttpServlet;

public class DaytimeServlet extends DaemonHttpServlet {

  public Date getDate() {
    return new Date();
  }

  public void init() throws ServletException {
    // As before, there's no need to call super.init() from the
    // no-arg init method, but you do need to call super.init(config) from
    // the older init(ServletConfig) method.  See Chapter 3 for details.
  }

  public void doGet(HttpServletRequest req, HttpServletResponse res)
                               throws ServletException, IOException {
    // If the client says "format=object" then
    // send the Date as a serialized object
    if ("object".equals(req.getParameter("format"))) {
      ObjectOutputStream out = new ObjectOutputStream(res.getOutputStream());
      out.writeObject(getDate());
    }
    // Otherwise send the Date as a normal ASCII string
    else {
      PrintWriter out = res.getWriter();
      out.println(getDate().toString());
    }
  }

  public void doPost(HttpServletRequest req, HttpServletResponse res)
                               throws ServletException, IOException {
```

Example 10-8. HTTP Server (continued)

```
    doGet(req, res);
  }

  public void destroy() {
    // Now, unlike before, if you override destroy() you have to call
    // super.destroy()
    super.destroy();
  }

  // Handle a client's socket connection by spawning a DaytimeConnection
  // thread.
  public void handleClient(Socket client) {
    new DaytimeConnection(this, client).start();
  }
}

class DaytimeConnection extends Thread {

  DaytimeServlet servlet;
  Socket client;

  DaytimeConnection(DaytimeServlet servlet, Socket client) {
    this.servlet = servlet;
    this.client = client;
    setPriority(NORM_PRIORITY - 1);
  }

  public void run() {
    try {
      // Read the first line sent by the client, as Latin-1 text
      BufferedReader in = new BufferedReader(
                          new InputStreamReader(
                          client.getInputStream(), "ISO-8859-1"));
      String line = in.readLine();

      // If it was "object" then return the Date as a serialized object
      if ("object".equals(line)) {
        ObjectOutputStream out =
          new ObjectOutputStream(client.getOutputStream());
        out.writeObject(servlet.getDate());
        out.close();
      }
      // Otherwise, send the Date as a normal string
      else {
        // Wrap a PrintStream around the Socket's OutputStream
        PrintStream out = new PrintStream(client.getOutputStream());
        out.println(servlet.getDate().toString());
```

Example 10-8. HTTP Server (continued)

```
        out.close();
      }

      // Be sure to close the connection
      client.close();
    }
    catch (IOException e) {
      servlet.log("IOException while handling client request", e);
    }
    catch (Exception e) {
      servlet.log("Exception while handling client request");
    }
  }
}
```

The `DaytimeServlet` class remains largely unchanged from its previous form. The major difference is that it extends `DaemonHttpServlet` and implements a `handleClient(Socket)` method that spawns a new `DaytimeConnection` thread. This `DaytimeConnection` instance bears the responsibility for handling a specific socket connection.

`DaytimeConnection` works as follows. When it is created, it saves a reference to the `DaytimeServlet`, so that it can call the servlet's `getDate()` method and a reference to the `Socket`, so that it can communicate with the client. `DaytimeConnection` also sets its running priority to one less than normal, to indicate that this communication can wait if necessary while other threads perform more time-critical work.

Immediately after it creates the `DaytimeConnection` thread, `DaytimeServlet` starts the thread, causing its `run()` method to be called. In this method, the `DaytimeConnection` communicates with the client using some unnamed (but definitely not HTTP) protocol. It begins by reading the first line sent by the client. If the line is `object`, it returns the current time as a serialized `Date` object. If the line is anything else, it returns the current time as a normal string. When it is done, it closes the connection.

The superclass

The low-level socket management is done in the `DaemonHttpServlet` class. Generally, this class can be used without modification, but it is useful to understand the internals. The code is shown in Example 10-9. Note it's written against Servlet API 2.0 to maintain backward compatibility.

Example 10-9. The DaemonHttpServlet Superclass

```
package com.oreilly.servlet;

import java.io.*;
import java.net.*;
import java.util.*;
import javax.servlet.*;
import javax.servlet.http.*;

public abstract class DaemonHttpServlet extends HttpServlet {

  protected int DEFAULT_PORT = 1313;  // not static or final
  private Thread daemonThread;

  public void init(ServletConfig config) throws ServletException {
    super.init(config);

    // Start a daemon thread
    try {
      daemonThread = new Daemon(this);
      daemonThread.start();
    }
    catch (Exception e) {
      getServletContext().log(e, "Problem starting socket server daemon thread");
    }
  }

  // Returns the socket port on which this servlet will listen.
  // A servlet can specify the port in three ways: by using the socketPort
  // init parameter, by setting the DEFAULT_PORT variable before calling
  // super.init(), or by overriding this method's implementation
  protected int getSocketPort() {
    try { return Integer.parseInt(getInitParameter("socketPort")); }
    catch (NumberFormatException e) { return DEFAULT_PORT; }
  }

  abstract public void handleClient(Socket client);

  public void destroy() {
    // Stop the daemon thread
    try {
      daemonThread.stop();
      daemonThread = null;
    }
    catch (Exception e) {
      getServletContext().log(e, "Problem stopping server socket daemon thread");
    }
  }
}
```

Example 10-9. The DaemonHttpServlet Superclass (continued)

```
// This work is broken into a helper class so that subclasses of
// DaemonHttpServlet can define their own run() method without problems.

class Daemon extends Thread {

  private ServerSocket serverSocket;
  private DaemonHttpServlet servlet;

  public Daemon(DaemonHttpServlet servlet) {
    this.servlet = servlet;
  }

  public void run() {
    try {
      // Create a server socket to accept connections
      serverSocket = new ServerSocket(servlet.getSocketPort());
    }
    catch (Exception e) {
      servlet.getServletContext().log(e, "Problem establishing server socket");
      return;
    }

    try {
      while (true) {
        // As each connection comes in, call the servlet's handleClient().
        // Note this method is blocking. It's the servlet's responsibility
        // to spawn a handler thread for long-running connections.
        try {
          servlet.handleClient(serverSocket.accept());
        }
        catch (IOException ioe) {
          servlet.getServletContext()
            .log(ioe, "Problem accepting client's socket connection");
        }
      }
    }
    catch (ThreadDeath e) {
      // When the thread is killed, close the server socket
      try {
        serverSocket.close();
      }
      catch (IOException ioe) {
        servlet.getServletContext().log(ioe, "Problem closing server socket");
      }
    }
  }
}
```

The `init()` method of `DaemonHttpServlet` creates and starts a new `Daemon` thread that is in charge of listening for incoming connections. The `destroy()` method stops the thread. This makes it imperative that any servlet subclassing `DaemonHttpServlet` call `super.init(config)` and `super.destroy()` if the servlet implements its own `init()` and `destroy()` methods. (A servlet written against Servlet API 2.1 and implementing the new no-argument `init()` doesn't need to call `super.init()`, but it does need to call `super.destroy()`.)

The `Daemon` thread begins by establishing a `ServerSocket` to listen on some specific socket port. Which socket port is determined with a call to the servlet's `getSocketPort()` method. The value returned is either the value of the init parameter `socketPort`, or, if that init parameter doesn't exist, the current value of the variable `DEFAULT_PORT`. A servlet may choose to override the `getSocketPort()` implementation if it so desires.

After establishing the `ServerSocket`, the `Daemon` thread waits for incoming requests with a call to `serverSocket.accept()`. This method is blocking—it stops this thread's execution until a client attaches to the server socket. When this happens, the `accept()` method returns a `Socket` object that the `Daemon` thread passes immediately to the servlet's `handleClient()` method. This `handleClient()` method usually spawns a handler thread and returns immediately, leaving the `Daemon` thread ready to accept another connection.

The server socket cleanup is equally as important as its setup. We have to be sure the server socket lives as long as the servlet, but no longer. To this end, the `destroy()` method of `DaemonHttpServlet` calls the `Daemon` thread's `stop()` method. This call doesn't immediately stop the `Daemon` thread, however. It just causes a `ThreadDeath` exception to be thrown in the `Daemon` thread at its current point of execution. The `Daemon` thread catches this exception and closes the server socket.

There are two caveats in writing a servlet that acts like a non-HTTP server. First, only one servlet at a time can listen to any particular socket port. This makes it vital that each daemon servlet choose its own socket port—by setting its `socketPort` init parameter, setting the `DEFAULT_PORT` variable before calling `super.init(config)`, or overriding `getSocketPort()` directly. Second, a daemon servlet must be loaded into its server and have its `init()` method called before it can accept incoming non-HTTP connections. Thus, you should either tell your server to load it at startup or be sure it is always accessed via HTTP before it is accessed directly.

The applet

The applet code to connect to the servlet using non-HTTP communication, primarily the `getDateUsingSocketText()` and `getDateUsingSocketObject()` methods, is shown in Example 10-10.

Example 10-10. The DaytimeApplet Getting the Time Using a Socket Connection

```
import java.net.Socket;                   // New addition

static final int DEFAULT_PORT = 1313;     // New addition

private int getSocketPort() {
  try { return Integer.parseInt(getParameter("socketPort")); }
  catch (NumberFormatException e) { return DEFAULT_PORT; }
}

private String getDateUsingSocketText() {
  Socket socket = null;
  try {
    // Establish a socket connection with the servlet
    socket = new Socket(getCodeBase().getHost(), getSocketPort());

    // Print an empty line, indicating we want the time as plain text
    PrintStream out = new PrintStream(socket.getOutputStream());
    out.print("\r\n");  // since println() behavior varies by system
    out.flush();

    // Read the first line of the response
    // It should contain the current time
    InputStream in = socket.getInputStream();
    DataInputStream result =
      new DataInputStream(new BufferedInputStream(in));
    String date = result.readLine();

    // Return the retrieved string
    return date;
  }
  catch (Exception e) {
    // If there was a problem, print to System.out
    // (typically the Java console) and return null
    e.printStackTrace();
    return null;
  }
  finally {
    // Always close the connection
    // This code executes no matter how the try block completes
    if (socket != null) {
      try { socket.close(); }
```

Example 10-10. The DaytimeApplet Getting the Time Using a Socket Connection (continued)

```
      catch (IOException ignored) { }
    }
  }
}

private String getDateUsingSocketObject() {
  Socket socket = null;
  try {
    // Establish a socket connection with the servlet
    Socket socket = new Socket(getCodeBase().getHost(), getSocketPort());

    // Print a line saying "object", indicating we want the time as
    // a serialized Date object
    PrintStream out = new PrintStream(socket.getOutputStream());
    out.print("object\r\n");  // since println() behavior varies by system
    out.flush();

    // Create an ObjectInputStream to read the response
    InputStream in = socket.getInputStream();
    ObjectInputStream result =
      new ObjectInputStream(new BufferedInputStream(in));

    // Read an object, and cast it to be a Date
    Object obj = result.readObject();
    Date date = (Date)obj;

    // Return a string representation of the retrieved Date
    return date.toString();
  }
  catch (Exception e) {
    // If there was a problem, print to System.out
    // (typically the Java console) and return null
    e.printStackTrace();
    return null;
  }
  finally {
    // Always close the connection
    // This code executes no matter how the try block completes
    if (socket != null) {
      try { socket.close(); }
      catch (IOException ignored) { }
    }
  }
}
```

For both these methods, the applet begins by creating a `Socket` that is used to communicate with the servlet. To do this, it needs to know both the hostname and the port number on which the servlet is listening. Determining the host is easy—it has to be the same host from which it was downloaded, accessible with a call to `getCodeBase().getHost()`. The port is harder, as it depends entirely on the servlet to which this applet is connecting. This applet uses the `getSocketPort()` method to make this determination. The implementation of `getSocketPort()` shown here returns the value of the applet's `socketPort` parameter or (if that parameter isn't given) returns the value of the `DEFAULT_PORT` variable.

Once it has established a socket connection, the applet follows an unnamed protocol to communicate with the servlet. This protocol requires that the applet send one line to indicate whether it wants the current time as text or as an object. If the line says `object`, it receives an object. If it says anything else, it receives plain text. After sending this line, the applet can read the response as appropriate.

The applet and servlet could continue to communicate using this socket. That's one of the major advantages of not using HTTP communication. But, in this case, the applet got what it wanted and just needs to close the connection. It performs this close in a `finally` block. Putting the close here guarantees that the connection is closed whether the `try` throws an exception or not.

With the addition of these two methods our applet is nearly complete. If you run it now, you should see that all of the fields except "RMI object" contain dates.

RMI Communication

Earlier in this chapter, we pointed out that one of the reasons not to use RMI communication is that it's complicated. Although that's true, it's also true that with the help of another servlet superclass, the code required for a servlet to make itself available via RMI communication can be ridiculously simple. First, we'll lead you through the step-by-step instructions on how to make a servlet a remote object. Then, after you've seen how simple and easy that is, we'll explain all the work going on behind the scenes.

The servlet

To begin with, all RMI remote objects must implement a specific interface. This interface does two things: it declares which methods of the remote object are to be made available to remote clients, and it extends the `Remote` interface to indicate it's an interface for a remote object. For our `DaytimeServlet`, we can write the `DaytimeServer` interface shown in Example 10-11.

Example 10-11. The DaytimeServer Interface

```
import java.util.Date;
import java.rmi.Remote;
import java.rmi.RemoteException;

public interface DaytimeServer extends Remote {
  public Date getDate() throws RemoteException;
}
```

This interface declares that our `DaytimeServlet` makes its `getDate()` method available to remote clients. Notice that the `getDate()` signature has been altered slightly—it now throws a `RemoteException`. Every method made available via RMI must declare that it throws this exception. Although the method itself may not throw the exception, it can be thrown by the system to indicate a network service failure.

The code for `DaytimeServlet` remains mostly unchanged from its original version. In fact, the only changes are that it now implements `DaytimeServer` and extends `com.oreilly.servlet.RemoteHttpServlet`, the superclass that allows this servlet to remain so unchanged. The servlet also implements a `destroy()` method that calls `super.destroy()`. It's true that this method is perfectly useless in this example, but it points out that any `destroy()` method implemented in a remote servlet must call `super.destroy()` to give the `RemoteHttpServlet` object's `destroy()` method a chance to terminate RMI communication. Example 10-12 shows the new `DaytimeServlet` code.

Example 10-12. The DaytimeServlet Now Supporting RMI Access

```
import java.io.*;
import java.net.*;
import java.util.*;
import javax.servlet.*;
import javax.servlet.http.*;

import com.oreilly.servlet.RemoteHttpServlet;          // New addition

public class DaytimeServlet extends RemoteHttpServlet  // New addition
                            implements DaytimeServer { // New addition

  // The single method from DaytimeServer
  // Note: the throws clause isn't necessary here
  public Date getDate() {
    return new Date();
  }

  public void init(ServletConfig config) throws ServletException {
    super.init(config);
```

Example 10-12. The DaytimeServlet Now Supporting RMI Access (continued)

```
    // Additional code could go here
  }

  public void doGet(HttpServletRequest req, HttpServletResponse res)
                              throws ServletException, IOException {
    // If the client says "format=object" then
    // send the Date as a serialized object
    if ("object".equals(req.getParameter("format"))) {
      ObjectOutputStream out = new ObjectOutputStream(res.getOutputStream());
      out.writeObject(getDate());
    }
    // Otherwise send the Date as a normal ASCII string
    else {
      PrintWriter out = res.getWriter();
      out.println(getDate().toString());
    }
  }

  public void doPost(HttpServletRequest req, HttpServletResponse res)
                                  throws ServletException, IOException {
    doGet(req, res);
  }

  public void destroy() {
    // If you override destroy() you have to call super.destroy()
    super.destroy();
  }
}
```

So that's how to write a remote object servlet. Compiling a remote object servlet is the same as for every other servlet, with one additional step. After compiling the servlet source code, you now have to compile the servlet class with the RMI compiler *rmic*. The RMI compiler takes a remote object's class file and generates stub and skeleton versions of the class. These classes work behind the scenes to enable RMI communication. You don't need to worry about the details, but you should know that the stub helps the client invoke methods on the remote object and the skeleton helps the server handle those invocations.

Using *rmic* is similar to using *javac*. For this example you can compile `DaytimeServlet` with the following command:

```
% rmic DaytimeServlet
```

Notice that you provide *rmic* with a Java class name—not a file—to compile. Thus, if the servlet to compile is part of a package it should be given to *rmic* as *`package.name.ServletName`*. The *rmic* program can take a classpath to search with the `-classpath` parameter, as well as a destination directory for the stub and skeleton files with the `-d` parameter.

After executing the preceding *rmic* command, you should see two new class files: `DaytimeServlet_Stub.class` and `DaytimeServlet_Skel.class`. We'll tell you what to do with these in just a minute. First, you should know that you don't have to rerun the RMI compiler every time you modify the remote servlet's code. This is because the stub and skeleton classes are built in terms of the servlet's interface, not its implementation of that interface. Accordingly, you need to regenerate them only when you modify the `DaytimeServer` interface (or your equivalent interface).

Now, for the final step in writing a remote servlet: copying a few class files to the server's document root, where they can be downloaded by an applet. There are two class files that need to be downloaded: the stub class `DaytimeServlet_Stub.class` and the remote interface class `DaytimeServer.class`. The client (in this case the applet) needs the stub class to perform its half of the RMI communication, and the stub class itself uses the remote interface class. Be aware that the servlet needs to use these classes, too, so copy them to the server's document root and leave them in the server's classpath.* Figure 10-2 shows where all the server files go.

That's it! If you follow these instructions you should be able to get a remote servlet operating in short order. Now let's look at the `RemoteHttpServlet` class and see what's going on behind the scenes.

The superclass

A remote object needs to do two things to prepare itself for RMI communication: it needs to export itself and register itself. When a remote object exports itself, it begins listening on a port for incoming method invocation requests. When a remote object registers itself, it tells a registry server its name and port number, so that clients can locate it (essentially, find out its port number) and communicate with it. These two tasks are handled by the `RemoteHttpServlet` class, shown in Example 10-13.

* Managing multiple class files can become a serious headache during development. On a Unix system, you can use soft links to simplify the task. Or, on any system, you can implement a more general-purpose solution: change the server's classpath to include *server_root/webapps/ROOT/classes*. (Notice that's not *WEB-INF/classes*.) Put the interface class and stub class in there. Then the server can find them in its new classpath and the applet's codebase can be set to */classes* to find them as well.

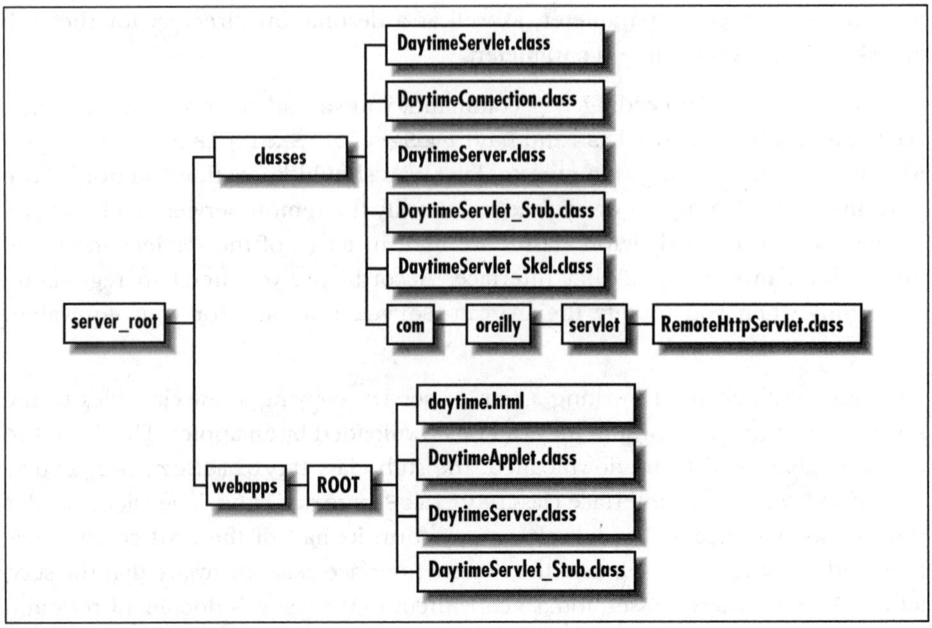

Figure 10-2. File locations for RMI communication

Example 10-13. The RemoteHttpServlet Superclass

```
package com.oreilly.servlet;

import java.io.*;
import java.net.*;
import java.rmi.*;
import java.rmi.server.*;
import java.rmi.registry.*;
import java.util.*;
import javax.servlet.*;
import javax.servlet.http.*;

public abstract class RemoteHttpServlet extends HttpServlet
                                       implements Remote {

  protected Registry registry;

  public void init(ServletConfig config) throws ServletException {
    super.init(config);
    try {
      // Export ourself
      UnicastRemoteObject.exportObject(this);
      // Register ourself
      bind();
    }
```

Example 10-13. The RemoteHttpServlet Superclass (continued)

```
    catch (RemoteException e) {
      getServletContext().log(e, "Problem binding to RMI registry");
    }
  }

  public void destroy() {
    // Unregister ourself
    unbind();
  }

  // Returns the name under which we are to be registered
  protected String getRegistryName() {
    // First name choice is the "registryName" init parameter
    String name = getInitParameter("registryName");
    if (name != null) return name;

    // Fallback choice is the name of this class
    return this.getClass().getName();
  }

  // Returns the port on which the registry server is listening
  // (or should be listening)
  protected int getRegistryPort() {
    // First port choice is the "registryPort" init parameter
    try { return Integer.parseInt(getInitParameter("registryPort")); }

    // Fallback choice is the default registry port (1099)
    catch (NumberFormatException e) { return Registry.REGISTRY_PORT; }
  }

  protected void bind() {
    // Try to find the appropriate registry already running
    try {
      registry = LocateRegistry.getRegistry(getRegistryPort());
      registry.list();  // Verify it's alive and well
    }
    catch (Exception e) {
      // Couldn't get a valid registry
      registry = null;
    }

    // If we couldn't find it, we need to create it.
    // (Equivalent to running "rmiregistry")
    if (registry == null) {
      try {
        registry = LocateRegistry.createRegistry(getRegistryPort());
      }
      catch (Exception e) {
```

Example 10-13. The RemoteHttpServlet Superclass (continued)

```
        log("Could not get or create RMI registry on port " +
            getRegistryPort() + ": " + e.getMessage());
        return;
      }
    }

    // If we get here, we must have a valid registry.
    // Now register this servlet instance with that registry.
    // "Rebind" to replace any other objects using our name.
    try {
      registry.rebind(getRegistryName(), this);
    }
    catch (Exception e) {
      log("Could not bind to RMI registry: " + e.getMessage());
      return;
    }
  }

  protected void unbind() {
    try {
      if (registry != null) registry.unbind(getRegistryName());
    }
    catch (Exception e) {
      getServletContext().log(e, "Problem unbinding from RMI registry");
    }
  }
}
```

If you've ever used or read about RMI before, you've probably seen remote objects that extend the `java.rmi.server.UnicastRemoteObject` class. This is the standard—and, in fact, recommended—way to write a remote object. The `RemoteHttpServlet` class, however, doesn't extend `UnicastRemoteObject`; it extends `HttpServlet`. As you may know, Java doesn't support multiple inheritance. This means that `RemoteHttpServlet` has to choose to extend either `UnicastRemoteObject` or `HttpServlet`—even though it needs functionality from both classes. It's a difficult choice. Whichever class `RemoteHttpServlet` doesn't extend it has to basically reimplement on its own. In the end, we have extended `HttpServlet` because it is easier to rewrite the functionality of `UnicastRemoteObject` than that of `HttpServlet`.

This rewrite requires `RemoteHttpServlet` to do two things it wouldn't have to if it extended `UnicastRemoteObject`. It must declare that it implements the `Remote` interface. All remote objects must implement this interface, but normally, by extending `UnicastRemoteObject`, a class gets this for free. The price for going it alone isn't bad, as the `Remote` interface doesn't actually define any methods. An object declares it implements `Remote` to be treated as a remote object.

The second thing RemoteHttpServlet has to do is manually export itself. Normally, this is performed automatically in the UnicastRemoteObject() constructor. But again, doing this without that constructor is not a problem. The UnicastRemoteObject class has a static exportObject(Remote) method that any Remote object can use to export itself. RemoteHttpServlet uses this method and exports itself with this single line:

```
UnicastRemoteObject.exportObject(this);
```

Those two steps, implementing Remote and exporting itself, are done by RemoteHttpServlet in lieu of extending UnicastRemoteObject.*

The rest of the RemoteHttpServlet code involves registering and unregistering itself with an RMI registry. As we said before, an RMI registry server acts as a location where clients can locate server objects. A remote object (server object) registers itself with the registry under a certain name. Clients can then go to the registry to look up the object by that name. To make itself available to clients then, our servlet has to find (or create) a registry server and register itself with that server under a specific name. In registry parlance, this is called *binding to the registry*. RemoteHttpServlet performs this binding with its bind() method, called from within its init() method.

The bind() method uses two support methods, getRegistryPort() and getRegistryName(), to determine the port on which the servlet should be running and the name under which the servlet should be registered. With the current implementations, the port is fetched from the registryPort init parameter, or it defaults to 1099. The name is taken from the registryName init parameter or defaults to the servlet's class name—in this case, DaytimeServlet.

Let's step through the bind() method. It begins by using the following code to try to find an appropriate registry that is already running:

```
registry = LocateRegistry.getRegistry(getRegistryPort());
registry.list();
```

The first line attempts to get the registry running on the given port. The second asks the registry to list its currently registered objects. If both calls succeed, we have a valid registry. If either call throws an Exception, the bind() method

* To be absolutely correct, there is more we need to do. According to the java.rmi.remote.UnicastRemoteObject documentation, "If UnicastRemoteObject is not extended, the implementation class must then assume the responsibility for the correct semantics of the hashCode, equals, and toString methods inherited from the Object class, so that they behave appropriately for remote objects." According to the java.rmi.remote.RemoteRef documentation, "These methods should guarantee that two remote object stubs that refer to the same remote object will have the same hashcode (in order to support remote objects as keys in hash tables)." Implementing the mechanism to support this guarantee is fairly difficult and, we believe, not commonly necessary for applet-servlet communication; thus, we've taken the liberty of shirking this responsibility with RemoteHttpServlet.

determines there is no valid registry and creates one itself. It does this with the following line of code:

```
registry = LocateRegistry.createRegistry(getRegistryPort());
```

After this, the `bind()` method should have either found or created a registry server. If it failed in getting the registry and failed again in creating it, it returns and the servlet remains unregistered. `RemoteHttpServlet` next binds itself to the registry using this line of code:

```
registry.rebind(getRegistryName(), this);
```

It uses the `Registry.rebind()` method instead of the `Registry.bind()` method to indicate that this binding should replace any previous binding using our name. This binding persists until the servlet is destroyed, at which time the `destroy()` method of `RemoteHttpServlet` calls its `unbind()` method. The code `unbind()` uses to unbind from the registry is remarkably simple:

```
if (registry != null) registry.unbind(getRegistryName());
```

It simply asks the registry to unbind its name.

Where to Run the Registry?

The commonly accepted way to run an RMI registry server is with the standalone Java program *rmiregistry*. We recommend, however, that you don't run *rmiregistry* and instead let the `RemoteHttpServlet` create the registry itself. It's easier and it's more efficient. The first servlet that needs the registry can create the registry. And, by starting the registry within a servlet, the registry runs using the same JVM as the servlet. That makes it possible to use just one JVM for the server, all of its servlets (the remote objects), and the registry. In fact, some application servers will automatically run a registry within their own JVM on startup.

It's also possible to avoid running a registry at all, using servlets. A client can connect to a special servlet using HTTP and request for a given remote object (using a parameter), and the servlet can return in its response data a serialized stub for the remote object—the same thing the registry would normally return. Using a servlet instead of *rmiregistry* allows the servlet to implement a security policy restricting who can look up objects, lets the servlet give each client a reference to a different remote object should it so choose, and (since the servlet can construct the remote object as part of the request handling) allows the remote object to be available even before it's created.

Please note that a remote servlet must be loaded into its server and have its `init()` method called before it is ready for RMI communication. Just as with a daemon servlet, you should either tell your server to load it at startup or be sure it is always accessed via HTTP before it is accessed directly.

The applet

Now let's turn our attention from the server and focus it on the client. The code our `DaytimeApplet` uses to invoke the `getDate()` method of our new `DaytimeServlet` is shown in Example 10-14.

Example 10-14. The DaytimeApplet Getting the Time Using RMI

```
import java.rmi.*;              // New addition
import java.rmi.registry.*;  // New addition

private String getRegistryHost() {
  return getCodeBase().getHost();
}

private int getRegistryPort() {
  try { return Integer.parseInt(getParameter("registryPort")); }
  catch (NumberFormatException e) { return Registry.REGISTRY_PORT; }
}

private String getRegistryName() {
  String name = getParameter("registryName");
  if (name == null) {
    name = "DaytimeServlet";  // default
  }
  return name;
}

private String getDateUsingRMIObject() {
  try {
    Registry registry =
      LocateRegistry.getRegistry(getRegistryHost(), getRegistryPort());
    DaytimeServer daytime =
      (DaytimeServer)registry.lookup(getRegistryName());
    return daytime.getDate().toString();
  }
  catch (ClassCastException e) {
    System.out.println("Retrieved object was not a DaytimeServer: " +
                       e.getMessage());
  }
  catch (NotBoundException e) {
    System.out.println(getRegistryName() + " not bound: " + e.getMessage());
  }
  catch (RemoteException e) {
    System.out.println("Hit remote exception: " + e.getMessage());
  }
```

Example 10-14. The DaytimeApplet Getting the Time Using RMI (continued)

```
  catch (Exception e) {
    System.out.println("Problem getting DaytimeServer reference: " +
                       e.getClass().getName() + ": " + e.getMessage());
  }
  return null;
}
```

The first three methods are support methods. `getRegistryHost()` returns the host on which the registry server should be running. This must always be the host from which the applet was downloaded. `getRegistryPort()` returns the port on which the registry server should be listening. It's normally the default registry port 1099, though it can be overridden with the `registryPort` parameter. `getRegistryName()` returns the name under which the servlet should have been registered. It defaults to `DaytimeServlet`, but it can be overridden with the `registryName` parameter.

The actual lookup of the remote servlet object and invocation of its `getDate()` method occur in these three lines of the `getDateUsingRMIObject()` method:

```
Registry registry =
  LocateRegistry.getRegistry(getRegistryHost(), getRegistryPort());
DaytimeServer daytime =
  (DaytimeServer)registry.lookup(getRegistryName());
return daytime.getDate().toString();
```

The first line locates the registry for the given host and the given port. The second line uses this registry to look up the remote object registered under the given name, in the process casting the object to a `DaytimeServer` object. The third line invokes this object's `getDate()` method and receives a serialized `Date` object in return. Then, in the same line, it returns the `String` representation of that `Date`.

The rest of the `getDateUsingRMIObject()` method handles the exceptions that could occur. It catches a `ClassCastException` if the retrieved object is not a `DaytimeServer`, a `NotBoundException` if the registry has no object registered under the given name, and a `RemoteException` if there's a network service failure. It catches a general `Exception`, in case there's some other problem.

You may be wondering why `DaytimeApplet` uses `Registry.lookup(String)` instead of `java.rmi.Naming.lookup(String)` to retrieve its reference to the remote servlet. There's really no reason: it's simply a matter of personal taste. It would work as well to replace the first two lines in `getDateUsingRMIObject()` with the following code:

```
DaytimeServer daytime =
  (DaytimeServer)Naming.lookup("rmi://" + getRegistryHost() +
                               ":" + getRegistryPort() +
                               "/" + getRegistryName());
```

That's it for the fifth and final method of `DaytimeApplet`. Go ahead and run the applet now. Do you see every date field nicely filled in? You shouldn't. You should instead see empty values for the socket communication options. If you remember, we removed support for socket communication when we made `DaytimeServlet` a remote object. Now let's put socket communication back in.

A full-service servlet

What we need now is a single servlet that can make itself available via HTTP communication, non-HTTP socket communication, and RMI communication. A servlet of this sort can extend a new superclass, `com.oreilly.servlet.RemoteDaemonHttpServlet`, implementing the capabilities discussed so far for both a `RemoteHttpServlet` and a `DaemonHttpServlet`.

Here's the code that declares this full-service servlet:

```
import java.io.*;
import java.net.*;
import java.util.*;
import javax.servlet.*;
import javax.servlet.http.*;

import com.oreilly.servlet.RemoteDaemonHttpServlet;

public class DaytimeServlet extends RemoteDaemonHttpServlet
                            implements DaytimeServer {

  public Date getDate() {
    return new Date();
  }

  // The rest is unchanged
```

This code is almost the same as Example 10-8. It's basically that example rewritten to declare that it extends `RemoteDaemonHttpServlet` and that it implements `DaytimeServer`.

The code for the `RemoteDaemonHttpServlet` superclass also nearly matches the code for `RemoteHttpServlet`. There are just two changes: it extends `DaemonHttpServlet` instead of `HttpServlet`, and its `destroy()` method first calls `super.destroy()`:

```
package com.oreilly.servlet;

import java.io.*;
import java.net.*;
import java.rmi.*;
import java.rmi.server.*;
```

```
import java.rmi.registry.*;
import java.util.*;
import javax.servlet.*;
import javax.servlet.http.*;

public abstract class RemoteDaemonHttpServlet extends DaemonHttpServlet
                                              implements Remote {

  public void destroy() {
    super.destroy();
    unbind();
  }

  // The rest is unchanged
```

Now our `DaytimeApplet` can connect to this revised remote daemon servlet and produce the full and complete output shown earlier in Figure 10-1.

Chat Server

The daytime server example from the last section demonstrated the nuts and bolts of using each of the three communication techniques for applet-servlet communication. It didn't take advantage, though, of the persistence gains when using socket communication. Nor did it show off the simplicity of RMI communication or the elegance of RMI callbacks (where the servlet can invoke methods of the applet). It also didn't provide a compelling reason for why one servlet should support all the communication techniques—there was no state to maintain or complicated code base to collect in one location. So, before we end our discussion of applet-servlet communication, let's look at a more sophisticated example: a chat server, implemented as a servlet, that supports clients connecting via HTTP, non-HTTP sockets, and RMI.

We'll build this chat server using all three communication techniques so that it can take advantage of the best, most efficient solution for each client. For example, when the client supports RMI, the servlet can be treated as a remote object, and (where possible) it can treat the applet as a remote object, too. When the client doesn't support RMI but can support direct socket communication, the chat server can utilize socket persistence and communicate with the client using a non-HTTP socket protocol. And, of course, when all else fails, the chat server can fall back to using HTTP. It would rather not fall back, because HTTP, being stateless, requires that the client poll for updates. But for many clients, HTTP is the only choice.

The chat server is implemented as a single class with a single instantiation because it has a large amount of associated state and a fair amount of code that would otherwise have to be repeated. To separate it into three classes, one for each protocol, would demand excessive interserver communication and replicate the core chat server code three times. Implementing the chat server as a servlet provides a simple way for one object to make itself available via all three communication techniques. By being an HTTP servlet, it has built-in HTTP support. And by extending the `RemoteDaemonHttpServlet` class, it can also easily gain support for non-HTTP socket and RMI communication.

Note that although you'll see the code in its entirety, we won't be fully explaining each and every line. To do so would extend this chapter beyond a reasonable length, assuming we aren't there already. Therefore, we'll explain the issues as they concern applet-servlet communication and rely on you to examine the code to understand all the details.

The Design

Figure 10-3 shows the chat applet in action. Notice that it uses a large `TextArea` component to display the running conversation, with a small `TextInput` component underneath where the user can post a new single-line message. As each contributor composes a message, it's sent to the chat server and distributed to the other chat clients in various ways.

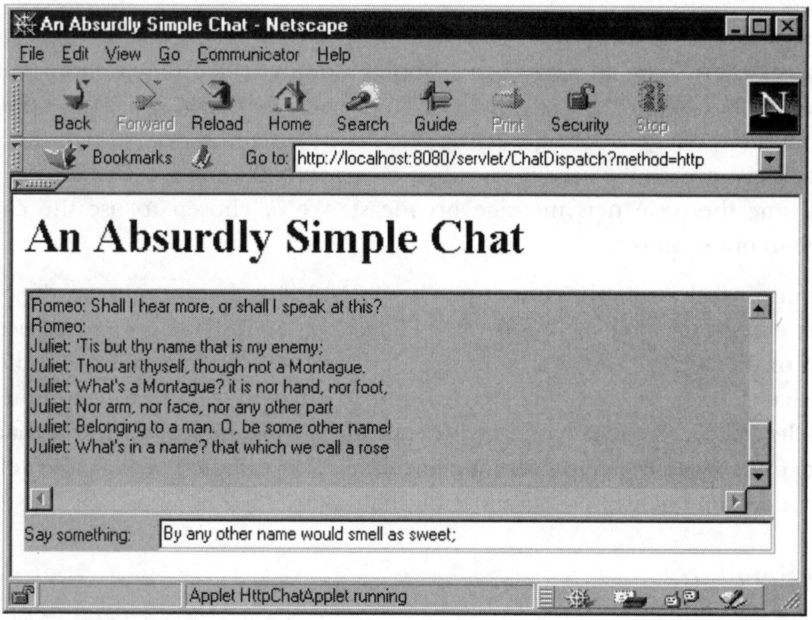

Figure 10-3. The chat applet in action

HTTP chat clients post their messages to the server using the HTTP POST method. The applet takes the new message from the `TextInput` component when the user hits Enter, URL-encodes the message, and posts it to the servlet as a message parameter. It's all very straightforward. What is a bit more complicated is how an HTTP chat client manages to get the other clients' messages. It uses the HTTP GET method to receive each message, but it has a problem: it doesn't know when exactly there's a new message to get. This is the problem with a unidirectional request/response communication paradigm. The client has to either periodically poll for updates or simulate bidirectional communication by making a series of blocking GET requests. By that we mean the chat client initiates a GET request that blocks until the server decides it's time to return something. For our example, we implement this simulated bidirectional communication.

Socket chat clients, for the sake of convenience, post their messages to the server the same way HTTP chat clients do, with the HTTP POST method. They could post their messages using raw socket connections, but only with a marginal gain in efficiency that, at least in this case, doesn't outweigh the increased complexity. These socket clients, however, do use raw sockets to get messages from the other clients, replacing the simulated bidirectional communication with actual bidirectional communication. As each new message comes in to the servlet, it's sent right away from the servlet to the socket chat clients across plain-text socket connections.

RMI chat clients perform their POSTs and their GETs using method invocations. To post each new message, the applet simply calls the remote servlet's `broadcastMessage(String)` method. To get new messages, it has two options. It can call the servlet's blocking `getNextMessage()` method or, through the use of callbacks, it can ask the servlet to call its own `setNextMessage(String)` method every time there's a new message broadcast. We've chosen to use the callback option in our example.

In front of all these applets is a dispatch servlet. It lets the user choose the applet-servlet communication technique (HTTP, socket, or RMI) she wants to use and, based on her choice, generates a page that contains the appropriate applet. It's true that a single applet could be written to support all three techniques and autoselect between them based on its runtime environment, but to do that here would unnecessarily complicate our example. The dispatch servlet also tells the applet the name of its user, but more on that later.

The Servlet

The full listings for the `ChatServer` interface and the `ChatServlet` class that implements it are given in Example 10-15 and Example 10-16.

Example 10-15. The ChatServer Interface, Implemented by ChatServlet

```
import java.rmi.Remote;
import java.rmi.RemoteException;

public interface ChatServer extends Remote {
  public String getNextMessage() throws RemoteException;
  public void broadcastMessage(String message) throws RemoteException;

  public void addClient(ChatClient client) throws RemoteException;
  public void deleteClient(ChatClient client) throws RemoteException;
}
```

Example 10-16. A Full-Service Chat Server/Servlet

```
import java.io.*;
import java.net.*;
import java.rmi.*;
import java.util.*;
import javax.servlet.*;
import javax.servlet.http.*;

import com.oreilly.servlet.RemoteDaemonHttpServlet;

public class ChatServlet extends RemoteDaemonHttpServlet
                         implements ChatServer {

  // source acts as the distributor of new messages
  MessageSource source = new MessageSource();

  // socketClients holds references to all the socket-connected clients
  Vector socketClients = new Vector();

  // rmiClients holds references to all the RMI clients
  Vector rmiClients = new Vector();

  // doGet() returns the next message. It blocks until there is one.
  public void doGet(HttpServletRequest req, HttpServletResponse res)
                               throws ServletException, IOException {
    res.setContentType("text/plain");
    PrintWriter out = res.getWriter();

    // Return the next message (blocking)
    out.println(getNextMessage());
  }

  // doPost() accepts a new message and broadcasts it to all
  // the currently listening HTTP, socket, and RMI clients.
  public void doPost(HttpServletRequest req, HttpServletResponse res)
                               throws ServletException, IOException {
```

Example 10-16. A Full-Service Chat Server/Servlet (continued)

```
    // Accept the new message as the "message" parameter
    String message = req.getParameter("message");

    // Broadcast it to all listening clients
    if (message != null) broadcastMessage(message);

    // Set the status code to indicate there will be no response
    res.setStatus(res.SC_NO_CONTENT);
  }

  // getNextMessage() returns the next new message.
  // It blocks until there is one.
  public String getNextMessage() {
    // Create a message sink to wait for a new message from the
    // message source.
    return new MessageSink().getNextMessage(source);
  }

  // broadcastMessage() informs all currently listening clients that there
  // is a new message. Causes all calls to getNextMessage() to unblock.
  public void broadcastMessage(String message) {
    // Send the message to all the HTTP-connected clients by giving the
    // message to the message source
    source.sendMessage(message);

    // Directly send the message to all the socket-connected clients
    Enumeration enum = socketClients.elements();
    while (enum.hasMoreElements()) {
      Socket client = null;
      try {
        client = (Socket)enum.nextElement();
        PrintStream out = new PrintStream(client.getOutputStream());
        out.println(message);
      }
      catch (IOException e) {
        // Problem with a client, close and remote it
        try {
          if (client != null) client.close();
        }
        catch (IOException ignored) { }
        socketClients.removeElement(client);
      }
    }

    // Directly send the message to all RMI clients
    enum = rmiClients.elements();
    while (enum.hasMoreElements()) {
      ChatClient chatClient = null;
```

Example 10-16. A Full-Service Chat Server/Servlet (continued)

```
      try {
        chatClient = (ChatClient)enum.nextElement();
        chatClient.setNextMessage(message);
      }
      catch (RemoteException e) {
        // Problem communicating with a client, remove it
        deleteClient(chatClient);
      }
    }
  }

  protected int getSocketPort() {
    // We listen on port 2428 (look at a phone to see why)
    return 2428;
  }

  public void handleClient(Socket client) {
    // We have a new socket client. Add it to our list.
    socketClients.addElement(client);
  }

  public void addClient(ChatClient client) {
    // We have a new RMI client. Add it to our list.
    rmiClients.addElement(client);
  }

  public void deleteClient(ChatClient client) {
    // Remote the specified client from our list.
    rmiClients.removeElement(client);
  }
}

// MessageSource acts as the source for new messages.
// Clients interested in receiving new messages can
// observe this object.
class MessageSource extends Observable {
  public void sendMessage(String message) {
    setChanged();
    notifyObservers(message);
  }
}

// MessageSink acts as the receiver of new messages.
// It listens to the source.
class MessageSink implements Observer {

  String message = null;  // set by update() and read by getNextMessage()
```

Example 10-16. A Full-Service Chat Server/Servlet (continued)

```
  // Called by the message source when it gets a new message
  synchronized public void update(Observable o, Object arg) {
    // Get the new message
    message = (String)arg;

    // Wake up our waiting thread
    notify();
  }

  // Gets the next message sent out from the message source
  synchronized public String getNextMessage(MessageSource source) {
    // Tell source we want to be told about new messages
    source.addObserver(this);

    // Wait until our update() method receives a message
    while (message == null) {
      try { wait(); } catch (Exception ignored) { }
    }

    // Tell source to stop telling us about new messages
    source.deleteObserver(this);

    // Now return the message we received
    // But first set the message instance variable to null
    // so update() and getNextMessage() can be called again.
    String messageCopy = message;
    message = null;
    return messageCopy;
  }
}
```

The `getNextMessage()` and `broadcastMessage(String message)` methods are the most interesting portions of `ChatServlet`. The `getNextMessage()` method returns the next new message as it comes in, blocking until there is one. To enable this blocking, it uses the `MessageSource` and `MessageSink` classes. Without getting too deep into the details of these two classes, we'll just say this: the servlet constructs a new `MessageSink` and asks this sink to get the next message from the source. To accomplish this, the sink registers itself as an observer of the source and calls `wait()` to block. When the source receives a new message, the sink (being an observer) is notified of the change with a call to its `update()` method. The sink's `update()` method saves the source's latest message in its message variable and then calls `notify()`. This causes its `getNextMessage()` method to unblock and return the message.

The `broadcastMessage()` method tells all listening clients when there's a new message. It notifies HTTP clients by sending the message to `MessageSource`; it notifies other clients directly by looping through its client list. For each of its socket-connected clients, it prints the message to the client's socket. For each of its RMI clients, it calls the client's `setNextMessage(String)` method. This is the callback we've been talking about. If, at any point, there's a problem with a socket or RMI client, it removes that client from its list.

The two lists, `socketClients` and `rmiClients`, are populated as the servlet hears from clients. When a socket client connects, the servlet's `handleClient(Socket)` method is called, and the new client is added to the `socketClients` `Vector`. RMI clients have to add themselves to the list by invoking the servlet's `addClient(ChatClient)` method.

The `doGet()` and `doPost()` methods of `ChatServlet` are essentially thin wrappers around the `getNextMessage()` and `broadcastMessage()` methods. The `doGet()` wrapper is so thin you can almost see through it: `doGet()` sends as its response whatever `String` is returned by `getNextMessage()`. The `doPost()` wrapper is a bit less transparent. It extracts the posted message from the POST form data's `message` parameter, broadcasts the message by passing it to the `broadcastMessage()` method, and sets its response's status code to `SC_NO_CONTENT` to indicate there is no content in the response. In a sense, making a GET request is equivalent to calling `getNextMessage()`, and making a POST request is equivalent to calling `broadcastMessage()`. The only problem is that with the HTTP design there's a small turnaround time between when the client gets a message and when it requests a new one, allowing some messages to be dropped under load. A better design (left to the reader) would use a client's `HttpSession` object to hold a queue of pending messages.

Did you notice which socket port `ChatServlet` listens on? It's 2428. Overriding the `getSocketPort()` method as `ChatServlet` does is an easy way to set the socket port when you don't want to use an init parameter.

The HTTP Applet

The code for our first applet, the HTTP chat applet, is shown in Example 10-17.

Example 10-17. A Chat Client Using HTTP Communication

```
import java.applet.*;
import java.awt.*;
import java.io.*;
import java.net.*;
import java.util.*;

import com.oreilly.servlet.HttpMessage;

public class HttpChatApplet extends Applet implements Runnable {
```

Example 10-17. A Chat Client Using HTTP Communication (continued)

```
  TextArea text;
  Label label;
  TextField input;
  Thread thread;
  String user;

  public void init() {
    // Check if this applet was loaded directly from the filesystem.
    // If so, explain to the user that this applet needs to be loaded
    // from a server in order to communicate with that server's servlets.
    URL codebase = getCodeBase();
    if (!"http".equals(codebase.getProtocol())) {
      System.out.println();
      System.out.println("*** Whoops! ***");
      System.out.println("This applet must be loaded from a web server.");
      System.out.println("Please try again, this time fetching the HTML");
      System.out.println("file containing this servlet as");
      System.out.println("\"http://server:port/file.html\".");
      System.out.println();
      System.exit(1);  // Works only from appletviewer
                       // Browsers throw an exception and muddle on
    }

    // Get this user's name from an applet parameter set by the servlet
    // We could just ask the user, but this demonstrates a
    // form of servlet->applet communication.
    user = getParameter("user");
    if (user == null) user = "anonymous";

    // Set up the user interface...
    // On top, a large TextArea showing what everyone's saying.
    // Underneath, a labeled TextField to accept this user's input.
    text = new TextArea();
    text.setEditable(false);
    label = new Label("Say something: ");
    input = new TextField();
    input.setEditable(true);

    setLayout(new BorderLayout());
    Panel panel = new Panel();
    panel.setLayout(new BorderLayout());

    add("Center", text);
    add("South", panel);

    panel.add("West", label);
```

Example 10-17. A Chat Client Using HTTP Communication (continued)

```
    panel.add("Center", input);
  }

  public void start() {
    thread = new Thread(this);
    thread.start();
  }

  String getNextMessage() {
    String nextMessage = null;
    while (nextMessage == null) {
      try {
        URL url = new URL(getCodeBase(), "/servlet/ChatServlet");
        HttpMessage msg = new HttpMessage(url);
        InputStream in = msg.sendGetMessage();
        DataInputStream data = new DataInputStream(
                               new BufferedInputStream(in));
        nextMessage = data.readLine();
      }
      catch (SocketException e) {
        // Can't connect to host, report it and wait before trying again
        System.out.println("Can't connect to host: " + e.getMessage());
        try { Thread.sleep(5000); } catch (InterruptedException ignored) { }
      }
      catch (FileNotFoundException e) {
        // Servlet doesn't exist, report it and wait before trying again
        System.out.println("Resource not found: " + e.getMessage());
        try { Thread.sleep(5000); } catch (InterruptedException ignored) { }
      }
      catch (Exception e) {
        // Some other problem, report it and wait before trying again
        System.out.println("General exception: " +
          e.getClass().getName() + ": " + e.getMessage());
        try { Thread.sleep(1000); } catch (InterruptedException ignored) { }
      }
    }
    return nextMessage + "\n";
  }

  public void run() {
    while (true) {
      text.appendText(getNextMessage());
    }
  }

  public void stop() {
    thread.stop();
    thread = null;
  }
```

Example 10-17. A Chat Client Using HTTP Communication (continued)

```
  void broadcastMessage(String message) {
    message = user + ": " + message;  // Pre-pend the speaker's name
    try {
      URL url = new URL(getCodeBase(), "/servlet/ChatServlet");
      HttpMessage msg = new HttpMessage(url);
      Properties props = new Properties();
      props.put("message", message);
      msg.sendPostMessage(props);
    }
    catch (SocketException e) {
      // Can't connect to host, report it and abandon the broadcast
      System.out.println("Can't connect to host: " + e.getMessage());
    }
    catch (FileNotFoundException e) {
      // Servlet doesn't exist, report it and abandon the broadcast
      System.out.println("Resource not found: " + e.getMessage());
    }
    catch (Exception e) {
      // Some other problem, report it and abandon the broadcast
      System.out.println("General exception: " +
        e.getClass().getName() + ": " + e.getMessage());
    }
  }

  public boolean handleEvent(Event event) {
    switch (event.id) {
      case Event.ACTION_EVENT:
        if (event.target == input) {
          broadcastMessage(input.getText());
          input.setText("");
          return true;
        }
    }
    return false;
  }
}
```

This applet has the same two workhorse methods as `ChatServlet`: `getNextMessage()` and `broadcastMessage()`. Its `getNextMessage()` method gets the next message from the servlet. It's called repeatedly to update the `TextArea`. It operates using an `HttpMessage` to make a GET request to the servlet, then interprets the first line of the response as the next new message. Its `broadcastMessage()` method sends a message to the servlet for distribution to the other clients. This method is called in the applet's `handleEvent()` method every time the user hits Enter in the `TextInput` component. It works similarly to `getNextMessage()`. It uses an `HttpMessage` to perform a POST request, passing the TextInput's text as the message parameter, and it doesn't bother to read the response.

The Socket-Connecting Applet

The only difference between the socket-based SocketChatApplet and the HTTP-based HttpChatApplet is a redesigned getNextMessage() method. This method is shown in Example 10-18.

Example 10-18. A Chat Client Using a Raw Socket Connection

```
static final int PORT = 2428;
DataInputStream serverStream;

String getNextMessage() {
  String nextMessage = null;
  while (nextMessage == null) {
    try {
      // Connect to the server if we haven't before
      if (serverStream == null) {
        Socket s = new Socket(getCodeBase().getHost(), PORT);
        serverStream = new DataInputStream(
                       new BufferedInputStream(
                       s.getInputStream()));
      }

      // Read a line
      nextMessage = serverStream.readLine();
    }
    catch (SocketException e) {
      // Can't connect to host, report it and wait before trying again
      System.out.println("Can't connect to host: " + e.getMessage());
      serverStream = null;
      try { Thread.sleep(5000); } catch (InterruptedException ignored) { }
    }
    catch (Exception e) {
      // Some other problem, report it and wait before trying again
      System.out.println("General exception: " +
        e.getClass().getName() + ": " + e.getMessage());
      try { Thread.sleep(1000); } catch (InterruptedException ignored) { }
    }
  }
  return nextMessage + "\n";
}
```

This method reads broadcast messages from a socket that's connected to the chat servlet. It uses a simple socket protocol: all content is plain text, one message per line. The first time this method is called, it establishes the socket connection and then uses the connection to get a `DataInputStream`, where it can read from the socket one line at a time. It reads the first line from this stream and returns the text as the next message. For each subsequent invocation, it reuses the same stream and simply returns the next line it reads. If there's ever a `SocketException`, it reestablishes the connection.

The RMI Applet

The code for the `ChatClient` interface is shown in Example 10-19; the RMI-based chat applet that implements it is shown in Example 10-20.

Example 10-19. The ChatClient Interface, Implemented by RMIChatApplet

```
import java.rmi.Remote;
import java.rmi.RemoteException;

public interface ChatClient extends Remote {
  public void setNextMessage(String message) throws RemoteException;
}
```

Example 10-20. A Chat Client Using RMI Communication

```
import java.applet.*;
import java.awt.*;
import java.io.*;
import java.net.*;
import java.rmi.*;
import java.rmi.registry.*;
import java.rmi.server.*;
import java.util.*;

public class RMIChatApplet extends Applet implements ChatClient {

  TextArea text;
  Label label;
  TextField input;
  Thread thread;
  String user;

  ChatServer chatServer;

  private int getRegistryPort() {
    try { return Integer.parseInt(getParameter("port")); }
    catch (NumberFormatException ignored) { return Registry.REGISTRY_PORT; }
  }

  private String getRegistryName() {
    String name = getParameter("name");
    return (name == null ? "ChatServlet" : name);
  }
```

Example 10-20. A Chat Client Using RMI Communication (continued)

```
// Returns a reference to the remote chat server/servlet
// Tries to exit if there's a problem.
private ChatServer getChatServer() {
  try {
    Registry registry =
      LocateRegistry.getRegistry(getCodeBase().getHost(), getRegistryPort());
    Object obj = registry.lookup(getRegistryName());
    return (ChatServer)obj;
  }
  catch (java.rmi.UnknownHostException e) {
    // Don't know the registry host, try to exit
    System.out.println("Host unknown in url: " + e.getMessage());
    System.exit(1);
  }
  catch (NotBoundException e) {
    // Can't find our object, try to exit
    System.out.println("Name not bound: " + e.getMessage());
    System.exit(1);
  }
  catch (ClassCastException e) {
    // The object wasn't a ChatServer, try to exit
    System.out.println(getRegistryName() + " was not a ChatServer:" +
                       e.getMessage());
    System.exit(1);
  }
  catch (RemoteException e) {
    // General RMI problem, try to exit
    System.out.println("Remote exception: " + e.getMessage());
    System.exit(1);
  }
  catch (Exception e) {
    // Some other problem, try to exit
    System.out.println("General exception: " +
      e.getClass().getName() + ": " + e.getMessage());
    System.exit(1);
  }
  return null;  // return null if the exit() doesn't work
}

// Add ourselves as a client of the chat server
// Notice there's no need for an RMI registry
private void registerWithChatServer(ChatServer server) {
  try {
    UnicastRemoteObject.exportObject(this);
    server.addClient(this);
  }
  catch (RemoteException e) {
```

Example 10-20. A Chat Client Using RMI Communication (continued)

```
      // General RMI problem, try to exit
      System.out.println("Remote exception: " + e.getMessage());
      System.exit(1);
    }
    catch (Exception e) {
      // Some other problem, try to exit
      System.out.println("General exception: " +
        e.getClass().getName() + ": " + e.getMessage());
      System.exit(1);
    }
  }

  public void init() {
    // Check if this applet was loaded directly from the filesystem.
    // If so, explain to the user that this applet needs to be loaded
    // from a server in order to communicate with that server's servlets.
    URL codebase = getCodeBase();
    if (!"http".equals(codebase.getProtocol())) {
      System.out.println();
      System.out.println("*** Whoops! ***");
      System.out.println("This applet must be loaded from a web server.");
      System.out.println("Please try again, this time fetching the HTML");
      System.out.println("file containing this servlet as");
      System.out.println("\"http://server:port/file.html\".");
      System.out.println();
      System.exit(1);  // Works only from appletviewer
                       // Browsers throw an exception and muddle on
    }

    // Get the remote chat server
    chatServer = getChatServer();

    // Register ourselves as one of its clients
    registerWithChatServer(chatServer);

    // Get this user's name from an applet parameter set by the dispatch servlet
    // We could just ask the user, but this demonstrates a
    // form of servlet->applet communication.
    user = getParameter("user");
    if (user == null) user = "anonymous";

    // Set up the user interface...
    // On top, a large TextArea showing what everyone's saying.
    // Underneath, a labeled TextField to accept this user's input.
    text = new TextArea();
    text.setEditable(false);
    label = new Label("Say something: ");
```

Example 10-20. A Chat Client Using RMI Communication (continued)

```
    input = new TextField();
    input.setEditable(true);

    setLayout(new BorderLayout());
    Panel panel = new Panel();
    panel.setLayout(new BorderLayout());

    add("Center", text);
    add("South", panel);

    panel.add("West", label);
    panel.add("Center", input);
  }

  String getNextMessage() {
    String nextMessage = null;
    while (nextMessage == null) {
      try {
        nextMessage = chatServer.getNextMessage();
      }
      catch (RemoteException e) {
        // Remote exception, report and wait before trying again
        System.out.println("Remote Exception:" + e.getMessage());
        try { Thread.sleep(1000); } catch (InterruptedException ignored) { }
      }
    }
    return nextMessage + "\n";
  }

  public void setNextMessage(String message) {
    text.appendText(message + "\n");
  }

  void broadcastMessage(String message) {
    message = user + ": " + message;  // Pre-pend the speaker's name
    try {
      chatServer.broadcastMessage(message);
    }
    catch (RemoteException e) {
      // Remote exception, report it and abandon the broadcast
      System.out.println("Remote exception: " + e.getMessage());
    }
    catch (Exception e) {
      // Some other exception, report it and abandon the broadcast
      System.out.println("General exception: " +
        e.getClass().getName() + ": " + e.getMessage());
    }
  }
```

Example 10-20. A Chat Client Using RMI Communication (continued)

```
  public boolean handleEvent(Event event) {
    switch (event.id) {
      case Event.ACTION_EVENT:
        if (event.target == input) {
          broadcastMessage(input.getText());
          input.setText("");
          return true;
        }
    }
    return false;
  }
}
```

This applet's `getNextMessage()` and `broadcastMessage()` implementations are as simple as any we've seen. They need call only the remote servlet's methods of the same name. But their simplicity comes with a cost: more complicated setup code. Specifically, the `init()` method now has to call the lengthy (but by now understandable) `getChatServer()` method to obtain a reference to the remote chat servlet.

If you look closely at `RMIChatApplet`, you'll notice that it doesn't actually use its `getNextMessage()` method. Instead, it asks the servlet to call its `setNextMessage()` method each time there's a new message being broadcast. `RMIChatApplet` makes this request in its `init()` method when it calls `registerWithChatServer(ChatServer)`. This method exports the applet as a remote object, then invokes the servlet's `addClient()` method passing a reference to itself. After this, the servlet's `broadcastMessage()` method sends a callback to the applet each time there's a new message.

If you try using callbacks on your own, don't forget the basics we covered earlier. You need to run the *rmic* RMI compiler on your remote applet to generate its stub and skeleton classes. And you need to be sure your server has the `RMIChatApplet_Stub.class` and `ChatClient.class` files somewhere in its classpath.

Another thing to watch out for is that modern browsers are more restrictive on allowing callbacks than browsers were in the past and often by default have the ability turned off. When this occurs you may see only cryptic error messages and sometimes no error messages, just silent failure. You can enable callbacks by digitally signing the applet (an action that differs depending on browser) and granting signed applets extra permissions or by accessing the applet using HTTPS from a trusted server. In general though, this can be considered yet another disadvantage of RMI and another reason to consider HTTP for applet-server communication.

The Dispatcher

Now, for this chapter's last code example, the `ChatDispatch` servlet is shown in Example 10-21. This servlet performs two duties. First, when this servlet is accessed without any request parameters, it prints a friendly welcome page asking the user which applet version he is interested in using, as shown in Figure 10-4. Second, when it's accessed with a request parameter, it prints a page that contains the appropriate applet, as you saw in Figure 10-3. Be aware that the URL used to access this dispatch servlet should contain the server's true name, not `localhost`, so as to avoid RMI security problems.

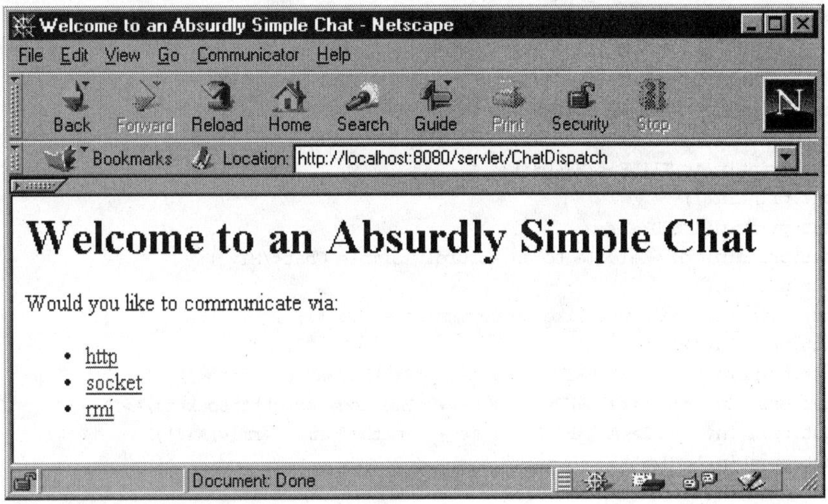

Figure 10-4. The chat dispatch welcome page

Example 10-21. The Front Door Dispatch Servlet

```
import java.io.*;
import javax.servlet.*;
import javax.servlet.http.*;

public class ChatDispatch extends HttpServlet {

  public void doGet(HttpServletRequest req, HttpServletResponse res)
                              throws IOException, ServletException {
    res.setContentType("text/html");

    if (!req.getParameterNames().hasMoreElements()) {
      // There were no request parameters. Print a welcome page.
      printWelcomePage(req, res);
    }
    else {
```

Example 10-21. The Front Door Dispatch Servlet (continued)

```
      // There was at least one request parameter.
      // Print a page containing the applet.
      printAppletPage(req, res);
    }
  }

  // The welcome page greets the reader and has a form where the user
  // can choose an applet-servlet communication method.
  private void printWelcomePage(HttpServletRequest req,
                                HttpServletResponse res)
                 throws IOException {
    PrintWriter out = res.getWriter();
    String me = req.getServletPath();

    out.println("<HTML>");
    out.println("<HEAD><TITLE>");
    out.println("Welcome to an Absurdly Simple Chat");
    out.println("</TITLE></HEAD>");
    out.println();
    out.println("<BODY>");
    out.println("<H1>Welcome to an Absurdly Simple Chat</H1>");
    out.println();
    out.println("Would you like to communicate via:");
    out.println("<UL>");
    out.println("  <LI><A HREF=\"" + me + "?method=http\">http</A>");
    out.println("  <LI><A HREF=\"" + me + "?method=socket\">socket</A>");
    out.println("  <LI><A HREF=\"" + me + "?method=rmi\">rmi</A>");
    out.println("</UL>");
    out.println("</BODY></HTML>");
  }

  // The applet page displays the chat applet.
  private void printAppletPage(HttpServletRequest req,
                               HttpServletResponse res)
                 throws IOException {
    PrintWriter out = res.getWriter();

    out.println("<HTML>");
    out.println("<HEAD><TITLE>An Absurdly Simple Chat</TITLE></HEAD>");
    out.println("<BODY>");
    out.println("<H1>An Absurdly Simple Chat</H1>");

    String method = req.getParameter("method");
    String user = req.getRemoteUser();
    String applet = null;
```

Example 10-21. The Front Door Dispatch Servlet (continued)

```
    if ("http".equals(method)) {
      applet = "HttpChatApplet";
    }
    else if ("socket".equals(method)) {
      applet = "SocketChatApplet";
    }
    else if ("rmi".equals(method)) {
      applet = "RMIChatApplet";
    }
    else {
      // No method given, or an invalid method given.
      // Explain to the user what we expect.
      out.println("Sorry, this servlet requires a <TT>method</TT> " +
                  "parameter with one of these values: " +
                  "http, socket, rmi");
      return;
    }

    // Print the HTML code to generate the applet.
    // Choose the applet code based on the method parameter.
    // Provide a user parameter if we know the remote user.
    out.println("<APPLET CODE=" + applet + " CODEBASE=/ " +
                "WIDTH=500 HEIGHT=170>");
    if (user != null)
      out.println("<PARAM NAME=user VALUE=\"" + user + "\">");
    out.println("</APPLET>");

    out.println("</BODY></HTML>");
  }
}
```

Nothing here should surprise you. In fact, we expect this code to appear refreshingly simple after the `ChatServlet` example. Still, this example does demonstrate one last form of applet-servlet communication: servlet-generated applet parameters. Using this technique, a servlet generates a page that contains an applet and passes information to the applet by manipulating the applet's `<PARAM>` tags. Any information the servlet wants to send to a new applet can be sent this way. In this example, the servlet sends the name returned by `req.getRemoteUser()`. In another example, a servlet could tell the applet its browser type by sending it the string returned by `req.getHeader("User-Agent")`. Or, to be more helpful, the servlet could use a database to determine the capabilities of the browser and tell the applet exactly what it needs to know. It could even tell the applet whether the browser supports RMI communication.

11

In this chapter:
- *Sharing Information*
- *Sharing Control*

Servlet Collaboration

Servlets running together in the same server have several ways to communicate with one another. There are two main styles of servlet collaboration:

Sharing information
: This involves two or more servlets sharing state or resources. For example, a set of servlets managing an online store could share the store's product inventory count or share a database connection. Session tracking (see Chapter 7, *Session Tracking*) is a special case of sharing information.

Sharing control
: This involves two or more servlets sharing control of the request. For example, one servlet could receive the request but let another servlet handle some or all of the request-handling responsibilities.

In the past (before Servlet API 2.1) we would have listed another style of collaboration: *direct manipulation.* With this style of collaboration, a servlet could obtain a direct reference to another through the `getServlet()` method and invoke methods on the other servlet. This style of collaboration is no longer supported; the `getServlet()` method has been deprecated and defined to return `null` for API 2.1 and later. The reason: a servlet may be destroyed by the web server at any time, so nothing but the server should hold a direct reference to a servlet. Everything that could be done with `getServlet()` can be accomplished better and safer using the alternatives we'll learn about in this chapter.

Sharing Information

Oftentimes servlets cooperate by sharing some information. The information may be state information, a shared resource, a resource factory, or anything. In Servlet API 2.0 and earlier there were no built-in mechanisms by which servlets could share information, and in the first edition of this book (written against API 2.0) we had to demonstrate several creative workarounds including putting information in the `System` properties list! Fortunately such workarounds are no longer necessary, because beginning with Servlet API 2.1 the `ServletContext` class has been enhanced to act as a shared information repository.

Sharing with the ServletContext

A servlet retrieves the `ServletContext` for its web application using the `getServletContext()` call. A servlet may use the context as if it were a `Hashtable` or `Map`, with the following methods.

```
public void ServletContext.setAttribute(String name, Object o)
public Object ServletContext.getAttribute(String name)
public Enumeration ServletContext.getAttributeNames()
public void ServletContext.removeAttribute(String name)
```

The `setAttribute()` method binds an object under a given name. Any existing binding with the same name is replaced. Attribute names should follow the same convention as package names to avoid overwriting one another. The package names `java.*`, `javax.*`, and `com.sun.*` are reserved.

The `getAttribute()` method retrieves the object bound under the given name or `null` if the attribute does not exist. The call may also retrieve server-specific hard-coded attributes (for example, `javax.servlet.context.tempdir`) as discussed in Chapter 4, *Retrieving Information.*

The `getAttributeNames()` method returns an `Enumeration`, which contains the names of all the bound attributes or an empty `Enumeration` if there are no bindings.

The `removeAttribute()` method removes the object bound under the given name or does nothing if the attribute does not exist. It's a good idea to remove attributes that are no longer needed to reduce memory bloat.

Using the context to sell burritos

As a fun example, imagine a set of servlets that sell burritos and share a special of the day. An administrative servlet could set the special of the day as shown in Example 11-1.

Example 11-1. Me Gustan Burritos

```
import java.io.*;
import java.util.*;
import javax.servlet.*;
import javax.servlet.http.*;
```

Example 11-1. Me Gustan Burritos (continued)

```
public class SpecialSetter extends HttpServlet {

  public void doGet(HttpServletRequest req, HttpServletResponse res)
                               throws ServletException, IOException {
    res.setContentType("text/plain");
    PrintWriter out = res.getWriter();

    ServletContext context = getServletContext();
    context.setAttribute("com.costena.special.burrito", "Pollo Adobado");
    context.setAttribute("com.costena.special.day", new Date());

    out.println("The burrito special has been set.");
  }
}
```

Thereafter, every other servlet on the server can access the special and display it using the code in Example 11-2.

Example 11-2. Especial Del Día

```
import java.io.*;
import java.text.*;
import java.util.*;
import javax.servlet.*;
import javax.servlet.http.*;

public class SpecialGetter extends HttpServlet {

  public void doGet(HttpServletRequest req, HttpServletResponse res)
                               throws ServletException, IOException {
    res.setContentType("text/html");
    PrintWriter out = res.getWriter();

    ServletContext context = getServletContext();
    String burrito = (String)
      context.getAttribute("com.costena.special.burrito");
    Date day = (Date)
      context.getAttribute("com.costena.special.day");

    DateFormat df = DateFormat.getDateInstance(DateFormat.MEDIUM);
    String today = df.format(day);

    out.println("Our burrito special today (" + today + ") is: " + burrito);
  }
}
```

Sharing with Another ServletContext

Using the `ServletContext` to share information has the beneficial effect that each web application has its own unique information store. There's no risk of accidental name collisions or even name collisions from the same application deployed twice on a server. However, sometimes information needs to be shared between web contexts. In this situation, there are two choices. First, use an external information repository such as a singleton or database, or, second, use special hooks to directly access another context. We'll explore the latter.

A servlet can obtain a handle to another context on the same server using the `getContext()` hook in its own context:

```
public ServletContext ServletContext.getContext(String uripath)
```

This method returns the `ServletContext` containing the specified URI path. The given path must be absolute (beginning with `/`) and is interpreted based on the server's document root. This method allows a servlet to gain access to a context outside its own. In a security-conscious or distributed environment (see Chapter 12, *Enterprise Servlets and J2EE*), the servlet container may return `null` for any and all paths.

To demonstrate, assume a servlet outside the burrito store context needs access to the special of the day. Furthermore, assume the burrito store context is rooted at */burritostore*. And finally, assume the server hasn't turned on security controls to disallow intercontext communication. Under these conditions the following code allows any servlet on the server to retrieve the special of the day from the burrito store application:

```
ServletContext myContext = getServletContext();
ServletContext otherContext = myContext.getContext("/burritostore/index.html");
String burrito = otherContext.getAttribute("com.costena.special.burrito");
Date day = (Date)otherContext.getAttribute("com.costena.special.day");
```

Currently the only way to obtain a reference to a different context is by path lookup, so our example here will break should the burrito store move to a different URL. In the future there may be a way to obtain a context by name.

Class loader issues

If the object placed into the context is a custom object, sharing the object between contexts becomes much more difficult due to class loader issues. Remember that each web application has its classes under *WEB-INF* loaded by a different class loader. Also remember that the class loader from one application cannot locate the classes stored within a different application. The unfortunate result: an object whose *.class* file exists only within *WEB-INF/classes* or *WEB-INF/lib* won't be easily usable from any other application. Any attempt to cast the object to its proper type results in a `NoClassDefFoundError`.

The solution of copying the *.class* file into both applications doesn't work either. Classes loaded by different class loaders are not the same class, even if their definitions match. If you try this, you'll only replace the `NoClassDefFoundError` with a `ClassCastException`.

There are three possible workarounds. First, copy the *.class* file for the shared object into the server's standard classpath (for Tomcat that's *server_root/classes*). This allows it to be found by the primordial class loader shared by all web applications. Second, avoid casting the returned object and invoke its methods using reflection (a technique whereby a Java class can inspect and manipulate itself at runtime). This isn't as elegant but works if you don't have full control over the server. Third, cast the returned object to an interface that declares the pertinent methods and place the interface in the server's standard classpath. Every class but the interface can remain in the individual web applications. This requires refactoring the shared object's class but works well if the implementation needs to remain in the original web applications.

Sharing Control

For more dynamic collaboration, servlets can share control of the request. First, a servlet can *forward* an entire request, doing some preliminary processing and then passing off the request to another component. Second, a servlet can *include* in its response a bit of content generated by another component, essentially creating a programmatic server-side include. Conceptually, if you think of the resulting page like a screen, a forward gives another servlet full control of the screen, while an include injects only a section of content into the screen at some point.

This delegation ability gives servlets more flexibility and allows for better abstraction. Using delegation, a servlet can construct its response as a collection of content generated by various web server components. This functionality is especially important to JavaServer Pages, where it often happens that one servlet preprocesses a request, then hands off the request to a JSP page for completion (see Chapter 18, *JavaServer Pages*).

Getting a Request Dispatcher

To support request delegation, Servlet API 2.1 introduced the `javax.servlet.RequestDispatcher` interface. A servlet gets a `RequestDispatcher` instance using the `getRequestDispatcher()` method on its request object. This method returns a `RequestDispatcher` that can dispatch to the component (servlet, JSP, static file, etc.) found at the given URI path:

```
public RequestDispatcher ServletRequest.getRequestDispatcher(String path)
```

The provided path may be relative, although it cannot extend outside the current servlet context. You can use the `getContext()` method as discussed in the previous section for dispatching outside the current context. There's no way to dispatch to a context on another server. If the path begins with a / it is interpreted as relative to the current context root. If the path contains a query string, the parameters are added to the beginning of the receiving component's parameter set. The method returns `null` if the servlet container cannot return a `RequestDispatcher` for any reason.

Curiously, there's a method by the same name in the `ServletContext` class:

```
public RequestDispatcher ServletContext.getRequestDispatcher(String path)
```

The difference here is that the version in `ServletContext` (introduced in API 2.1) accepts only absolute URLs (beginning with a slash) while the version in `ServletRequest` (introduced in API 2.2) accepts both absolute URLs and relative URLs. Consequently, there's no reason to use the method in `ServletContext`. It exists only for historical reasons and can be considered deprecated although officially it's not.

It's also possible to get a `RequestDispatcher` for a resource specified by name instead of by path, using `getNamedDispatcher()` in `ServletContext`:

```
public RequestDispatcher ServletContext.getNamedDispatcher(String name)
```

This allows dispatching to resources that are not necessarily publicly available. Servlets (and JSP pages also) may be given names via the web application deployment descriptor, as discussed in Chapter 3, *The Servlet Lifecycle*. The method returns `null` if the context cannot return a dispatcher for any reason.

`RequestDispatcher` has two methods, `forward()` and `include()`. The `forward()` method hands off the entire request to the delegate. The `include()` method adds the delegate's output to the calling servlet's response but leaves the calling servlet in control.

Dispatching a Forward

The `forward()` method forwards a request from a servlet to another resource on the server. The method allows one servlet to do preliminary processing of a request and another resource to generate the response. Unlike a `sendRedirect()`, a `forward()` operates entirely within the server, and the client cannot tell the forward occurred. Information can be passed to the delegate using an attached query string or using request attributes set with the `setAttribute()` method. Example 11-3 demonstrates a servlet that performs a search, then forwards the search results to another page for rendering.

Example 11-3. A Search Engine Backend

```
import java.io.*;
import javax.servlet.*;
import javax.servlet.http.*;

public class SearchLogic extends HttpServlet {

  public void doGet(HttpServletRequest req, HttpServletResponse res)
                               throws ServletException, IOException {
    // We don't set the content type or get a writer

    // Get the string to search for
    String search = req.getParameter("search");

    // Calculate the URLs containing the string
    String[] results = getResults(search);

    // Specify the results as a request attribute
    req.setAttribute("results", results);

    // Forward to a display page
    String display = "/servlet/SearchView";
    RequestDispatcher dispatcher = req.getRequestDispatcher(display);
    dispatcher.forward(req, res);
  }

  // In real use this method would call actual search engine logic
  // and return more information about each result than a URL
  String[] getResults(String search) {
    return new String[] { "http://www.abc.com",
                          "http://www.xyz.com" };
  }
}
```

This servlet's job is to be the brains of an online search engine. It does a search for the text given by the `search` parameter, then stores the resulting URLs into a `results` attribute of the request. Then the servlet forwards the request to a display component for rendering. Here that's hard coded as */servlet/SearchView*, but the path could be made to change depending on user preferences for language, site colors, beginner or advanced display, and so on.

The rules a forwarding servlet must follow are relatively strict:

- It may set headers and the status code but may not send any response body to the client (that's the job for an include). Consequently, the `forward()` must be called before the response has been committed.

- If the response already has been committed, the `forward()` call throws an `IllegalStateException`.
- If the response has not been committed but there's content within the response buffer, the buffer is automatically cleared as part of the forward.
- In addition, you can't get creative by substituting new request and response objects. The `forward()` method must be called with the same request and response objects as were passed to the calling servlet's service method, and the `forward()` must be called from within the same handler thread.

The receiving component may be written as any other component, as Example 11-4 demonstrates.

Example 11-4. A Search Engine Frontend

```
import java.io.*;
import javax.servlet.*;
import javax.servlet.http.*;

public class SearchView extends HttpServlet {

  public void doGet(HttpServletRequest req, HttpServletResponse res)
                               throws ServletException, IOException {
    res.setContentType("text/plain");
    PrintWriter out = res.getWriter();

    // Get the search results from a request attribute
    String[] results = (String[]) req.getAttribute("results");

    if (results == null) {
      out.println("No results.");
      out.println("Did you accidentally access this servlet directly?");
    }
    else {
      out.println("Results:");
      for (int i = 0; i < results.length; i++) {
        out.println(results[i]);
      }
    }

    out.println();
    out.println("Request URI: " + req.getRequestURI());
    out.println("Context Path: " + req.getContextPath());
    out.println("Servlet Path: " + req.getServletPath());
    out.println("Path Info: " + req.getPathInfo());
    out.println("Query String: " + req.getQueryString());
  }
}
```

When you try this servlet yourself, notice the path information printed by the servlet has been adjusted. It doesn't match the original request information; instead, it matches the path used to obtain the dispatcher:

```
Request URI: /servlet/SearchView
Context Path:
Servlet Path: /servlet/SearchView
Path Info: null
Query String: null
```

The reason for this path adjustment is that, if you forward to a servlet, that servlet should get the same path info as if it were invoked directly; it has full control over the request from this point. That's also why it's important that the response buffer is flushed before it's invoked and that the response has not been committed.

Dispatching by name

One problem with dispatching by path is that if the target component is available to server components on some path, it's also available to clients at the same path. For safety you may consider making a component not publicly available (by disabling the */servlet* invoker logic, for example) and dispatching requests by name instead of path. The `getNamedDispatcher()` method makes this possible. Example 11-3 could be rewritten with dispatch logic as follows:

```
// Forward to a display page
String display = "searchView";
RequestDispatcher dispatcher = req.getNamedDispatcher(display);
dispatcher.forward(req, res);
```

One thing to be aware of with `getNamedDispatcher()` is that, because there's no URI path used, no query strings may be appended and there's no path adjustment.

Forward Versus Redirect

Is it better to use `forward()` or `sendRedirect()`? Both methods have their uses. `forward()` works best when one component must perform business logic and share the results with another component. `sendRedirect()` works best when the client should be redirected from one page to another. It's tempting to use `forward()` instead of `sendRedirect()` for simple redirect duties, because a `forward()` operates within the server and executes faster than a `sendRedirect()` which requires round-trip communication with the client. Unfortunately, that causes problems with relative URL handling, as demonstrated by Example 11-5, a servlet that forwards a request to the site home page.

Example 11-5. Go Directly to Home, Do Not Pass Go

```
import java.io.*;
import javax.servlet.*;
import javax.servlet.http.*;

public class HomePageForward extends HttpServlet {

  public void doGet(HttpServletRequest req, HttpServletResponse res)
                               throws ServletException, IOException {
    RequestDispatcher dispatcher = req.getRequestDispatcher("/index.html");
    dispatcher.forward(req, res);
  }
}
```

If you use Tomcat to access this servlet at the URL *http://localhost:8080/servlet/HomePageForward*, you'll notice all images within the page are broken. The reason is that the page contains <IMG> tags with relative paths to the image files, and while a `sendRedirect()` would have given the client notice that the file was served from the document root directory, the `forward()` gave the client no such notice, and all relative URLs end up broken. The `sendRedirect()` method also makes it easier to dispatch to resources within other contexts, because no `getContext()` lookup is required. Our advice is to use `sendRedirect()` whenever possible and to use `forward()` only when required.

Dispatching an Include

The `RequestDispatcher`'s `include()` method includes the content of a resource into the current response. It enables what could be considered a programmatic server-side include. It's different than a `forward()` because the calling servlet retains control of the response and may include content both before and after the included content. Example 11-6 demonstrates a servlet that includes a catalog item display into the current response.

Example 11-6. Including a Catalog Item

```
import java.io.*;
import javax.servlet.*;
import javax.servlet.http.*;

public class NileBooks extends HttpServlet {

  public void doGet(HttpServletRequest req, HttpServletResponse res)
                               throws ServletException, IOException {
    res.setContentType("text/html");
    PrintWriter out = res.getWriter();
```

Example 11-6. Including a Catalog Item (continued)

```
    out.println("<HTML><HEAD><TITLE>Welcome to Nile</TITLE></HEAD>");
    out.println("<BODY>");

    // Show an item in an online catalog
    out.println("Feast your eyes on this beauty:");

    RequestDispatcher dispatcher =
      req.getRequestDispatcher("/servlet/NileItem?item=0596000405");
    dispatcher.include(req, res);

    out.println("And, since I like you, it's 20% off!");

    out.println("</BODY></HTML>");
  }
}
```

As with `forward()`, information can be passed to the called resource using an attached query string or using request attributes set with the `setAttribute()` method. Using attributes instead of parameters gives you the ability to pass objects instead of simple strings, as shown in Example 11-7.

Example 11-7. Including Several Catalog Items

```
import java.io.*;
import javax.servlet.*;
import javax.servlet.http.*;

public class NileBooks extends HttpServlet {

  public void doGet(HttpServletRequest req, HttpServletResponse res)
                               throws ServletException, IOException {
    res.setContentType("text/html");
    PrintWriter out = res.getWriter();

    out.println("<HTML><HEAD><TITLE>Welcome to Nile</TITLE></HEAD>");
    out.println("<BODY>");

    // Show items in an online catalog
    RequestDispatcher dispatcher =
      req.getRequestDispatcher("/servlet/NileItem");

    out.println("Feast your eyes on this beauty:");
    req.setAttribute("item", Book.getBook("0596000405"));
    dispatcher.include(req, res);

    // Remove the "item" attribute after use
    req.removeAttribute("item");
```

Example 11-7. Including Several Catalog Items (continued)

```
    out.println("Or how about this one:");
    req.setAttribute("item", Book.getBook("0395282659"));
    dispatcher.include(req, res);

    out.println("And, since I like you, they're all 20% off!");

    out.println("</BODY></HTML>");
  }
}

// A simple Book class
class Book {
  String isbn;
  String title;
  String author;

  private static Book JSERVLET =
    new Book("0596000405", "Java Servlet Programming", "Hunter");

  private static Book HOBBIT =
    new Book("0395282659", "The Hobbit", "Tolkien");

  // Here we simulate a database lookup
  public static Book getBook(String isbn) {
    if (JSERVLET.getISBN().equals(isbn)) {
      return JSERVLET;
    }
    else if (HOBBIT.getISBN().equals(isbn)) {
      return HOBBIT;
    }
    else {
      return null;
    }
  }

  private Book(String isbn, String title, String author) {
    this.isbn = isbn;
    this.title = title;
    this.author = author;
  }

  public String getISBN() {
    return isbn;
  }

  public String getTitle() {
    return title;
  }
```

Example 11-7. Including Several Catalog Items (continued)

```
  public String getAuthor() {
    return author;
  }
}
```

Here instead of passing just an ISBN, the servlet passes a complete Book object. In production use, the book information would come from an ISBN lookup on a database. Here we simply hard coded a pair of books.

The `NileItem` servlet can receive the `item` request attribute by calling `req.getAttribute("item")`, as shown in Example 11-8.

Example 11-8. Displaying a Catalog Item

```
import java.io.*;
import javax.servlet.*;
import javax.servlet.http.*;

public class NileItem extends HttpServlet {

  public void doGet(HttpServletRequest req, HttpServletResponse res)
                               throws ServletException, IOException {

    // We do not set the content type

    PrintWriter out = res.getWriter();

    Book book = (Book) req.getAttribute("item");

    out.println("<BR>");
    if (book != null) {
      out.println("<I>" + book.getTitle() + "</I>");
      out.println(" by " + book.getAuthor());
    }
    else {
      out.println("<I>No book record found</I>");
    }
    out.println("<BR>");
  }
}
```

An included servlet may have its content placed anywhere in a page, and because of that it has no ability to change the status code or HTTP headers sent in the response. Any attempt to make a change is ignored.

Unlike a `forward()`, the path elements and parameters of the request remain unchanged from the caller's. If the included component requires access to its own path elements and parameters, it may retrieve them using the following server-assigned request attributes:

```
javax.servlet.include.request_uri
javax.servlet.include.context_path
javax.servlet.include.servlet_path
javax.servlet.include.path_info
javax.servlet.include.query_string
```

The request and response parameters must be the same objects as were passed to the calling servlet's service method, and the `include()` must be called from within the same handler thread.

The included resource must use an output mechanism that matches the caller's. If the caller uses a `PrintWriter`, then the included resource must use a `PrintWriter`. If the caller uses an `OutputStream`, then the included resource must use an `OutputStream`. If the mechanisms don't match, the included servlet throws an `IllegalStateException`. If you can, make sure to use the `PrintWriter` for all text output, and this won't be a problem.

12

In this chapter:
- *Distributing Load*
- *Integrating with J2EE*

Enterprise Servlets and J2EE

This chapter discusses enterprise servlets. The term *enterprise* is used all the time with Java these days, but what does it mean? According to my trusty and beat-up copy of *The American Heritage Dictionary* (so old it's priced at $1.95) the word *enterprise* has three definitions:

1. An undertaking, esp. one of some scope and risk
2. A business
3. Readiness to venture; initiative

It's a surprisingly close definition to what people mean when they say *enterprise Java* and *enterprise servlets.* We can merge the traditional definitions to create a modern definition:

1. Readiness to support a business undertaking of large scope

In other words, *enterprise servlets* are servlets designed to support business-oriented large-scale web sites—high-traffic, high-reliability sites that have extra demands for scalability, load balancing, failover support, and integration with other Java 2, Enterprise Edition (J2EE) technologies.

As servlets have become increasingly popular and robust, and as servlet containers have become more solid and featureful, a growing number of enterprise sites are being built using servlets. Writing servlets for these sites differs from writing servlets for traditional sites, and in this chapter we'll discuss the special requirements and abilities of these enterprise servlets.

Distributing Load

For high-traffic and/or high-reliability sites, it's often desirable to distribute the site's content and processing duties across multiple backend servers. This distribution allows multiple servers to share the load, increasing the number of simultaneous requests that can be handled and providing failover so the site can remain up even when one particular component crashes.

Distribution isn't appropriate for every site. Creating and maintaining a distributed site can be significantly more complicated than doing the same for a standalone site and can be more costly as well in terms of load-balancing hardware and/or software requirements. Distribution also doesn't tend to provide a significant performance benefit until the server is under extreme load. When presented with a performance problem, it's often easiest to "throw hardware at the problem" by installing a single higher-end machine rather than trying to share the load between two underperforming machines.

Still, there are many sites that need to scale beyond the capabilities of a single machine and that need a level of reliability no single machine can offer. These are the sites that need to be distributed.

How to Be Distributable

The programming requirements for a distributable servlet are much stricter than the requirements for a nondistributable servlet. A distributable servlet must be written following certain rules so that different instances of the servlet can execute on multiple backend machines. Any programmer assumptions that there's only one servlet instance, one servlet context, one JVM, or one filesystem have the potential to cause serious problems.

To learn how servlets can be distributed, look at Enterprise JavaBeans (EJB) technology, a server-side component model for implementing distributed business objects and the technology that's at the heart of J2EE. EJB is designed from the ground up as distributable objects. An EJB implements business logic and lets the *container* (essentially the server) in which it runs manage services such as transactions, persistence, concurrency, and security. An EJB may be distributed across a number of backend machines and may be moved between machines at the container's discretion. To enable this distribution model, EJB must follow a strict specification-defined ruleset for what they can and cannot do.*

* For more information on Enterprise JavaBeans see *http://java.sun.com/products/ejb* and *Enterprise JavaBeans* by Richard Monson-Haefel (O'Reilly).

Servlets have no such specification-defined ruleset. This stems from their heritage as frontend server-side components, used to communicate with the client and call on the distributed EJB and not be distributed themselves. However, for high-traffic sites or sites that need high reliability, servlets too need to be distributed. We expect upcoming Servlet API versions to include a tighter definition for the implementation of distributed servlet containers.

The following are our own rules of thumb for writing servlets to be deployed in a distributed environment:

- Consider that different instances of the servlet may exist on each different JVM and/or machine. Therefore, instance variables and static variables should not be used to store state. Any state should be held in an external resource such as a database or EJB (the servlet's name can be used in the lookup).
- Consider that a different instances of the `ServletContext` may exist on each different JVM and/or machine. Therefore, the context should not be used to store application state. Any state should be held in an external resource such as a database or EJB (the context's path can be used in the lookup).
- Consider that any object placed into an `HttpSession` should be capable of being moved to (or accessed from) a different machine. For example, the object can implement `java.io.Serializable`. Be aware that because sessions may migrate, the session unbind event may occur on a different machine than the session bind event!
- Consider that files may not exist on all backend machines. Therefore, you should avoid using the `java.io` package for file access and use the `getServletContext().getResource()` mechanism instead—or make sure all accessed files are replicated across all backend machines.
- Consider that synchronization is not global and works only for the local JVM.

A web application whose components follow these rules can be marked *distributable*, and that marking allows the server to deploy the application across multiple backend machines. The distributable mark is placed within the *web.xml* deployment descriptor as an empty `<distributable/>` tag located between the application's description and its context parameters:

```
<web-app>
  <description>
    All servlets and JSPs are ready for distributed deployment
  </description>

  <distributable/>

  <context-param>
    <!-- ... -->
```

```
    </context-param>
</web-app>
```

Applications are nondistributable by default, to allow the casual servlet programmer to author servlets without worrying about the extra rules for distributed deployment. Marking an application distributable does not necessarily mean the application will be split across different machines. It only indicates the capability of the application to be split. Think of it as a programmer-provided certification.

Servers do not enforce most of the preceding rules given for a distributed application. For example, a servlet is not barred from using instance and static variables nor barred from storing objects in its `ServletContext`, and a servlet may still directly access files using the `java.io` package. It's up to the programmer to ensure these abilities aren't abused. The only enforcement that the server may perform is throwing an `IllegalArgumentException` if an object bound to the `HttpSession` does not implement `java.io.Serializable` (and even that's optional because, as we'll see later, a J2EE-compliant server must allow additional types of objects to be stored in the session).

Many Styles of Distribution

Servlet distribution (often called *clustering*) is an optional feature of a servlet container, and servlet containers that do support clustering are free to do so in several different ways. There are four standard architectures, listed here from simplest to most advanced.

1. No clustering. All servlets execute within a single JVM, and the `<distributable/>` marker is essentially ignored. This design is simple, and works fine for a standard site. The standalone Tomcat server works this way.
2. Clustering support, no session migration, and no session failover. Servlets in a web application marked `<distributable/>` may execute across multiple machines. Nonsession requests are randomly distributed (modulo some weighting perhaps). Session requests are "sticky" and tied to the particular backend server on which they first start. Session data does not move between machines, and this has the advantage that sessions may hold nontransferable (non-`Serializable`) data and the disadvantage that sessions may not migrate to underutilized servers and a server crash may result in broken sessions. This is the architecture used by Apache/JServ and Apache/Tomcat. Sessions are tied to a particular host through a mechanism where the `mod_jserv`/`mod_jk` connector in Apache uses a portion of the session ID to indicate which backend JServ or Tomcat owns the session. Multiple instances of Apache may be used as well, with the support of load-balancing hardware or software.

3. Clustering support, with session migration, no session failover. This architecture works the same as the former, except a session may migrate from one server to another to improve the load balance. To avoid concurrency issues, any session migration is guaranteed to occur between user requests. The Servlet Specification makes this guarantee: "Within an application that is marked as distributable, all requests that are part of a session can only be handled on a single VM at any one time." All objects placed into a session that may be migrated must implement `java.io.Serializable` or be transferable in some other way.
4. Clustering support, with session migration and with session failover. A server implementing this architecture has the additional ability to duplicate the contents of a session so the crash of any individual component does not necessarily break a user's session. The challenge with this architecture is coordinating efficient and effective information flow. Most high-end servers follow this architecture.

The details on how to implement clustering vary by server and are a point on which server vendors actively compete. Look to your server's documentation for details on what level of clustering it supports. Another useful feature to watch for is *session persistence*, the background saving of session information to disk or database, which allows the information to survive server restarts and crashes.

Integrating with J2EE

Throughout the rest of this book, servlets have been used as a standalone technology built upon the standard Java base. Servlets have another life, however, where they act as an integral piece of what's known as *Java 2, Enterprise Edition*, or *J2EE* for short.* J2EE 1.2 collects together several server-side APIs including Servlet API 2.2, JSP 1.1, EJB, JavaMail, the Java Messaging Service (JMS), Java Transactions (JTA), CORBA, JDBC, the Java API for XML Parsing (JAXP), and the Java Naming and Directory Interface (JNDI). J2EE makes the whole greater than the sum of its parts by defining how these technologies can interoperate and make use of one another, and providing certification that certain application servers are J2EE compliant, meaning they provide all the required services as well as the extra connection glue.

* Most pronounce J2EE as J-2-E-E but those who know it best at Sun just say "jah-too-ee."

J2EE Division of Labor

J2EE breaks enterprise application development into six distinct roles. Of course, an individual may participate in more than one role and multiple individuals may work together in a given role.

J2EE product provider
: The operating system vendor, database system vendor, application server vendor, and/or web server vendor. The product provider provides an implementation of the J2EE APIs and tools for application deployment and management.

Application component provider
: The author of the application's servlets, EJB, and other code as well as general content such as HTML. (In other words, you.)

Application assembler
: Takes the application's components and (using tools from the product provider) places them in a form appropriate for deployment. As part of this the assembler describes the external dependencies of the application that may change from deployment to deployment, like database or user login information.

Deployer
: Takes the output of the assembler and (using tools from the product provider) installs, configures, and executes the application. The configuration task requires satisfying the external dependencies outlined by the assembler.

System administrator
: Configures and administers the network infrastructure to keep the application alive.

Tool provider
: Creates tools to support J2EE development, beyond those provided by the product provider.

The division of labor between component provider, assembler, and deployer has an impact on how we (as servlet programmers in the content provider role) behave. Specifically, we should design our code to make external dependencies clear for the assembler, and furthermore we should use mechanisms that allow the deployer to satisfy these dependencies without modifying the files received from the assembler. That means no deployer edits to the *web.xml* file! Why not? Because J2EE applications are assembled into Enterprise Archive (*.ear*) files of which a contained web application's *web.xml* file is but one uneditable part.

This sounds more difficult than it actually is. J2EE provides a standard mechanism to achieve this abstraction using JNDI and a few special tags in the *web.xml* deployment descriptor. JNDI is an object lookup mechanism, a way to bind objects under certain paths and locate them later using that path. You can think of it like an RMI registry, except it's more general with support for accessing a range of services including LDAP and NIS (and even, in fact, the RMI registry!). An assembler declares external dependencies within the *web.xml* using special tags, a deployer satisfies these dependencies using server-specific tools, and at runtime our Java code uses the JNDI API to access the external resources—kindly placed there by the J2EE-compliant server. All goals are satisfied: our Java code remains portable between J2EE-compliant servers, and the deployer can satisfy the code's external dependencies without modifying the files received from the assembler. There's even enough flexibility left over for server vendors to compete on implementations of the standard.

Environment Entries

Context init parameters serve a useful purpose with servlets, but there's a problem with context init parameters in the J2EE model: any change to a parameter value requires a modification to the *web.xml* file. For parameter values that may need to change during deployment, it's better to use environment entries instead, as indicated by the `<env-entry>` tag. The `<env-entry>` tag may contain a `<description>`, `<env-entry-name>`, `<env-entry-value>`, and `<env-entry-type>`. The following `<env-entry>` specifies whether the application should enable sending of PIN codes by mail:

```
<env-entry>
  <description>Send pincode by mail</description>
  <env-entry-name>mailPincode</env-entry-name>
  <env-entry-value>false</env-entry-value>
  <env-entry-type>java.lang.Boolean</env-entry-type> <!-- FQCN -->
</env-entry>
```

The `<description>` explains to the deployer the purpose of this entry. It's optional but a good idea to provide. The `<env-entry-name>` is used by Java code as part of the JNDI lookup. The `<env-entry-value>` defines the default value to be presented to the deployer. It's optional, but not specifying a value requires the deployer to provide one. The `<env-entry-type>` represents the fully qualified class name (FQCN) of the entry. The type may be a `String`, `Byte`, `Short`, `Integer`, `Long`, `Boolean`, `Double`, or `Float` (all with their full `java.lang` qualification). The type helps the deployer know what's expected. If you're familiar with the EJB deployment descriptor, these tags may look familiar; they have the same names and semantics in EJB as well.

Java code can retrieve the `<env-entry>` values using JNDI:

```
Context initCtx = new InitialContext();
Boolean mailPincode = (Boolean) initCtx.lookup("java:comp/env/mailPincode");
```

All entries are placed by the server into the `java:comp/env` context. If you're new to JNDI, you can think of this as a URL base or filesystem directory. The `java:comp/env` context is read-only and unique per web application, so if two different web applications define the same environment entry, the entries do not collide. The context abbreviations, by the way, stand for *component environment.*

Example 12-1 shows a servlet that displays all its environment entries, using the JNDI API to browse the `java:comp/env` context.

Example 12-1. Snooping the java:comp/env Context

```
import java.io.*;
import java.util.*;
import javax.servlet.*;
import javax.servlet.http.*;

import javax.naming.*;

public class EnvEntrySnoop extends HttpServlet {

  public void doGet(HttpServletRequest req, HttpServletResponse res)
                               throws ServletException, IOException {
    res.setContentType("text/plain");
    PrintWriter out = res.getWriter();

    try {
      Context initCtx = new InitialContext();
      NamingEnumeration enum = initCtx.listBindings("java:comp/env");

      // We're using JDK 1.2 methods; that's OK since J2EE requires JDK 1.2
      while (enum.hasMore()) {
        Binding binding = (Binding) enum.next();
        out.println("Name: " + binding.getName());
        out.println("Type: " + binding.getClassName());
        out.println("Value: " + binding.getObject());
        out.println();
      }
    }
    catch (NamingException e) {
      e.printStackTrace(out);
    }
  }
}
```

Assuming the previous *web.xml* entry, the servlet would generate:

```
Name: mailPincode
Type: java.lang.Boolean
Value: false
```

Remember, a server that does not support J2EE is not required to support these tags or any of the tags we talk about in this section.

References to EJB Components

When the environment entry object is an EJB component, there's a special `<ejb-ref>` tag that must be used. It provides a way for servlets to get a handle to an EJB using an abstract name. The deployer ensures the availability of an appropriate bean at runtime based on the constraints given by the `<ejb-ref>` tag. The tag may contain a `<description>`, `<ejb-ref-name>`, `<ejb-ref-type>`, `<home>`, `<remote>`, and `<ejb-link>`. Here's a typical `<ejb-ref>`:

```
<ejb-ref>
  <description>Cruise ship cabin</description>
  <ejb-ref-name>ejb/CabinHome</ejb-ref-name>
  <ejb-ref-type>Entity</ejb-ref-type>
  <home>com.titan.cabin.CabinHome</home>
  <remote>com.titan.cabin.Cabin</remote>
</ejb-ref>
```

These tags also have similar counterparts in EJB, and in fact this example is borrowed from the book *Enterprise JavaBeans* by Richard Monson-Haefel (O'Reilly). The `<description>` supports the deployer and is optional but recommended. The `<ejb-ref-name>` dictates the JNDI lookup name. It's recommended (but not required) that the name be placed within the `ejb/` subcontext, making the full path to the bean `java:comp/env/ejb/CabinHome`. The `<ejb-ref-type>` must have a value of either `Entity` or `Session`, the two types of EJB components.* Finally, the `<home>` element specifies the fully qualified class name of the EJB's home interface, while the `<remote>` element specifies the FQCN of the EJB's remote interface.

A servlet would obtain a reference to the `Cabin` bean with the following code:

```
InitialContext initCtx = new InitialContext();
Object ref = initCtx.lookup("java:comp/env/ejb/CabinHome");
CabinHome home =
  (CabinHome) PortableRemoteObject.narrow(ref, CabinHome.class);
```

If the assembler writing the *web.xml* file has a specific EJB component in mind for an EJB reference, that information can be conveyed to the deployer with the addition of the optional `<ejb-link>` element. The `<ejb-link>` element should refer to the `<ejb-name>` of an EJB component registered in an EJB deployment

* The Servlet API 2.2 Specification states, "The `ejb-ref-type` element contains the expected Java class type of the referenced EJB." This is a confirmed mistake. The actual purpose is as stated here.

descriptor within the same J2EE application. The deployer has the option to use the suggestion or override it. Here's an updated *web.xml* entry:

```
<ejb-ref>
  <description>Cruise ship cabin</description>
  <ejb-ref-name>ejb/CabinHome</ejb-ref-name>
  <ejb-ref-type>Entity</ejb-ref-type>
  <home>com.titan.cabin.CabinHome</home>
  <remote>com.titan.cabin.Cabin</remote>
  <ejb-link>CabinBean</ejb-link>
</ejb-ref>
```

References to External Resource Factories

Finally, for those times when the environment entry is a resource factory, there's a `<resource-ref>` tag to use. A factory is an object that creates other objects on demand. A resource factory creates resource objects, such as database connections or message queues.

The `<resource-ref>` tag may contain a `<description>`, `<res-ref-name>`, `<res-type>`, and `<res-auth>`. Here's a typical `<resource-ref>`:

```
<resource-ref>
  <description>Primary database</description>
  <res-ref-name>jdbc/primaryDB</res-ref-name>
  <res-type>javax.sql.DataSource</res-type>
  <res-auth>CONTAINER</res-auth>
</resource-ref>
```

The `<description>` again supports the deployer and is optional but recommended. The `<res-ref-name>` dictates the JNDI lookup name. It's recommended but not required to place the resource factories under a subcontext that describes the resource type:

- `jdbc/` for a JDBC `javax.sql.DataSource` factory
- `jms/` for a JMS `javax.jms.QueueConnectionFactory` or `javax.jms.TopicConnectionFactory`
- `mail/` for a JavaMail `javax.mail.Session` factory
- `url/` for a `java.net.URL` factory

The `<res-type>` element specifies the FQCN of the resource factory (not the created resource). The factory types in the preceding list are the standard types. A server has the option to support additional types; user factories cannot be used. The upcoming J2EE 1.3 specification proposes a "connector" mechanism to extend this model for user-defined factories.

The `<res-auth>` tells the server who is responsible for authentication. It can have two values: `CONTAINER` or `SERVLET`. If `CONTAINER` is specified, the servlet container (the J2EE server) handles authentication before binding the factory to JNDI, using credentials provided by the deployer. If `SERVLET` is specified, the servlet must handle authentication duties programmatically. To demonstrate:

```
InitialContext initCtx = new InitialContext();
DataSource source =
  (DataSource) initCtx.lookup("java:comp/env/jdbc/primaryDB");

// If "CONTAINER"
Connection con1 = source.getConnection();

// If "SERVLET"
Connection con2 = source.getConnection("user", "password");
```

These tags too have similar counterparts in the EJB deployment descriptor. The only difference is that in EJB the two possible values for `<res-auth>` are `Container` and `Application` (note the inexplicable case difference).

Servlet Distribution in a J2EE Environment

The final difference between servlets in a standalone environment and servlets in a J2EE environment involves a subtle change to the rules for session distribution. While a standard web server is required to support only `java.io.Serializable` objects in the session for a distributable application, a J2EE-compliant server that supports a distributed servlet container must also support several additional types of objects:

- Any `javax.ejb.EJBObject`
- Any `javax.ejb.EJBHome`
- Any `javax.transaction.UserTransaction`
- The `javax.naming.Context` for `java:comp/env`

All these are interfaces that do not implement `Serializable`. For transferring the objects the container may use its own custom mechanism, perhaps based on serialization or perhaps not. Additional class types may be supported at the server's discretion, but these are the only guaranteed types.

In this chapter:
- *Western European Languages*
- *Conforming to Local Customs*
- *Non–Western European Languages*
- *Multiple Languages*
- *Dynamic Language Negotiation*
- *HTML Forms*

13
Internationalization

Despite its name, the World Wide Web has a long way to go before it can be considered to truly extend worldwide. Sure, physical wires carry web content to nearly every country across the globe. But to be considered a true worldwide resource, that web content has to be readable to the person receiving it—something that often doesn't occur with today's large number of English-only web pages.

The situation is starting to change, however. Many of the largest web sites have established areas designed for non-English languages. For example, the Netscape home page is available to English speakers at *http://home.netscape.com/index.html*, to French speakers at *http://home.netscape.com/fr/index.html*, and to speakers of a dozen other languages at a dozen other URLs.

It's also possible for web servers to support a transparent solution, in which a single URL can be used to view the same content in several languages, with the language chosen based on the preference of the client. Which language you see depends on how you've configured your browser.* Although this technique creates the impression that a dynamic translation is occurring, in reality the server just has several specially named versions of the static document at its disposal.

While these techniques work well for static documents, they don't address the problem of how to internationalize and localize dynamic content. That's the topic of this chapter. Here we explore how servlets can use the internationalization capabilities added to JDK 1.1 to truly extend the Web worldwide.

First, let's discuss terminology. *Internationalization* (a word that's often mercifully shortened to *I18N* because it begins with an *I*, ends with an *N*, and has 18 letters in

* Many older browsers do not support language customization, however. For example, the feature was added first in Netscape Navigator 4 and Microsoft Internet Explorer 4.

between) is the task of making a program flexible enough to run in any locale. *Localization* (often shortened to *L10N*) is the process of arranging for a program to run in a specific locale. This chapter, for the most part, covers servlet internationalization. We'll cover localization only in the case of dates, times, numbers, and other objects for which Java has built-in localization support.

Western European Languages

Let's begin with a look at how a servlet outputs a page written in a Western European language such as English, Spanish, German, French, Italian, Dutch, Norwegian, Finnish, or Swedish. As our example, we'll say "Hello World!" in Spanish, generating a page similar to the one shown in Figure 13-1.

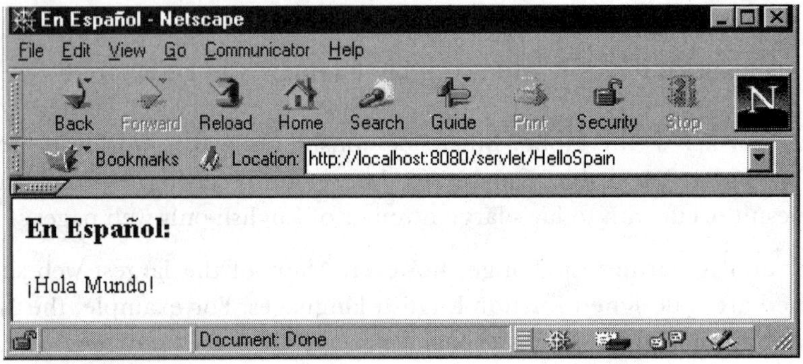

Figure 13-1. En Español: ¡Hola Mundo!

Notice the use of the special characters *ñ* and *¡*. Characters such as these, while scarce in English, are prevalent in Western European languages. Servlets have two ways to generate these characters: with HTML character entities or Unicode escape sequences.

HTML Character Entities

HTML 2.0 introduced the ability for specific sequences of characters in an HTML page to be displayed as a single character. The sequences, called *character entities*, begin with an ampersand (&) and end with a semicolon (;). Character entities can either be named or numbered. For example, the named character entity `ñ` represents *ñ*, while `¡` represents *¡*. A complete listing of special characters and their names is given in Appendix E, *Character Entities*. Example 13-1 shows a servlet that uses named entities to say "Hello World" in Spanish.

Example 13-1. Hello to Spanish Speakers, Using Named Character Entities

```
import java.io.*;
import javax.servlet.*;
import javax.servlet.http.*;

public class HelloSpain extends HttpServlet {

  public void doGet(HttpServletRequest req, HttpServletResponse res)
                               throws ServletException, IOException {
    res.setContentType("text/html");
    PrintWriter out = res.getWriter();
    res.setHeader("Content-Language", "es");

    out.println("<HTML><HEAD><TITLE>En Espa&ntilde;ol</TITLE></HEAD>");
    out.println("<BODY>");
    out.println("<H3>En Espa&ntilde;ol:</H3>");
    out.println("&iexcl;Hola Mundo!");
    out.println("</BODY></HTML>");
  }
}
```

You may have noticed that, in addition to using character entities, this servlet sets its `Content-Language` header to the value `es`. The `Content-Language` header is used to specify the language of the following entity body. In this case, the servlet uses the header to indicate to the client that the page is written in Spanish (Español). Most clients ignore this information, but it's polite to send it anyway. Languages are always represented using two-character lowercase abbreviations. For a complete listing, see the ISO-639 standard at *http://www.ics.uci.edu/pub/ietf/http/related/iso639.txt.*

Character entities can also be referenced by number. For example, `ñ` represents *ñ*, and `¡` represents *¡*. The number corresponds to the character's ISO-8859-1 (Latin-1) decimal value, which will be discussed later in this chapter. A complete listing of the numeric values for character entities can also be found in Appendix E. Example 13-2 shows `HelloSpain` rewritten using numeric entities.

Example 13-2. Hello to Spanish Speakers, Using Numbered Character Entities

```
import java.io.*;
import javax.servlet.*;
import javax.servlet.http.*;

public class HelloSpain extends HttpServlet {

  public void doGet(HttpServletRequest req, HttpServletResponse res)
                               throws ServletException, IOException {
    res.setContentType("text/html");
```

Example 13-2. Hello to Spanish Speakers, Using Numbered Character Entities (continued)

```
    PrintWriter out = res.getWriter();
    res.setHeader("Content-Language", "es");

    out.println("<HTML><HEAD><TITLE>En Espa&#241;ol</TITLE></HEAD>");
    out.println("<BODY>");
    out.println("<H3>En Espa&241;ol:</H3>");
    out.println("&#161;Hola Mundo!");
    out.println("</BODY></HTML>");
  }
}
```

Unfortunately, there's one major problem with the use of character entities: they work only for HTML pages. If the servlet's output isn't HTML, the page looks something like Figure 13-2. To handle non-HTML output, we need to use *Unicode escapes*.

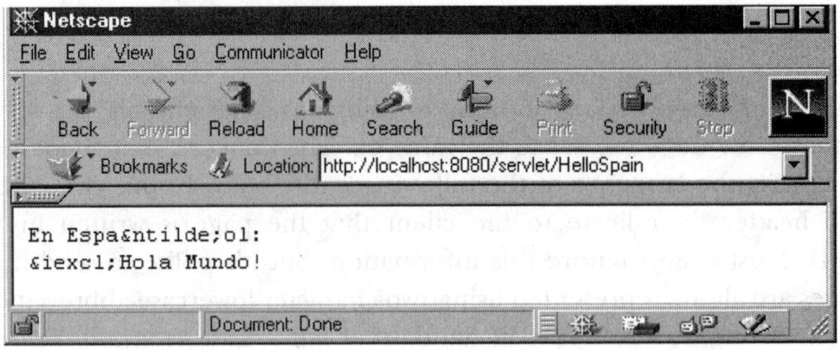

Figure 13-2. Not quite Spanish

Unicode Escapes

In Java, characters, strings, and identifiers are internally composed of 16-bit (2-byte) Unicode 2.0 characters. Unicode was established by the Unicode Consortium, which describes the standard as follows (see *http://www.unicode.org*):

> The Unicode Worldwide Character Standard is a character coding system designed to support the interchange, processing, and display of the written texts of the diverse languages of the modern world. In addition, it supports classical and historical texts of many written languages.
>
> In its current version (2.0), the Unicode standard contains 38,885 distinct coded characters derived from the Supported Scripts. These characters cover the principal written languages of the Americas, Europe, the Middle East, Africa, India, Asia, and Pacifica.

For more information on Unicode see *http://www.unicode.org*. Also see *The Unicode Standard, Version 2.0* (Addison-Wesley). Note that although Unicode 3.0 has become available, Java continues to support Version 2.0.

Java's use of Unicode is very important to this chapter because it means a servlet can internally represent essentially any character in any commonly used written language. We can represent 16-bit Unicode characters in 7-bit US-ASCII source code using Unicode escapes of the form \uxxxx, where *xxxx* is a sequence of four hexadecimal digits. The Java compiler interprets each Unicode escape sequence as a single character.

Conveniently, and not coincidentally, the first 256 characters of Unicode (`\u0000` to `\u00ff`) correspond to the 256 characters of ISO-8859-1 (Latin-1). Thus, the *ñ* character can be written as `\u00f1` and the *¡* character can be written as `\u00a1`. A complete listing of the Unicode escape sequences for ISO-8859-1 characters is also included in Appendix E. Example 13-3 shows `HelloSpain` rewritten using Unicode escapes.

Example 13-3. Hello to Spanish Speakers, Using Unicode Escapes

```
import java.io.*;
import javax.servlet.*;
import javax.servlet.http.*;

public class HelloSpain extends HttpServlet {

  public void doGet(HttpServletRequest req, HttpServletResponse res)
                               throws ServletException, IOException {
    res.setContentType("text/plain");
    PrintWriter out = res.getWriter();
    res.setHeader("Content-Language", "es");

    out.println("En Espa\u00f1ol:");
    out.println("\u00a1Hola Mundo!");
  }
}
```

The output from this servlet displays correctly when used as part of an HTML page or when used for plain-text output.

Conforming to Local Customs

Now we know how to use HTML character entities and Unicode escapes to display the characters in Western European languages. The question remains, what do we say with these languages? In general, this is a translation problem best left to a dedicated localization team. In some instances, however, Java provides some help.

For example, let's assume that in addition to saying "Hello World," we need our example servlet to tell the current time in a format naturally understood by the recipient. What could be a difficult formatting problem is actually quite easy because JDK 1.1 provides built-in support for localizing dynamic objects such as dates and times.

The trick is to use a `java.text.DateFormat` instance appropriate for the target audience. A `DateFormat` object can convert a `Date` to a correctly localized `String`. For example, a timestamp written in English as "February 16, 1998 12:36:18 PM PST" would be written in Spanish as "16 de febrero de 1998 12:36:18 GMT-08:00."

A `DateFormat` object is created using a factory method that accepts a formatting style (short, medium, long, full) and a `java.util.Locale` object that identifies the target audience (U.S. English, Mainland Chinese, etc.). The most common `Locale` constructor accepts two parameters: a two-character lowercase language abbreviation (as we saw earlier) and a two-character uppercase country code as defined by ISO-3166 (available at *http://www.chemie.fu-berlin.de/diverse/doc/ISO_3166.html*). An empty string for the country code indicates the default country for the language.

Example 13-4 shows the `HelloSpain` servlet using a `DateFormat` object to print the current time in a format naturally understood by a Spanish-speaking recipient.

Example 13-4. Hello to Spanish Speakers, with the Localized Time

```
import java.io.*;
import java.text.*;
import java.util.*;
import javax.servlet.*;
import javax.servlet.http.*;

public class HelloSpain extends HttpServlet {

  public void doGet(HttpServletRequest req, HttpServletResponse res)
                               throws ServletException, IOException {
    res.setContentType("text/plain");
    PrintWriter out = res.getWriter();
    res.setHeader("Content-Language", "es");

    Locale locale = new Locale("es", "");
    DateFormat fmt = DateFormat.getDateTimeInstance(DateFormat.LONG,
                                                    DateFormat.LONG,
                                                    locale);
    fmt.setTimeZone(TimeZone.getDefault());

    out.println("En Espa\u00f1ol:");
```

Example 13-4. Hello to Spanish Speakers, with the Localized Time (continued)

```
    out.println("\u00a1Hola Mundo!");
    out.println(fmt.format(new Date()));
  }
}
```

This servlet first creates a `Locale` that represents a generic Spanish environment. Then it uses that `Locale` to create a `DateFormat` instance that formats dates in Spanish. Next, it sets the time zone to the default time zone (the time zone of the server). The reason is that, by default, a `DateFormat` object formats its times to match the time zone in which it assumes the intended recipient is located, in this case Spain. Because this servlet can't be sure that's a correct assumption, it overrides the default and sets the time zone to match the server's. It would be better, of course, to set the time zone to accurately match the client's location, but that's not currently possible without additional user-provided information. Finally, after saying its "Hello World," this servlet prints the correctly formatted date and time. The output is shown in Figure 13-3.

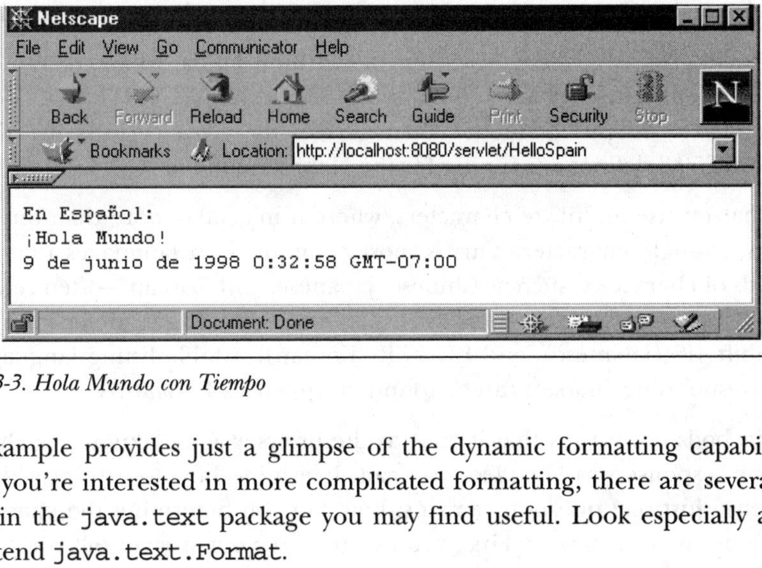

Figure 13-3. Hola Mundo con Tiempo

This example provides just a glimpse of the dynamic formatting capabilities of Java. If you're interested in more complicated formatting, there are several other classes in the `java.text` package you may find useful. Look especially at those that extend `java.text.Format`.

Non-Western European Languages

Let's continue now with a look at how a servlet outputs a page written in a non-Western European language, such as Russian, Japanese, Chinese, Korean, or Hebrew. To understand how to work with these languages, we must first understand how things work behind the scenes of our previous examples.

Charsets

Let's begin looking at the situation from the perspective of the browser. Imagine having the browser's job. You make an HTTP request to some URL and receive a response. That response, in the basest terms, is nothing more than a long sequence of bytes. How do you know how to display that response?

A common way, and in fact the default way, is to assume that every byte represents one of 256 possible characters and to further assume that the character a byte represents can be determined by looking up the byte value in some table. The default table is specified by the ISO-8859-1 standard, also called Latin-1. It contains byte-to-character mappings for the characters most commonly used in Western European languages. So, by default, you (acting as the browser) can receive a sequence of bytes and convert them to a sequence of Western European characters.

Now what do you do if you want to receive text that isn't written in a Western European language? You have to take the long sequence of bytes in the response and interpret it differently, using some other byte-sequence-to-character mapping. Technically put, you need to use a different *charset.** There are an infinite number of potential charsets. Fortunately, there are only a few dozen that are commonly used.

Some charsets use single-byte characters in a fashion similar to ISO-8859-1, though with a different byte-to-character mapping. For example, ISO-8859-5 defines a byte-to-character mapping for the characters of the Cyrillic (Russian) alphabet, while ISO-8859-8 defines a mapping for the Hebrew alphabet.†

Other charsets use multibyte characters, where it may take more than one byte to represent a single character. This is most common with languages that contain thousands of characters, such as Chinese, Japanese, and Korean—often referred to collectively as *CJK*. Charsets used to display these languages include Big5 (Chinese), Shift_JIS (Japanese), and EUC-KR (Korean). A table listing languages and their corresponding charsets can be found in Appendix F, *Charsets*.

What this boils down to is that if you (as the browser again) know the charset in which the response was encoded, you can determine how to interpret the bytes you receive. Just one question remains: how can you determine the charset? You can do it in one of two ways. First, you can require your user to tell you the charset. With Netscape Navigator 4, this is done through View → Encoding; with Netscape Navigator 6, it is done through View → Character Coding. With Microsoft Internet Explorer 4, it's done through View → Fonts; with Microsoft Internet

* A *charset* (a byte-sequence-to-character mapping) is not the same as a *character set* (a set of characters). See RFC 2278 at *http://www.ietf.org/rfc/rfc2278.txt* for a full explanation.

† It's useful to note that, for nearly all charsets, the byte values between 0 and 127 decimal represent the standard US-ASCII characters, allowing English text to be added to a page written in nearly any language.

Explorer 5, it's View → Encoding. This approach often requires the user to try a few charsets until the display makes sense. The second possibility is that the server (or servlet) specifies the charset in the `Content-Type` header you receive. For example, the following `Content-Type` value:

```
text/html; charset=Shift_JIS
```

indicates that the charset is Shift_JIS. Unfortunately, a few older browsers can be confused by the inclusion of a charset in the `Content-Type` header.

Writing Encoded Output

Now that we understand charsets from the perspective of the browser, it's time to return to the perspective of the servlet. A servlet's role is to do the following:

1. Choose a charset and set it for the servlet.
2. Get a `PrintWriter` for that charset.
3. Output characters that can be displayed using that charset.

Example 13-5 demonstrates with a servlet that says "Hello World" and displays the current date and time in Japanese.

Example 13-5. Hello to Japanese Speakers

```
import java.io.*;
import java.text.*;
import java.util.*;
import javax.servlet.*;
import javax.servlet.http.*;

public class HelloJapan extends HttpServlet {

  public void doGet(HttpServletRequest req, HttpServletResponse res)
                               throws ServletException, IOException {
    res.setContentType("text/plain; charset=Shift_JIS");
    PrintWriter out = res.getWriter();
    res.setHeader("Content-Language", "ja");

    Locale locale = new Locale("ja", "");
    DateFormat full = DateFormat.getDateTimeInstance(DateFormat.LONG,
                                                     DateFormat.LONG,
                                                     locale);
    out.println("In Japanese:");
    out.println("\u4eca\u65e5\u306f\u4e16\u754c"); // Hello World
    out.println(full.format(new Date()));
  }
}
```

Figure 13-4 shows a screen shot of Example 13-5.

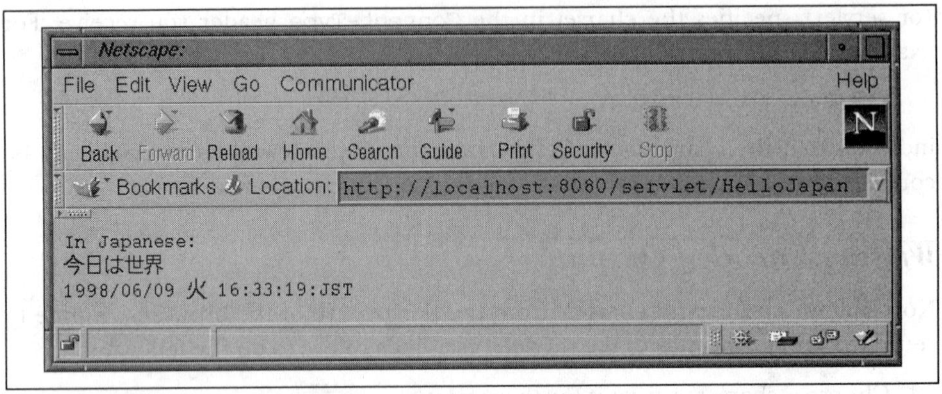

Figure 13-4. A Japanese hello

This servlet starts by setting the content type to `text/plain` and the charset to `Shift_JIS`. Then it calls `res.getWriter()` just like always—except in this case the `PrintWriter` it receives is special. This `PrintWriter` encodes all the servlet's output in the Shift_JIS charset because that charset is specified in the `Content-Type` header. This second line is therefore equivalent to the following:

```
PrintWriter out = new PrintWriter(
  new OutputStreamWriter(res.getOutputStream(), "Shift_JIS"), true);
```

Also, be sure to note that the call to `res.getWriter()` may throw an `UnsupportedEncodingException` if the charset is not recognized by Java* or an `IllegalStateException` if `getOutputStream()` has been called already on this request.

The servlet next creates a `Locale` with the language `ja` to represent a generic Japanese environment and then creates a `DateFormat` to match. Finally, it prints the equivalent of "Hello World" in Japanese, using Unicode escapes for the characters, and outputs the current date and time.

For this servlet to work, your server's classpath must include the `sun.io.CharToByte*` converter classes or their equivalent. On some platforms, these are not always included by default. Also, for the Japanese glyphs (or glyphs from other languages) to display correctly in the browser, the browser has to support the charset and have access to the necessary fonts to display the charset.

* With some early versions of Java, it may in some situations erroneously throw an `IllegalArgumentException` if the charset is not recognized.

For more information on the internationalization capabilities of Netscape Navigator, see *http://home.netscape.com/eng/intl/index.html*. For more information on the capabilities of Microsoft Internet Explorer, see *http://www.microsoft.com/ie/intlhome.htm*.

Reading and Writing Encoded Output

It can often be prohibitively slow to enter hundreds or thousands of Unicode escapes manually in Java source files. An easier option is to write the servlet using an internationalized text editor, saving the file in an appropriate charset. So long as the charset is one recognized by Java, the source can be compiled with almost any modern Java compiler. For example, with the *javac* that comes with the JDK a servlet source file encoded with Shift_JIS would be compiled like this:

```
javac -encoding Shift_JIS HelloJapan.java
```

The *HelloJapan.java* source file should look nearly identical to Example 13-5, the only difference being than the Unicode escapes can be replaced by native Japanese characters. If you looked at the encoded file with a Japanese text editor, you would see Japanese characters between the `out.println()` double quotes. If you used any other text editor, those characters—and depending on the encoding sometimes the whole file—would look like gibberish. Interestingly, the contents of the *.class* file are identical whether compiling with Unicode escapes or encoded source files.

Another option, useful when the programmer doesn't understand the language of the output page, is to write the servlet using standard ASCII but read localized text from an encoded file. For example, let's assume the "Hello World" Japanese text we want to output is saved by someone on the localization team in a file named *HelloWorld.ISO-2022-JP*, using the ISO-2022-JP encoding to make things more interesting. A servlet can read this file and send the content to the browser using the Shift_JIS encoding, as shown in Example 13-6.

Example 13-6. Sending Localized Output Read from a File

```
import java.io.*;
import java.text.*;
import java.util.*;
import javax.servlet.*;
import javax.servlet.http.*;

public class HelloJapanReader extends HttpServlet {

  public void doGet(HttpServletRequest req, HttpServletResponse res)
                               throws ServletException, IOException {
    res.setContentType("text/plain; charset=Shift_JIS");
    PrintWriter out = res.getWriter();
    res.setHeader("Content-Language", "ja");
```

Example 13-6. Sending Localized Output Read from a File (continued)

```
    Locale locale = new Locale("ja", "");
    DateFormat full = DateFormat.getDateTimeInstance(DateFormat.LONG,
                                                     DateFormat.LONG,
                                                     locale);
    out.println("In Japanese:");

    try {
      FileInputStream fis = new FileInputStream(
        getServletContext().getRealPath("/HelloWorld.ISO-2022-JP"));
      InputStreamReader isr = new InputStreamReader(fis, "ISO-2022-JP");
      BufferedReader reader = new BufferedReader(isr);
      String line = null;
      while ((line = reader.readLine()) != null) {
        out.println(line);
      }
    }
    catch (FileNotFoundException e) {
      // No Hello for you
    }

    out.println(full.format(new Date()));
  }
}
```

This servlet is essentially a character-encoding converter. It reads the *HelloWorld.ISO-2022-JP* text encoded with ISO-2022-JP and internally converts it to Unicode. Then, it outputs the same text by converting from Unicode to Shift_JIS.

Multiple Languages

Now it's time to push the envelope a little and attempt something that has only recently become possible. Let's write a servlet that includes several languages on the same page. In a sense, we have already written such a servlet. Our last example, `HelloJapan`, included both English and Japanese text. It should be observed, however, that this is a special case. Adding English text to a page is almost always possible, due to the convenient fact that nearly all charsets include the 128 US-ASCII characters. In the more general case, when the text on a page contains a mix of languages and none of the previously mentioned charsets contains all the necessary characters, we require an alternate technique.

UCS-2 and UTF-8

The best way to generate a page containing multiple languages is to output 16-bit Unicode characters to the client. There are two common ways to do this: UCS-2 and UTF-8. UCS-2 (Universal Character Set, 2-byte form) sends Unicode characters in what could be called their natural format, 2 bytes per character. All characters, including US-ASCII characters, require 2 bytes. UTF-8 (UCS Transformation Format, 8-bit form) is a variable-length encoding. With UTF-8, a Unicode character is transformed into a 1-, 2-, or 3-byte representation. In general, UTF-8 tends to be more efficient than UCS-2 because it can encode a character from the US-ASCII charset using just 1 byte. For this reason, the use of UTF-8 on the Web far exceeds UCS-2. For more information on UTF-8, see RFC 2279 at *http://www.ietf.org/rfc/rfc2279.txt.*

Before we proceed, you should know that support for UTF-8 is not yet guaranteed. Netscape first added support for the UTF-8 encoding in Netscape Navigator 4, and Microsoft first added support in Internet Explorer 4.

Writing UTF-8

Example 13-7 shows a servlet that uses the UTF-8 encoding to say "Hello World!" and tell the current time (in the local time zone) in English, Spanish, Japanese, Chinese, Korean, and Russian.

Example 13-7. A Servlet Version of the Rosetta Stone

```
import java.io.*;
import java.text.*;
import java.util.*;
import javax.servlet.*;
import javax.servlet.http.*;

import com.oreilly.servlet.ServletUtils;

public class HelloRosetta extends HttpServlet {

  public void doGet(HttpServletRequest req, HttpServletResponse res)
                               throws ServletException, IOException {
    Locale locale;
    DateFormat full;

    try {
      res.setContentType("text/plain; charset=UTF-8");
      PrintWriter out = res.getWriter();

      locale = new Locale("en", "US");
      full = DateFormat.getDateTimeInstance(DateFormat.LONG,
                                            DateFormat.LONG,
                                            locale);
      out.println("In English appropriate for the US:");
      out.println("Hello World!");
```

Example 13-7. A Servlet Version of the Rosetta Stone (continued)

```
    out.println(full.format(new Date()));
    out.println();

    locale = new Locale("es", "");
    full = DateFormat.getDateTimeInstance(DateFormat.LONG,
                                          DateFormat.LONG,
                                          locale);
    out.println("En Espa\u00f1ol:");
    out.println("\u00a1Hola Mundo!");
    out.println(full.format(new Date()));
    out.println();

    locale = new Locale("ja", "");
    full = DateFormat.getDateTimeInstance(DateFormat.LONG,
                                          DateFormat.LONG,
                                          locale);
    out.println("In Japanese:");
    out.println("\u4eca\u65e5\u306f\u4e16\u754c");
    out.println(full.format(new Date()));
    out.println();

    locale = new Locale("zh", "");
    full = DateFormat.getDateTimeInstance(DateFormat.LONG,
                                          DateFormat.LONG,
                                          locale);
    out.println("In Chinese:");
    out.println("\u4f60\u597d\u4e16\u754c");
    out.println(full.format(new Date()));
    out.println();

    locale = new Locale("ko", "");
    full = DateFormat.getDateTimeInstance(DateFormat.LONG,
                                          DateFormat.LONG,
                                          locale);
    out.println("In Korean:");
    out.println("\uc548\ub155\ud558\uc138\uc694\uc138\uacc4");
    out.println(full.format(new Date()));
    out.println();

    locale = new Locale("ru", "");
    full = DateFormat.getDateTimeInstance(DateFormat.LONG,
                                          DateFormat.LONG,
                                          locale);
    out.println("In Russian (Cyrillic):");
    out.print("\u0417\u0434\u0440\u0430\u0432\u0441\u0442");
    out.println("\u0432\u0443\u0439, \u041c\u0438\u0440");
    out.println(full.format(new Date()));
    out.println();
```

Example 13-7. A Servlet Version of the Rosetta Stone (continued)

```
      }
      catch (Exception e) {
        log(ServletUtils.getStackTraceAsString(e));
      }
    }
}
```

Figure 13-5 shows a screen shot of the servlet's output.

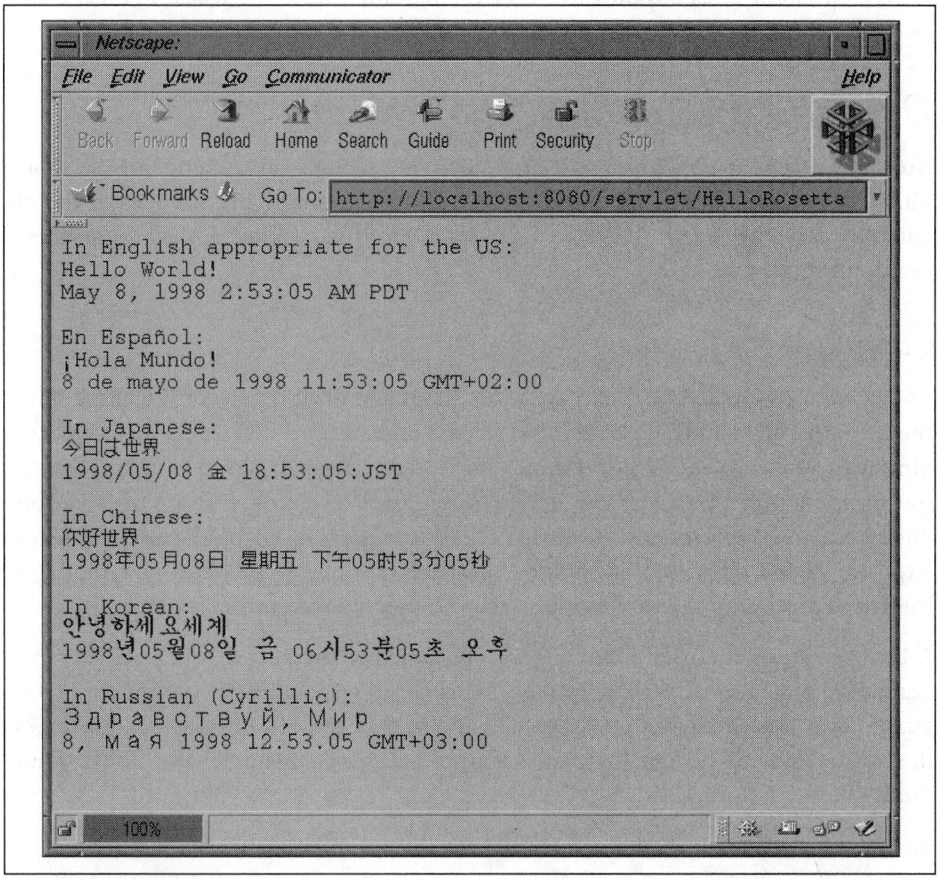

Figure 13-5. A true Hello World

For this servlet to work as written, your server must support JDK 1.1.6 or later. Earlier versions of Java throw an `UnsupportedEncodingException` when trying to get the `PrintWriter`, and the page is left blank. The problem is a missing charset alias. Java has had support for the UTF-8 encoding since JDK 1.1 was first introduced. Unfortunately, the JDK used the name `UTF8` for the encoding, while browsers expect the name `UTF-8`. So, who's right? It wasn't clear until early 1998, when the IANA (Internet Assigned Numbers Authority) declared UTF-8 to be the preferred name. (See *http://www.isi.edu/in-notes/iana/assignments/character-sets*.) Shortly thereafter, JDK 1.1.6 added UTF-8 as an alternate alias for the UTF8 encoding. For maximum portability across Java versions, you can use the UTF8 name directly with the following code:

```
res.setContentType("text/html; charset=UTF-8");
PrintWriter out = new PrintWriter(
  new OutputStreamWriter(res.getOutputStream(), "UTF8"), true);
```

Also, your client must support the UTF-8 encoding and have access to all the necessary fonts. Otherwise, some of your output is likely to appear garbled.

Dynamic Language Negotiation

Now let's push the envelope yet a little farther (perhaps off the edge of the table) with a servlet that tailors its output to match the language preferences of the client. This allows the same URL to serve its content to readers across the globe in their native tongues.

Language Preferences

There are two ways a servlet can know the language preferences of the client. First, the browser can send the information as part of its request. Newer browsers, beginning with Netscape Navigator 4 and Microsoft Internet Explorer 4, allow users to specify their preferred languages. With Netscape Navigator 4 and 6, this is done under Edit → Preferences → Navigator → Languages. With Microsoft Internet Explorer 4, it's done under View → Internet Options → General → Languages; Internet Explorer 5 moves the option from under View to under Tools.

A browser sends the user's language preferences to the server using the Accept-Language HTTP header. The value of this header specifies the language or languages that the client prefers to receive. Note that the HTTP specification allows this preference to be ignored. An Accept-Language header value looks something like the following:

```
en, es, de, ja, zh-TW
```

This indicates the client user reads English, Spanish, German, Japanese, and Chinese appropriate for Taiwan. By convention, languages are listed in order of preference. Each language may also include a *q-value* that indicates, on a scale from 0.0 to 1.0, an estimate of the user's preference for that language. The default q-value is 1.0 (maximum preference). An Accept-Language header value including q-values looks like this:

```
en, es;q=0.8, de;q=0.7, ja;q=0.3, zh-TW;q=0.1
```

This header value means essentially the same thing as the previous example.

The second way a servlet can know the language preferences of the client is by asking. For example, a servlet might generate a form that asks which language the client prefers. Thereafter, it can remember and use the answer, perhaps using the session-tracking techniques discussed in Chapter 7, *Session Tracking*.

Charset Preferences

In addition to an `Accept-Language` HTTP header, a browser may send an `Accept-Charset` header that tells the server which charsets it understands. An `Accept-Charset` header value may look something like this:

```
iso-8859-1, utf-8
```

This indicates the browser understands ISO-8859-1 and UTF-8. If the `Accept-Charset` isn't sent or if its value contains an asterisk (`*`), it can be assumed the client accepts all charsets. Note that the current usefulness of this header is limited: few browsers yet send the header, and those browsers that do tend to send a value that contains an asterisk.

Resource Bundles

Using `Accept-Language` (and, in some cases, `Accept-Charset`), a servlet can determine the language in which it will speak to each client. But how can a servlet efficiently manage several localized versions of a page? One answer is to use Java's built-in support for resource bundles.

A resource bundle holds a set of localized resources appropriate for a given locale. For example, a resource bundle for the French locale might contain a French translation of all the phrases output by a servlet. Then, when the servlet determines it wants to speak French, it can load that resource bundle and use the stored phrases. All resource bundles extend `java.util.ResourceBundle`. A servlet can load a resource bundle using the static method `ResourceBundle.getBundle()`:

```
public static final
  ResourceBundle ResourceBundle.getBundle(String bundleName, Locale locale)
```

A servlet can pull phrases from a resource bundle using the `getString()` method of `ResourceBundle`:

```
public final String ResourceBundle.getString(String key)
```

A resource bundle can be created in several ways. For servlets, the most useful technique is to put a special properties file in the server's classpath that contains the translated phrases. The file should be specially named according to the pattern *bundlename_language.properties* or *bundlename_language_country.properties*. For example, use *Messages_fr.properties* for a French bundle or *Messages_zh_TW.properties* for a Chinese/Taiwan bundle. The file should contain US-ASCII characters in the following format:

```
name1=value1
name2=value2
...
```

Each line may also contain whitespace and Unicode escapes. The information in this file can be loaded automatically by the `getBundle()` method.

Writing to Each His Own

Example 13-8 demonstrates the use of `Accept-Language`, `Accept-Charset`, and resource bundles with a servlet that says "Hello World" to each client in that client's own preferred language. Here's a sample resource bundle properties file for English, which you would store in *HelloBabel_en.properties* somewhere searched by the server's class loader (such as *WEB-INF/classes*):

```
greeting=Hello world
```

And here's a resource bundle for Japanese, to be stored in *HelloBabel_ja.properties*:

```
greeting=\u4eca\u65e5\u306f\u4e16\u754c
```

This `HelloBabel` servlet uses the `com.oreilly.servlet.LocaleNegotiator` class that contains the black box logic to determine which `Locale`, charset, and `ResourceBundle` should be used. Its code is shown in the next section.

Example 13-8. A Servlet Version of the Tower of Babel

```
import java.io.*;
import java.util.*;
import java.text.*;
import javax.servlet.*;
import javax.servlet.http.*;

import com.oreilly.servlet.LocaleNegotiator;
import com.oreilly.servlet.ServletUtils;

public class HelloBabel extends HttpServlet {

  public void doGet(HttpServletRequest req, HttpServletResponse res)
                               throws ServletException, IOException {
    try {
      String bundleName = "HelloBabel";
      String acceptLanguage = req.getHeader("Accept-Language");
      String acceptCharset = req.getHeader("Accept-Charset");

      LocaleNegotiator negotiator =
```

Example 13-8. A Servlet Version of the Tower of Babel (continued)

```
        new LocaleNegotiator(bundleName, acceptLanguage, acceptCharset);

      Locale locale = negotiator.getLocale();
      String charset = negotiator.getCharset();
      ResourceBundle bundle = negotiator.getBundle();  // may be null

      res.setContentType("text/plain; charset=" + charset);
      res.setHeader("Content-Language", locale.getLanguage());
      res.setHeader("Vary", "Accept-Language");

      PrintWriter out = res.getWriter();

      DateFormat fmt = DateFormat.getDateTimeInstance(DateFormat.LONG,
                                                       DateFormat.LONG,
                                                       locale);
      if (bundle != null) {
        out.println("In " + locale.getDisplayLanguage() + ":");
        out.println(bundle.getString("greeting"));
        out.println(fmt.format(new Date()));
      }
      else {
        out.println("Bundle could not be found.");
      }
    }
    catch (Exception e) {
      log(ServletUtils.getStackTraceAsString(e));
    }
  }
}
```

This servlet begins by setting the name of the bundle it wants to use, and then it retrieves its `Accept-Language` and `Accept-Charset` headers. It creates a `LocaleNegotiator`, passing in this information, and quickly asks the negotiator which `Locale`, charset, and `ResourceBundle` it is to use. Notice that a servlet may ignore the returned charset in favor of the UTF-8 encoding. And just remember, UTF-8 is not as widely supported as the charsets normally returned by `LocaleNegotiator`. Next, the servlet sets its headers: its `Content-Type` header specifies the charset, `Content-Language` specifies the locale's language, and the `Vary` header indicates to the client (if by some chance it should care) that this servlet can vary its output based on the client's `Accept-Language` header.

Once the headers are set, the servlet generates its output. It first gets a `PrintWriter` to match the charset. Then it says—in the default language, usually English—which language the greeting is to be in. Next, it retrieves and outputs the appropriate greeting from the resource bundle. And lastly, it prints the date and time appropriate to the client's locale. If the resource bundle is `null`, as happens when there are no resource bundles to match the client's preferences, the servlet simply reports that no bundle could be found.

The LocaleNegotiator Class

The code for `LocaleNegotiator` is shown in Example 13-9. Its helper class, `LocaleToCharsetMap`, is shown in Example 13-10. If you are happy to treat the locale negotiator as a black box, feel free to skip this section.

`LocaleNegotiator` works by scanning through the client's language preferences looking for any language for which there is a corresponding resource bundle. Once it finds a correspondence, it uses `LocaleToCharsetMap` to determine the charset. If there's any problem, it tries to fall back to U.S. English. The logic ignores the client's charset preferences.

The most complicated aspect of the `LocaleNegotiator` code is having to deal with the unfortunate behavior of `ResourceBundle.getBundle()`. The `getBundle()` method attempts to act intelligently. If it can't find a resource bundle that is an exact match to the specified locale, it tries to find a close match. The problem, for our purposes, is that `getBundle()` considers the resource bundle for the default locale to be a close match. Thus, as we loop through client languages, it's difficult to determine when we have an exact resource bundle match and when we don't. The workaround is to first fetch the ultimate fallback resource bundle, then use that reference later to determine when there is an exact match. This logic is encapsulated in the `getBundleNoFallback()` method.

Example 13-9. The LocaleNegotiator Class

```
package com.oreilly.servlet;

import java.io.*;
import java.util.*;

import com.oreilly.servlet.LocaleToCharsetMap;

public class LocaleNegotiator {

  private ResourceBundle chosenBundle;
  private Locale chosenLocale;
  private String chosenCharset;

  public LocaleNegotiator(String bundleName,
                          String languages,
                          String charsets) {

    // Specify default values:
    //   English language, ISO-8859-1 (Latin-1) charset, English bundle
```

Example 13-9. The LocaleNegotiator Class (continued)

```
    Locale defaultLocale = new Locale("en", "US");
    String defaultCharset = "ISO-8859-1";
    ResourceBundle defaultBundle = null;
    try {
      defaultBundle = ResourceBundle.getBundle(bundleName, defaultLocale);
    }
    catch (MissingResourceException e) {
      // No default bundle was found. Flying without a net.
    }

    // If the client didn't specify acceptable languages, we can keep
    // the defaults.
    if (languages == null) {
      chosenLocale = defaultLocale;
      chosenCharset = defaultCharset;
      chosenBundle = defaultBundle;
      return;  // quick exit
    }

    // Use a tokenizer to separate acceptable languages
    StringTokenizer tokenizer = new StringTokenizer(languages, ",");

    while (tokenizer.hasMoreTokens()) {
      // Get the next acceptable language.
      // (The language can look something like "en; qvalue=0.91")
      String lang = tokenizer.nextToken();

      // Get the locale for that language
      Locale loc = getLocaleForLanguage(lang);

      // Get the bundle for this locale. Don't let the search fallback
      // to match other languages!
      ResourceBundle bundle = getBundleNoFallback(bundleName, loc);

      // The returned bundle is null if there's no match. In that case
      // we can't use this language since the servlet can't speak it.
      if (bundle == null) continue;  // on to the next language

      // Find a charset we can use to display that locale's language.
      String charset = getCharsetForLocale(loc, charsets);

      // The returned charset is null if there's no match. In that case
      // we can't use this language since the servlet can't encode it.
      if (charset == null) continue;  // on to the next language

      // If we get here, there are no problems with this language.
      chosenLocale = loc;
      chosenBundle = bundle;
```

Example 13-9. The LocaleNegotiator Class (continued)

```
        chosenCharset = charset;
        return;  // we're done
      }

      // No matches, so we let the defaults stand
      chosenLocale = defaultLocale;
      chosenCharset = defaultCharset;
      chosenBundle = defaultBundle;
    }

    public ResourceBundle getBundle() {
      return chosenBundle;
    }

    public Locale getLocale() {
      return chosenLocale;
    }

    public String getCharset() {
      return chosenCharset;
    }

    private Locale getLocaleForLanguage(String lang) {
      Locale loc;
      int semi, dash;

      // Cut off any q-value that might come after a semi-colon
      if ((semi = lang.indexOf(';')) != -1) {
        lang = lang.substring(0, semi);
      }

      // Trim any whitespace
      lang = lang.trim();

      // Create a Locale from the language. A dash may separate the
      // language from the country.
      if ((dash = lang.indexOf('-')) == -1) {
        loc = new Locale(lang, "");  // No dash, no country
      }
      else {
        loc = new Locale(lang.substring(0, dash), lang.substring(dash+1));
      }

      return loc;
    }

    private ResourceBundle getBundleNoFallback(String bundleName, Locale loc) {
```

Example 13-9. The LocaleNegotiator Class (continued)

```
    // First get the fallback bundle -- the bundle that will be selected
    // if getBundle() can't find a direct match. This bundle can be
    // compared to the bundles returned by later calls to getBundle() in
    // order to detect when getBundle() finds a direct match.
    ResourceBundle fallback = null;
    try {
      fallback =
        ResourceBundle.getBundle(bundleName, new Locale("bogus", ""));
    }
    catch (MissingResourceException e) {
      // No fallback bundle was found.
    }

    try {
      // Get the bundle for the specified locale
      ResourceBundle bundle = ResourceBundle.getBundle(bundleName, loc);

      // Is the bundle different than our fallback bundle?
      if (bundle != fallback) {
        // We have a real match!
        return bundle;
      }
      // So the bundle is the same as our fallback bundle.
      // We can still have a match, but only if our locale's language
      // matches the default locale's language.
      else if (bundle == fallback &&
            loc.getLanguage().equals(Locale.getDefault().getLanguage())) {
        // Another way to match
        return bundle;
      }
      else {
        // No match, keep looking
      }
    }
    catch (MissingResourceException e) {
      // No bundle available for this locale
    }

    return null;  // no match
  }

  protected String getCharsetForLocale(Locale loc, String charsets) {
    // Note: This method ignores the client-specified charsets
    return LocaleToCharsetMap.getCharset(loc);
  }
}
```

Example 13-10. The LocaleToCharsetMap Class

```
package com.oreilly.servlet;

import java.util.*;

public class LocaleToCharsetMap {

  private static Hashtable map;

  static {
    map = new Hashtable();

    map.put("ar", "ISO-8859-6");
    map.put("be", "ISO-8859-5");
    map.put("bg", "ISO-8859-5");
    map.put("ca", "ISO-8859-1");
    map.put("cs", "ISO-8859-2");
    map.put("da", "ISO-8859-1");
    map.put("de", "ISO-8859-1");
    map.put("el", "ISO-8859-7");
    map.put("en", "ISO-8859-1");
    map.put("es", "ISO-8859-1");
    map.put("et", "ISO-8859-1");
    map.put("fi", "ISO-8859-1");
    map.put("fr", "ISO-8859-1");
    map.put("he", "ISO-8859-8");
    map.put("hr", "ISO-8859-2");
    map.put("hu", "ISO-8859-2");
    map.put("is", "ISO-8859-1");
    map.put("it", "ISO-8859-1");
    map.put("iw", "ISO-8859-8");
    map.put("ja", "Shift_JIS");
    map.put("ko", "EUC-KR");     // Requires JDK 1.1.6
    map.put("lt", "ISO-8859-2");
    map.put("lv", "ISO-8859-2");
    map.put("mk", "ISO-8859-5");
    map.put("nl", "ISO-8859-1");
    map.put("no", "ISO-8859-1");
    map.put("pl", "ISO-8859-2");
    map.put("pt", "ISO-8859-1");
    map.put("ro", "ISO-8859-2");
    map.put("ru", "ISO-8859-5");
    map.put("sh", "ISO-8859-5");
    map.put("sk", "ISO-8859-2");
    map.put("sl", "ISO-8859-2");
    map.put("sq", "ISO-8859-2");
    map.put("sr", "ISO-8859-5");
    map.put("sv", "ISO-8859-1");
    map.put("tr", "ISO-8859-9");
```

Example 13-10. The LocaleToCharsetMap Class (continued)

```
    map.put("uk", "ISO-8859-5");
    map.put("zh", "GB2312");
    map.put("zh_TW", "Big5");
  }

  public static String getCharset(Locale loc) {
    String charset;

    // Try for a full name match (may include country)
    charset = (String) map.get(loc.toString());
    if (charset != null) return charset;

    // If a full name didn't match, try just the language
    charset = (String) map.get(loc.getLanguage());
    return charset;  // may be null
  }
}
```

System-Provided Locales

Beginning with Servlet API 2.2 a servlet can get and set the preferred locale of the client using a few convenience methods. `ServletRequest` has a new `getLocale()` method that returns a `Locale` object indicating the client's most preferred locale. For HTTP servlets, the preference is based on the `Accept-Language` header. There's also a `getLocales()` method that returns an `Enumeration` of `Locale` objects indicating all the acceptable locales for the client, with the most preferred first. Accompanying these methods is a `setLocale(Locale loc)` method added to `ServletResponse` that allows a servlet to specify the locale of the response. The method automatically sets the `Content-Language` header and the `Content-Type` charset value. The `setLocale()` method should be called after `setContentType()` and before `getWriter()` (because it modifies the content type and impacts the `PrintWriter` creation). For example:

```
public void doGet(HttpServletRequest req, httpServletResponse res)
               throws ServletException, IOException {
  res.setContentType("text/html");
  Locale locale = req.getLocale();
  res.setLocale(locale);
  PrintWriter out = res.getWriter();

  // Write output based on locale.getLanguage()
}
```

While these methods allow for appealing code, they provide no assistance in determining whether or not a `Locale` is supported by the web application. To make this determination, you need extra logic like `LocaleNegotiator`.

HTML Forms

Managing HTML forms requires a little extra work and a few special tricks when you're dealing with localized content. To understand the problem, imagine this situation. An HTML form is sent as part of a Japanese page. It asks the user for his name, which he enters as a string of Japanese characters. How is that name submitted to the servlet? And, more importantly, how can the servlet read it?

The answer to the first question is that all HTML form data is sent as a sequence of bytes. Those bytes are an encoded representation of the original characters. With Western European languages, the encoding is the default, ISO-8859-1, with one byte per character. For other languages, there can be other encodings. Browsers tend to encode form data using the same encoding that was applied to the page containing the form. Thus, if the Japanese page mentioned was encoded using Shift_JIS, the submitted form data would also be encoded using Shift_JIS. Note that if the page did not specify a charset and the user had to manually choose Shift_JIS encoding for viewing, many browsers stubbornly submit the form data using ISO-8859-1.* Generally, the encoded byte string contains a large number of special bytes that have to be URL-encoded. If we assume the Japanese form sends the user's name using a GET request, the resulting URL might look like this:

http://server:port/servlet/NameHandler?name=%8CK%8C%B4%90%B3%8E%9F

The answer to the second question, how can a servlet read the submitted information, is a bit more complicated. A servlet has two choices. First, a servlet can leave the form data in its raw encoded format, treating it essentially like a sequence of bytes—with each byte awkwardly stored as a character in the parameter string. This tactic is useful only if the servlet does not need to manipulate the data and can be sure that the data is output only to the same user using the same charset. Alternatively, a servlet can convert the form data from its native encoded format to a Java-friendly Unicode string. This allows the servlet to freely manipulate the text and output the text using alternate charsets. There is one problem with this plan, however. Browsers currently provide no information to indicate which encoding was used on the form data. Browsers may provide that information in the future (using the `Content-Type` header in a POST, most likely), but for now, the servlet is left responsible for tracking that information.

The Hidden Charset

The commonly accepted technique for tracking the charset of submitted form data is to use a hidden charset form field.† Its value should be set to the charset of

* For more information on the internationalization of HTML and HTML forms, please see RFC 2070 at *http://www.ietf.org/rfc/rfc2070.txt.*

† Hidden form fields were first discussed in Chapter 7, where they were used for session tracking.

the page in which it is contained. Then, any servlet receiving the form can read the value of the charset field and know how to decode the submitted form data.

Example 13-11 demonstrates this technique with a form generator that sets the charset to match the charset of the page. Here's an English resource bundle that might accompany the servlet, stored as *CharsetForm_en.properties*:

```
title=CharsetForm
header=<H1>Charset Form</H1>
prompt=Enter text:
```

And here's a Japanese resource, to be stored as *CharsetForm_ja.properties*:

```
title=CharsetForm
header=<H1>\u6587\u5b57\u30bb\u30c3\u30c8\u30fb\u30d5\u30a9\u30fc\u30e0</H1>
prompt=\u30c6\u30ad\u30b9\u30c8\u3092\u5165\u529b\u3057\u3066\u304f\u3060\
\u3055\u3044
```

Example 13-11. Saving the Charset in a Hidden Form Field

```
import java.io.*;
import java.util.*;
import javax.servlet.*;
import javax.servlet.http.*;

import com.oreilly.servlet.LocaleNegotiator;
import com.oreilly.servlet.ServletUtils;

public class CharsetForm extends HttpServlet {

  public void doGet(HttpServletRequest req, HttpServletResponse res)
                               throws ServletException, IOException {
    try {
      String bundleName = "CharsetForm";
      String acceptLanguage = req.getHeader("Accept-Language");
      String acceptCharset = req.getHeader("Accept-Charset");

      LocaleNegotiator negotiator =
        new LocaleNegotiator(bundleName, acceptLanguage, acceptCharset);

      Locale locale = negotiator.getLocale();
      String charset = negotiator.getCharset();
      ResourceBundle bundle = negotiator.getBundle();  // may be null

      res.setContentType("text/html; charset=" + charset);
      res.setHeader("Content-Language", locale.getLanguage());
      res.setHeader("Vary", "Accept-Language");

      PrintWriter out = res.getWriter();
```

Example 13-11. Saving the Charset in a Hidden Form Field (continued)

```
        if (bundle != null) {
          out.println("<HTML><HEAD><TITLE>");
          out.println(bundle.getString("title"));
          out.println("</TITLE></HEAD>");
          out.println("<BODY>");
          out.println(bundle.getString("header"));
          out.println("<FORM ACTION=CharsetAction METHOD=get>");
          out.println("<INPUT TYPE=hidden NAME=charset value=" + charset + ">");
          out.println(bundle.getString("prompt"));
          out.println("<INPUT TYPE=text NAME=text>");
          out.println("</FORM>");
          out.println("</BODY></HTML>");
        }
        else {
          out.println("Bundle could not be found.");
        }
      }
      catch (Exception e) {
        log(ServletUtils.getStackTraceAsString(e));
      }
    }
}
```

A screen shot of the Japanese version is shown in Figure 13-6.

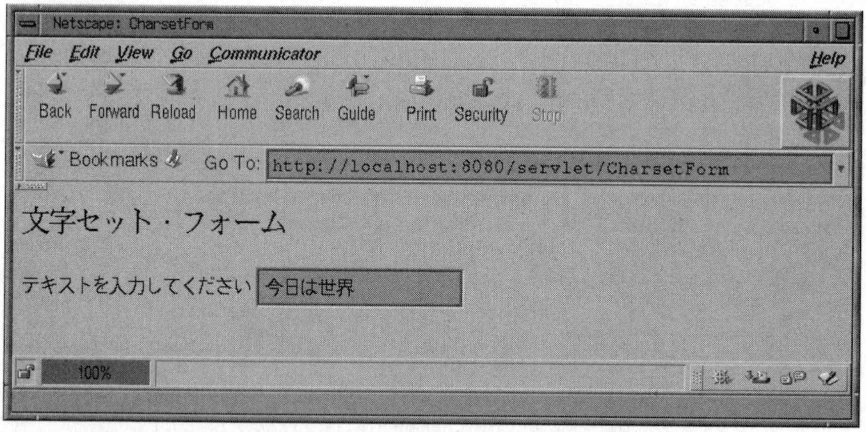

Figure 13-6. A Japanese form, with the user entering text

The servlet responsible for handling the submitted form is shown in Example 13-12. This servlet reads the submitted text and converts it to Unicode, then outputs the characters using the UTF-8 encoding. As a bonus, it also displays the received string as a Unicode escape string, showing what you would have to enter in a Java source file or resource bundle to create the same output. This lets the servlet act as a web-based native-charset-to-Unicode-string translator.

Example 13-12. Receiving the Charset in a Hidden Form Field

```
import java.io.*;
import java.text.*;
import java.util.*;
import javax.servlet.*;
import javax.servlet.http.*;

public class CharsetAction extends HttpServlet {

  public void doGet(HttpServletRequest req, HttpServletResponse res)
                               throws ServletException, IOException {
    try {
      res.setContentType("text/plain; charset=UTF-8");
      PrintWriter out = res.getWriter();

      String charset = req.getParameter("charset");

      // Get the text parameter
      String text = req.getParameter("text");

      // Now convert it from an array of bytes to an array of characters.
      // Do this using the charset that was sent as a hidden field.
      // Treat the original value as raw 8-bit bytes held within a String.
      text = new String(text.getBytes("ISO-8859-1"), charset);

      out.println("Received charset: " + charset);
      out.println("Received text: " + text);
      out.println("Received text (escaped): " + toUnicodeEscapeString(text));
    }
    catch (Exception e) {
      e.printStackTrace();
    }
  }

  public void doPost(HttpServletRequest req, HttpServletResponse res)
                               throws ServletException, IOException {
    doGet(req, res);
  }

  private static String toUnicodeEscapeString(String str) {
    // Modeled after the code in java.util.Properties.save()
    StringBuffer buf = new StringBuffer();
    int len = str.length();
    char ch;
    for (int i = 0; i < len; i++) {
```

Example 13-12. Receiving the Charset in a Hidden Form Field (continued)

```
        ch = str.charAt(i);
        switch (ch) {
          case '\\': buf.append("\\\\"); break;
          case '\t': buf.append("\\t"); break;
          case '\n': buf.append("\\n"); break;
          case '\r': buf.append("\\r"); break;

          default:
            if (ch >= ' ' && ch <= 127) {
              buf.append(ch);
            }
            else {
              buf.append('\\');
              buf.append('u');
              buf.append(toHex((ch >> 12) & 0xF));
              buf.append(toHex((ch >>  8) & 0xF));
              buf.append(toHex((ch >>  4) & 0xF));
              buf.append(toHex((ch >>  0) & 0xF));
            }
        }
      }
      return buf.toString();
    }

    private static char toHex(int nibble) {
      return hexDigit[(nibble & 0xF)];
    }

    private static char[] hexDigit = {
      '0','1','2','3','4','5','6','7','8','9','a','b','c','d','e','f'
    };
}
```

Sample output is shown in Figure 13-7.

Figure 13-7. Handling a Japanese form

The most interesting part of this servlet is the bit that receives and converts the submitted text:

```
text = new String(text.getBytes("ISO-8859-1"), charset);
```

The `text.getBytes("ISO-8859-1")` call converts the text to its raw `byte` format. Although the parameter value is returned as a `String`, it's not a true `String`. Each character in the `String` actually stores one byte of the encoded text, requiring this special conversion. The surrounding `String` constructor then creates a `String` from the raw bytes using the encoding specified by the charset field. It's ugly, but it works. For a more elegant solution, there's the `com.oreilly.servlet.ParameterParser` class introduced in Chapter 19, *Odds and Ends*.

14

In this chapter:
- *The Tea Language*
- *Getting Started*
- *Request Information*
- *Tea Administration*
- *Tea Applications*
- *A Tool Application*
- *Final Words*

The Tea Framework

Now we're ready to discuss servlet-based content creation frameworks. We'll postpone our discussion of JSP because it's the most complicated content creation alternative and start instead with a look at Tea. TeaServlet (colloquially known as *Tea*) is a product from the Walt Disney Internet Group (WDIG)—formerly GO.com—developed internally over the years to aid in the creation of high-traffic web sites such as ESPN.com, NFL.com, Disney.com, DisneyLand.com, Movies.com, ABC.com, and GO.com. It was recently released as open source in the hopes that others would find Tea useful and continue to enhance the tool. The strategy makes business sense; you share your tools in the hope that others will help sharpen them. Here we discuss TeaServlet 1.1.0, available at *http://opensource.go.com*. It requires Servlet API 2.1 or 2.2 and JDK 1.2 or later. TeaServlet's license is Apache-style, one of the least-restrictive licenses and most appealing to developers because it means you can use Tea in creating new products and sites without releasing those products as open source. This is the license model used by all Apache projects, including the Apache web server and the Tomcat server.

Tea was designed for projects run by small teams of developers and *technical producers*. The developer's role is the creation of "applications" written in Java and installed into the TeaServlet. A producer creates and maintains the final appearance of dynamic web pages by writing Tea templates that call upon functions provided by the developer's applications. For example, on an ESPN web site, one developer creates an application for team statistics, one developer (working independently) creates an application for player statistics, and a technical producer posts the data to the web using Tea templates. In fact, several producers working independently can use the same backend data to create targeted sites for different audiences—something WDIG has done for their sites including Disney.com, Movies.com, ESPN.com, and GO.com. The templates are written in the Tea language to enforce an excellent separation of content from presentation.

The Tea Language

Tea is a programming language designed for text formatting. It is strongly typed, compiled, and designed to work within a Java-based hosting environment. The TeaServlet is that hosting environment, making use of Tea for web page creation and providing a standard hook into servlet engines with which to call Tea template files.*

The main goal of the Tea language is to enforce separation between content and presentation, without sacrificing basic programming constructs. To this end, Tea was created with four basic constraints:

- Data or datatypes cannot be directly created; they are acquired.
- Acquired data cannot be directly modified in any way.
- A template cannot directly cause harm to its hosting environment.
- Only the minimum amount of programming constructs is provided.

These constraints additionally protect the system from a buggy or poorly written template, something that's extremely desirable when you have a site accepting new templates by the dozen, as occurs on popular news sites. This design also benefits web hosting companies that need to provide clients with the ability to create dynamic pages but don't want any particular client's mistake to negatively impact the rest of the server.

But do we need another language, especially a language that does *less* than Java? The *Tea Template Language Manual* answers this question:

> Tea resulted from several years of experience with other web page building mechanisms. Most web-based applications start out with HTML tags embedded in code, whether it be C, Perl, or Java. This approach is adequate for small or first-time projects because it doesn't take very long to develop.
>
> Because changes to page formatting can occur frequently, and developers don't wish to make these changes, they inevitably evolve into using some kind of token replacement templating mechanism. Each token is just a placeholder for a string, which contains application-created data. These template systems further evolve into supporting special constructs for formatting tables, forms, and simple conditional logic.
>
> When introducing programming constructs into a template, the challenge is to come up with something that is powerful enough, yet at the same time be simple and safe. If it's too powerful, then complete applications could be developed in

* Although Tea was designed for text formatting, it's actually possible for a Tea template to control an image-producing application class and easily script together a dynamic image. Unlike other content creation tools we'll discuss, Tea templates may output binary data as well as character data.

templates. If it is too weak, then HTML formatting ends up in the application. If it isn't simple or safe, then application developers end up writing and maintaining templates.

Rather than embedding an existing language into something like an ASP or JSP, Tea is a language specially designed to meet the requirements of a templating system. It is safe, simple, efficient, and powerful.

In one instance, Tea is integrated with a special servlet. This servlet gives Tea templates control over page building, while retaining strong ties to a backend application written by a Java developer. While this servlet provides functionality similar to that of JSPs, Tea enforces correct model-view separation because of the intentional language limitations. Although this is also the suggested separation model in JSPs, it cannot be enforced. In addition, Tea templates don't support programming features that can be used irresponsibly. Modifications need not go through a strict review and testing phase, which would still be required for JSPs.

Everyone working on a project should be empowered to do their job the most effectively, and Tea does its part by letting you do exactly what you need, as easily as possible, and no more. Even on projects run by just developers, using Tea is still beneficial. It encourages good development practices and it makes applications easier to maintain.

Readers of this book should also remember, Tea isn't a language intended for *you*; it's a language to be used by technical producers. It's a simpler language than Java, a safer language than Java, and equally as efficient as Java.

Getting Started

To get familiar with Tea, let's start simple by looking at a few standalone templates. These templates aren't going to take advantage of any supporting "application" Java classes and thus won't be able to do very much. Here is our first template:

```
<% template SimplePage() %>
This is a simple page that does nothing special.
```

This template simply outputs "This is a simple page that does nothing special." to everyone who accesses it. Templates are composed of code and text regions. Code regions are delimited by `<%` and `%>` (no other special delimiters are required). Text outside a code region is output by the template as is, which is why this template prints the simple statement.

To run the template, you must first save it to a file named *SimplePage.tea*. Similar to Java classes, the name of the file must match the name of the template as declared by the constructor (case sensitive), and the file must end with a *.tea* suffix. The location in which to save the template is configurable; we recommend a directory under *WEB-INF* such as *WEB-INF/templates*.

The next step to running the template is installing Tea itself. Download the distribution from *http://opensource.go.com* and follow their instructions for install: place the *TeaServlet.jar* file from the distribution into the web server's classpath. Then edit your web application's *web.xml* deployment descriptor to register the `TeaServlet` under the name `tea` with an init parameter specifying a location for configuration information. Also set up a prefix mapping rule that `/tea/*` invokes the `tea` servlet. An example *web.xml* addition is shown in Example 14-1.

Example 14-1. Installing TeaServlet

```
<!-- ... -->
<servlet>
    <servlet-name>
        tea
    </servlet-name>
    <servlet-class>
        com.go.teaservlet.TeaServlet
    </servlet-class>
    <init-param>
        <param-name>
            properties.file
        </param-name>
        <param-value>
            <!-- Edit this to be an absolute path to your prop file -->
            /tomcat/webapps/teatime/WEB-INF/TeaServlet.properties
        </param-value>
    </init-param>
</servlet>
<servlet-mapping>
    <servlet-name>
        tea
    </servlet-name>
    <url-pattern>
        /tea/*
    </url-pattern>
</servlet-mapping>
<!-- ... -->
```

The only thing you must customize is the path to the *TeaServlet.properties* file. It should be an absolute path. The *TeaServlet.properties* file configures the behavior of the `TeaServlet`. It can be quite long, which is why the *web.xml* file points to an external file instead of including the configuration information directly. We'll postpone a full discussion of the properties file for now and use the most simple *TeaServlet.properties* file possible:

```
# TeaServlet.properties
#
# Specify the location of Tea templates
template.path = /tomcat/webapps/teatime/WEB-INF/templates
```

Make sure to save the properties file at the location stated in the *web.xml* file. The final step is to restart your server so it reads the new *web.xml* file (with some servers this isn't necessary).

Once `TeaServlet` has been properly installed, the `SimplePage` can be accessed at a location such as *http://localhost:8080/teatime/tea/SimplePage.* The */teatime* portion of the path specifies the web application being accessed. The following */tea* portion matches the prefix mapping given in the `teatime` *web.xml*, causing the `TeaServlet` to be invoked to handle the request. Templates can be placed in subdirectories under `template.path`, in which case they're invoked using a path that includes the subdirectory name such as */teatime/tea/subdir/SimplePage.*

Request Information

That's a lot of work to create static content, so let's create something more dynamic. The template constructor can accept any number of parameters, whose values are passed in automatically from the request's parameters (through the query string and POST data). The parameters can be of type `String`, `Integer`, `Float`, `Double`, and any other `java.lang.Number` subclass. The conversion to numeric types happens automatically. If no parameter by a given name is sent, or the type conversion fails, the template receives a `null` parameter value. The template shown in Example 14-2 uses its constructor to accept a parameter called `name`:

```
<% template SimplePage(String name) %>
This is a simple page that does nothing special
except show a name: <% name %>
```

If you access the template as */teatime/tea/SimplePage?name=Waldo,* it will show "Waldo" in the page. If the template is accessed without a name parameter, it prints "null" in the page. Example 14-2 shows a template that checks for this case.

Example 14-2. A Template to Check Names

```
<% template SimplePage(String name) %>
This is a simple page that does nothing special
except show a name: <% name %>
<P>

<%
if (name == null) {
  "You gave a null name"
}
if (name == "Slim Shady") {
  "Please stand up"
}
%>
```

This new template checks if the name was `null` and if so prints a warning to the user. The template also checks if the name was `Slim Shady` and if so gives the user special treatment. It's important to notice two things from the `Slim Shady` comparison: first, string values in Tea can be equivalence-checked with the == operator (as can all objects). This means there's no need to explain to a technical producer the purpose of the `.equals()` method. Second, a `null` string can be compared to another string without risk of a `NullPointerException`, something that could happen with `.equals()`.

Digging Deeper

Other request information is available with TeaServlet. For example, a Tea template can access request headers and cookies, as well as parameters directly. Example 14-3 shows a Tea template that snoops request information. In practical use, it's fairly rare that a Tea template would need to access this information directly, choosing instead to let the application provide a processed version of the information to be displayed.

Example 14-3. A Template to Snoop Request Information

```
<% template Snoop() %>

<HTML><HEAD><TITLE>Let's Snoop!</TITLE></HEAD><BODY>

<% request = getRequest()  // Object type is implied %>

<H1>Miscellaneous Info</H1>
QueryString: <% request.queryString %> <BR>
RemoteUser: <% request.remoteUser %> <BR>

<H1>Parameter Info</H1>
<%
foreach (paramName in request.parameters.names) {
  paramName ": " request.parameters[paramName] "<BR>"
}
%>

<H1>Request Attribute Info</H1>
<%
foreach (attribName in request.attributes.names) {
  attribName ': ' request.attributes[attribName] '<BR>'
}
%>
```

Example 14-3. A Template to Snoop Request Information (continued)

```
<H1>Header Info</H1>
<%
foreach (headerName in request.headers.names) {
  headerName ': ' request.headers[headerName] '<BR>'
}
%>

<h1>Cookie Info</h1>
<%
foreach (cookie in request.cookies.all) {
  cookie.name ': ' cookie.value '<BR>'
}
%>
The session id cookie value is <% request.cookies["JSESSIONID"].value %>.

<% // Some things we can't do in Tea... %>
<%/*
"<H1>Read from the User's Session</H1>"
request.session["may"] = "work later"

"<H1>Set an Attribute</H1>"
request.attributes["will"] = "not work"

"<H1>Set a Cookie</H1>"
// Response manipulations are through application functions
*/%>

</BODY></HTML>
```

We can learn quite a lot about Tea from this simple example. First, local variables (such as the `request`) don't need to declared against an object type. They are strongly typed, but the type assignment is implicit. There's an `isa` keyword in the language to handle casting duties if necessary.

We use a `foreach` statement that handles the frequent task of looping over a collection of objects. It's a flexible device, able to iterate over arrays as well as any object that implements `java.util.Collection`. The `foreach` statement also supports iterating over a range and iterating in reverse. For example:

```
foreach (count in 1 .. 10 reverse) { count '<BR>' }
```

prints a countdown starting with 10. The `foreach` statement handles all looping duties in Tea; there is no `for` or `while` statement. (Thus there are also no infinite loops in Tea.)

Tea statements need not terminate with a semicolon as they do in Java, nor are statements separated by new lines. Instead, the Tea compiler uses the carefully designed Tea grammar to calculate the end of statements! Semicolons are still supported for the rare circumstance where a semicolon is required to disambiguate statement separation and as a convenience for Java programmers who instinctively add semicolons.

Much of the time there's no need for a string concatenation operator in Tea. The presence of a "double-quoted" or 'single-quoted' string within a Tea code block usually provides enough of a hint that there should be a string concatenation. For more explicit concatenation, use the `&` character. The `+` character isn't used because overloading the + operator causes typing ambiguities.

Comments in Tea follow the Java standard where `/*` and `*/` denote multiline comments and `//` begins a single-line comment. These comments aren't sent to the client, so long as you remember to place them within a Tea code block.

We used a multiline comment to comment out the final code block demonstrating things that can't be done: reading from a user's session, setting a request attribute, setting a cookie, and in fact setting anything on the request. The ability to access the session may be added later as part of the open source effort behind Tea; it's currently not supported only because WDIG internally uses another user-session-tracking mechanism. The other abilities are intentionally unsupported and would need to be done by Java code in a supporting application, due to the design constraint that "Acquired data cannot be directly modified in any way."

Tea Administration

The TeaServlet framework provides a centralized administration web page (written in Tea of course) with which a site administrator can manage all the Tea templates and supporting application classes. The administration screen makes it possible to view the currently loaded templates, view the currently enabled applications, and peruse the functions made available by those applications in a Javadoc-like style. It also provides access to runtime logs for the templates, letting the administrator view all logs or be more selective based on template and log level (`debug`, `info`, `warn`, or `error`). The administration screen also provides a mechanism for controlled template reloading, as we'll talk about later in detail. A screen shot of the Templates page is shown in Figure 14-1.

To run the TeaServlet administration application we must first flesh out the *TeaServlet.properties* file. An example configuration file is shown in Example 14-4.

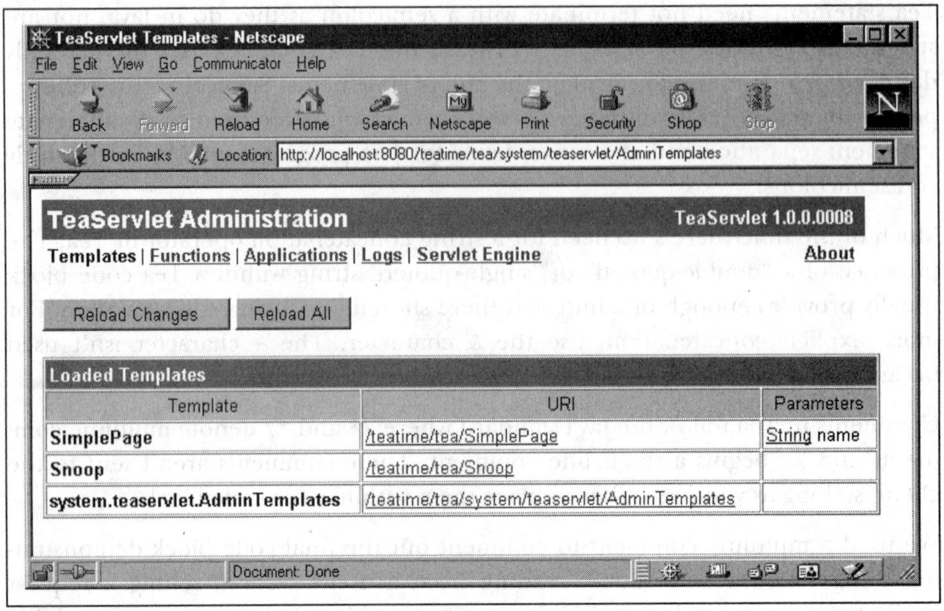

Figure 14-1. Administering the currently loaded templates

Example 14-4. A Starter TeaServlet.properties File

```
# TeaServlet.properties

# Specify the location of Tea templates (the .tea files)
template.path = /tomcat/webapps/teatime/WEB-INF/templates

# Specify an optional path for where the system will write compiled
# templates, as .class files
template.classes = /tomcat/webapps/teatime/WEB-INF/templateClasses

# Specify an optional default template to load if none is given
template.default = Index

# Specify the supporting applications to load into the TeaServlet system
applications {
    "System" {
        # The SystemApplication provides TeaServlet administration support
        class = com.go.teaservlet.AdminApplication
        init {
            # The security key for the Admin page
            admin.key = admin
            admin.value = true
        }
    }
    "Other" {
        class = MoreOnApplicationsLater
```

Example 14-4. A Starter TeaServlet.properties File (continued)

```
    }
}

# Specify what application messages are printed to the log file
log.debug = true
log.info = true
log.warn = true
log.error = true
```

The *TeaServlet.properties* file configures the TeaServlet system much like the *web.xml* file configures a web application. This file tells the `TeaServlet` where to find template files, where to place compiled template classes so they can be saved between server restarts, which applications should be loaded to support templates, and what level of log messages should be written by default. Each application must be registered in *TeaServlet.properties* with a specified class file and optionally specified init parameter name/value pairs.

The structure of *TeaServlet.properties* operates like a traditional `java.util.Properties` file with several important enhancements: ordering of elements is preserved, quotation marks (single or double) can be used to define keys that have embedded spaces, and properties may be nested using curly braces. Example 14-4 could be written using a normal Java properties file using the longhand shown in the following code (although if read by the `java.util.Properties` class the order between elements would be lost). The file could have been written using XML, although for simple uses such as this, XML may be buzzword-compliant overkill:

```
template.path=/tomcat/webapps/teatime/WEB-INF/templates
template.classes=/tomcat/webapps/teatime/WEB-INF/templatesClasses
applications.System.class=com.go.teaservlet.AdminApplication
applications.System.init.admin.key=admin
applications.System.init.admin.value=true
applications.Other.class=MoreOnApplicationsLater
log.debug=true
log.info=true
log.warn=true
log.error=true
```

After editing the *TeaServlet.properties* file and restarting your server, the system is ready for administration. The default location for the admin application (assuming it's installed in the */teatime* context) is *http://localhost:8080/teatime/tea/system/teaservlet/Admin?admin=true.* The *?admin=true* operates as a primitive security precaution; the name and value must match the `admin.key`/`admin.value` from the *TeaServlet.properties* file. There's really nothing significant an outsider could gain by accessing the admin pages, but having a wide-open front door isn't wise either, so this provides a primitive lock. The odds are good the open source community will quickly improve this security mechanism.

The most common use of the admin application is the reloading of template files. Templates do not automatically reload on access as do JSP pages. Changes to templates aren't seen until the Reload Changes button is clicked on the Templates admin screen. Compiling templates only on demand is more efficient than performing a file timestamp check during a request and also allows for a more explicit "publish" step to occur on an active site. The admin application rejects all changes if a template fails to compile, allowing the previous version to persist so clients *absolutely cannot* ever see a compile error. All errors occurring during the compile are listed in the administration application, as shown in Figure 14-2.

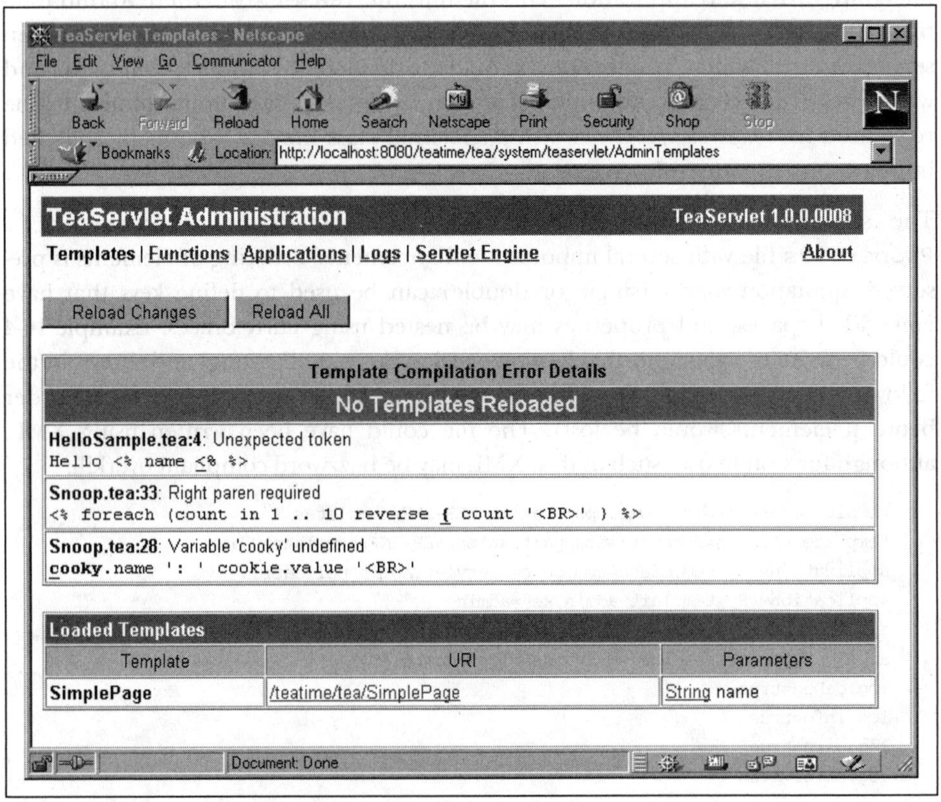

Figure 14-2. Comprehensive and precise compile error messages

Notice how the error location and description are perfectly precise. The TeaServlet can do this because Tea templates compile directly to Java bytecode! There's no interim *.java* file created and no Java compiler needed. Compiling templates directly to bytecode takes advantage of JIT and HotSpot technologies for maximizing performance, but unlike JSP pages, the compiler works directly on source written by the human and can better diagnose errors without the intermediary file adding a level of indirection. Also, Tea doesn't require bundling a Java compiler with the web server as is needed with JSP, a requirement that can be fraught with licensing difficulties. Tea can precompile templates as well, allowing the distribution of templates without the template source.

Compiled Templates: a Business Opportunity

The ability to distribute precompiled Tea templates opens up an interesting new business model. A vendor creating a web application using Tea has the option to sell the web application without giving away the original source code for the templates. All that's needed is the Tea library, which is portable across servers and can ship with the application. Being able to ship product without shipping code may encourage some vendors to produce new web applications for sale.

Note that JSP also supports precompiling pages. Unfortunately, the bytecode generated by JSP often has dependencies on container-specific classes and the generated class must follow a container-specific name-mangling convention (see Example 18-2 from Chapter 18, *JavaServer Pages*). This tends to tie the precompiled JSPs to a particular container.

Tea also handles runtime errors elegantly. Exceptions thrown from within Tea contain stack traces that include Tea template line numbers, like this:

```
2000/07/10 19:29:12.105 PDT> java.lang.NullPointerException:
    at com.go.teaservlet.template.SimplePage.execute(SimplePage.tea:5)
    at java.lang.reflect.Method.invoke(Native Method)
   at com.go.tea.runtime.TemplateLoader$TemplateImpl.execute(TemplateLoader.java,
Compiled Code)
    at com.go.teaservlet.TeaServlet.processTemplate(TeaServlet.java, Compiled
Code)
    at com.go.teaservlet.TeaServlet.doGet(TeaServlet.java:238)
    <etc>
```

Messages such as this can be viewed using the TeaServlet administration application. When they occur the client by default receives a 500 status code error page, intentionally without a stack trace for security reasons.

Tea also has an "exception guardian" feature. This feature enables Tea to continue to process the page while logging the exception. Tea renders whatever parts of the page it can while omitting the small section that is affected by the exception. For many sites, a page that is missing a small section is better than a server error being returned to the user.

Tea Applications

So far we've been looking at Tea templates alone, and they are very weak—*intentionally* weak. But Tea templates are like frontline infantry soldiers—when alone they are weak but when teamed with advanced backend air support, they become extremely powerful. Here are some ways to make Tea templates more powerful.

Templates may access any function from any "application" installed into the TeaServlet via the *TeaServlet.properties* file. (Each web application can have a different *TeaServlet.properties* file and thus a different set of installed applications.) Templates call functions by specifying within a Tea code block the function name followed by open and close parentheses. Functions may accept parameters and may return values:

```
<% list = getRecords() %>
<% removeRecord(8086) %>
```

The TeaServlet administration screen shows a list of all available functions from all installed applications. Should two applications declare the same function, a template can prefix the function call with the application name to remove the ambiguity:

```
<% list = RecordListApp.getRecords() %>
```

There's a set of utility functions available across all templates intended to help with basic text-processing chores. The following sections list some of the most frequently called utility functions.

Text Processing

Here are some common text-processing functions.

`Date currentDate()`
: Returns the current date.

`void dateFormat(String format)`
: Alters the format of all dates later output by this template.

`void numberFormat(String format)`
: Alters the format of all numbers later output by this template (not including string literal numbers).

`void nullFormat(String format)`
: Assigns a string to be used in place of null when printing a variable with a null value.

`void setLocale(String language, String country)`
: Alters the locale for all dates, numbers, and so forth later output by this template.

`boolean startsWith(String str, String prefix)`
: Returns `true` if the string starts with the prefix specified.

`boolean endsWith(String str, String suffix)`
: Returns `true` if the string ends with the suffix specified.

`String substring(String str, int startIndex, int endIndex)`
: Returns the section of the string from the start index to the end index (exclusive).

`String trim(String str)`
: Returns the string with leading and trailing whitespace removed.

`int[] find(String str, String search)`
`int[] find(String str, String search, int fromIndex)`
: Return the indexes at which the given string contains the search string, with an optional starting index.

`String replace(String source, String pattern, String replacement)`
`String replace(String source, String pattern, String replacement, int fromIndex)`
`String replace(String source, String pattern, String replacement, int fromIndex, int toIndex)`
: Replace all exact matches of the pattern within the source with the given replacement string, with an optional starting and ending index.

Content Handling

Here are some common content-handling methods.

`void insertFile(String filename)`
: Inserts the contents of the given file into the page output. Inserts nothing if the file can't be read. The filename can be relative or absolute. If absolute, the path is offset from the template root (usually the web application document root).

`void insertURL(String url)`
: Inserts the contents of the URL into the page output. If the URL can't be read, it inserts nothing. The URL can be relative or absolute.

`boolean fileExists(String filename)`
: Returns `true` if a file by the given name exists.

`boolean URLExists(String url)`
: Returns `true` if the given URL exists.

Request/Response Handling

In addition, here are some frequently-used request/response methods.

`com.go.teaservlet.HttpContext.Request getRequest()`
`com.go.teaservlet.HttpContext.Request getRequest(String encoding)`
: Get an object that contains request information, with an optional encoding to allow automatic parameter value conversion.

`void setContentType(String contentType)`
Sets the content type of the response.

`void setHeader(String name, String value)`
Sets a response header.

`void setStatus(int sc)`
Sets the status code of the response.

`void sendRedirect(String url)`
Redirects the request to the given URL.

`void sendError(int sc)`
`void sendError(int sc, String message)`
Send an error page for the given status code with an optional error message.

The template in Example 14-5 demonstrates how a template may call on the utility functions to print an ad-click-through percentage for a given day. The date and percentage are formatted in the French style.

Example 14-5. French Clicks

```
<% template clicks() %>

<HTML><HEAD><TITLE>Testing the Tea Built-In Functions</TITLE></HEAD><BODY>

<%
// Set the locale; it remains for all later template output
setLocale("fr", "CA")  // Quebec

// Specify how time and numbers should be formatted
dateFormat("d MMMM yyyy")
numberFormat("#0.00%")

// Some fake data
clicks = 485.0
accesses = 7673.0
%>

<H2><% currentDate() %></H2>
Le pourcentage: <% clicks/accesses %>

</BODY></HTML>
```

The template writes something like this, with the date and percentage appropriate for someone living in Quebec:

```
16 juillet 2000
Le pourcentage: 6,32%
```

Writing a Tea Application

Now let's look at how to write a custom Tea application. It's easy: just write an application class and a context class. All application classes implement the `com.go.teaservlet.Application` interface. Just like a servlet, the `Application` interface has `init()` and `destroy()` methods to handle lifecycle issues. Instead of a `service()` method the `Application` has a `createContext()` and `getContextType()` pair of methods. The `createContext()` method returns a context object whose methods are made available to templates as functions. The `getContextType()` method returns the `java.lang.Class` of the object returned by `createContext()` to facilitate type checking.

The following two examples show a simple application that attempts to determine the name of the user through various means. The `NameApp` class is the application class (Example 14-6); the `NameContext` class is the context object created by `NameApp` and made available to templates (Example 14-7).

Example 14-6. The NameApp Class

```
import com.go.teaservlet.*;
import javax.servlet.*;

public class NameApp implements Application {

  // Both init(ApplicationConfig) and destroy() must be implemented because
  // they are declared in the Application interface.  They can be left empty.
  public void init(ApplicationConfig config) throws ServletException {
  }

  // Creating a context provides functions accesible from the templates.
  public Object createContext(ApplicationRequest request,
                              ApplicationResponse response) {
    // You often pass on the request and response even if
    // they are not used, since they may be used later
    return new NameContext(request, response);
  }

  // This method must be implemented to return the class of the object
  // returned by createContext()
  public Class getContextType() {
    return NameContext.class;
  }

  public void destroy() {
  }
}
```

The TeaServlet calls the `init()` method a single time when the application is first loaded to give the application an opportunity to perform initialization. It calls `destroy()` a single time on shutdown to give the application a chance to clean up. The `init()` method accepts an `ApplicationConfig` parameter, which is a subinterface of `ServletConfig` with three additional methods—`getLog()`, `getName()`, and `getProperties()`—to retrieve the application log, name, and initialization properties.

The TeaServlet calls the `createContext()` method before request handling and makes available all the methods of the returned context object as functions for the requested Tea template. If there needs to be a different context per user, that can be easily managed using standard session-tracking code in the `createContext()` method. The `createContext()` method accepts `ApplicationRequest` and `ApplicationResponse` as parameters. These are subinterfaces of `HttpServletRequest` and `HttpServletResponse` with the addition of a few Tea methods.

Example 14-7. The NameContext Class

```
import com.go.teaservlet.*;
import javax.servlet.*;
import javax.servlet.http.*;

public class NameContext {

  ApplicationRequest request;
  ApplicationResponse response;
  String name;

  public NameContext(ApplicationRequest request,
                     ApplicationResponse response) {
    this.request = request;
    this.response = response;
  }

  public String getName() {
    // If we already determined the user's name, return it
    if (name != null) {
      return name;
    }

    // Try to determine the name of the user
    name = request.getRemoteUser();

    // If the login name isn't available, try reading a parameter
    if (name == null) {
      name = request.getParameter("name");
    }
```

Example 14-7. The NameContext Class (continued)

```
    // If the name isn't available as a parameter, try the session
    if (name == null) {
      name = (String) request.getSession().getAttribute("name");
    }

    // If the name isn't in the session, try a cookie
    if (name == null) {
      Cookie[] cookies = request.getCookies();
      for (int i = 0; i < cookies.length; i++) {
        if (cookies[i].getName().equals("name")) {
          name = cookies[i].getValue();
        }
      }
    }

    // If the name isn't in a cookie either, give up
    return name;
  }
}
```

The `getName()` method attempts to determine the name of the client user by searching the client's login credentials, parameter list, session data, and request cookies. It returns `null` if no name information could be found. Templates access the name by calling the `getName()` function. Notice the context calculates the client's name in `getName()`and not in the constructor. This is a performance trick. If the logic were in the constructor it would be executed during the handling of each request, whether or not any template actually called `getName()`.

To make the `NameApp` application available requires the following short addition to the *TeaServlet.properties* file:

```
"NameApp" {
    class = NameApp
}
```

You can verify the application was properly loaded by browsing the Applications link of the TeaServlet administration application.* With this application loaded, any template can display the client's name using the `getName()` function:

```
<% template names() %>
```

* If the application classes aren't found even though it appears they should be, the cause may be a class loader issue. There can be problems if the *TeaServlet.jar* and application classes are loaded by different class loaders. Either put both in the system classpath where they'll be found by the primordial class loader or put both under the *WEB-INF* directory where they'll be found by the web application class loader. (Put *TeaServlet.jar* in the *WEB-INF/lib* directory; put the application classes in the *WEB-INF/classes* directory.) Also remember that because of class loader issues, support classes aren't necessarily reloaded even when selecting Reload All from the TeaServlet administration page.

```
<%
setContentType("text/plain")
nullFormat("Unknown")
%>

Your name is <% getName() %>.
```

A Tool Application

Determining a user's name is hardly a realistic application, so let's continue now with something closer. We'll create an application that displays a list of the various content creation tools available (an application much like what Servlets.com requires). The tool information will come from an XML file, although it could just as well come from a database. Example 14-8 shows the `ToolApp` class.

Example 14-8. The Brains of a Tool Application

```
import com.go.teaservlet.*;
import com.go.trove.log.*;
import java.sql.Timestamp;
import java.util.*;
import javax.servlet.*;

public class ToolApp implements Application {

  private Log log;
  private Tool[] tools;

  public void init(ApplicationConfig config) throws ServletException {
    // Keep a log of events specific to this application
    log = config.getLog();

    // Load the tool data in our init for simplicity
    String toolsFile = config.getInitParameter("toolsFile");
    if (toolsFile == null) {
      throw new ServletException(
        "A tools data file must be specified as the toolsFile init parameter");
    }
    log.debug("Loading tools from " + toolsFile);
    try {
      tools = Tool.loadTools(toolsFile);
      if (tools.length == 0) {
        log.warn("No tools found in " + toolsFile);
      }
    }
    catch (Exception e) {
      log.error(e);
      throw new ServletException(e);
```

Example 14-8. The Brains of a Tool Application (continued)

```
    }
  }

  public Object createContext(ApplicationRequest request,
                              ApplicationResponse response) {
    return new ToolContext(request, response, this);
  }

  public Class getContextType() {
    return ToolContext.class;
  }

  public void destroy() {
  }

  public Tool[] getTools() {
    // Normally the "application" would maintain or have access to a
    // pre-existing database connection.  Here, for simplicity, we use XML.
    return tools;
  }

  public Tool[] getTools(String state) {
    // Return only tools of a given state
    // (submitted, live, rejected, or dead)
    List list = new LinkedList();
    for (int i = 0; i < tools.length; i++) {
      if (tools[i].getStateFlag().equalsIgnoreCase(state)) {
        list.add(tools[i]);
      }
    }
    return (Tool[]) list.toArray(new Tool[0]);
  }
}
```

The `init()` method of `ToolApp` uses the passed-in `ApplicationConfig` to retrieve and save a reference to the log, then uses the `config` to get the value of the init parameter `toolsFile`. This parameter value must be specified in the *TeaServlet.properties* file:

```
"ToolApp" {
    class = ToolApp
    init {
        toolsFile = /tomcat/webapps/teatime/WEB-INF/tools.xml
    }
}
```

The `init()` method then calls `loadTools()` to load the tool information from the XML file into the tools array. The XML file should look something like Example 14-9.

Example 14-9. Sample Data

```
<?xml version="1.0"?>

<tools>
  <tool id="1">
    <name>JavaServer Pages</name>
    <homeURL>http://java.sun.com/products/jsp</homeURL>
    <comments>
      JavaServer Pages (JSP) is a technology created by Sun Microsystems
      and closely tied to servlets.  As with servlets, Sun releases a JSP
      specification, and third-party vendors compete on their implementation
      of that standard.  Being released by Sun puts JSPs in a very privileged
      position, and had JSP solved a sufficient number of user problems it
      would probably have won the market before there were any other viable
      entries.  As is, a surprising number of users are disenchanted with JSP
      and alternatives are gaining popularity.
    </comments>
    <stateFlag>LIVE</stateFlag>
    <createdTime>1998-03-17 00:00:00.000</createdTime>
    <modifiedTime>1999-12-16 00:00:00.000</modifiedTime>
  </tool>
  <tool id="2">
    <name>Tea</name>
    <homeURL>http://opensource.go.com</homeURL>
    <comments>
      Tea is a newly open sourced product from the Walt Disney Internet Group,
      created internally over the years to solve their tremendous web production
      needs for sites such as ESPN.com.  It's similar to JSP although it avoids
      many of JSPs problems, and already has terrific tools support.
    </comments>
    <stateFlag>LIVE</stateFlag>
    <createdTime>2000-07-12 00:00:00.000</createdTime>
    <modifiedTime>2000-07-12 00:00:00.000</modifiedTime>
  </tool>
  <tool id="3">
    <name>WebMacro</name>
    <homeURL>http://jakarta.apache.org</homeURL>
    <comments>
      WebMacro is a template engine created by Semiotek as part of the Shimari
      project and now merged into the Apache Jakarta Project.  WebMacro has
      been used on commercial sites such as AltaVista.com, has been integrated
      in open source frameworks such as Turbine and Melati, and has been used
      in prominent open source projects such as JetSpeed.
    </comments>
```

Example 14-9. Sample Data (continued)

```
    <stateFlag>LIVE</stateFlag>
    <createdTime>1998-11-19 00:00:00.000</createdTime>
    <modifiedTime>2000-08-31 00:00:00.000</modifiedTime>
  </tool>
  <tool id="4">
    <name>Element Construction Set</name>
    <homeURL>http://java.apache.org/ecs</homeURL>
    <comments>
      The Element Construction Set (ECS) package from the Java Apache Project
      is a set of classes modeled after the htmlKona product from WebLogic
      (now BEA Systems).  ECS has many limitations, but it solves a certain
      class of problems.
    </comments>
    <stateFlag>LIVE</stateFlag>
    <createdTime>1999-03-31 00:00:00.000</createdTime>
    <modifiedTime>2000-06-16 00:00:00.000</modifiedTime>
  </tool>
  <tool id="5">
    <name>XMLC</name>
    <homeURL>http://xmlc.enhydra.org</homeURL>
    <comments>
      XMLC makes use of XML to get nearly all the power of ECS without many of
      its limitations.  It was created by Lutris as part of their Open Source
      Enhydra Application Server, and can be used as a separate component.
    </comments>
    <stateFlag>LIVE</stateFlag>
    <createdTime>1998-10-11 00:00:00.000</createdTime>
    <modifiedTime>2000-03-09 00:00:00.000</modifiedTime>
  </tool>
  <!-- etc -->
</tools>
```

The app reads this file using the JDOM API, an open source API for reading, writing, and manipulating XML from Java. If we wanted to read the results from a database instead, we could do this by simply replacing the JDOM `SAXBuilder` (which builds a `Document` from a file or stream using a SAX parser) with a JDOM `ResultSetBuilder` (which builds a `Document` from a `java.sql.ResultSet`, a contributed class to JDOM).* At the time of this writing, JDOM was still under development. This example uses JDOM Beta 5. Some minor changes may be required to work with the final JDOM release.

The `createContext()` method constructs a new `ToolContext` instance. The code for `ToolContext` is shown in Example 14-10.

* Jason is one of the co-creators of JDOM, along with Brett McLaughlin. More information on JDOM can be found at *http://jdom.org*.

Example 14-10. The Context Containing All Accessible Functions

```
import com.go.teaservlet.*;

public class ToolContext {

  ApplicationRequest request;
  ApplicationResponse response;
  ToolApp app;

  public ToolContext(ApplicationRequest request,
                     ApplicationResponse response,
                     ToolApp app) {
    this.request = request;
    this.response = response;
    this.app = app;
  }

  public Tool[] getTools() {
    return app.getTools();
  }

  public Tool[] getTools(String state) {
    return app.getTools(state);
  }
}
```

The public methods on the context are the functions made available to Tea templates. Here the methods call back to the application, something considered good style because contexts should be as lightweight as possible; state should be held in the application. The `Tool` class itself acts as a holder of `Tool` information. Example 14-11 shows its code.

Example 14-11. A Class to Load and Hold Tool Data

```
import java.io.*;
import java.sql.*;
import java.util.*;
import org.jdom.*;
import org.jdom.input.*;

public class Tool {
  // Data about this tool record
  public int id;
  public String name;
  public String homeURL;
  public String comments;
  public String stateFlag;
  public Timestamp createdTime;
```

Example 14-11. A Class to Load and Hold Tool Data (continued)

```
  public Timestamp modifiedTime;

  // Tea can only access bean properties, so accessor methods are required
  public int getId() { return id; }
  public String getName() { return name; }
  public String getHomeURL() { return homeURL; }
  public String getComments() { return comments; }
  public String getStateFlag() { return stateFlag; }
  public Timestamp getCreatedTime() { return createdTime; }
  public Timestamp getModifiedTime() { return modifiedTime; }


  public int getCreatedAgeInDays() {
    return (int) ((System.currentTimeMillis() - createdTime.getTime()) /
            (24 * 60 * 60 * 1000));  // millis in a day
  }

  public int getModifiedAgeInDays() {
    return (int) ((System.currentTimeMillis() - modifiedTime.getTime()) /
            (24 * 60 * 60 * 1000));  // millis in a day
  }


  // Ideally we'd use methods like these, but Tea only allows property
  // access on an object.  These won't be visible.
  public boolean isNewWithin(int days) {
    return getCreatedAgeInDays() < days;
  }

  public boolean isUpdatedWithin(int days) {
    return getModifiedAgeInDays() < days;
  }



  public static Tool[] loadTools(String toolsFile) throws Exception {
    // Read the tool data from an XML file containing <tool> elements
    // Use the JDOM API to keep things simple (http://jdom.org)
    List toolObjects = new LinkedList();

    SAXBuilder builder = new SAXBuilder();
    Document document = builder.build(new File(toolsFile));
    Element root = document.getRootElement();
    List toolElements = root.getChildren("tool");
    Iterator i = toolElements.iterator();
    while (i.hasNext()) {
      Element tool = (Element) i.next();
      Tool t = new Tool();
      t.id = tool.getAttribute("id").getIntValue();
```

Example 14-11. A Class to Load and Hold Tool Data (continued)

```
      t.name = tool.getChild("name").getTextTrim();
      t.homeURL = tool.getChild("homeURL").getTextTrim();
      t.comments = tool.getChild("comments").getTextTrim();
      t.stateFlag = tool.getChild("stateFlag").getTextTrim();
      t.createdTime = Timestamp.valueOf(
                      tool.getChild("createdTime").getTextTrim());
      t.modifiedTime = Timestamp.valueOf(
                       tool.getChild("modifiedTime").getTextTrim());
      toolObjects.add(t);
    }

    return (Tool[]) toolObjects.toArray(new Tool[0]);
  }
}
```

Notice that although the class has public variables holding its state, they aren't visible from Tea templates. Tea templates have access only to the functions declared by the installed contexts and to the bean properties of the objects returned by those functions. That's why the `Tool` class has various accessor methods. `Tool` also has two convenience methods to return the number of days since the record was created and modified. One might be tempted to use an `isNewWithin(int days)` or `isUpdatedWithin(int days)` method. However, the template cannot see the method because this does not appear as a bean property.

Example 14-12 shows a simple template frontend for this application. It's named `toolview1` and accepts an optional `state` parameter so views can be limited to tools of a particular state. A screen shot of its output is given in Figure 14-3.

Example 14-12. A Simple View of the Tools

```
<% template toolview1(String state) %>

<%
  if (state == null) {
    tools = getTools("live");
  }
  else {
    tools = getTools(state)
  }
%>

<% foreach (tool in tools) { %>

  <HR SIZE=2 ALIGN=LEFT>

  <H3>
  <% tool.name %>
```

Example 14-12. A Simple View of the Tools (continued)

```
  <%
  if (tool.createdAgeInDays < 45) {
    '<FONT COLOR=#FF0000><B> (New!) </B></FONT>'
  }
  else if (tool.modifiedAgeInDays < 45) {
    '<FONT COLOR=#FF0000><B> (Updated!) </B></FONT>'
  }
  %>
  </H3>
  <A HREF="<% tool.homeURL %>"><% tool.homeURL %></A><BR>

  <% tool.comments %>

<% } %>
```

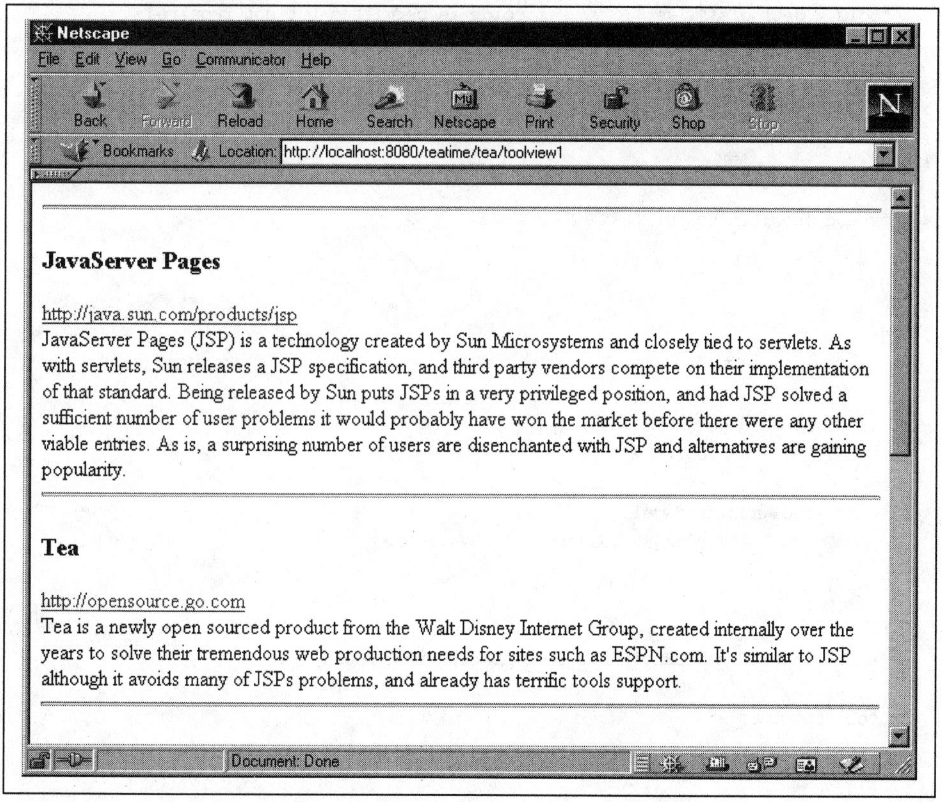

Figure 14-3. A tools listing with no surrounding content

As you can see, the output lacks the decoration (header, sidebar, footer) needed for a professional page. We can add such decoration by calling on other templates, as shown in the revised `toolview2` in Example 14-13.

Example 14-13. A More Complete View of the Tools

```
<% template toolview2(String state) %>

<%
    title = "Tool Listing"
    deck = "A list of content creation tools"
    desc = "Without tools, people are nothing more than animals.  And " &
           "pretty weak ones at that.  Here's a list of servlet-based " &
           "content creation tools you can use so you won't be a servlet " &
           "weakling."
%>

<% call header(title, deck, desc) %>

<%
  if (state == null) {
    tools = getTools("live");  // semicolon is permitted but not required
  }
  else {
    tools = getTools(state)
  }
%>

<% foreach (tool in tools) { %>

  <HR SIZE=2 ALIGN=LEFT>

  <H3>
  <% tool.name %>
  <%
  if (tool.createdAgeInDays < 45) {
    '<FONT COLOR=#FF0000><B> (New!) </B></FONT>'
  }
  else if (tool.modifiedAgeInDays < 45) {
    '<FONT COLOR=#FF0000><B> (Updated!) </B></FONT>'
  }
  %>
  </H3>
  <A HREF="<% tool.homeURL %>"><% tool.homeURL %></A><BR>

  <% tool.comments %>

<% } %>

<% call footer() %>
```

This new template defines variables for the page title, deck, and description. Then it calls a header template passing along these values. The header template generates the header and sidebar content, then lets the `toolview2` template add the core content. At the end of the page, the footer template adds the page footer. Sample header and footer templates are shown in Example 14-14 and Example 14-15. The improved output can be seen in Figure 14-4.

Example 14-14. The Header File

```
<% template header(String title, String deck, String desc) %>

<HTML><HEAD><TITLE><% title %></TITLE></HEAD>

<BODY BGCOLOR="#FFFFFF" BACKGROUND="/images/background.gif"
      LINK="#003333" ALINK="#669999" VLINK="#333333">

<IMG SRC="/images/banner.gif" WIDTH=600 HEIGHT=87 BORDER=0><BR>

<TABLE>
<TR>
<TD WIDTH=125 VALIGN=TOP>
 <BR><BR><BR>
 <FONT FACE="Arial,Helvetica" SIZE="+1" COLOR="#FF0000">
 <A HREF="/index.html">Home</A><BR>
 <A HREF="/hosting.html">Hosting</A><BR>
 <A HREF="/engines.html">Engines</A><BR>
 </FONT>
</TD>

<TD WIDTH=475>

  <TABLE CELLPADDING=5><TR><TD WIDTH=600 BGCOLOR="#006699" VALIGN=TOP>
  <B><FONT FACE="Arial,Helvetica" SIZE="+2">
  <% title %>
  </FONT></B>
  </TD></TR></TABLE>

  <B><FONT FACE="Arial,Helvetica" SIZE="+1" COLOR="#003366">
  <% deck %>
  </FONT></B><P>

  <P>
  <FONT FACE="Arial,Helvetica">

  <% desc %>
```

Example 14-15. The Footer File

```
<% template footer() %>

 </FONT>

</TD>
</TR>

<TR>
<TD></TD>
<TD WIDTH=475 ALIGN=CENTER COLSPAN=3>
<HR>
<FONT FACE="Arial,Helvetica">
<A HREF="/index.html">Home</A>  
<A HREF="/hosting.html">Hosting</A>  
<A HREF="/engines.html">Engines</A>  <P>
</FONT>

<TABLE WIDTH=100%>
<TR>
<TD WIDTH=260 ALIGN=LEFT VALIGN=TOP>
<FONT FACE="Arial,Helvetica">
<A HREF="/copyright.html">Copyright</A> &copy; 2000 Jason Hunter<BR>
All Rights Reserved.</TD>
<TD WIDTH=5></FONT></TD>
<TD WIDTH=230 ALIGN=RIGHT VALIGN=TOP>
<FONT FACE="Arial,Helvetica">
Contact: <A HREF="mailto:webmaster@servlets.com">webmaster@servlets.com</A>
</FONT></TD>
</TR>
</TABLE>

</TD>
</TR>
</TABLE>

</BODY>
</HTML>
```

Following this design, changes to the header, sidebar, or footer are isolated to single files. It also is possible to use a single file to lay out the entire page, inserting core content using the `<% ... %>` command. This approach provides more power and allows the core section of the page to not know about its outside formatting, although it takes a little getting used to. Be sure to read the TeaServlet documentation for more information.

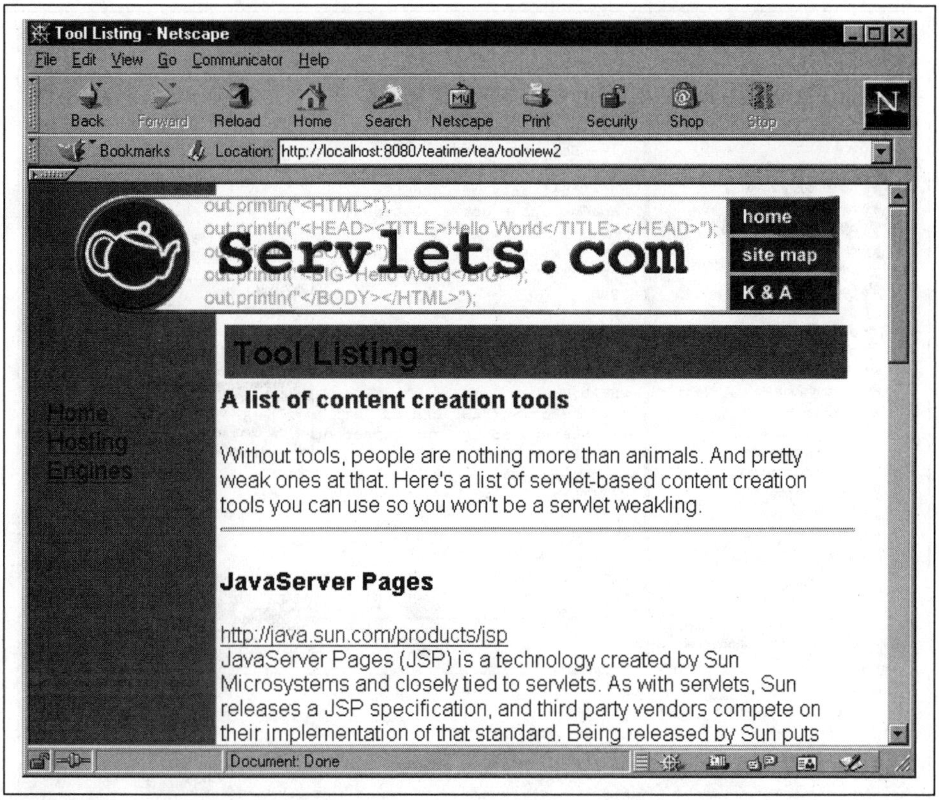

Figure 14-4. A tools listing with surrounding content

Final Words

One of the most useful features of Tea is hard to demonstrate in a book: its graphical authoring environment named Kettle, shown in Figure 14-5. In addition to the traditional IDE features, Kettle provides real-time feedback on the template authoring process—underlining as you type all syntax errors in green, semantic errors in red, and compilation errors in blue. Similar functionality in tools supporting other content creation mechanisms would be wonderful but nearly impossible to provide. Kettle also offers pop-up property examination to help the template creator immediately see what properties are available on any given object. Kettle is available for free but runs only on Windows and is not open source. In addition, there are plans to do an open source reimplementation based on Java Swing.

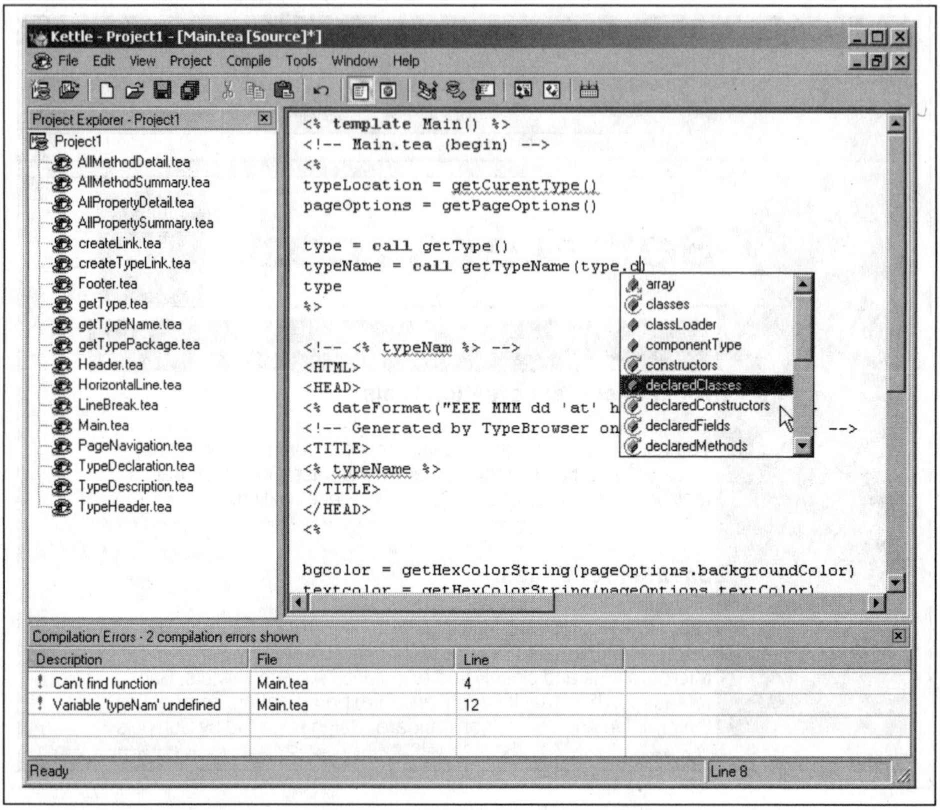

Figure 14-5. It's best to make Tea in a Kettle

As you explore Tea and the TeaServlet, you may notice support for special kinds of features are lacking because its creators (WDIG) didn't need them. Being newly open sourced, other users will input their needs and ideas, and the product will grow. Although the Tea language has matured, the TeaServlet is still quite new and there's lots of potential.

In this chapter:

- *The WebMacro Framework*
- *Installing WebMacro*
- *WebMacro Directives*
- *WebMacro Templates*
- *A Tool Application*
- *Filters*

15

WebMacro

In the same family as Tea, but following a more servlet-driven approach, is a development framework named WebMacro, available from *http://www.webmacro.org*. WebMacro was created by Justin Wells at Semiotek as part of the company's site creation contract service and released as open source to improve the tool and increase the company's exposure. There are talks of merging WebMacro into the Apache Jakarta Project at *http://jakarta.apache.org* to gain wider community-based development. Currently there's a clone of WebMacro named Velocity being developed within Jakarta.

WebMacro is commonly referred to as a *template engine*, the generic name for systems that perform text replacement operations inside web page templates. There are other open source template engines available, most notably FreeMarker (*http://freemarker.sourceforge.net*); however, we look at WebMacro here because at the time of this writing it has the largest mindshare, has been used on large commercial sites such as AltaVista, has been integrated in open source frameworks such as Turbine (*http://java.apache.org/turbine*) and Melati (*http://www.melati.org*), and has been used as a base for prominent open source projects such as JetSpeed (*http://java.apache.org/jetspeed*). Like Tea, WebMacro is licensed under an Apache-style license so it can be used in conjunction with commercial applications without any problem.

This section covers WebMacro 0.94, a prerelease snapshot from October 2000. Things are subject to change and are going to change. If the example code listed here doesn't work with the final release, be sure to read the documentation provided with the WebMacro release to determine what changed. WebMacro requires Servlet API 2.0 or later and JDK 1.1.7 or later.

The WebMacro Framework

The WebMacro framework works like this: a servlet receives a client request, the servlet does the business logic required to handle the request (likely using supporting classes or components such as EJBs), and the servlet creates a context object full of "answer objects" containing the results of the business logic that should be displayed to the client. The servlet then selects a template file (perhaps based on the business logic results) and pushes the answer objects through the template file generating content for the client.

A Java programmer creates the servlet and the business logic in pure Java, and a template engineer creates the template file for rendering. The template consists of HTML or XML content filled with a simple substitution syntax and minor scripting abilities. The syntax is HTML and XML-editor friendly, explicitly avoiding the use of angle brackets to ensure HTML and XML parsers don't get confused. The programmer provides to the template engineer a list of variables that will be present, as well as a list of the properties and methods of those variables.

The model has some similarity to the TeaServlet architecture, with the difference that WebMacro by default uses more of a servlet-driven push model, provides no sandboxing of the template, and uses a more simplified scripting syntax. We suspect that WebMacro has an advantage over Tea for highly functional web applications that have a completion point, and Tea has an advantage over WebMacro for sites that continuously add new template content and need template sandboxing and less programmer involvement.

Saying Hello with WebMacro

Example 15-1 demonstrates a simple servlet making use of the WebMacro templating system. Example 15-2 shows the *hello.wm* template file. Together they print the current date and time. We'll talk about where to place the files in the next section.

Example 15-1. A Simple Servlet to Drive the Hello Template

```
import java.io.*;
import java.util.*;
import javax.servlet.*;
import javax.servlet.http.*;

import org.webmacro.*;
import org.webmacro.servlet.*;

public class WMHello extends HttpServlet {

  public void doGet(HttpServletRequest req, HttpServletResponse res)
                               throws ServletException, IOException {
```

Example 15-1. A Simple Servlet to Drive the Hello Template (continued)

```
    FastWriter out = new FastWriter(res.getOutputStream(),
                                    res.getCharacterEncoding());

    try {
      WebMacro wm = new WM(); // optionally WM("/path/to/config/file")
      Context c = wm.getWebContext(req, res);
      c.put("date", new Date());
      Template tmpl = wm.getTemplate("hello.wm");
      tmpl.write(out, c);
      out.flush();
    }
    catch (WebMacroException e) {
      throw new ServletException(e);
    }
  }
}
```

Example 15-2. A Simple Hello Template

```
## hello.wm

#set $Response.ContentType = "text/html"

<HTML><HEAD><TITLE>Testing WebMacro</TITLE></HEAD><BODY>

Hello! <P>

The current time is $date. <BR>
(For you nerds, that's $date.Time milliseconds.) <P>

</BODY></HTML>
```

Let's look first at the servlet. It's a normal servlet, extending `HttpServlet` and implementing the `doGet()` method. You'll notice right away that its logic is different. It retrieves a `FastWriter` instead of a normal `PrintWriter`. This allows special optimizations to avoid the cost of Unicode conversion for static content. It works like an ordinary writer with the improvement that WebMacro can push preencoded bytes through it and also call `setAsciiHack(true)` to gain speed when outputting Latin-1 or US-ASCII data. Just be aware that (at least currently) you must call the writer's `flush()` method to send the writer's buffered content to the client.

The code within the `try` block creates a new `WebMacro` object, to act as its primary hook into the WebMacro system. `WebMacro` is an interface, so the servlet actually constructs an instance of the concrete class `WM` that implements the `WebMacro` interface. The servlet then calls `wm.getWebContext(req, res)` to retrieve a WebContext in which to put answer objects to be passed to the template. The context operates like a Hashtable. It has a put(Object, Object) method which the servlet uses to place a Date object in the context under the name date. That object will then be available to the template executing within this context. For power users, it's interesting to note that the WebContext class extends Context, and the servlet could retrieve a non–web-aware Context by calling getContext(). This comes in handy for some situations, such as for offline or nonservlet use.

To retrieve a template, the servlet calls wm.getTemplate("hello.wm"). The method accepts the name of the template to retrieve, including the file extension. A template can use any file extension, but most people use *.wm* by standard convention. With the template in hand, the servlet can call the template's write() method and pass as its parameters the FastWriter to write to and the WebContext full of answer objects. The output could be captured as a String also, using a Template's String evaluate(Context context) method.

If any method throws a WebMacroException, the servlet has been written to rethrow the exception wrapped within a ServletException. Nearly every WebMacro method can throw a WebMacroException or some subclass. The WM() constructor may throw an InitException if, for example, a required configuration file could not be found. The getTemplate() method may throw a NotFoundException if the template could not be found. And the write() method may throw a ContextException if the template required data that was missing from the context, and it may also throw an IOException if there was a problem writing to the client. All WebMacro-defined exceptions extend WebMacroException, a checked (nonruntime) exception, and it's common to catch and handle the generic exception class at the bottom of a doGet() method.

As another approach, you can write a WebMacro-enabled servlet by extending the org.webmacro.servlet.WMServlet superclass, a convenience demonstrated in Example 15-3.

Example 15-3. Another Approach to WebMacro Servlet Design

```
import java.io.*;
import java.util.*;
import javax.servlet.*;
import javax.servlet.http.*;

import org.webmacro.*;
import org.webmacro.servlet.*;

public class WMServletHello extends WMServlet {

  public Template handle(WebContext context) throws HandlerException {
```

Example 15-3. Another Approach to WebMacro Servlet Design (continued)

```
    try {
      context.put("date", new Date());
      return getTemplate("hello.wm");
    }
    catch (NotFoundException e) {
      throw new HandlerException(e.getMessage());
    }
  }
}
```

Following this style, a servlet extends `WMServlet` and implements a single `handle()` method. The superclass creates the `WebMacro` object automatically and passes `WebContext` in as a parameter. The servlet need only perform its business logic, fill the `WebContext` with appropriate answer objects, and return the template to use for page creation (or return `null` if the servlet handled the page creation itself internally). The methods `start()` and `stop()` may be implemented by the servlet as well, taking the place of a typical servlet's `init()` and `destroy()` methods. Should the `HttpServletRequest` and `HttpServletResponse` objects be needed, they can be retrieved from `WebContext` using the `getRequest()` and `getResponse()` methods.

Using the `WMServlet` superclass can be more convenient than handling the WebMacro objects manually. The price is a loss of power. You must use the manual approach to put two independent templates in a page, run the output through a filter such as a `GZIPOutputStream`, perform offline generation, differentiate between GET and POST requests, and determine whether the servlet has to extend another custom superclass.

Now let's take a look at the template. The template looks like a normal HTML page except for a little markup. In the body of the page we see the `Date` object, previously added to the context under the name `date`, has been included in the page using the syntax `$date`. We also see on the next line that the `time` property of the `Date` object (which holds the current time as a millisecond count) has been included using the syntax `$date.Time`. That's the simple substitution syntax used by WebMacro: `$`*`varname`* prints the variable value (converted to a `String` if necessary) and `$`*`varname.Property`* prints the property value. Property subproperties are also available using the syntax `$`*`varname.Property.Subproperty`*, and in fact far more than just bean properties can be accessed due to the advanced reflection work WebMacro performs, as we'll see later. For now, just remember that when accessing bean properties the property name must be capitalized.

Looking more at the template, at the beginning of the file there's a comment telling us the name of the file. Comments in WebMacro begin with `##` and continue to the end of the line. Right below the comment there's a `#set` command, what

WebMacro calls a *directive*. This sets the ContentType property on the Response object to the value "text/html", which is equivalent to calling response.setContentType("text/html"). The $Response variable represents the servlet response and, along with $Request, is implicitly made available in all WebContext objects. WebMacro has a handful of directives for handling variable manipulation, file inclusion, conditional logic, and looping. We'll look at these in more detail later.

Installing WebMacro

To execute a WebMacro servlet and template requires a little installation work. First, download the distribution from *http://www.webmacro.org* and unpack it. Include *webmacro.jar* and *collections.jar* in your server's classpath.* Then locate the *WebMacro.properties* file found within the distribution and copy it to a directory in your server's classpath. Note that because the classes in *webmacro.jar* rely on their class loader to locate the file, the file must be in the classpath of the class loader that loads *webmacro.jar*. To ensure you have this right, either put both in the system classpath where they'll be found by the primordial class loader, or put both under the *WEB-INF* directory where they'll be found by the web application class loader. (Put *webmacro.jar* in the *WEB-INF/lib* directory; put the *WebMacro.properties* file in the *WEB-INF/classes* directory.)

The default *WebMacro.properties* in the distribution contains a long list of configuration options, the first portion of which is shown in Example 15-4. Most aspects of this file are well documented within the file. All you need to configure for now is the TemplatePath parameter, specifying the directory or directories where your templates are stored.

Example 15-4. A Standard WebMacro.properties File

```
# NOTE FOR NT USERS
#
# Beware that the \ character is the escape character in a Java
# properties file. You must either double it (\\) or use the Unix
# style (/) file separator in this file. Both should work. Also
# when you set TemplatePath, be sure and use the NT path
# separator (;) rather than the Unix separator (:).

###########################################################
#
```

* The *collections.jar* archive contains the Java Collections classes (introduced in JDK 1.2) built for use with the earlier JDK 1.1. This JAR isn't required if you're using a build of WebMacro compiled specifically for JDK 1.2; however, at the time of this writing the default build held in the *webmacro.jar* archive was built for JDK 1.1.7 and therefore this JAR is required even when running JDK 1.2 or later.

Example 15-4. A Standard WebMacro.properties File (continued)

```
# BASIC CONFIGURATION:
#


# You should set TemplatePath, at the very least! It is a list of
# directories which will be searched for your templates, if you
# give a relative filename. It is a list of directories separated
# by a : (on Unix) or a ; (on NT).

TemplatePath = /tomcat/webapps/webmacro/WEB-INF/templates;/local/webmacro/templates


# WebMacro compiles and caches templates for efficiency. During development
# you will want to turn this off by setting the following value to 0, so
# that your template changes are immediately reflected on the website. In
# production systems, this it the number of milliseconds of idle time
# that a cached template will be retained, ie: 600000 is ten minutes.

TemplateExpireTime = 0
# TemplateExpireTime == 600000


# LogLevel can be: ALL, DEBUG, EXCEPTION, ERROR, WARNING, INFO, or NONE
# in order of most information to least information displayed.

LogLevel = EXCEPTION


# LogTraceExceptions causes exception stack traces to be included in the log,
# this causes exceptions to be verbose, but may point out the exact line
# or method which is causing a fault.

LogTraceExceptions = TRUE


# Uncomment the following to log to a file rather than stderr. If your
# standard error writes to a useful log already, you don't need this,
# but many servlet runners simply eat standard error.

# LogFile = /usr/local/webmacro/wm.log


# Set the template (relative to TemplateDirectory) used for errors. You
# can edit this template to customize the way script failures appear

ErrorTemplate = error.wm
# The file continues with "ADVANCED CONFIGURATION" features...
```

A power user can create multiple versions of this file and swap between versions to quickly and completely alter the look and feel of a site (changing `TemplatePath`)

or to just move from development to production mode (changing things like `TemplateExpireTime`). This swap-out can be done at a servlet-by-servlet level as well because the `WM()` constructor takes an optional `String` argument that specifies the location of the configuration file it should read. If a servlet needs direct access to the properties in this file, that's available through the `getConfig(String key)` method present in both the `WebMacro` interface and the `WMServlet` class. This lets the config file hold the equivalent of context init parameters, except these parameters are tied to a particular configuration—perhaps pointing during development at a test database and on deployment at a production database.

Once everything has been properly installed, invoking WebMacro-enabled servlets is done like invoking any other servlet. Invoke the servlet as *http://localhost:8080/servlet/WMHello* or, with the servlets and templates that are placed under the */webmacro* context as shown in the *WebMacro.properties* file, the URL would be *http://localhost:8080/webmacro/servlet/WMHello*. See Figure 15-1.

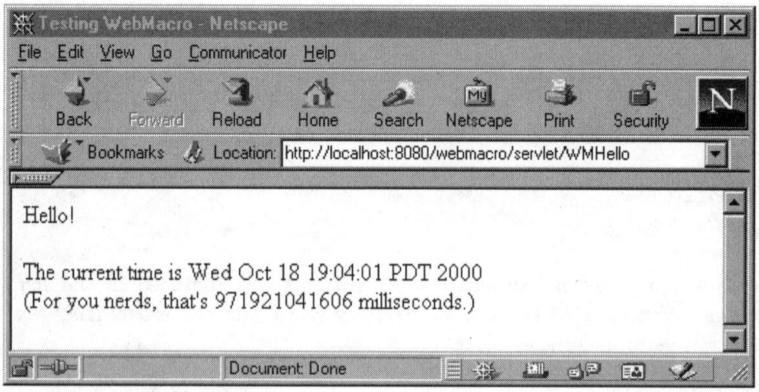

Figure 15-1. Testing WebMacro

The WebMacro Template Language

The WebMacro template language leverages the syntax of Perl and the C preprocessor to create a markup that looks familiar to many. Variables begin with a dollar sign (`$`) and end implicitly with whitespace or various punctuation characters like `<`, `/`, and `"`. This lets you write fairly readable substitutions, for example:

```
$Request.ContextPath/servlet/WMHello
<A HREF="$url">$url</A>
```

Where needed, you can use parentheses to explicitly surround a variable name and disambiguate the parsing. The parentheses are consumed and not printed.

For example:

```
#set $prefix = "for"
#set $suffix = "give"
To err is human, to $(prefix)$suffix divine.
```

The WebMacro engine doesn't use the `java.beans.Introspector` class to access object properties; instead, it performs a more exhaustive reflective search. When you write `$Request.ContextPath`, the WebMacro engine first locates the object referred to by `$Request`, then attempts to locate the property using the following search pattern:

```
request.ContextPath
request.getContextPath()
request.get("ContextPath");
```

If you write a longer substitution, such as `$Request.Header.Accept`, WebMacro adds the following search pattern to the end of the list:

```
request.getHeader("Accept")
```

Variable assignment follows a similar search pattern.

You have the ability with WebMacro to directly invoke methods on all the objects in scope (something you explicitly couldn't do in Tea). For example, the following substitution locates the list of products in inventory, looks up the `hinge` product, and returns its part number:

```
$Inventory.Products.findProduct("hinge").PartNumber
```

This can prove useful when accessor methods don't follow the naming pattern expected by WebMacro. On the other hand, the direct invocation of methods means there can be no complete sandboxing of a WebMacro template.

WebMacro Context Tools

One powerful trait of WebMacro is that the `WebContext` can make available a small number of variables, called *context tools*, to all templates, and these tools are always included without the calling servlet having to place them within the context. The list of which tools to include is maintained in the *WebMacro.properties* file as *WebContextTools*. By default, WebMacro provides the following tools:

`$Request`
: A reference to the servlet `HttpServletRequest`. Can be used to access the request's Accept header with `$Request.Header.Accept` or equivalently `$Request.getHeader("Accept")`.

`$Response`
: A reference to the servlet `HttpServletResponse`. Can be used to set the response's `Content-Type` with `#set $Response.ContentType = "text/html"`.

`$Session`
: A reference to the user's `HttpSession`. Can be used to retrieve a value from the session with `$Session.Attribute.Count` or equivalently `$Session.getAttribute("Count")`.

`$Form`
: A tool for accessing the request's form data. Can be used to retrieve the `partnumber` parameter as `$Form.partnumber`. Shorthand for `$Request.getParameter("partnumber")` or `$Request.Parameter.partnumber`.

`$FormList`
: A tool for accessing the request's form data, when the form data has values with more than one value. Used in conjunction with the `#foreach` directive.

`$Cookie`
: A tool for retrieving and setting cookies. Can be used to set a cookie with `$Cookie.set("name", "value")` or `#set $Cookie.name = "value"`. Cookies are retrieved as `$Cookie.get("name").Value` or `$Cookie.name.Value`.

`$CGI`
: A tool for accessing request information using CGI-style names. Can be used by template engineers familiar with CGI to access variables like the document root: `$CGI.DOCUMENT_ROOT`.

Additional context tools can be made available by simply writing a class that implements `org.webmacro.ContextTool` and adding the class to the `WebContextTools` list. One could write or download tools to do math, internationalization, database access, or even create HTML objects using ECS from the next section. In many ways, context tools behave for WebMacro like tag libraries behave for JSP.

Example 15-5 shows a simple context tool that performs integer arithmetic. This `MathTool` often comes in handy because the WebMacro template language has been so simplified that it doesn't include even basic arithmetic operations.*

* Although due to popular demand, arithmetic operations are being added and may be available by the time you read this.

Example 15-5. A Context Tool for Integer Arithmetic (A Complicated Calculator)

```
import org.webmacro.*;

public class MathTool implements ContextTool {
  /**
   * A new tool object will be instantiated per-request by calling
   * this method.  A ContextTool is effectively a factory used to
   * create objects for use in templates.  Some tools may simply return
   * themselves from this method; others may instantiate new objects
   * to hold the per-request state.
   */
  public Object init(Context c) {
    return this;
  }

  public static int add(int x, int y) {
    return x + y;
  }

  public static int subtract(int x, int y) {
    return x - y;
  }

  public static int multiply(int x, int y) {
    return x * y;
  }

  public static int divide(int x, int y) {
    return x / y;
  }

  public static int mod(int x, int y) {
    return x % y;
  }

  public static boolean lessThan(int x, int y) {
    return (x < y);
  }

  public static boolean greaterThan(int x, int y) {
    return (x > y);
  }
}
```

With this tool added to the `WebContextTools` list (don't forget that step), all templates can perform basic math. For example, to print the year of a `Date` object requires adding 1900 to the `Year` property:

```
The current year is $Math.add($date.Year, 1900).
```

WebMacro Directives

Directives are WebMacro statements that perform some operation, conditionally include text, or repeat a block within a template. The list of available directives is maintained in the *WebMacro.properties* file as the `Directives` property. Directives all begin with a `#` character. Some directives operate on a block, and such blocks can be demarcated with curly braces, `{` and `}`, or with `#begin` and `#end` keywords. The keywords aren't as convenient to type as curly braces but cause less trouble with included JavaScript.

There are seven commonly used default directives. As with context tools, you can write your own directives to supplement the defaults, although with directives it's not as common. Let's look at the seven defaults.

#if

```
#if (condition) { ... } #else { ... }
```

The `#if` directive, alone or in conjunction with the `#else` directive, can be used to conditionally include text. The text is included if the condition is true and not included if the condition is false. A condition is considered true if it has a non-null value other than the Boolean false. The `#if` condition can make use of the familiar Boolean operators `&&`, `||`, and `!`, as well as parentheses to specify ordering. Objects can be compared as part of the condition using the `==` and `!=` operators, which actually invoke the `.equals()` method to do the comparison. No operators exist for less-than or greater-than comparisons, because objects are not required to be comparable in this manner. The `MathTool` includes such comparisons for use with integers.

```
#if ($Customer.owesMoney() && $Customer.Name != "Jason") {
  Pay up, or else!
}
#else {
  Welcome!
}
```

#set

```
#set $property = value
```

The `#set` directive assigns a value to the given variable or variable property. The property must be successfully located using the WebMacro reflection logic and must be publicly settable in some manner. If no such variable is in scope, a new variable is created and assigned the given value. Variables are implicitly assigned either a `String` or `Integer` type. A `String` type is the default unless the value can be parsed as an `Integer` and is not surrounded by double quotes. For convenience,

`Integer` values can be converted to `String` values as necessary. Arrays can also be set using square brackets. Use a backslash to escape a dollar sign:

```
#set $num1 = 4
#set $num2 = 7
#set $price = "90"
#set $invoice = "You owe \$$price"
#set $quote = "$num1 score and $num2 years ago..."
#set $all = [ $num1, $num2, $quote ]  ## array syntax
```

#foreach

```
#foreach $thing in $list { ... }
```

The `#foreach` directive iterates through a list, including its output block once for each element in the list. Each time through the loop the variable `$thing` takes on the value of the next term in the `$list`. The list can be an array declared from within WebMacro or a Java object that satisfies one of the following conditions (searched for via reflection in this order):

1. The object itself is an array.
2. The object itself is an `Iterator`.
3. The object itself is an `Enumeration`.
4. The object has an `Iterator iterator()` method.
5. The object has an `Enumeration elements()` method.

The following code prints the client's preferred locales (if any):

```
#set $array = $Request.Locales
<UL>
#foreach $item in $array {
  <LI>$item
}
</UL>
```

#parse

```
#parse file
```

The `#parse` directive includes the contents of the target file at the location of the directive and parses it as though it were part of the current template. This provides a convenient mechanism to include template code that's common between template files. The file can be specified as an absolute path or as a relative path located within the `TemplatePath`:

```
#set $title = "Page title"
#parse "header.wm"  ## The $title variable is visible in header.wm
```

#include

```
#include url
```

The `#include` directive includes the contents of the target URL at the location of the directive but does not attempt to parse its contents. This provides an easy mechanism to include JavaScript and other things whose syntax might conflict with WebMacro. If the URL has no protocol, `file:` is assumed:

```
#include "http://webmacro.org/CREDITS"  ## Raw text include
```

#param

```
#param $name = value
```

The `#param` directive specifies values within the template that can be examined by the servlet calling the template. They provide a way for the template author to pass information to the backend Java programmer that may be used to determine what kind of information to put into the context:

```
#param $author = "Susan Kelley"
#param $require = [ "user", "document", "session" ]
```

The servlet can retrieve the value by calling `Object getParam(String)` on the `Template` object. The method returns a `String` or `Integer` if there's one value and an `Object[]` containing `String` and/or `Integer` objects if the value is a list:

```
String author = (String) tmpl.getParam("author");
Object[] require = (Object[]) tmpl.getParam("require");
```

#use

```
#use 'parser'
#begin
  ...
#end
```

Finally, the `#use` directive allows a block of template text (denoted by the `#begin` and `#end` markers) to be parsed by an alternate parser. This feature allows enhancement or even wholesale replacement of the WebMacro syntax. Generally it's not used for nearly such grandiose endeavors, however. Its two most common uses are to literally include a block of text (using the `text` parser) or to remove a block of text (using the `null` parser):

```
#use 'text'
#begin
  All text here is included raw
  ## Comments too since the comment format is a parser issue
#end
```

```
#use 'null'
#begin
  Text here can be considered to be "commented out"
#end
```

The *WebMacro.properties* file maintains the list of available default parsers in the `Parsers` property.*

WebMacro Templates

To demonstrate the context tools and directives available to WebMacro templates, Example 15-6 shows a simple template that prints information from the request.

Example 15-6. Snooping the Request with WebMacro

```
## snoop.wm

#set $Response.ContentType = "text/html"

<HTML><HEAD><TITLE>Let's Snoop!</TITLE></HEAD>
<BODY>

## A snoop template to get comfortable with WebMacro

<H1>Miscellaneous Info</H1>
QueryString: $Request.QueryString<BR>
RemoteUser: $Request.RemoteUser<BR>

## WebMacro does not yet recognize isXXX() properties; must use a method call
## It doesn't currently have elseif either (it's being added)

#if ($Request.isRequestedSessionIdFromCookie())  {
  You're in a session thanks to cookies!
}
#else {
  #if ($Request.isRequestedSessionIdFromURL()) {
    You're in a session thanks to URL rewriting!
  }
  #else {
    You're not in a session, poor guy.
  }
}

<H1>Parameter Info</H1>
#foreach $paramName in $Request.ParameterNames {
```

* The pluggable parser mechanism may be replaced by targeted directives. For example, `#use 'text'` may be replaced by `#text`, and `#use 'null'` may be replaced by `#comment`.

Example 15-6. Snooping the Request with WebMacro (continued)

```
  $paramName: $Request.getParameter($paramName) <BR>
}

<H1>Header Info</H1>
#foreach $headerName in $Request.HeaderNames {
  $headerName: $Request.getHeader($headerName) <BR>
}

<H1>Cookie Info</H1>
#foreach $cookie in $Request.Cookies {
  $cookie.Name: $cookie.Value <BR>
}

</BODY></HTML>
```

Figure 15-2 shows a screen shot.

This template demonstrates the `#set` directive to set the content type of the response. It uses the `#if` and `#else` directives to determine if the client joined a session using a cookie or URL rewriting or isn't part of the session, and it uses the `#foreach` directive to loop over the parameter, header, and cookie values present in the request.

Some tricks to notice: first, a bean accessor method following the naming pattern `isProperty()` isn't located automatically by WebMacro and must be called explicitly through method invocation. Second, there's no `#elseif` directive currently, so an if/elseif/else construct has to be done through nesting.

A Reusable MacroView Servlet

The template from Example 15-6 can be considered "standalone" because it uses no servlet-provided variables. Standalone templates can't be invoked directly and require a servlet to call them, but because the template has no special needs, that servlet can be a generic and reusable `MacroView` servlet, as shown in Example 15-7.

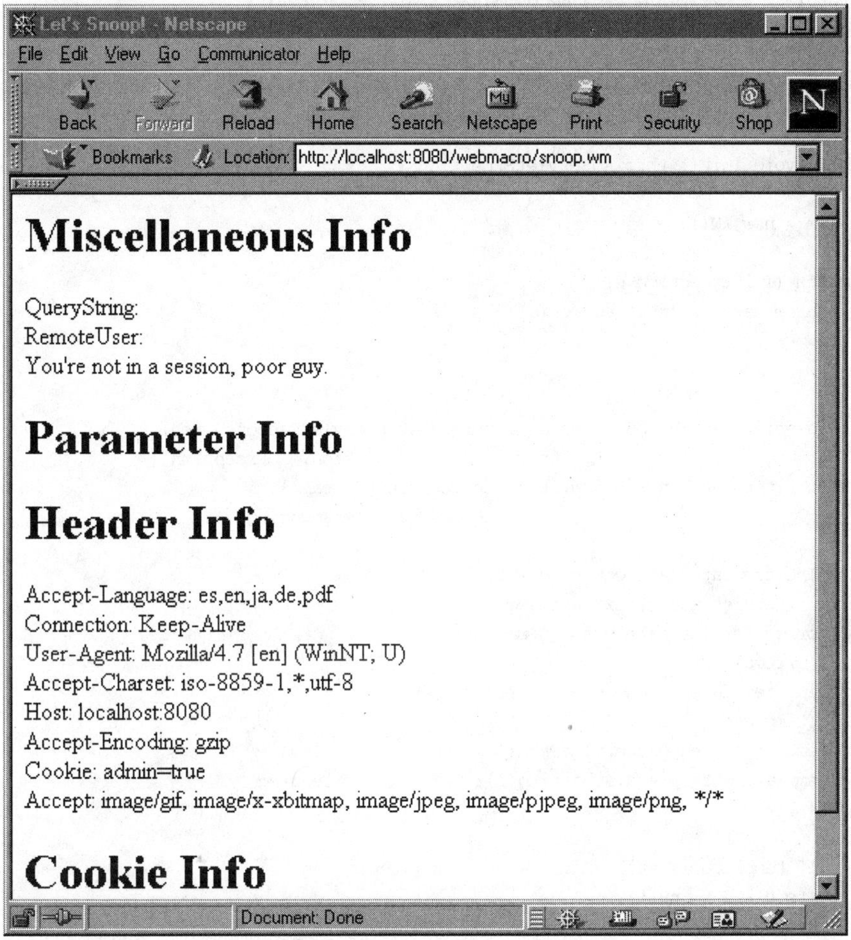

Figure 15-2. Snooping with WebMacro

Example 15-7. A Generically Reusable WebMacro Servlet

```
import java.io.*;
import javax.servlet.*;
import javax.servlet.http.*;

import org.webmacro.*;
import org.webmacro.servlet.*;
import org.webmacro.engine.*;
import org.webmacro.broker.*;

// Extending com.oreilly.servlet.CacheHttpServlet can improve response time
```

Example 15-7. A Generically Reusable WebMacro Servlet (continued)

```
public class MacroView extends HttpServlet {

  WebMacro wm;  // WebMacro main hook

  public void init() throws ServletException {
    try {
      wm = new WM();
    }
    catch (InitException e) {
      throw new ServletException(e);
    }
  }

  public void doGet(HttpServletRequest req, HttpServletResponse res)
                              throws ServletException, IOException {
    FastWriter out = new FastWriter(res.getOutputStream(),
                                    res.getCharacterEncoding());

    // The template name comes as extra path info
    //   /servlet/MacroView/templ.wm
    // or as servlet path via a *.wm rule
    //   /templ.wm
    String template = req.getPathInfo();
    if (template == null) {
      template = req.getServletPath();
      template = template.substring(1);  // cut off leading "/"
    }

    // If template is still null, we have a problem
    if (template == null) {
      throw new ServletException(
        "No template specified as extra path info or servlet path");
    }

    try {
      Template tmpl = wm.getTemplate(template);
      WebContext context = wm.getWebContext(req, res);
      tmpl.write(out, context);
    }
    catch (WebMacroException e) {
      throw new ServletException(e);
    }
    finally {
      out.flush();
    }
  }

  public void destroy() {
```

Example 15-7. A Generically Reusable WebMacro Servlet (continued)

```
    super.destroy();
    if (wm != null) wm.destroy();
  }
}
```

This servlet calls on whichever template name was passed as extra path info, or if there's no extra path info, then it calls on the template name pointed to by the servlet path (through a file extension match). It can be convenient to register this servlet to handle all **.wm* requests using the *web.xml* snippet in Example 15-8. This allows WebMacro template files to appear to be requested directly using URLs like */snoop.wm* or */webmacro/snoop.wm*, while in reality the `MacroView` servlet handles the processing behind the scenes.

*Example 15-8. Registering MacroView to Handle *.wm*

```
<servlet>
    <servlet-name>
        mv
    </servlet-name>
    <servlet-class>
        MacroView
    </servlet-class>
</servlet>
<servlet-mapping>
    <servlet-name>
        mv
    </servlet-name>
    <url-pattern>
        *.wm
    </url-pattern>
</servlet-mapping>
```

You may find it useful to enhance the `MacroView` servlet to perform some standard business logic on each request and perhaps make a set of common objects available in the context for all system templates. A servlet like this, combined with the context tools discussed later, lets WebMacro templates operate with a pull model similar to Tea (and in fact that's how AltaVista uses WebMacro).

Template Processing

WebMacro does quite a lot of template parsing work behind the scenes that programmers and designers don't generally need to think about but whose mechanisms should be understood to make the most of the tool. WebMacro parses templates on their first use and after that stores a representation of the template suitable in memory for fast execution. WebMacro automatically reloads and reparses the template content after template file changes but for efficiency checks timestamps only after a timeout period, specified as the `TemplateExpireTime` in *WebMacro.properties*. By default the timeout is 0 milliseconds so that timestamps are checked on every request. That's convenient for development, but make sure you increase the timeout for production use. For power users, template objects have a `parse()` method that forces a load and parse. You can use this method to parse all your templates at startup or to force an early reparse if you know a template has changed.

When templates have errors, various things can occur. If a referenced variable or property has a `null` value or doesn't exist, WebMacro treats that failed substitution as a noncatastrophic error. WebMacro generates the page as best it can but writes a `WARN` message to the log and in the generated page places an HTML/XML comment at the location of the error (this approach has some shortcomings if the generated page is not HTML or XML):

```
<!-- warning: attempt to write out undefined variable Request.ContentType: java.
lang.NullPointerException -->.
```

If a template has a syntax error, WebMacro does treat that as a catastrophic failure and writes an `ERROR` message to the log and in the generated page displays an error description.* For certain types of errors, such as a template not being found by a servlet, WebMacro has the notion of a default error template to display, configured with the `ErrorTemplate` property in *WebMacro.properties*.

Of course, most of the error handling within a WebMacro site—dealing with invalid parameters, crashed databases, missing files, and all the other errors that should be checked before control passes to the template—should occur in servlet code. WebMacro works well for this. A servlet can use a set of standard WebMacro templates to display these error cases, choosing which template to pass control to and what to include in the context depending on the error. For example, if a database error occurred, control could be rerouted to a *sqlException.wm* file along with the exception stack trace for display.

A Tool Application

To conclude our discussion of WebMacro, let's look at how we would rewrite the tool application from the previous chapter using WebMacro now instead of Tea. It's easiest to understand if we look at the template first, shown in Example 15-9.

* There's a bug in WebMacro 0.94 (the version against which the code in this chapter was tested) where a template syntax error can cause WebMacro to generate an empty page instead of a page with an error description. No doubt this bug will be fixed in later versions.

Example 15-9. The Tool Application WebMacro Template

```
## toolview.wm

#set $Response.ContentType = "text/html"

#set $title = "Tool Listing"
#set $deck = "A list of content creation tools"
#set $desc = "Without tools, people are nothing more than animals.  And \
              pretty weak ones at that.  Here's a list of servlet-based \
              content creation tools you can use so you won't be a servlet \
              weakling."

#parse "header.wm"

## Define a value to be read by the servlet
#param $defaultState = "LIVE"

#foreach $tool in $tools {

  <HR SIZE=2 ALIGN=LEFT>

  <H3>
  $tool.Name

  #if ($tool.isNewWithin(45)) {
    <FONT COLOR=#FF0000><B> (New!) </B></FONT>
  }
  #else {
    #if ($tool.isUpdatedWithin(45)) {
      <FONT COLOR=#ff0000><B> (Updated!) </B></FONT>
    }
  }
  </H3>
  <A HREF="$tool.HomeURL">$tool.HomeURL</A><BR>

  $tool.Comments

}

#parse "footer.wm"
```

The beginning of this template assigns values for the page's title, deck, and description (using \ characters as line continuators for the description). These variables are used within the parsed *header.wm* template to create the page structure surrounding the core tools list. The variables are also visible within the *footer.wm* template parsed at the bottom of the template, although the footer doesn't make use of them. The header and footer templates are shown in Example 15-10 and Example 15-11, respectively.

The *toolview.wm* template uses the `#param` directive to define `LIVE` as a constant value for the template parameter `defaultState`, allowing the servlet calling this template to know the default tool state this page should display.

Then the template uses a `#foreach` directive to iterate over the `tools` list the servlet passed in. The tools variable may be an array, `Iterator`, `Enumeration`, or an object like `Vector` or `List` with either an `iterator()` or `elements()` method—the template doesn't care. For each tool entry, the template prints its name, whether it's new or updated, its URL, and finally the comments about the tool. The template invokes the `isNewWithin(int)` and `isUpdatedWithin(int)` methods to determine if the content should count as new or updated. The template could access `$tool.CreatedAgeInDays` and `$tool.ModifiedAgeInDays`, however it would need the support of the `MathTool` context tool from Example 15-5 to perform the less-than comparison.

Example 15-10. The header.wm File

```
## header.wm

<HTML><HEAD><TITLE>$title</TITLE></HEAD>

<BODY BGCOLOR="#FFFFFF" BACKGROUND="/images/background.gif"
      LINK="#003333" ALINK="#669999" VLINK="#333333">

<IMG SRC="/images/banner.gif" WIDTH=600 HEIGHT=87 BORDER=0><BR>

<TABLE>
<TR>
<TD WIDTH=125 ROWS=10 VALIGN=TOP>
 <BR><BR><BR>
 <FONT FACE="Arial,Helvetica" SIZE="+1" COLOR="#FF0000">
 <A HREF="/index.html">Home</A><BR>
 <A HREF="/hosting.html">Hosting</A><BR>
 <A HREF="/engines.html">Engines</A><BR>
 </FONT>
</TD>

<TD WIDTH=475>

  <TABLE CELLPADDING=5><TR><TD WIDTH=600 BGCOLOR="#006699" VALIGN=TOP>
  <B><FONT FACE="Arial,Helvetica" SIZE="+2">
  $title
  </FONT></B>
  </TD></TR></TABLE>

  <B><FONT FACE="Arial,Helvetica" SIZE="+1" COLOR="#003366">
  $deck
  </FONT></B><P>
```

Example 15-10. The header.wm File (continued)

```
  <P>

  <FONT FACE="Arial,Helvetica">

  $desc
```

Example 15-11. The footer.wm File

```
## footer.wm

 </FONT>

</TD>
</TR>

<TR>
<TD></TD>
<TD WIDTH=475 ALIGN=CENTER COLSPAN=3>
<HR>
<FONT FACE="Arial,Helvetica">
<A HREF="/index.html">Home</A>  
<A HREF="/hosting.html">Hosting</A>  
<A HREF="/engines.html">Engines</A>  <P>
</FONT>

<TABLE WIDTH=100%>
<TR>
<TD WIDTH=260 ALIGN=LEFT VALIGN=TOP>
<FONT FACE="Arial,Helvetica">
<A HREF="/copyright.html">Copyright</A> &copy; 2000 Jason Hunter<BR>
All Rights Reserved.</TD>
<TD WIDTH=5></FONT></TD>
<TD WIDTH=230 ALIGN=RIGHT VALIGN=TOP>
<FONT FACE="Arial,Helvetica">
Contact: <A HREF="mailto:webmaster@servlets.com">webmaster@servlets.com</a>
</FONT></TD>
</TR>
</TABLE>

</TD>
</TR>
</TABLE>

</BODY>
</HTML>
```

The code for the `Tool` class remains the same as for the Tea application, although with WebMacro the bean accessor methods aren't necessary and the isNewWithin(int) and isUpdatedWithin(int) are visible from the template. The code for the ToolServlet class is listed in Example 15-12.

Example 15-12. The Servlet Driving the Tool Application

```
import org.webmacro.*;
import org.webmacro.servlet.*;
import org.webmacro.util.*;
import java.io.*;
import java.sql.*;
import java.util.*;
import javax.servlet.*;

public class ToolServlet extends WMServlet {

  private Log log;
  private Tool[] tools;

  public void start() throws ServletException {
    // Load the tool data in our init for simplicity
    String toolsFile = getInitParameter("toolsFile"); // from web.xml
    if (toolsFile == null) {
      throw new ServletException(
        "A tools data file must be specified as the toolsFile init parameter");
    }
    log = new Log(getServletName(), "Tool example debugging log");
    log.debug("Loading tools from " + toolsFile);
    try {
      tools = Tool.loadTools(toolsFile);
      if (tools.length == 0) {
        log.warning("No tools found in " + toolsFile);
      }
      else {
        log.info(tools.length + " tools found in " + toolsFile);
      }
    }
    catch (Exception e) {
      log.error(e);
      throw new ServletException(e);
    }
  }

  // Creating a context provides functions accessible from the templates.
  public Template handle(WebContext context) throws HandlerException {
    // You often pass on the request, response, and application even if
    // not all the objects are used, since they may be used later
    try {
      Template view = getTemplate("toolview.wm");
      String state = context.getRequest().getParameter("state");
```

Example 15-12. The Servlet Driving the Tool Application (continued)

```
      if (state == null) {
        state = (String)view.getParam("defaultState");
      }

      if (state == null) {
        context.put("tools", getTools());
      }
      else {
        context.put("tools", getTools(state));
      }
      return view;
    }
    catch (WebMacroException e) {
      log.exception(e);
      throw new HandlerException(e.getMessage());
    }
    catch (IOException e) {
      log.exception(e);
      throw new HandlerException(e.getMessage());
    }
  }

  public Tool[] getTools() {
    return tools;
  }

  public Tool[] getTools(String state) {
    List list = new LinkedList();
    for (int i = 0; i < tools.length; i++) {
      if (tools[i].getStateFlag().equalsIgnoreCase(state)) {
        list.add(tools[i]);
      }
    }
    return (Tool[]) list.toArray(new Tool[0]);
  }
}
```

The servlet extends `WMServlet` and thus defines a `start()` method instead of `init()` and a `handle()` method instead of `doGet()` and `doPost()`. The `start()` method retrieves the init parameter `toolsFile` and loads the tool data from the file using `Tool.loadTools(toolsFile)`. The method also creates a `Log` instance and uses it to report on its progress writing info, debug, warning, and error messages.

The `handle()` method loads the *toolview.wm* template, then reads the request's `state` parameter to determine tools of which state to display. If no such parameter exists, the servlet uses the default value specified within the template itself. The servlet then places into the WebContext the appropriate tools list under the variable name tools and returns the template. Any exception thrown is logged and passed on as a HandlerException.

The getTools() methods at the end of the servlet are only supporting methods. They aren't accessible by the template, although they could be made visible by including a lookup object containing these methods within the context. Then a template could do its own handling of the state parameter:

```
#set $state = $Form.state;
#if (!state) {
  #set $tools = $lookup.getTools("live")
}
#else {
  #set $tools = $lookup.getTools($state)
}
```

Whether you prefer this pull approach or the push model presented earlier is mostly a matter of taste. WebMacro tends to encourage the push model, and Tea tends to encourage the pull model; yet both can easily support either model.

You can use the com.oreilly.servlet.CacheHttpServlet class from Chapter 3, *The Servlet Lifecycle*, to cache the output and improve the performance of templates. The technique works best for templates whose output takes a significant time to produce but changes only rarely, such as templates that display database results. To take advantage of the caching you need to write your servlet to extend CacheHttpServlet (you'll have to avoid the convenience of WMServlet and handle templates manually) and implement getLastModified(). If the data comes from a database, the getLastModified() method can return the time the database was last updated (as notes in a context-wide variable by the servlet doing the update) or, if the update time can't be determined, the method can simply return the current time modulo some value so updates occur on regular intervals. If the data comes from a file, the method can return the time the datafile was last updated (perhaps checking only every once in a while for efficiency).

Filters

At the time of this writing, WebMacro has just opened up its development process to a wider audience and moved from the relatively restrictive GPL license to the less restrictive Apache-style license. As a result of the increased developer resources, many interesting and useful enhancements are now in the works.

The most substantial enhancement involves a pluggable filter mechanism. The idea is for a variable to go through a filter when output, with the filter controlling how the variable is displayed. Standard filters are likely to perform:

HTML escaping
: Filter a user-entered comment field to prohibit special characters from accidentally or maliciously causing problems.

Localization
: Filter a date through some localized display logic.

URL rewriting
: Filter a URL to add the `jsessionid` session-tracking value.

Display of null values
: Filter the display of null variables to output an error message or silently ignore the variable.

Custom Filters

Custom filters hold particular promise. For example, a `customer` variable could be filtered through a customer template designed to render the variable and its properties based on an external template file. The customer template might even filter the customer's address through an external address template. This allows easy reuse and customization of display logic. Filters may support being chained as well. That would allow, for example, a variable to be both localized and escaped, with a predetermined output value should the variable be `null`.

The possible uses for filters are still purely in people's imaginations. It will be interesting to see what uses for WebMacro filters actually become popular.

16

In this chapter:

- *Page Components as Objects*
- *Displaying a Result Set*

Element Construction Set

The Element Construction Set (ECS) package takes a dramatically different approach to content generation than JSP, Tea, and WebMacro. ECS abstracts away the HTML text and treats HTML as just another set of Java objects. A web page in ECS is manipulated as an object that can contain other HTML objects (such as lists and tables) that can contain yet more HTML objects (such as list items and table cells). This "object-oriented HTML generation" model proves to be very powerful, but also very programmer-centric.

Stephan Nagy and Jon Stevens wrote ECS and released it as open source as part of the Java Apache Project, using the Apache license of course. They modeled the library after the commercial htmlKona product from WebLogic, a product which lost support when WebLogic was purchased by BEA Systems. Here we talk about ECS Version 1.3.3, available at *http://jakarta.apache.org/ecs*.

Page Components as Objects

ECS includes classes for all HTML 4.0 constructs. Example 16-1 shows how a simple HTML page can be constructed with ECS.

Example 16-1. A Page as a Set of Objects

```
import java.io.*;
import java.util.*;
import javax.servlet.*;
import javax.servlet.http.*;

import org.apache.ecs.*;
import org.apache.ecs.html.*;

public class ECSHello extends HttpServlet {
```

Example 16-1. A Page as a Set of Objects (continued)

```
  public void doGet(HttpServletRequest req, HttpServletResponse res)
                               throws ServletException, IOException {

    res.setContentType("text/html");
    PrintWriter out = res.getWriter();

    Document doc = new Document();
    doc.appendTitle("Testing ECS");
    doc.appendBody(new Big("Hello!"))
       .appendBody(new P())
       .appendBody("The current time is " + new Date());
    doc.output(out);
  }
}
```

Notice how all the HTML tags have been replaced with objects. This servlet creates a new `Document` object that represents the web page it will return. Then, it adds a "Hello World" title to the page and appends to the page body a big "Hello!" plus a paragraph break and a printing of the current time. Finally, the servlet outputs the page to its `PrintWriter`. That's how object-oriented HTML generation works: get a `Document` object, add component objects to it, and send it to the client.

To execute this servlet, you need to install ECS by putting the ECS JAR file into your server's classpath (or into the *WEB-INF/lib* directory of your web application). For ECS 1.3.3 the JAR file is named *ecs-1.3.3.jar*. You may have to restart your server for it to find the new JAR. With ECS installed you can invoke the servlet as usual, and the servlet will generate output like this:

```
<html><head><title>Testing ECS</title></head><body><big>Hello!</big><p>The
current time is Thu Aug 03 17:58:37 PDT 2000</body></html>
```

By default all the ECS output appears on one line with no indentation or carriage returns. This saves bandwidth when communicating with a browser client. If you want more human-readable content, edit the *ecs.properties* file that comes with the distribution and change the `pretty_print` value to `true`. Then the tricky part: make sure your *ecs.properties* file is found in the server's classpath *before* the ECS JAR file, so that your edited file overrides the *ecs.properties* file included in the JAR. The *ecs.properties* file is searched for as *org/apache/ecs/ecs.properties* so the file needs to be placed not directly in the classpath but in an *org/apache/ecs* subdirectory of a directory within the classpath (like *WEB-INF/classes/org/apache/ecs/ecs.properties*).

The servlet imports two ECS packages: `org.apache.ecs` for the core ECS classes and `org.apache.ecs.html` for the HTML-specific classes. (There are other packages for XML, WML, and RTF.)* The `org.apache.ecs.html` package contains

* If you're interested in programatically creating XML from Java, you'll be better off using JDOM (*http://jdom.org*) because JDOM has better integration with XML technologies.

nearly a hundred classes representing all the HTML 4.0 components. Most of the HTML classes are named to match their HTML tag names: `Big`, `Small`, `P`, `Table`, `TR`, `TD`, `TH`, `H1`, `H2`, `H3`, `Frame`, `A`, `Head`, `Body`, and so on. Each HTML class has methods for configuring the component. For example, the `TD` class has a `setBackground(String url)` method that sets the background of that table cell. The `Body` class has a similar method as well, to set the background of the entire page. No other ECS component has a `setBackground()` method, because no other component can set its background, and that allows ECS to ensure that documents programatically created are always well-formed HTML.

To append the body elements, the servlet makes use of method chaining, in which several methods are invoked on the same object. You see this a lot in ECS. For example, to construct a table:

```
Table tab = new Table()
            .setCellPadding(0)
            .setCellSpacing(0);
```

The whitespace is irrelevant. The previous code is equivalent to:

```
Table tab = new Table().setCellPadding(0).setCellSpacing(0);
```

This chaining is possible because each `set` and `append` method returns a reference to the object on which it was invoked—that reference is used to invoke the next method. This trick comes in handy when using ECS.

Displaying a Result Set

The use of ECS for full page creation has fallen out of favor as servlet-based templating technologies have improved. It's simply too much work to dynamically create what tends to be mostly static page content. However, ECS still has its place. ECS works well for those sections of a page that are *extremely* dynamic, where you need the full power of Java to determine what content to produce. As Jon Stevens, one of its creators, said, "Use ECS when you would otherwise have to use `out.println()`."

For example, picture having a web application that lets clients execute ad hoc queries against a database. Perhaps you've implemented an online bug-tracking system and want a servlet that gives power users the option of running their own queries against the data (using a connection with read-only privileges). ECS works well for writing the page to display the database results, programmatically generating a table customized for the data. Example 16-2 demonstrates a simple `ResultSet` view component. It's reminiscent of the `HtmlSQLResult` class from Chapter 9, *Database Connectivity*, that used `out.println()`. Using ECS instead of `out.println()` allows the code to be simpler and, as we'll see in the next section, more customizable.

Example 16-2. An Improved ResultSet Table

```
import java.io.*;
import java.sql.*;
import java.util.*;
import javax.servlet.*;
import javax.servlet.http.*;

import org.apache.ecs.*;
import org.apache.ecs.html.*;

public class SimpleResultSetTable extends Table {

  public SimpleResultSetTable(ResultSet rs) throws SQLException {
    setBorder(1);

    ResultSetMetaData rsmd = rs.getMetaData();
    int colCount = rsmd.getColumnCount();

    TR row = new TR();
    for (int i = 1; i <= colCount; i++) {
      addElement(new TH().addElement(rsmd.getColumnName(i)));
    }
    addElement(row);

    while (rs.next()) {
      row = new TR();
      for (int i = 1; i <= colCount; i++) {
        addElement(new TD().addElement(rs.getString(i)));
      }
      addElement(row);
    }
  }
}
```

This class extends `org.apache.ecs.html.Table`, thus representing an HTML <TABLE> element. It performs all its work in its constructor, reading the `ResultSet` and its `ResultSetMetaData` to generate a simple table of results. The constructor first calls `setBorder(1)` to set the border attribute of the table. Then it creates a row (`TR`) full of table header elements (`TH`) with each table head displaying the column name retrieved from the meta data. Finally the constructor loops over the result set and creates a row for each entry, filling the row with table data elements (`TD`) containing the simple `String` representation of the result set data.

The `SimpleResultSetTable` class can be used directly within a servlet using the snippet of code shown in Example 16-3.

Example 16-3. Using SimpleResultSetTable

```
Statement stmt = con.createStatement();
boolean gotResultSet = stmt.execute(sql);  // SQL from user

if (!gotResultSet) {
  out.println(stmt.getUpdateCount() + " rows updated.");
}
else {
  out.println(new SimpleResultSetTable(stmt.getResultSet()));
}
```

It generates a table as shown in Figure 16-1.

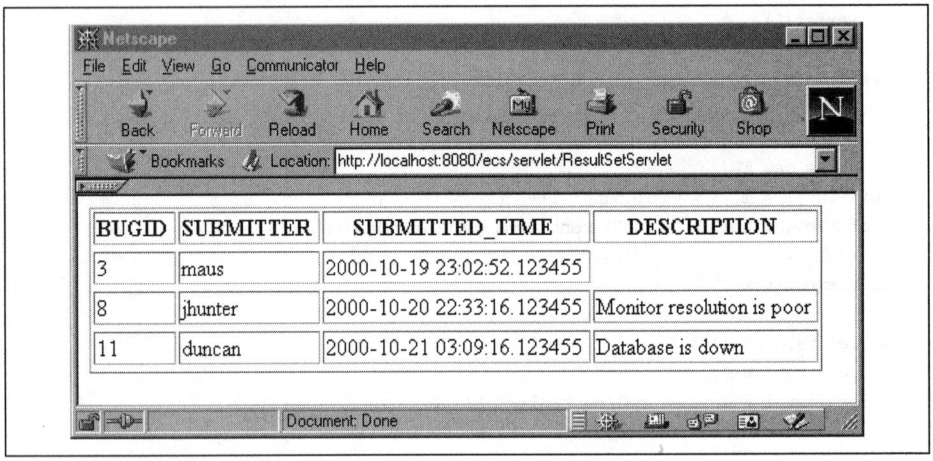

Figure 16-1. A raw result set veiw

The class can be used in conjunction with templating technologies. There's no reason a template needs to produce all the HTML content itself; if some page section requires the power of ECS, the template can include the ECS component's output into the page at the appropriate location.

What happens if the text returned by the `ResultSet` contains characters that HTML treats as special, like <, >, and &? By default, they're included directly and can potentially break the structure of the HTML. To solve this problem, ECS includes an `org.apache.ecs.filter.CharacterFilter` class that converts special HTML characters into their corresponding character entities. Every element uses this filter as its default filter, but all filtering is turned off by default for speed. You can turn on filtering on a per-element basis by calling `setFilterState(true)`, or you can turn it on for the entire system by editing *ecs.properties* and setting the `filter_state` and `filter_attribute_state` values to `true`. Then all special characters in any text output will be automatically converted to character entities.

Customizing the Display

ECS uses the object-oriented nature of Java to provide highly customizable data display. With a little Java coding we can build on the `SimpleResultSetTable` class and create a less "simplistic" `ResultSetTable` class. This new table class will accept an array of `TableCustomizer` objects to control the content added to the table. Example 16-4 shows the `TableCustomizer` interface.

Example 16-4. The TableCustomizer Class

```
import java.sql.*;
import org.apache.ecs.*;
import org.apache.ecs.html.*;

public interface TableCustomizer {
  public boolean accept(int columnType, String columnTypeName,
                        String columnName, ResultSet rs, int index)
                                           throws SQLException;

  public Element display(int columnType, String columnTypeName,
                        String columnName, ResultSet rs, int index)
                                           throws SQLException;
}
```

For customizers that implement this interface, the `accept()` method should return `true` if the customizer has an interest in handling the current table cell and `false` if not. The `accept()` method has access to the column type, column type name, column name, `ResultSet` object, and column index to help it decide. The `display()` method gets called if `accept()` returns `true`; it creates and returns an `Element` containing the table cell data to be added to the table. All HTML components implement the `Element` interface, so by returning `Element` the `display()` method allows for any type of component to be returned.

We can write customizers to better display null values, dates, and numbers, as shown in Example 16-5, Example 16-6, and Example 16-7. Creating HTML component objects instead of strings keeps the code simpler and more extensible. It would also be possible for the table to programmatically limit the sort of elements that could be returned.

Example 16-5. A Customizer for Null Values

```
import java.sql.*;
import org.apache.ecs.*;
import org.apache.ecs.html.*;

public class NullCustomizer implements TableCustomizer {
  public boolean accept(int columnType, String columnTypeName,
                        String columnName, ResultSet rs, int index)
                                                throws SQLException {
    rs.getObject(index);
    return rs.wasNull();
  }

  public Element display(int columnType, String columnTypeName,
                         String columnName, ResultSet rs, int index)
                                                throws SQLException {
    // Print an "N/A" for null entries
    return new StringElement("N/A");
  }
}
```

Example 16-6. A Customizer for Date Values

```
import java.sql.*;
import java.text.*;
import java.util.*;
import org.apache.ecs.*;
import org.apache.ecs.html.*;

public class DateCustomizer implements TableCustomizer {

  DateFormat fmt;

  public DateCustomizer(Locale loc) {
    fmt = DateFormat.getDateTimeInstance(
                    DateFormat.SHORT, DateFormat.SHORT, loc);
  }

  public boolean accept(int columnType, String columnTypeName,
                        String columnName, ResultSet rs, int index)
                                                throws SQLException {
    return (columnType == Types.DATE || columnType == Types.TIMESTAMP);
  }

  public Element display(int columnType, String columnTypeName,
                         String columnName, ResultSet rs, int index)
                                                throws SQLException {
```

Example 16-6. A Customizer for Date Values (continued)

```
    // Print a short date and time using the specified locale
    return new StringElement(fmt.format(rs.getDate(index)));
  }
}
```

Example 16-7. A Customizer for Number Values

```
import java.sql.*;
import java.text.*;
import java.util.*;
import org.apache.ecs.*;
import org.apache.ecs.html.*;

public class NumberCustomizer implements TableCustomizer {

  NumberFormat fmt;

  public NumberCustomizer(Locale loc) {
    fmt = NumberFormat.getNumberInstance(loc);
  }

  public boolean accept(int columnType, String columnTypeName,
                        String columnName, ResultSet rs, int index)
                                                throws SQLException {
    return (columnType == Types.TINYINT ||
            columnType == Types.SMALLINT ||
            columnType == Types.INTEGER ||
            columnType == Types.BIGINT ||
            columnType == Types.REAL ||
            columnType == Types.FLOAT ||
            columnType == Types.DOUBLE);
  }

  public Element display(int columnType, String columnTypeName,
                         String columnName, ResultSet rs, int index)
                                                throws SQLException {
    // Print the number using the specified locale
    if (columnType == Types.TINYINT ||
        columnType == Types.SMALLINT ||
        columnType == Types.INTEGER ||
        columnType == Types.BIGINT) {
      return new StringElement(fmt.format(rs.getLong(index)));
    }
    else {
      return new StringElement(fmt.format(rs.getDouble(index)));
    }
  }
}
```

We can also write a more advanced customizer to make all bug IDs in the table into hyperlinks to a "bug view" servlet. Then no matter what query a user might enter, bug IDs will automatically be created as hyperlinks. Example 16-8 shows this customizer.

Example 16-8. A Customizer for Bug IDs

```
import java.sql.*;
import java.text.*;
import org.apache.ecs.*;
import org.apache.ecs.html.*;

public class BugIdCustomizer implements TableCustomizer {

  String bugViewServlet;

  public BugIdCustomizer(String bugViewServlet) {
    this.bugViewServlet = bugViewServlet;
  }

  public boolean accept(int columnType, String columnTypeName,
                        String columnName, ResultSet rs, int index)
                                               throws SQLException {
    return ((columnType == Types.CHAR ||
             columnType == Types.VARCHAR ||
             columnType == Types.LONGVARCHAR) &&
            "bugid".equalsIgnoreCase(columnName));
  }

  public Element display(int columnType, String columnTypeName,
                        String columnName, ResultSet rs, int index)
                                               throws SQLException {
    // Create a link to a servlet to display this bug
    String bugid = rs.getString(index);
    return new A(bugViewServlet + "?bugid=" + bugid, bugid);
  }
}
```

The `ResultSetTable` class accepts in its constructor an array of `TableCustomizer` objects. For each cell the customizers in the array are given the opportunity to control the creation of each table cell. The customizers will be called in the order they are placed in the array, and the first customizer to accept the table cell wins. The code for the `ResultSetTable` class can be found in Example 16-9.

Example 16-9. A Customizable Result Set Table

```
import java.io.*;
import java.sql.*;
import java.util.*;
import javax.servlet.*;
import javax.servlet.http.*;

import org.apache.ecs.*;
import org.apache.ecs.html.*;

public class ResultSetTable extends Table {

  public ResultSetTable(ResultSet rs) throws SQLException {
    this(rs, null);
  }

  public ResultSetTable(ResultSet rs, TableCustomizer[] customizers)
                                      throws SQLException {
    setBorder(1);

    if (customizers == null) {
      customizers = new TableCustomizer[0];
    }

    ResultSetMetaData rsmd = rs.getMetaData();
    int colCount = rsmd.getColumnCount();

    TR row = new TR();
    for (int i = 1; i <= colCount; i++) {
      addElement(new TH().addElement(rsmd.getColumnName(i)));
    }
    addElement(row);

    while (rs.next()) {
      row = new TR();
      for (int i = 1; i <= colCount; i++) {
        TD td = new TD();
        int columnType = rsmd.getColumnType(i);
        String columnTypeName = rsmd.getColumnTypeName(i);
        String columnName = rsmd.getColumnName(i);

        // Give each customizer a chance to control output
        boolean customized = false;
        for (int c = 0; c < customizers.length; c++) {
          TableCustomizer customizer = customizers[c];
          if (customizer.accept(columnType, columnTypeName,
                                columnName, rs, i)) {
            td.addElement(customizer.display(columnType, columnTypeName,
                                             columnName, rs, i));
```

Example 16-9. A Customizable Result Set Table (continued)

```
              customized = true;
              break;
            }
          }

          // If no customizer wanted the job, display the value as a String
          if (!customized) {
            td.addElement(rs.getString(i));
          }

          addElement(td);
        }
        addElement(row);
      }
    }
}
```

The outer `while` loop iterates through table rows, the outer `for` loop iterates over table columns, and the inner `for` loop manages the new customizer logic. The first customizer that "accepts" the cell handles the display for the cell. If no customizer accepts the cell, the table displays a simple `String` value. The servlet to call `ResultSetTable` is shown in Example 16-10.

Example 16-10. A Servlet to Exercise the ResultSetTable

```
import java.io.*;
import java.sql.*;
import java.text.*;
import java.util.*;
import javax.servlet.*;
import javax.servlet.http.*;

import org.apache.ecs.*;
import org.apache.ecs.html.*;

import com.oreilly.servlet.*;

public class ResultSetServlet extends HttpServlet {

  public void doPost(HttpServletRequest req, HttpServletResponse res)
                                throws ServletException, IOException {

    res.setContentType("text/html");
    PrintWriter out = res.getWriter();

    String url = req.getParameter("url");
    String driver = req.getParameter("driver");
    String sql = req.getParameter("sql");
```

Example 16-10. A Servlet to Exercise the ResultSetTable (continued)

```
    // Quickly verify url/driver/sql exist
    ParameterParser parser = new ParameterParser(req);
    String[] required = { "url", "driver", "sql" };
    String[] missing = parser.getMissingParameters(required);
    if (missing != null && missing.length > 0) {
      res.sendError(res.SC_BAD_REQUEST,
                   "URL, Driver, and SQL string must all be provided");
      return;
    }

    String param1 = req.getParameter("param1");
    String param2 = req.getParameter("param2");
    String param3 = req.getParameter("param3");
    String param4 = req.getParameter("param4");
    String param5 = req.getParameter("param5");
    String param6 = req.getParameter("param6");
    String val1 = req.getParameter("val1");
    String val2 = req.getParameter("val2");
    String val3 = req.getParameter("val3");
    String val4 = req.getParameter("val4");
    String val5 = req.getParameter("val5");
    String val6 = req.getParameter("val6");

    Properties props = new Properties();
    if (param1 != null && val1 != null) { props.put(param1, val1); }
    if (param2 != null && val2 != null) { props.put(param2, val2); }
    if (param3 != null && val3 != null) { props.put(param3, val3); }
    if (param4 != null && val4 != null) { props.put(param4, val4); }
    if (param5 != null && val5 != null) { props.put(param5, val5); }
    if (param6 != null && val6 != null) { props.put(param6, val6); }

    Connection con = null;

    try {
      Class.forName(driver);
      con = DriverManager.getConnection(url, props);

      Statement stmt = con.createStatement();
      boolean gotResultSet = stmt.execute(sql);

      if (!gotResultSet) {
        out.println(stmt.getUpdateCount() + " rows updated.");
      }
      else {
        TableCustomizer[] customizers = {
          new NullCustomizer(),
          new DateCustomizer(req.getLocale()),
          new BugIdCustomizer(req.getContextPath() + "/servlet/BugView"),
```

Example 16-10. A Servlet to Exercise the ResultSetTable (continued)

```
          new NumberCustomizer(req.getLocale()),
        };
        out.println(new ResultSetTable(stmt.getResultSet(), customizers));
      }
    }
    catch (Exception e) {
      throw new ServletException(e);
    }
  }
}
```

Figure 16-2 shows sample output. Notice now the bug ID is a hyperlink, the date is nicely formatted, and the null description displays "N/A."

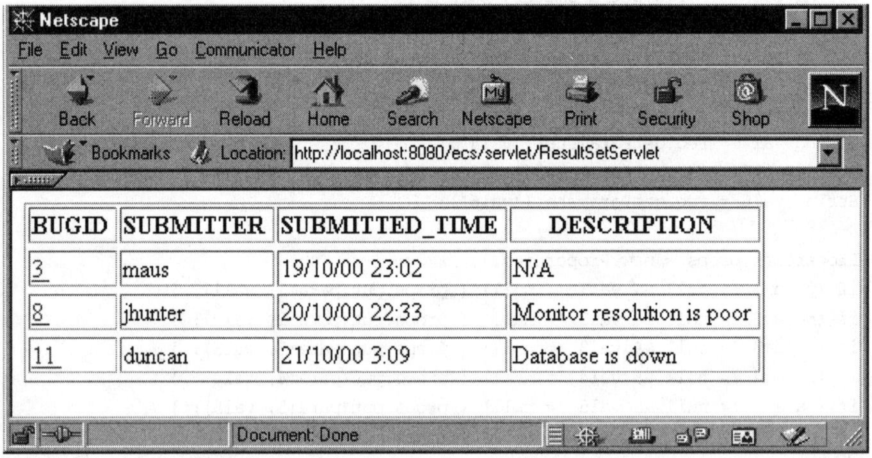

Figure 16-2. A customized result set view (European date)

Example 16-11 gives a simple HTML frontend for the servlet.

Example 16-11. A Simple HTML Frontend for ResultSetServlet

```
<HTML><HEAD><TITLE>SQL Query</TITLE></HEAD><BODY>

<P>
  This application executes a SQL query or update
  against any database on the public Internet.
</P>

<FORM METHOD="POST" ACTION="servlet/ResultSetServlet">
  <TABLE WIDTH="75%" BORDER="1">
    <TR>
      <TD WIDTH="35%">Database URL:</TD>
```

Example 16-11. A Simple HTML Frontend for ResultSetServlet (continued)

```
      <TD WIDTH="65%"><INPUT TYPE=TEXT NAME="url" SIZE="60"></TD>
    </TR>
    <TR>
      <TD WIDTH="35%">Database Driver:</TD>
      <TD WIDTH="65%"><INPUT TYPE=TEXT NAME="driver" SIZE="60"></TD>
    </TR>
    <TR>
      <TD COLSPAN="2"><P ALIGN=CENTER> -- Database Properties -- </p></TD>
    </TR>
    <TR>
      <TD WIDTH="35%"><INPUT TYPE=TEXT NAME="prop1" VALUE="username"></TD>
      <TD WIDTH="65%"><INPUT TYPE=TEXT NAME="val1"></TD>
    </TR>
    <TR>
      <TD WIDTH="35%"><INPUT TYPE=TEXT NAME="prop2" VALUE="password"></TD>
      <TD WIDTH="65%"><INPUT TYPE=TEXT NAME="val2"></TD>
    </TR>
    <TR>
      <TD WIDTH="35%"><INPUT TYPE=TEXT NAME="prop3" VALUE="cacherows"></TD>
      <TD WIDTH="65%"><INPUT TYPE=TEXT NAME="val3"></TD>
    </TR>
    <TR>
      <TD WIDTH="35%"><INPUT TYPE=TEXT NAME="prop4"></TD>
      <TD WIDTH="65%"><INPUT TYPE=TEXT NAME="val4"></TD>
    </TR>
    <TR>
      <TD WIDTH="35%"><INPUT TYPE=TEXT NAME="prop5"></TD>
      <TD WIDTH="65%"><INPUT TYPE=TEXT NAME="val5"></TD>
    </TR>
    <TR>
      <TD WIDTH="35%"><INPUT TYPE=TEXT NAME="prop6"></TD>
      <TD WIDTH="65%"><INPUT TYPE=TEXT NAME="val6"></TD>
    </TR>
  </TABLE>
  <P>
    <TEXTAREA NAME="sql" COLS="80" ROWS="5"></TEXTAREA>
    <BR>
    <INPUT TYPE=SUBMIT VALUE="Submit SQL">
  </P>
</FORM>
```

This demonstration of ECS has only scratched the surface of what's possible. With the full power of Java at your disposal, you can create pages or sections of pages that are customized perfectly for the data, and by taking advantage of the object-oriented nature of ECS, you can use inheritance, polymorphism, and strong type checking to make your job easier.

17

In this chapter:
- *A Simple XML Compile*
- *The Manipulation Class*
- *A Tool Application*

XMLC

XMLC uses XML technology to make HTML files into resources for Java. It was created by Lutris as part of their open source Enhydra Application Server and can be downloaded separately for use with any other servlet container.* Here we talk about XMLC 1.2b1, available for download at *http://xmlc.enhydra.org*. XMLC requires JDK 1.1 or later and any version of the Servlet API. It's released under the Enhydra Public License (EPL), an open source license similar to the Mozilla Public License (MPL). Basically, it requires changes to the existing code to be contributed back but allows private extensions, even commercial ones.

XMLC stands for *XML Compiler*. The tool takes a standard HTML or XML document and "compiles" it into a Java class. That class contains the Java instructions necessary to create an XML DOM (Document Object Model) tree representation of the document in memory. A programmer can manipulate the in-memory tree to add dynamic content and after manipulation can output the modified tree as HTML, XHTML, or any other XML.

In traditional use, a page designer creates one or more "mock-up" versions of the web page being developed. The mock-ups are pure HTML files. They are reviewed by interested parties, discussed, debated, and fine-tuned as necessary. The designer doesn't need to add any XMLC instructions into the file, only HTML 4.0-compliant `ID` attributes to the areas in the page to be replaced with dynamic content.

Offline, the XMLC tool compiles the mock-up page into a Java class containing the DOM tree representation of the document. The Java programmer makes use of the public API of this class to write a *manipulation class* that creates an instance of the tree, locates the sections of the document that need to be changed, and

* Enhydra Lutris is the scientific name for a sea otter, a fitting corporate identity for a company based in Santa Cruz with sea otters swimming in the nearby Monterey Bay.

modifies each section as necessary. The sections to change are located using accessor methods added to the tree by XMLC for every `ID` attribute in the document. The HTML files become, essentially, resources for Java.

If the page should contain a list of items, the mock-up can include maybe five or ten items to make the page look realistic. The Java programmer can delete all but the first item, then construct the actual list by repeatedly cloning the first item—thus matching the style of the mock-up but using data generated dynamically. It's even possible to tell the XMLC compiler to remove all but the first item automatically, improving performance at runtime.

XMLC achieves a high level of separation between content and presentation. HTML files are pure HTML, Java files are pure Java, and the files connect only through agreed-upon `ID` markers. As new mock-ups are created, they can be used directly with no retrofitting, and if a relied-upon tag is absent in the new mock-up, it triggers a compile error when the manipulation class tries to invoke the method to retrieve the `ID` that no longer exists.

A Simple XML Compile

To learn how to use XMLC, we'll start with a simple substitution application. Example 17-1 shows a simple *hello.html* mock-up web page that greets a user by name and tells her how many messages she has waiting for her. The HTML 4.0-compliant <SPAN> tags surround the text to be replaced.

Example 17-1. A Simple XMLC Substitution

```
<!-- hello.html -->
<HTML>
<HEAD><TITLE>Hello</TITLE></HEAD>
<BODY>

<H2><SPAN ID="Greeting">Hello, Kathlyn</SPAN></H2>
You have <SPAN ID="Messages">103</SPAN> new messages.

</BODY>
</HTML>
```

To run XMLC on this file you must first install XMLC. Download the tool from *http://xmlc.enhydra.org*, unpack the archive, and follow the instructions in the *README* for running *xmlc-config*. Then you're ready to run the *xmlc* compiler:

```
xmlc -class Hello -keep hello.html
```

This tells XMLC to compile the *hello.html* file into a class named `Hello`, keeping the generated *Hello.java* file for our examination. Because standard HTML files don't have to be well-formed XML, the XMLC compiler uses the Tidy parser to handle the conversion from HTML to the DOM. Beware, though, Tidy can get confused with HTML files that stray too far from valid HTML, and when this occurs you'll see a long list of warnings and errors during the XMLC compile. To eliminate this concern, you can use HTML design tools (like Dreamweaver) to create the HTML for XMLC processing. You can learn more about Tidy at *http://www.w3.org/People/Raggett/tidy* and the Java port named JTidy at *http://www3.sympatico.ca/ac.quick/jtidy.html*.

XMLC accepts dozens of compile options. The most commonly used options are listed below.* Here is the command-line syntax:

```
xmlc [options] docfile
```

`-class Classname`
: Specifies the fully qualified name for the generated class. For example, `Hello` or `com.servlets.xmlc.Hello`.

`-keep`
: Says to keep the generated Java source. Handy when getting started with XMLC.

`-methods`
: Prints the signature of each generated access method. Also handy when getting started.

`-verbose`
: Generates extra output about the compile process.

`-urlmapping` *`oldURL newURL`*
: Specifies a URL replacement rule. All instances of *`oldURL`* will become *`newURL`*. Allows a change in URL between the mock-up and production phases. This option may be specified multiple times.

`-urlregexpmapping` *`regexp subst`*
: Specifies an advanced URL replacement rule, using regular expressions. This option may be specified multiple times.

`-urlsetting` *`id newURL`*
: Specifies a URL to modify in the DOM by its tag ID. The URL with the ID *`id`* will be changed to *`newURL`*.

`-javac` *`prog`*
: Specifies the Java compiler to use.

* XMLC is also available as an Ant task, for those using the excellent Ant build tool. See *http://jakarta.apache.org*.

`-d directory`
: Specifies the output directory. Passed directly to the Java compiler during the compile phase.

`-delete-class classname`
: Deletes all document elements that have the `CLASS` attribute of *`classname`*. This is useful for removing mock-up data as we'll see later. The option may be specified multiple times.

`-version`
: Prints the XMLC version.

When you run XMLC with the `-keep` flag you can examine the generated source. The source for *Hello.java* is shown in Example 17-2.

Example 17-2. The Autogenerated Hello.java Source

```
/*
 ************************************
 * XMLC GENERATED CODE, DO NOT EDIT *
 ************************************
 */
import org.w3c.dom.*;
import org.enhydra.xml.xmlc.XMLCUtil;
import org.enhydra.xml.xmlc.XMLCError;
import org.enhydra.xml.xmlc.dom.XMLCDomFactory;

public class Hello extends org.enhydra.xml.xmlc.html.HTMLObjectImpl {
    /**
     * Field that is used to identify this as an XMLC
     * generated class.  Contains an reference to the
     * class object.
     */
    public static final Class XMLC_GENERATED_CLASS = Hello.class;

    /**
     * Field containing CLASSPATH relative name of the source file
     * that this class was generated from.
     */
    public static final String XMLC_SOURCE_FILE = "hello.html";

    /**
     * Get the element with id <CODE>Greeting</CODE>.
     * @see org.w3c.dom.html.HTMLElement
     */
    public org.w3c.dom.html.HTMLElement getElementGreeting() {
        return $elementGreeting;
    }
    private org.w3c.dom.html.HTMLElement $elementGreeting;

    /**
```

Example 17-2. The Autogenerated Hello.java Source (continued)

```
     * Get the value of text child of element <CODE>Greeting</CODE>.
     * @see org.w3c.dom.Text
     */
    public void setTextGreeting(String text) {
        XMLCUtil.getFirstText($elementGreeting).setData(text);
    }

    /**
     * Get the element with id <CODE>Messages</CODE>.
     * @see org.w3c.dom.html.HTMLElement
     */
    public org.w3c.dom.html.HTMLElement getElementMessages() {
        return $elementMessages;
    }
    private org.w3c.dom.html.HTMLElement $elementMessages;

    /**
     * Get the value of text child of element <CODE>Messages</CODE>.
     * @see org.w3c.dom.Text
     */
    public void setTextMessages(String text) {
        XMLCUtil.getFirstText($elementMessages).setData(text);
    }

    /**
     * Create document object.
     */
    private static Document createDocument() {
        XMLCDomFactory domFactory =
            new org.enhydra.xml.xmlc.dom.DefaultHTMLDomFactory();
        Document document = domFactory.createDocument(null, null);
        return document;
    }

    /**
     * Create document as a DOM and initialize accessor method fields.
     */
    public void buildDocument() {
        Document document = createDocument();
        setDocument(document);
        Node $node0, $node1, $node2, $node3, $node4;
        Element $elem0, $elem1, $elem2, $elem3;
        Attr $attr0, $attr1, $attr2, $attr3;

        $elem0 = document.getDocumentElement();
        $elem1 = document.createElement("HEAD");;
        $elem0.appendChild($elem1);
```

Example 17-2. The Autogenerated Hello.java Source (continued)

```
        $elem2 = document.createElement("TITLE");;
        $elem1.appendChild($elem2);

        $node3 = document.createTextNode("Hello");;
        $elem2.appendChild($node3);

        $elem1 = document.createElement("BODY");;
        $elem0.appendChild($elem1);

        $elem2 = document.createElement("H2");;
        $elem1.appendChild($elem2);

        $elem3 = document.createElement("SPAN");;
        $elem2.appendChild($elem3);

        $elementGreeting = (org.w3c.dom.html.HTMLElement)$elem3;
        $attr3 = document.createAttribute("id");
        $attr3.setValue("Greeting");
        $elem3.setAttributeNode($attr3);

        $node4 = document.createTextNode("Hello, Jason");;
        $elem3.appendChild($node4);

        $node2 = document.createTextNode("You have ");;
        $elem1.appendChild($node2);

        $elem2 = document.createElement("SPAN");;
        $elem1.appendChild($elem2);

        $elementMessages = (org.w3c.dom.html.HTMLElement)$elem2;
        $attr2 = document.createAttribute("id");
        $attr2.setValue("Messages");
        $elem2.setAttributeNode($attr2);

        $node3 = document.createTextNode("103");;
        $elem2.appendChild($node3);

        $node2 = document.createTextNode(" new messages.");;
        $elem1.appendChild($node2);

        $node1 = document.createComment(" hello.html ");;
        $elem0.appendChild($node1);
    }

    /**
     * Recursive function to do set access method fields from the DOM.
     * Missing ids have fields set to null.
     */
```

Example 17-2. The Autogenerated Hello.java Source (continued)

```
    protected void syncWithDocument(Node node) {
        if (node instanceof Element) {
            String id = ((Element)node).getAttribute("id");
            if (id.length() == 0) {
            } else if (id.equals("Greeting")) {
                $elementGreeting = (org.w3c.dom.html.HTMLElement)node;
            } else if (id.equals("Messages")) {
                $elementMessages = (org.w3c.dom.html.HTMLElement)node;
            }
        }
    }

    /**
     * Default constructor.
     */
    public Hello() {
        buildDocument();
    }

    /**
     * Constructor with optional building of the DOM.
     *
     * @param buildDOM If false, the DOM will not be built until
     * buildDocument() is called by the derived class.  If true,
     * the DOM is built immediately.
     */
    public Hello(boolean buildDOM) {
        if (buildDOM) {
            buildDocument();
        }
    }

    /**
     * Copy constructor.
     * @param src The document to clone.
     */
    public Hello(Hello src) {
        setDocument((Document)src.getDocument().cloneNode(true));
        syncAccessMethods();
    }

    /**
      * Clone the document.
      * @param deep Must be true, only deep clone is supported.
      */
    public Node cloneNode(boolean deep) {
```

Example 17-2. The Autogenerated Hello.java Source (continued)

```
        cloneDeepCheck(deep);
        return new Hello(this);
    }
}
```

This example contains a lot of code, but it's fairly simple. The class is named `Hello` as we dictated with the `-class` option. It extends `org.enhydra.xml.xmlc.html.HTMLObjectImpl`, the XMLC superclass for all HTML objects, and implements `org.w3c.dom.html.HTMLDocument`, the standard DOM interface representing an HTML document. The `Hello` constructor calls the `buildDocument()` method to populate the DOM tree with the content from the HTML file. DOM is just a set of interfaces, and there are many possible DOM implementations to choose from. We can see in the `createDocument()` method that this class uses the XMLC default implementation as returned by `DefaultHTMLDomFactory`, which in 1.2b1 is Apache Xerces (see *http://xml.apache.org*).

If you run *xmlc* with the `-methods` option you can see a summary of the generated access methods in the source:

```
% xmlc -class Hello -keep -methods hello.html
public org.w3c.dom.html.HTMLElement getElementGreeting();
public void setTextGreeting(String text);
public org.w3c.dom.html.HTMLElement getElementMessages();
public void setTextMessages(String text);
```

The getter methods return the `HTMLElement` DOM object representing the HTML element marked with the `ID` attribute. The setter methods set the text content of those elements. Notice the value of the `ID` attribute is encoded into the method names. Values that cannot be converted to legal Java identifiers will not have access methods generated for them, so be careful to use only letters, numbers, and underscores. Also remember ID values are supposed to be unique within the scope of the page.

The Manipulation Class

Once you have compiled your HTML file into a Java-based XML representation, the next step is to write what's called a *manipulation class*. This class creates an instance of the document, modifies its content, and outputs the document to its final destination. Example 17-3 demonstrates a simple manipulation class for our `Hello` page. Notice that it's a standalone program. The manipulation class tends to be a servlet or a class called by a servlet, but it doesn't have to be. XMLC has no dependencies on the Servlet API.

Example 17-3. The Manipulation Class for the Hello Page

```
import java.io.*;
import org.w3c.dom.*;
import org.w3c.dom.html.*;

import org.enhydra.xml.io.DOMFormatter;

public class HelloManipulation {

  public static void main(String[] args) {
    // Some pseudodynamic content
    String username = "Mark Diekhans";
    int numMessages = 43;

    // Create the DOM tree
    Hello hello = new Hello();

    // Set the title, using a standard DOM method
    hello.setTitle("Hello XMLC!");

    // Set the value for "greeting"
    hello.setTextGreeting("Hello, " + username);

    // Set the value for "messages"
    hello.setTextMessages("" + numMessages);

    try {
      DOMFormatter formatter = new DOMFormatter();  // can be heavily tweaked
      formatter.write(hello, System.out);
    }
    catch (IOException e) {
      e.printStackTrace();
    }
  }
}
```

The class first sets the pseudodynamic values to be added to the page: the username, and number of messages. Then it creates an instance of the `Hello` class that holds the contents of the HTML document. If the `hello` instance were output at this point, it would generate a faithful representation of the original HTML file. The manipulation class then proceeds to set the page title, the value for the greeting, and the value for the number of messages. It sets the greeting and number of messages using the accessor methods added by XMLC. It sets the title using a standard DOM method. There are many interesting accessor methods standard to the HTML DOM classes such as `getApplets()`, `getImages()`, `getLinks()`, `getForms()`, `getAnchors()`, and so on. For more information on the capabilities of the DOM classes, see the documentation bundled with XMLC. Finally, the manipulation class uses an `org.enhydra.xml.io.DOMFormatter` to write the `hello` instance to `System.out`. The `DOMFormatter` can accept an `OutputOptions` class in its constructor to tweak how the XML is output, but for standard web browsers the default behavior works fine and produces:

```
<HTML><HEAD><TITLE>Hello XMLC!</TITLE></HEAD><BODY><H2><SPAN id='Greeting'>Hello,
Mark Diekhans</SPAN></H2>You have <SPAN id='Messages'>43</SPAN> new messages.
</BODY><!-- hello.html --></HTML>
```

Notice the mock-up values have been replaced with new values and that all extraneous whitespace has been removed for efficiency. Also notice the comment has been placed at the end of the file. That's a harmless Xerces bug.

To run the manipulation class yourself you'll need to make sure the *xmlc.jar* file containing the XMLC classes can be found in your classpath (or your server's classpath if calling XMLC from a servlet). Be aware that *xmlc.jar* contains several supporting packages that can cause conflicts if you have installed different versions of these same packages. With XMLC 1.2b1, watch out for external collisions with Apache Xerces 1.0.2, SAX 1.0, DOM Level 2, GNU RegExp 1.0.8, and JTidy 26jul1999. Package collisions can result in cryptic error messages. For example, when running *xmlc* the compiler might report the XMLC-generated class is abstract and can't be instantiated because the class does not define a particular method from a particular class. The true problem: you have a mismatch between DOM versions. The solution is to make sure the newest version comes first in the classpath. This works as long as package versions are backward compatible.

Modifying a List

Now let's move on to a more advanced operation, modifying a list. First, we create the prototype page containing a mock-up list as shown in Example 17-4.

Example 17-4. A Mock-up List of Languages

```
<!-- snoop.html -->
<HTML><HEAD><TITLE>XMLC Snoop</TITLE></HEAD>

<H1>Client Locales</H1>

<UL>
<LI ID="locale">en
<LI CLASS="mockup">es
<LI CLASS="mockup">jp
</UL>

</BODY></HTML>
```

In production use this list would be part of a much larger page but it doesn't matter to XMLC at all. We compile the page using the XMLC compiler, and we specify `-delete-class mockup` to have the elements marked `mockup` automatically removed during the compile phase:

```
% xmlc -class Snoop -keep -delete-class mockup -methods snoop.html
public org.w3c.dom.html.HTMLLIElement getElementLocale();
```

Notice only one accessor method was added to the document: `getElementLocale()` was added to return the <ID> element marked `locale` as an `HTMLLIElement` object. The manipulation class to dynamically alter this document is given in Example 17-5.

Example 17-5. The Manipulation Class for the List of Languages

```
import java.io.*;
import java.util.*;
import javax.servlet.*;
import javax.servlet.http.*;

import org.w3c.dom.*;
import org.w3c.dom.html.*;

import org.enhydra.xml.io.DOMFormatter;

public class SnoopManipulation extends HttpServlet {

  public void doGet(HttpServletRequest req, HttpServletResponse res)
                               throws ServletException, IOException {
    res.setContentType("text/html");
    PrintWriter out = res.getWriter();

    // Get some dynamic data to display
    Enumeration locales = req.getLocales();

    // Create the DOM tree
    Snoop snoop = new Snoop();

    // Get the first "prototype" list item
    // The rest were removed during the xmlc compile
    HTMLLIElement item = snoop.getElementLocale();

    // Get the prototype's parent so we can manage the children
    Node parent = item.getParentNode();

    // Loop over the locales adding a node for each
    while (locales.hasMoreElements()) {
      Locale loc = (Locale)locales.nextElement();
      HTMLLIElement newItem = (HTMLLIElement) item.cloneNode(true);
```

Example 17-5. The Manipulation Class for the List of Languages (continued)

```
      Text text = snoop.createTextNode(loc.toString());
      newItem.replaceChild(text, newItem.getLastChild());
      parent.insertBefore(newItem, null);
    }

    // Remove the prototype item
    parent.removeChild(item);

    // Output the document
    DOMFormatter formatter = new DOMFormatter();  // can be heavily tweaked
    formatter.write(snoop, out);
  }
}
```

The interesting part of this servlet is the `while` loop. For each locale the servlet clones the prototype item, changes the text held by the clone, and inserts the clone to the end of the list. After the `while` loop the servlet removes the prototype item, leaving the list full of clones containing the actual data. The result is shown in Figure 17-1.*

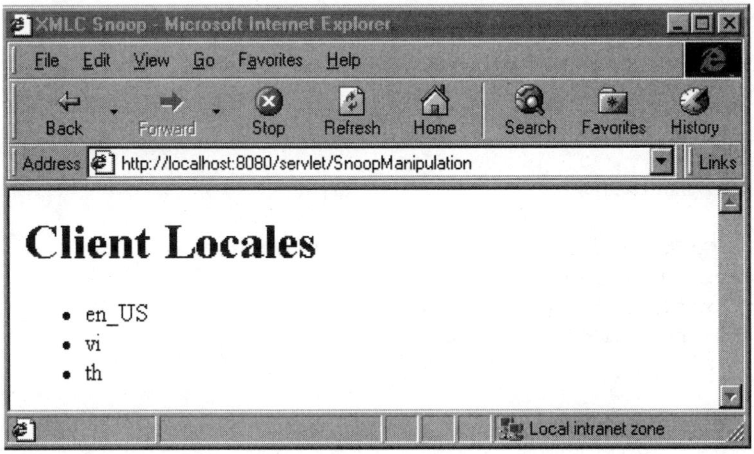

Figure 17-1. English (U.S.), Vietnamese, and Thai Locale Abbreviations

With this example we can see that one of the difficulties of XMLC is dealing with the less-than-intuitive DOM object model. There are some tricks to using DOM. For example, you see here that `String` content can only be created using the factory

* Beware of classpath interactions when running this example. We have XML libraries needed by XMLC, JDOM, and possibly the server itself. Satisfying the XML library version requirements of all three components without conflict can involve a fair amount of black magic and isn't always possible.

method `createTextNode()` called on the document to which the text will be added, and once you have the content created, the model for adding the text to the document requires adding the text as a child node of its containing element and removing the existing child. Under consideration is that a future version of XMLC may include support for the much easier to use JDOM object model. Also, toolkits being developed for XMLC layer on top of the DOM and abstract away some of its more cumbersome requirements.

A Tool Application

To conclude our discussion of XMLC, let's look at how the tool application used to demonstrate Tea and WebMacro can be rewritten using XMLC. We'll look first at the HTML template file that represents the common look and feel for our site but has no content relating to our tool listing. It's shown in Example 17-6.

Example 17-6. The Tool Application Template File

```
<!-- template.html -->
<HTML><HEAD><TITLE>Example Title</TITLE></HEAD>

<BODY BGCOLOR="#FFFFFF" BACKGROUND="/images/background.gif"
      LINK="#003333" ALINK="#669999" VLINK="#333333">

<IMG SRC="/images/banner.gif" WIDTH=600 HEIGHT=87 BORDER=0><BR>

<TABLE>
<TR>
<TD WIDTH=125 VALIGN=TOP>
 <BR><BR><BR>
 <FONT FACE="Arial,Helvetica" SIZE="+1" COLOR="#FF0000">
 <A HREF="/index.html">Home</A><BR>
 <A HREF="/hosting.html">Hosting</A><BR>
 <A HREF="/engines.html">Engines</A><BR>
 </FONT>
</TD>

<TD WIDTH=475>

  <TABLE CELLPADDING=5><TR><TD WIDTH=600 BGCOLOR="#006699" VALIGN=TOP>
  <B><FONT FACE="Arial,Helvetica" SIZE="+2">
  <SPAN ID="title">Example Title</SPAN>
  </FONT></B>
  </TD></TR></TABLE>

  <B><FONT FACE="Arial,Helvetica" SIZE="+1" COLOR="#003366">
  <SPAN ID="deck">Example Deck</SPAN>
  </FONT></B><P>
```

Example 17-6. The Tool Application Template File (continued)

```
  <P>

  <FONT FACE="Arial,Helvetica">

  <SPAN ID="desc">Example Description</SPAN>

  <DIV id="content">True content here</DIV>

  </FONT>

</TD>
</TR>

<TR>
<TD></TD>
<TD WIDTH=475 ALIGN=CENTER COLSPAN=3>
<HR>
<FONT FACE="Arial,Helvetica">
<A HREF="/index.html">Home</A>  
<A HREF="/hosting.html">Hosting</A>  
<A HREF="/engines.html">Engines</A>  <P>
</FONT>

<TABLE WIDTH=100%>
<TR>
<TD WIDTH=260 ALIGN=LEFT VALIGN=TOP>
<FONT FACE="Arial,Helvetica">
<A HREF="/copyright.html">Copyright</A> &copy; 2000 Jason Hunter<BR>
All Rights Reserved.</TD>
<TD WIDTH=5></FONT></TD>
<TD WIDTH=230 ALIGN=RIGHT VALIGN=TOP>
<FONT FACE="Arial,Helvetica">
Contact: <A HREF="mailto:webmaster@servlets.com">webmaster@servlets.com</a>
</FONT></TD>
</TR>
</TABLE>

</TD>
</TR>
</TABLE>

</BODY>
</HTML>
```

Notice the title of the page is a placeholder, and there are three <SPAN> elements named `title`, `deck`, and `desc` holding mock-up text intended for replacement. Also, there's a <DIV> element named `content` marking the location where the true content for the page should be displayed. The HTML file that will be used to generate the tool application content is shown in Example 17-7.

Example 17-7. The Tool Application Content File

```
<!-- toolview.html -->
<HTML><HEAD><TITLE>Tool Listing</TITLE></HEAD>

<BODY BGCOLOR="#FFFFFF" BACKGROUND="/images/background.gif"
      LINK="#003333" ALINK="#669999" VLINK="#333333">

<IMG SRC="/images/banner.gif" WIDTH=600 HEIGHT=87 BORDER=0><BR>

<TABLE>
<TR>
<TD WIDTH=125 VALIGN=TOP>
 <BR><BR><BR>
 <FONT FACE="Arial,Helvetica" SIZE="+1" COLOR="#FF0000">
 <A HREF="/index.html">Home</A><BR>
 <A HREF="/hosting.html">Hosting</A><BR>
 <A HREF="/engines.html">Engines</A><BR>
 </FONT>
</TD>

<TD WIDTH=475>

  <TABLE CELLPADDING=5><TR><TD WIDTH=600 BGCOLOR="#006699" VALIGN=TOP>
  <B><FONT FACE="Arial,Helvetica" SIZE="+2">
  <SPAN ID="title">Tool Listing</SPAN>
  </FONT></B>
  </TD></TR></TABLE>

  <B><FONT FACE="Arial,Helvetica" SIZE="+1" COLOR="#003366">
  <SPAN ID="deck">A list of content creation tools</SPAN>
  </FONT></B><P>

  <P>

  <FONT FACE="Arial,Helvetica">

  <SPAN ID="desc">
  Without tools, people are nothing more than animals.  And pretty weak ones
  at that.  Here's a list of servlet-based content creation tools you can use
  so you won't be a servlet weakling.
  </SPAN>

  <DIV ID="record">
    <HR SIZE=2 ALIGN=LEFT>
```

Example 17-7. The Tool Application Content File (continued)

```
    <FONT FACE="Arial,Helvetica">
    <H3>
    <SPAN ID="toolName">Some Tool Name</SPAN>
    <FONT COLOR=#FF0000><B> <SPAN ID="toolStatus">(New!)</SPAN> </B></FONT>
    </H3>
    <A ID="toolLink" HREF="http://toolhome.com">http://toolhome.com</A><BR>

    <SPAN ID="toolComments">
      Here go comments for this tool.
    </SPAN>
    </FONT>
  </DIV>

  <DIV>
    <HR SIZE=2 ALIGN=LEFT>

    <FONT FACE="Arial,Helvetica">
    <H3>
    Another Tool Name
    <FONT COLOR=#FF0000><B> (Updated!) </B></FONT>
    </H3>
    <A HREF="http://toolhome.com">http://toolhome.com</A><BR>

      Here go comments for this tool.

    </FONT>
  </DIV>

  </FONT>

</TD>
</TR>

<TR>
<TD></TD>
<TD WIDTH=475 ALIGN=CENTER COLSPAN=3>
<HR>
<FONT FACE="Arial,Helvetica">
<A HREF="/index.html">Home</A>  
<A HREF="/hosting.html">Hosting</A>  
<A HREF="/engines.html">Engines</A>  <P>
</FONT>

<TABLE WIDTH=100%>
<TR>
<TD WIDTH=260 ALIGN=LEFT VALIGN=TOP>
<FONT FACE="Arial,Helvetica">
<A HREF="/copyright.html">Copyright</A> &copy; 2000 Jason Hunter<BR>
```

Example 17-7. The Tool Application Content File (continued)

```
All Rights Reserved.</TD>
<TD WIDTH=5></FONT></TD>
<TD WIDTH=230 ALIGN=RIGHT VALIGN=TOP>
<FONT FACE="Arial,Helvetica">
Contact: <A HREF="mailto:webmaster@servlets.com">webmaster@servlets.com</a>
</FONT></TD>
</TR>
</TABLE>

</TD>
</TR>
</TABLE>

</BODY>
</HTML>
```

This file looks a lot like the template file, but we have replaced the placeholder values with realistic values and filled in the content area with some prototype tool records. Here's how we'll use this file: we'll programmatically take its key components (its title, deck, description, and prototype record), copy them, and place them into the template file to create the final page.

Why do we need two files? Couldn't we just modify the *toolview.html* file directly? Yes, we could, but we use the template so that if we update the header, sidebar, or footer in the future, we can update just the *template.html* file and have that change affect all pages. In other words, the template dictates the overall layout of the page. The *toolview.html* file is used only for its critical parts.

We run the HTML files through the XMLC compiler using commands like the following. There will be some warnings because the HTML is not valid XML:

```
% xmlc -class Template -keep -methods template.html
% xmlc -class ToolView -keep -methods toolview.html
```

Then we're ready to write the servlet that acts as the manipulation class. It's listed in Example 17-8.

Example 17-8. The Tool Application Manipulation Class

```
import java.io.*;
import java.util.*;
import javax.servlet.*;
import javax.servlet.http.*;

import org.w3c.dom.*;
import org.w3c.dom.html.*;

import org.enhydra.xml.io.DOMFormatter;
```

Example 17-8. The Tool Application Manipulation Class (continued)

```
public class ToolViewServlet extends HttpServlet {

  private Tool[] tools;

  public void init() throws ServletException {
    // Load the tool data in our init for simplicity
    String toolsFile = getInitParameter("toolsFile"); // from web.xml
    if (toolsFile == null) {
      throw new ServletException(
        "A tools data file must be specified as the toolsFile init parameter");
    }
    log("Loading tools from " + toolsFile);
    try {
      tools = Tool.loadTools(toolsFile);
      if (tools.length == 0) {
        log("No tools found in " + toolsFile);
      }
      else {
        log(tools.length + " tools found in " + toolsFile);
      }
    }
    catch (Exception e) {
      throw new ServletException(e);
    }
  }

  public void doGet(HttpServletRequest req, HttpServletResponse res)
                              throws ServletException, IOException {
    res.setContentType("text/html");
    PrintWriter out = res.getWriter();

    // Create the DOM tree for the full document
    Template template = new Template();

    // Create the DOM Tree that contains the internal content
    ToolView toolview = new ToolView();

    // Get the prototype tool view record
    HTMLDivElement record = toolview.getElementRecord();

    // Get a reference to the insertion point for the tool list
    HTMLDivElement insertionPoint = template.getElementContent();
    Node insertionParent = insertionPoint.getParentNode();

    // Set the template title, deck, and desc
    // Pull the data from the toolview.html file
    String title = ((Text)toolview.getElementTitle().getFirstChild()).getData();
    String deck = ((Text)toolview.getElementDeck().getFirstChild()).getData();
```

Example 17-8. The Tool Application Manipulation Class (continued)

```
    String desc = ((Text)toolview.getElementDesc().getFirstChild()).getData();
    template.setTitle(title);       // the page title
    template.setTextTitle(title); // the element marked "title"
    template.setTextDeck(deck);    // the element marked "deck"
    template.setTextDesc(desc);    // the element marked "desc"

    // Loop over the tools adding a record for each
    for (int i = 0; i < tools.length; i++) {
      Tool tool = tools[i];

      toolview.setTextToolName(tool.name);
      toolview.setTextToolComments(tool.comments);

      if (tool.isNewWithin(45)) {
        toolview.setTextToolStatus(" (New!) ");
      }
      else if (tool.isUpdatedWithin(45)) {
        toolview.setTextToolStatus(" (Updated!) ");
      }
      else {
        toolview.setTextToolStatus("");
      }

      HTMLAnchorElement link = toolview.getElementToolLink();
      link.setHref(tool.homeURL);
      Text linkText = toolview.createTextNode(tool.homeURL);
      link.replaceChild(linkText, link.getLastChild());

      // importNode() is DOM Level 2
      insertionParent.insertBefore(template.importNode(record, true), null);
    }

    // Remove insertion placeholder
    insertionParent.removeChild(insertionPoint);

    // Output the document
    DOMFormatter formatter = new DOMFormatter();  // can be heavily tweaked
    formatter.write(template, out);
  }
}
```

The `init()` method of the servlet loads the tool data from the file specified in the `toolsFile` init parameter, using the `Tool` class from Chapter 14, *The Tea Framework*. In the `doGet()` method we do the interesting work. We create an instance of the `Template` document and an instance of the `ToolView` document. Then we locate the prototype tool record in the `ToolView` and the insertion point for tool records in the `Template`. Next we retrieve the title, deck, and description from the `ToolView` document and copy over those values to the `Template`.

In the `for` loop we handle the task of creating the list of tool records. For each tool, we assign appropriate values to the prototype record: first the name and comments, then the status, and finally the link. After the record has been modified, we add the record to the template at the insertion point. In DOM, nodes are tied to the document that created them, so we use the `importNode()` method to enable the record to move from the `ToolView` document to the `Template`. The `importNode()` method performs a deep copy (because we passed `true` as the second argument) so each iteration of the `for` loop adds a different copy of the record contents. After the `for` loop we remove the insertion point from the template and output the document to the client.

When running this servlet be aware that the `importNode()` method is new in DOM Level 2, so for this servlet to execute, your server must have a classpath that includes the DOM Level 2 classes before any DOM Level 1 classes. The *xmlc.jar* archive contains DOM Level 2, so you wouldn't think this would be a problem, but some servers (including Tomcat 3.2) have a DOM Level 1 implementation in their default classpath to help them read *web.xml* files. For this servlet to work on such servers you must edit the server classpath to ensure XMLC's *xmlc.jar* is located before the server's own XML libraries. (Tomcat 3.2 autoloads JAR files in alphabetical order, so you may need to rename JAR files.)

One problem inherent to XMLC shown by this example is that conditionally included blocks of text whose contents vary, like the (*New!*) and (*Updated!*) remarks, can be difficult to incorporate into pages because the template can declare only one possible block of text for inclusion. In this example it's clear the Java code knows more than it should about the rendering of the remarks.

A nice perk of XMLC is that any special characters in the included element content like <, >, and & are automatically escaped as they're sent to the client, because the formatter outputting the document can easily recognize what's structure and what's content. This knowledge of document structure also makes it possible for the formatter to perform advanced tasks like modifying all links to encode session IDs, although that particular feature hasn't yet been implemented.

The page generated by this servlet looks the same as the page generated by the Tea and WebMacro examples.

18

In this chapter:

- *Using JavaServer Pages*
- *Behind the Scenes*
- *Expressions and Declarations*
- *Directives*
- *JSP and JavaBeans*
- *Includes and Forwards*
- *A Tool Application*
- *Custom Tag Libraries*

JavaServer Pages

JavaServer Pages, commonly known as JSP, is a technology created by Sun Microsystems and closely tied to servlets. JSP was one of the first efforts to create a non-proprietary servlet-based content creation system. If you've been following servlets long, you may remember JSP was first announced in the spring of 1998—early enough in fact for the first edition of this book to include a short tutorial on JSP's prerelease 0.91 version. Of course, JSP has changed significantly since then. In this section, we cover JSP 1.1, built on top of Servlet API 2.2.

As with servlets, Sun releases a JSP specification (created by an expert group consisting of outside vendors and individuals), and then third-party vendors compete on their implementation of that standard. Unlike the other technologies discussed that build on top of pure servlets, JSP is a specification, not a product, and requires support from the server in order to work. Most servlet container vendors are providing this support, including Tomcat where the JSP engine is named Jasper and JSP is a core component of Java 2, Enterprise Edition (J2EE).

One stated purpose of JSP (quoting from the specification) is to "enable the separation of dynamic and static content." Another purpose is to "enable the authoring of Web pages that create dynamic content easily but with maximum power and flexibility." JSP accomplishes both of these goals fairly well. However, because of the "maximum power" inherent in the JSP design, the JSP page author always has complete control of the system, and thus one could say JSP *enables* separation of content from presentation but doesn't *enforce* or *encourage* it as alternatives do. It's similar to how C++ allows good object-oriented design but doesn't structurally promote that good design as much as Java does.

JSP is also a very flexible technology, and there are many different ways to make use of JSP. One way is as a "shorthand" way to write a servlet: a servlet programmer, comfortable with Java, can put Java code directly in a JSP page instead of writing a full servlet—and by that gains niceties like eliminating `out.println()` calls, being able to point at JSP files directly, and taking advantage of JSP's autocompile feature. By writing a JSP page instead of a servlet, however, the programmer loses full contact with the code and loses the ability to control the true execution environment to do things like extend `com.oreilly.servlet.CacheHttpServlet` or generate binary (image) output. For this reason real coding is best left to regular servlets, with JSPs used primarily for presentation logic.

Even when used just for presentation logic, JSP pages can be used many different ways. One way involves the use of JavaBeans embedded within the page. Another way involves creating custom tags that look like HTML but are actually hooks into supporting Java code. Yet another way involves sending all requests to a servlet that performs business logic and having that servlet forward the request for rendering to a JSP page using the `RequestDispatcher` mechanism. This technique is often called the *Model 2 architecture,* a name taken from the JSP 0.92 specification. Then there are other architectures, some given whimsical names like *Model 1½*, *Model 2½*, or *Model 2 + 1.* There's no shortage to ideas for the best way to use JSP.

In this chapter we'll look at the various ways to use JSPs, everything from "servlet shorthand" to custom tags. The coverage will be fast and furious but should provide enough of a base for you to compare JSP against the alternatives. We will not discuss all the various architecture options and will instead concentrate on the technical nuts and bolts. For architecture options and more information on JavaServer Pages, see the JSP home page at *http://java.sun.com/products/jsp* (a syntax "cheat sheet" for JSP 1.0 is available at *http://java.sun.com/products/jsp/syntax.pdf*) and the book *JavaServer Pages* by Hans Bergsten (O'Reilly).

Using JavaServer Pages

At its most basic, JSP allows for the direct insertion of servlet code into an otherwise static HTML file.* Each block of servlet code (called a *scriptlet*) is surrounded by a leading `<%` tag and a closing `%>` tag. For convenience, a scriptlet can use a number of predefined variables. The six most frequently used variables are:

`HttpServletRequest request`
: The servlet request.

`HttpServletResponse response`
: The servlet response.

* Before we start, it's worth pointing out that putting Java code within a JSP page is considered by many to be poor style. We cover more advanced uses of JSP later that are commonly considered better style.

`javax.servlet.jsp.JspWriter out`
: The output writer, used like a `PrintWriter` but it has different buffering characteristics.

`HttpSession session`
: The user's session.

`ServletContext application`
: The web application.

`javax.servlet.jsp.PageContext pageContext`
: An object primarily used to abstract the implementation of the server but sometimes used directly to share variables between JSP pages and supporting beans and tags.

You'll notice that core JSP classes reside under the `javax.servlet.jsp` package.

Example 18-1 shows a simple JSP page that says a personalized "Hello" using the predefined `request` and `out` variables. If you have a server that supports Java-Server Pages and want to test this page, you should place the file under the server's document root and save it with a *.jsp* extension. Assuming you have saved the page as *hello1.jsp*, you can then access it at the URL *http://server:port/hello1.jsp*, or if you put the file in a context path of *jsp*, then the URL would be *http://server:port/jsp/hello1.jsp*.

Example 18-1. Saying "Hello" with JSP

```
<HTML>
<HEAD><TITLE>Hello</TITLE></HEAD>
<BODY>
<H1>
<%
if (request.getParameter("name") == null) {
   out.println("Hello World");
}
else {
  out.println("Hello, " + request.getParameter("name"));
}
%>
</H1>
</BODY></HTML>
```

A screen shot is shown in Figure 18-1.

Behind the Scenes

How does JSP work? Behind the scenes, the server automatically creates, compiles, loads, and runs a special servlet to generate the page's content, as shown in

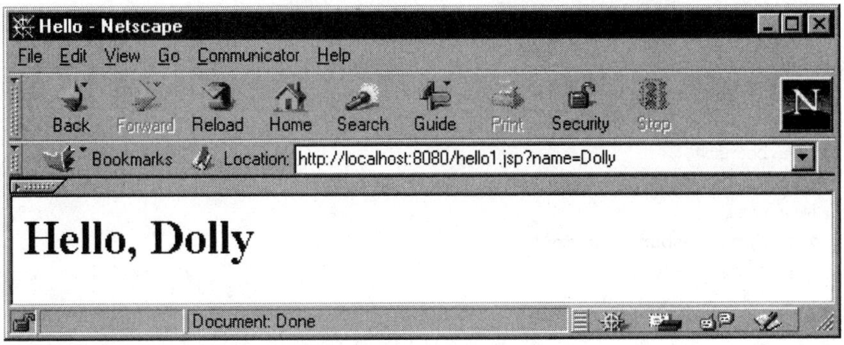

Figure 18-1. Saying Hello using JavaServer Pages

Figure 18-2. You can think of this special servlet as a background, workhorse servlet. The static portions of the HTML page are generated by the workhorse servlet using the equivalent of `out.println()` calls, while the dynamic portions are included directly. For example, the servlet shown in Example 18-2 might be the background workhorse for *hello1.jsp* running under Tomcat.*

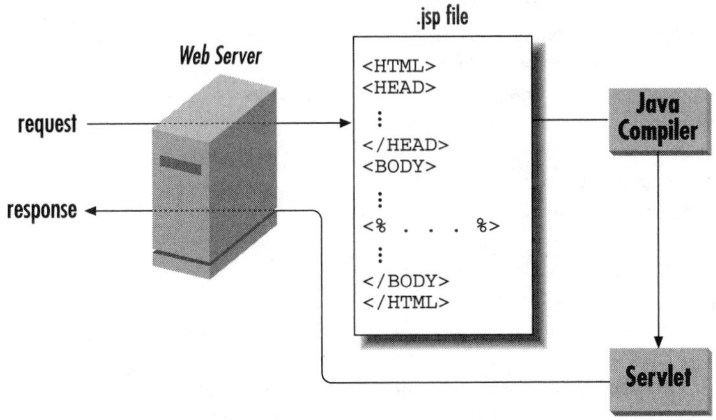

Figure 18-2. Generating JavaServer Pages

* If you're interested in seeing the true servlet source code for a JSP page, it's generally placed somewhere under the temporary directory specified in the context attribute `javax.servlet.context.tempdir` (see Chapter 4, *Retrieving Information*). When you find the true servlet source, you're likely to see that it is more complicated and convoluted than what is shown here.

Example 18-2. The Autogenerated Workhorse Servlet for hello1.jsp

```
import javax.servlet.*;
import javax.servlet.http.*;
import javax.servlet.jsp.*;
import javax.servlet.jsp.tagext.*;
import java.beans.*;
import java.io.*;
import java.util.*;
import org.apache.jasper.runtime.*;
import org.apache.jasper.*;

public class _0002fhello_00031_0002ejsphello1_jsp_0 extends HttpJspBase {
    private static boolean _jspx_inited = false;

    public _0002fhello_00031_0002ejsphello1_jsp_0() { }

    public final void _jspx_init() throws JasperException { }

    public void _jspService(HttpServletRequest request,
                            HttpServletResponse response)
                                throws IOException, ServletException {

        JspFactory _jspxFactory = null;
        PageContext pageContext = null;
        HttpSession session = null;
        ServletContext application = null;
        ServletConfig config = null;
        JspWriter out = null;
        Object page = this;
        String  _value = null;
        try {
            if (_jspx_inited == false) {
                _jspx_init();
                _jspx_inited = true;
            }
            _jspxFactory = JspFactory.getDefaultFactory();
            response.setContentType("text/html;charset=8859_1");
            pageContext = _jspxFactory.getPageContext(this, request, response,
                        "", true, 8192, true);

            application = pageContext.getServletContext();
            config = pageContext.getServletConfig();
            session = pageContext.getSession();
            out = pageContext.getOut();

            // HTML // begin [file="C:\\hello1.jsp";from=(0,0);to=(4,0)]
            out.write("<HTML>\r\n<HEAD><TITLE>Hello</TITLE></HEAD>\r\n<BODY>");
            out.write("\r\n<H1>\r\n");
            // end
```

Example 18-2. The Autogenerated Workhorse Servlet for hello1.jsp (continued)

```
          // begin [file="C:\\hello1.jsp";from=(4,2);to=(11,0)]
          if (request.getParameter("name") == null) {
             out.println("Hello World");
          }
          else {
            out.println("Hello, " + request.getParameter("name"));
          }
          // end

          // HTML // begin [file="C:\\hello1.jsp";from=(11,2);to=(15,0)]
          out.write("\r\n</H1>\r\n</BODY></HTML>\r\n\r\n");
          // end
      } catch (Exception ex) {
          if (out.getBufferSize() != 0)
              out.clearBuffer();
          pageContext.handlePageException(ex);
      } finally {
          out.flush();
          _jspxFactory.releasePageContext(pageContext);
      }
   }
}
```

The first time you access a JSP page, you may notice that it takes a short time to respond. This is the time necessary for the server to create and compile the background servlet, what has been called the *first-person penalty*. Subsequent requests should be as fast as ever because the server can reuse the servlet in memory. The one exception is when the *.jsp* file changes, in which case the server notices during the next request for that page and recompiles a new background servlet. If there's ever an error in compiling, you can expect the server to somehow report the problem, usually in the page returned to the client and/or a server log file.

You can avoid the first-person penalty by precompiling your JSPs. This can be done manually by making a request to each JSP page passing a query string of *?jsp_precompile="true"*. The request causes the server to compile the JSPs, but the special query string tells the server not to bother passing the request through to the JSP for handling. Servlet container vendors can make this process more automated and easier.

Expressions and Declarations

In addition to scriptlets, JavaServer Pages allows code to be placed into a page using expressions and declarations. A JSP expression begins with `<%=` and ends with `%>`. Any Java expression between the two tags is evaluated, the result is converted to a

String, and the text is included directly in the page. This technique eliminates the clutter of an out.println() call. For example, <%= foo %> includes the value of the foo variable.

A declaration begins with <%! and ends with %>. In between the tags, you can include any servlet code that should be placed outside the servlet's service method. You may declare static or instance variables or define new methods. Example 18-3 demonstrates with a JSP page that uses a declaration to define the getName() method and an expression to print it. The comment at the top of the file shows that JSP comments are surrounded by <%-- --%> tags.

Example 18-3. Saying "Hello" Using a JSP Declaration

```
<%-- hello2.jsp --%>
<HTML>
<HEAD><TITLE>Hello</TITLE></HEAD>
<BODY>
<H1>
Hello, <%= getName(request) %>
</H1>
</BODY>
</HTML>

<%!
private static final String DEFAULT_NAME = "World";

private String getName(HttpServletRequest req) {
  String name = req.getParameter("name");
  if (name == null)
    return DEFAULT_NAME;
  else
    return name;
}
%>
```

This JSP behaves the same as *hello1.jsp*.

The special methods jspInit() and jspDestroy() can be implemented within a declaration. They are called by the background servlet's init() and destroy() methods and give the JSP page an opportunity to declare code to be executed on initialization and destruction. A JSP page cannot override the standard init() and destroy() methods because the methods are declared final by the background servlet.

Directives

A JSP directive allows a JSP page to control certain aspects of its workhorse servlet. Directives can be used to have the workhorse servlet set its content type, import a package, control its output buffering and session management, extend a different superclass, and give special handling to errors. A directive can even specify the use of a non-Java scripting language.

The directive syntax requires a directive name along with an attribute name/value pair, all surrounded by `<%@ %>` tags. The quotes around the attribute value are mandatory:

```
<%@ directiveName attribName="attribValue" %>
```

The `page` directive allows the JSP to control the generated servlet through the setting of special attributes, as listed here:

`contentType`
: Specifies the content type of the generated page. For example:

```
<%@ page contentType="text/plain" %>
```

The default content type is `text/html; charset=8859_1`.

`import`
: Specifies a list of classes and packages the generated servlet should import. Multiple classes can be given in a comma-separated list. For example:

```
<%@ page import="java.io.*,java.util.Hashtable" %>
```

The implicit include list is `java.lang.*,javax.servlet.*,javax.servlet.http.*,javax.servlet.jsp.*`.

`buffer`
: Specifies the minimum required size of the response buffer in kilobytes, similar to the servlet method `setBufferSize()`. The value should be written as ##kb. A special value of `none` indicates that content should be passed directly to the underlying `PrintWriter` in the `ServletResponse` (which may or may not pass the content directly to the client). For example:

```
<%@ page buffer="12kb" %>
```

The default is `8kb`.

`autoFlush`
: Specifies if the buffer should be flushed when it's filled or if instead an `IOException` should be thrown. A `true` indicates to flush, a `false` indicates to throw. For example:

```
<%@ page autoFlush="true" %>
```

The default is `true`.

`session`
: Indicates the page wants to have access to the user's session. A `true` puts the `session` variable in scope and may set a client cookie to manage the session. A `false` disables access to the `session` variable. For example:

```
<%@ page session="false" %>
```

The default is `true`.

`errorPage`
: Specifies a page to display if a `Throwable` is thrown from within the JSP page and is not caught before reaching the server. This proves useful because it's difficult to do `try/catch` blocks when writing JSP pages. For example:

```
<%@ page errorPage="/error.jsp" %>
```

The default behavior is implementation dependent. The path is context relative, so you don't need to worry about prepending the current context path. The target may be a JSP but doesn't have to be. If the target is a servlet, the servlet may retrieve the `Throwable` as the context attribute `javax.servlet.jsp.jspException`.

`isErrorPage`
: Indicates the page is intended to be used as the target of an `errorPage`. If the value is `true` the page can access an implicit variable named `exception` to retrieve the `Throwable`.

`language`
: Specifies the scripting language used in the code sections of the page. The language used must interact with Java well enough to expose the necessary Java objects to the script environment. For example:

```
<%@ page language="javascript" %>
```

The default is `java`, the only language blessed by the specification.

Using Directives

Example 18-4 shows a JSP page named *errorMaker.jsp* that uses several directives. First it sets the page directive `session` attribute to `false` because the page doesn't use the session object and there's no need for the server to create a session needlessly. Then it sets the `errorPage` attribute to `/errorTaker.jsp` so if the page throws an uncaught exception the *errorTaker.jsp* page will handle the display of the error message. The body of the page is simple. It throws an exception to trigger the `errorPage` behavior. (We'll talk about why it uses the `if` check a little later.)

Example 18-4. Born to Be Bad

```
<%-- errorMaker.jsp --%>

<%@ page session="false" %>              <%-- Don't send needless cookies --%>
<%@ page errorPage="/errorTaker.jsp" %> <%-- General error handling page --%>

<%-- All we're good for is throwing an exception --%>
<%
  if (System.currentTimeMillis() > 0) {
    throw new Exception("oops");
  }
%>
```

The *errorTaker.jsp* page is shown in Example 18-5. It sets the page directive `isErrorPage` attribute to `true` to indicate this page handles errors, and it uses the import attribute to import the `com.oreilly.servlet` classes. The JSP uses a scriptlet to set the status code of the response to `500`, then it writes the body of the page with the exception class name, a stack trace, and a message suggesting the user contact the webmaster to report the problem.

Example 18-5. And Your Problem Is...

```
<%-- errorTaker.jsp --%>

<%@ page isErrorPage="true" %>
<%@ page import="com.oreilly.servlet.*" %>

<% response.setStatus(500); %>

<HTML>
<HEAD><TITLE>Error: <%= exception.getClass().getName() %></TITLE></HEAD>
<BODY>

<H1>
<%= exception.getClass().getName() %>
</H1>

We encountered an error while executing your page:

<PRE>
<%= ServletUtils.getStackTraceAsString(exception) %>
</PRE>

<% String name = request.getServerName(); %>
Please contact <A HREF="mailto:webmaster@<%= name %>">webmaster@<%= name %></A>
to report the problem.

</BODY>
</HTML>
```

On any request to *errorMaker.jsp*, an exception is thrown, control is transferred to *errorTaker.jsp*, and *errorTaker.jsp* displays a nice error-reporting page. See Figure 18-3.

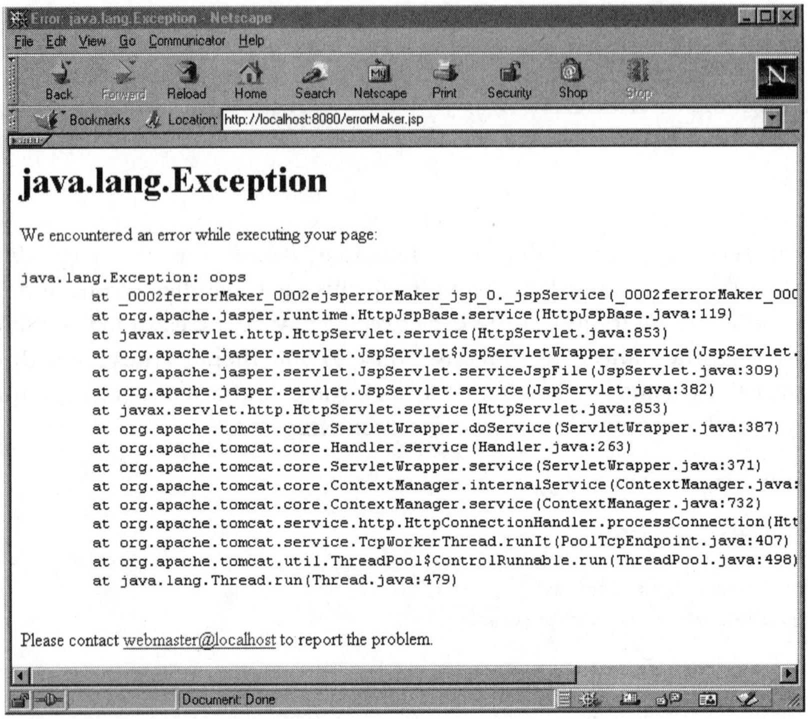

Figure 18-3. A customizable error page

So why did we have the `System.currentTimeMillis()` call in *errorMaker.jsp*? That stems from the fact that JSP pages are required to preserve all whitespace from the body text of the document. This allows JSP to be used to create not only HTML but also XML, where whitespace can be very important. Unfortunately, preserving all whitespace means that the simple scriptlet:

```
<% throw new Exception("oops"); %>
```

must generate code to print a new line after the throw—code that can never be reached! Compiling this scriptlet on Tomcat generates this error message:

```
org.apache.jasper.JasperException: Unable to compile class for
  JSPC:\engines\jakarta-tomcat\work\localhost_8080%2Fjsp\
  _0002ferrorMaker_0002ejsperrorMaker_jsp_3.java:75:
Statement not reached.
                out.write("\r\n");
                ^
```

By adding the check as to whether `System.currentTimeMillis()` is greater than zero, the compiler assumes there's a possibility the exception won't be thrown and thus there's no compile error. Similar problems happen with return and throw statements inside scriptlets.

In fact, there are many such "gotchas" when using scriptlets with JSP. If you accidentally write a scriptlet instead of an expression (by forgetting the equals sign), declare a static variable inside a scriptlet (where statics aren't allowed), forget a semicolon (they're not needed in expressions but are needed in scriptlets), or write anything but perfect Java code, you're likely to get a confusing error message because the compiler is acting on the generated Java code, not on the JSP file. To demonstrate the problem, picture if `<%= name %>` were replaced by `<% name %>` in *errorTaker.jsp*. Tomcat generates this error:

```
org.apache.jasper.JasperException: Unable to compile class for
  JSPC:\engines\jakarta-tomcat\work\localhost_8080%2Fjsp\
  _0002ferrorTaker_0002ejsperrorTaker_jsp_6.java:91:
Class name not found.
                    name
                    ^
```

Debugging an error like this often requires a programmer to look at the generated code to reconstruct what caused the error.

Avoid Java Code in JSP Pages

Scriptlets, expressions, and declarations allow the placement of Java code within a JSP page. They are powerful tools, yet we discourage their use. Even in the hands of a skilled programmer, placing code in the page is "secondhand" programming. You're writing Java code but not directly, and when errors occur the extra level of indirection makes the problem hard to diagnose.

When put into the hands on nonprogrammers, the situation becomes even worse. The nonprogrammers must learn some amount of Java, a language not designed for scripting and not intended for nonprogrammers. A language like JavaScript—simpler, more forgiving, and better known by web designers—could work better than Java, but JavaScript support is nonstandard and not widely implemented.

And finally, it's a matter of design. Having designers and developers working on the same file creates a bottleneck and extra opportunities for error. The content and presentation should be separated. To enable this and to move Java code out of the page, JSP allows the use of JavaBeans and custom tag libraries. We'll look at JavaBeans next.

JSP and JavaBeans

One of the most interesting and powerful ways to use JavaServer Pages is in cooperation with JavaBeans components. JavaBeans are reusable Java classes whose methods and variables follow specific naming conventions to give them added abilities. They can be embedded directly in a JSP page using the `<jsp:useBean>` tag, or what JSP calls an *action*. A JavaBean component can perform a well-defined task (execute database queries, connect to a mail server, maintain information about the client, etc.) and make its resulting information available to the JSP page through simple accessor methods. For more information on JavaBeans, see *http://java.sun.com/bean* and the book *Developing Java Beans* by Robert Englander (O'Reilly).

The difference between a JavaBeans component embedded in a JSP page and a normal third-party class used by the generated servlet is that the web server can give JavaBeans embedded in a page special treatment. For example, a server can automatically set a bean's properties (essentially instance variables) using the parameter values in the client's request. In other words, if the request includes a `name` parameter and the server detects through introspection (a technique in which the methods and variables of a Java class can be programmatically determined at runtime) that the bean has a `name` property and a `setName(String name)` method, the server can automatically call `setName()` with the value of the `name` parameter. There's no need for `getParameter()`.

A bean can also have its scope managed automatically by the server. A bean can be assigned to a specific page (where it is used once and destroyed), a specific request (similar to page scope except the bean persists between internal include and forward calls), to a client session (where the bean is automatically made available every time the same client reconnects), or to an application scope (where the same bean is available to the entire web application).

Embedding a Bean

Beans are embedded in a JSP page using the `<jsp:useBean>` action. It has the following syntax (case sensitive, and the quotes are mandatory):

```
<jsp:useBean id="name" scope="page|request|session|application"
             class="className" type="typeName">
</jsp:useBean>
```

You can set the following attributes of the `<jsp:useBean>` action:

`id`

Specifies the name of the bean. This is the key under which the bean is saved if its scope extends beyond the page. If a bean instance saved under this name already exists in the given scope, that instance is used with this page. Otherwise a new bean is created. For example:

```
id="userPreferences"
```

`scope`

Specifies the scope of the bean's visibility. The value must be `page`, `request`, `session`, or `application`. If `page`, the variable is created essentially as an instance variable; if `request`, the variable is stored as a request attribute; if `session`, the bean is stored in the user's session; and if `application`, the bean is stored in the servlet context. For example:

```
scope="session"
```

The default value is `page`.

`class`

Specifies the class name of the bean. This is used when initially constructing the bean. The class name must be fully qualified. For example:

```
class="com.company.tracking.UserPreferencesImpl"
```

The `class` attribute is not necessary if the bean already exists in the current scope, but there must still be a `type` attribute to allow the system to cast the object to the proper type. If there's a problem constructing the given class, the JSP page throws an `InstantiationException`.

`type`

Specifies the type of the bean as it should be held by the system, used for casting when the object is retrieved from the request, session, or context. The type value should be the fully qualified name of a superclass or an interface of the actual class. For example:

```
type="com.company.tracking.UserPreferences"
```

If unspecified, the value defaults to be the same as the `class` attribute. If the type does not match the object's true type, the JSP page throws a `ClassCastException`.

`beanName`

The `class` attribute may be replaced by a `beanName` attribute. The difference between the two is that `beanName` uses `Beans.instantiate()` to create the bean instance, which looks for a serialized version of the bean (a *.ser* file) before creating an instance from scratch. This allows the use of preconfigured beans. See the `Beans.instantiate()` Javadoc documentation for more information. For example:

```
beanName="com.company.tracking.UserPreferencesImpl"
```

The body of the `<jsp:useBean>` element—everything between the opening `<jsp:useBean>` and the closing `</jsp:useBean>`—is interpreted after the bean's creation. If the bean is not created (because an existing instance was found in the given scope) then the body is ignored. To demonstrate:

```
<jsp:useBean id="prefs" class="com.company.tracking.UserPreferencesImpl">
If you see this we must have created a new bean!
</jsp:useBean>
```

If no body is needed, the XML shorthand for an empty tag /> can be used:

```
<jsp:useBean id="prefs" class="com.company.tracking.UserPreferencesImpl" />
```

Controlling Bean Properties

The `<jsp:setProperty>` action provides the ability for request parameters to automatically (via introspection) set properties on the beans embedded within a page. This gives beans automatic access to the parameters of the request without having to call `getParameter()`. This feature can be used in several ways. First:

```
<jsp:setProperty name="beanName" property="*" />
```

This says that any request parameter with the same name and type as a property on the given bean should be used to set that property on the bean. For example, if a bean has a `setSize(int size)` method and the request has a parameter `size` with a value of `12`, the server will automatically call `bean.setSize(12)` at the beginning of the request handling. If the parameter value can't be converted to the proper type, the parameter is ignored. (Note that an empty string parameter value is treated as if the parameter does not exist and will not assign an empty string value to a `String` property.)

Notice that the action uses the XML shorthand for an empty tag. This is very important. The JSP specification requires all JSP actions to be well-formed XML, even when placed in HTML files. Here's the second `<jsp:setProperty>` usage:

```
<jsp:setProperty name="beanName" property="propertyName" />
```

This says that the given property should be set, if there's a request parameter with the same name and type. For example, to set the `size` property but no other property, use this action:

```
<jsp:setProperty name="prefs" property="size" />
```

Here's a third `<jsp:setProperty>` usage:

```
<jsp:setProperty name="beanName" property="propertyName" param="paramName" />
```

This says that the given property should be set, if there's a request parameter with the given name and the same type. This lets a parameter with one name set a property with another name. For example, to set the `size` property from the `fontSize` parameter:

```
<jsp:setProperty name="prefs" property="size" param="fontSize" />
```

This is the final usage:

```
<jsp:setProperty name="beanName" property="propertyName" value="constant" />
```

This says that the given property should be set to the given value, which will be converted to the appropriate type if necessary. For example, to set the default size to 18 with a parameter override:

```
<jsp:setProperty name="prefs" property="size" value="18" />
<jsp:setProperty name="prefs" property="size" param="fontSize" />
```

For advanced users, the value attribute does not need to be a constant; it can be specified using an expression with what's called a *request-time attribute expression*. For example, to ensure the size never drops below 6:

```
<jsp:setProperty name="prefs" property="size" param="fontSize" />
<jsp:setProperty name="prefs" property="size"
    value="<%= Math.max(6, prefs.getSize()) %>" />
```

Finally, the `<jsp:getProperty>` action provides a mechanism for retrieving property values without using Java code in the page. Its usage looks much like that of `<jsp:setProperty>`:

```
<jsp:getProperty name="beanName" property="propertyName" />
```

This says to include at this location the value of the given property on the given bean. It's longer to type than an expression but eliminates the need to place Java code in the page. Whether to use `<jsp:getProperty>` or an expression is a matter of personal taste. Note that `<jsp:getProperty>` embeds the property value directly, so if it contains characters that HTML treats as special, that will cause problems. The Apache Struts project has a solution using a custom `<property>` tag, as we'll discuss later.

Saying "Hello" Using a Bean

Example 18-6 demonstrates the use of a JavaBeans component with a JSP page; it says "Hello" with the help of a `HelloBean`.

Example 18-6. Saying "Hello" Using a JavaBean

```
<%-- hello3.jsp --%>

<%@ page import="HelloBean" %>

<jsp:useBean id="hello" class="HelloBean">
  <jsp:setProperty name="hello" property="*" />
</jsp:useBean>

<HTML>
<HEAD><TITLE>Hello</TITLE></HEAD>
```

Example 18-6. Saying "Hello" Using a JavaBean (continued)

```
<BODY>
<H1>
Hello, <jsp:getProperty name="hello" property="name" />
</H1>
</BODY>
</HTML>
```

As you can see, using a JavaBeans component with JavaServer Pages can reduce the amount of code placed into the page. The `HelloBean` class contains the business logic for determining a user's name, while the JSP page acts only as a template.

The code for `HelloBean` is shown in Example 18-7. Its class file should be placed in the standard directory for support classes (*WEB-INF/classes*).

Example 18-7. The HelloBean Class

```
public class HelloBean {
  private String name = "World";

  public void setName(String name) {
    this.name = name;
  }

  public String getName() {
    return name;
  }
}
```

This is about as simple a bean as you'll ever see. It has a single `name` property that is set using `setName()` and retrieved using `getName()`. The default value of `name` is `World`, but when a request comes in that includes a `name` parameter, the property is set automatically by the server with a call to `setName()`. To test the mechanism, try browsing to *http://server:port/hello3.jsp*. You should see something similar to the screen shot in Figure 18-4.

One thing to watch out for: on some servers (including Tomcat 3.2) if you have a bean with a scope of `session` or `application` and you change the bean class implementation, you may get a `ClassCastException` on a later request. This exception occurs because the generated servlet code has to do a cast on the bean instance as it's retrieved from the session or application, and the old bean type stored in the session or application doesn't match the new bean type expected. The simplest solution is to restart the server.

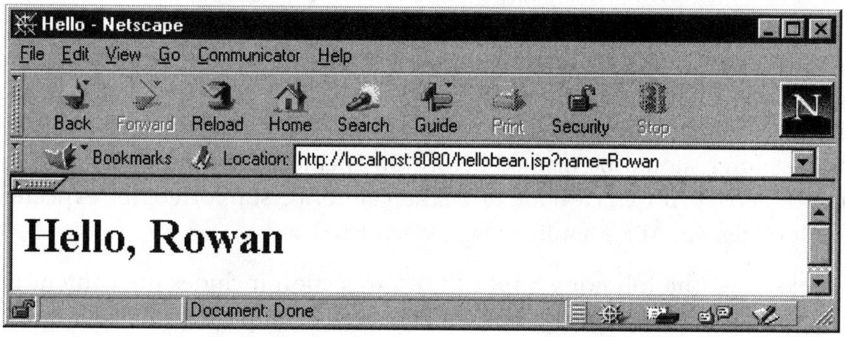

Figure 18-4. Saying "Hello" using JavaServer pages in cooperation with a JavaBeans component

Includes and Forwards

Through a combination of directives and actions, JSP provides support for includes and forwards. There are two kinds of include, and one kind of forward. The first include is an `include` directive:

```
<%@ include file="pathFoFile" %>
```

This include occurs at *translation time* which means it happens during the creation of the background servlet. All content from the external file is included as if it were typed into the JSP page directly. For C programmers, this works like a `#include`. The file path is rooted at the context root (so */index.jsp* refers to the *index.jsp* for the current web application) and the path may not extend outside the context root (don't try *../../../otherContext*). The content within the file is typically a page fragment, not a full page, so you may want to use the *.inc* or *.jin* file extension to indicate this. The following JSP page uses several include directives to construct a page from a set of components (the components aren't shown):

```
<%@ include file = "/header.html" %>
<%@ include file = "/nameCalculation.inc" %>
Hello, <%= name %>
<%@ include file = "/footer.html" %>
```

Where does the `name` variable come from? It's created by the *nameCalculation.inc* file. Because the included file's content is included directly, there's no separation of variable scope.

The second kind of include is a `<jsp:include>` action:

```
<jsp:include page="pathToDynamicResource" flush="true" />
```

This include occurs at *request time.* It's not a raw include like the `include` directive; instead the server executes the specified dynamic resource and includes its output into the content sent to the client. Behind the scenes the `<jsp:include>`

action generates code that calls the RequestDispatcher's include() method, and so the same usage rules apply for <jsp:include> as apply for include()—the included page must be dynamic, cannot set the status code, and cannot set any headers, and the path to the page is rooted at the context root.* The flush attribute is required and in JSP 1.1 must always be set to true. This indicates the response buffer should be flushed before the include takes place. Given the capabilities of Servlet API 2.2, a value of false cannot be supported; it's expected JSP 1.2 built on Servlet API 2.3 will allow a value of false.

As an example, the following <jsp:include> action includes the content generated by a call to the *greeting.jsp* page. The *greeting.jsp* page could look a lot like *hello1.jsp*, except you'd want to remove the surrounding HTML that makes *hello1.jsp* a complete HTML page:

```
<jsp:include page="/greeting.jsp" />
```

The <jsp:include> directive can optionally take any number of <jsp:param> tags within its body. These tags add request parameters to the include request. For example, the following action passes the greeting a default name:

```
<jsp:include page="/greeting.jsp">
  <jsp:param name="defaultName" value="New User" />
</jsp:include>
```

Finally, a JSP may forward a request using the <jsp:forward> action:

```
<jsp:forward page="pathToDynamicResource" />
```

The forward causes control of the request handling to be passed to the specified resource. As with the <jsp:include> action it's executed at request time and is built on the RequestDispatcher's forward() method. The forward() usage rules apply—at the time of the forward all buffered output is cleared and if output has already been flushed, the system throws an exception. The following action forwards the request to a special page if the user is not logged in:

```
<% if (session.getAttribute("user") == null) { %>
  <jsp:forward page="/login.jsp" />
<% } %>
```

The <jsp:forward> action accepts <jsp:param> tags as well.

* One minor difference between the include() method and the <jsp:include> action: the include() method requires the page path to begin with a /. The <jsp:include> action additionally allows relative paths, like ../index.jsp, as long as the path doesn't extend outside the current context.

A Tool Application

Now that we have the ability to execute includes and embed JavaBeans into our JSP pages, let's look at how we might use these features to write the tool view application. We'll embed a bean into the JSP page that gives the page access to the tool information and let the page act as the view onto that data. Example 18-8 shows the JSP page, called *toolview.jsp.*

Example 18-8. A Tool View Application Using JSP

```
<%-- toolview.jsp --%>

<%
  String title = "Tool Listing";
  String deck = "A list of content creation tools";
  String desc = "Without tools, people are nothing more than animals.  And " +
                "pretty weak ones at that.  Here's a list of servlet-based " +
                "content creation tools you can use so you won't be a " +
                "servlet weakling.";
%>

<%@ include file="/header.jsp" %>

<%@ page session="false" %>
<%@ page errorPage="/errorTaker.jsp" %>

<jsp:useBean id="toolbean" class="ToolBean" scope="application">
  <jsp:setProperty name="toolbean" property="toolsFile"
                value='<%= application.getInitParameter("toolsFile") %>' />
</jsp:useBean>

<%
  Tool[] tools = toolbean.getTools(request.getParameter("state"));

  for (int i = 0; i < tools.length; i++) {
    Tool tool = tools[i];
%>
  <HR SIZE=2 ALIGN=LEFT>

  <H3>
  <%= tool.name %>

  <% if (tool.isNewWithin(45)) { %>
    <FONT COLOR=#FF0000><B> (New!) </B></FONT>
  <% } else if (tool.isUpdatedWithin(45)) { %>
    <FONT COLOR=#FF0000><B> (Updated!) </B></FONT>
  <% } %>

  </H3>
```

Example 18-8. A Tool View Application Using JSP (continued)

```
  <A HREF="<%= tool.homeURL %>"><%= tool.homeURL %></A><BR>

  <%= tool.comments %>

<% } %>

<%@ include file="/footer.jsp" %>
```

First we define the title, deck, and description of the page as `Strings` within a scriptlet. We then use the `include` directive to include standard header content from *header.jsp* and standard footer content (at the end of the file) from *footer.jsp*. The `include` directive places the content of the header and footer files into this file during the translation phase, so the `title`, `deck`, and `desc` variables are visible from within the included files, and in fact *header.jsp* does make use of these variables. The *header.jsp* and *footer.jsp* files are shown in Example 18-9 and Example 18-10.

Example 18-9. The header.jsp File

```
<%-- header.jsp --%>
<%-- Depends on variables title, deck, and desc being present --%>

<HTML><HEAD><TITLE><%= title %></TITLE></HEAD>

<BODY BGCOLOR="#FFFFFF" BACKGROUND="/images/background.gif"
      LINK="#003333" ALINK="#669999" VLINK="#333333">

<IMG SRC="/images/banner.gif" WIDTH=600 HEIGHT=87 BORDER=0><BR>

<TABLE>
<TR>
<TD WIDTH=125 ROWS=10 VALIGN=TOP>
 <BR><BR><BR>
 <FONT FACE="Arial,Helvetica" SIZE="+1" COLOR="#FF0000">
 <A HREF="/index.html">Home</A><BR>
 <A HREF="/hosting.html">Hosting</A><BR>
 <A HREF="/engines.html">Engines</A><BR>
 </FONT>
</TD>

<TD WIDTH=475>

  <TABLE CELLPADDING=5><TR><TD WIDTH=600 BGCOLOR="#006699" VALIGN=TOP>
  <B><FONT FACE="Arial,Helvetica" SIZE="+2">
  <%= title %>
  </FONT></B>
  </TD></TR></TABLE>
```

Example 18-9. The header.jsp File (continued)

```
  <B><FONT FACE="Arial,Helvetica" SIZE="+1" COLOR="#003366">
  <%= deck %>
  </FONT></B><P>

  <P>

  <FONT FACE="Arial,Helvetica">

  <%= desc %>
```

Example 18-10. The footer.jsp File

```
<%-- footer.jsp --%>
<%-- Has no dependencies on any variables being present --%>

 </FONT>

</TD>
</TR>

<TR>
<TD></TD>
<TD WIDTH=475 ALIGN=CENTER COLSPAN=3>
<HR>
<FONT FACE="Arial,Helvetica">
<A HREF="/index.html">Home</A>  
<A HREF="/hosting.html">Hosting</A>  
<A HREF="/engines.html">Engines</A>  <P>
</FONT>

<TABLE WIDTH=100%>
<TR>
<TD WIDTH=260 ALIGN=LEFT VALIGN=TOP>
<FONT FACE="Arial,Helvetica">
<A HREF="/copyright.html">Copyright</A> &copy; 2000 Jason Hunter<BR>
All Rights Reserved.</TD>
<TD WIDTH=5></FONT></TD>
<TD WIDTH=230 ALIGN=RIGHT VALIGN=TOP>
<FONT FACE="Arial,Helvetica">
Contact: <A HREF="mailto:webmaster@servlets.com">webmaster@servlets.com</a>
</FONT></TD>
</TR>
</TABLE>

</TD>
</TR>
```

Example 18-10. The footer.jsp File (continued)

```
</TABLE>

</BODY>
</HTML>
```

Next in the *toolview.jsp* page we use the `<jsp:useBean>` action to embed a JavaBean named `toolbean` that's an instance of the class `ToolBean`. The bean is scoped to `application` so a single instance of the data will be automatically stored in the context and made available to all pages.

Within the body of the `<jsp:useBean>` tag we place a `<jsp:setProperty>` action that sets the `toolsFile` property on the bean to the value of the context init parameter `toolsFile`, using a request-time attribute expression to extract the value. This tells the bean the file from which it can load the tool information. It would be ideal if the bean could access the application variable directly to retrieve this information, but beans have access only to what the JSP page provides. It would be elegant if perhaps the bean could accept the filename as a parameter to its constructor, but beans are instantiated using the default no-argument constructor, so this isn't possible either. The approach we take is to include the `<jsp:setProperty>` action within the body of the `<jsp:useBean>` tag so the first time the bean is constructed, it's directly given the filename to load from.

Two things to notice about the request-time attribute expression. First, we had to use single quotes around the value because we used double quotes inside the expression. This keeps the JSP parser from becoming confused. We could also have escaped the double quotes within the expression using backslashes. Second, if the init parameter does not exist and the `getInitParameter()` call returns `null`, that causes a `JspException` to be thrown, because a null value is not legal in a request-time attribute expression.*

After the `<jsp:useBean>` tag we use a scriptlet to extract the array of tools from the bean, calling the `getTools()` method with the value of the `state` parameter in case the user wants to view only tools with a certain state. It's tempting to want to write a `<jsp:setProperty>` action that would let the bean access the `state` parameter value directly, but because we gave the bean `application` scope we cannot—to do so would cause concurrency issues as multiple requests tried to set the same property on the bean's single shared instance.

Once we retrieve the array of tools, we use a little more scriptlet code to start a `for` loop iterating over the array. Inside the `for` loop we place the logic that displays

* Technically the JSP specification makes no comment on what should happen with a null request-time attribute expression. The Tomcat reference implementation therefore becomes the arbitrator, and Tomcat 3.2 throws an exception.

each individual tool. We use expressions to print simple values like the tool's name, URL, and comments. We use scriptlets to handle the printing of the New or Updated status remark.* The code for the `ToolBean` class is in Example 18-11. The code for the `Tool` class is the same as shown in Chapter 14, *The Tea Framework*.

Example 18-11. The Supporting ToolBean Class

```
import java.util.*;

public class ToolBean {

  private Tool[] tools;
  private String state;

  public ToolBean() { }

  public void setToolsFile(String toolsFile) throws Exception {
    // No way to gain access to the application context directly from a bean
    tools = Tool.loadTools(toolsFile);
  }

  public Tool[] getTools(String state) throws Exception {
    if (tools == null) {
      throw new IllegalStateException(
        "You must always set the toolsFile property on a ToolBean");
    }

    if (state == null) {
      return tools;
    }
    else {
      // Return only tools matching the given "state"
      List list = new LinkedList();
      for (int i = 0; i < tools.length; i++) {
        if (tools[i].getStateFlag().equalsIgnoreCase(state)) {
          list.add(tools[i]);
        }
```

* Because of JSP whitespace-preservation rules you must be careful when writing `if/else` statements with scriptlets. The following code would *not* work:

```
<% if (tool.isNewWithin(45)) { %>
  <FONT COLOR=#FF0000><B> (New!) </B></FONT>
<% } %>
<% else if (tool.isUpdatedWithin(45)) { %>
  <FONT COLOR=#FF0000><B> (Updated!) </B></FONT>
<% } %>
```

With this code, the background servlet would attempt to print a new line between the `if` and `else` clauses, causing the obscure compile error: `'else' without 'if'`.

Example 18-11. The Supporting ToolBean Class (continued)

```
      }
      return (Tool[]) list.toArray(new Tool[0]);
    }
  }
}
```

The `setToolsFile()` method is called automatically by the `<jsp:setProperty>` action right after the bean is constructed. It loads the tool information from the specified file.

The `getTools()` method is called by the JSP page directly from within a scriptlet. The method accepts as a parameter the `state` of the tools to match against; if the state is `null` it returns the full list. If the tools variable is `null`, then `setToolsFile()` must not have completed successfully, and the bean throws an `IllegalStateException` warning the user of the problem.

Custom Tag Libraries

To conclude, let's look at the most interesting aspect of JavaServer Pages: the support for *custom tag libraries.* Custom tags (aka *custom actions*) let a JSP page contain XML tags that, although they look like HTML, actually cause specific Java code to be executed when a tag is encountered. The possible uses for custom tag libraries are quite exciting. For example, Live Software (creators of JRun) used JSP custom tags to implement a 100% portable version of the Allaire Cold Fusion tags called CF_Anywhere. (Shortly thereafter, Live Software was purchased by Allaire.)

The details on how to write a custom tag library are fairly involved and extend beyond the scope of this chapter. Fortunately, several open source tag libraries are under development and already useful. The two most prominent are Apache Taglibs and Apache Struts, both from the Apache Jakarta project at *http://jakarta.apache.org.* Apache Taglibs holds general-purpose tag libraries; Apache Struts holds a tag libary intended to support a Model 2–style architecture, but many of the tags are generally useful. For a list of JSP tag libraries see *http://jsptags.com.* There's also an effort to create a standard tag library as a formal Java specification request process as JSR-052. For more information on JSR-052 see *http://java.sun.com/aboutJava/communityprocess/jsr/jsr_052_jsptaglib.html.*

Using Custom Tag Libraries

Custom actions allow the embedding of application logic into JSP pages using HTML-like tags. With the right set of tags, logic that previously had to be written using scriptlets can instead be written using tags. For example, the Apache Struts project has an `<iterate>` tag we can use to replace a `for` loop. The `<iterate>`

tag repeats the body of the tag once for each element of a collection (`List`, `Set`, `Vector`, `Map`, array, etc.). During each iteration it puts the element into `page` scope for use within the body.* Struts also has a `<property>` tag that operates like `<jsp:getProperty>` with the extra enhancement that it filters the content for HTML display by converting all HTML special characters into their appropriate character entities. For example, < becomes `%lt;`.

Using `<iterate>` and `<property>` together we can write the following page snippet to display all the cookies sent in the request—with all special characters properly filtered:

```
<%@ taglib uri="/WEB-INF/struts.tld" prefix="struts" %>

<struts:iterate id="cookie" collection="<%= request.getCookies() %>">
  <struts:property name="cookie" property="name" /> =
  <struts:property name="cookie" property="value" /> <BR>
</struts:iterate>
```

To install and use a tag library like Struts you must do several things:

1. Download and unpack the tag library distribution. For example, Struts is available at *http://jakarta.apache.org*.
2. Place the tag library Java classes so they will be found by the server. For example, place the *struts.jar* file in *WEB-INF/lib* or place the compiled classes in *WEB-INF/classes*.
3. Place the Tag Library Descriptor (TLD) file into a location under the *WEB-INF* directory. It's common to use either *WEB-INF/tlds* or *WEB-INF* directly, the exact location isn't important. For example, place *struts.tld* into *WEB-INF*. The TLD file is an XML datafile providing the server with information about each tag in the library—its name, class, how to use its attributes, how to use its body, and so on. There's an extra bonus to having TLDs: based on the TLD a web page documenting the tag library can be generated (perhaps using an XSL stylesheet).
4. Add a `<taglib>` entry to the *web.xml* file. Then within the entry place a `<taglib-uri>` entry giving the lookup name for the taglib, and also a `<taglib-location>` entry giving the location of the TLD. This step is would not be required if the `<taglib-uri>` entry would exactly match the `<taglib-location>` entry. To demonstrate:

```
<taglib> <!-- since the uri matches the location this is optional -->
    <taglib-uri>/WEB-INF/struts.tld</taglib-uri>
    <taglib-location>/WEB-INF/struts.tld</taglib-location>
</taglib>
```

* The `<iterate>` tag requires JDK 1.2 or later. There's an `<enumerate>` tag for JDK 1.1.

The <taglib-uri> entry must be a URI path, so legal values include `struts`, `http://jakarta.apache.org/struts`, and `/WEB-INF/struts.tld`. A URI path traditionally refers to an actual resource location, but here it's used only as a unique identifier for the tag library.

5. In every JSP page using the custom tag library, add the following `taglib` directive. This tells the server to load the tag library with the given "lookup URI" and to put those tags in the XML namespace prefix `struts`:

   ```
   <%@ taglib uri="/WEB-INF/struts.tld" prefix="struts" %>
   ```

6. Use the tags within the JSP page, making sure the XML namespace prefix matches that declared in the taglib directive:

   ```
   <struts:property name="beanname" property="propname" />
   ```

   It is possible for the tag library creator to bundle the TLD within the tag library's JAR file. In this event, instead of pointing at the *.tld,* you then point at the *.jar* itself.

A Tool Application Using Custom Tag Libraries

Using the `<iterate>` and `<property>` tags from Struts we can simplify our *toolview.jsp* page. We'll also take this opportunity to demonstrate the servlet-driven Model 2 architecture in which a servlet receives the request, adds attributes to the request object, then dispatches the request to a JSP that acts like a template. Example 18-12 shows the controller servlet.

Example 18-12. A Model 2 Servlet Controller

```
import java.io.*;
import java.util.*;
import javax.servlet.*;
import javax.servlet.http.*;

public class ToolServlet extends HttpServlet {

  Tool[] tools = null;

  public void init() throws ServletException {
    // Load the tool data in our init for simplicity
    String toolsFile =
      getServletContext().getInitParameter("toolsFile"); // from web.xml
    if (toolsFile == null) {
      throw new ServletException("A tools data file must be specified as " +
                                 "the toolsFile context init parameter");
    }
    log("Loading tools from " + toolsFile);
    try {
      tools = Tool.loadTools(toolsFile);
```

Example 18-12. A Model 2 Servlet Controller (continued)

```
      if (tools.length == 0) {
        log("No tools found in " + toolsFile);
      }
      else {
        log(tools.length + " tools found in " + toolsFile);
      }
    }
    catch (Exception e) {
      throw new ServletException(e);
    }
  }

  public void doGet(HttpServletRequest req, HttpServletResponse res)
                               throws ServletException, IOException {
    Tool[] tools = null;

    // Place an appropriate "tools" attribute in the request
    String state = req.getParameter("state");
    if (state == null) {
      req.setAttribute("tools", getTools());
    }
    else {
      req.setAttribute("tools", getTools(state));
    }

    // Send the request to the JSP for processing
    RequestDispatcher disp = req.getRequestDispatcher("/toolview-tag.jsp");
    disp.forward(req, res);
  }

  public Tool[] getTools() {
    return tools;
  }

  public Tool[] getTools(String state) {
    List list = new LinkedList();
    for (int i = 0; i < tools.length; i++) {
      if (tools[i].getStateFlag().equalsIgnoreCase(state)) {
        list.add(tools[i]);
      }
    }
    return (Tool[]) list.toArray(new Tool[0]);
  }
}
```

This servlet behaves similarly to the `ToolApp` in Tea and `ToolServlet` in WebMacro. It loads the tool information in its `init()` method, and on each request places an appropriate subset of tools into the request object. The servlet forwards each request to a JSP for actual rendering, and the JSP can gain access to the tools in the request object using the `<jsp:useBean>` tag. Example 18-13 demonstrates the JSP named *toolview-tag.jsp*.

Example 18-13. The Tool Application Rewritten Using Tag Libraries

```
<%-- toolview-tag.jsp --%>

<%@ taglib uri="/WEB-INF/struts.tld" prefix="struts" %>

<%
  String title = "Tool Listing";
  String deck = "A list of content creation tools";
  String desc = "Without tools, people are nothing more than animals.  And " +
                "pretty weak ones at that.  Here's a list of servlet-based " +
                "content creation tools you can use so you won't be a " +
                "servlet weakling.";
%>

<%@ include file="/header.jsp" %>

<%@ page session="false" %>
<%@ page errorPage="/errorTaker.jsp" %>

<%-- Fetch the tools array as a request attribute --%>
<jsp:useBean id="tools" class="Tool[]" scope="request"/>

<struts:iterate id="tool" collection="<%= tools %>">
  <HR SIZE=2 ALIGN=LEFT>

  <H3>
  <%-- Automatically HTML-escapes values --%>
  <struts:property name="tool" property="name" />

  <% if (((Tool)tool).isNewWithin(45)) { %>
    <FONT COLOR=#FF0000><B> (New!) </B></FONT>
  <% } else if (((Tool)tool).isUpdatedWithin(45)) { %>
    <FONT COLOR=#FF0000><B> (Updated!) </B></FONT>
  <% } %>

  </H3>
  <A HREF="<struts:property name="tool" property="homeURL"/>">
           <struts:property name="tool" property="homeURL"/></A><BR>

  <%-- Assume don't want HTML in comments --%>
  <struts:property name="tool" property="comments" />

</struts:iterate>

<%@ include file="/footer.jsp" %>
```

This page first uses the `taglib` directive to load the Struts custom tag library. Don't forget this step! If you do forget, you won't get a direct error message but things won't work. The reason is that without the `taglib` directive the `<struts:iterate>` and `<struts:property>` tags look to the server like any other HTML tags and they're treated like page content to be output instead of page logic to be executed!

The body of the page uses the `<struts:iterate>` tag to loop over the array of tools and the `<struts:property>` tag to display each tool's name, URL, and comments. If the comments are allowed to contain HTML markup then the proper tag to use would be `<jsp:getProperty>` so the HTML markup isn't filtered away.

Using the common tags from Apache Struts removes some more code from the HMTL page, but a few scriptlets remain. To remove all the scriptlets would require creating a custom tag to perform the timestamp comparison. Unfortunately, because of the many details involved in writing custom tags, we can't include a tutorial here. If you're interested in learning more on creating custom tags, see Hans Bergsten's book *JavaServer Pages* (O'Reilly).

19

In this chapter:

- *Parsing Parameters*
- *Sending Email*
- *Using Regular Expressions*
- *Executing Programs*
- *Using Native Methods*
- *Acting as an RMI Client*
- *Debugging*
- *Performance Tuning*

Odds and Ends

Every house has a junk drawer—a drawer loaded to the brim with odds and ends that don't exactly fit into any organized drawer and yet can't be thrown away because when they're needed they're really needed. This chapter is like that drawer. It holds a whole slew of useful servlet examples and tips that don't really fit anywhere else. Included are servlets that parse parameters, send email, execute programs, use regular expression engines, use native methods, and act as RMI clients. There's also a demonstration of basic debugging techniques, along with some suggestions for servlet performance tuning.

Parsing Parameters

If you've tried your hand at writing your own servlets as you have been reading through this book, you've probably noticed how awkward it can be to get and parse request parameters, especially when the parameters have to be converted to some non-`String` format. For example, let's assume you want to fetch the `count` parameter and get its value as an `int`. Furthermore, let's also assume that you want to handle error conditions by calling `handleNoCount()` if `count` isn't given and `handleMalformedCount()` if `count` cannot be parsed as an integer. To do this using the standard Servlet API requires the following code:

```
int count;

String param = req.getParameter("count");
if (param == null || param.length() == 0) {
  handleNoCount();
}
else {
  try {
    count = Integer.parseInt(param);
  }
```

```
    catch (NumberFormatException e) {
      handleMalformedCount();
    }
  }
```

Does this look like any code you've written? It's not very pretty, is it? A better solution is to hand off the responsibility for getting and parsing parameters to a utility class. The com.oreilly.servlet.ParameterParser class is just such a class. By using ParameterParser, we can rewrite the previous code to be more elegant:

```
int count;

ParameterParser parser = new ParameterParser(req);
try {
  count = parser.getIntParameter("count");
}
catch (NumberFormatException e) {
  handleMalformedCount();
}
catch (ParameterNotFoundException e) {
  handleNoCount();
}
```

The parameter parser's getIntParameter() method returns the specified parameter's value as an int. It throws a NumberFormatException if the parameter cannot be converted to an int and a ParameterNotFoundException if the parameter isn't part of the request. It also throws ParameterNotFoundException if the parameter had a value of the empty string. This often happens with form submissions for text fields when nothing is entered, something that for all intents and purposes should be treated the same as a missing parameter.

If it's enough that a servlet use a default value if there's a problem with a parameter, as is often the case, the code can be simplified even further:

```
ParameterParser parser = new ParameterParser(req);
int count = parser.getIntParameter("count", 0);
```

This second version of getIntParameter() takes a default value of 0 that is returned in lieu of throwing an exception.

There's also a capability to find out if any required parameters are missing from a request:

```
ParameterParser parser = new ParameterParser(req);
String[] required = { "fname", "lname", "account" };
String[] missing = parser.getMissingParameters(required);
```

The method returns null if no parameters are missing.

And finally, `ParameterParser` supports internationalization using the `setCharacterEncoding()` method. This specifies the charset to be used in interpreting parameter values. The value may come from a user cookie, a hidden form field, or the user's session:

```
ParameterParser parser = new ParameterParser(req);
parser.setCharacterEncoding("Shift_JIS");
String japaneseValue = parser.getStringParameter("latinName");
```

Internally `ParameterParser` uses the `getBytes()` trick demonstrated in Chapter 13, *Internationalization*, to handle the conversion. Parameter names must still be given in the Latin-1 charset because the value lookup uses the not-yet-internationalized Servlet API `getParameter()` and `getParameterValues()` methods.

ParameterParser Code

The `ParameterParser` class contains more than a dozen methods that return request parameters—two for each of Java's native types. It also has two `getStringParameter()` methods in case you want to get the parameter in its raw `String` format. The code for `ParameterParser` is provided in Example 19-1; `ParameterNotFoundException` is in Example 19-2.

Example 19-1. The ParameterParser Class

```
package com.oreilly.servlet;

import java.io.*;
import java.util.*;
import javax.servlet.*;

public class ParameterParser {

  private ServletRequest req;
  private String encoding;

  public ParameterParser(ServletRequest req) {
    this.req = req;
  }

  public void setCharacterEncoding(String encoding)
                 throws UnsupportedEncodingException {
    // Test the encoding is valid
    "".getBytes(encoding);
    // Getting here means we're valid, so set the encoding
    this.encoding = encoding;
  }

  public String getStringParameter(String name)
```

Example 19-1. The ParameterParser Class (continued)

```
      throws ParameterNotFoundException {
    String[] values = req.getParameterValues(name);
    if (values == null) {
      throw new ParameterNotFoundException(name + " not found");
    }
    else if (values[0].length() == 0) {
      throw new ParameterNotFoundException(name + " was empty");
    }
    else {
      if (encoding == null) {
        return values[0];
      }
      else {
        try {
          return new String(values[0].getBytes("8859_1"), encoding);
        }
        catch (UnsupportedEncodingException e) {
          return values[0];  // should never happen
        }
      }
    }
  }

  public String getStringParameter(String name, String def) {
    try { return getStringParameter(name); }
    catch (Exception e) { return def; }
  }

  public boolean getBooleanParameter(String name)
      throws ParameterNotFoundException, NumberFormatException {
    String value = getStringParameter(name).toLowerCase();
    if ((value.equalsIgnoreCase("true")) ||
        (value.equalsIgnoreCase("on")) ||
        (value.equalsIgnoreCase("yes"))) {
        return true;
    }
    else if ((value.equalsIgnoreCase("false")) ||
             (value.equalsIgnoreCase("off")) ||
             (value.equalsIgnoreCase("no"))) {
        return false;
    }
    else {
      throw new NumberFormatException("Parameter " + name + " value " + value +
                                      " is not a boolean");
    }
  }

  public boolean getBooleanParameter(String name, boolean def) {
```

Example 19-1. The ParameterParser Class (continued)

```
    try { return getBooleanParameter(name); }
    catch (Exception e) { return def; }
  }

  public byte getByteParameter(String name)
      throws ParameterNotFoundException, NumberFormatException {
    return Byte.parseByte(getStringParameter(name));
  }

  public byte getByteParameter(String name, byte def) {
    try { return getByteParameter(name); }
    catch (Exception e) { return def; }
  }

  public char getCharParameter(String name)
      throws ParameterNotFoundException {
    String param = getStringParameter(name);
    if (param.length() == 0)
      throw new ParameterNotFoundException(name + " is empty string");
    else
      return (param.charAt(0));
  }

  public char getCharParameter(String name, char def) {
    try { return getCharParameter(name); }
    catch (Exception e) { return def; }
  }

  public double getDoubleParameter(String name)
      throws ParameterNotFoundException, NumberFormatException {
    return new Double(getStringParameter(name)).doubleValue();
  }

  public double getDoubleParameter(String name, double def) {
    try { return getDoubleParameter(name); }
    catch (Exception e) { return def; }
  }

  public float getFloatParameter(String name)
      throws ParameterNotFoundException, NumberFormatException {
    return new Float(getStringParameter(name)).floatValue();
  }

  public float getFloatParameter(String name, float def) {
    try { return getFloatParameter(name); }
    catch (Exception e) { return def; }
  }
```

Example 19-1. The ParameterParser Class (continued)

```
  public int getIntParameter(String name)
      throws ParameterNotFoundException, NumberFormatException {
    return Integer.parseInt(getStringParameter(name));
  }

  public int getIntParameter(String name, int def) {
    try { return getIntParameter(name); }
    catch (Exception e) { return def; }
  }

  public long getLongParameter(String name)
      throws ParameterNotFoundException, NumberFormatException {
    return Long.parseLong(getStringParameter(name));
  }

  public long getLongParameter(String name, long def) {
    try { return getLongParameter(name); }
    catch (Exception e) { return def; }
  }

  public short getShortParameter(String name)
      throws ParameterNotFoundException, NumberFormatException {
    return Short.parseShort(getStringParameter(name));
  }

  public short getShortParameter(String name, short def) {
    try { return getShortParameter(name); }
    catch (Exception e) { return def; }
  }

  public String[] getMissingParameters(String[] required) {
    Vector missing = new Vector();
    for (int i = 0; i < required.length; i++) {
      String val = getStringParameter(required[i], null);
      if (val == null) {
        missing.addElement(required[i]);
      }
    }
    if (missing.size() == 0) {
      return null;
    }
    else {
      String[] ret = new String[missing.size()];
      missing.copyInto(ret);
      return ret;
    }
  }
}
```

Example 19-2. The ParameterNotFoundException Class

```
package com.oreilly.servlet;

public class ParameterNotFoundException extends Exception {

  public ParameterNotFoundException() {
    super();
  }

  public ParameterNotFoundException(String s) {
    super(s);
  }
}
```

Sending Email

Sometimes it's necessary, or just convenient, for a servlet to fire off an email message. For example, imagine a servlet that receives data from a user feedback form. The servlet might want to send the feedback data to a mailing list of interested parties. Or imagine a servlet that encounters an unexpected problem and knows to send an email page to its administrator asking for help.

A servlet has four choices for sending email:

- It can manage the details itself—establishing a raw socket connection to a mail server and speaking a low-level mail transport protocol, usually the so-called Simple Mail Transfer Protocol (SMTP).
- It can run an external command-line email program, if the server system has such a program.
- It can use the JavaMail API, designed to support complicated mail handling, filing, and processing (see *http://java.sun.com/products/javamail*).
- It can use one of the many freely available mail classes that abstracts the details of sending email into simple, convenient method calls.

For simple email sending, we recommend the final approach for its simplicity. For more complicated uses, we recommend JavaMail—especially for servlets running inside a J2EE server where the two JAR files needed by JavaMail are sure to be available.

Using the MailMessage Class

For the purposes of this example, we will demonstrate a servlet that uses the `com.oreilly.servlet.MailMessage` class, which is not shown here but available at *http://www.servlets.com*. It is modeled after the `sun.net.smtp.SmtpClient` class provided with Sun's JDK but can be used without the political problem of using an "unsupported and subject to change" `sun.*` class. It also has a few nice usability improvements. Using it is simple:

1. Call `MailMessage msg = new MailMessage()`. Optionally, pass the constructor the name of a host to use as the mail server, which replaces the default of `localhost`. Most Unix machines can act as SMTP mail servers.
2. Call `msg.from(fromAddress)`, specifying the address of the sender. The address doesn't have to be valid.
3. Call `msg.to(toAddress)`, specifying the address of the receiver. This method may be called multiple times if there are additional recipients. There are `cc()` and `bcc()` methods as well.
4. Call `msg.setSubject(subject)` to set the subject. Technically this isn't required, but providing a subject is always a good idea.
5. Call `msg.setHeader(name, value)` if there are any additional headers to be set. The `To:`, `Cc:`, and `Subject:` headers don't need to be set as they are assigned automatically in the `to()`, `cc()`, and `setSubject()` methods. (The `bcc()` method of course doesn't set any headers.) You can use `setHeader()` to override the defaults. The header names and values should conform to the rules given in RFC 822 at *http://www.ietf.org/rfc/rfc0822.txt.*
6. Call `PrintStream msg = msg.getPrintStream()` to get an output stream for the message.
7. Write the body of the mail message to the `PrintStream`.
8. Call `msg.sendAndClose()` to send the message and close the connection to the server.

Emailing Form Data

Example 19-3 shows a servlet that emails the form data it receives to a mailing list. Notice the extensive use of the `ParameterParser` class.

Example 19-3. Sending Mail from a Servlet

```
import java.io.*;
import java.util.*;
import javax.servlet.*;
import javax.servlet.http.*;

import com.oreilly.servlet.MailMessage;
import com.oreilly.servlet.ParameterParser;
import com.oreilly.servlet.ServletUtils;

public class MailServlet extends HttpServlet {
```

Example 19-3. Sending Mail from a Servlet (continued)

```
  static final String FROM = "MailServlet";
  static final String TO = "feedback-folks@attentive-company.com";

  public void doGet(HttpServletRequest req, HttpServletResponse res)
                               throws ServletException, IOException {
    res.setContentType("text/plain");
    PrintWriter out = res.getWriter();

    ParameterParser parser = new ParameterParser(req);
    String from = parser.getStringParameter("from", FROM);
    String to = parser.getStringParameter("to", TO);

    try {
      MailMessage msg = new MailMessage();  // assume localhost
      msg.from(from);
      msg.to(to);
      msg.setSubject("Customer feedback");

      PrintStream body = msg.getPrintStream();

      Enumeration enum = req.getParameterNames();
      while (enum.hasMoreElements()) {
        String name = (String)enum.nextElement();
        if (name.equals("to") || name.equals("from")) continue; // Skip to/from
        String value = parser.getStringParameter(name, null);
        body.println(name + " = " + value);
      }

      body.println();
      body.println("---");
      body.println("Sent by " + HttpUtils.getRequestURL(req));

      msg.sendAndClose();

      out.println("Thanks for the submission...");
    }
    catch (IOException e) {
      out.println("There was a problem handling the submission...");
      log("There was a problem sending email", e);
    }
  }
}
```

This servlet first determines the "from" and "to" addresses for the message. The default values are set in the `FROM` and `TO` variables, although a submitted form can include (probably hidden) fields that specify alternate from and to addresses. The servlet then begins an SMTP email message. It connects to the local host and addresses the message. Next, it sets the subject and fills the body with the form data, ignoring the `TO` and `FROM` variables. Finally, it sends the message and thanks the user for the submission. If there's a problem, it informs the user and logs the exception.

The `MailMessage` class does not currently support attachments (although support could easily be added). For more advanced uses such as this, JavaMail is a good alternative.

Using Regular Expressions

If you're a servlet programmer with a background in Perl-based CGI scripting and you're still smitten with Perl's regular expression capabilities, this section is for you. Here we show how to use regular expressions from within Java. For those of you who are unfamiliar with regular expressions, they are a mechanism for allowing extremely advanced string manipulation with minimal code. Regular expressions are wonderfully explained in all their glory in the book *Mastering Regular Expressions* by Jeffrey E. F. Friedl (O'Reilly).

With all the classes and capabilities Sun has added in to the JDK throughout the years, one feature still absent is a regular expression engine. Ah, well, not to worry. As with most Java features, if you can't get it from Sun, a third-party vendor is probably offering what you need at a reasonable price, or when it's something as generally useful as regular expressions, the odds are good it's available as a open source library. And in fact there's an open source regular expression engine available as part of Apache's Jakarta Project, originally developed by Jonathan Locke and available under the Apache license. The Apache license is a much more forgiving license than the GNU General Public License (GPL) because it allows developers to use the regular expression engine in creating new products without requiring them to release their own products as open source.

Finding Links with Regular Expressions

To demonstrate the use of regular expressions, let's use Apache's regular expression engine to write a servlet that extracts and displays in a list all the HTML `<A HREF>` links found on a web page. The code is shown in Example 19-4.

Example 19-4. Searching for All Links

```
import java.io.*;
import java.net.*;
import java.util.*;
import javax.servlet.*;
import javax.servlet.http.*;
```

Example 19-4. Searching for All Links (continued)

```
import com.oreilly.servlet.*;

import org.apache.regexp.*;

public class Links extends HttpServlet {

  public void doGet(HttpServletRequest req, HttpServletResponse res)
                               throws ServletException, IOException {
    res.setContentType("text/html");
    PrintWriter out = res.getWriter();

    // We accept the URL to process as extra path info
    // http://localhost:8080/servlet/Links/http://www.servlets.com/
    String url = req.getPathInfo();
    if (url == null || url.length() == 0) {
      res.sendError(res.SC_BAD_REQUEST,
                    "Please pass a URL to read from as extra path info");
      return;
    }
    url = url.substring(1);  // cut off leading '/'

    String page = null;
    try {
      // Request the page
      HttpMessage msg = new HttpMessage(new URL(url));
      BufferedReader in =
        new BufferedReader(new InputStreamReader(msg.sendGetMessage()));

      // Read the entire response into a String
      StringBuffer buf = new StringBuffer(10240);
      char[] chars = new char[10240];
      int charsRead = 0;
      while ((charsRead = in.read(chars, 0, chars.length)) != -1) {
        buf.append(chars, 0, charsRead);
      }
      page = buf.toString();
    }
    catch (IOException e) {
      res.sendError(res.SC_NOT_FOUND,
                    "Link Extractor could not read from " + url + ":<BR>" +
                    ServletUtils.getStackTraceAsString(e));
      return;
    }

    out.println("<HTML><HEAD><TITLE>Link Extractor</TITLE>");

    try {
      // We need to specify a <BASE> so relative links work correctly
```

Example 19-4. Searching for All Links (continued)

```
      // If the page already has one, we can use that
      RE re = new RE("<base[^>]*>", RE.MATCH_CASEINDEPENDENT);
      boolean hasBase = re.match(page);

      if (hasBase) {
        // Use the existing <BASE>
        out.println(re.getParen(0));
      }
      else {
        // Calculate the base from the URL, use everything up to last '/'
        re = new RE("http://.*/", RE.MATCH_CASEINDEPENDENT);
        boolean extractedBase = re.match(url);
        if (extractedBase) {
          // Success, print the calculated base
          out.println("<BASE HREF=\"" + re.getParen(0) + "\">");
        }
        else {
          // No trailing slash, add one ourselves
          out.println("<BASE HREF=\"" + url + "/" + "\">");
        }
      }

      out.println("</HEAD><BODY>");

      out.println("The links on <A HREF=\"" + url + "\">" + url + "</A>" +
                  " are: <BR>");
      out.println("<UL>");

      String search = "<a\\s+[^<]*</a\\s*>";
      re = new RE(search, RE.MATCH_CASEINDEPENDENT);

      int index = 0;
      while (re.match(page, index)) {
        String match = re.getParen(0);
        index = re.getParenEnd(0);
        out.println("<LI>" + match + "<BR>");
      }

      out.println("</UL>");
      out.println("</BODY></HTML>");
    }
    catch (RESyntaxException e) {
      // Should never happen as the search strings are hard coded
      e.printStackTrace(out);
    }
  }
}
```

A screen shot is shown in Figure 19-1.

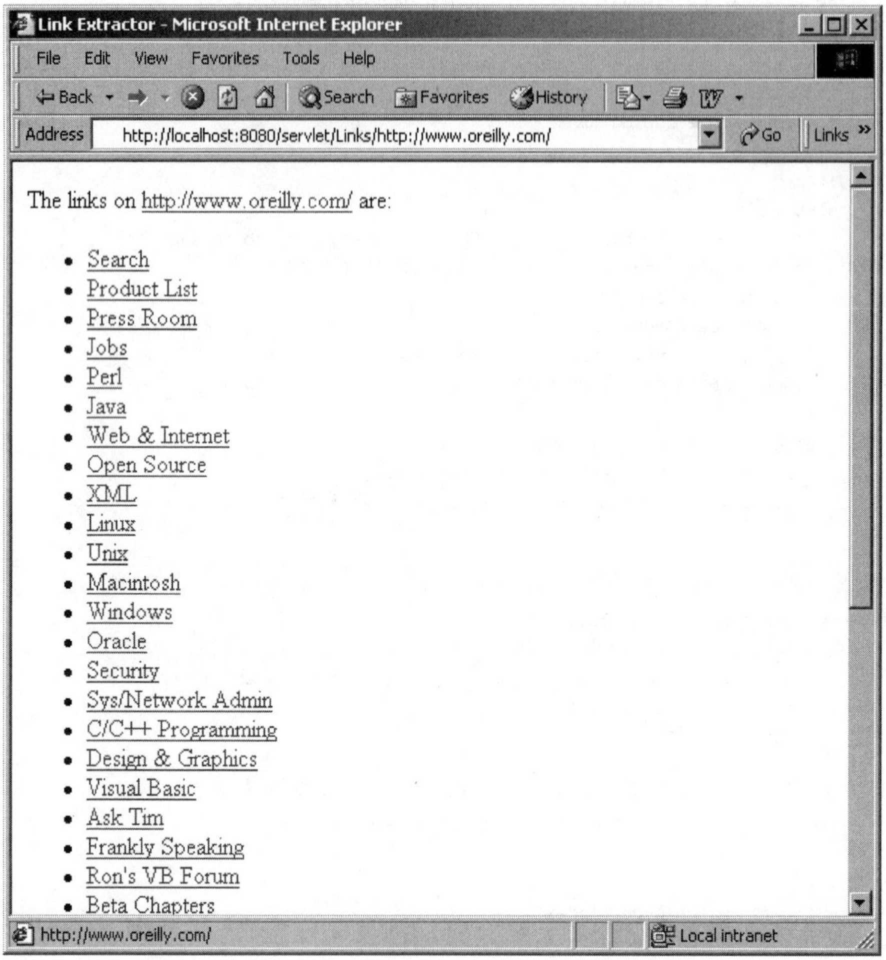

Figure 19-1. Ultralow-bandwidth browsing

Let's walk through the code. First, the servlet determines the URL whose links are to be extracted by looking at its extra path info. This means that this servlet should be invoked like this: *http://localhost:8080/servlet/Links/http://www.servlets.com*. Then the servlet reads the contents at that URL using the `HttpMessage` class and stores the page as a `String`. For extremely large pages this approach is not efficient, but it makes for a good book example.

The next step is to make sure the output page has a proper `<BASE>` tag so that any relative links in our list will be interpreted correctly by the browser. If there's a preexisting `<BASE>` tag on the input page we can use that, so we search for such a tag using the regular expression `<base[^>]*>` We pass that string to the `org.apache.regexp.RE` constructor along with a case-insensitivity flag. This regexp syntax is standard and exactly like Perl. It says to match the text `<base>`, followed by any number of characters that aren't >, followed by the text >. If we have a match, we extract the match using `re.getParen(0)` which gets the most outside match (matches may be nested by parentheses).

If there's no `<BASE>` tag in the page, we need to construct one. The `<BASE>` should be everything in the source URL up to and including the last slash.* We can extract this information using the simple regular expression `http://.*/`. This says to match the text `http://`, followed by any number of characters, followed by a /. The `.*` pattern reads as many characters as possible while still satisfying the rest of the regexp condition (what regexp terminology calls being *greedy*) so this expression returns everything up to and including the trailing slash. If there's no trailing slash, we simply add one.

Finally we extract the `<A HREF>` tags from the page using the fairly complicated regular expression `<a\s+[^<]*</a\s*>`. (You'll notice the code has escaped the \ characters with an additional \ character.) This says to match the text `<a`, followed by one or more whitespace characters (`\s` indicates whitespace), followed by any number of chracters that aren't <, followed by the text `</a`, followed by any number of whitespace characters, followed by >. Put together, this extracts `<A HREF>` tags from the beginning `<A` to the trailing `</A>`, all nicely case insensitive and whitespace forgiving, and making sure not to erroneously match tags like `<APPLET>`. As each match is found, it's displayed in the list, and the search continues using an index to record the next starting point.

For more information on what can be done with regular expressions in Java, see the documentation that comes with the library.

Executing Programs

Sometimes a servlet needs to execute an external program. This is generally important in situations in which an external program offers functionality that isn't easily available from within Java. For example, a servlet could call an external program to perform an image manipulation or to check the status of the server. Launching an external program raises portability and security concerns. It's an action that should be taken only when necessary and only by servlets running with a fairly lenient security manager—specifically, a security manager that grants permission for the servlet to call the `exec()` method of `java.lang.Runtime`.

---

* Without extra logic not shown here (involving preconnecting to the server), this approach can fail for URLs like *http://www.jdom.org/news* that redirect to *http://www.jdom.org/news/*. To be safe, make explicit any trailing slash in the URL passed to this servlet.

Finger

The *finger* program queries a (possibly remote) computer for a list of currently logged-in users. It's available on virtually all Unix systems and some Windows NT machines with networking capabilities. The *finger* program works by connecting to a *finger* daemon (usually named *fingerd*) that listens on port 79. *finger* makes its request of *fingerd* using a custom "finger" protocol, and *fingerd* replies with the appropriate information. Most Unix systems run *fingerd*, though many security-conscious administrators turn it off to limit information that could be used for break-in attempts. It's still fairly rare to find *fingerd* on Windows systems. Run without any arguments, *finger* reports all users of the local machine. The local machine must be running *fingerd*. Here's an example:

```
% finger
Login      Name                  TTY Idle When        Office
jhunter    Jason Hunter          q0  3:13 Thu 12:13
kbautista  Kathlyn Bautista      q1       Thu 12:18
```

Run with a username as an argument, *finger* reports on just that user:

```
% finger jhunter
Login name: jhunter                      In real life: Jason Hunter
Directory: /usr/people/jhunter           Shell: /bin/tcsh
On since Jan  1 12:13:28 on ttyq0 from :0.0
3 hours 13 minutes Idle Time
On since Jan  1 12:13:30 on ttyq2 from :0.0
```

Run with a hostname as an argument, *finger* reports all the users of the specified host. The remote host must be running *fingerd*:

```
% finger @deimos
Login    Name                  TTY Idle When        Office
bday     Bill Day              q0   17d Mon 10:45
```

And, of course, run with a username and hostname, *finger* reports on the specified user on the specified host:

```
% finger bday@deimos
[deimos.engr.sgi.com]
Login name: bday                         In real life: Bill Day
Directory: /usr/people/bday              Shell: /bin/tcsh
On since Dec 15 10:45:22 on ttyq0 from :0.0
17 days Idle Time
```

Executing the finger Command

Let's assume that a servlet wants access to the information retrieved by *finger*. It has two options: it can establish a socket connection to *fingerd* and make a request for information just like any other *finger* client, or it can execute the command-line *finger* program to make the connection on its behalf and read the information from *finger*'s output. We'll show the second technique here.

Example 19-5 shows how a servlet can execute the `finger` command to see who's logged into the local machine. It reads the command's output and prints it to its output stream.

Example 19-5. Executing the finger Command from a Servlet

```
import java.io.*;
import java.util.*;
import javax.servlet.*;
import javax.servlet.http.*;

import com.oreilly.servlet.ServletUtils;

public class Finger extends HttpServlet {

  public void doGet(HttpServletRequest req, HttpServletResponse res)
                               throws ServletException, IOException {
    res.setContentType("text/plain");
    PrintWriter out = res.getWriter();

    String command = "finger";

    Runtime runtime = Runtime.getRuntime();
    Process process = null;
    try {
      process = runtime.exec(command);
      BufferedReader in =
        new BufferedReader(new InputStreamReader(process.getInputStream()));

      // Read and print the output
      String line = null;
      while ((line = in.readLine()) != null) {
        out.println(line);
      }
    }
    catch (Exception e) {
      out.println("Problem with finger: " +
                  ServletUtils.getStackTraceAsString(e));
    }
  }
}
```

This servlet uses the `exec()` command just like any other Java class would. It executes the *finger* command, then reads and prints the output. If there's a problem, the servlet catches an exception and prints the stack trace to the user. This servlet assumes the *finger* command exists in the default search path. If that isn't the case, change the command string to specify the path where *finger* can be found.

We should point out that, although Java is executing native code when it executes the *finger* program, it doesn't open itself up to the risks that normally exist when executing native code. The reason is that the *finger* program executes as a separate process. It can crash or be killed without impacting the server executing the servlet.

Executing finger with Arguments

Now let's assume we want to pass an argument to the *finger* command. The usage is slightly different. The exec() method takes either a single string that specifies a command or an array of strings that specifies a command and the arguments to pass to that command. To run *finger jhunter* the code looks like Example 19-6.

Example 19-6. Adding a Parameter to the Executed Command

```
import java.io.*;
import java.util.*;
import javax.servlet.*;
import javax.servlet.http.*;

import com.oreilly.servlet.ServletUtils;

public class Finger extends HttpServlet {

  public void doGet(HttpServletRequest req, HttpServletResponse res)
                              throws ServletException, IOException {
    res.setContentType("text/plain");
    PrintWriter out = res.getWriter();

    String[] command = { "finger", "jhunter" };  // Only change!

    Runtime runtime = Runtime.getRuntime();
    Process process = null;
    try {
      process = runtime.exec(command);
      BufferedReader in =
        new BufferedReader(new InputStreamReader(process.getInputStream()));

      // Read and print the output
      String line = null;
      while ((line = in.readLine()) != null) {
        out.println(line);
      }
    }
    catch (Exception e) {
```

Example 19-6. Adding a Parameter to the Executed Command (continued)

```
        out.println("Problem with finger: " +
                    ServletUtils.getStackTraceAsString(e));
    }
  }
}
```

The command variable is now the string array `{"finger", "jhunter"}`. The command would not work as the single string `"finger jhunter"`.

Executing finger with Redirected Output

And finally, let's assume we want to redirect the output from our *finger* command. We may want to redirect the output to a file for later use, as in `finger jhunter > /tmp/jhunter`. Or we may want to redirect the output to the *grep* program to remove any references to some user, as in `finger | grep -v jhunter`.

This task is harder than it may appear. If the command variable is set to the string `finger | grep -v jhunter`, Java treats this string as the name of a single program—one that it most assuredly won't find. If the command variable is set to the string array `{"finger", "|", "grep", "-v", "jhunter"}`, Java executes the `finger` command and pass it the next four strings as parameters, no doubt thoroughly confusing *finger*.

The solution requires an understanding that redirection is a feature of the *shell*. The shell is the program into which you normally type commands. On Unix the most common shells are *csh*, *tcsh*, *bash*, and *sh*. On Windows 95/98, the shell is usually *command.com*. On Windows NT and Windows 2000, the shell is either *command.com* or *cmd.exe*.

Instead of executing *finger* directly, we can execute a shell and tell it the command string we want run. That string can contain the *finger* command and any sort of redirection. The shell can parse the command and correctly recognize and perform the redirection. The exact command needed to execute a shell and program depends on the shell and thus on the operating system. This technique therefore limits the platform independence of the servlets that use it. On a Unix system, the following command variable asks *csh* to execute the command `finger | grep -v jhunter`:

```
String[] command = { "/bin/csh", "-c", "finger | grep -v jhunter" };
```

The program Java executes is */bin/csh*. *csh* is passed two arguments: `-c`, which asks the shell to execute the next parameter, and `finger | grep -v jhunter`, which is executed by the shell.

On a Windows system, the command variable looks like this:

```
String[] command = { "command.com", "/c", "finger | grep -v jhunter" };
```

The `/c` argument for *command.com* works the same way `-c` did for *csh* and—yes, the *.com* suffix is necessary. Windows NT users should note that using *cmd.exe* is problematic because it redirects its output to a new window instead of to the Java runtime that spawned it. In fact, even launching your server from a *cmd.exe* shell can cause the *command.com* command to fail.

Using Native Methods

Despite Sun's push for 100% Pure Java, native code still has its place. You need native code to do things that Java (and external programs launched by Java) cannot do: locking files, accessing user IDs, accessing shared memory, sending faxes, and so on. Native code is also useful when accessing legacy data through non-Java gateways. Last, in situations in which every last bit of performance is vital, native code libraries can give a servlet a big boost.

Native code, however, should not be used except when absolutely necessary, since if the native code run by a servlet goes south, the entire server goes down with it! The security protections in Java can't protect the server from native code crashes. For this reason, it's wise not to use the native JDBC-ODBC bridge from a servlet because many ODBC drivers seem to have problems with multithreaded access. Native code also limits the platform independence of a servlet. While this may not matter for custom-built servlets tied to a particular server, it's something to remember.

How a servlet accesses native methods depends on the web server and JVM in which it's running. To take a risk and speak in broad generalities, let us say that you can pretty much expect your web server and JVM to support the standard *Java Native Interface (JNI)*. Using JNI is fairly involved, and even a basic introduction extends beyond the scope of this chapter.

When using JNI with servlets, remember these things:

- Only the most liberal server security managers allow a servlet to execute native code.
- There is a JDK 1.1.x bug that doesn't allow native code to be loaded by a class that was loaded with a custom class loader (such as the class loader that loads servlets from the default servlet directory). Servlets using native code may therefore need to reside in the server's classpath (such as *server_root/classes*).
- The directory where the shared library (or dynamic load library or DLL) that contains the native code is placed depends on the web server and JVM. Some servers have specific locations where they look for shared libraries. If the server doesn't provide a specific shared library directory, try placing the library

in a JVM-specific location such as *jdk_root\bin* or under *jdk_root/lib* (where *jdk_root* is the root of the JDK install), or try an operating system–specific location such as *windows_root\system32* or */usr/lib.*

Acting as an RMI Client

In Chapter 10, *Applet-Servlet Communication,* we saw how a servlet can act as an RMI server. Here we turn the tables and see a servlet acting as an RMI client. By taking the role of an RMI client, a servlet can leverage the services of other servers to accomplish its task, coordinate its efforts with other servers or servlets on those servers, and/or act as a proxy on behalf of applets that can't communicate with RMI servers themselves.

Example 19-7 shows `DaytimeClientServlet`, a servlet that gets the current time of day from the `DaytimeServlet` RMI server shown in Chapter 10.

Example 19-7. A Servlet as an RMI Client

```
import java.io.*;
import java.rmi.*;
import java.rmi.registry.*;
import javax.servlet.*;
import javax.servlet.http.*;

public class DaytimeClientServlet extends HttpServlet {

  DaytimeServer daytime;

  // Returns a reference to a DaytimeServer or null if there was a problem.
  protected DaytimeServer getDaytimeServer() {
    // If you use RMI's dynamic code loading feature, you have to
    // set a security manager such as RMISecurityManager
    //if (System.getSecurityManager() == null) {
    //  System.setSecurityManager(new RMISecurityManager());
    //}

    try {
      Registry registry =
        LocateRegistry.getRegistry(getRegistryHost(), getRegistryPort());
      return (DaytimeServer)registry.lookup(getRegistryName());
    }
    catch (Exception e) {
      log("Problem getting DaytimeServer reference", e);
      return null;
    }
  }

  private String getRegistryName() {
```

Example 19-7. A Servlet as an RMI Client (continued)

```
    String name = getInitParameter("registryName");
    return (name == null ? "DaytimeServlet" : name);
  }

  private String getRegistryHost() {
    // Return either the hostname given by "registryHost" or
    // if no name was given return null to imply localhost
    return getInitParameter("registryHost");
  }

  private int getRegistryPort() {
    try { return Integer.parseInt(getInitParameter("registryPort")); }
    catch (NumberFormatException e) { return Registry.REGISTRY_PORT; }
  }

  public void doGet(HttpServletRequest req, HttpServletResponse res)
                               throws ServletException, IOException {
    res.setContentType("text/plain");
    PrintWriter out = res.getWriter();

    // Get a daytime object if we haven't before
    if (daytime == null) {
      daytime = getDaytimeServer();
      if (daytime == null) {
        // Couldn't get it, so report we're unavailable.
        throw new UnavailableException("Could not locate daytime");
      }
    }

    // Get and print the current time on the (possibly remote) daytime host
    out.println(daytime.getDate().toString());
  }
}
```

This servlet should remind you of the applet you saw in Chapter 10. Both servlets and applets perform the same basic steps to access an RMI server. They both locate a registry using a hostname and port number, then use that registry to look up a reference to the remote object. The only possible difference is that a servlet, if it's taking advantage of RMI's dynamic code loading feature to automatically download the stub class file from another host, must first ensure it's running under the watch of a security manager to protect itself from the potentially hostile remotely loaded stub. An applet is guaranteed to run under an applet security manager, so this step isn't necessary. A servlet, however, can operate without a default security manager, so before acting as an RMI client it may need to assign one.

Debugging

The testing/debugging phase can be one of the hardest aspects of developing servlets. Servlets tend to involve a large amount of client/server interaction, making errors likely—but hard to reproduce. It can also be hard to track down the cause of nonobvious errors because servlets don't work well with standard debuggers, since they run inside a heavily multithreaded and generally complex web server. Here are a few hints and suggestions that may aid you in your debugging.

Check the Logs

When you first think there might be a problem, check the logs. Most servers output an error log where you can find a list of all the errors observed by the server and an event log where you can find a list of interesting servlet events. The event log may also hold the messages logged by servlets through the `log()` method, but not always.

Note that many servers buffer their output to these logs to improve performance. When hunting down a problem, you may want to stop this buffering (usually by reducing the server's buffer size to zero bytes), so you can see problems as they occur. Be sure to reset the buffer size to a reasonable value afterward.

Output Extra Information

If you don't see an indication of the problem in the server's logs, try having your servlet log extra information with the `log()` method. As you've seen in examples elsewhere in this book, we habitually log stack traces and other error situations. During debugging, you can add a few temporary `log()` commands as a poor man's debugger, to get a general idea of the code execution path and the values of the servlet's variables. Sometimes it's convenient to leave the `log()` commands in a servlet surrounded by `if` clauses so they trigger only when a specific debug init parameter is set to `true`.

Extracting the extra information from the server's logs can at times be unwieldy. To make the temporary debugging information easier to find, you can have a servlet output its debug information to the client (through the `PrintWriter`) or to a console on the server (through `System.out`). Not all servers have a console associated with a servlet's `System.out`; some redirect the output to a file instead.

Use a Standard Debugger

It's also possible to use a standard debugger to track down servlet problems, although exactly how might not be intuitively obvious. After all, you can't debug a servlet directly because servlets aren't standalone programs. Servlets are server extensions, and, as such, they need to run inside a server.

Fortunately, Tomcat is a pure Java web server perfect for debugging servlets. The only trick is that Tomcat must be started from within a debugger. The exact procedures vary depending on the version of Tomcat (or other Java-based web server) you're using, but the idea is always the same:

1. Set your debugger's classpath so that it can find the classes and JARs needed to run Tomcat. You can look to the output emitted on startup and the server startup scripts (*tomcat.sh* and *tomcat.bat*) for help in determining this classpath.
2. Set your debugger's classpath so that it can also find your servlets and support classes, typically the directory *WEB-INF/classes* and the files in *WEB-INF/lib*. You normally wouldn't want these directories and JARs in your classpath because that disables servlet reloading. This inclusion, however, is useful for debugging. It allows your debugger to set breakpoints in a servlet before the custom servlet loader responsible for loading classes from *WEB-INF* loads the servlet.
3. Once you have set the proper classpath, start debugging the server by running the server class containing the primary `main()` method. For Tomcat 3.2 the class is `org.apache.tomcat.startup.Tomcat`. Other Java-based servers, and future versions of Tomcat, may use a different class. Look to the startup script for clues to the primary class name.
4. Tomcat may complain about certain system properties or environment variables needing to be set. For example, Tomcat 3.2 looks to the system property `tomcat.home` or the environment variable `TOMCAT_HOME` to determine its base directory. Set these as necessary.
5. Set breakpoints in whatever servlet you're interested in debugging, then use a web browser to make a request to the `HttpServer` for the given servlet (*http://localhost:8080/servlet/ServletToDebug*). You should see execution stop at your breakpoints.

Many IDE debuggers hide these details and allow integrated servlet debugging using a built-in server to execute the servlets. It's often good to know the manual procedure, however, because the servers provided with IDE debuggers are usually a revision or two behind.

Some servlet container plug-ins (that normally work only in conjunction with a non-Java web server) have standalone pure Java versions created explicitly for use in debugging as described here. The advantage to using these servers, when they're available, is that you can easily move any custom web server configuration files from the production server to the test environment and back again.

Examine the Client Request

Sometimes when a servlet doesn't behave as expected, it's useful to look at the raw HTTP request to which it's responding. If you're familiar with the structure of HTTP, you can read the request and see exactly where a servlet might get confused.* One way to see the raw request is to replace the web server process with a custom server application that prints out everything it receives. Example 19-8 shows such a server.

Example 19-8. Catching a Client Request

```
import java.io.*;
import java.net.*;
import java.util.*;

public class SocketWatch {

  private static void printUsage() {
    System.out.println("usage: java SocketWatch port");
  }

  public static void main(String[] args) {
    if (args.length < 1) {
      printUsage();
      return;
    }

    // The first argument is the port to listen on
    int port;
    try {
      port = Integer.parseInt(args[0]);
    }
    catch (NumberFormatException e) {
      printUsage();
      return;
    }

    try {
      // Establish a server socket to accept client connections
      // As each connection comes in, pass it to a handler thread
      ServerSocket ss = new ServerSocket(port);
      while (true) {
        Socket request = ss.accept();
        new HandlerThread(request).start();
```

* Of course, if you're not familiar with the structure of HTTP, it may be you who is getting confused. In that case, we recommend reading the HTTP primer in Chapter 2, *HTTP Servlet Basics*, and the book *HTTP Pocket Reference* by Clinton Wong (O'Reilly).

Example 19-8. Catching a Client Request (continued)

```
      }
    }
    catch (Exception e) {
      e.printStackTrace();
    }
  }
}

class HandlerThread extends Thread {

  Socket s;

  public HandlerThread(Socket s) {
    this.s = s;
  }

  public void run() {
    try {
      // Print each byte as it comes in from the socket
      InputStream in = s.getInputStream();
      byte[] bytes = new byte[1];
      while ((in.read(bytes)) != -1) {
        System.out.print((char)bytes[0]);
      }
    }
    catch (Exception e) {
      e.printStackTrace();
    }
  }
}
```

Start this server listening on port 8080 by typing the following command in a shell:

```
java SocketWatch 8080
```

Note that two applications can't listen to the same socket at the same time, so first make sure there's no other server listening on your chosen port. Once you have the server running, you can make HTTP requests to it as if it were a normal web server. For example, you can use a web browser to surf to *http://localhost:8080*. When `SocketWatch` receives the browser's HTTP request, it sends the request to its standard out for your examination. The browser is likely to be busy waiting for a response that will never come. End its wait by clicking the Stop button.

Here is some sample output from `SocketWatch` that shows the details of a GET request made to *http://localhost:8080*:

```
GET / HTTP/1.0
Connection: Keep-Alive
```

```
User-Agent: Mozilla/4.7 [en] (X11; U; IRIX 6.2 IP22)
Pragma: no-cache
Host: localhost:8080
Accept: image/gif, image/x-xbitmap, image/jpeg, image/pjpeg, */*
Cookie: JSESSIONIN=To1010mC10934500694587412At
```

Create a Custom Client Request

In addition to catching and examining a client's HTTP request, you may find it useful to create your own HTTP request. You can do this by connecting to the server socket on which the web server is listening, then manually entering a properly structured HTTP request. To establish the connection, you can use the *telnet* program, available on all Unix machines and most Windows machines with networking. The *telnet* program accepts as arguments the host and port number to which it should connect. Once you're connected, you can make a request that looks like what you saw in the last section. Fortunately, your request can be far simpler—all you need to specify is the first line, saying what to get, and the last line, which must be an empty line that indicates the end of the request. For example:

```
% telnet localhost 8080
Trying 127.0.0.1...
Connected to localhost.
Escape character is '^]'.
GET /servlet/ParameterSnoop?name=value HTTP/1.0

HTTP/1.1 200 OK
Server: Tomcat Web Server/3.2
Content-Type: text/plain
Connection: close
Date: Sun, 25 Jun 2000 20:29:06 GMT

Query String:
name=value

Request Parameters:
name (0): value
Connection closed by foreign host.
```

As is too often the case, Windows behaves a little differently than you'd like. The default Windows 95/98/NT *telnet.exe* program misformats many web server responses because it doesn't understand that on the Web, a line feed should be treated the same as a line feed and carriage return. In lieu of *telnet.exe*, Windows programmers can use the better-behaved Java program shown in Example 19-9.

Example 19-9. Another Way to Connect to a Web Server

```
import java.io.*;
import java.net.*;
import java.util.*;

public class HttpClient {

  private static void printUsage() {
    System.out.println("usage: java HttpClient host port");
  }

  public static void main(String[] args) {
    if (args.length < 2) {
      printUsage();
      return;
    }

    // Host is the first parameter, port is the second
    String host = args[0];
    int port;
    try {
      port = Integer.parseInt(args[1]);
    }
    catch (NumberFormatException e) {
      printUsage();
      return;
    }

    try {
      // Open a socket to the server
      Socket s = new Socket(host, port);

      // Start a thread to send keyboard input to the server
      new KeyboardInputManager(System.in, s).start();

      // Now print everything we receive from the socket
      BufferedReader in =
        new BufferedReader(new InputStreamReader(s.getInputStream()));
      String line;
      while ((line = in.readLine()) != null) {
        System.out.println(line);
      }
    }
    catch (Exception e) {
      e.printStackTrace();
    }
  }
}
```

Example 19-9. Another Way to Connect to a Web Server (continued)

```
class KeyboardInputManager extends Thread {

  InputStream in;
  Socket s;

  public KeyboardInputManager(InputStream in, Socket s) {
    this.in = in;
    this.s = s;
    setPriority(MIN_PRIORITY);  // socket reads should have a higher priority
                                // Wish I could use a select() !
    setDaemon(true);  // let the app die even when this thread is running
  }

  public void run() {
    try {
      BufferedReader keyb = new BufferedReader(new InputStreamReader(in));
      PrintWriter server = new PrintWriter(s.getOutputStream());

      String line;
      System.out.println("Connected... Type your manual HTTP request");
      System.out.println("------------------------------------------");
      while ((line = keyb.readLine()) != null) {
        server.print(line);
        server.print("\r\n");  // HTTP lines end with \r\n
        server.flush();
      }
    }
    catch (Exception e) {
      e.printStackTrace();
    }
  }
}
```

This HttpClient program operates similarly to *telnet*:

```
% java HttpClient localhost 8080
Connected... Type your manual HTTP request
------------------------------------------
GET /index.html HTTP/1.0

HTTP/1.0 200 OK
Content-Type: text/html
Content-Length: 2582
Last-Modified: Fri, 15 Sep 2000 22:20:15 GMT
Servlet-Engine: Tomcat Web Server/3.2 (JSP 1.1; Servlet 2.2; Java 1.2.2;
Windows NT 4.0 x86; java.vendor=Sun Microsystems Inc.)

<!doctype html public "-//w3c//dtd html 4.0 transitional//en">
```

```
<html>
<head>
  <meta http-equiv="Content-Type" content="text/html; charset=iso-8859-1">
  <title>Tomcat v3.2</title>
</head>
...
```

Use a Third-Party Tool

Third-party tools are bringing new capabilities and ease of use to the task of servlet debugging. IBM AlphaWorks produces a program called Distributed Application Tester (DAT) that snoops HTTP and HTTPS requests and responses, making it possible to view and record both sides of client/server traffic. DAT includes the ability to do functional tests and performance tests of your web application by autogenerating requests and scanning the responses. The program is pure Java but comes with an install tool that works only on Windows. Its only license is a free 90-day evaluation because the software is "alpha," and curiously has been since January 1999. DAT is available at *http://www.alphaworks.ibm.com.*

Allaire, maker of the popular JRun servlet plug-in (after their purchase of Live Software), has a little-known tool for servlet debugging named ServletDebugger. It's designed to help programmatically test and debug a servlet. ServletDebugger doesn't require using a web server or a browser to make a request. Instead, you use a set of classes to write a small stub class that prepares and executes a servlet request. The stub specifies everything: the servlet's init parameters, the request's HTTP headers, and the request's parameters. ServletDebugger is fairly straightforward and is well suited to automated testing. The largest drawback is that it takes extra effort to properly prepare a realistic request. ServletDebugger is hidden deep on Allaire's price sheet at *http://www.allaire.com.**

Some Final Tips

If all the advice so far hasn't helped track down your bug, here are some final tips on servlet debugging:

- Use `System.getProperty("java.class.path")` from your servlet to help debug classpath problems. Because servlets are often run from web servers with embedded JVMs, it can be hard at times to identify exactly what classpath the JVM is searching. The property `java.class.path` will tell you.
- Be aware that classes found in the server's direct classpath (*server_root/classes*) probably don't reload, nor on most servers do nonservlet support classes in

* We wouldn't be surprised if Allaire drops support for ServletDebugger in the not too distant future. If that happens, or maybe even if it doesn't happen, keep an eye out for an open source version.

the web application classes directory (*WEB-INF/classes*). Normally only servlet classes under the web application classes directory will reload.

- Ask a browser to show the raw content of the page it is displaying. This can help identify formatting problems. It's usually an option under the View menu.
- Make sure the browser isn't caching a previous request's output by forcing a full reload of the page. With Netscape Navigator, use Shift-Reload; with Internet Explorer use Shift-Refresh.
- If you override the version of `init()` that takes a `ServletConfig`, verify that the overriding method calls `super.init(config)` right away.

Performance Tuning

Performance tuning servlets requires a slightly different mindset than performance tuning normal Java applications or applets. The reason is that the JVM running the servlets is expected to simultaneously handle dozens, if not hundreds, of threads, each executing a servlet. These coexisting servlets have to share the resources of the JVM in a way that normal applications do not. The traditional performance-tuning tricks still apply, of course, but they have a different impact when used in a heavily multithreaded system. What follows are some of the tricks that have the largest special impact on servlet developers.

Go Forth, but Don't Prosper

Avoid the unnecessary creation of objects. This has always been good advice—creating unnecessary objects wastes memory and wastes a fair amount of time as the objects are created. With servlets, it's even better advice. Traditionally many JVMs have used a global object heap that must be locked for each new memory allocation. While any servlet is creating a new object or allocating additional memory, no other servlet can do so.

Don't Append by Concatenation

Avoid concatenating several strings together. Use the `append()` method of `StringBuffer` instead. This too has always been good advice, but with servlets it's particularly tempting to write code like this to prepare a string for later output:

```
String output;
output += "<TITLE>";
output += "Hello, " + user;
output += "</TITLE>";
```

Although this code looks nice and neat, when it runs it executes as if written roughly as follows, with a new `StringBuffer` and new `String` created on each line:

```
String output;
output = new StringBuffer().append("<TITLE>").toString();
output = new StringBuffer(output).append("Hello, ").toString();
output = new StringBuffer(output).append(user).toString();
output = new StringBuffer(output).append("</TITLE>").toString();
```

When efficiency counts, rewrite the original code to look like the following, so just one `StringBuffer` and one `String` are created:

```
StringBuffer buf = new StringBuffer();
buf.append("<TITLE>");
buf.append("Hello, ").append(user);
buf.append("</TITLE);
output = buf.toString();
```

Note that using an array of bytes is even more efficient.

Limit Synchronization

Synchronize whenever necessary, but no more. Every synchronized block in a servlet slows the servlet's response time. Because the same servlet instance may handle multiple concurrent requests, it must, of course, take care to protect its class and instance variables with synchronized blocks. All the time one request thread is in a servlet's synchronized block, however, no other thread can enter the block. Therefore, it's generally best to keep these blocks as small as possible.

You should also take a look at the worst-case result of thread contention. If the worst case is bearable (as with the counter example from Chapter 3, *The Servlet Lifecycle*), you can consider removing synchronization blocks entirely. Also consider using the `SingleThreadModel` tag interface, where the server manages a pool of servlet instances to guarantee each instance is used at most by one thread at a time. Servlets that implement `SingleThreadModel` don't need to synchronize access to their instance variables.

Finally, remember that `java.util.Vector` and `java.util.Hashtable` are always internally synchronized, while the equivalent `java.util.ArrayList` and `java.util.HashMap`, introduced in JDK 1.2, are not synchronized unless requested. So if your `Vector` or `Hashtable` doesn't need synchronization and you're running on JDK 1.2, try the unsynchronized `ArrayList` or `HashMap` instead.

Buffer Your Input and Output

Buffer your input and your output, all your storage files, any streams loaded from a database, and so on. This almost always improves performance, but the improvement can be especially profound with servlets. The reason is reading and writing one unit at a time can slow down the entire server due to the frequent context switches that have to be made. Fortunately, you generally don't need to buffer when writing to a servlet's `PrintWriter` or `ServletOutputStream` or when reading from a servlet's `BufferedReader` or `ServletInputStream`. Most server implementations already buffer these streams.

Try Using an OutputStream

For web pages using the Latin-1 character encoding, it's technically possible to use either a `PrintWriter` or a `ServletOutputStream` to write to the client. Using a `PrintWriter` is the recommended approach because it supports internationalization, but on some servers using a `ServletOutputStream` provides a noticeable performance increase, and `ServletOutputStream` conveniently has a long list of `print()` and `println()` methods left over from Servlet API 1.0 when there was no `PrintWriter` option. Just be careful. Many servers are just the opposite and with them using a `PrintWriter` provides higher performance. Unless you're sure of your deployment platform and have run comparable time trials, stick with `PrintWriter`.

Use a Profiling Tool

There are a number of Java profiling tools available that can help identify bottlenecks in your code. After all, most performance problems in server-side Java are caused not by the language or JVM but rather by a handful of bottlenecks; the trick is locating those bottlenecks. These analysis tools run in the background, observing as your web server handles requests, reporting a detailed summary of where time was spent as well as how memory was allocated. Two popular tools are OptimizeIt! from Intuitive Systems (*http://www.optimizeit.com*) and JProbe from Sitraka, formerly the KL Group (*http://www.sitraka.com/jprobe*). Many JVMs also accept command-line flags (`-prof` under JDK 1.1 and `-Xrunhprof` under JDK 1.2) to report some basic profiling information. To run the server under load you can use a tool such as Apache JMeter (*http://java.apache.org/jmeter*).

20

In this chapter:
- *Changes in the Servlet API 2.3*
- *Conclusion*

What's New in the Servlet 2.3 API

Shortly before this book went to print, Sun Microsystems published the Proposed Final Draft of the Servlet API 2.3 specification.* This is not the specification's final form; the Proposed Final Draft is one step away from a formal Final Release and technical details are still subject to change. However, those changes should not be significant—in fact, server vendors have already begun to implement the new features. In this chapter, I will review in detail everything that changed between API 2.2 and API 2.3. I will also explain the reasons for the changes and demonstrate how to write servlets using the new features.†

Changes in the Servlet API 2.3

Servlet API 2.3 actually leaves the core of servlets relatively untouched, which indicates that servlets have reached a high level of maturity. Most of the action has involved adding new features outside the core. Among the changes:

- Servlets now require JDK 1.2 or later.
- A filter mechanism has (finally) been created.
- Application lifecycle events have been added.
- New internationalization support has been added.
- The technique to express inter-JAR dependencies has been formalized.

* Although this specification was published by Sun, Servlet API 2.3 was actually developed by the many individuals and companies working on the JSR-053 expert group, in accordance with the Java Community Process (JCP) Version 2.0. This expert group was led by Danny Coward of Sun Microsystems.

† This material originally appeared in the article "Servlet 2.3: New Features Exposed" by Jason Hunter, published by JavaWorld (*http://www.javaworld.com*), copyright ITworld.com, Inc., January 2001. Reprinted with permission. (See also *http://www.javaworld.com/jw-01-2001/jw-0126-servletapi.html*).

- Rules for class loading have been clarified.
- New error and security attributes have been added.
- The `HttpUtils` class has been deprecated.
- Various new helpful methods have been added.
- Several DTD behaviors have been expanded and clarified.

Other clarifications have been made, but they mostly concern server vendors, not general servlet programmers (except for the fact that programmers will see improved portability), so I'll omit those details.

Before I begin my examination, let me point out that Version 2.3 has been released as a draft specification only. Most of the features discussed here won't yet work with all servers. If you want to test those features, I recommend downloading the official reference implementation server, Apache Tomcat 4.0. It's open source, and you can download the server for free. Tomcat 4.0 is currently in beta release; its support for API 2.3 is getting better, but is still incomplete. Read the `NEW_SPECS.txt` file that comes with Tomcat 4.0 to learn its level of support for all new specification features.

Servlets in J2SE and J2EE

One of the first things you should note about Servlet API 2.3 is that servlets now depend on the Java 2 Platform, Standard Edition 1.2 (also known as J2SE 1.2 or JDK 1.2). This small, but important, change means you can now use J2SE 1.2 features in your servlets and be guaranteed that the servlets will work across all servlet containers. Previously, you could use J2SE 1.2 features, but servers were not required to support them.

The Servlet API 2.3 is slated to become a core part of Java 2 Platform, Enterprise Edition 1.3 (J2EE 1.3). The previous version, Servlet API 2.2, was part of J2EE 1.2. The only noticeable difference is the addition of a few relatively obscure J2EE-related deployment descriptor tags in the *web.xml* DTD: `<resource-env-ref>` to support "administered objects," such as those required by the Java Messaging System (JMS), `<res-ref-sharing-scope>` to allow either shared or exclusive access to a resource reference, and `<run-as>` to specify the security identity of a caller to an EJB. Most servlet authors need not concern themselves with those J2EE tags; you can get a full description from the J2EE 1.3 specification.

Filters

The most significant part of API 2.3 is the addition of *filters*. Filters are objects that can transform a request or modify a response. Note that they are not servlets; they do not actually create a response. They are preprocessors of the request before it reaches a servlet, and/or postprocessors of the response leaving a servlet. In a sense, filters are a mature version of the old "servlet chaining" concept. A filter can:

- Intercept a servlet's invocation before the servlet is called.
- Examine a request before a servlet is called.
- Modify the request headers and request data by providing a customized version of the request object that wraps the real request.
- Modify the response headers and response data by providing a customized version of the response object that wraps the real response.
- Intercept a servlet's invocation after the servlet is called.

You can configure a filter to act on a servlet or group of servlets; that servlet or group can be filtered by zero or more filters. Some practical filter ideas include authentication filters, logging and auditing filters, image conversion filters, data compression filters, encryption filters, tokenizing filters, filters that trigger resource access events, XSLT filters that transform XML content, or MIME-type chain filters (just like servlet chaining).

A filter implements `javax.servlet.Filter` and defines its three methods:

`void setFilterConfig(FilterConfig config)`
: This method sets the filter's configuration object.

`FilterConfig getFilterConfig()`
: This method returns the filter's configuration object.

`void doFilter(ServletRequest req, ServletResponse res, FilterChain chain)`
: This method performs the actual filtering work

The server calls `setFilterConfig()` once to prepare the filter for service, then calls `doFilter()` any number of times for various requests. The `FilterConfig` interface has methods to retrieve the filter's name, its init parameters, and the active servlet context. The server can also pass `null` to `setFilterConfig()` to indicate that the filter is being taken out of service.

NOTE It's anticipated that in the Final Release of 2.3 the `getFilterConfig()` method will be removed and the `setFilterConfig(FilterConfig config)` method will be replaced by `init(FilterConfig)` and `destroy()`.

Each filter receives the current request and response in its `doFilter()` method, as well as a `FilterChain` containing the filters that still must be processed. In the `doFilter()` method, a filter may do what it wants with the request and response. (For example, it could gather data by calling their methods, or wrap the objects to give them new behavior, as discussed next.) The filter then calls `chain.doFilter()` to transfer control to the next filter. When that call returns, a filter can, at the end of its own `doFilter()` method, perform additional work on the response; for instance, it can log information about the response. If the filter wants to halt the request processing and gain full control of the response, it can intentionally not call the next filter.

A filter may wrap the request and/or response objects to provide custom behavior, changing certain method call implementation to influence later request handling actions. The Servlet API 2.3 provides new `HttpServletRequestWrapper` and `HttpServletResponseWrapper` classes to help with this. They provide default implementations of all request and response methods, and delegate the calls to the original request or response by default. Changing one method's behavior just requires extending the wrapper and reimplementing one method. Wrappers give filters great control over the request-handling and response-generating process. The code for a simple logging filter that records the duration of all requests is shown here:

```
public class LogFilter implements Filter {

  FilterConfig config;

  public void setFilterConfig(FilterConfig config) {
    this.config = config;
  }

  public FilterConfig getFilterConfig() {
    return config;
  }

  public void doFilter(ServletRequest req,
                       ServletResponse res,
                       FilterChain chain) {
    ServletContext context = getFilterConfig().getServletContext();
    long bef = System.currentTimeMillis();
    chain.doFilter(req, res); // no chain parameter needed here
    long aft = System.currentTimeMillis();
    context.log("Request to " + req.getRequestURI() + ": " +
                                                   (aft-bef));
  }
}
```

When the server calls `setFilterConfig()`, the filter saves a reference to the filter configuration in its `config` variable, which is later used in the `doFilter()` method to retrieve the `ServletContext`. The logic in `doFilter()` is simple: time how long request handling takes and log the time once processing has been completed. To use this filter, you must declare it in the *web.xml* deployment descriptor using the `<filter>` tag, as shown here:

```
<filter>
  <filter-name>
    log
  </filter-name>
  <filter-class>
    LogFilter
  </filter-class>
</filter>
```

This tells the server a filter named log is implemented in the `LogFilter` class. You can apply a registered filter to certain URL patterns or servlet names using the `<filter-mapping>` tag:

```
<filter-mapping>
  <filter-name>log</filter-name>
  <url-pattern>/*</url-pattern>
</filter-mapping>
```

This configures the filter to operate on all requests to the server (static or dynamic), just what we want for our logging filter. If you connect to a simple page, the log output might look like this:

```
Request to /index.jsp: 10
```

Lifecycle Events

Servlet API 2.3's second most significant change is the addition of application lifecycle events, which let "listener" objects be notified when servlet contexts and sessions are initialized and destroyed, as well as when attributes are added or removed from a context or session.

Servlet lifecycle events work like Swing events. Any listener interested in observing the `ServletContext` lifecycle can implement the `ServletContextListener` interface. The interface has two methods:

`void contextInitialized(ServletContextEvent e)`
: Called when a web application is first ready to process requests (i.e., on web server startup and when a context is added or reloaded). Requests will not be handled until this method returns.

`void contextDestroyed(ServletContextEvent e)`
: Called when a web application is about to be shut down (i.e., on web server shutdown or when a context is removed or reloaded). Request handling will be stopped before this method is called.

The `ServletContextEvent` class passed to both methods consists only of a `getServletContext()` method that returns the context being initialized or destroyed.

A listener interested in observing the `ServletContext` attribute lifecycle can implement the `ServletContextAttributesListener` interface, which has three methods:

`void attributeAdded(ServletContextAttributeEvent e)`
: Called when an attribute is added to a servlet context.

`void attributeRemoved(ServletContextAttributeEvent e)`
: Called when an attribute is removed from a servlet context.

`void attributeReplaced(ServletContextAttributeEvent e)`
: Called when an attribute is replaced by another attribute in a servlet context.

The `ServletContextAttributeEvent` class extends `ServletContextEvent`, and adds `getName()` and `getValue()` methods so the listener can learn about the attribute being changed. That is useful because web applications that need to synchronize application state (context attributes) with something like a database can now do it in one place.

The session listener model is similar to the context listener model. In the session model, there's an `HttpSessionListener` interface with two methods:

`void sessionCreated(HttpSessionEvent e)`
: Called when a session is created.

`void sessionDestroyed(HttpSessionEvent e)`
: Called when a session is destroyed (invalidated).

The methods accept an `HttpSessionEvent` instance with a `getSession()` accessor to return the session being created or destroyed. You can use all these methods when implementing an administrator interface that keeps track of all active users in a web application.

The session model also has an `HttpSessionAttributesListener` interface with three methods. Those methods tell the listener when attributes change, and could be used, for example, by an application that synchronizes profile data held in sessions into a database:

`void attributeAdded(HttpSessionBindingEvent e)`
: Called when an attribute is added to a session.

`void attributeRemoved(HttpSessionBindingEvent e)`
: Called when an attribute is removed from a session.

`void attributeReplaced(HttpSessionBindingEvent e)`
Called when an attribute replaces another attribute in a session.

As you might expect, the `HttpSessionBindingEvent` class extends `HttpSessionEvent` and adds `getName()` and `getValue()` methods. The only somewhat abnormal thing is that the event class is named `HttpSessionBindingEvent`, not `HttpSessionAttributeEvent`. That's for legacy reasons; the API already had an `HttpSessionBindingEvent` class, so it was reused. This confusing aspect of the API may be ironed out before final release.

A possible practical use of lifecycle events is a shared database connection managed by a context listener. You declare the listener in the *web.xml* file as follows:

```
<listener>
 <listener-class>
   com.acme.MyConnectionManager
 </listener-class>
</listener>
```

The server creates an instance of the listener class to receive events and uses introspection to determine what listener interface (or interfaces) the class implements. Bear in mind that because the listener is configured in the deployment descriptor, you can add new listeners without any code change. You could write the listener itself as something like this:

```
public class MyConnectionManager implements ServletContextListener {

  public void contextInitialized(ServletContextEvent e) {
    Connection con =       // create connection
      e.getServletContext().setAttribute("con", con);
  }

  public void contextDestroyed(ServletContextEvent e) {
    Connection con =
       (Connection) e.getServletContext().getAttribute("con");
    try { con.close(); }
    catch (SQLException ignored) { } // close connection
  }
}
```

This listener ensures that a database connection is available in every new servlet context, and that all connections are closed when the context shuts down.

The `HttpSessionActivationListener` interface, another new listener interface in API 2.3, is designed to handle sessions that migrate from one server to another. A listener implementing `HttpSessionActivationListener` is notified when any session is about to passivate (move) and when the session is about to activate (become live) on the second host. These methods give an application the chance to persist nonserializable data across JVMs, or to glue or unglue serialized objects back into some kind of object model before or after migration. The interface has two methods:

`void sessionWillPassivate(HttpSessionEvent e)`
: The session is about to passivate. The session will already be out of service when this call is made.

`void sessionDidActivate(HttpSessionEvent e)`
: The session has been activated. The session will not yet be in service when this call is made.

You register this listener just like the others. However, unlike the others, the passivate and activate calls here will most likely occur on two different servers!

Selecting Character Encodings

The Servlet API 2.3 provides much-needed support for handling foreign language form submittals. A new method, `request.setCharacterEncoding(String encoding)`, allows you to tell the server a request's character encoding. A character encoding (also known as a *charset*) is a way to map bytes to characters. The server can use the specified charset to correctly parse the parameters and POST data.

By default, a server parses parameters using the common Latin-1 (ISO 8859-1) charset. Unfortunately, that only works for Western European languages. When a browser uses another charset, it is supposed to send the encoding information in the `Content-Type` header of the request, but virtually no browsers adhere to this. The `setCharacterEncoding()` method lets a servlet tell the server what charset is in use (it is typically the charset of the page that contains the form); the server takes care of the rest. For example, a servlet receiving Japanese parameters from a `Shift_JIS` encoded form could read the parameters like this:

```
// Set the charset as Shift_JIS
req.setCharacterEncoding("Shift_JIS");

// Read a parameter using that charset
String name = req.getParameter("name");
```

Remember to set the encoding before calling `getParameter()` or `getReader()`. The `setCharacterEncoding()` call may throw a `java.io.UnsupportedEncodingException` if the encoding is not supported. This functionality is also available for users of API 2.2 and earlier, as part of the `com.oreilly.servlet.ParameterParser` class.

JAR Dependencies

A WAR file (*Web Application Archive* file, added in Servlet API 2.2) often requires various other JAR libraries to exist on the server and operate correctly. For example, a web application using the `ParameterParser` class needs `cos.jar` in the classpath. A web application using WebMacro needs `webmacro.jar`.

Before API 2.3, either those dependencies had to be documented (as if anyone actually reads documentation!) or each web application had to include all its required JAR files in its own *WEB-INF/lib* directory (unnecessarily bloating each web application). Servlet API 2.3 lets you express JAR dependencies within the WAR using the WAR's *META-INF/MANIFEST.MF* entry. That is the standard way for JAR files to declare dependencies, but with API 2.3, WAR files must officially support the same mechanism. If a dependency can't be satisfied, a server can politely reject the web application at deployment time instead of causing an obscure error message at runtime. The mechanism allows a high degree of granularity. For example, you can express a dependency on a particular version of an optional package, and the server has to find the right one with a search algorithm.

Class Loaders

Here's a small change with a big impact: in API 2.3, a servlet container (a.k.a. the server) will ensure that classes in a web application not be allowed to see the server's implementation classes. In other words, the class loaders should be kept separate.

That doesn't sound like much, but it eliminates the possibility of a collision between Web application classes and server classes. That had become a serious problem because of XML parser conflicts. Each server needs an XML parser to parse *web.xml* files, and many web applications these days also use an XML parser to handle reading, manipulation, and writing of XML data. If the parsers supported different DOM or SAX versions, that could cause an irreparable conflict. The separation of class scope solves this issue nicely.

New Error Attributes

The previous API version, Servlet API 2.2, introduced several request attributes that could be used by servlets and JSPs acting as targets of an `<error-page>` rule. Recall from earlier in the book that `<error-page>` rules let you configure a web application so that certain error status codes or exception types cause specific pages to be displayed:

```
<web-app>
    <!-- ..... -->
    <error-page>
```

```
        <error-code>
            404
        </error-code>
        <location>
            /404.html
        </location>
    </error-page>
    <error-page>
        <exception-type>
            javax.servlet.ServletException
        </exception-type>
        <location>
            /servlet/ErrorDisplay
        </location>
    </error-page>
    <!-- ..... -->
</web-app>
```

A servlet in the `<location>` for an `<error-page>` rule could receive the following three attributes:

`javax.servlet.error.status_code`
: An `Integer` telling the error status code, if any.

`javax.servlet.error.exception_type`
: A `Class` instance indicating the type of exception that caused the error, if any.

`javax.servlet.error.message`
: A `String` telling the exception message, passed to the exception constructor.

Using those attributes, a servlet could generate an error page customized to the error, as shown here:

```
import java.io.*;
import javax.servlet.*;
import javax.servlet.http.*;

public class ErrorDisplay extends HttpServlet {

  public void doGet(HttpServletRequest req,
      HttpServletResponse res)
      throws ServletException, IOException {

    res.setContentType("text/html");
    PrintWriter out = res.getWriter();

    String code = null, message = null, type = null;
    Object codeObj, messageObj, typeObj;

    // Retrieve the three possible error attributes.
    // Some may be null
```

```
        codeObj = req.getAttribute("javax.servlet.error.status_code");
        messageObj = req.getAttribute("javax.servlet.error.message");
        typeObj = req.
            getAttribute("javax.servlet.error.exception_type");

        // Convert the attributes to string values
        // We do things this way because some old servers return String
        // types while new servers return Integer, String, and Class
        // types. This works for all.

        if (codeObj != null) code = codeObj.toString();
        if (messageObj != null) message = messageObj.toString();
        if (typeObj != null) type = typeObj.toString();

        // The error reason is either the status code or exception type
        String reason = (code != null ? code : type);

        out.println("<HTML>");
        out.println("<HEAD><TITLE>" + reason + ": " + message +
            "</TITLE></HEAD>");
        out.println("<BODY>");
        out.println("<H1>" + reason + "</H1>");
        out.println("<H2>" + message + "</H2>");
        out.println("<HR>");
        out.println("<I>Error accessing " + req.getRequestURI() +
            "</I>");
        out.println("</BODY></HTML>");
    }
}
```

But what if the error page could contain the exception stack trace or the URI of the servlet that truly caused the problem (since it's not always the originally requested URI)? With API 2.2, that wasn't possible. With API 2.3, that information is available with two new attributes:

`javax.servlet.error.exception`
: A `Throwable` object that is the actual exception thrown.

`javax.servlet.error.request_uri`
: A `String` telling the URI of the resource causing problems.

Those attributes let the error page include the stack trace of the exception and the URI of the problem resource. The servlet below has been rewritten to use the new attributes. Note that it fails gracefully if they don't exist, for backward compatibility:

```
import java.io.*;
import javax.servlet.*;
import javax.servlet.http.*;
```

```
public class ErrorDisplay extends HttpServlet {

  public void doGet(HttpServletRequest req, HttpServletResponse res)
                               throws ServletException, IOException {
    res.setContentType("text/html");
    PrintWriter out = res.getWriter();

    String code = null, message = null, type = null, uri = null;
    Object codeObj, messageObj, typeObj;
    Throwable throwable;

    // Retrieve the three possible error attributes, some may be null
    codeObj = req.getAttribute("javax.servlet.error.status_code");
    messageObj = req.getAttribute("javax.servlet.error.message");
    typeObj = req.getAttribute("javax.servlet.error.exception_type");
    throwable = (Throwable)
      req.getAttribute("javax.servlet.error.exception");
    uri = (String)
      req.getAttribute("javax.servlet.error.request_uri");

    if (uri == null) {
      uri = req.getRequestURI(); // in case there's no URI given
    }

    // Convert the attributes to string values
    if (codeObj != null) code = codeObj.toString();
    if (messageObj != null) message = messageObj.toString();
    if (typeObj != null) type = typeObj.toString();

    // The error reason is either the status code or exception type
    String reason = (code != null ? code : type);

    out.println("<HTML>");
    out.println("<HEAD><TITLE>" + reason + ": " + message +
                "</TITLE></HEAD>");
    out.println("<BODY>");
    out.println("<H1>" + reason + "</H1>");
    out.println("<H2>" + message + "</H2>");
    out.println("<PRE>");
    if (throwable != null) {
      throwable.printStackTrace(out);
    }
    out.println("</PRE>");
    out.println("<HR>");
    out.println("<I>Error accessing " + uri + "</I>");
    out.println("</BODY></HTML>");
  }
}
```

New Security Attributes

Servlet API 2.3 also adds two new request attributes that can help a servlet make an informed decision about how to handle secure HTTPS connections. For requests made using HTTPS, the server will provide these new request attributes:

`javax.servlet.request.cipher_suite`
: A `String` representing the cipher suite used by HTTPS, if any.

`javax.servlet.request.key_size`
: An `Integer` representing the bit size of the algorithm, if any.

A servlet can use those attributes to programmatically decide if the connection is secure enough to proceed. An application may reject connections with small bit-sizes or untrusted algorithms. For example, a servlet could use the following method to ensure that its connection uses at least a 128-bit key size:

```
public boolean isAbove128(HttpServletRequest req) {
  Integer size = (Integer)
    req.getAttribute("javax.servlet.request.key_size");

  if (size == null || size.intValue() < 128) {
    return false;
  }
  else {
    return true;
  }
}
```

NOTE The attribute names in the Proposed Final Draft use dashes instead of underscores; however, they're being changed, as shown here before the Final Release, to be more consistent with existing attribute names.

Little Tweaks

A number of small changes also made it into the API 2.3 release. First, the `getAuthType()` method that returns the type of authentication used to identify a client has been defined to return one of the four new static final `String` constants in the `HttpServletRequest` class: `BASIC_AUTH`, `DIGEST_AUTH`, `CLIENT_CERT_AUTH`, and `FORM_AUTH`. This allows simplified code like:

```
if (req.getAuthType() == req.BASIC_AUTH) {
  // handle basic authentication
}
```

Of course, the four constants still have traditional `String` values, so the following code from API 2.2 works too, but is not as fast or as elegant. Notice the reverse `equals()` check to avoid a `NullPointerException` if `getAuthType()` returns `null`:

```
if ("BASIC".equals(req.getAuthType())) {
  // handle basic authentication
}
```

Another change in API 2.3 is that `HttpUtils` has been deprecated. `HttpUtils` has always stood out as an odd collection of static methods—calls that were useful sometimes, but might have been better placed elsewhere. As you may recall, the class contained methods to reconstruct an original URL from a request object and to parse parameter data into a hashtable. API 2.3 moves this functionality into the request object where it more properly belongs, and deprecates `HttpUtils`. The new methods on the request object are:

`StringBuffer req.getRequestURL()`
: Returns a `StringBuffer` containing the original request URL, rebuilt from the request information.

`java.util.Map req.getParameterMap()`
: Returns an immutable `Map` of the request's parameters. The parameter names act as keys and the parameter values act as map values. It has not been decided how parameters with multiple values will be handled; most likely, all values will be returned as a `String[]`. These methods use the new `req.setCharacterEncoding()` method to handle character conversions.

API 2.3 also adds two new methods to `ServletContext` that let you obtain the name of the context and a list of all the resources it holds:

`String context.getServletContextName()`
: Returns the name of the context as declared in the *web.xml* file.

`java.util.Set context.getResourcePaths()`
: Returns all the resource paths available in the context, as an immutable set of `String` objects. Each `String` has a leading slash (`/`) and should be considered relative to the context root.

There is also a new method on the response object to increase programmer control of the response buffer. API 2.2 introduced a `res.reset()` method to reset the response and clear the response body, headers, and status code. API 2.3 adds a `res.resetBuffer()` that clears just the response body:

`void resetBuffer()`
: Clears the response buffer without clearing headers or the status code. If the response has already been committed, it throws an `IllegalStateException`.

And finally, after a lengthy debate by a group of experts, Servlet API 2.3 has clarified once and for all exactly what happens on a `res.sendRedirect("/index.html")` call for a servlet executing within a non-root context. The issue is that Servlet API 2.2 requires an incomplete path like `"/index.html"` to be translated by the servlet container into a complete path, but it does not say how context paths are to be handled. If the servlet making the call is in a context at the path `"/contextpath"`, should the redirect URI translate relative to the container root (`http://server:port/index.html`) or the context root (`http://server:port/contextpath/index.html`)? For maximum portability, it's imperative to define the behavior; after lengthy debate, the experts chose to translate relative to the container root. For those who want context relative, you can prepend the output from `getContextPath()` to your URI.

DTD Clarifications

The Servlet API 2.3 ties up a few loose ends regarding the *web.xml* deployment descriptor behavior. It's now mandated that you trim text values in the *web.xml* file before use. (In standard non-validated XML, all white space is generally preserved.) This rule ensures that the following two entries can be treated identically:

```
<servlet-name>hello<servlet-name>
```

and

```
<servlet-name>
  hello
</servlet-name>
```

The Servlet API 2.3 also allows an `<auth-constraint>` rule, so the special value `"*"` can be used as a `<role-name>` wildcard to allow all roles. This allows you to write a rule like the following that lets all users enter as soon as they've been properly identified as belonging to any role in the web application:

```
<auth-constraint>
  <role-name>*</role-name> <!-- allow all recognized roles -->
</auth-constraint>
```

Finally, it's been clarified that you can use a role name declared by a `<security-role>` rule as a parameter to the `isUserInRole()` method. For example, look at the following snippet of a *web.xml* entry:

```
<servlet>
    <servlet-name>
        secret
    </servlet-name>
    <servlet-class>
        SalaryViewer
    </servlet-class>
```

```
    <security-role-ref>
        <role-name>
            mgr <!-- name used by servlet -->
        </role-name>
        <role-link>
            manager <!-- name used in deployment descriptor -->
        </role-link>
    </security-role-ref>
</servlet>

<!-- ... -->

<security-role>
    <role-name>
        manager
    </role-name>
</security-role>
```

With this, the servlet secret can call either `isUserInRole("mgr")` or `isUserInRole("manager")`; both will give the same behavior. Basically, `security-role-ref` acts to create an alias, but isn't necessary. That is what you'd naturally expect, but the API 2.2 specification could be interpreted as implying that you could only use roles explicitly declared in a <security-role-ref> alias rule. (If that doesn't make sense to you, don't worry about it; just be aware that things are now guaranteed to work as they should.)

Conclusion

The Servlet API 2.3 includes an exciting new filter mechanism, an expanded lifecycle model, and new functionality to support internationalization, error handling, secure connections, and user roles. The specification document has also been tightened to remove ambiguities that could interfere with cross-platform deployment.

A

Servlet API Quick Reference

The `javax.servlet` package is the core of the Servlet API. It includes the basic `Servlet` interface, which all servlets must implement in one form or another, and an abstract `GenericServlet` class for developing basic servlets. It also includes classes for communicating with the host server and client (`ServletRequest` and `ServletResponse`) and communicating with the client (`ServletInputStream` and `ServletOutputStream`). The class hierarchy of the `javax.servlet` package is shown in Figure A-1. Servlets should confine themselves to the classes in this package in situations in which the underlying protocol is unknown.

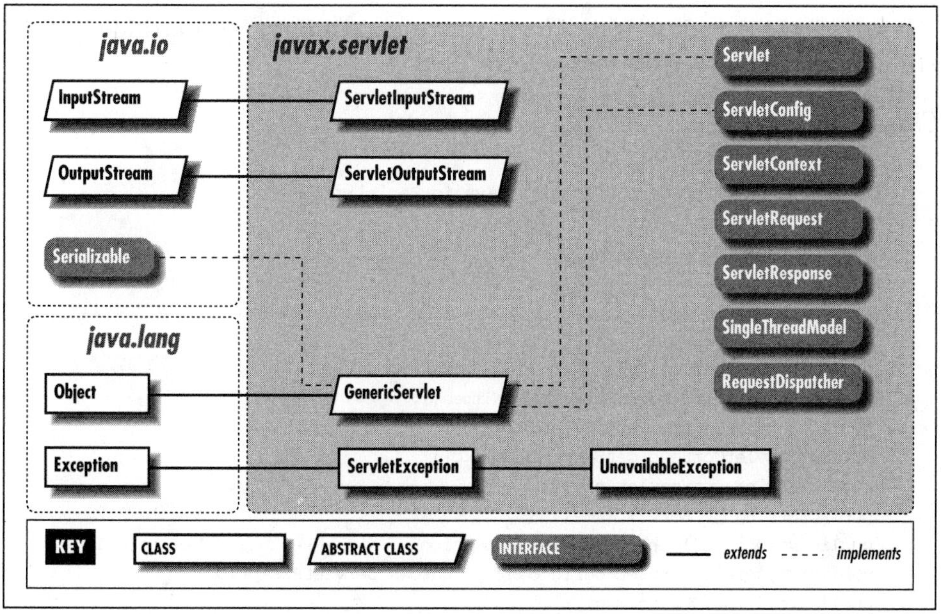

Figure A-1. The java.servlet package

GenericServlet

Synopsis

Class Name: `javax.servlet.GenericServlet`
Superclass: `java.lang.Object`
Immediate Subclasses: `javax.servlet.http.HttpServlet`
Interfaces Implemented: `javax.servlet.Servlet`, `javax.servlet.ServletConfig`, `java.io.Serializable`
Availability: Servlet API 1.0 and later

Description

`GenericServlet` provides a basic implementation of the `Servlet` interface for protocol-independent servlets. As a convenience, it also implements the `ServletConfig` interface. Most servlet developers subclass this class or `HttpServlet`, rather than implement the `Servlet` interface directly.

`GenericServlet` includes basic versions of the `init()` and `destroy()` methods, which perform basic setup and cleanup tasks, such as managing the server's `ServletConfig` object. It's good form for a servlet that overrides one of these methods to call the superclass version of the method. `GenericServlet` also includes `log()` methods that provide easy access to the logging functions from `ServletContext`.

The `service()` method is declared as abstract and must be overridden. Well-written servlets also override `getServletInfo()`.

Class Summary

```
public abstract class GenericServlet
 implements Servlet, ServletConfig, java.io.Serializable {
  // Constructors
  public GenericServlet();

  // Instance Methods
  public void destroy();
  public String getInitParameter(String name);
  public Enumeration getInitParameterNames();
  public ServletConfig getServletConfig();
  public ServletContext getServletContext();
  public String getServletInfo();
  public String getServletName();                          // New in 2.2
  public void init() throws ServletException;              // New in 2.1
  public void init(ServletConfig config) throws ServletException;
  public void log(String msg);
  public void log(String msg, Throwable t);                // New in 2.1
```

```
  public abstract void service(ServletRequest req, ServletResponse res)
    throws ServletException, IOException;
}
```

Constructors

GenericServlet()

```
public GenericServlet()
```

Description

The default `GenericServlet` constructor does no work. Any servlet initialization tasks should be performed in `init()`, rather than in the constructor.

Instance Methods

destroy()

```
public void destroy()
```

Description

Called by the servlet container to indicate to a servlet that the servlet has been taken out of service. This method is called only after all threads within the servlet's service method have exited or after a timeout period has passed. After the servlet container calls this method, the container will not call the service method again on the servlet. The default implementation logs the servlet's destruction using the `log()` method. A servlet can override this method to save its state, free its resources (database connections, threads, file handles, etc.), and so forth.

getInitParameter()

```
public String getInitParameter(String name)
```

Description

Returns the value of the named servlet initialization parameter or `null` if no matching parameter is found. From the `ServletConfig` interface.

getInitParameterNames()

```
public Enumeration getInitParameterNames()
```

Description

Returns all the servlet's init parameter names as an `Enumeration` of `String` objects or an empty `Enumeration` if no parameters exist. From the `ServletConfig` interface.

getServletConfig()

```
public ServletConfig getServletConfig()
```

Description

Returns the servlet's `ServletConfig` object. In practice, this method is rarely called by a `GenericServlet` because all of the `ServletConfig` methods are duplicated internally.

getServletContext()

```
public ServletContext getServletContext()
```

Description

Returns the servlet's `ServletContext` object. From the `ServletConfig` interface.

getServletInfo()

```
public String getServletInfo()
```

Description

Returns a programmer-defined `String` that describes the servlet. A servlet should override this method and provide a customized identity string (e.g., "Al's Message Board Servlet v1.21"), but it is not required.

getServletName()

```
public String getServletName()
```

Description

Returns the name of this servlet instance. The name may be provided via server administration, may be assigned in the web application deployment descriptor, or for an unregistered (and thus unnamed) servlet instance will be the servlet's class name. From the `ServletConfig` interface. This method was introduced in Servlet API 2.2.

init()

```
public void init() throws ServletException;
public void init(ServletConfig config) throws ServletException
```

Description

Called by the servlet container after the servlet is first loaded and before the servlet's `service()` method is called. A servlet can override this method to perform one-time setup, creation of resources, and so on. Servlets written against Servlet API 2.1 or later can implement the no-argument version. Servlets that must be backward compatible with Servlet API 2.0 should implement the version that takes a `ServletConfig` parameter. Do not implement both versions. The default implementation of `init()` logs the servlet's initialization and stores the `ServletConfig` object for use by the methods in the `ServletConfig` interface. A servlet implementing the version that takes a `ServletConfig` parameter must call `super.init(config)` before executing any custom initialization code. Servlets taking advantage of the new no-argument version do not need to worry about this.

log()

```
public void log(String msg)
public void log(String msg, Throwable t)
```

Description

Writes the given message to a servlet log, prepended by the calling servlet's name. The output location is server-specific, usually an event log file.

service()

```
public abstract void service(ServletRequest req, ServletResponse res)
  throws ServletException, IOException
```

Description

Called to handle a single client request. A servlet receives request information via a `ServletRequest` object and sends data back to the client via a `ServletResponse` object. This is the only method that must be overridden when extending `GenericServlet`.

RequestDispatcher

Synopsis

Interface Name:	`javax.servlet.RequestDispatcher`
Superinterface:	None
Immediate Subinterfaces:	None
Implemented By:	None
Availability:	Servlet API 2.1 and later

Description

The interface for an object that can internally dispatch requests to any resource (such as a servlet, HTML file, or JSP file) on the server. The servlet container creates the `RequestDispatcher` object that is then used as a wrapper around a server resource located at a particular path or given by a particular name. This interface is intended to wrap servlets and JSP pages, but a servlet container can create `RequestDispatcher` objects to wrap any type of resource. The dispatching can be used to forward a request to the resource or to include the content of that resource into the current response. This class was introduced in Servlet API 2.1.

Interface Declaration

```
public interface RequestDispatcher {
  // Methods
  public abstract void forward(ServletRequest req, ServletResponse res)
    throws ServletException, java.io.IOException          // New in 2.1
  public abstract void include(ServletRequest req, ServletResponse res)
    throws ServletException, java.io.IOException          // New in 2.1
}
```

Methods

forward()

```
public abstract void forward(ServletRequest req, ServletResponse res)
  throws ServletException, IOException, IllegalStateException
```

Description

Forwards a request from a servlet to another resource on the server. This method allows one servlet to do preliminary processing of a request and another resource to generate the response. For a `RequestDispatcher` obtained via `getRequestDispatcher()`, the `ServletRequest` object has its path elements and parameters adjusted to match the path of the target resource. This method should be called before the response has been committed to the client; if the response already has been committed, this method throws an `IllegalStateException`. Uncommitted output in the response buffer is automatically cleared before the forward. The request and response parameters must be the same objects as were passed to the calling servlet's service method. This method was introduced in Servlet API 2.1.

include()

```
public abstract void include(ServletRequest req, ServletResponse res)
  throws ServletException, IOException
```

Description

Includes the content of a resource into the current response. The path elements and parameters of the `ServletRequest` remain unchanged from the caller's; if the included resource requires access to its own path elements and parameters, it may retrieve them using the server-assigned request attributes `javax.servlet.include.request_uri`, `javax.servlet.include.context_path`, `javax.servlet.include.servlet_path`, `javax.servlet.include.path_info`, and `javax.servlet.include.query_string`. The included servlet cannot change the response status code or set headers; any attempt to make a change is ignored. The request and response parameters must be the same objects as were passed to the calling servlet's service method. This method was introduced in Servlet API 2.1.

Servlet

Synopsis

Interface Name: `javax.servlet.Servlet`
Superinterface: None

Immediate Subinterfaces: None
Implemented By: `javax.servlet.GenericServlet`
Availability: Servlet API 1.0 and later

Description

All servlets implement the `Servlet` interface, either directly or by subclassing the `GenericServlet` or `HttpServlet` class. Most servlet developers find it easier to subclass one of the two existing servlet classes than to implement this interface directly. The interface declares the basic servlet functionality—initializing a servlet, handling a client request, and destroying a servlet.

Interface Declaration

```
public interface Servlet {
  // Methods
  public abstract void destroy();
  public abstract ServletConfig getServletConfig();
  public abstract String getServletInfo();
  public abstract void init(ServletConfig config) throws ServletException;
  public abstract void service(ServletRequest req, ServletResponse res)
    throws ServletException, IOException;
}
```

Methods

`destroy()`

```
public abstract void destroy()
```

Description

Called by the servlet container to indicate to a servlet that the servlet has been taken out of service. See the full description under `GenericServlet`.

`getServletConfig()`

```
public abstract ServletConfig getServletConfig()
```

Description

Returns the `ServletConfig` object saved by the `init()` method.

`getServletInfo()`

```
public abstract String getServletInfo()
```

Description

Returns a programmer-defined `String` that describes the servlet.

`init()`

```
public abstract void init(ServletConfig config) throws ServletException
```

Description

Called by the servlet container after the servlet is first loaded and before the servlet's `service()` method is called. See the full description under `GenericServlet`.

service()

```
public abstract void service(ServletRequest req, ServletResponse res)
  throws ServletException, IOException
```

Description

Called to handle a single client request. A servlet receives request information via the `ServletRequest` object and sends data back to the client via the `ServletResponse` object.

ServletConfig

Synopsis

Interface Name:	`javax.servlet.ServletConfig`
Superinterface:	None
Immediate Subinterfaces:	None
Implemented By:	`javax.servlet.GenericServlet`
Availability:	Servlet API 1.0 and later

Description

Servlet containers use `ServletConfig` objects to pass initialization and context information to servlets. The initialization information generally consists of a series of initialization parameters (init parameters) and a `ServletContext` object, which provides information about the server environment. A servlet can implement `ServletConfig` to allow easy access to init parameters and context information, as `GenericServlet` does.

Interface Declaration

```
public interface ServletConfig {
  // Methods
  public abstract String getInitParameter(String name);
  public abstract Enumeration getInitParameterNames();
  public abstract ServletContext getServletContext();
  public abstract String getServletName();                // New in 2.2
}
```

Methods

`getInitParameter()`

```
public abstract String getInitParameter(String name)
```

Description

Returns the value of the named servlet initialization parameter or `null` if no matching parameter is found.

`getInitParameterNames()`

```
public abstract Enumeration getInitParameterNames()
```

Description

Returns the names of all the servlet's initialization parameters as an `Enumeration` of `String` objects or an empty `Enumeration` if no parameters exist.

`getServletContext()`

```
public abstract ServletContext getServletContext()
```

Description

Returns the `ServletContext` object for this servlet, allowing interaction with the servlet container.

`getServletName()`

```
public String getServletName()
```

Description

Returns the name of this servlet instance. The name may be provided via server administration, may be assigned in the web application deployment descriptor, or for an unregistered (and thus unnamed) servlet instance will be the servlet's class name. This method was introduced in Servlet API 2.2.

ServletContext

Synopsis

Interface Name:	`javax.servlet.ServletContext`
Superinterface:	None
Immediate Subinterfaces:	None
Implemented By:	None
Availability:	Servlet API 1.0 and later

Description

The `ServletContext` interface defines a set of methods that can be used to communicate with the servlet container in a non-request-specific manner. This includes finding path information, accessing other servlets running on the server, and writing to the server log file. Each web application has a different servlet context.

Interface Declaration

```
public interface ServletContext {
  // Methods
  public abstract Object getAttribute(String name);
  public abstract Enumeration getAttributeNames();           // New in 2.1
  public abstract ServletContext getContext(String uripath); // New in 2.1
  public abstract String getInitParameter(String name);      // New in 2.2
  public abstract Enumeration getInitParameterNames();       // New in 2.2
  public abstract int getMajorVersion();                     // New in 2.1
  public abstract String getMimeType(String file);
  public abstract int getMinorVersion();                     // New in 2.1
  public abstract
    RequestDispatcher getNamedDispatcher(String name);       // New in 2.2
  public abstract String getRealPath(String path);
  public abstract URL getResource(String path)               // New in 2.1
    throws MalformedURLException;
  public abstract InputStream getResourceAsStream(String path); // New in 2.1
  public abstract String getServerInfo();
  public abstract Servlet getServlet(String name)            // Deprecated
    throws ServletException;
  public abstract Enumeration getServletNames();             // Deprecated
  public abstract Enumeration getServlets();                 // Deprecated
  public abstract void log(Exception exception, String msg); // Deprecated
  public abstract void log(String msg);
  public abstract void log(String msg, Throwable t);         // New in 2.1
  public abstract void removeAttribute(String name);         // New in 2.1
  public abstract void setAttribute(String name, Object o);  // New in 2.1
}
```

Methods

getAttribute()

```
public abstract Object getAttribute(String name)
```

Description

Returns the value of the named context attribute as an `Object` or `null` if the attribute does not exist. Server-specific attributes may be autoset by the servlet container to provide servlets with information above and beyond that provided for by the base Servlet API. Attributes can also be set programmatically by servlets as a way of sharing information throughout the web application represented by this context. Attribute names should follow the same convention as package names. The package names `java.*` and `javax.*` are reserved for use by the Java Software division of Sun Microsystems (formerly known as JavaSoft), and `com.sun.*` is reserved for use by Sun Microsystems. See your server's documentation for a list of its built-in attributes. Remember that servlets relying on server-specific attributes are not portable.

getAttributeNames()

```
public abstract Enumeration getAttributeNames()
```

Description

Returns the names of all the current context attributes as an `Enumeration` of `String` objects. It returns an empty `Enumeration` if the context has no attributes. This method was introduced in Servlet API 2.1.

getContext()

```
public abstract ServletContext getContext(String uripath)
```

Description

Returns the `ServletContext` instance assigned to the specified URI path. The given path must be absolute (beginning with `/`) and is interpreted based on the server's root. This method allows a servlet to gain access to a context outside its own, letting it view data inside that context or obtain a `RequestDispatcher` to resources within that context. In a security-conscious or distributed environment, the servlet container may return `null` for any and all paths. This method was introduced in Servlet API 2.1.

getInitParameter()

```
public abstract String getInitParameter(String name)
```

Description

Returns the value of the named context initialization parameter or `null` if no matching parameter is found. This method can make available configuration information useful to an entire web application. For example, it can provide a webmaster's email address or the name of a system that holds critical data. Context init parameters are assigned in the web application deployment descriptor. This method was introduced in Servlet API 2.2.

getInitParameterNames()

```
public abstract Enumeration getInitParameterNames()
```

Description

Returns the names of all the init parameters for this context as an `Enumeration` of `String` objects. It returns an empty `Enumeration` if the context has no attributes. Context init parameters are assigned in the web application deployment descriptor. This method was introduced in Servlet API 2.2.

getMajorVersion()

```
public abstract int getMajorVersion()
```

Description

Returns the major version of the Servlet API that this container supports. For example, a container implementing 2.1 returns 2. This method was introduced in Servlet API 2.1.

getMimeType()

```
public abstract String getMimeType(String file)
```

Description

Returns the MIME type of the given file or `null` if it is not known. Some implementations return `text/plain` if the specified file does not exist. Common MIME types are `text/html`, `text/plain`, `image/gif`, and `image/jpeg`.

getMinorVersion()

```
public abstract int getMinorVersion()
```

Description

Returns the minor version of the Servlet API that this container supports. For example, a container implementing 2.1 returns 1. This method was introduced in Servlet API 2.1.

getNamedDispatcher()

```
public abstract RequestDispatcher getNamedDispatcher(String name)
```

Description

Returns a `RequestDispatcher` to dispatch to a resource given by name, instead of by path. This allows dispatching to resources that are not necessarily publicly available. Servlets (and JSP pages also) may be given names via server administration or via the web application deployment descriptor. The method returns `null` if the context cannot return a dispatcher for any reason. This method was introduced in Servlet API 2.2.

getRealPath()

```
public abstract String getRealPath(String path)
```

Description

Returns the real filesystem path of any given "virtual path" or `null` if the translation cannot be performed (such as when the file is on a remote filesystem or is found only inside a *.war* archive). If the given path is `/`, the method returns the document root for the context. If the given path is the same as the one returned by `getPathInfo()`, the method returns the same real path as would be returned by `getPathTranslated()`. There is no CGI counterpart.

getResource()

`public abstract URL getResource(String path)`

Description

Returns a URL to the resource mapped to the specified path. The path must begin with a `/`, and is interpreted as relative to the context root. The method may return `null` if no resource could be associated with the path. This method allows the servlet container to make a resource available to servlets from any source. Resources can be located on a local or remote filesystem, in a database, or in a *.war* file. Some containers may also allow writing to the URL object using the methods of the URL class. This method should be used when not all resources are local files—such as in a distributed environment (where a servlet container may be on a different host than the resource) or when content is coming from a *.war* file (where the files cannot be accessed directly). The resource content is returned raw, so be aware that requesting a *.jsp* page returns the JSP source code. Use a `RequestDispatcher` instead to include results of a JSP execution. This method has a different purpose than `Class.getResource()`, which looks up resources based on a class loader. This method does not use class loaders. This method was introduced in Servlet API 2.1.

getResourceAsStream()

`public abstract InputStream getResourceAsStream(String path)`

Description

Returns an `InputStream` to read the content of the resource mapped to the specified path. The path must begin with a `/`, and is interpreted as relative to the context root. The method may return `null` if no resource could be associated with the path. Using this method is often more convenient than using `getResource()`; however, metainformation about the resource such as content length and content type that is available via `getResource()` is lost when using this method. This method was introduced in Servlet API 2.1.

getServerInfo()

`public abstract String getServerInfo()`

Description

Returns the name and version of the server software, separated by a forward slash (`/`). The value is the same as the CGI variable `SERVER_SOFTWARE`.

getServlet()

```
public abstract Servlet getServlet(String name) throws ServletException
```

Description

Returns `null` in Servlet API 2.1 and later. Previously returned the loaded servlet matching the given name or `null` if the servlet was not found. This method has been deprecated and defined to return `null` as of Servlet API 2.1 because direct access to another servlet instance opens up too many opportunities for error. The reasoning goes that servlets may be destroyed by the servlet container at any time, so no object but the container should hold a direct reference to a servlet. Also, on a server that supports load balancing where servlets are distributed across a number of servers, it may be impossible even to return a local servlet reference. Servlets instead should collaborate by using shared `ServletContext` attributes. Technically, defining this method to return `null` does not break backward compatibility because the servlet container always had the option of returning `null` on this method for any reason.

getServletNames()

```
public abstract Enumeration getServletNames()
```

Description

Returns an empty `Enumeration` in Servlet API 2.1 and later. Previously returned an `Enumeration` of the names of the servlet objects loaded in this context. This method has been deprecated and defined to return an empty `Enumeration` as of Servlet API 2.1 for the same reasons `getServlet()` was deprecated and defined to return `null`. This method was introduced in Servlet API 2.0.

getServlets()

```
public abstract Enumeration getServlets() throws ServletException
```

Description

Returns an empty `Enumeration` in Servlet API 2.1 and later. Previously returned an `Enumeration` of the `Servlet` objects loaded in this context. This method was deprecated in Servlet API 2.0 in favor of `getServletNames()`. It was defined to return an empty `Enumeration` in Servlet API 2.1 following the behavior of `getServletNames()`.

log()

```
public abstract void log(String msg)
```

Description

Writes the given message to a servlet log. The output location is server-specific, usually an event log file.

```
public abstract void log(String msg, Throwable t)
```

Description

Writes the given message and the stack trace of the `Throwable` to a servlet log. The output location is server-specific, usually an event log file. This method was introduced in Servlet API 2.1.

```
public abstract void log(Exception exception, String msg)
```

Description

Writes the given message and the stack trace of the `Exception` to a servlet log. The output location is server-specific. Notice the nonstandard placement of the optional `Exception` parameter as the first parameter instead of the last. This method was deprecated in Servlet API 2.1 in favor of `log(String msg, Throwable t)`, a method which follows the standard parameter ordering and also allows any `Throwable` to be logged, not just an `Exception`. This method was introduced in Servlet API 2.0.

removeAttribute()

```
public abstract void removeAttribute(String name)
```

Description

Removes the attribute with the given name from the context. Attributes should be removed when no longer needed to eliminate memory bloat. This method was introduced in Servlet API 2.1.

setAttribute()

```
public abstract void setAttribute(String name, Object o)
```

Description

Binds an object under a given name in this servlet context. Any existing binding with the same name is replaced. This method was introduced in Servlet API 2.1.

ServletException

Synopsis

Class Name:	`javax.servlet.ServletException`
Superclass:	`java.lang.Exception`
Immediate Subclasses:	`javax.servlet.UnavailableException`
Interfaces Implemented:	None
Availability:	Servlet API 1.0 and later

Description

A generic exception thrown by servlets encountering difficulties.

Class Summary

```
public class ServletException extends java.lang.Exception {
  // Constructors
  public ServletException();                                      // New in 2.0
  public ServletException(String msg);
  public ServletException(String msg, Throwable rootCause);   // New in 2.1
  public ServletException(Throwable rootCause);                   // New in 2.1
  public Throwable getRootCause();                                // New in 2.1
}
```

Constructors

public ServletException()

```
public ServletException()
public ServletException(String msg)
public ServletException(String msg, Throwable rootCause)
public ServletException(Throwable rootCause)
```

Description

Constructs a new `ServletException`, with an optional descriptive message and an optional "root cause" for the exception. If a message is specified, it can be retrieved by calling `getMessage()`; if a root cause is specified, it can be retrieved by calling `getRootCause()`. The messages and root cause are usually included in server logs and user error messages. The constructor versions taking a root cause were introduced in Servlet API 2.1.

Instance Methods

getRootCause()

```
public Throwable getRootCause()
```

Description

Returns the `Throwable` object that caused the servlet exception or `null` if there was no root cause. This method was introduced in Servlet API 2.1.

ServletInputStream

Synopsis

Class Name:	`javax.servlet.ServletInputStream`
Superclass:	`java.io.InputStream`
Immediate Subclasses:	None
Interfaces Implemented:	None
Availability:	Servlet API 1.0 and later

Description

Provides an input stream for reading binary data from a client request, including a `readLine()` method for reading data one line at a time. A `ServletInputStream` is returned by the `getInputStream()` method of `ServletRequest`. For HTTP servlets the `ServletInputStream` provides access to the submitted POST data.

Class Summary

```
public abstract class ServletInputStream extends java.io.InputStream {
  // Constructors
  protected ServletInputStream();

  // Instance methods
  public int readLine(byte b[], int off, int len) throws IOException;
}
```

Constructors

ServletInputStream()

```
protected ServletInputStream()
```

Description

The default constructor does nothing. A servlet should never construct its own `ServletInputStream`.

Instance Methods

readLine()

```
public int readLine(byte b[], int off, int len) throws IOException
```

Description

Reads bytes from the input stream into the byte array `b`, starting at an offset in the array given by `off`. It stops reading when it encounters an `\n` or it has read `len` number of bytes. The ending `\n` character is read into the buffer as well. Returns the number of bytes read or `-1` if the end of the stream is reached. The version of this class provided with Servlet API 2.0 had a bug where the `len` parameter was ignored, causing an `ArrayIndexOutOfBoundsException` when reading a line longer than the buffer. This was fixed in Servlet API 2.1.

ServletOutputStream

Synopsis

Class Name:	`javax.servlet.ServletOutputStream`
Superclass:	`java.io.OutputStream`

Immediate Subclasses:	None
Interfaces Implemented:	None
Availability:	Servlet API 1.0 and later

Description

Provides an output stream for sending binary data back to a client. A servlet obtains a `ServletOutputStream` object from the `getOutputStream()` method of `ServletResponse`. Although it includes a range of `print()` and `println()` methods for sending text or HTML, the `ServletOutputStream` has been superseded by `PrintWriter`. It should be used only for sending binary data. If you subclass `ServletOutputStream`, you must provide an implementation of the `write(int)` method.

Class Summary

```
public abstract class ServletOutputStream extends java.io.OutputStream {
  // Constructors
  protected ServletOutputStream();

  // Instance methods
  public void print(boolean b) throws IOException;
  public void print(char c) throws IOException;
  public void print(double d) throws IOException;
  public void print(float f) throws IOException;
  public void print(int i) throws IOException;
  public void print(long l) throws IOException;
  public void print(String s) throws IOException;
  public void println() throws IOException;
  public void println(boolean b) throws IOException;
  public void println(char c) throws IOException;
  public void println(double d) throws IOException;
  public void println(float f) throws IOException;
  public void println(int i) throws IOException;
  public void println(long l) throws IOException;
  public void println(String s) throws IOException;
}
```

Constructors

ServletOutputStream()

```
protected ServletOutputStream()
```

Description

The default constructor does nothing.

Instance Methods

print()

```
public void print(boolean b) throws IOException
public void print(char c) throws IOException
public void print(double d) throws IOException
public void print(float f) throws IOException
public void print(int i) throws IOException
public void print(long l) throws IOException
public void print(String s) throws IOException
```

Description

Writes the given data to the client, without a trailing carriage return/line feed (CRLF).

println()

```
public void println() throws IOException
public void println(boolean b) throws IOException
public void println(char c) throws IOException
public void println(double d) throws IOException
public void println(float f) throws IOException
public void println(int i) throws IOException
public void println(long l) throws IOException
public void println(String s) throws IOException
```

Description

Writes the given data to the client, with a trailing CRLF. The method with no parameters simply writes a CRLF.

ServletRequest

Synopsis

Interface Name:	`javax.servlet.ServletRequest`
Superinterface:	None
Immediate Subinterfaces:	`javax.servlet.http.HttpServletRequest`
Implemented By:	None
Availability:	Servlet API 1.0 and later

Description

A `ServletRequest` object encapsulates information about a single client request, including request parameters, request attributes, client locales, and an input stream for reading binary data from the request body. `ServletRequest` can be subclassed to provide additional protocol-specific information. `HttpServletRequest`, for instance, includes methods to manipulate HTTP headers.

Interface Declaration

```
public interface ServletRequest {
  // Methods
  public abstract Object getAttribute(String name);
  public abstract Enumeration getAttributeNames();              // New in 2.1
  public abstract String getCharacterEncoding();                // New in 2.0
  public abstract int getContentLength();
  public abstract String getContentType();
  public abstract ServletInputStream getInputStream() throws IOException;
  public abstract Locale getLocale();                           // New in 2.2
  public abstract Enumeration getLocales();                     // New in 2.2
  public abstract String getParameter(String name);
  public abstract Enumeration getParameterNames();
  public abstract String[] getParameterValues(String name);
  public abstract String getProtocol();
  public abstract BufferedReader getReader() throws IOException;// New in 2.0
  public abstract String getRealPath(String path);              // Deprecated
  public abstract String getRemoteAddr();
  public abstract String getRemoteHost();
  public abstract RequestDispatcher getRequestDispatcher(String path); // New
  public abstract String getScheme();
  public abstract String getServerName();
  public abstract int getServerPort();
  public abstract boolean isSecure();                           // New in 2.2
  public abstract void removeAttribute(String name);            // New in 2.2
  public abstract void setAttribute(String name, Object o);     // New in 2.1
}
```

Methods

getAttribute()

```
public abstract Object getAttribute(String name)
```

Description

Returns the value of the named request attribute as an `Object` or `null` if the attribute does not exist. Server-specific request attributes may be autoset by the servlet container to provide servlets with information above and beyond that provided for by the base Servlet API. Attributes can also be set programmatically by servlets as a way of passing information from one servlet to another when using a `RequestDispatcher`. Attribute names should follow the same convention as package names. The package names `java.*` and `javax.*` are reserved for use by the Java Software division of Sun Microsystems (formerly known as JavaSoft), and `com.sun.*` is reserved for use by Sun Microsystems. See your server's documentation for a list of its built-in attributes. Remember that servlets relying on server-specific attributes are not portable.

getAttributeNames()

```
public abstract Enumeration getAttributeNames()
```

Description

Returns the names of all the current request attributes as an `Enumeration` of `String` objects. It returns an empty `Enumeration` if the request has no attributes. This method was introduced in Servlet API 2.1.

getCharacterEncoding()

```
public abstract String getCharacterEncoding()
```

Description

Returns the charset encoding for the servlet's input stream or `null` if not known. This method was introduced in Servlet API 2.0.

getContentLength()

```
public abstract int getContentLength()
```

Description

Returns the length, in bytes, of the content being sent via the input stream or `-1` if the length is not known (such as when there is no data). Equivalent to the CGI variable `CONTENT_LENGTH`.

getContentType()

```
public abstract String getContentType()
```

Description

Returns the media type of the content being sent via the input stream or `null` if the type is not known or there is no data. The same as the CGI variable `CONTENT_TYPE`.

getInputStream()

```
public abstract ServletInputStream getInputStream()
  throws IOException, IllegalStateException
```

Description

Retrieves the input stream as a `ServletInputStream` object. `ServletInputStream` is a direct subclass of `InputStream` and can be treated identically to a normal `InputStream`, with the added ability to efficiently read input a line at a time into an array of bytes. This method should be used for reading binary input. It throws an `IllegalStateException` if `getReader()` has been called before on the request. The `IllegalStateException` does not need to be explicitly caught.

getLocale()

```
public abstract Locale getLocale()
```

Description

Returns the client's preferred `Locale`, as extracted from the client's `Accept-Language` request header. If the client request does not provide an `Accept-Language` header, this method returns the default locale for the server. Use the `com.oreilly.servlet.LocaleNegotiator` class for more robust locale detection. This method was introduced in Servlet API 2.2.

getLocales()

```
public abstract Enumeration getLocales()
```

Description

Returns an `Enumeration` of `Locale` objects indicating the locales that are acceptable to the client based on the `Accept-Language` header, from most preferred to least preferred. If the client request doesn't provide an `Accept-Language` header, this method returns an `Enumeration` containing one `Locale`, the default locale for the server. Use the `com.oreilly.servlet.LocaleNegotiator` class for more robust locale detection. This method was introduced in Servlet API 2.2.

getParameter()

```
public abstract String getParameter(String name)
```

Description

Returns the value of the named parameter as a `String`. Returns `null` if the parameter does not exist or an empty string if the parameter exists but has no value. The value is guaranteed to be in its normal, decoded form. If the parameter has multiple values, use the `getParameterValues()` method to retrieve an array of values. If this method is called on a parameter with multiple values, the value returned is the same as the first element in the array returned by `getParameterValues()`. If the parameter information came in as encoded POST data, it may not be available if the POST data has already been manually read using the `getReader()` or `getInputStream()` methods. This method was deprecated momentarily in favor of `getParameterValues()`, but thanks to an overwhelming flood of support from the developer community, it was restored in Servlet API 2.0.

getParameterNames()

```
public abstract Enumeration getParameterNames()
```

Description

Returns all the parameter names as an `Enumeration` of `String` objects. It returns an empty `Enumeration` if the servlet has no parameters.

getParameterValues()

```
public abstract String[] getParameterValues(String name)
```

Description

Returns all the values of the named parameter as an array of `String` objects or `null` if the parameter does not exist. A single value is returned in an array of length 1.

getProtocol()

```
public abstract String getProtocol()
```

Description

Returns the name and version of the protocol used by the request as a `String` in the form *`protocol/major-version.minor-version`*. Equivalent to the CGI variable SERVER_PROTOCOL.

getReader()

```
public abstract BufferedReader getReader()
  throws IOException, IllegalStateException
```

Description

This method retrieves the input stream as a `BufferedReader` object, which should be used for reading character-based input, since the reader translates charsets as appropriate. This method throws an `IllegalStateException` if `getInputStream()` has been called before on this same request. It throws an `UnsupportedEncodingException` if the character encoding of the input is unsupported or unknown. This method was introduced in Servlet API 2.0.

getRealPath()

```
public abstract String getRealPath(String path)
```

Description

Returns the real filesystem path of any given "virtual path" or `null` if the translation cannot be performed. If the given path is / it returns the document root for the server. If the given path is the same as the one returned by `getPathInfo()`, it returns the same real path as would be returned by `getPathTranslated()`. There is no CGI counterpart. This method has been deprecated as of Servlet API 2.1 in favor of the `getRealPath()` method in `ServletContext`.

getRemoteAddr()

```
public abstract String getRemoteAddr()
```

Description

Returns the IP address of the client machine as a `String`. This information comes from the socket connecting the server to the client, so the remote address may be that of a proxy server. It is the same as the CGI variable `REMOTE_ADDR`.

`getRemoteHost()`

```
public abstract String getRemoteHost()
```

Description

Returns the name of the client host. This comes from the socket connecting the server to the client and may be the name of a proxy server. It is the same as the CGI variable `REMOTE_HOST`.

`getRequestDispatcher()`

```
public abstract RequestDispatcher getRequestDispatcher(String path)
```

Description

Returns a `RequestDispatcher` capable of dispatching the request to the given path. A `RequestDispatcher` can be used to forward a request to the resource or to include the content of that resource into the current response. The resource can be dynamic or static. The pathname specified may be relative, although it cannot extend outside the current servlet context. If the path begins with a `/`, it is interpreted as relative to the current context root. This method returns `null` if the servlet container cannot return a `RequestDispatcher` for any reason. The difference between this method and the `getRequestDispatcher()` method in `ServletContext` is that this method can take a relative path. This method was introduced in Servlet API 2.2.

`getScheme()`

```
public abstract String getScheme()
```

Description

This method returns the scheme used to make this request. Examples include `http`, `https`, and `ftp`, as well as the newer Java-specific schemes `jdbc` and `rmi`.

`getServerName()`

```
public abstract String getServerName()
```

Description

Returns the name of the server that received the request. It is an attribute of the `ServletRequest` because it can change for different requests depending on how the client refers to the server. Similar to the CGI variable `SERVER_NAME`.

`getServerPort()`

```
public abstract int getServerPort()
```

Description

Returns the port number on which this request was received. The same as the CGI variable `SERVER_PORT`.

`isSecure()`

```
public abstract boolean isSecure()
```

Description

Returns whether this request was made using a secure channel, such as HTTPS. This method was introduced in Servlet API 2.2.

`removeAttribute()`

```
public abstract void removeAttribute(String name)
```

Description

Removes the attribute with the given name from the request. Server-specific attributes generally cannot be removed. This method was introduced in Servlet API 2.2.

`setAttribute()`

```
public abstract void setAttribute(String name, Object o)
```

Description

Binds an object under a given name in this request. Any existing binding with the same name is replaced. Request attributes most often are set as a way of passing information from one servlet to another when using a `RequestDispatcher`. Attribute names should follow the same convention as package names. The package names `java.*` and `javax.*` are reserved for use by the Java Software division of Sun Microsystems (formerly known as JavaSoft), and `com.sun.*` is reserved for use by Sun Microsystems. This method was introduced in Servlet API 2.1.

ServletResponse

Synopsis

Interface Name:	`javax.servlet.ServletResponse`
Superinterface:	None
Immediate Subinterfaces:	`javax.servlet.http.HttpServletResponse`
Interfaces Implemented:	None
Availability:	Servlet API 1.0 and later

Description

Servlets use `ServletResponse` objects to send MIME-encoded data back to the client. To send binary data, use the `ServletOutputStream` returned by `getOutputStream()`. In order to send character data, use the `PrintWriter` returned by `getWriter()`. You can explicitly set the output's MIME type using the `setContentType()` method and can set the response locale using the `setLocale()` method. Make these calls before calling `getWriter()`, as `getWriter()` consults the content type and locale to determine which charset to use. Consult RFC 2045 at *http:/www.ietf.org/rfc/rfc2045.txt* for more information on MIME.

Interface Declaration

```
public interface ServletResponse {
  // Methods
  public abstract void flushBuffer() throws IOException;       // New in 2.2
  public abstract int getBufferSize();                         // New in 2.2
  public abstract String getCharacterEncoding();               // New in 2.0
  public abstract Locale getLocale();                          // New in 2.2
  public abstract ServletOutputStream getOutputStream()
    throws IOException, IllegalStateException;
  public abstract PrintWriter getWriter()                      // New in 2.0
    throws IOException, IllegalStateException;
  public abstract boolean isCommitted();                       // New in 2.2
  public abstract void reset() throws IllegalStateException;   // New in 2.2
  public abstract void setBufferSize(int size)                 // New in 2.2
    throws IllegalStateException;
  public abstract void setContentLength(int len);
  public abstract void setContentType(String type);
  public abstract void setLocale(Locale loc);                  // New in 2.2
}
```

Methods

flushBuffer()

```
public abstract void flushBuffer() throws IOException
```

Description

Forces any content in the buffer to be written to the client. Calling this method automatically commits the response, meaning the status code and headers will be written and a `reset()` will no longer be possible. This method was introduced in Servlet API 2.2.

getBufferSize()

```
public abstract int getBufferSize()
```

Description

Returns an int indicating how large the current buffer actually is or 0 in the unlikely event no buffering is used. This method was introduced in Servlet API 2.2.

getCharacterEncoding()

```
public abstract String getCharacterEncoding()
```

Description

Returns the charset encoding used for this MIME body. This is the charset specified by the assigned content type or ISO-8859-1 if no charset has been specified. This method was introduced in Servlet API 2.0.

getLocale()

```
public abstract Locale getLocale()
```

Description

Returns the Locale currently assigned to the response. This method was introduced in Servlet API 2.2.

getOutputStream()

```
public abstract ServletOutputStream getOutputStream()
  throws IOException, IllegalStateException
```

Description

Returns a ServletOutputStream for writing binary (byte-at-a-time) response data. No encoding is performed. Throws an IllegalStateException if getWriter() has already been called on this response.

getWriter()

```
public abstract PrintWriter getWriter() throws IOException
```

Description

Returns a PrintWriter for writing character-based response data. The writer encodes the characters according to whatever charset is given in the content type. If no charset is specified in the content type, as is generally the case, the writer uses the ISO-8859-1 (Latin-1) encoding appropriate for Western European languages. Throws an IllegalStateException if getOutputStream() has already been called on this response and an UnsupportedEncodingException if the encoding of the output stream is unsupported or unknown. This was introduced in Servlet API 2.0.

isCommitted()

```
public abstract boolean isCommitted()
```

Description

Returns a `boolean` indicating whether any part of the response has actually been sent. If this method returns `true`, it's too late to change the status code and headers. This method was introduced in Servlet API 2.2.

`reset()`

```
public abstract void reset() throws IllegalStateException
```

Description

Clears the response buffer as well as the currently assigned status code and response headers. This method must be called before the response has been committed, otherwise it throws an `IllegalStateException`. `reset()` is automatically called by the methods `sendError()` and `sendRedirect()`. This method was introduced in Servlet API 2.2.

`setBufferSize()`

```
public abstract void setBufferSize(int size) throws IllegalStateException
```

Description

Tells the server the minimum response buffer size, in bytes, that the servlet will accept. The server may provide a larger buffer than requested—to keep buffers in 8K blocks, for example, to facilitate reuse. A larger buffer allows more content to be written before anything is actually sent, thus providing the servlet with more time to set appropriate status codes and headers. A smaller buffer decreases server memory load and allows the client to start receiving data more quickly. This method must be called before any response body content is written; if content has been written, this method throws an `IllegalStateException`. This method was introduced in Servlet API 2.2.

`setContentLength()`

```
public abstract void setContentLength(int len)
```

Description

Sets the length of the content being returned by the server. In HTTP servlets, it sets the HTTP `Content-Length` header. HTTP servlets use this method to enable persistent connections and help client progress monitors. Its use is optional. If the response content fits entirely within the assigned response buffer size, the server can automatically set the content length.

`setContentType()`

```
public abstract void setContentType(String type)
```

Description

This method sets the content type of the response to be the specified type. In HTTP servlets, it sets the `Content-Type` HTTP header.

setLocale()

```
public abstract void setLocale(Locale loc)
```

Description

Sets the locale of the response. The server modifies the `Content-Language` and `Content-Type` headers as appropriate for the given locale. This method should be called after setting the `Content-Type` and before calling `getWriter()`. By default, the response locale is the default locale for the server. This method was introduced in Servlet API 2.2.

SingleThreadModel

Synopsis

Interface Name:	`javax.servlet.SingleThreadModel`
Superinterface:	None
Immediate Subinterfaces:	None
Implemented By:	None
Availability:	Servlet API 2.0 and later

Description

`SingleThreadModel` is a tag interface with no methods. If a servlet implements this interface, the servlet container ensures that each instance of the servlet handles only one service request at a time. For example, a servlet container may implement this functionality by maintaining a pool of servlet instances and dispatching incoming requests to free servlets within the pool. Using `SingleThreadModel` makes the servlet itself thread safe; however, using this interface does not prevent synchronization problems that result from servlets accessing shared resources such as static class variables or variables not local to the servlet. There are very few situations in which this interface is useful.

Interface Declaration

```
public interface SingleThreadModel {
}
```

UnavailableException

Synopsis

Class Name:	`javax.servlet.UnavailableException`
Superclass:	`javax.servlet.ServletException`

Immediate Subclasses:	None
Interfaces Implemented:	None
Availability:	Servlet API 1.0 and later

Description

A servlet can throw an `UnavailableException` at any time to indicate that it is not available to service client requests. There are two types of unavailability: permanent (where the problem will not correct itself and administrative action needs to be taken) and temporary (where the problem will likely correct itself after some length of time). To mark a servlet as temporarily unavailable, specify a duration (in seconds) when constructing the exception. Well-written servlet containers will use the duration to provide better error messages to the client. Servlet implementations are allowed to treat temporary unavailability as permanent unavailability.

Class Summary

```
public class UnavailableException extends ServletException {
  // Constructors
  public UnavailableException(int seconds, Servlet servlet, String msg);  //
Deprecated
  public UnavailableException(Servlet servlet, String msg);  // Deprecated
  public UnavailableException(String msg);                   // New in 2.2
  public UnavailableException(String msg, int seconds);      // New in 2.2

  // Instance methods
  public Servlet getServlet();                               // Deprecated
  public int getUnavailableSeconds();
  public boolean isPermanent();
}
```

Constructors

UnavailableException()

```
public UnavailableException(String msg)
public UnavailableException(String msg, int seconds)
public UnavailableException(Servlet servlet, String msg)
public UnavailableException(int seconds, Servlet servlet, String msg)
```

Description

Constructs an `UnavailableException` with a given explanatory message. A period of unavailability may optionally be provided, given in seconds. The two constructors with signatures that accept a `Servlet` parameter were deprecated in Servlet API 2.2 in favor of the simpler and safer constructor versions that do not accept a servlet instance.

Instance Methods

getServlet()

```
public Servlet getServlet()
```

Description

Returns the servlet that threw this exception or `null` if the servlet instance was not provided to the constructor. This method was deprecated as of Servlet API 2.2 for safety reasons.

getUnavailableSeconds()

```
public int getUnavailableSeconds()
```

Description

Returns the number of seconds for which this servlet will be unavailable. A nonpositive number indicates permanent unavailability. No attempt is made to compensate for the time elapsed since the exception was thrown.

isPermanent()

```
public boolean isPermanent()
```

Description

Returns `true` if the servlet is unavailable indefinitely, `false` otherwise.

B

HTTP Servlet API Quick Reference

The `javax.servlet.http` package provides support for servlets that speak the HTTP protocol. The classes in this package build upon the core functionality provided by the `javax.servlet` package to provide servlets access to HTTP-specific features such as status codes, request and response headers, sessions, and cookies. Figure B-1 shows the class hierarchy of the `javax.servlet.http` package.

Cookie

Synopsis

Class Name:	`javax.servlet.http.Cookie`
Superclass:	`java.lang.Object`
Immediate Subclasses:	None
Interfaces Implemented:	`java.lang.Cloneable`
Availability:	Servlet API 2.0 and later

Description

The `Cookie` class provides an easy way for servlets to read, create, and manipulate HTTP-style cookies, which allow servlets to store small amounts of data on the client. Cookies are generally used for session tracking or storing small amounts of user-specific configuration information. For more information, consult Chapter 7, *Session Tracking*.

A servlet uses the `getCookies()` method of `HttpServletRequest` to retrieve cookies submitted as part of a client request. The `addCookie()` method of `HttpServletResponse` sends a new cookie to the browser. Because cookies are

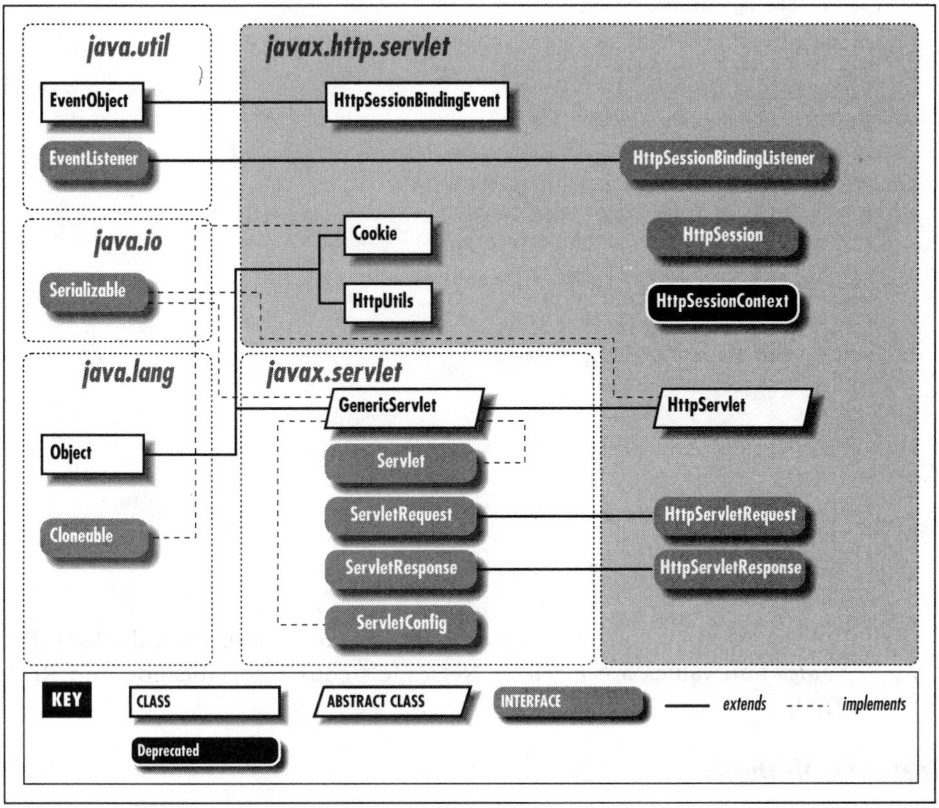

Figure B-1. The javax.servlet.http package

set using HTTP headers, `addCookie()` must be called before the response is committed.

The `getXXX()` methods are rarely used because when a cookie is sent to the server, it contains only its name, value, and version. If you set an attribute on a cookie received from the client, you must add it to the response for the change to take effect, and you should take care that all attributes except name, value, and version are reset on the cookie as well.

This class supports both the Netscape cookie specification and RFC 2109.

Class Summary

```
public class Cookie implements java.lang.Cloneable {
  // Constructors
  public Cookie(String name, String value);

  // Instance methods
  public Object clone();
  public String getComment();
```

```
    public String getDomain();
    public int getMaxAge();
    public String getName();
    public String getPath();
    public boolean getSecure();
    public String getValue();
    public int getVersion();
    public void setComment(String purpose);
    public void setDomain(String pattern);
    public void setMaxAge(int expiry);
    public void setPath(String uri);
    public void setSecure(boolean flag);
    public void setValue(String newValue);
    public void setVersion(int v);
}
```

Constructors

Cookie()

```
public Cookie(String name, String value)
```

Description

Constructs a new cookie with an initial name and value. The rules for valid names and values are given in Netscape's cookie specification and RFC 2109.

Instance Methods

clone()

```
public Object clone()
```

Description

Overrides the standard `clone()` method to return a copy of this object (a duplicate cookie).

getComment()

```
public String getComment()
```

Description

Returns the comment associated with the cookie. This information is available only right after the comment has been set; when the cookie is returned by the client this information is not included.

getDomain()

```
public String getDomain()
```

Description

Returns the domain limitation associated with this cookie. This information is available only right after the domain has been set; when the cookie is returned by the client this information is not included.

getMaxAge()

`public int getMaxAge()`

Description

Returns the maximum age allowed for this cookie. This information is available only right after the maximum age has been set; when the cookie is returned by the client this information is not included.

getName()

`public String getName()`

Description

Returns the name of this cookie.

getPath()

`public String getPath()`

Description

Returns the path limitation for this servlet. This information is available only right after the path has been set; when the cookie is returned by the client this information is not included.

getSecure()

`public boolean getSecure()`

Description

Returns `true` if this cookie requires a secure connection, `false` otherwise. This information is available only right after the flag has been set; when the cookie is returned by the client this information is not included.

getValue()

`public String getValue()`

Description

Returns the value of this cookie, in string format.

getVersion()

`public int getVersion()`

Description

Returns the version of this cookie.

setComment()

`public void setComment(String purpose)`

Description

Sets the comment field of the cookie. A comment describes the intended purpose of a cookie. A web browser may choose to display this text to the user. Comments are not supported by Version 0 cookies.

setDomain()

```
public void setDomain(String pattern)
```

Description

Specifies a domain restriction pattern. A domain pattern specifies the servers that should see a cookie. By default, cookies are returned only to the host that saved them. Specifying a domain name pattern overrides this. The pattern must begin with a dot and must contain at least two dots. A pattern matches only one entry beyond the initial dot. For example, `.foo.com` is valid and matches `www.foo.com` and `upload.foo.com` but not `www.upload.foo.com`. For details on domain patterns, see Netscape's cookie specification and RFC 2109.

setMaxAge()

```
public void setMaxAge(int expiry)
```

Description

Specifies the maximum age of the cookie in seconds before it expires. A negative value indicates the default, that the cookie should expire when the browser exits. A zero value tells the browser to delete the cookie immediately.

setPath()

```
public void setPath(String uri)
```

Description

Specifies a path for the cookie, which is the subset of URIs to which a cookie should be sent. By default, cookies are sent to the page that set the cookie and to all the pages in that directory or under that directory. For example, if */servlet/CookieMonster* sets a cookie, the default path is `/servlet`. That path indicates the cookie should be sent to */servlet/Elmo* and to */servlet/subdir/BigBird*—but not to the */Oscar.html* servlet alias or to any CGI programs under */cgi-bin*. A path set to "`/`" causes a cookie to be sent to all the pages on a server. A cookie's path must be such that it includes the servlet that set the cookie.

setSecure()

```
public void setSecure(boolean flag)
```

Description

The secure flag indicates whether the cookie should be sent only over a secure channel, such as SSL. This value defaults to `false`.

setValue()

```
public void setValue(String newValue)
```

Description

Assigns a new value to a cookie. With Version 0 cookies, values should not contain the following: whitespace, brackets, parentheses, equals signs, commas, double quotes, slashes, question marks, at signs, colons, or semicolons. Empty values may not behave the same way on all browsers.

setVersion()

```
public void setVersion(int v)
```

Description

Servlets can send and receive cookies formatted to match either Netscape persistent cookies (Version 0) or the newer, somewhat experimental, RFC 2109 cookies (Version 1). Newly constructed cookies default to Version 0 to maximize interoperability. When using Version 1 cookies the servlet container may also send a Version 0 style cookie with the same name and value for backward compatibility.

HttpServlet

Synopsis

Class Name:	`javax.servlet.http.HttpServlet`
Superclass:	`javax.servlet.GenericServlet`
Immediate Subclasses:	None
Interfaces Implemented:	`javax.servlet.Servlet`, `java.io.Serializable`
Availability:	Servlet API 1.0 and later

Description

`HttpServlet` is an abstract class that serves as the base class for HTTP (World Wide Web) servlets. The public `service()` method dispatches requests to an HTTP-specific, protected `service()` method, which then dispatches requests to particular handler functions for each HTTP submission type: `doGet()`, `doPost()`, and so on. Because the default HTTP servlet implementation handles dispatching to these methods, if you override the protected `service()` method, you must either handle the dispatching manually or not use the handler functions for HTTP request methods.

Class Summary

```
public abstract class HttpServlet extends javax.servlet.GenericServlet
  implements javax.servlet.Servlet, java.io.Serializable {
```

```
    // Constructors
    public HttpServlet();

    // Public instance method
    public void service(ServletRequest req, ServletResponse res)
      throws ServletException, IOException;

    // Protected instance methods
    protected void doDelete(HttpServletRequest req, HttpServletResponse res)
      throws ServletException, IOException;                 // New in 2.0
    protected void doGet(HttpServletRequest req, HttpServletResponse res)
      throws ServletException, IOException;
    protected void doOptions(HttpServletRequest req, HttpServletResponse res)
      throws ServletException, IOException;                 // New in 2.0
    protected void doPost(HttpServletRequest req,  HttpServletResponse res)
      throws ServletException, IOException;
    protected void doPut(HttpServletRequest req, HttpServletResponse res)
      throws ServletException, IOException;                 // New in 2.0
    protected void doTrace(HttpServletRequest req, HttpServletResponse res)
      throws ServletException, IOException;                 // New in 2.0
    protected long getLastModified(HttpServletRequest req);
    protected void service(HttpServletRequest req, HttpServletResponse res)
      throws ServletException, IOException;
}
```

Constructors

HttpServlet()

```
public HttpServlet()
```

Description

The default constructor does nothing. Because you cannot be sure of how and when classes will be loaded, it is not advisable to override this constructor to perform startup tasks. Use `init()` instead.

Public Instance Methods

service()

```
public void service(ServletRequest req, ServletResponse res)
  throws ServletException, IOException
```

Description

This `service()` method handles dispatching requests to the protected, HTTP-specific `service()` method; it should generally not be overridden.

Protected Instance Methods

doDelete()

```
protected void doDelete(HttpServletRequest req, HttpServletResponse res)
```

```
  throws ServletException, IOException
```

Description

The default `service()` implementation in `HttpServlet` dispatches all HTTP DELETE requests to this method. Servlets implement this method to handle DELETE requests. The default implementation returns an HTTP `SC_BAD_REQUEST` error. This method was introduced in the Servlet API 2.0.

`doGet()`

```
protected void doGet(HttpServletRequest req, HttpServletResponse res)
  throws ServletException, IOException
```

Description

The default `service()` implementation in `HttpServlet` dispatches all HTTP GET requests to this method. Servlets implement this method to handle GET requests. The default implementation returns an HTTP `SC_BAD_REQUEST` error.

`doOptions()`

```
protected void doOptions(HttpServletRequest req, HttpServletResponse res)
  throws ServletException, IOException
```

Description

The default `service()` implementation in `HttpServlet` dispatches all HTTP OPTIONS requests to this method. The default implementation determines which options are supported and returns an appropriate header. For example, if a servlet overrides `doGet()` and `doPost()`, the browser is informed that GET, POST, HEAD, TRACE, and OPTIONS are supported. There is almost never any reason to override this method. This method was introduced in Servlet API 2.0.

`doPost()`

```
protected void doPost(HttpServletRequest req, HttpServletResponse res)
  throws ServletException, IOException
```

Description

The default `service()` implementation in `HttpServlet` dispatches all HTTP POST requests to this method. Servlets implement this method to handle POST requests. The default implementation returns an HTTP `SC_BAD_REQUEST` error.

`doPut()`

```
protected void doPut(HttpServletRequest req, HttpServletResponse res)
  throws ServletException, IOException
```

Description

The default `service()` implementation in `HttpServlet` dispatches all HTTP PUT requests to this method. Servlets implement this to handle PUT requests. The default implementation returns an HTTP `SC_BAD_REQUEST` error. See RFC 2068 at *http://www.ietf.org/rfc/rfc2068.txt* for more on HTTP PUT requests. This method was introduced in Servlet API 2.0.

doTrace()

```
protected void doTrace(HttpServletRequest req, HttpServletResponse res)
  throws ServletException, IOException
```

Description

The default `service()` implementation in `HttpServlet` dispatches all HTTP TRACE requests to this method. The default implementation returns a message listing all of the headers sent in the TRACE request. There is almost never any reason to override this method. This method was introduced in Servlet API 2.0.

getLastModified()

```
protected long getLastModified(HttpServletRequest req)
```

Description

Returns the date and time (expressed as milliseconds since midnight, January 1, 1970, GMT) that the content produced by the servlet was last modified. Negative values indicate that the time is not known. The default implementation returns `-1`. Called by servers in support of conditional HTTP GET requests and to manage response caches. See Chapter 4, *Retrieving Information*, for more information.

service()

```
protected void service(HttpServletRequest req, HttpServletResponse res)
  throws ServletException, IOException
```

Description

The public `service()` method dispatches requests to this `service()` method. The method handles dispatching requests to `doGet()`, `doPost()`, and the other handler functions based on the type of request. If this method is overridden, no handlers are called.

HttpServletRequest

Synopsis

Interface Name:	`javax.servlet.http.HttpServletRequest`
Superinterface:	`javax.servlet.ServletRequest`
Immediate Subinterfaces:	None

Implemented By: None
Availability: Servlet API 1.0 and later

Description

`HttpServletRequest` extends the basic `ServletRequest` class, providing additional functionality for HTTP (World Wide Web) servlets. It includes support for cookies and session tracking and access to HTTP header information. `HttpServletRequest` also parses incoming HTTP form data and stores it as servlet parameters. The server passes an `HttpServletRequest` object to the service method of an `HttpServlet`.

Certain methods in this interface have suffered from documentation and implementation inconsistencies. Discrepancies have been noted where possible.

Interface Declaration

```
public interface HttpServletRequest extends javax.servlet.ServletRequest {
  // Methods
  public abstract String getAuthType();
  public abstract String getContextPath();                  // New in 2.2
  public abstract Cookie[] getCookies();                    // New in 2.0
  public abstract long getDateHeader(String name);
  public abstract String getHeader(String name);
  public abstract Enumeration getHeaderNames();
  public abstract Enumeration getHeaders(String name);      // New in 2.2
  public abstract int getIntHeader(String name);
  public abstract String getMethod();
  public abstract String getPathInfo();
  public abstract String getPathTranslated();
  public abstract String getQueryString();
  public abstract String getRemoteUser();
  public abstract String getRequestedSessionId();           // New in 2.0
  public abstract String getRequestURI();
  public abstract String getServletPath();
  public abstract HttpSession getSession();                 // New in 2.1
  public abstract HttpSession getSession(boolean create);   // New in 2.0
  public abstract java.security.Principal getUserPrincipal(); // New in 2.2
  public abstract boolean isRequestedSessionIdFromCookie(); // New in 2.0
  public abstract boolean isRequestedSessionIdFromUrl();    // Deprecated
  public abstract boolean isRequestedSessionIdFromURL();    // New in 2.1
  public abstract boolean isRequestedSessionIdValid();      // New in 2.0
  public abstract boolean isUserInRole(String role);        // New in 2.2
}
```

Methods

getAuthType()

```
public abstract String getAuthType()
```

Description

Returns the servlet's authentication scheme or `null` if the servlet was not protected by an access control mechanism. Possible schemes are `BASIC`, `DIGEST`, `FORM`, and `CLIENT-CERT`. Same as the CGI variable `AUTH_TYPE`.

getContextPath()

```
public abstract String getContextPath()
```

Description

Returns the portion of the request URI that indicates the context (web application) of the request. The context path always comes first in a request URI. The path starts with a / character but does not end with a / character and is returned directly without being URL-decoded. For servlets in the default (root) context, this method returns an empty string. This method was introduced in Servlet API 2.2.

getCookies()

```
public abstract Cookie[] getCookies()
```

Description

Returns an array of `Cookie` objects that contains all the cookies sent by the browser as part of the request or `null` if no cookies were sent. This method was introduced in Servlet API 2.0.

getDateHeader()

```
public abstract long getDateHeader(String name)
```

Description

Returns the value of the named header as a long value that represents a `Date` (the number of milliseconds since midnight, January 1, 1970, GMT) or `-1` if the header was not sent as part of the request. The name is case insensitive. Throws an `IllegalArgumentException` when called on a header whose value cannot be converted to a `Date`. This method is useful for handling headers like `Last-Modified` and `If-Modified-Since`.

getHeader()

```
public abstract String getHeader(String name)
```

Description

Returns the value of the named header as a `String` or `null` if the header was not sent as part of the request. The name is case insensitive. This method can retrieve all header types.

getHeaderNames()

```
public abstract Enumeration getHeaderNames()
```

Description

Returns the names of all the headers a servlet can access as an `Enumeration` of `String` objects or an empty `Enumeration` if there were no headers. Some servlet implementations may not allow headers to be accessed in this way, in which case this method returns `null`.

getHeaders()

```
public abstract Enumeration getHeaders(String name)
```

Description

Returns all the values of the named header as an `Enumeration` of `String` objects. Some headers, such as `Accept-Language`, can be sent by clients as several headers, each with a different value. This method allows all values to be retrieved. If the request did not include any headers of the specified name, this method returns an empty `Enumeration`. The name is case insensitive. This method can retrieve all header types. This method was introduced in Servlet API 2.2.

getIntHeader()

```
public abstract int getIntHeader(String name)
```

Description

Returns the value of the named header as an `int` or `-1` if the header was not sent as part of the request. The name is case insensitive. Throws a `NumberFormatException` when called on a header with a value that cannot be converted to an `int`.

getMethod()

```
public abstract String getMethod()
```

Description

Returns the HTTP method used to make the request. Example methods include `GET`, `POST`, and `HEAD`. The same as the CGI variable `REQUEST_METHOD`. The `HttpServlet` implementation of `service()` uses this method when dispatching requests.

getPathInfo()

```
public abstract String getPathInfo()
```

Description

Returns the extra path information associated with the request or `null` if none was provided. The path is URL-decoded before being returned. The same as the CGI variable `PATH_INFO`.

getPathTranslated()

```
public abstract String getPathTranslated()
```

Description

Returns the extra path information translated to a filesystem path or `null` if there was no extra path information or if the servlet container cannot create a valid file path (such as when the file is on a remote filesystem or is found only inside a *.war* archive). The path returned does not necessarily point to an existing file or directory. The path is URL-decoded before being returned. The call is similar to the CGI variable `PATH_TRANSLATED`. Also the same as `getServletContext().getRealPath(req.getPathInfo())`.

getQueryString()

```
public abstract String getQueryString()
```

Description

Returns the query string from the request's URL. This value is the same as the CGI variable `QUERY_STRING`. Because `HttpServletRequest` parses this string into a set of servlet parameters available through `getParameter()`, most servlets can ignore this method.

getRemoteUser()

```
public abstract String getRemoteUser()
```

Description

Returns the name of the user making the request as a `String` or `null` if access to the servlet was not restricted. The same as the CGI variable `REMOTE_USER`. This generally requires that the user has logged in using HTTP authentication. There is no comparable method to directly retrieve the remote user's password.

getRequestedSessionId()

```
public abstract String getRequestedSessionId()
```

Description

This method returns the session ID specified by the client. This may not be the actual session identifier currently in use—for example, if the session expired before the request occurred, the server creates a new session ID and uses that one instead. This method was introduced in Servlet API 2.0.

getRequestURI()

```
public abstract String getRequestURI()
```

Description

Returns the Universal Resource Identifier (URI) of the request. This is the resource requested by the client in the first line of its HTTP request, everything after the protocol and before the query string. For normal HTTP servlets, the request URI is the request URL minus the scheme, host, port, and query string but including extra path information. The path is returned directly, without being URL-decoded. Early versions of the Servlet API defined and implemented this method in different ways. When writing code that depends on this method, make sure you know what you're actually getting.

`getServletPath()`

```
public abstract String getServletPath()
```

Description

Returns the part of the URI that refers to the servlet. The path is URL-decoded before being returned and does not include any extra path information or the query string. For file extension matches the path does include the extension. This is the same as the CGI variable `SCRIPT_NAME`.

`getSession()`

```
public abstract HttpSession getSession()
public abstract HttpSession getSession(boolean create)
```

Description

Returns the current session associated with the user making the request. If the user has no current valid session, this method creates one if `create` is `true` or returns `null` if `create` is `false`. The no-argument version has `create` set implicitly to `true`. To ensure the session is properly maintained, this method should be called at least once before any output is written to the response. Servlets not using session tracking may ignore this method. This method was introduced in Servlet API 2.0. The no-argument version was introduced in Servlet API 2.1.

`getUserPrincipal()`

```
public abstract java.security.Principal getUserPrincipal()
```

Description

Returns a `java.security.Principal` object containing the name of the current authenticated user. If the user has not been authenticated, the method returns `null`. This method was introduced in Servlet API 2.2.

`isRequestedSessionIdFromCookie()`

```
public abstract boolean isRequestedSessionIdFromCookie()
```

Description

Returns `true` if the client submitted a session identifier via a cookie, `false` otherwise. This method was introduced in Servlet API 2.0.

`isRequestedSessionIdFromURL()`

```
public abstract boolean isRequestedSessionIdFromUrl()
public abstract boolean isRequestedSessionIdFromURL()
```

Description

Returns `true` if the requested session ID was submitted via a rewritten URL, `false` otherwise. The `isRequestedSessionIdFromUrl()` method was introduced in Servlet API 2.0, then deprecated in Servlet API 2.1 with the introduction of the more standardly named `isRequestedSessionIdFromURL()` method.

`isRequestedSessionIdValid()`

```
public abstract boolean isRequestedSessionIdValid()
```

Description

Returns `true` if the session requested by the client is a valid session and is therefore the session currently in use. For new sessions and expired sessions, it returns `false`. This method was introduced in Servlet API 2.0.

`isUserInRole()`

```
public abstract boolean isUserInRole(String role)
```

Description

Returns a `boolean` indicating whether the authenticated user is included in the specified logical "role." Roles and role membership can be defined using deployment descriptors, and roles can be mapped to users and groups using server administration tools. If the user has not been authenticated, the method always returns `false`. This method was introduced in Servlet API 2.2.

HttpServletResponse

Synopsis

Interface Name:	`javax.servlet.http.HttpServletResponse`
Superinterface:	`javax.servlet.ServletResponse`
Immediate Subinterfaces:	None
Implemented By:	None
Availability:	Servlet API 1.0 and later

Description

`HttpServletResponse` extends the `ServletResponse` class to allow manipulation of HTTP protocol-specific data, including response headers and status codes. It also defines a series of constants that represent various HTTP status codes and includes helper functions for session-tracking operations.

Interface Declaration

```
public interface HttpServletResponse extends javax.servlet.ServletResponse {
  // Constants
  public static final int SC_ACCEPTED;
  public static final int SC_BAD_GATEWAY;
  public static final int SC_BAD_REQUEST;
  public static final int SC_CONFLICT;
  public static final int SC_CONTINUE;                       // New in 2.0
  public static final int SC_CREATED;
  public static final int SC_EXPECTATION_FAILED;             // New in 2.2
  public static final int SC_FORBIDDEN;
  public static final int SC_GATEWAY_TIMEOUT;                // New in 2.0
  public static final int SC_GONE;                           // New in 2.0
  public static final int SC_HTTP_VERSION_NOT_SUPPORTED;     // New in 2.0
  public static final int SC_INTERNAL_SERVER_ERROR;
  public static final int SC_LENGTH_REQUIRED;                // New in 2.0
  public static final int SC_METHOD_NOT_ALLOWED;             // New in 2.0
  public static final int SC_MOVED_PERMANENTLY;
  public static final int SC_MOVED_TEMPORARILY;
  public static final int SC_MULTIPLE_CHOICES;               // New in 2.0
  public static final int SC_NO_CONTENT;
  public static final int SC_NON_AUTHORITATIVE_INFORMATION; // New in 2.0
  public static final int SC_NOT_ACCEPTABLE;                 // New in 2.0
  public static final int SC_NOT_FOUND;
  public static final int SC_NOT_IMPLEMENTED;
  public static final int SC_NOT_MODIFIED;
  public static final int SC_OK;
  public static final int SC_PARTIAL_CONTENT;                // New in 2.0
  public static final int SC_PAYMENT_REQUIRED;               // New in 2.0
  public static final int SC_PRECONDITION_FAILED;            // New in 2.0
  public static final int SC_PROXY_AUTHENTICATION_REQUIRED; // New in 2.0
  public static final int SC_REQUEST_ENTITY_TOO_LARGE;       // New in 2.0
  public static final int SC_REQUEST_TIMEOUT;                // New in 2.0
  public static final int SC_REQUEST_URI_TOO_LONG;           // New in 2.0
  public static final int SC_REQUESTED_RANGE_NOT_SATISFIABLE;// New in 2.2
  public static final int SC_RESET_CONTENT;                  // New in 2.0
  public static final int SC_SEE_OTHER;                      // New in 2.0
  public static final int SC_SERVICE_UNAVAILABLE;
  public static final int SC_SWITCHING_PROTOCOLS;            // New in 2.0
  public static final int SC_UNAUTHORIZED;
  public static final int SC_UNSUPPORTED_MEDIA_TYPE;         // New in 2.0
  public static final int SC_USE_PROXY;                      // New in 2.0

  // Methods
  public abstract void addCookie(Cookie cookie);             // New in 2.0
  public abstract void addDateHeader(String name, long date);// New in 2.2
  public abstract void addHeader(String name, String value);// New in 2.2
  public abstract void addIntHeader(String name, int value);// New in 2.2
  public abstract boolean containsHeader(String name);
```

```
    public abstract String encodeRedirectUrl(String url);     // Deprecated
    public abstract String encodeRedirectURL(String url);     // New in 2.1
    public abstract String encodeUrl(String url);             // Deprecated
    public abstract String encodeURL(String url);             // New in 2.1
    public abstract void sendError(int sc)
      throws IOException, IllegalStateException;
    public abstract void sendError(int sc, String msg)
      throws IOException, IllegalStateException;
    public abstract void sendRedirect(String location)
      throws IOException, IllegalStateException;
    public abstract void setDateHeader(String name, long date);
    public abstract void setHeader(String name, String value);
    public abstract void setIntHeader(String name, int value);
    public abstract void setStatus(int sc);
    public abstract void setStatus(int sc, String sm);        // Deprecated
}
```

Constants

Appendix D, *HTTP Status Codes*, contains complete descriptions of all the SC_*XXX* status codes.

Methods

`addCookie()`

```
public abstract void addCookie(Cookie cookie)
```

Description

Adds the specified cookie to the response. Additional cookies can be added with repeated calls to `addCookie()`. Because cookies are sent using HTTP headers, they should be added to the response before the response is committed. Browsers are required to accept only 20 cookies per site, 300 total per user, and they can limit each cookie's size to 4096 bytes.

`addDateHeader()`

```
public abstract void addDateHeader(String name, long date)
```

Description

Adds a header with the given name and date value. The method accepts the date as a long that represents the number of milliseconds since midnight, January 1, 1970, GMT. This method allows response headers to have multiple values. This method was introduced in Servlet API 2.2.

`addHeader()`

```
public abstract void addHeader(String name, String value)
```

Description

Adds a header with the given name and value. This method allows response headers to have multiple values. This method was introduced in Servlet API 2.2.

addIntHeader()

```
public abstract void addIntHeader(String name, int value)
```

Description

Adds a header with the given name and `int` value. The method accepts the date as a `long` that represents the number of milliseconds since midnight, January 1, 1970, GMT. This method allows response headers to have multiple values. This method was introduced in Servlet API 2.2.

containsHeader()

```
public abstract boolean containsHeader(String name)
```

Description

Returns `true` if the named header has already been set, `false` if not.

encodeRedirectURL()

```
public abstract String encodeRedirectUrl(String url)
public abstract String encodeRedirectURL(String url)
```

Description

Returns the specified URL encoded (rewritten) to include the session ID. If encoding is not needed or not supported, the method leaves the URL unchanged. The rules used to decide when and how to encode a URL are server-specific. This method may use different rules than `encodeURL()`. To enable session tracking, all URLs passed to the `sendRedirect()` method should be run through this method. The `encodeRedirectUrl()` method was introduced in Servlet API 2.0, then deprecated in Servlet API 2.1 with the introduction of the more standardly named `encodeRedirectURL()` method.

encodeURL()

```
public abstract String encodeUrl(String url)
public abstract String encodeURL(String url)
```

Description

Returns the specified URL encoded (rewritten) to include the session ID. If encoding is not needed or not supported, the method leaves the URL unchanged. The rules used to decide when and how to encode a URL are server-specific. To enable session tracking, all URLs emitted by a servlet should be run through this method. The `encodeUrl()` method was introduced in Servlet API 2.0, then deprecated in Servlet API 2.1 with the introduction of the more standardly named `encodeURL()` method.

sendError()

```
public abstract void sendError(int sc)
  throws IOException, IllegalStateException
public abstract void sendError(int sc, String msg)
  throws IOException, IllegalStateException
```

Description

These methods are similar to `setStatus()`, except that they are used when the status code indicates an error during the handling of the request and the servlet would like the server to generate an appropriate error page. This method should be called before the response is committed, otherwise it will throw an `IllegalStateException`. This method performs an implicit reset on the response buffer before generating the error page. Headers set before `sendError()` should remain set.

sendRedirect()

```
public abstract void sendRedirect(String location)
  throws IOException, IllegalStateException
```

Description

Redirects the response to the specified location, automatically setting the status code and `Location` header. The default implementation also writes a short response body that contains a hyperlink to the new location, to support browsers without redirect capabilities. Consequently, do not write your own response body when using this method. The HTTP specification dictates that all redirect URLs must be absolute; however, beginning with Servlet API 2.2 this method can accept a relative URL—the server will transform the URL to an absolute form (automatically prepending the current protocol, server, and port—but not the context path; do that yourself if necessary) before sending it to the client. This method should be called before the response is committed, otherwise it will throw an `IllegalStateException`. This method performs an implicit reset on the response buffer before generating the redirect page. Headers set before `sendRedirect()` should remain set.

setDateHeader()

```
public abstract void setDateHeader(String name, long date)
```

Description

Sets the value of the named header as a `String` specifying a particular date and time. The method accepts the date value as a long that represents the number of milliseconds since midnight, January 1, 1970, GMT. If the header has already been set, the new value overwrites all previous values.

setHeader()

```
public abstract void setHeader(String name, String value)
```

Description

Sets the value of the named header as a `String`. The name is case insensitive (as with all header-related methods). If the header has already been set, the new value overwrites all previous values. This method can set any header type. Headers should always be set before the response is committed.

setIntHeader()

```
public abstract void setIntHeader(String name, int value)
```

Description

Sets the value of the named header as an `int`. If the header has already been set, the new value overwrites all previous values.

setStatus()

```
public abstract void setStatus(int sc)
public abstract void setStatus(int sc, String sm)
```

Description

Sets the HTTP status code. The code can be specified using a numeric value or by using the `SC_XXX` codes defined within `HttpServletResponse`. A custom HTTP protocol error message can be provided as a second parameter; however, this should never be done and the version of this method that accepts a `String` has been deprecated as of Servlet API 2.1. The status code should be set before the response is committed, otherwise the call is ignored.

HttpSession

Synopsis

Interface Name:	`javax.servlet.http.HttpSession`
Superinterface:	None
Immediate Subinterfaces:	None
Implemented By:	None
Availability:	Servlet API 2.0 and later

Description

The `HttpSession` interface provides a mechanism for holding temporary information about visitors to a web site. For a detailed introduction to session tracking, see Chapter 7. The `HttpSession` interface itself allows servlets to view and manipulate session-specific information, such as creation time and the unique session identifier. It also includes methods to bind objects to the session for later retrieval, allowing "shopping cart" and other applications to hold onto data between client requests.

A servlet obtains an HttpSession object from the getSession() method of HttpServletRequest. Session behavior, such as the amount of idle time before a session is destroyed, can be configured programmatically and via the web application deployment descriptor.

For sessions inside a nondistributed web application, any object may be bound to the session. Objects that implement java.io.Serializable may be written to disk to save memory and to persist between server restarts.

For sessions inside a distributed web application, objects placed into the session *must* implement java.io.Serializable. The server may throw an IllegalArgumentException when this requirement is not met. Servers use *session affinity* to efficiently manage sessions in a distributed environment where there are multiple backend servers. This means that all requests that are part of a single session from a particular user are handled by only one JVM at a time. This eliminates the need to constantly replicate session information across all the back-end servers. Responsibility for the session can be moved to another server between user requests, and to enable the moving of a session all objects placed into a session must be Serializable.

Interface Declaration

```
public interface HttpSession {
  // Methods
  // Most methods may throw IllegalStateException
  public abstract Object getAttribute(String name);          // New in 2.2
  public abstract Enumeration getAttributeNames();           // New in 2.2
  public abstract long getCreationTime();
  public abstract String getId();
  public abstract long getLastAccessedTime();
  public abstract int getMaxInactiveInterval();              // New in 2.1
  public abstract HttpSessionContext getSessionContext();    // Deprecated
  public abstract Object getValue(String name);              // Deprecated
  public abstract String[] getValueNames();                  // Deprecated
  public abstract void invalidate();
  public abstract boolean isNew();
  public abstract void putValue(String name, Object value); // Deprecated
  public abstract void removeAttribute(String name);         // New in 2.2
  public abstract void removeValue(String name);             // Deprecated
  public abstract void setAttribute(String name, Object value);// New in 2.2
  public abstract void setMaxInactiveInterval(int secs);     // New in 2.1
}
```

Methods

getAttribute()

```
public abstract Object getAttribute(String name)
  throws IllegalStateException
```

Description

Returns the object bound in the session under the specified name or `null` if there is no matching binding. Throws an `IllegalStateException` if the session is invalid.

getAttributeNames()

```
public abstract Enumeration getAttributeNames()
  throws IllegalStateException
```

Description

Returns an `Enumeration` containing the names of all objects bound to this session as `String` objects or an empty `Enumeration` if there are no bindings. Throws an `IllegalStateException` if the session is invalid.

getCreationTime()

```
public abstract long getCreationTime()
  throws IllegalStateException
```

Description

Returns the time at which the session was created, as a long representing the number of milliseconds since midnight, January 1, 1970, GMT. Throws an `IllegalStateException` if the session is invalid.

getId()

```
public abstract String getId()
  throws IllegalStateException
```

Description

Returns the unique `String` identifier assigned to this session. The structure of the ID is implementation dependent; it should simply be difficult for anyone else to guess. For example, a Tomcat ID might be something like `awj4qyhsn2`. Throws an `IllegalStateException` if the session is invalid.

getLastAccessedTime()

```
public abstract long getLastAccessedTime()
  throws IllegalStateException
```

Description

Returns the time at which the client last sent a request associated with this session (not including the current request), as a long representing the number of milliseconds since midnight, January 1, 1970, GMT. Throws an `IllegalStateException` if the session is invalid.

getMaxInactiveInterval()

```
public abstract int getMaxInactiveInterval()
  throws IllegalStateException
```

Description

Returns the time, in seconds, between client requests before the servlet container will invalidate this session. A negative time indicates the session should never time out. The default timeout is set inside the web application's deployment descriptor. Throws an `IllegalStateException` if the session is invalid. This method was introduced in Servlet API 2.1.

getSessionContext()

```
public abstract HttpSessionContext getSessionContext()
```

Description

Returns an empty context for security reasons, as of Servlet API 2.1. Also deprecated as of Servlet API 2.1. See `HttpSessionContext` for more information.

getValue()

```
public abstract Object getValue(String name)
  throws IllegalStateException
```

Description

Returns the object bound in the session under the specified name or `null` if there is no matching binding. Throws an `IllegalStateException` if the session is invalid. Deprecated as of Servlet API 2.2 in favor of `getAttribute()`.

getValueNames()

```
public abstract String[] getValueNames()
  throws IllegalStateException
```

Description

Returns an array containing the names of all objects bound to this session or an empty (zero length) array if there are no bindings. Throws an `IllegalStateException` if the session is invalid. Deprecated as of Servlet API 2.2 in favor of `getAttributeNames()`.

invalidate()

```
public abstract void invalidate()
  throws IllegalStateException
```

Description

Causes the session to be immediately invalidated. All objects stored in the session are unbound. Throws an `IllegalStateException` if the session is already invalid.

isNew()

```
public abstract boolean isNew()
  throws IllegalStateException
```

Description

Returns whether the session is new. A session is considered new if it has been created by the server but the client has not yet acknowledged joining the session. For example, if a server supports only cookie-based sessions and a client has completely disabled the use of cookies, calls to `getSession()` always return new sessions. Throws an `IllegalStateException` if the session is invalid.

putValue()

```
public abstract void putValue(String name, Object value)
  throws IllegalStateException
```

Description

Binds the specified object value under the specified name in the session. Any existing binding with the same name is replaced. Throws an `IllegalStateException` if the session is invalid. Deprecated as of Servlet API 2.2 in favor of `setAttribute()`.

removeAttribute()

```
public abstract void removeAttribute(String name)
  throws IllegalStateException
```

Description

Removes the object bound to the specified name or does nothing if there is no binding. Throws an `IllegalStateException` if the session is invalid.

removeValue()

```
public abstract void removeValue(String name)
  throws IllegalStateException
```

Description

Removes the object bound to the specified name or does nothing if there is no binding. Throws an `IllegalStateException` if the session is invalid. Deprecated as of Servlet API 2.2 in favor of `removeAttribute()`.

setAttribute()

```
public abstract void setAttribute(String name, Object value)
  throws IllegalStateException
```

Description

Binds the specified object value under the specified name in the session. Any existing binding with the same name is replaced. Throws an

`IllegalStateException` if the session is invalid. This method was introduced in Servlet API 2.2.

`setMaxInactiveInterval()`

```
public abstract void setMaxInactiveInterval(int secs)
```

Description

Specifies the time, in seconds, between client requests before the servlet container will invalidate this session. A negative time indicates the session should never time out. A default timeout can be set inside a web application's deployment descriptor. This method was introduced in Servlet API 2.1.

HttpSessionBindingEvent

Synopsis

Class Name:	`javax.servlet.http.HttpSessionBindingEvent`
Superclass:	`java.util.EventObject`
Immediate Subclasses:	None
Interfaces Implemented:	None
Availability:	Servlet API 2.0 and later

Description

An `HttpSessionBindingEvent` is passed to an `HttpSessionBindingListener` when the listener object is bound to or unbound from a session.

Class Summary

```
public class HttpSessionBindingEvent extends java.util.EventObject {
  // Constructors
  public HttpSessionBindingEvent(HttpSession session, String name);

  // Instance methods
  public String getName();
  public HttpSession getSession();
}
```

Constructors

`HttpSessionBindingEvent()`

```
public HttpSessionBindingEvent(HttpSession session, String name)
```

Description

Constructs a new `HttpSessionBindingEvent` using the session being bound and the name that this object is being assigned (this is the same name passed to the `setAttribute()` method of `HttpSession`). Servlet programmers should never need to use this constructor.

Instance Methods

`getName()`

```
public String getName()
```

Description

Returns the name this object has been assigned within the session.

`getSession()`

```
public HttpSession getSession()
```

Description

Returns the session this object is being bound to or unbound from.

HttpSessionBindingListener

Synopsis

Interface Name:	`javax.servlet.http.HttpSessionBindingListener`
Superinterface:	`java.util.EventListener`
Immediate Subinterfaces:	None
Implemented By:	None
Availability:	Servlet API 2.0 and later

Description

An object that implements `HttpSessionBindingListener` is notified via calls to `valueBound()` and `valueUnbound()` when it is bound to or unbound from an `HttpSession`. Among other things, this interface allows orderly cleanup session-specific resources, such as database connections. Note that in a distributed environment the `valueBound()` call may be made inside a different JVM than the `valueUnbound()` call.

Interface Declaration

```
public interface HttpSessionBindingListener extends java.util.EventListener {
  // Methods
  public abstract void valueBound(HttpSessionBindingEvent event);
```

```
    public abstract void valueUnbound(HttpSessionBindingEvent event);
}
```

Methods

`valueBound()`

```
public abstract void valueBound(HttpSessionBindingEvent event)
```

Description

Called when the listener is bound to a session.

`valueUnbound()`

```
public abstract void valueUnbound(HttpSessionBindingEvent event)
```

Description

Called when the listener is unbound from a session (including at session destruction).

HttpSessionContext

Synopsis

Interface Name:	`javax.servlet.http.HttpSessionContext`
Superinterface:	None
Immediate Subinterfaces:	None
Implemented By:	None
Availability:	Servlet API 2.0 and later; deprecated in Servlet API 2.1

Description

`HttpSessionContext` is deprecated as of Servlet API 2.1. Previously this class provided access to all of the currently active sessions inside the servlet container. This provided a potential security hole where a servlet could use this class to display all the session IDs found inside the context, and that information could then be used by unscrupulous clients to forge their way into another's session. Because the ability to access all sessions at once is almost never needed, this class was deprecated for security's sake.

Interface Declaration

```
public interface HttpSessionContext {
  // Methods
  public abstract Enumeration getIds();                         // Deprecated
  public abstract HttpSession getSession(String sessionId); // Deprecated
}
```

Methods

`getIds()`

```
public abstract Enumeration getIds()
```

Description

Deprecated as of Servlet API 2.1. In Servlet API 2.0, returns an `Enumeration` that contained the session IDs for all the currently valid sessions in this context, or an empty `Enumeration` if there are no valid sessions. The session IDs returned by `getIds()` must be held as a server secret because any client with knowledge of another client's session ID can, with a forged cookie or URL, join the second client's session.

`getSession()`

```
public abstract HttpSession getSession(String sessionId)
```

Description

Deprecated as of Servlet API 2.1. In Servlet API 2.0, returns the session associated with the given session identifier. A list of valid session IDs can be obtained from the `getIds()` method.

HttpUtils

Synopsis

Class Name:	`javax.servlet.http.HttpUtils`
Superclass:	`java.lang.Object`
Immediate Subclasses:	None
Interfaces Implemented:	None
Availability:	Servlet API 1.0 and later

Description

A container object for a handful of potentially useful HTTP-oriented methods.

Class Summary

```
public class HttpUtils {
  // Constructors
  public HttpUtils();

  // Class methods
  public static StringBuffer getRequestURL(HttpServletRequest req);
  public static Hashtable parsePostData(int len, ServletInputStream in);
  public static Hashtable parseQueryString(String s);
}
```

Constructors

HttpUtils()

```
public HttpUtils()
```

Description

The default constructor does nothing.

Class Methods

getRequestURL()

```
public static StringBuffer getRequestURL(HttpServletRequest req)
```

Description

Reconstitutes the request URL based on information available in the `HttpServletRequest` object. Returns a `StringBuffer` that includes the scheme, server name, server port, and extra path information, but not the query string. The reconstituted URL should look almost identical to the URL used by the client. This method can be used for error reporting, redirecting, and URL creation. For applications that need to uniquely identify particular servlets, the `getRequestURI()` method of `HttpServletRequest` is generally a better choice.

parsePostData()

```
public static Hashtable parsePostData(int len, ServletInputStream in)
```

Description

Parses `len` characters of parameter data from a `ServletInputStream` (usually sent as part of a POST operation). Throws an `IllegalArgumentException` if the parameter data is invalid. Most servlets use `getParameterNames()`, `getParameter()`, and `getParameterValues()` instead of this method.

parseQueryString()

```
public static Hashtable parseQueryString(String s)
```

Description

Returns a `Hashtable` where the hashtable keys are the parameter names taken from the query string and each hashtable value is a `String` array that contains the parameter's decoded value(s). Throws an `IllegalArgumentException` if the query string is invalid. Most servlets use `getParameterNames()`, `getParameter()`, and `getParameterValues()` instead. It is not safe to use both.

C

Deployment Descriptor DTD Reference

A *Document Type Definition* (*DTD*) file dictates what is valid content within an XML file. This appendix provides the official DTD for the Servlet API 2.2 web application deployment descriptor. DTD files are not XML, but the syntax is easy to follow: each `<!ELEMENT>` tag defines in parentheses which child elements it may have, how many of each child it may have, and in what order. A question mark (`?`) after a child's name means the child is optional (*0* – *1*), an asterisk (`*`) means the child may appear any number of times (*0* – *n*), a plus sign (`+`) means some number of children must appear (*1* – *n*), and no following character means the child is simply required (*1*). The syntax `(x|y)` means either `x` or `y`. The children of an element must follow the exact order listed within the parentheses.

Figures C-1 through C-4 graphically demonstrate the element structure; Example C-1 shows the DTD itself. Each `<!ATTLIST>` tag controls the allowed attributes for an element. In this DTD, the tag is used only to provide default `id` values. The rest of this appendix is reference material for the elements in the DTD.

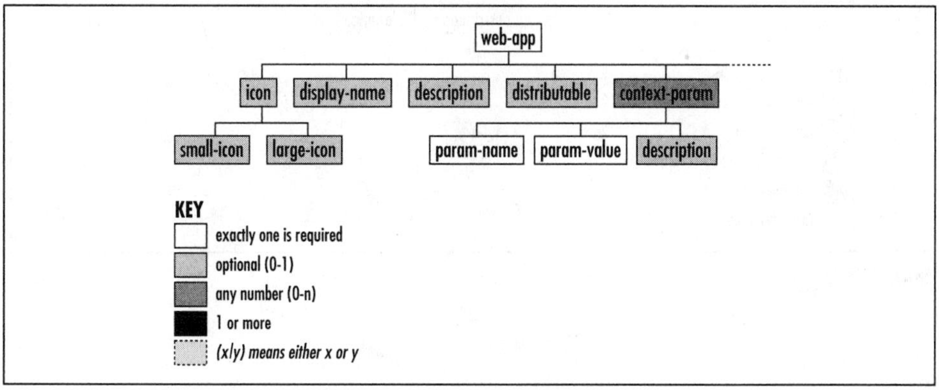

Figure C-1. The element structure of the deployment descriptor DTD

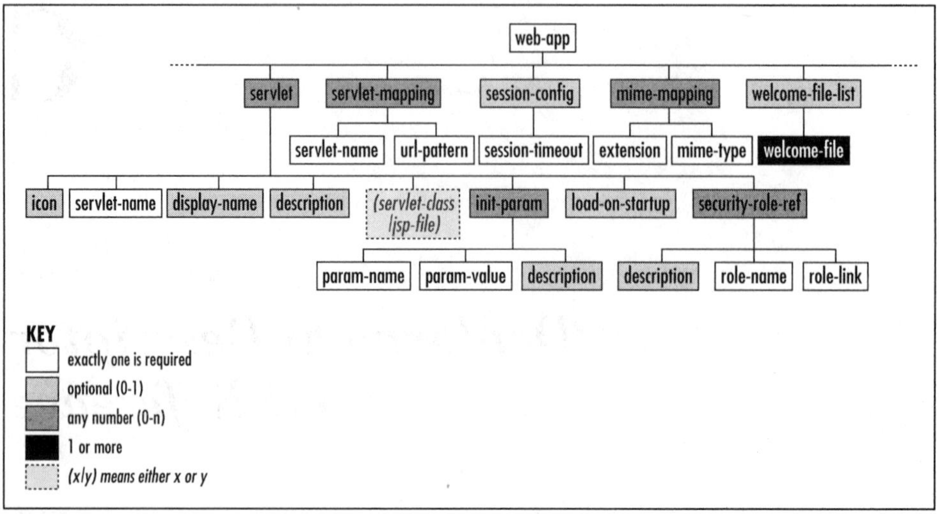

Figure C-2.

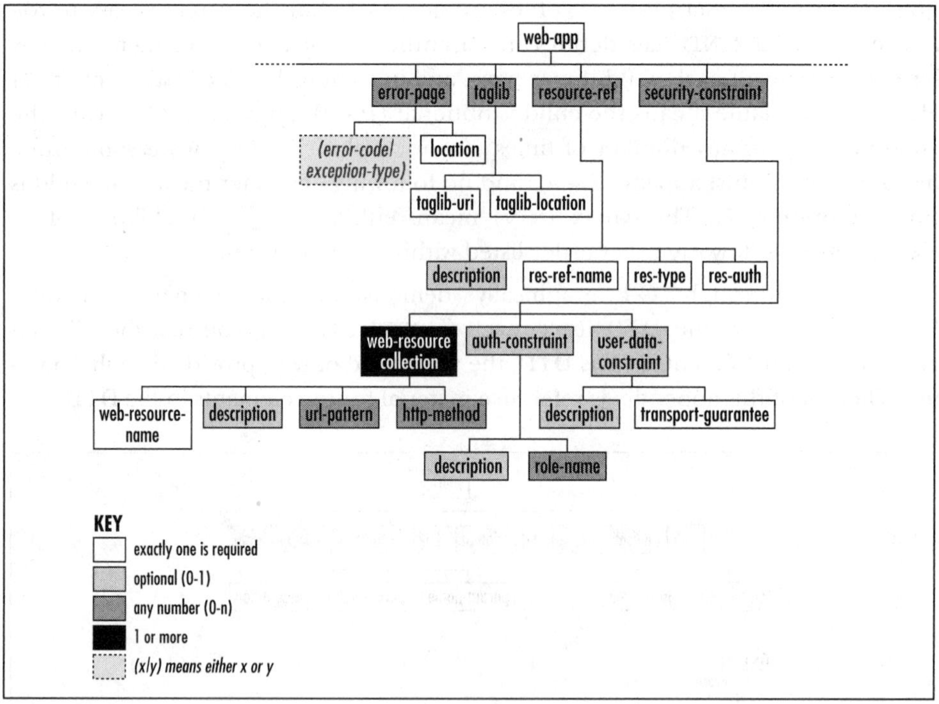

Figure C-3.

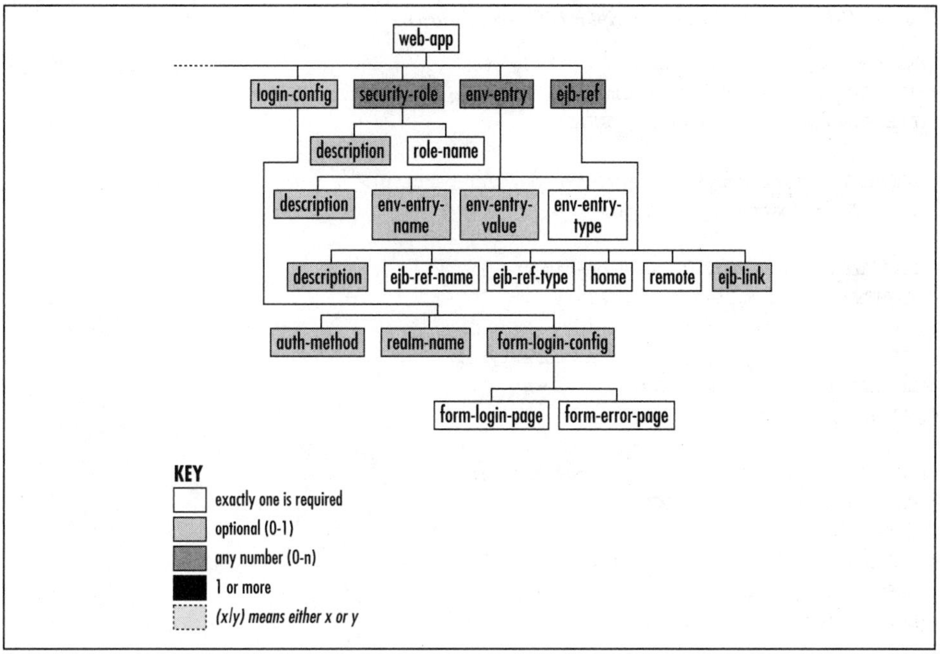

Figure C-4.

Example C-1. The Deployment Descriptor DTD

```
<!ELEMENT web-app (icon?, display-name?, description?, distributable?,
                   context-param*, servlet*, servlet-mapping*, session-config?,
                   mime-mapping*, welcome-file-list?, error-page*, taglib*,
                   resource-ref*, security-constraint*, login-config?,
                   security-role*, env-entry*, ejb-ref*)>

<!ELEMENT icon (small-icon?, large-icon?)>
<!ELEMENT small-icon (#PCDATA)>
<!ELEMENT large-icon (#PCDATA)>
<!ELEMENT display-name (#PCDATA)>
<!ELEMENT description (#PCDATA)>

<!ELEMENT distributable EMPTY>

<!ELEMENT context-param (param-name, param-value, description?)>
<!ELEMENT param-name (#PCDATA)>
<!ELEMENT param-value (#PCDATA)>

<!ELEMENT servlet (icon?, servlet-name, display-name?, description?,
                  (servlet-class|jsp-file), init-param*, load-on-startup?,
                   security-role-ref*)>
<!ELEMENT servlet-name (#PCDATA)>
<!ELEMENT servlet-class (#PCDATA)>
```

Example C-1. The Deployment Descriptor DTD (continued)

```
<!ELEMENT jsp-file (#PCDATA)>
<!ELEMENT init-param (param-name, param-value, description?)>
<!ELEMENT load-on-startup (#PCDATA)>

<!ELEMENT servlet-mapping (servlet-name, url-pattern)>
<!ELEMENT url-pattern (#PCDATA)>

<!ELEMENT session-config (session-timeout?)>
<!ELEMENT session-timeout (#PCDATA)>

<!ELEMENT mime-mapping (extension, mime-type)>
<!ELEMENT extension (#PCDATA)>
<!ELEMENT mime-type (#PCDATA)>

<!ELEMENT welcome-file-list (welcome-file+)>
<!ELEMENT welcome-file (#PCDATA)>

<!ELEMENT taglib (taglib-uri, taglib-location)>
<!ELEMENT taglib-uri (#PCDATA)>
<!ELEMENT taglib-location (#PCDATA)>

<!ELEMENT error-page ((error-code | exception-type), location)>
<!ELEMENT error-code (#PCDATA)>
<!ELEMENT exception-type (#PCDATA)>
<!ELEMENT location (#PCDATA)>

<!ELEMENT resource-ref (description?, res-ref-name, res-type, res-auth)>
<!ELEMENT res-ref-name (#PCDATA)>
<!ELEMENT res-type (#PCDATA)>
<!ELEMENT res-auth (#PCDATA)>

<!ELEMENT security-constraint (web-resource-collection+,
                              auth-constraint?, user-data-constraint?)>
<!ELEMENT web-resource-collection (web-resource-name, description?,
                                  url-pattern*, http-method*)>
<!ELEMENT web-resource-name (#PCDATA)>
<!ELEMENT http-method (#PCDATA)>
<!ELEMENT user-data-constraint (description?, transport-guarantee)>
<!ELEMENT transport-guarantee (#PCDATA)>
<!ELEMENT auth-constraint (description?, role-name*)>
<!ELEMENT role-name (#PCDATA)>

<!ELEMENT login-config (auth-method?, realm-name?, form-login-config?)>
<!ELEMENT realm-name (#PCDATA)>
<!ELEMENT form-login-config (form-login-page, form-error-page)>
<!ELEMENT form-login-page (#PCDATA)>
<!ELEMENT form-error-page (#PCDATA)>
<!ELEMENT auth-method (#PCDATA)>
```

Example C-1. The Deployment Descriptor DTD (continued)

```
<!ELEMENT security-role (description?, role-name)>
<!ELEMENT security-role-ref (description?, role-name, role-link)>
<!ELEMENT role-link (#PCDATA)>

<!ELEMENT env-entry (description?, env-entry-name, env-entry-value?,
                     env-entry-type)>
<!ELEMENT env-entry-name (#PCDATA)>
<!ELEMENT env-entry-value (#PCDATA)>
<!ELEMENT env-entry-type (#PCDATA)>

<!ELEMENT ejb-ref (description?, ejb-ref-name, ejb-ref-type, home, remote,
                   ejb-link?)>
<!ELEMENT ejb-ref-name (#PCDATA)>
<!ELEMENT ejb-ref-type (#PCDATA)>
<!ELEMENT home (#PCDATA)>
<!ELEMENT remote (#PCDATA)>
<!ELEMENT ejb-link (#PCDATA)>

<!-- The ID mechanism is to allow tools to easily make tool-specific
references to the elements of the deployment descriptor.  This allows tools
that produce additional deployment information (i.e., information beyond the
standard deployment descriptor information) to store the nonstandard
information in a separate file and easily refer from these tools-specific
files to the information in the standard web-app deployment descriptor. -->

<!ATTLIST web-app id ID #IMPLIED>
<!ATTLIST icon id ID #IMPLIED>
<!ATTLIST small-icon id ID #IMPLIED>
<!ATTLIST large-icon id ID #IMPLIED>
<!ATTLIST display-name id ID #IMPLIED>
<!ATTLIST description id ID #IMPLIED>
<!ATTLIST distributable id ID #IMPLIED>
<!ATTLIST context-param id ID #IMPLIED>
<!ATTLIST param-name id ID #IMPLIED>
<!ATTLIST param-value id ID #IMPLIED>
<!ATTLIST servlet id ID #IMPLIED>
<!ATTLIST servlet-name id ID #IMPLIED>
<!ATTLIST servlet-class id ID #IMPLIED>
<!ATTLIST jsp-file id ID #IMPLIED>
<!ATTLIST init-param id ID #IMPLIED>
<!ATTLIST load-on-startup id ID #IMPLIED>
<!ATTLIST servlet-mapping id ID #IMPLIED>
<!ATTLIST url-pattern id ID #IMPLIED>
<!ATTLIST session-config id ID #IMPLIED>
<!ATTLIST session-timeout id ID #IMPLIED>
<!ATTLIST mime-mapping id ID #IMPLIED>
<!ATTLIST extension id ID #IMPLIED>
<!ATTLIST mime-type id ID #IMPLIED>
```

Example C-1. The Deployment Descriptor DTD (continued)

```
<!ATTLIST welcome-file-list id ID #IMPLIED>
<!ATTLIST welcome-file id ID #IMPLIED>
<!ATTLIST error-page id ID #IMPLIED>
<!ATTLIST error-code id ID #IMPLIED>
<!ATTLIST exception-type id ID #IMPLIED>
<!ATTLIST location id ID #IMPLIED>
<!ATTLIST resource-ref id ID #IMPLIED>
<!ATTLIST res-ref-name id ID #IMPLIED>
<!ATTLIST res-type id ID #IMPLIED>
<!ATTLIST res-auth id ID #IMPLIED>
<!ATTLIST security-constraint id ID #IMPLIED>
<!ATTLIST web-resource-collection id ID #IMPLIED>
<!ATTLIST web-resource-name id ID #IMPLIED>
<!ATTLIST http-method id ID #IMPLIED>
<!ATTLIST user-data-constraint id ID #IMPLIED>
<!ATTLIST transport-guarantee id ID #IMPLIED>
<!ATTLIST auth-constraint id ID #IMPLIED>
<!ATTLIST role-name id ID #IMPLIED>
<!ATTLIST auth-method id ID #IMPLIED>
<!ATTLIST basic-auth id ID #IMPLIED>
<!ATTLIST form-auth id ID #IMPLIED>
<!ATTLIST form-login-page id ID #IMPLIED>
<!ATTLIST form-error-page id ID #IMPLIED>
<!ATTLIST form-login-config id ID #IMPLIED>
<!ATTLIST realm-name id ID #IMPLIED>
<!ATTLIST login-config id ID #IMPLIED>
<!ATTLIST security-role id ID #IMPLIED>
<!ATTLIST security-role-ref id ID #IMPLIED>
<!ATTLIST role-link id ID #IMPLIED>
<!ATTLIST env-entry id ID #IMPLIED>
<!ATTLIST env-entry-name id ID #IMPLIED>
<!ATTLIST env-entry-value id ID #IMPLIED>
<!ATTLIST env-entry-type id ID #IMPLIED>
<!ATTLIST mutual-auth id ID #IMPLIED>
<!ATTLIST ejb-ref id ID #IMPLIED>
<!ATTLIST ejb-ref-name id ID #IMPLIED>
<!ATTLIST ejb-ref-type id ID #IMPLIED>
<!ATTLIST home id ID #IMPLIED>
<!ATTLIST remote id ID #IMPLIED>
<!ATTLIST ejb-link id ID #IMPLIED>
```

<auth-constraint>

Synopsis

```
<!ELEMENT auth-constraint (description?, role-name*)>
```

Description

The <auth-constraint> element indicates the user roles that should be permitted access to a resource collection. The role names used here must appear in a <security-role-ref> element.

```
<security-constraint>
    <web-resource-collection>
        ...
    </web-resource-collection>
    <auth-constraint>
        <role-name>manager</role-name>
    </auth-constraint>
</security-constraint>
```

<auth-method>

Synopsis

```
<!ELEMENT auth-method (#PCDATA)>
```

Description

The <auth-method> element is used to configure the authentication mechanism for the web application. As a prerequisite to gaining access to any web resources that are protected by an authorization constraint, a user must have authenticated using the configured mechanism. Legal values for this element are BASIC, DIGEST, FORM, and CLIENT-CERT.

```
<login-config>
    <auth-method>BASIC</auth-method>
    <realm-name>Default</realm-name>
</login-config>
```

<context-param>

Synopsis

```
<!ELEMENT context-param (param-name, param-value, description?)>
```

Description

The <context-param> element contains the declaration of a web application's servlet context initialization parameters.

```
<context-param>
    <param-name>rmihost</param-name>
    <param-value>localhost</param-value>
</context-param>
```

<description>

Synopsis

```
<!ELEMENT description (#PCDATA)>
```

Description

The `<description>` element is used to provide descriptive text about the parent element.

```
<description>Don't forget to say Hello!</description>
```

<display-name>

Synopsis

```
<!ELEMENT display-name (#PCDATA)>
```

Description

The `<display-name>` element contains a short name for a servlet that is intended to be displayed by GUI tools.

```
<servlet>
    <servlet-name>hi</servlet-name>
    <display-name>HelloWorld</display-name>
    <servlet-class>HelloWorld</servlet-class>
</servlet>
```

<distributable>

Synopsis

```
<!ELEMENT distributable EMPTY>
```

Description

The <distributable> element, by its presence in a web application deployment descriptor, indicates that the web application is programmed appropriately to be deployed into a distributed servlet container.

```
<web-app>
    <description>
        All servlets and JSPs are ready for distributed deployment
    </description>

    <distributable/>
...
```

<ejb-link>

Synopsis

```
<!ELEMENT ejb-link (#PCDATA)>
```

Description

The <ejb-link> element is used in the <ejb-ref> element to specify that an EJB reference is linked to an EJB in an encompassing Java 2, Enterprise Edition (J2EE) application package. The value of the <ejb-link> element must be the <ejb-name> of the EJB in the J2EE application package.

```
<ejb-ref>
    <description>Cruise ship cabin</description>
    <ejb-ref-name>ejb/CabinHome</ejb-ref-name>
    <ejb-ref-type>Entity</ejb-ref-type>
    <home>com.titan.cabin.CabinHome</home>
    <remote>com.titan.cabin.Cabin</remote>
    <ejb-link>CabinBean</ejb-link>
</ejb-ref>
```

<ejb-ref>

Synopsis

```
<!ELEMENT ejb-ref (description?, ejb-ref-name, ejb-ref-type, home, remote,
                   ejb-link?)>
```

Description

The <ejb-ref> element is used to declare a reference to an enterprise bean.

```
<ejb-ref>
    <description>Cruise ship cabin</description>
    <ejb-ref-name>ejb/CabinHome</ejb-ref-name>
    <ejb-ref-type>Entity</ejb-ref-type>
    <home>com.titan.cabin.CabinHome</home>
    <remote>com.titan.cabin.Cabin</remote>
</ejb-ref>
```

<ejb-ref-name>

Synopsis

```
<!ELEMENT ejb-ref-name (#PCDATA)>
```

Description

The `<ejb-ref-name>` element contains the name of an EJB reference. This is the JNDI name that the servlet code uses to get a reference to the enterprise bean.

```
<ejb-ref>
    <description>Cruise ship cabin</description>
    <ejb-ref-name>ejb/CabinHome</ejb-ref-name>
    <ejb-ref-type>Entity</ejb-ref-type>
    <home>com.titan.cabin.CabinHome</home>
    <remote>com.titan.cabin.Cabin</remote>
</ejb-ref>
```

<ejb-ref-type>

Synopsis

```
<!ELEMENT ejb-ref-type (#PCDATA)>
```

Description

The `<ejb-ref-type>` element contains the bean type. Its value must be either `Entity` or `Session`.*

```
<ejb-ref>
    <description>Cruise ship cabin</description>
    <ejb-ref-name>ejb/CabinHome</ejb-ref-name>
    <ejb-ref-type>Entity</ejb-ref-type>
```

* The original comment for this tag erroneously declares that the tag "contains the expected Java class type of the referenced EJB."

```
        <home>com.titan.cabin.CabinHome</home>
        <remote>com.titan.cabin.Cabin</remote>
    </ejb-ref>
```

<env-entry>

Synopsis

```
<!ELEMENT env-entry (description?, env-entry-name, env-entry-value?,
                     env-entry-type)>
```

Description

The <env-entry> element contains the declaration of an application's environment entry, available through a JNDI lookup in the `java:comp/env` context.

```
<env-entry>
    <description>Send pincode by mail</description>
    <env-entry-name>mailPincode</env-entry-name>
    <env-entry-value>false</env-entry-value>
    <env-entry-type>java.lang.Boolean</env-entry-type> <!-- FQCN -->
</env-entry>
```

<env-entry-name>

Synopsis

```
<!ELEMENT env-entry-name (#PCDATA)>
```

Description

The <env-entry-name> element specifies the lookup name of an application's environment entry.

```
<env-entry>
    <description>Send pincode by mail</description>
    <env-entry-name>mailPincode</env-entry-name>
    <env-entry-value>false</env-entry-value>
    <env-entry-type>java.lang.Boolean</env-entry-type> <!-- FQCN -->
</env-entry>
```

<env-entry-type>

Synopsis

```
<!ELEMENT env-entry-type (#PCDATA)>
```

Description

The <env-entry-type> element contains the fully qualified Java type of the environment entry value that is expected by the application code. The following are the legal values of <env-entry-type>: `java.lang.Boolean`, `java.lang.String`, `java.lang.Integer`, `java.lang.Double`, and `java.lang.Float`.

```
<env-entry>
    <description>Send pincode by mail</description>
    <env-entry-name>mailPincode</env-entry-name>
    <env-entry-value>false</env-entry-value>
    <env-entry-type>java.lang.Boolean</env-entry-type> <!-- FQCN -->
</env-entry>
```

<env-entry-value>

Synopsis

```
<!ELEMENT env-entry-value (#PCDATA)>
```

Description

The <env-entry-value> element contains the default value of an application's environment entry.

```
<env-entry>
    <description>Send pincode by mail</description>
    <env-entry-name>mailPincode</env-entry-name>
    <env-entry-value>false</env-entry-value>
    <env-entry-type>java.lang.Boolean</env-entry-type> <!-- FQCN -->
</env-entry>
```

<error-code>

Synopsis

```
<!ELEMENT error-code (#PCDATA)>
```

Description

The <error-code> element contains an HTTP error code.

```
<error-page>
    <error-code>400</error-code>
    <location>/400.html</location>
</error-page>
```

<error-page>

Synopsis

```
<!ELEMENT error-page ((error-code | exception-type), location)>
```

Description

The <error-page> element contains a mapping between an error code or exception type and the path of a resource in the web application.

```
<error-page>
    <error-code>400</error-code>
    <location>/400.html</location>
</error-page>
```

<exception-type>

Synopsis

```
<!ELEMENT exception-type (#PCDATA)>
```

Description

The <exception-type> element contains a fully qualified class name of a Java exception type.

```
<error-page>
    <exception-type>javax.servlet.ServletException</exception-type>
    <location>/servlet/ErrorDisplay</location>
</error-page>
```

<extension>

Synopsis

```
<!ELEMENT extension (#PCDATA)>
```

Description

The `<extension>` element contains a string describing a file extension.

```
<mime-mapping>
    <extension>wml</extension>
    <mime-type>text/vnd.wap.wml</mime-type>
</mime-mapping>
```

<form-error-page>

Synopsis

```
<!ELEMENT form-error-page (#PCDATA)>
```

Description

The `<form-error-page>` element defines the location in the web application of the error page that is displayed when login is not successful.

```
<form-login-config>
    <form-login-page>/loginpage.html</form-login-page>
    <form-error-page>/errorpage.html</form-error-page>
</form-login-config>
```

<form-login-config>

Synopsis

```
<!ELEMENT form-login-config (form-login-page, form-error-page)>
```

Description

The `<form-login-config>` element specifies the login and error pages that should be used in form-based login. If form-based authentication is not used, these elements are ignored.

```
<login-config>
    <auth-method>FORM</auth-method>
```

```
    <form-login-config>
        <form-login-page>/loginpage.html</form-login-page>
        <form-error-page>/errorpage.html</form-error-page>
    </form-login-config>
</login-config>
```

<form-login-page>

Synopsis

```
<!ELEMENT form-login-page (#PCDATA)>
```

Description

The <form-login-page> element defines the location in the web application of the login page.

```
<form-login-config>
    <form-login-page>/loginpage.html</form-login-page>
    <form-error-page>/errorpage.html</form-error-page>
</form-login-config>
```

<home>

Synopsis

```
<!ELEMENT home (#PCDATA)>
```

Description

The <home> element contains the fully qualified name of the EJB's home interface.

```
<ejb-ref>
    <description>Cruise ship cabin</description>
    <ejb-ref-name>ejb/CabinHome</ejb-ref-name>
    <ejb-ref-type>Entity</ejb-ref-type>
    <home>com.titan.cabin.CabinHome</home>
    <remote>com.titan.cabin.Cabin</remote>
</ejb-ref>
```

<http-method>

Synopsis

```
<!ELEMENT http-method (#PCDATA)>
```

Description

The <http-method> element specifies an HTTP method.

```
<web-resource-collection>
    <web-resource-name>SecretProtection</web-resource-name>
    <url-pattern>/servlet/SalaryServer</url-pattern>
    <url-pattern>/servlet/secret</url-pattern>
    <http-method>GET</http-method>
    <http-method>POST</http-method>
</web-resource-collection>
```

<icon>

Synopsis

```
<!ELEMENT icon (small-icon?, large-icon?)>
```

Description

The <icon> element can contain <small-icon> and <large-icon> elements that specify the location within the web application file structure for small and large images used to represent the web application in a GUI tool.

```
<icon>
    <small-icon>/images/little.gif</small-icon>
    <large-icon>/images/big.gif</large-icon>
</icon>
```

<init-param>

Synopsis

```
<!ELEMENT init-param (param-name, param-value, description?)>
```

Description

The <init-param> element contains a name/value pair that specifies an initialization parameter for the servlet.

```
<init-param>
    <param-name>key</param-name>
    <param-value>-9151314447111823249</param-value>
</init-param>
```

<jsp-file>

Synopsis

```
<!ELEMENT jsp-file (#PCDATA)>
```

Description

The `<jsp-file>` element contains the path to a JSP file within the web application.

```
<servlet>
    <servlet-name>catalog-order</servlet-name>
    <servlet-class>Catalog</servlet-class>
    <jsp-file>/orderform.jsp</jsp-file>
</servlet>
```

<large-icon>

Synopsis

```
<!ELEMENT large-icon (#PCDATA)>
```

Description

The `<large-icon>` element specifies the location within the web application of a file containing a large (32×32 pixel) icon image. At a minimum, tools will accept GIF and JPEG format images.

```
<icon>
    <small-icon>/images/little.gif</small-icon>
    <large-icon>/images/big.gif</large-icon>
</icon>
```

<load-on-startup>

Synopsis

```
<!ELEMENT load-on-startup (#PCDATA)>
```

Description

The <load-on-startup> element indicates that the servlet should be loaded on the startup of the web application. The optional contents of this element must be a positive integer that specifies the order in which the servlet should be loaded. Servlets with lower values are loaded before servlets with higher values. If no value is specified or if the value specified is not a positive integer, the container is free to load the servlet at any time in the startup sequence.

```
<servlet>
    <servlet-name>ps</servlet-name>
    <servlet-class>PrimeSearcher</servlet-class>
    <load-on-startup/>
</servlet>
```

<location>

Synopsis

```
<!ELEMENT location (#PCDATA)>
```

Description

The <location> element contains the location of a resource in the web application.

```
<error-page>
    <exception-type>javax.servlet.ServletException</exception-type>
    <location>/servlet/ErrorDisplay</location>
</error-page>
```

<login-config>

Synopsis

```
<!ELEMENT login-config (auth-method?, realm-name?, form-login-config?)>
```

Description

The <login-config> element is used to configure the authentication method and the realm name that should be used for the application, as well as the attributes for form-based login, if it is used.

```
<login-config>
    <auth-method>BASIC</auth-method>
    <realm-name>Default</realm-name>
</login-config>
```

<mime-mapping>

Synopsis

```
<!ELEMENT mime-mapping (extension, mime-type)>
```

Description

The <mime-mapping> element defines a mapping between an extension and a MIME type.

```
<mime-mapping>
    <extension>wml</extension>
    <mime-type>text/vnd.wap.wml</mime-type>
</mime-mapping>
```

<mime-type>

Synopsis

```
<!ELEMENT mime-type (#PCDATA)>
```

Description

The <mime-type> element contains a defined MIME type.

```
<mime-mapping>
    <extension>wml</extension>
    <mime-type>text/vnd.wap.wml</mime-type>
</mime-mapping>
```

<param-name>

Synopsis

```
<!ELEMENT param-name (#PCDATA)>
```

Description

The <param-name> element contains the name of a parameter.

```
<context-param>
    <param-name>rmihost</param-name>
    <param-value>localhost</param-value>
</context-param>
```

<param-value>

Synopsis

```
<!ELEMENT param-value (#PCDATA)>
```

Description

The <param-value> element contains the value of a parameter.

```
<init-param>
    <param-name>key</param-name>
    <param-value>-9151314447111823249</param-value>
</init-param>
```

<realm-name>

Synopsis

```
<!ELEMENT realm-name (#PCDATA)>
```

Description

The <realm-name> element specifies the realm name to use in HTTP basic authentication.

```
<login-config>
    <auth-method>BASIC</auth-method>
    <realm-name>Default</realm-name>
</login-config>
```

<remote>

Synopsis

```
<!ELEMENT remote (#PCDATA)>
```

Description

The <remote> element contains the fully qualified name of the EJB's remote interface.

```
<ejb-ref>
    <description>Cruise ship cabin</description>
    <ejb-ref-name>ejb/CabinHome</ejb-ref-name>
```

```
    <ejb-ref-type>Entity</ejb-ref-type>
    <home>com.titan.cabin.CabinHome</home>
    <remote>com.titan.cabin.Cabin</remote>
</ejb-ref>
```

<res-auth>

Synopsis

```
<!ELEMENT res-auth (#PCDATA)>
```

Description

The <res-auth> element indicates whether the application component code performs resource sign-on programmatically or whether the container signs onto the resource based on the principal mapping information supplied by the deployer. Must be CONTAINER or SERVLET.

```
<resource-ref>
    <description>Primary database</description>
    <res-ref-name>jdbc/primaryDB</res-ref-name>
    <res-type>javax.sql.DataSource</res-type>
    <res-auth>CONTAINER</res-auth>
</resource-ref>
```

<res-ref-name>

Synopsis

```
<!ELEMENT res-ref-name (#PCDATA)>
```

Description

The <res-ref-name> element specifies the name of a resource factory reference.

```
<resource-ref>
    <description>Primary database</description>
    <res-ref-name>jdbc/primaryDB</res-ref-name>
    <res-type>javax.sql.DataSource</res-type>
    <res-auth>CONTAINER</res-auth>
</resource-ref>
```

<res-type>

Synopsis

```
<!ELEMENT res-type (#PCDATA)>
```

Description

The `<res-type>` element specifies the (Java class) type of the data source.

```
<resource-ref>
    <description>Primary database</description>
    <res-ref-name>jdbc/primaryDB</res-ref-name>
    <res-type>javax.sql.DataSource</res-type>
    <res-auth>CONTAINER</res-auth>
</resource-ref>
```

<resource-ref>

Synopsis

```
<!ELEMENT resource-ref (description?, res-ref-name, res-type, res-auth)>
```

Description

The `<resource-ref>` element contains a declaration of a web application's reference to an external resource, such as an Enterprise JavaBeans component or a JDBC `DataSource` object.

```
<resource-ref>
    <description>Primary database</description>
    <res-ref-name>jdbc/primaryDB</res-ref-name>
    <res-type>javax.sql.DataSource</res-type>
    <res-auth>CONTAINER</res-auth>
</resource-ref>
```

<role-link>

Synopsis

```
<!ELEMENT role-link (#PCDATA)>
```

Description

The <role-link> element is used to link a security role reference to a defined security role. The element must contain the name of one of the security roles defined in the <security-role> elements.

```
<security-role-ref>
    <role-name>mgr</role-name>
    <role-link>manager</role-link>
</security-role-ref>
```

<role-name>

Synopsis

```
<!ELEMENT role-name (#PCDATA)>
```

Description

The <role-name> element contains the name of a security role.

```
<auth-constraint>
    <role-name>manager</role-name>
</auth-constraint>
```

<security-constraint>

Synopsis

```
<!ELEMENT security-constraint (web-resource-collection+,
                               auth-constraint?, user-data-constraint?)>
```

Description

The <security-constraint> element is used to associate security constraints with one or more web resource collections.

```
<security-constraint>
    <web-resource-collection>
        <web-resource-name>SecretProtection</web-resource-name>
        <url-pattern>/servlet/SalaryServer</url-pattern>
        <url-pattern>/servlet/secret</url-pattern>
        <http-method>GET</http-method>
        <http-method>POST</http-method>
    </web-resource-collection>
    <auth-constraint>
```

```
        <role-name>manager</role-name>
    </auth-constraint>
</security-constraint>
```

<security-role>

Synopsis

```
<!ELEMENT security-role (description?, role-name)>
```

Description

The <security-role> element contains the declaration of a security role that is used in the security constraints placed on the web application.

```
<security-role>
    <role-name>manager</role-name>
</security-role>
```

<security-role-ref>

Synopsis

```
<!ELEMENT security-role-ref (description?, role-name, role-link)>
```

Description

The <security-role-ref> element specifies an alias for a security role, mapping between the name used by a servlet and the name used in the deployment descriptor.

```
<security-role-ref>
    <role-name>mgr</role-name>
    <role-link>manager</role-link>
</security-role-ref>
```

<servlet>

Synopsis

```
<!ELEMENT servlet (icon?, servlet-name, display-name?, description?,
                  (servlet-class|jsp-file), init-param*, load-on-startup?,
                   security-role-ref*)>
```

Description

The <servlet> element contains the declarative data of a servlet, such as its registered name and its class file.

```
<servlet>
    <servlet-name>hi</servlet-name>
    <display-name>hi</display-name>
    <description>Don't forget to say hello!</description>
    <servlet-class>HelloWorld</servlet-class>
    <init-param>
        <param-name>defaultName</param-name>
        <param-value>World</param-value>
    </init-param>
    <load-on-startup/>
    <security-role-ref>
        <role-name>mgr</role-name>
        <role-link>manager</role-link>
    </security-role-ref>
</servlet>
```

<servlet-class>

Synopsis

```
<!ELEMENT servlet-class (#PCDATA)>
```

Description

<servlet-class> contains the fully qualified class name of the servlet.

```
<servlet>
    <servlet-name>hi</servlet-name>
    <servlet-class>HelloWorld</servlet-class>
</servlet>
```

<servlet-mapping>

Synopsis

```
<!ELEMENT servlet-mapping (servlet-name, url-pattern)>
```

Description

The <servlet-mapping> element defines a mapping between a servlet and a URL pattern.

```
<servlet-mapping>
    <servlet-name>hi</servlet-name>
    <url-pattern>/hello.html</url-pattern>
</servlet-mapping>
```

<servlet-name>

Synopsis

```
<!ELEMENT servlet-name (#PCDATA)>
```

Description

The <servlet-name> element specifies the canonical name of the servlet.

```
<servlet>
    <servlet-name>hi</servlet-name>
    <servlet-class>HelloWorld</servlet-class>
</servlet>
```

<session-config>

Synopsis

```
<!ELEMENT session-config (session-timeout?)>
```

Description

The <session-config> element defines the session parameters for the web application.

```
<session-config>
    <session-timeout>60 <!-- minutes --></session-timeout>
</session-config>
```

<session-timeout>

Synopsis

```
<!ELEMENT session-timeout (#PCDATA)>
```

Description

The <session-timeout> element defines the default session timeout interval for all sessions created in the web application. The specified timeout must be expressed in a whole number of minutes.

```
<session-config>
    <session-timeout>60 <!-- minutes --></session-timeout>
</session-config>
```

<small-icon>

Synopsis

```
<!ELEMENT small-icon (#PCDATA)>
```

Description

The <small-icon> element specifies the location within the web application of a file containing a small (16×16 pixel) icon image. At a minimum, tools will accept GIF and JPEG format images.

```
<icon>
    <small-icon>/images/little.gif</small-icon>
    <large-icon>/images/big.gif</large-icon>
</icon>
```

<taglib>

Synopsis

```
<!ELEMENT taglib (taglib-uri, taglib-location)>
```

Description

The <taglib> element is used to describe a JSP tag library.

```
<taglib>
    <taglib-uri>/WEB-INF/struts.tld</taglib-uri>
    <taglib-location>/WEB-INF/struts.tld</taglib-location>
</taglib>
```

<taglib-location>

Synopsis

```
<!ELEMENT taglib-location (#PCDATA)>
```

Description

The <taglib-location> element contains the location (as a resource relative to the root of the web application) of the Tag Library Description file for the tag library.

```
<taglib>
    <taglib-uri>/WEB-INF/struts.tld</taglib-uri>
    <taglib-location>/WEB-INF/struts.tld</taglib-location>
</taglib>
```

<taglib-uri>

Synopsis

```
<!ELEMENT taglib-uri (#PCDATA)>
```

Description

The <taglib-uri> element describes a URI, relative to the location of the *web.xml* document, that identifies a tag library used in the web application.

```
<taglib>
    <taglib-uri>/WEB-INF/struts.tld</taglib-uri>
    <taglib-location>/WEB-INF/struts.tld</taglib-location>
</taglib>
```

<transport-guarantee>

Synopsis

```
<!ELEMENT transport-guarantee (#PCDATA)>
```

Description

The <transport-guarantee> element specifies that the communication between client and server should be NONE, INTEGRAL, or CONFIDENTIAL. NONE means that the application does not require any transport guarantees. A value of INTEGRAL means that the application requires that the data sent between the client and server be sent in such a way that it can't be changed in transit. CONFIDENTIAL means that the application requires that the data be transmitted in a fashion that prevents other entities from observing the contents of the transmission. In most cases, the presence of the INTEGRAL or CONFIDENTIAL flag will indicate that the use of SSL is required.

```
<user-data-constraint>
    <transport-guarantee>CONFIDENTIAL</transport-guarantee>
</user-data-constraint>
```

<url-pattern>

Synopsis

```
<!ELEMENT url-pattern (#PCDATA)>
```

Description

The <url-pattern> element contains the URL pattern of a mapping for a servlet. This pattern must follow the rules specified in Section 10 of the Servlet API specification and explained in Chapter 2, *HTTP Servlet Basics.*

```
<servlet-mapping>
    <servlet-name>hi</servlet-name>
    <url-pattern>/hello.html</url-pattern>
</servlet-mapping>
```

<user-data-constraint>

Synopsis

```
<!ELEMENT user-data-constraint (description?, transport-guarantee)>
```

Description

The <user-data-constraint> element is used to indicate how data communicated between the client and container should be protected.

```
<security-constraint>
    <web-resource-collection>
        ...
    </web-resource-collection>
```

```
    <user-data-constraint>
        <transport-guarantee>CONFIDENTIAL</transport-guarantee>
    </user-data-constraint>
</security-constraint>
```

<web-app>

Synopsis

```
<!ELEMENT web-app (icon?, display-name?, description?, distributable?,
                   context-param*, servlet*, servlet-mapping*, session-config?,
                   mime-mapping*, welcome-file-list?, error-page*, taglib*,
                   resource-ref*, security-constraint*, login-config?,
                   security-role*, env-entry*, ejb-ref*)>
```

Description

The <web-app> element is the root element of the deployment descriptor for a web application.

```
<?xml version="1.0" encoding="ISO-8859-1"?>

<!DOCTYPE web-app
    PUBLIC "-//Sun Microsystems, Inc.//DTD Web Application 2.2//EN"
    "http://java.sun.com/j2ee/dtds/web-app_2_2.dtd">

<web-app>
    <servlet>
        <servlet-name>hi</servlet-name>
        <servlet-class>HelloWorld</servlet-class>
    </servlet>
</web-app>
```

<web-resource-collection>

Synopsis

```
<!ELEMENT web-resource-collection (web-resource-name, description?,
                                   url-pattern*, http-method*)>
```

Description

The <web-resource-collection> element is used to identify a subset of the resources and HTTP methods on those resources within a web application to which a security constraint applies. If no HTTP methods are specified, the security constraint applies to all HTTP methods.

```
<security-constraint>
    <web-resource-collection>
        <web-resource-name>SecretProtection</web-resource-name>
        <url-pattern>/servlet/SalaryServer</url-pattern>
        <url-pattern>/servlet/secret</url-pattern>
        <http-method>GET</http-method>
        <http-method>POST</http-method>
    </web-resource-collection>
</security-constraint>
```

<web-resource-name>

Synopsis

```
<!ELEMENT web-resource-name (#PCDATA)>
```

Description

The `<web-resource-name>` specifies the name of the web resource collection.

```
<web-resource-collection>
    <web-resource-name>SecretProtection</web-resource-name>
    <url-pattern>/servlet/SalaryServer</url-pattern>
    <url-pattern>/servlet/secret</url-pattern>
    <http-method>GET</http-method>
    <http-method>POST</http-method>
</web-resource-collection>
```

<welcome-file>

Synopsis

```
<!ELEMENT welcome-file (#PCDATA)>
```

Description

The `<welcome-file>` element contains a filename to use as a default welcome file.

```
<welcome-file-list>
    <welcome-file>index.html</welcome-file>
    <welcome-file>index.htm</welcome-file>
</welcome-file-list>
```

<welcome-file-list>

Synopsis

```
<!ELEMENT welcome-file-list (welcome-file+)>
```

Description

The `<welcome-file-list>` specifies a list of files that the container should search for when a browser requests a directory, rather than a web page or a servlet.

```
<welcome-file-list>
    <welcome-file>index.html</welcome-file>
    <welcome-file>index.htm</welcome-file>
</welcome-file-list>
```

D

HTTP Status Codes

HTTP status codes are grouped as shown in Table D-1.

Table D-1. HTTP Status Code Groupings

Code Range	Response Meaning
`100-199`	Informational
`200-299`	Client request successful
`300-399`	Client request redirected, further action necessary
`400-499`	Client request incomplete
`500-599`	Server error

Table D-2 lists the HTTP status code constants defined by the `HttpServletResponse` interface and used as parameters to its `setStatus()` and `sendError()` methods. The version number in the last column refers to the HTTP protocol version that first defined the status code. Servlet API 2.0 added constants for HTTP Version 1.1 status codes as specified in the *proposed standard* RFC 2068; Servlet API 2.2 added status codes 416 and 417 as specified in the *draft standard* RFC 2616. Note that HTTP/1.1 status codes require an HTTP/1.1-compliant browser.

For more information on HTTP, see the book *Web Client Programming* by Clinton Wong (O'Reilly). The latest HTTP/1.1 specification is available in RFC 2616 at *http://www.ietf.org/rfc/rfc2616.txt.*

Table D-2. HTTP Status Code Constants

Constant	Code	Default Message	Meaning	HTTP Version
`SC_CONTINUE`	100	Continue	The server has received the initial part of the request and the client can continue with the remainder of its request.	1.1
`SC_SWITCHING_PROTOCOLS`	101	Switching Protocols	The server is willing to comply with the client's request to switch protocols to the one specified in the request's `Upgrade` header. This might include switching to a newer HTTP version or to a custom synchronous video streaming protocol.	1.1
`SC_OK`	200	OK	The client's request was successful and the server's response contains the requested data. This is the default status code.	1.0
`SC_CREATED`	201	Created	A resource has been created on the server, presumably in response to a client request. The response body should include the URL(s) where the new resource can be found, with the most specific URL set in the `Location` header. If the resource cannot be created immediately, an `SC_ACCEPTED` status code should be returned instead.	1.0
`SC_ACCEPTED`	202	Accepted	The request has been accepted for processing but has not yet completed. The server should describe the current status of the request in the response body. The server is under no obligation to act on or complete the request.	1.0
`SC_NON_AUTHORITATIVE_INFORMATION`	203	Non-Authoritative Information	The HTTP response headers came from a local or third-party source, rather than the original server. Normal servlets have no reason to use this status code.	1.1

Table D-2. HTTP Status Code Constants (continued)

Constant	Code	Default Message	Meaning	HTTP Version
SC_NO_CONTENT	204	No Content	The request succeeded but there was no new response body to return. Browsers receiving this code should retain their current document view. This is a useful code for a servlet when it accepts data from a form but wants the browser view to stay at the form, as it avoids the "Document contains no data" error message.	1.0
SC_RESET_ CONTENT	205	Reset Content	The request succeeded and the browser should reset (reload) the current document view. This is a useful code for a servlet when it accepts data from a form and wants the form redisplayed in a fresh state.	1.1
SC_PARTIAL_ CONTENT	206	Partial Content	The server has completed a partial GET request and returned the portion of the document specified in the client's `Range` header.	1.1
SC_MULTIPLE_ CHOICES	300	Multiple Choices	The requested URL refers to more than one resource. For example, the URL may refer to a document translated into many languages. The response body should explain the client's options in a format appropriate for the response content type. The server can suggest a choice with the `Location` header.	1.1
SC_MOVED_ PERMANENTLY	301	Moved Permanently	The requested resource has permanently moved to a new location. Future references should use the new URL in requests. The new location is given by the `Location` header. Most browsers automatically access the new location.	1.0

Table D-2. HTTP Status Code Constants (continued)

Constant	Code	Default Message	Meaning	HTTP Version
SC_MOVED_TEMPORARILY	302	Moved Temporarily	The requested resource has temporarily moved to another location, but future references should still use the original URI to access the resource. The new location is given by the `Location` header. Most browsers automatically access the new location.	1.0
SC_SEE_OTHER	303	See Other	The requested resource processed the request but the client should get its response by performing a GET on the URL specified in the `Location` header. This code is useful for a servlet that wants to receive POST data then redirect the client to another resource for the response.	1.1
SC_NOT_MODIFIED	304	Not Modified	The requested document has not changed since the date specified in the request's `If-Modified-Since` header. Normal servlets should not need to use this status code. They implement `getLastModified()` instead.	1.0
SC_USE_PROXY	305	Use Proxy	The requested resource must be accessed via the proxy given in the `Location` header.	1.1
SC_BAD_REQUEST	400	Bad Request	The server could not understand the request, probably due to a syntax error.	1.0
SC_UNAUTHORIZED	401	Unauthorized	The request lacked proper authorization. Used in conjunction with the `WWW-Authenticate` and `Authorization` headers.	1.0
SC_PAYMENT_REQUIRED	402	Payment Required	Reserved for future use. Proposals exist to use this code in conjunction with a `Charge-To` header, but this has not been standardized as of press time.	1.1

Table D-2. HTTP Status Code Constants (continued)

Constant	Code	Default Message	Meaning	HTTP Version
SC_FORBIDDEN	403	Forbidden	The request was understood, but the server is not willing to fulfill it. The server can explain the reason for its unwillingness in the response body.	1.0
SC_NOT_FOUND	404	Not Found	The requested resource was not found or is not available.	1.0
SC_METHOD_NOT_ALLOWED	405	Method Not Allowed	The method used by the client is not supported by this URL. The methods that are supported must be listed in the response's `Allow` header.	1.1
SC_NOT_ACCEPTABLE	406	Not Acceptable	The requested resource exists, but not in a format acceptable to the client (as indicated by the `Accept` header(s) in the request).	1.1
SC_PROXY_AUTHENTICATION_REQUIRED	407	Proxy Authentication Required	The proxy server needs authorization before it can proceed. Used with the `Proxy-Authenticate` header. Normal servlets should not need to use this status code.	1.1
SC_REQUEST_TIMEOUT	408	Request Timeout	The client did not completely finish its request within the time that the server was willing to listen.	1.1
SC_CONFLICT	409	Conflict	The request could not be completed because it conflicted with another request or the server's configuration. This code is most likely to occur with HTTP PUT requests, where the file being put is under revision control and the new version conflicts with some previous changes. The server can send a description of the conflict in the response body.	1.0

Table D-2. HTTP Status Code Constants (continued)

Constant	Code	Default Message	Meaning	HTTP Version
SC_GONE	410	Gone	The resource is no longer available at this server and no alternate address is known. This code should be used only when the resource has been permanently removed. Normal servlets have no reason to use this status code.	1.1
SC_LENGTH_REQUIRED	411	Length Required	The server will not accept the request without a `Content-Length` header.	1.1
SC_PRECONDITION_FAILED	412	Precondition Failed	A precondition specified by one or more `If...` headers in the request evaluated to `false`.	1.1
SC_REQUEST_ENTITY_TOO_LARGE	413	Request Entity Too Large	The server will not process the request because the request content is too large. If this limitation is temporary, the server can include a `Retry-After` header.	1.1
SC_REQUEST_URI_TOO_LONG	414	Request-URI Too Long	The server will not process the request because the request URI is longer than the server is willing to interpret. This can occur when a client has accidentally converted a POST request into a GET request. Normal servlets have no reason to use this status code.	1.1
SC_UNSUPPORTED_MEDIA_TYPE	415	Unsupported Media Type	The server will not process the request because the request body is in a format unsupported by the requested resource.	1.1
SC_REQUESTED_RANGE_NOT_SATISFYABLE	416	Requested Range Not Satisfiable	The range of content requested by the client via the `Range` header does not overlap with the size of the requested resource.	1.1 (RFC 2616)
SC_EXPECTATION_FAILED	417	Expectation Failed	The expectation given by the client via the `Expect` header could not be met.	1.1 (RFC 2616)
SC_INTERNAL_SERVER_ERROR	500	Internal Server Error	An unexpected error occurred inside the server that prevented it from fulfilling the request.	1.0

Table D-2. HTTP Status Code Constants (continued)

Constant	Code	Default Message	Meaning	HTTP Version
SC_NOT_ IMPLEMENTED	501	Not Implemented	The server does not support the functionality needed to fulfill the request.	1.0
SC_BAD_GATEWAY	502	Bad Gateway	A server acting as a gateway or proxy did not receive a valid response from an upstream server.	1.0
SC_SERVICE_ UNAVAILABLE	503	Service Unavailable	The service (server) is temporarily unavailable but should be restored in the future. If the server knows when it will be available again, a `Retry-After` header may also be supplied.	1.0
SC_GATEWAY_ TIMEOUT	504	Gateway Timeout	A server acting as a gateway or proxy did not receive a valid response from an upstream server during the time it was prepared to wait.	1.1
SC_HTTP_ VERSION_NOT_ SUPPORTED	505	HTTP Version Not Supported	The server does not support the version of the HTTP protocol used in the request. The response body should specify the protocols supported by the server. Normal servlets should not need to use this status code.	1.1

E

Character Entities

The following table lists the various Unicode escapes, HTML numeric entities, and HTML named entites for all printable ISO-8859-1 (Latin-1) characters.

The numeric and named entities may be used within HTML pages; they are converted to symbols by web browsers. Unicode escapes may be used within servlet code; they are interpreted by the Java compiler. For example, a pound sign (£) can be embedded in an HTML page as `£` or `£`. It can be embedded directly in Java code as `\u00A3`.

Note that not every HTML character entity is universally supported. The Support column indicates its level of support. An *S* value means the numeric and named entity values for the symbol are part of the HTML standard. A *P* indicates the entity values are proposed standards—not part of the HTML standard but in most cases widely supported. An *N* in the column indicates the entity values are nonstandard and poorly supported. For these symbols, it's often best to use Unicode escapes.

Unicode Escape	Numeric Entity	Named Entity	Symbol	Description	Support
\u0009			\t	Horizontal tab	S
\u000A
	\n	Line feed	S
\u000D
	\r	Carriage return	S
\u0020				Space	S
\u0021	!		!	Exclamation point	S
\u0022	"	"	"	Quotation mark	S
\u0023	#		#	Hash mark	S
\u0024	$		$	Dollar sign	S
\u0025	%		%	Percent sign	S

Unicode Escape	Numeric Entity	Named Entity	Symbol	Description	Support
\u0026	&	&	&	Ampersand	S
\u0027	'		'	Apostrophe	S
\u0028	(		(	Left parenthesis	S
\u0029	)		)	Right parenthesis	S
\u002A	*		*	Asterisk	S
\u002B	+		+	Plus sign	S
\u002C	,		,	Comma	S
\u002D	-		-	Hyphen	S
\u002E	.		.	Period	S
\u002F	/		/	Slash	S
\u0030-\u0039	0-9		0–9	Digits 0–9	S
\u003A	:		:	Colon	S
\u003B	;		;	Semicolon	S
\u003C	<	<	<	Less than	S
\u003D	=		=	Equals sign	S
\u003E	>	>	>	Greater than	S
\u003F	?		?	Question mark	S
\u0040	@		@	Commercial at sign	S
\u0041-\u005A	A-Z		A–Z	Letters A–Z	S
\u005B	[		[	Left square bracket	S
\u005C	\		\	Backslash	S
\u005D	]		]	Right square bracket	S
\u005E	^		^	Caret	S
\u005F	_		_	Underscore	S
\u0060	`		`	Grave accent	S
\u0061-\u007A	a-z		a–z	Letters a–z	S
\u007B	{		{	Left curly brace	S
\u007C				|	Vertical bar	S
\u007D	}		}	Right curly brace	S
\u007E	~		~	Tilde	S
\u0082	‚		‚	Low left single quote	N
\u0083	ƒ		ƒ	Florin	N
\u0084	„		„	Low left double quote	N
\u0085	…		…	Ellipsis	N
\u0086	†		†	Dagger	N

Unicode Escape	Numeric Entity	Named Entity	Symbol	Description	Support
\u0087	‡		‡	Double dagger	N
\u0088	ˆ		ˆ	Circumflex	N
\u0089	‰		‰	Permil	N
\u008A	Š		Š	Capital S, caron	N
\u008B	‹		<	Less-than sign	N
\u008C	Œ		Œ	Capital OE ligature	N
\u0091	‘		'	Left single quote	N
\u0092	’		'	Right single quote	N
\u0093	“		"	Left double quote	N
\u0094	”		"	Right double quote	N
\u0095	•		•	Bullet	N
\u0096	–		–	En dash	N
\u0097	—		—	Em dash	N
\u0098	˜		˜	Tilde	N
\u0099	™		™	Trademark	N
\u009A	š		š	Small s, caron	N
\u009B	›		>	Greater-than sign	N
\u009C	œ		œ	Small oe ligature	N
\u009F	Ÿ		Ÿ	Capital Y, umlaut	N
\u00A0				Nonbreaking space	P
\u00A1	¡	¡	¡	Inverted exclamation point	P
\u00A2	¢	¢	¢	Cent sign	P
\u00A3	£	£	£	Pound sign	P
\u00A4	¤	¤	¤	General currency sign	P
\u00A5	¥	¥	¥	Yen sign	P
\u00A6	¦	¦	¦	Broken vertical bar	P
\u00A7	§	§	§	Section sign	P
\u00A8	¨	¨	¨	Umlaut	P
\u00A9	©	©	©	Copyright	P
\u00AA	ª	ª	ª	Feminine ordinal	P
\u00AB	«	«	«	Left angle quote	P
\u00AC	¬	¬	¬	Not sign	P
\u00AD			-	Soft hyphen	P
\u00AE	®	®	®	Registered trademark	P

Unicode Escape	Numeric Entity	Named Entity	Symbol	Description	Support
\u00AF	¯	¯	¯	Macron accent	P
\u00B0	°	°	°	Degree sign	P
\u00B1	±	±	±	Plus or minus	P
\u00B2	²	²	^{2}	Superscript 2	P
\u00B3	³	³	^{3}	Superscript 3	P
\u00B4	´	´	´	Acute accent	P
\u00B5	µ	µ	µ	Micro sign (Greek mu)	P
\u00B6	¶	¶	¶	Paragraph sign	P
\u00B7	·	·	·	Middle dot	P
\u00B8	¸	¸	¸	Cedilla	P
\u00B9	¹	¹	^{1}	Superscript 1	P
\u00BA	º	º	º	Masculine ordinal	P
\u00BB	»	»	»	Right angle quote	P
\u00BC	¼	¼	$^{1}/_{4}$	Fraction one-fourth	P
\u00BD	½	½	$^{1}/_{2}$	Fraction one-half	P
\u00BE	¾	¾	$^{3}/_{4}$	Fraction three-fourths	P
\u00BF	¿	¿	¿	Inverted question mark	P
\u00C0	À	À	À	Capital A, grave accent	S
\u00C1	Á	Á	Á	Capital A, acute accent	S
\u00C2	Â	Â	Â	Capital A, circumflex accent	S
\u00C3	Ã	Ã	Ã	Capital A, tilde	S
\u00C4	Ä	Ä	Ä	Capital A, umlaut	S
\u00C5	Å	Å	Å	Capital A, ring	S
\u00C6	Æ	Æ	Æ	Capital AE ligature	S
\u00C7	Ç	Ç	Ç	Capital C, cedilla	S
\u00C8	È	È	È	Capital E, grave accent	S
\u00C9	É	É	É	Capital E, acute accent	S
\u00CA	Ê	Ê	Ê	Capital E, circumflex accent	S
\u00CB	Ë	Ë	Ë	Capital E, umlaut	S
\u00CC	Ì	Ì	Ì	Capital I, grave accent	S
\u00CD	Í	Í	Í	Capital I, acute accent	S
\u00CE	Î	Î	Î	Capital I, circumflex accent	S
\u00CF	Ï	Ï	Ï	Capital I, umlaut	S

Unicode Escape	Numeric Entity	Named Entity	Symbol	Description	Support
\u00D0	Ð	Ð	Ð	Capital eth, Icelandic	S
\u00D1	Ñ	Ñ	Ñ	Capital N, tilde	S
\u00D2	Ò	Ò	Ò	Capital O, grave accent	S
\u00D3	Ó	Ó	Ó	Capital O, acute accent	S
\u00D4	Ô	Ô	Ô	Capital O, circumflex accent	S
\u00D5	Õ	Õ	Õ	Capital O, tilde	S
\u00D6	Ö	Ö	Ö	Capital O, umlaut	S
\u00D7	×	×	×	Multiply sign	P
\u00D8	Ø	Ø	Ø	Capital O, slash	S
\u00D9	Ù	Ù	Ù	Capital U, grave accent	S
\u00DA	Ú	Ú	Ú	Capital U, acute accent	S
\u00DB	Û	Û	Û	Capital U, circumflex accent	S
\u00DC	Ü	Ü	Ü	Capital U, umlaut	S
\u00DD	Ý	Ý	Ý	Capital Y, acute accent	S
\u00DE	Þ	Þ	Þ	Capital thorn, Icelandic	S
\u00DF	ß	ß	ß	Small sz ligature, German	S
\u00E0	à	à	à	Small a, grave accent	S
\u00E1	á	á	á	Small a, acute accent	S
\u00E2	â	â	â	Small a, circumflex accent	S
\u00E3	ã	ã	ã	Small a, tilde	S
\u00E4	ä	ä	ä	Small a, umlaut	S
\u00E5	å	å	å	Small a, ring	S
\u00E6	æ	æ	æ	Small ae ligature	S
\u00E7	ç	ç	ç	Small c, cedilla	S
\u00E8	è	è	è	Small e, grave accent	S
\u00E9	é	é	é	Small e, acute accent	S
\u00EA	ê	ê	ê	Small e, circumflex accent	S
\u00EB	ë	ë	ë	Small e, umlaut	S
\u00EC	ì	ì	ì	Small i, grave accent	S
\u00ED	í	í	í	Small i, acute accent	S
\u00EE	î	î	î	Small i, circumflex accent	S
\u00EF	ï	ï	ï	Small i, umlaut	S

Unicode Escape	Numeric Entity	Named Entity	Symbol	Description	Support
\u00F0	ð	ð	ð	Small eth, Icelandic	S
\u00F1	ñ	ñ	ñ	Small n, tilde	S
\u00F2	ò	ò	ò	Small o, grave accent	S
\u00F3	ó	ó	ó	Small o, acute accent	S
\u00F4	ô	ô	ô	Small o, circumflex accent	S
\u00F5	õ	õ	õ	Small o, tilde	S
\u00F6	ö	ö	ö	Small o, umlaut	S
\u00F7	÷	÷	÷	Division sign	P
\u00F8	ø	ø	ø	Small o, slash	S
\u00F9	ù	ù	ù	Small u, grave accent	S
\u00FA	ú	ú	ú	Small u, acute accent	S
\u00FB	û	û	û	Small u, circumflex accent	S
\u00FC	ü	ü	ü	Small u, umlaut	S
\u00FD	ý	ý	ý	Small y, acute accent	S
\u00FE	þ	þ	þ	Small thorn, Icelandic	S
\u00FF	ÿ	ÿ	ÿ	Small y, umlaut	S

F

Charsets

The following table lists the suggested charset(s) for a number of languages. Charsets are used by servlets that generate multilingual output; they determine which character encoding a servlet's `PrintWriter` is to use. By default, the `PrintWriter` uses the ISO-8859-1 (Latin-1) charset, appropriate for most Western European languages. To specify an alternate charset, the charset value must be passed to the `setContentType()` method before the servlet retrieves its `PrintWriter`, for example:

```
res.setContentType("text/html; charset=Shift_JIS");  // A Japanese charset
PrintWriter out = res.getWriter();  // Writes Shift_JIS Japanese
```

The charset can also be set implicitly using the `setLocale()` method, for example:

```
res.setContentType("text/html");
res.setLocale(new Locale("ja", ""));  // Sets charset to Shift_JIS
PrintWriter out = res.getWriter();    // Writes Shift_JIS Japanese
```

The `setLocale()` method assigns a charset to the response according to the table listed here. Where multiple charsets are possible, the first listed charset is chosen.

Note that not all web browsers support all charsets or have the fonts available to represent all characters, although at minimum all clients support ISO-8859-1. Further note that the UTF-8 charset can represent all Unicode characters and may be assumed a viable alternative for all languages.

Language	Language Code	Suggested Charsets
Albanian	sq	ISO-8859-2
Arabic	ar	ISO-8859-6
Bulgarian	bg	ISO-8859-5

Language	Language Code	Suggested Charsets
Byelorussian	be	ISO-8859-5
Catalan (Spanish)	ca	ISO-8859-1
Chinese (Simplified/Mainland)	zh	GB2312
Chinese (Traditional/Taiwan)	zh (country TW)	Big5
Croatian	hr	ISO-8859-2
Czech	cs	ISO-8859-2
Danish	da	ISO-8859-1
Dutch	nl	ISO-8859-1
English	en	ISO-8859-1
Estonian	et	ISO-8859-1
Finnish	fi	ISO-8859-1
French	fr	ISO-8859-1
German	de	ISO-8859-1
Greek	el	ISO-8859-7
Hebrew	he (formerly iw)	ISO-8859-8
Hungarian	hu	ISO-8859-2
Icelandic	is	ISO-8859-1
Italian	it	ISO-8859-1
Japanese	ja	Shift_JIS, ISO-2022-JP, EUC-JP[a]
Korean	ko	EUC-KR[b]
Latvian, Lettish	lv	ISO-8859-2
Lithuanian	lt	ISO-8859-2
Macedonian	mk	ISO-8859-5
Norwegian	no	ISO-8859-1
Polish	pl	ISO-8859-2
Portuguese	pt	ISO-8859-1
Romanian	ro	ISO-8859-2
Russian	ru	ISO-8859-5, KOI8-R
Serbian	sr	ISO-8859-5, KOI8-R
Serbo-Croatian	sh	ISO-8859-5, ISO-8859-2, KOI8-R
Slovak	sk	ISO-8859-2
Slovenian	sl	ISO-8859-2
Spanish	es	ISO-8859-1

Language	Language Code	Suggested Charsets
Swedish	sv	ISO-8859-1
Turkish	tr	ISO-8859-9
Ukranian	uk	ISO-8859-5, KOI8-R

[a] First supported in JDK 1.1.6. Earlier versions of the JDK know the EUC-JP character set by the name EUCJIS, so for portability you can set the character set to EUC-JP and manually construct an EUCJIS `PrintWriter`.

[b] First supported in JDK 1.1.6. Earlier versions of the JDK know the EUC-KR character set by the name KSC_5601, so for portability you can set the character set to EUC-KR and manually construct a KSC_5601 `PrintWriter`.

Index

We'd like to hear your suggestions for improving our indexes. Send email to *index@oreilly.com.*

C

E

J

K

L

N

T

X

Y

Z

About the Authors

Jason Hunter is Senior Technologist with CollabNet (*http://collab.net*), a company that provides tools and services for open source collaboration. In addition to authoring *Java Servlet Programming*, he is publisher of Servlets.com, creator of the com.oreilly.servlet library, a contributor to the Apache Jakarta project that creates Tomcat (starting on the project when it was still Sun internal), a member of the expert groups responsible for Servlet/JSP and JAXP API development, and he holds a seat on the JCP Executive Committee overseeing the Java platform, as a representative of the Apache Software Foundation. He also writes columns for JavaWorld and speaks at many programming and open source conferences. Most recently he co-created the open source JDOM library (*http://jdom.org*) to enable optimized Java and XML integration, and he leads the expert group responsible for JDOM development.

Jason previously held the position of Chief Technology Officer at K&A Software, a company specializing in Java training and consulting, where he acted as hired gun Java guru for dozens of companies including Sun Microsystems. Before that he worked at Silicon Graphics where he was responsible for developing (and breaking) all sorts of web technologies.

Jason graduated summa cum laude from Willamette University (Salem, Oregon) in 1995 with a degree in computer science. He began programming in Java in the summer of 1995 and has been involved with servlets and related server-side technologies since December 1996. If by some miracle you don't find him at work, he's probably out hiking in the mountains.

William "Will" Crawford got involved with web development back in 1995. He has worked at the Children's Hospital Informatics Program in Boston, where he helped develop the first web-based electronic medical record system and was involved in some of the first uses of Java at the enterprise level. He has consulted on Intranet development projects for, among others, Children's Hospital, Massachusetts General Hospital, Brigham and Women's Hospital, the Boston Anesthesia Education Foundation, and Harvard Medical Center.

Will currently heads the product development team at Invantage, Inc., a Cambridge, Massachusetts, startup developing Java-based intranet tools for the pharmaceutical industry. In his spare time, he is an avid amateur photographer, writer, and pursuer of a Bachelor's of Economics at Yale University.

Colophon

Our look is the result of reader comments, our own experimentation, and feedback from distribution channels. Distinctive covers complement our distinctive approach to technical topics, breathing personality and life into potentially dry subjects.

The image on the cover of *Java Servlet Programming, Second Edition* is a common European bear.

Colleen Gorman was the production editor, and Norma Emory was the copyeditor for *Java Servlet Programming, Second Edition*. Catherine Morris and Leanne Soylemez provided quality control. Frameworks Consulting provided production support. Ellen Troutman-Zaig wrote the index.

Hanna Dyer designed the cover of this book, based on a series design by Edie Freedman. The cover image is a 19th-century engraving from the Dover Pictorial Archive. Emma Colby produced the cover layout with QuarkXPress 4.1 using Adobe's ITC Garamond font.

David Futato designed the interior layout based on a series design by Nancy Priest. Judy Hoer converted the Microsoft Word files to FrameMaker 5.5.6, using tools created by Mike Sierra. The heading font is Bodoni BT, the text font is New Baskerville, and the code font is Constant Willison. The illustrations that appear in the book were produced by Robert Romano using Macromedia FreeHand 8 and Adobe Photoshop 5.

Whenever possible, our books use a durable and flexible lay-flat binding. If the page count exceeds this binding's limit, perfect binding is used.

Other Titles Available from O'Reilly

Java

Java Extreme Programming Cookbook

By Eric M. Burke & Brian M. Coyner
1st Edition March 2003
288 pages, ISBN0-596-00387-0

Brimming with over 100 "recipes" for getting down to business and actually doing XP, the *Java Extreme Programming Cookbook* doesn't try to "sell" you on XP; it succinctly documents the most important features of popular open source tools for XP in Java—including Ant, Junit, HttpUnit, Cactus, Tomcat, XDoclet—and then digs right in, providing recipes for implementing the tools in real-world environments.

Java Enterprise Best Practices

By The O'Reilly Java Authors, edited by Robert Eckstein
1st Edition December 2002
288 pages, ISBN 0-596-00384-6

This book is for intermediate and advanced Java developers, the ones who have been around the block enough times to understand just how complex—and unruly—an enterprise system can get. Each chapter in this collection contains several rules that provide insight into the "best practices" for creating and maintaining projects using the Java Enterprise APIs. Written by the world's leading Java experts, this book covers JDBC, RMI/CORBA, Servlets, JavaServer Pages and custom tag libraries, XML, Internationalization, JavaMail, Enterprise JavaBeans, and performance tuning.

Java Cookbook

By Ian Darwin
1st Edition June 2001
882 pages, ISBN 0-59600-170-3

This book offers Java developers short, focused pieces of code that are easy to incorporate into other programs. The idea is to focus on things that are useful, tricky, or both. The book's code segments cover all of the dominant APIs and many specialized APIs and should serve as a great "jumping-off place" for Java developers who want to get started in areas outside their specialization.

Learning Java, 2nd Edition

By Pat Niemeyer & Jonathan Knudsen
2nd Edition June 2002
832 pages, ISBN 0-596-00285-8

This new edition of *Learning Java* comprehensively addresses important topics such as web applications, servlets, and XML. It provides full coverage of all Java 1.4 language features including assertions and exception chaining as well as new APIs such as regular expressions and NIO, the new I/O package. New Swing features and components are described along with updated coverage of the JavaBeans component architecture using the open source NetBeans IDE the latest information about Applets and the Java Plug-in for all major browsers.

Mac OS X for Java Geeks

By Will Iverson
1st Edition April 2003
304 pages, ISBN 0-596-00400-1

Mac OS X for Java Geeks delivers a complete and detailed look at the OS X platform for Java development. Based on the new 1.4 JDK and the 10.2 release of Mac OS X from Apple Computer, this is the most thorough guide available for both new and experienced Java developers who want to create cross-platform applications that take advantage of Mac OS X's unique functionality.

Java Management Extensions

By J. Steven Perry
1st Edition June 2002
312 pages, ISBN 0-596-00245-9

Java Management Extensions is a practical, hands-on guide to using the JMX APIs. This one-of-a kind book is a complete treatment of the JMX architecture (both the instrumentation level and the agent level), and it's loaded with real-world examples for implementing Management Extensions. It also contains useful information at the higher level about JMX (the "big picture") to help technical managers and architects who are evaluating various application management approaches and are considering JMX.

Java

Java & XML, 2nd Edition

By Brett McLaughlin
2nd Edition September 2001
528 pages, ISBN 0-596-000197-5

New chapters on Advanced SAX, Advanced DOM, SOAP, and data binding, as well as new examples throughout, bring the second edition of *Java & XML* thoroughly up to date. Except for a concise introduction to XML basics, the book focuses entirely on using XML from Java applications. It's a worthy companion for Java developers working with XML or involved in messaging, web services, or the new peer-to-peer movement.

JavaServer Pages, 2nd Edition

By Hans Bergsten
2nd Edition August 2002
712 pages, ISBN 0-596-00317-X

Filled with useful examples and the depth, clarity, and attention to detail that made the first edition so popular with web developers, *JavaServer Pages*, 2nd Edition is completely revised and updated to cover the substantial changes in the 1.2 version of the JSP specifications, and includes coverage of the new JSTL Tag libraries—an eagerly anticipated standard set of JSP elements for the tasks needed in most JSP applications, as well as thorough coverage of Custom Tag Libraries.

J2EE Design Patterns

By William C.R. Crawford
& Jonathan Kaplan
1st Edition September 2003
352 pages, ISBN 0-596-00427-3

Crawford and Kaplan's *J2EE Design Patterns* takes a different approach than just simply presenting another catalog of design patterns. The authors broaden the scope by discussing ways to choose design patterns when building an enterprise application from scratch, looking closely at the real world tradeoffs that Java developers must weigh when architecting their applications. They also extend design patterns into areas not covered in other books, presenting original patterns for data modeling, transaction/process modeling, and interoperability. This design pattern book breaks the mold.

Enterprise JavaBeans, 3rd Edition

By Richard Monson-Haefel
3rd Edition September 2001
592 pages, ISBN 0-596-00226-2

Enterprise JavaBeans has been thoroughly updated for the new EJB Specification. Important changes in Version 2.0 include a completely new CMP (container-managed persistence) model that allows for much more complex business function modeling; local interfaces that will significantly improve performance of EJB applications; and the "message driven bean," an entirely new kind of Java bean based on asynchronous messaging and the Java Message Service.

Java Message Service

By Richard Monson-Haefel &
David Chappell
1st Edition December 2000
238 pages, ISBN 0-596-00068-5

This book is a thorough introduction to Java Message Service (JMS) from Sun Microsystems. It shows how to build applications using the point-to-point and publish-and-subscribe models; use features like transactions and durable subscriptions to make applications reliable; and use messaging within Enterprise JavaBeans. It also introduces a new EJB type, the MessageDrivenBean, that is part of EJB 2.0, and discusses integration of messaging into J2EE.